CANNON FINANCIAL INSTITUTE
CONCEPTS
FOR PROFESSIONALS

A COMPLETE LIBRARY OF ESSENTIAL FINANCIAL CONCEPTS

Content Meets Current FINRA Guidelines

Substantially similar material that meet current FINRA guidelines can be found in the current version of the Back Room Technician software.

CANNON FINANCIAL INSTITUTE

649-4 S. Milledge Avenue
Athens, GA 30605

Phone: 706-353-3346
Fax: 706.353-3994

www.cannonfinancial.com

2008

This publication is designed to provide accurate and authoritative information in regard to the subject matter covered. It is sold with the understanding that the publisher is not engaged in rendering legal, accounting, or other professional services. If legal advice or other expert assistance is required, the services of a competent professional should be sought. – **From a Declaration of Principles jointly adopted by the Committee of the American Bar Association and a Committee of Publishers and Associations.**

Licensed to
Cannon Financial Institute, Inc.
649-4 South Milledge Avenue
Post Office Box 6447
Athens, Georgia 306004
Phone   706-353-3346 • Fax 706-353-3994

ISBN 978-097021865-0
Copyright © 2008
Advisys, Inc.
20271 SW Birch Street #200
Newport Beach, California
Sales 800-777-3162 • Fax 949-250-0794

Printed in the U.S.A.

Table of Contents

i

ACCUMULATION AND INVESTMENTS

CURRENT INCOME TAX

PROPERTY AND CASUALTY

LIFE INSURANCE AND ANNUITIES

EMPLOYEE BENEFITS

THE RETIREMENT PLANNING PROBLEM

INDIVIDUAL RETIREMENT ACCOUNTS

EMPLOYER SPONSORED RETIREMENT PLANS

DISTRIBUTIONS FROM IRAS AND QUALIFIED PLANS

BUSINESS PLANNING GENERALLY

BUSINESS USES OF LIFE INSURANCE

BUSINESS CONTINUATION

THE ESTATE PLANNING PROBLEM

BASIC ESTATE PLANNING

LIFE INSURANCE AND ESTATE TAXATION

ADVANCED ESTATE PLANNING

ESTATE FREEZING TECHNIQUES

CHARITABLE ALTERNATIVES

PLANNER SUPPORT REPORTS

The Financial Planning Puzzle

Our financial lives often have many scattered pieces.

A coordinated financial plan provides a framework for achieving financial security.

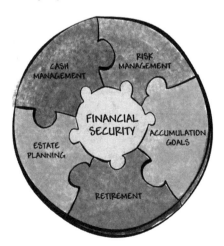

The Need for Financial Planning

Building a successful financial plan can be confusing. As we construct a plan, we find that our financial lives have many scattered pieces.

The Pieces of the Puzzle

Some of the financial issues that each of us can expect to face during life include:

- **Cash management:** More than just balancing the checkbook, cash management includes preparing (and following) a budget, using credit wisely, and keeping the income tax burden to the lowest level possible.

- **Risk management:** There is risk of loss of both life and property. Life insurance can be used to protect a family against the risk of premature death. Disability insurance can protect against the loss of a person's ability to earn a living. Property and casualty insurance can protect our worldly goods against accident and such perils as fire, flood, earthquake and theft. Health insurance can help pay the cost of needed medical care.

- **Accumulation goals:** We all need to save money for some reason. Educating our children is one very common goal. Buying a home and building an investment portfolio are two other typical accumulation goals.

- **Retirement:** Taking action today to insure that the later years are as comfortable and worry-free as possible.

- **Estate planning:** Recognizing that death is inevitable and planning for the ultimate transfer of our assets to our heirs.

Continued

The Need for Financial Planning

A coordinated financial plan provides a framework for achieving financial security.

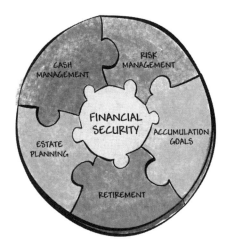

Steps to Achieving Financial Security

Solving financial problems in today's world takes work. Two basic steps are involved:

- **Step 1 – Choose Your Financial Planning Team:** In our complex, ever-changing world, expert help is needed. Trained professionals such as your attorney, CPA, IRS enrolled agent, life insurance agent, health insurance agent, securities broker, and financial planner are generally members of your team.

- **Step 2 – Develop Your Plan:** With the help of your team, the second step can be taken: the development of a systematic, integrated plan for dealing with each of these issues. This is called developing a financial plan.

You can choose to ignore these problems until it is too late. Or, you can take steps to put the puzzle together and achieve your financial security. The most important step is the first one.

Basic Steps in the Financial Planning Process

The Basic Steps

1. **Choose your team:** Choose, as needed, your financial planner, tax advisor, life insurance agent, property & casualty agent, health insurance agent, investment broker, attorney, charitable giving advisor, trust officer, or banker.
2. **Gather information:** A completed fact finder serves to list your goals and objectives, shows your assets and liabilities, measures cash flow, and notes the current status of your retirement, estate, and risk management planning.
3. **Analyze data:** To determine if current and future needs are met.
4. **Team makes recommendations:** Review the suggestions made by your team.
5. **Decide and implement:** Select the plan that best fits your needs and goals. Sign essential documents, purchase needed insurance, and re-allocate investments as necessary.
6. **Periodic review:** Starting the cycle over. Because the world is constantly changing, many advisors recommend an annual planning review.

Choose the Financial Planning Team

Financial planning is a complex field which covers many areas including investments, education planning, retirement planning, wills, trusts, insurance, accounting, business continuation, and estate, gift, and income taxes.

It would be difficult to find one person who is a trained and licensed expert in all of these areas. Most often, the needed skills and knowledge are available only by bringing together a financial planning team. The various members of your chosen team can then work closely with you to create an estate, to preserve it, and to and pass it on to your heirs with the least amount of expense and aggravation.

Potential members of the team may include the following:

The Captain of the Team

You are the captain of the team. The final decisions must be made by you after carefully reviewing the recommendations of the other members of your financial planning team.

Financial Planner

Often a member of the team will have special training in financial planning. A qualified financial planner should take a very active part in directing the formation of the overall financial plan.

Investment Specialist

Investors face a confusing range of investment tools, each with different characteristics and uses. Professional investment guidance is essential.

Tax Professional

Taxes consume a large part of our income and must be considered in all aspects of a financial plan.

Life Underwriter

Life insurance contracts differ greatly and are issued by companies with varying degrees of financial strength. A professional life underwriter will help you choose a financially strong company, the correct type of policy for your situation, and the correct amount of insurance.

Continued...

Choose the Financial Planning Team

Property & Casualty Agent

Property & casualty insurance helps protect the physical assets an individual owns from loss or damage.

Health and Disability Specialist

Health insurance can pay much of the cost of needed medical care. Disability insurance can help replace lost income if you are unable to work for a period of time. Long-term care insurance aids in paying for needed care if a disability or other severe health problem will continue for an extended period of time.

Estate Planning Attorney

Most attorneys can draft a basic will. However, one who specializes in estate planning law will be more familiar with the various tools and techniques available to save you and your heirs thousands of dollars in taxes, probate and administration expenses.

Trust Administrator

If you select a corporate fiduciary (a bank or trust company) as executor of your will or trustee of your trust, you should consider involving them in the development of the estate planning portion of your financial plan.

Planned-Giving Specialist

Charitable organizations often have planned-giving specialists who are well versed in methods of making lifetime gifts or bequests at the time of death, which can benefit you and your heirs.

Annual Review Checklist

An annual review of your financial situation typically involves the examination of a number of topics. The review is designed to catch problems before they occur, measure progress toward established goals and make necessary adjustments in response to changed conditions.

Review Topics

- ❑ **Cash flow management:** Includes budgeting, emergency cash reserves and debt management.

- ❑ **Risk management – Property and casualty:** Ensures that the appropriate level and type of property and personal liability insurance is in place.

- ❑ **Risk management – Health and disability:** Checks for suitable health, disability and long-term care coverage.

- ❑ **Risk management – Life insurance:** Reviews current life insurance planning, including the most appropriate amount and type of insurance.

- ❑ **Income tax:** Looks for appropriate strategies to keep the income tax burden to the lowest level possible.

- ❑ **Accumulation – General:** Establishes goals and methods of accumulating funds for general savings goals such as college education.

- ❑ **Accumulation – Retirement:** Evaluates current plans to accumulate the resources necessary to ensure a comfortable retirement.

- ❑ **Estate planning:** Checks to see if the appropriate tools and strategies are being used to ensure that the estate will pass to the chosen heirs with minimum delay and costs.

Notes

_____

_____

_____

_____

_____

_____

_____

Life Events Checklist

Change is a constant part of every life. In order to determine how we may best serve you, please complete the form below and return it to us at your earliest convenience.

Common Life Events

❑ New child or grandchild ❑ Change in marital status ❑ Death of family member

❑ New job or promotion ❑ Change in estate plan ❑ New investments or insurance

❑ Receipt of an inheritance ❑ Sale or purchase of home ❑ Retirement

❑ Major investment gain/loss ❑ Start/purchase a business ❑ Gain/loss business partner

❑ Health concerns ❑ Sold or acquired assets ❑ Other: _____

Areas of Interest or Concern

❑ Retirement planning ❑ Education funding ❑ Investment review

❑ Estate planning ❑ Income tax planning ❑ Survivor benefit planning

❑ Major asset purchase/lease ❑ Planning for parents ❑ Health/LTC planning

❑ Business/exec. benefits ❑ Business continuation ❑ Charitable giving

❑ Pers. property/liability ins. ❑ Disability income ❑ Other: _____

Additional Comments and Notes

_____

_____

_____

Contacting You

Name: _____ Address: _____

Telephone: _____ _____

Best time to call: _____ _____

❑ Please contact me as soon as possible Email: _____

Accumulation Goals
Four Key Factors

A savings plan to reach an accumulation goal has four distinct, yet interrelated, factors, each of which contributes to the success or failure of the plan.

1. **Contribution amount:** How much is being saved? Should more or less be put aside? Is inflation being considered in future contribution amounts?

2. **Rate of return (ROR):** How much is being earned in interest, dividends or capital growth? Can a higher return be earned, without greater risk? How is the growth taxed?

3. **Time frame:** How much time remains to reach the goal? Can the time frame be shortened or should it be extended? Compound interest will have its greatest impact in later years. Adding a year or two (or more) can be a tremendous help.

4. **Amount of the goal:** Can the goal amount be adjusted? How much is really needed? Sometimes the most difficult factor to adjust is the goal amount, due to an emotional attachment.

A Hypothetical Example[1]

Consider the following example, illustrated graphically below. A couple wants to accumulate $100,000, 20 years from now, to purchase a vacation home. They are currently saving $1,000 per year and earning 7% per year on their savings. At this rate of savings and growth, at the end of 20 years they will have accumulated $43,865 – well short of the goal. As the graph indicates, they could achieve their goal by continuing to save for 10 more years. They don't, however, wish to wait that long.

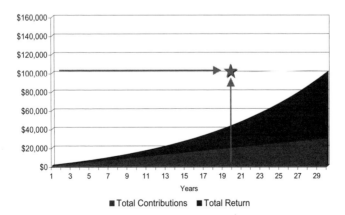

■ Total Contributions ■ Total Return

---

[1] The rates of return shown are not indicative of any particular investment and will fluctuate over time.

Continued...

Accumulation Goals
Four Key Factors

Small Changes

Now consider how a few coordinated changes can make a difference to the success of the plan. If the couple makes relatively small changes to each of the four factors, the goal can be met. The graph below illustrates the effect of making the following four adjustments.

- Increase their annual contribution to $1,200 – a 20% increase;

- Reallocate their savings to earn an 8% ROR – a 14.3% increase;[1]

- Plan to save for an additional four years – a 20% increase; and

- Reduce the goal from $100,000 to $85,000 – a 15% decrease.

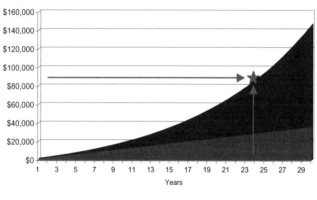

■ Total Contributions ■ Total Return

The couple is now on track to meeting their goal. There are, of course, any number of change combinations that can be applied to this example. The right combination will depend on the individuals involved and the importance of the objective.

---

[1] A higher rate of return generally involves a greater degree of volatility and risk.

An Overview of Social Security Benefits

What Is Social Security?

Social Security is a system of social insurance benefits available to all covered workers in the United States. Begun in 1937, the Social Security system covers a wide range of social programs. The term "Social Security," as it is commonly used, refers to the benefits provided under one part of the system, known by its acronym, OASDI, or Old-Age, Survivors and Disability Insurance.

OASDI benefits are funded primarily by payroll taxes paid by covered employees, employers, and self-employed individuals. Both the OASDI portion of the payroll tax, as well as that part of the tax that goes to finance hospital insurance, HI (Medicare), are provided for under the Federal Insurance Contributions Act, FICA.

Insured Status

In general, to be eligible to receive benefits, a worker must first be insured (either fully insured or currently insured). An individual acquires an insured status by completing a certain number of quarters of covered employment. For example, a worker may become fully insured by completing 40 calendar quarters (10 years) in covered employment.[1] To be considered currently insured, a worker must have at least six quarters of coverage in the last 13 calendar quarters, ending with the quarter in which he or she became entitled to benefits. All benefits are available if a worker is fully insured. Some benefits are not available if the worker is only currently insured. Special requirements apply to disability benefits.

Who Receives Benefits?

In general, the following individuals are entitled to receive OASDI benefits through their relationship to a covered worker.

- **Worker's benefit:** This is a monthly income for a retired or disabled worker.

- **Spouse's benefit:** Refers to monthly income for the spouse or former spouse of a retired or disabled worker.

- **Widow(er)'s benefit:** Refers to monthly retirement income for the surviving spouse or former spouse of a deceased worker.

- **Child's benefit:** A monthly income for the dependent child of a deceased, disabled, or retired worker. To qualify, a child must be under age 18, or 18 or 19 and a full-time elementary or high school student, or 18 or over and disabled before 22.

- **Mother's or father's benefit:** Monthly income paid to a surviving spouse who is caring for a worker's dependent child who is under age 16 or over age 16 but disabled before age 22. If under age 62, the spouse of a retired worker receives the same benefit.

---

[1] For those working less than 10 years, an alternative test to determine fully-insured status might apply.

Continued...

An Overview of Social Security Benefits

On What Is the Amount of a Social Security Benefit Based?

In general, a covered worker's benefits, and those of his or her family members, are based on the worker's earnings record. The earnings taken into account are only those reported to the Social Security Administration (SSA), up to a certain annual maximum known as the "wage base." The wage base is indexed for inflation each year and effectively places a cap on the amount of Social Security benefits a worker can receive, regardless of earnings. The wage base for 2008 is $102,000.[1]

Using a worker's earnings record, the SSA calculates a number known as the Primary Insurance Amount, or PIA. The PIA is the basic value used to determine the dollar amount of benefits available to a worker and his or her family.

What Is the Benefit Amount?

The table below summarizes the benefit amounts generally payable under OASDI in the event of a worker's death, disability, or retirement. All monthly benefit amounts are subject to reduction to meet a "family maximum" limit. Individual benefits may also be reduced if the recipient has earned income in excess of specified limits.

	Death[2]	Disability[3]	Retirement[4]
Worker's benefit		100% of PIA	100% of PIA
Spouse's benefit	N/A	50% of PIA	50% of PIA
Widow(er)'s benefit	100% of PIA	N/A	N/A
Child's benefit	75% of PIA	50% of PIA	50% of PIA
Mother's or father's benefit	75% of PIA	50% of PIA	50% of PIA

The Social Security Administration (SSA) automatically sends annual benefit estimates to workers age 25 and older who are not currently receiving Social Security benefits. The annual statement is generally sent three months before a worker's birthday, and contains estimated retirement, disability and survivors' benefits.

---

[1] The wage base for 2007 was $97,500.
[2] Reduced widow(er)'s benefits are available at age 60.
[3] Disability benefits are subject to a very strict definition of disability. At normal retirement age (NRA), disability benefits cease and retirement benefits begin.
[4] Unreduced benefits are available at NRA. For those born before 1938, NRA is age 65. For individuals born after 1937, NRA gradually increases from age 65 to age 67. For example, for baby boomers born between 1943 -1954, NRA is age 66. A larger retirement benefit is available to those who continue to work past NRA.

Who Receives Social Security Benefits?

Social Security, also known by its acronym OASDI, or "Old Age, Survivors, and Disability Insurance", pays benefits to many individuals.

Who Receives Benefits?

- **Worker's benefit:** A monthly income for a retired or disabled worker.

- **Spouse's benefit:** Monthly income for the spouse or former spouse of a retired or disabled worker.

- **Widow(er)'s benefit:** Monthly retirement income for the surviving spouse or former spouse of a deceased worker.

- **Child's benefit:** Monthly income for the dependent child of a deceased, disabled or retired worker. To receive benefits, the child must be under age 18, over age 18 and attending elementary or high school full-time, or over age 18 and disabled before age 22.

- **Mother's or father's benefit:** Monthly income paid to a surviving spouse who is caring for a worker's dependent child who is under age 16 or over age 16 but disabled before age 22. If under age 62, the spouse of a retired worker receives the same benefit.

The Benefits of a College Education

For many, accumulating funds for the children's education is a savings goal that is often thought about, but seldom acted upon. There are numerous reasons why saving for college is an essential need.

- **Economics:** Statistically, the average worker with a 4-year college education earns far more than the average worker with only a high school diploma.

- **Increasing costs:** In recent years, college costs have increased at a rate greater than the general rate of inflation.[1]

- **Years of study:** Four years of study may not be sufficient. In many professions, six or even eight years of study are required.

What Is a College Education Worth?

College educated, full-time workers statistically enjoy a higher median income than those with less education. In a recent report on education and earnings,[2] the Census Bureau found that those with four years of college could expect to have substantially higher annual earnings than high school graduates.

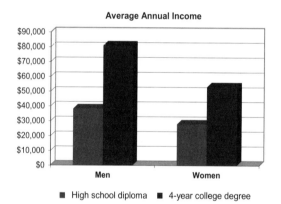

Average Annual Income

■ High school diploma   ■ 4-year college degree

Over a lifetime of work, 39 years on average, a four-year college education can increase a man's total income by over $1,664,364. Because of time spent raising children, the average woman spends 28 years in the workforce. A college education could increase her lifetime earnings by over $707,252.[3]

---

[1] See "Trends in College Pricing – 2006," published by The College Board, page 4.
[2] U.S. Statistical Abstract, 2007; Table No. 684, Average Earnings of Year-Round, Full-Time workers, by Educational Attainment: 2003.
[3] Figures do not take inflation into account.

Continued

The Benefits of a College Education

What Does a College Education Cost?

In recent years, college costs have often exceeded the general rate of inflation. The table below projects college costs for a small group of well-known institutions.

	Annual Costs[1] (Assumes inflation is 4% per year.)			
Private Institutions	**2007**	**2012**	**2017**	**2022**
Yale University New Haven, Connecticut	$43,050	$52,377	$63,725	$77,531
Northwestern University Evanston, Illinois	$43,674	$53,136	$64,648	$78,654
Stanford University Stanford, California	$43,361	$52,755	$64,185	$78,091
Public Institutions	**2007**	**2012**	**2017**	**2022**
State University of New York Stony Brook, New York	$13,998	$17,031	$20,720	$25,210
University of Michigan Ann Arbor, Michigan	$17,562	$21,367	$25,996	$31,628
University of Colorado Boulder, Colorado	$13,943	$16,964	$20,639	$25,111

---

[1] Annual costs are for the 2006-2007 academic year and include tuition and fees, and on campus room and board. Books, transportation and personal expenses are additional. Costs for out-of-state students at public institutions are higher.

Saving for College

Funding a college education for a child is generally the largest purchase a family will make, aside from buying a home. And college is expensive. In 2005, for example, the average one-year cost of tuition and fees, and room and board, at four-year public colleges in the U.S. was $12,605.[1] If this annual figure is multiplied for four years of study, the total reaches $50,420. And that's not everything – these figures do not include books, transportation to and from school, other incidentals, and continuing cost inflation.

Not only is college expensive today, the cost of a college education keeps going up as each year passes. Even worse, higher education costs have been increasing at a rate faster than inflation. The average annual tuition and required fees charged at four-year public colleges in the U.S. in 1985 was $1,386. By 2005 that figure had grown to $5,948[1], a compound annual growth rate of 7.55%. In comparison, inflation, as measured by the Consumer Price Index (CPI-W),[2] increased from 1985 to 2005 by an annual compound rate of only 2.90%. Many expect that college costs will continue to outpace inflation.

Start Planning Early

With college costs high and rising, a family needs to begin the college planning process as early as possible. Taking key steps now makes it easier to reach the goal:

- **Start a savings program:** Start by estimating the cost of college. Once the cost is known, the needed savings can be calculated. Then compare available cash flow with the savings required. If current cash flow is not enough to save the full amount, at least a partial savings program can be started.

- **Consider tax-advantaged approaches:** 529 Prepaid Tuition Plans, 529 Higher Education Savings Plans,[3] and Coverdell Savings Accounts all have significant tax advantages.

- **If there's a shortage:** If personal savings will not be enough, the family can plan for the need to apply for financial aid or begin the search for scholarship funds.

> ### Savings Example
>
> *Assume a family has a new born child. College costs are currently estimated to be $15,000 per year, and are expected to increase at 6% per year over the next 18 years. The total amount needed at the start of college for four years will be almost $169,000. If the family can earn 7% (after-tax) on their savings, monthly deposits of approximately $390 will be needed to pay for the child's education.*

---

[1] Statistical Abstract of the United States: 2007. Table No. 282 Institutions of Higher Education – Charges: 1985 to 2005.
[2] The CPI is the Consumer Price Index for Urban Wage Earners and Clerical Workers, calculated by the U.S. Bureau of Labor Statistics.
[3] Federal law does not allow deductions for contributions to 529 plans, although growth inside a plan is tax deferred and qualified distributions are tax-exempt. The earnings portion of a non-qualified distribution is subject to federal income tax, including a 10% tax penalty. State or local tax law, however, can vary widely. 529 plans involve investment risk, including possible loss of funds, and there is no guarantee a college-funding goal will be met. The fees, expenses, and features of 529 plans vary from state to state.

Ways to Save for College

In accumulating funds for college, one of the first questions a family will face is, "Where do we invest the money?" Many financial professionals will recommend to their clients that money saved for college should be placed in relatively low-risk investments. If there is a long enough time frame, the savings may be placed initially in higher risk (and potentially higher return) investments. As the time for college gets closer, the accumulated funds can be shifted into more conservative choices.

The ultimate decision will depend on a range of factors such as the number of years until college begins, the amount of money available to invest, a family's income tax bracket, risk tolerance, and investment experience. A few of the more traditional approaches are:

- **Savings accounts:** Including CDs, money market accounts, and regular savings.

- **Tax-free municipal bonds:** Held either directly or through a mutual fund.

- **U.S. Treasury securities:** Such as treasury bills or treasury bonds.

- **Growth stocks/growth mutual funds:** For the long-term investor.

Tax-Advantaged Strategies

There are a number of tax-advantaged[1] strategies available to accumulate funds for college expenses. The rules surrounding these strategies can be complicated and they should only be used after careful review with a tax or other financial professional.

- **IRC Sec. 529 qualified tuition program:** These plans allow an individual to either prepay a student's tuition, or contribute to a savings account established to pay the student's "qualified higher education expenses." Contributions are not tax deductible, but growth in an account is tax-deferred. If certain requirements are met, distributions to pay qualified higher expenses are excluded from income.[2]

- **Coverdell education savings account:** Through 2010, up to $2,000 per year may be contributed to a Coverdell ESA for an individual. Contributions are not tax-deductible, but growth is tax-deferred. Distributions are excluded from income if used for qualifying educational expenses. Other restrictions may apply.[3]

- **U.S. savings bonds:** Interest on series EE savings bonds issued after 1989, or Series I savings bonds, may (certain limits apply) be excluded from income if qualifying education expenses are paid in the year the bonds are redeemed. The exclusion also applies to savings bond interest contributed to an IRC Sec. 529 qualified tuition program or a Coverdell ESA.

---

[1] The rules described here concern federal income tax law. State or local income tax law may vary.
[2] 529 plans involve investment risk, including possible loss of funds, and there is no guarantee a college-funding goal will be met. The fees, expenses, and features of 529 plans vary from state to state.
[3] Under current federal income tax law, many of the tax benefits of Coverdell accounts expire after 2010.

Continued...

Ways to Save for College

Who Owns the Funds?

A second issue facing families planning for college is the question of "Who will own the funds?" The answer to this question involves issues of control, income and gift taxes, and can impact a future application for financial aid.

- **Parents:** Either in accounts specifically earmarked for college or as a part of a general family portfolio.

- **Child:** Often a custodial account is used, under either the Uniform Gifts to Minors Act (UGMA) or the Uniform Transfers to Minors Act (UTMA).

- **Trust:** In certain situations, usually involving wealthy families, specialized types of trusts may be used, such as a Crummey trust or charitable remainder trust.

Impact On Financial Aid

For need-based financial aid purposes, assets considered to be owned by the parents have a relatively small negative impact. Assets considered to be owned by the child have a much greater negative impact. Trust assets are generally considered to be owned by the child. Frequently, trust provisions restrict access to principal, thus forcing inclusion of the trust assets in the eligibility process each year that a student is in school. Non-trust assets can be "spent down" in a year or two, limiting their financial aid impact.

Other Resources

There are a number of excellent references and guides to investments and college planning available in bookstores and public libraries. State and federal agencies involved in higher education also are excellent sources of information. In addition, there are a number of sites on the Internet which can provide information, including the following.

- **The College Board** – http://www.collegeboard.com

- **FinAid! The SmartStudent® Guide To Financial Aid** – http://www.finaid.org

- **College Savings Plan Network** – links to state-run web pages on prepaid tuition or college savings plans, at: http://www.collegesavings.org

- **U.S. Department of Education – student aid website** – http://www.studentaid.ed.gov

Begin Early and Seek Professional Advice

Developing a plan to save for a child's college education can be complicated. Questions can arise involving income tax, estate and gift taxes, investment issues, and the impact of asset ownership on financial aid eligibility. Individuals are strongly advised to begin a savings program as early as possible, and seek professional advice before implementation.

Section 529 Qualified Tuition Plans

To encourage saving for higher education, Congress created Section 529 of the Internal Revenue Code. This law provides for two tax-advantaged programs that parents and others can use to accumulate some or all of the resources needed to pay for college.

- **Prepaid tuition plans:** Cash contributions are made to a qualified trust to "prepay," at today's prices, a beneficiary's future tuition costs. This approach allows you to purchase a number of course units or academic periods that are redeemed when the beneficiary is old enough to attend college.

- **Higher education savings plans:** Cash contributions are made to an account established for a named beneficiary. An investment management firm typically directs the investments. The amount of money available for higher education expenses depends on growth in the account between contribution and withdrawal.

Under federal tax law, contributions are not tax deductible and any growth in an account is tax-deferred. Distributions used solely to pay for qualified higher education expenses are federally tax-exempt. The earnings portion of a "non-qualified" distribution is taxable to the beneficiary and may be subject to a 10% tax penalty. State or local law can vary.

Issues to Consider

Which type of plan is best? As a starting point, consider the following issues:

- **Investment risk:** Prepaid tuition plans are generally seen as having a lower level of market risk, along with a lower rate of return. Higher education savings plans combine the potential for gain with the possibility of losing money.

- **Home state plans:** Does the plan in your (or the beneficiary's) home state offer any tax or other benefits that are only available to participants in such state's plan?

- **Expenses covered:** Funds in a savings plan can typically be used for any qualified higher education expenses. Tuition, fees, books, supplies, and equipment required for attendance generally qualify, as do reasonable costs for room and board if the student is attending school at least half time. Also qualifying are costs incurred to allow a special-needs beneficiary to enroll at and attend an eligible institution. Prepaid tuition plans, however, are generally limited to payment of required tuition and fees; in a few plans, room and board is also included.

- **Flexibility:** What happens if a beneficiary decides not to attend college? How easy is it to change the beneficiary, so that the assets may be used for someone else? What expenses or fees are involved if the account owner wants to terminate the plan? Is there a different rate of return if the beneficiary attends college in a different state or if the account owner terminates the plan?

Seek Professional Guidance

Individuals and families considering a qualified tuition plan are faced with a number of complex income, gift, estate, and investment questions. The advice of appropriate tax, legal, need-based student aid, and financial professionals is highly recommended.

"529" Higher Education Savings Plan

Federal tax law[1] allows the states to establish tax-advantaged savings programs to pay for a student's qualified higher education expenses. In these programs, cash contributions are made to an account established for a named beneficiary. An investment management firm typically manages account funds. The amount ultimately available to pay for the beneficiary's education depends on growth in the account between contribution and withdrawal. Higher education savings accounts are not insured and losses are possible.

Under federal tax law, contributions are not tax deductible and any growth in an account is tax-deferred. Distributions used solely to pay for qualified higher education expenses are federally tax-exempt. State or local law, however, can vary widely; contributions may or may not be tax deductible, and distributions may or may not be tax exempt.

Key Definitions Under IRC Sec. 529

- **Qualified higher education expenses:** Tuition, fees, books, supplies, and equipment required for attendance generally qualify. Reasonable costs of room and board are also included if the student is attending school at least half time. Qualified higher education expenses also include costs incurred to allow a special needs beneficiary to enroll at and attend an eligible institution.

- **Eligible educational institution:** Accredited post-high school educational institutions offering associate's, bachelor's, graduate level, or professional degrees typically qualify as eligible. Certain vocational schools are also included.

Contributions

Contributions to a savings plan must be in cash and may not exceed the amount necessary to provide the beneficiary's qualified higher education expenses. Program sponsors will specify the maximum allowable contribution . In many programs, more than $250,000 may be contributed for a single beneficiary. While some donors contribute lump-sum amounts, many 529 savings plan accounts are set up with automatic monthly payments. Other considerations include:

- For federal gift tax purposes, contributions are considered completed gifts of a present interest. Generally, no federal gift tax will be payable if a contribution is limited to the annual gift tax exclusion amount. For 2008, this is $12,000. A married couple can elect to "split" gifts for a total annual contribution of $24,000.

- If a contribution for a single beneficiary in one calendar year exceeds the annual exclusion amount, the donor may elect to treat the contribution as having been made ratably over a five-year period.[2] Thus, for 2008, an individual could contribute up to $60,000 for a single beneficiary in one calendar year. If a married couple elects gift splitting, $120,000 could be contributed.

- Contributions may be made to both a savings plan and a Coverdell Education Savings Account (Coverdell ESA) for the same beneficiary in the same year.

---

[1] "529" refers to Section 529 of the Internal Revenue Code, the section of federal law which authorizes these plans.
[2] If the donor dies before the end of the five years, a pro-rata portion of the contribution is included in his or her estate. Any amounts in a savings plan when the *beneficiary* dies will generally be includable in the beneficiary's estate.

Continued

"529" Higher Education Savings Plan

Distributions

For federal income tax purposes, distributions used to pay for qualified higher education expenses are generally excluded from income if the amount distributed does not exceed the amount of qualified education expenses. If a distribution is greater than the amount of qualified education expenses, a portion of the earnings may be subject to federal income tax and a 10% penalty tax may also apply.

- **Distributions due to the death or disability of the beneficiary, or the receipt of certain scholarships:** The earnings portion of the distribution is taxable as ordinary income to the recipient of the payment.

- **Rollover distributions:** Federal law allows one tax-free transfer every twelve months, from one savings plan to another, for the same beneficiary. Funds may be rolled from a 529 higher education savings plan to a 529 prepaid tuition plan and vice versa. If there is a change of beneficiary within the same family, the rollover must be completed within 60 days or the earnings portion will be subject to tax. If a new beneficiary is not part of the same family as the original beneficiary, the earnings portion of the transfer is subject to current income tax.

- **Other distributions:** If a distribution is made from a savings plan for any other reason, the earnings portion of the distribution is included in the taxable income of the recipient. A 10% penalty tax is also applied against the distributed earnings.

- **State and local law:** State and local law can vary widely from federal law with regard to the income tax treatment of contributions and withdrawals.

- **Coordination with other programs:** A savings plan beneficiary may generally also claim either the Hope Scholarship Credit or Lifetime Learning Credit (not both in the same tax year), receive a distribution from a Coverdell ESA, or claim the tuition and fees deduction, as long as the qualifying educational expenses are not the same.

Higher Education Savings Account Characteristics

Higher education savings plans have a number of characteristics that a potential donor should clearly understand.

- The beneficiary must be identified at the time an account is created.[1] Generally, the account owner is the primary contributor. However, others, such as grandparents, may also contribute.

- The account owner may change the beneficiary. If the new beneficiary is a member of the same family[2] as the original beneficiary, there is generally no current federal income tax.

- Amounts accumulated in a savings plan operated by one state generally may be used at educational institutions in a different state.

---

[1] An exception exists for organizations accumulating funds for future scholarships.
[2] Generally, siblings, children, grandchildren, parents, grandparents, nieces or nephews, uncles or aunts, their spouses, and first cousins are considered members of the same family.

Continued...

"529" Higher Education Savings Plan

- A higher education savings plan involves investment risk, including the potential to lose money. Contributing to a higher education saving plan does not ensure that your college funding goals will be met. Further, there is no guarantee that a beneficiary will be admitted to college.

- Neither the beneficiary nor the account owner is permitted to direct the investments in the account. Account owners are, however, permitted to choose among broad investment strategies established by the program sponsor. A change in investment strategy is generally permitted at least once each year or if a new beneficiary is named.

- Most savings plans require that funds in a custodial account become the property of the beneficiary when the beneficiary reaches his or her majority. A custodial account is one set up under the Uniform Gifts to Minors Act (UGMA), the Uniform Transfers to Minors Act (UTMA) or the local state version.

Other Issues to Consider

- **Home State Plans:** The fees, expenses, and features of higher education savings plans vary widely from state to state; some states have more than one plan. Consider whether the plan in your (or the beneficiary's) home state offers any tax or other benefits that are only available to participants in that particular state's plan.

- **Effect on financial aid:** Assets in a 529 savings plan are considered in the "Expected Family contribution" calculations only if the account is owned by an independent student or the parent of a dependent student.[1] Tax-free distributions from a 529 savings account (those used to pay for qualified education expenses) are not counted as income to either the parent or student in the financial aid determination process.[2]

Internet Resources

- **The College Board** – http://www.collegeboard.com

- **FinAid! The SmartStudent® Guide To Financial Aid** – http://www.finaid.org

- **College Savings Plan Network** – links to state-run web pages on prepaid tuition or college savings plans, at: http://www.collegesavings.org

- **U.S. Department of Education – student aid website** – http://www.studentaid.ed.gov

Seek Professional Advice

Individuals considering a higher education savings plan are faced with a number of income, gift, estate tax, and investment questions. The advice of appropriate tax, legal, need-based student aid, and financial professionals is highly recommended.

---

[1] Through a legislative drafting error, assets owned by a dependent student (i.e. arrangements where a dependent student is both owner and beneficiary) are not currently reported as an asset for financial aid purposes. This oversight was corrected by the College Cost Reduction and Access Act of 2007, with an effective date of July 1, 2009.
[2] See the U.S. Department of Education "Dear Colleague" letter of January 22, 2004, GEN-04-02.

How a "529" Higher Education Savings Plan Works

A "529" higher education savings plan is a tax-favored program operated by a state designed to help families save for future college costs. While the fees, expenses, and features of these plans will vary from state to state, as long as a plan satisfies the requirements of Section 529 of the Internal Revenue Code,[1] federal tax law provides tax benefits for both the contributor and the beneficiary.

How Does It Work?

Makes contributions to plan

Contributor

Higher Education Savings Plan

- A tax-advantaged account to save for higher education.
- Earnings accumulate tax deferred.
- Does not guarantee admission.
- If a beneficiary does not use funds, new beneficiary can be designated.

Tax-free withdrawals

Beneficiary

Taxable withdrawals

Withdrawals for Education

- Withdrawals for qualified expenses are generally tax-free.
- Qualified expenses generally include tuition, books, fees, supplies, equipment, and room and board.

Non-Qualified

- Any part of a withdrawal that is not applied to a qualified expense is considered non-qualified.
- The earnings portion of non-qualified amounts is taxable and a 10% penalty is generally applied.

---

[1] Federal law does not allow income tax deductions for contributions to 529 plans, although growth inside a plan is tax-deferred and qualified distributions are tax-exempt. State or local tax law can vary widely. 529 plans involve investment risk, including possible loss of funds, and there is no guarantee a college-funding goal will be met.

"529" Prepaid Tuition Plan

Federal law[1] allows the states and qualifying private colleges to establish tax-advantaged prepaid tuition plans. Under these plans, contributions are made into a qualified trust to prepay, at today's prices, some or all of a beneficiary's tuition costs. There are two general types of prepaid plans:

- **Contract plans:** Most prepaid plans are contract plans, which commit the account owner to purchase a specified number of years of tuition in exchange for a lump-sum or periodic payments. Generally speaking, contract plans offer lower prices for younger beneficiaries since the state or college will have more time to invest the money.

- **Unit plans:** Unit plans allow the account owner to purchase a fixed percentage of tuition. In a typical unit plan, one unit represents 1% of a year's tuition. All participants in the plan pay the same price for a unit.

Independent 529 Plan

A number of private colleges and universities have joined together to form the Independent 529 Plan. Under this arrangement, an account owner purchases tuition certificates (similar to units in a state-run plan) guaranteeing payment of a specified percentage of future tuition. These certificates can be "redeemed" at a participating college or university when the beneficiary reaches college age.

Key Definitions Under IRC Sec. 529

- **Qualified higher education expenses:** Tuition, fees, books, supplies, and equipment required for attendance typically qualify. Reasonable costs of room and board are also included if the student is attending school at least half time. Qualified higher education expenses include costs incurred to allow a special needs beneficiary to enroll at and attend an eligible institution.

- **Eligible educational institution:** Accredited post-high school educational institutions offering associate's, bachelor's, graduate level, or professional degrees qualify as eligible. Certain vocational schools are also included.

Contributions

Contributions to a prepaid plan must be in cash. Broadly speaking, anyone (parents, grandparents, friends, etc.) can contribute to a plan. Many state plans require that either the account owner or beneficiary be a state resident, either at the time an account is opened, or at the time the beneficiary begins school. Under federal law, contributions are not tax deductible and any growth in an account is tax-deferred.

- Contributions may be made to both a prepaid plan and a Coverdell Education Savings Account (Coverdell ESA) for the same beneficiary in the same year.

---

[1] "529" refers to Section 529 of the Internal Revenue Code, the section of federal law which authorizes these plans.

Continued

"529" Prepaid Tuition Plan

- For federal gift tax purposes, contributions are considered completed gifts of a present interest. Generally, no federal gift tax will be payable if a contribution is limited to the annual gift tax exclusion amount. For 2008, this amount is $12,000. A married couple can elect to "split" gifts for a total annual contribution of $24,000.

- If a contribution for a single beneficiary in one calendar year exceeds the annual gift tax exclusion amount, the donor may elect to treat the contribution as having been made ratably over a five-year period.[1] Thus, for 2008, an individual could contribute up to $60,000 for a single beneficiary in one calendar year. If a married couple elects gift splitting, $120,000 could be contributed.

Distributions

For federal income tax purposes, distributions used to pay for qualified higher-education expenses are generally excluded from income if the amount distributed does not exceed the amount of qualified education expenses. If the distribution from a prepaid plan is greater than the amount of qualified education expenses, a portion of the earnings may be subject to federal income tax and a 10% penalty tax may also apply.

- **Distributions due to the death or disability of the beneficiary, or the receipt of certain scholarships:** The earnings portion of the distribution is taxable as ordinary income to the recipient of the payment.

- **Rollover distributions:** If there is a change of beneficiary within the same family,[2] the rollover must be completed within 60 days or the earnings portion will be subject to tax. If a new beneficiary is not part of the same family as the original beneficiary, the earnings portion of the transfer is subject to current income tax. Funds may be rolled from a 529 prepaid tuition plan to a 529 higher education savings plan and vice versa.

- **Other distributions:** If a distribution is made from a plan for any other reason, the earnings portion of the distribution is included in the taxable income of the recipient. A 10% penalty tax is also applied against the distributed earnings.

- **State and local law can vary:** State and local law can vary widely from federal law with regard to the income tax treatment of contributions and withdrawals.

Other Issues to Consider

- **Limited use of funds:** Although the federal law governing prepaid plans has a very broad definition of "qualified higher education expenses," most prepaid tuition plans are limited to paying for tuition and required fees for undergraduate study; in a few programs, room and board is also covered. Costs that are not covered by the prepaid tuition plan must be paid for from other resources.

- **Increased tuition costs:** Many prepaid plans agree to cover all future increases in tuition costs. However, some plans limit that promise; if tuition costs increase more than the limit, will you have to contribute more money to the plan?

---

[1] If the donor dies before the end of the five years, a pro-rata portion of the contribution is included in his or her estate.
[2] Generally, siblings, children, grandchildren, parents, grandparents, nieces or nephews, uncles or aunts, their spouses, and first cousins are considered members of the same family.

Continued...

"529" Prepaid Tuition Plan

- **No guaranteed admission:** A prepaid tuition plan does not guarantee that a beneficiary will be admitted to college.

- **Change in plans:** If the beneficiary does not attend college, or does not complete the full course of study, what does it cost to cancel or withdraw from a prepaid plan? Does the plan allow the account owner to "roll over" the funds to another beneficiary? If a beneficiary attends an out-of-state school, what amount of tuition credit is allowed at the out-of-state school?

- **Home state plans:** Prepaid plans will vary widely from state to state. Consider whether the plan in your (or the beneficiary's) home state offers any tax or other benefits that are only available to participants in that particular state's plan.

- **Effect on financial aid eligibility:** Assets in a 529 prepaid tuition plan are considered in the "Expected Family Contribution" calculations only if the account is owned by an independent student or the parent of a dependent student.[1] Tax-free distributions from a 529 prepaid tuition plan (those used to pay for qualified educational expenses) are not counted as income to either the parent or student in the financial aid process.[2]

- **Ownership:** The donor is generally the owner of the funds. However, funds in a custodial account (an account set up under the Uniform Gifts to Minors Act (UGMA) or the Uniform Transfers to Minors Act (UTMA) become the property of the beneficiary when the beneficiary reaches his or her majority, or the age defined in state law.

- **Coordination with other programs:** A prepaid tuition plan beneficiary may generally also claim either the Hope Scholarship Credit or Lifetime Learning Credit (not both in the same tax year), receive a distribution from a Coverdell ESA, or claim the tuition and fees deduction, as long as the qualifying educational expenses are not the same.

Internet Resources

- **The College Board** – http://www.collegeboard.com

- **FinAid! The SmartStudent® Guide To Financial Aid** – http://www.finaid.org

- **College Savings Plan Network** – links to state-run web pages on prepaid tuition or college savings plans, at: http://www.collegesavings.org

- **Independent 529 Plan** - http://www.independent529plan.org

- **U.S. Department of Education – student aid website** – http://www.studentaid.ed.gov

Seek Professional Advice

Individuals considering a prepaid tuition plan are faced with a number of income tax, gift tax, estate tax and financial aid issues. Contributing to a prepaid plan does not guarantee that a college funding goal will be completely met. The advice of appropriate tax and financial professionals is highly recommended.

---

[1] Through a legislative drafting error, assets owned by a dependent student (i.e. arrangements where a dependent student is both owner and beneficiary) are not currently reported as an asset for financial aid purposes. This oversight was corrected by the College Cost Reduction and Access Act of 2007, with an effective date of July 1, 2009.

[2] See the U.S. Department of Education "Dear Colleague" letter of January 22, 2004, GEN-04-02.

How a "529" Prepaid Tuition Plan Works

A "529" prepaid tuition plan is a tax-favored program operated by a state or eligible private institution designed to help families prepay future college costs. While the specific details of these plans will vary, as long as a plan satisfies the requirements of Section 529 of the Internal Revenue Code,[1] federal tax law provides tax benefits for both the contributor and the beneficiary.

How Does It Work?

Makes contributions to plan.

Contributor

Prepaid Tuition Plan

- A program to prepay tomorrow's tuition at today's prices.
- Earnings accumulate tax deferred.
- Does not guarantee admission.
- If a beneficiary does not use funds, a new beneficiary can be designated.

Tax-Free Withdrawals

Taxable Withdrawals

Beneficiary

Withdrawals for Education

- Withdrawals for qualified expenses are generally tax-free.
- Generally covers only tuition and fees. In a few plans, also pays for room and board. Remaining costs must be paid for from other resources.

Non-Qualified

- Any part of a withdrawal that is not applied to a qualified expense is considered non-qualified.
- The earnings portion of non-qualified amounts is taxable and a 10% penalty is generally applied.

---

[1] Federal law does not allow deductions for contributions to 529 plans; growth inside a plan is tax-deferred and qualified distributions are tax-exempt. State or local income tax law can vary widely. The fees, expenses, and features of 529 plans will vary from state to state and from institution to institution and should be carefully considered. 529 plans involve risk, including the possible loss of funds or the need to make additional contributions. There is no guarantee a college-funding goal will be met.

Coverdell Education Savings Account

The Taxpayer Relief Act of 1997 (TRA '97) created a tax-favored education individual retirement account designed to help certain taxpayers save for a child's education. These plans have been renamed as Coverdell Education Savings Accounts. Money contributed to a Coverdell ESA is nondeductible, but earnings accumulate tax-deferred.

Contributions to a Coverdell ESA are treated as nontaxable gifts to the beneficiary. In general, to the extent that earnings are distributed to pay qualified educational expenses, the earnings are excluded from the beneficiary's income and are received free of federal income tax.[1]

The contributor need not be related to the beneficiary and there is no limit on the number of individual beneficiaries for whom one contributor may set up a Coverdell ESA.

Contributions

Federal income tax law currently limits contributions to a Coverdell ESA to $2,000 per beneficiary per year. Under existing legislation, this contribution limit will decrease to $500 per beneficiary per year beginning in 2011. Contributions must be in cash and must generally be made before the beneficiary reaches age 18. Other considerations include:

- **Due date for contributions:** Contributions must be made by the due date (not including extensions) of the contributor's return for the tax year of the contribution, generally April 15 of the following year.

- **Special needs beneficiaries:** Contributions to accounts for special needs beneficiaries may be made past the age of 18. See IRC Sec. 530(b)(1)(E).[2]

- **Multiple accounts:** May not be used to exceed the $2,000 limit for any one beneficiary.

- **Excess contributions:** Excess contributions are subject to a 6% excise tax paid by the beneficiary for each year that any excess remains in the account. See IRC Sec. 4973.

- **Contribution phase out:** The $2,000 per year limit is phased out for taxpayers with an adjusted gross income (AGI) above certain levels. For single filers, the contribution phases out when AGI is between $95,000 and $110,000. For married couples filing jointly, the phase-out range is between $190,000 and $220,000.

---

[1] The income tax treatment of Coverdell ESAs discussed here reflects federal law; state or local law may differ.
[2] A special needs beneficiary, generally, is an individual who, because of a physical, mental or emotional condition, needs extra time to complete his or her education.

Continued.

Coverdell Education Savings Account

- **Qualified tuition programs:** Contributions to a Coverdell ESA for a beneficiary are permitted in the same year in which a contribution is made for the same beneficiary to a qualified tuition program (QTP).[1]

- **Contributions by other entities:** Contributions to Coverdell ESA may be made by entities such as corporations or tax-exempt organizations.

Key Definitions

Coverdell Education Savings Accounts provide a tax-favored framework within which funds may be accumulated to pay for a beneficiary's "qualified education expenses." Depending on the educational level involved, the definition of qualified education expenses will change, as will the allowable educational institutions.

- **Kindergarten - Grade 12:** Qualified elementary and secondary education expenses refers to tuition, fees, academic tutoring, services for special needs individuals, books, supplies, and equipment. The term also includes room and board, uniforms, transportation, and supplemental services such as extended day programs. In specified circumstances, computer equipment and technology, including software and Internet connections, are qualified expenses. Contributions to a Qualified Tuition Plan, under IRC Sec. 529 are considered allowable expenses. The term "school" refers to an institution that provides elementary or secondary education (kindergarten through grade 12), under state law. This may be a public, private, or religious school.

- **Post-secondary:** Qualified higher education expenses include tuition, fees, books, and supplies and equipment needed for attendance. Room and board is included for students attending half time or greater. The term also encompasses the expenses incurred to allow a special needs beneficiary to enroll at and attend an eligible institution. Contributions to a Qualified Tuition Plan, under IRC Sec. 529, are also considered allowable expenses. The term "eligible educational institution" refers, generally, to accredited post-high school educational institutions offering associates, bachelors, graduate level, or professional degrees. Certain vocational schools are also included.

- **Family member:** Certain tax-free transfers of Coverdell ESA assets are permitted between family members. In addition to the spouse, family members include:

Family Members
Son or daughter, or their descendents
Stepson or stepdaughter
Brother, sister, stepbrother, or stepsister
Father or mother or ancestor of either
Stepfather or stepmother
Son or daughter of a brother or sister
Brother or sister of father or mother
Spouse of any person listed above
First cousins

---

[1] See IRC Sec. 529 for more detail.

Continued...

Coverdell Education Savings Account

Distributions

Distributions from a Coverdell ESA are considered to be part principal (the original contributions) and part earnings. If qualified education expenses exceed the total amount distributed from the account for the year, all of the distributed earnings are excluded from the beneficiary's income. If qualified education expenses are less than the amount distributed, a portion of the distributed earnings will be included in the beneficiary's taxable income for the year. An additional 10% tax may be added to the portion included in taxable income.

- **Additional tax:** Any earnings distributions included in a beneficiary's income because they are not used for qualified educational expenses are subject to an additional 10% tax. Certain exceptions apply, including the death or disability of the beneficiary, or the receipt of certain scholarships.

- **Rollovers/change of beneficiary:** If a beneficiary does not use the funds held for him or her in a Coverdell ESA, the money may be distributed and rolled over into a new account for a different beneficiary. If the rollover occurs within 60 days of the distribution, and if the new beneficiary is a member of the original beneficiary's family[1] and has not yet attained age 30, the distribution is not taxable to the original beneficiary. The same objective may be reached by simply changing the beneficiary of a Coverdell ESA. As long as the new beneficiary is a member of the original beneficiary's family, and has not reached age 30, the change is not treated as a taxable distribution.

- **Beneficiary reaches age 30:** If a beneficiary reaches the age of 30 and there are still funds remaining in the Coverdell ESA, federal tax law deems the remaining funds to be distributed and, therefore, subject to tax for that year. The 10% additional tax also applies to amounts so distributed because of the beneficiary reaching age 30. If a beneficiary dies before age 30, any remaining account balance must be distributed to the beneficiary's estate (and thus become taxable) within 30 days of death.

- **Special needs beneficiaries:** The requirement that any funds left in a Coverdell ESA must be distributed when the beneficiary reaches age 30 does not apply to a special needs beneficiary. Similarly, a special needs individual may be the beneficiary of an account rollover even though he or she is age 30 or older.

- **Coordination with other programs:** A Coverdell ESA beneficiary may generally also claim either the Hope Scholarship Credit or the Lifetime Learning Credit (not both in the same tax year), receive a distribution from a qualified tuition plan, or claim the tuition and fees deduction, as long as the qualifying educational expenses are not the same.

---

[1] As defined in IRC Sec. 529 (e)(2)

Continued

Coverdell Education Savings Account

Other Issues

- **Effect on financial aid eligibility:** Assets in a Coverdell ESA are considered in the "Expected Family Contribution" calculations only if the account is owned by an independent student or the parent of a dependent student.[1] Tax-free distributions from a Coverdell ESA (those used to pay for qualified education expenses) are not counted as income to either the parent or student in the financial aid determination process.[2]

  Private institutions, however, may consider Coverdell ESA assets and income into consideration when awarding school-based financial aid, regardless of who is listed as the account owner.

- **Loss of control:** Ownership of the funds contributed to a Coverdell ESA will eventually pass to the beneficiary. A donor may not simply "take back" the account, as can be done with IRC Sec. 529 qualified tuition plans.

- **Federal bankruptcy impact:** If certain requirements are met, federal bankruptcy law can protect a portion (in some cases all) of the assets in a Coverdell ESA from creditors.

- **Future federal legislative changes:** A number of the provisions in federal law affecting Coverdell ESAs came into being with the Economic Growth and Tax Relief Reconciliation Act (EGTRRA) of 2001. Unless the law is changed, most of the provisions of the EGTRRA, including those affecting Coverdell ESAs, will expire after 2010, when prior law will be reinstated.

Seek Professional Guidance

TRA '97 presented each taxpayer with a wide range of tax-favored tools for funding a child's education. The Economic Growth and Tax Relief Reconciliation Act of 2001 further enhanced these tools. A qualified tax or financial professional can help select the best approach.

---

[1] Through a legislative drafting error, assets owned by a dependent student (i.e. arrangements where a dependent student is both owner and beneficiary) are not currently reported as an asset for financial aid purposes. This oversight was corrected by the College Cost Reduction and Access Act of 2007, with an effective date of July 1, 2009.

[2] See the U.S. Department of Education "Dear Colleague" letter of January 22, 2004, GEN-04-02.

How a Coverdell ESA Works

A Coverdell Education Savings Account is a tax-favored account designed to help families accumulate funds for future education costs. While contributions (limited to $2,000 per beneficiary per year) are not deductible, earnings accumulate tax deferred, and qualified withdrawals are tax-free[1].

How Does It Work?

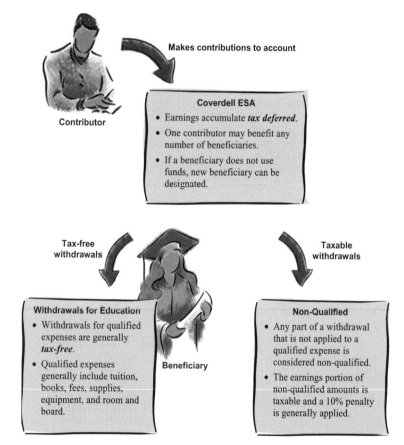

Makes contributions to account

Contributor

Coverdell ESA
- Earnings accumulate *tax deferred*.
- One contributor may benefit any number of beneficiaries.
- If a beneficiary does not use funds, new beneficiary can be designated.

Tax-free withdrawals

Taxable withdrawals

Beneficiary

Withdrawals for Education
- Withdrawals for qualified expenses are generally *tax-free*.
- Qualified expenses generally include tuition, books, fees, supplies, equipment, and room and board.

Non-Qualified
- Any part of a withdrawal that is not applied to a qualified expense is considered non-qualified.
- The earnings portion of non-qualified amounts is taxable and a 10% penalty is generally applied.

---

[1] The rules discussed here concern federal tax law; state or local law may vary.

Education Savings Plans Compared

Benefit or Feature	"529" Prepaid Tuition Plan[1]	"529" Higher Education Savings Plan[1]	Coverdell Education Savings Account
Basic concept	Buy tomorrow's tuition at today's prices.	Tax-advantaged savings account to accumulate funds for higher education.	Tax-advantaged savings account to accumulate funds for education.
Federal income tax treatment	Contributions are not deductible; growth is tax-deferred; withdrawals for qualified higher education expenses are exempt from tax.	Contributions are not deductible; growth is tax-deferred; withdrawals for qualified higher education expenses are exempt from tax.	Contributions are not deductible; growth is tax-deferred; withdrawals for qualified education expenses are exempt from tax.
State or local income tax treatment	Varies. Some states follow federal income tax law, while others do not.	Varies. Some states follow federal income tax law, while others do not.	Varies. Some states follow federal income tax law, while others do not.
Level of investment risk	Generally a low level of risk. Sponsoring state or organization typically promises to invest funds to match tuition increases. Later contributions may be required.	Varies, depending on the underlying investments. An investment manager typically manages the funds. Both gains and losses are possible.	Varies, depending on the underlying investment. A wide range of self-directed investments is available. Both gains and losses are possible.
Where to purchase	Directly from the state or private institution involved.	Investment brokers, banks, credit unions, or directly from the state involved.	Investment brokers, banks, credit unions.
Who can contribute?	Generally, anyone. Residency restrictions may apply.	Generally, anyone. Residents in one state can usually invest in another state's plan.	Generally, anyone.
How much can be contributed?	Contributions must be in cash and may not exceed what is needed to fund the beneficiary's higher education expenses. The program sponsor will specify the maximum amount.	Contributions must be in cash and may not exceed what is needed to fund the beneficiary's higher education expenses. The program sponsor will specify the maximum amount.[2]	Contributions must be in cash and may not exceed $2,000 per beneficiary per year.
Beneficiary age limits for contributions?	None	None	Before age 18 unless a special needs student.
How are payments made?	In a lump-sum or periodic payments.	In a lump-sum or periodic payments.	Typically, in annual contributions.

[1] "529" refers to Section 529 of the Internal Revenue Code, the section of federal law which authorizes these plans.
[2] In some higher education savings programs, more than $250,000 may be contributed for a single beneficiary.

Continued...

Education Savings Plans Compared

Benefit or Feature	"529" Prepaid Tuition Plan	"529" Higher Education Savings Plan	Coverdell Education Savings Account
Do income limitations apply to the donor?	No	No	Yes. The allowable contribution is phased out for donors whose AGI exceeds certain limits.[1]
Who controls the funds?	Generally, the donor.[2] If the account is a custodial account, the beneficiary becomes the owner when he or she reaches age 21 (18 in some states).	Generally, the donor.[2] If the account is a custodial account, the beneficiary becomes the owner when he or she reaches age 21 (18 in some states).	Generally, the donor.[2] If the account is a custodial account, the beneficiary becomes the owner when he or she reaches age 21 (18 in some states).
What expenses are covered?	Typically, tuition only. In a few programs room and board is also included.	Generally, most costs required to attend a qualified post-high school educational institution. May includes tuition, fees, books, supplies, and equipment as well as reasonable costs for room and board.	A wide range of expenses are allowed, to attend Kindergarten thru 12th grade, as well as post-high school educational institutions. May includes tuition, fees, books, supplies, and equipment, as well as reasonable costs for room and board.
What schools may the beneficiary attend?	Prepaid tuition plans typically limit attendance to same-state post-high school institutions.	Funds accumulated in the savings plan of one state may usually be used at institutions of higher education throughout the U.S. Some foreign schools also qualify.	For K-12, any school that qualifies under state law, including public, private, or religious schools. For post-high school, most institutions in the U.S. qualify.
Effect on financial aid?	Generally reduces financial aid. Account owned by student penalized more than parent-owned account.	Generally reduces financial aid. Account owned by student penalized more than parent-owned account.	Generally reduces financial aid. Account owned by student penalized more than parent-owned account.
May account be rolled-over to other family members?	Yes	Yes	Yes
Legislative issues	Key federal law is permanent.	Key federal law is permanent.	Key federal law expires after 2010.

---

[1] For unmarried individuals, the contribution is phased out when adjusted gross income (AGI) is between $95,000 - $110,000. For married couples filing jointly, the phase-out range is an AGI of $190,000 - $220,000.

[2] With a "529" prepaid tuition plan or a "529" savings plan, if the assets are not used for higher education they may be returned to the donor. In a Coverdell Education Savings Account, if the assets are not used for higher education, they will ultimately become the property of the beneficiary.

Paying for College Today

For many Americans, providing a college education for their children has long been an important family goal. Paying for that education, however, has never been easy. Over the past few years it has become even more of a challenge as college costs have risen faster than the general level of inflation.[1]

Few families seem able to save enough to fully fund four or more years of higher education. For many students, some type of financial aid, in the form of grants, scholarships, loans, or work-study, is needed to make the dream a reality.

And such financial aid is available. The federal government, through the Department of Education, provides approximately $78 billion a year[2] in student aid, through a variety of programs. Private organizations and foundations, state governments, as well as the schools and universities themselves, are additional sources of financial aid.

Applying for Financial Aid

The vast majority of financial aid is awarded through a standardized process which, in general, proceeds as follows.

- **Free Application for Federal Student Aid (FAFSA):** The student and his or her family complete the Free Application for Federal Student Aid, the single form used to apply for all types of federal aid; it is also used to apply for state financial aid at many public and private colleges. The FAFSA collects information such as family size and number of family members in college, in addition to financial data such as income and benefits, and net assets.

- **Student Aid Report (SAR):** Using the information supplied on the FAFSA, the government calculates the amount a family is expected to contribute toward a student's education, known as the Expected Family Contribution (EFC). This information is reported on the SAR and is sent to the student. The same information is sent to the financial aid offices of the colleges the student listed on the FAFSA.

- **CSS/Financial Aid PROFILE:** A few schools will require a prospective student to complete an additional standardized financial questionnaire known as PROFILE. The data collected on this form is used to award a college's institutional aid.

- **Cost of attendance:** To calculate financial aid eligibility, colleges need to first determine the cost of attendance at the institution. The cost of attendance includes, in addition to tuition, fees and books, general living expenses such as rent or dormitory costs, transportation, and personal expenses a student could be expected to incur during the nine-month academic year.

---

[1] See "Trends in College Pricing – 2007," published by The College Board, page 4.
[2] Source: Department of Education website: http://studentaid.ed.gov/, accessed 11/28/07.

Continued...

Paying for College Today

- **Financial aid eligibility or financial need:** Eligibility for need-based financial aid is determined by taking the college's calculated cost of attendance and subtracting the EFC. The difference, if any, is the amount the student may receive in need-based forms of financial aid, including grants, scholarships, and loans.

- **Financial aid package:** Once the need-based eligibility is determined, a college's financial aid office will attempt to provide for that need with a combination or package of financial aid funds that may include grants, loans, scholarships, and work-study funds. The amount and type of financial aid will vary between colleges. In some cases a financial aid package may not cover all costs, leaving a gap that the student and his or her family must cover from other sources.

Federal Financial Aid

The largest source[1] of financial aid provided to college students in the U.S. is from programs funded and/or administered by the federal government, with much of the support coming in the form of student loans. The major elements in federal student aid are:

- **Federal Pell Grants:** Pell Grants are designed to assist very low-income undergraduate students and are awarded based on expected family contribution (EFC). Only students with very low EFCs are awarded Pell Grants. Pell Grants do not have to be repaid.

- **Federal Supplemental Educational Opportunity Grant (FSEOG):** Like Pell grants, FSEOGs do not have to be repaid. They are awarded to undergraduate students with exceptional financial need.

- **Federal Perkins Loans:** Perkins loans are federal low-interest loans. They are awarded based on need and on the availability of funds. No interest accrues while the student is attending school at least halftime. Repayment begins nine months after the student ceases to attend at least half time.

- **Federal subsidized and unsubsidized loan programs, Stafford loans:** There are two different loan programs currently available, with the same interest rates and repayment terms. Direct loans are loans made by the federal government; FFEL loans are made by private lenders, such as banks or credit unions, and are guaranteed by the federal government. A school will usually offer one program or the other. Subsidized loans, made on the basis of financial need, do not accrue interest, nor require repayment, until six months after the student ceases to attend college at least half time. Unsubsidized loans differ in that they are not need-based and interest accrues from the date the loan is disbursed.

- **PLUS loans:** There are two versions of this program: (1) Parent PLUS, allowing parents of undergraduate students to borrow on behalf of their student, and (2) Grad PLUS, allowing graduate and professional students to borrow funds for their own education. PLUS loans require that the borrower not have an "adverse credit history."

- **Federal Work-Study Program (FWS):** The FWS program provides federally funded employment for qualified students in both on-campus and off-campus positions. The amount a student can earn is limited to the amount of the award.

---

[1] Source: Department of Education website: http://studentaid.ed.gov, accessed 11/28/07.

Continued

Paying for College Today

Other Financial Aid Programs

In addition to the financial aid programs provided through the federal government, there is a wide range of aid available through other organizations.

- **State programs:** Many state governments have their own financial aid programs. Such programs include need-based grants (the family has to show financial aid eligibility), as well as work-study programs, loan-forgiveness programs for targeted careers, and merit-based scholarship programs.

- **Institutional aid programs:** To supplement federal and state financial aid, many schools have additional means of making college affordable. Scholarships, based on either academic or athletic ability, are one example. Some schools have their own student loan programs to replace or supplement federal loan programs. Some institutions offer installment or deferred payment plans for tuition, or a discount may be offered if more than one child from the same family is enrolled, or if the parents are alumni.

- **Military aid programs:** The Armed Forces have available a number of programs to enable prospective, active duty, and former service personnel to attend college. Reserve Officer Training Corps (ROTC) scholarships are available at a number of schools. A ROTC/NROTC Scholarship or an appointment to one of the service academies, West Point, Annapolis, or the Air Force Academy effectively ends any concerns about paying for college. Current active duty personnel can apply for tuition assistance through their education officer. For former service people, the various GI Bills and the Army or Navy college savings funds are additional sources of college financing.

- **Private scholarships:** Many private organizations make available scholarships, based on both need and merit. Many scholarships are for relatively small amounts of money or for only a single year and a student may need to apply to many different scholarship programs. Scholarship information is widely available at bookstores and libraries, in high school and college financial aid offices and on the Internet.

Tax Advantaged Strategies

Congress has passed legislation[1] designed to lighten the burden of paying for higher education. Because the rules surrounding these strategies can be complicated, the counsel of a qualified tax or financial advisor is recommended.

- **Education tax credits:** Two separate tax credits are available: (1) the Hope Scholarship Credit, of up to $1,800[2] per student, for tuition and fees paid during the first two calendar years of college, and (2) the Lifetime Learning Credit, providing a credit of up to $2,000 per return for qualified education expenses. A taxpayer may not take both credits in the same tax year. Other limitations apply.

---

[1] The rules discussed here concern federal income tax law; state or local law may vary.
[2] 2008 value. The credit amount is subject to adjustment for inflation in future years.

Continued...

Paying for College Today

- **Interest deduction on education loans:** A deduction of up to $2,500, taken as an adjustment to gross income, is available for interest paid on student loans. Certain restrictions and requirements apply.

- **Tuition and fees deduction:** Through 2007, a taxpayer could deduct, as an adjustment to gross income, up to $4,000 for qualified higher education tuition and related expenses for a qualifying individual at an eligible educational institution. At press time, Congress was considering extending this deduction to future tax years.

- **Exclusion of U.S. Savings Bond interest:** Interest earned on U.S. Savings Bonds is normally taxable. However, if a taxpayer pays qualified education expenses, the interest earned on qualified U.S. savings bonds may be excluded from income. Certain income level and filing status requirements apply.

- **Withdrawals from Traditional IRAs before age 59½:** Withdrawals from traditional IRAs used to pay qualified education expenses are exempt from the 10% penalty on withdrawals before age 59-1/2. Amounts withdrawn, however, will generally be subject to regular income tax.

Other Approaches

A number of other approaches can be used to help pay for college expenses. Consider carefully the pros and cons of each suggestion, including the income tax ramifications, the impact on any possible financial aid, the likelihood that a student might not complete college, and any effect on your long-term financial goals.

- **Home equity loan:** Parents with equity in the family home may want to consider taking out a home equity loan. If certain conditions are met, the interest on such a loan can be tax deductible.

- **Life insurance cash values:** Cash-value life insurance policies can provide another source of low-cost loans.[1]

- **Borrow from qualified plans:** Some types of employer-sponsored qualified plans allow a participant to borrow from the plan. There are generally strict rules regarding the repayment of such loans.

- **Skip a year:** Some colleges will admit a student and defer admission allowing the student to live at home, work full-time and save the earnings for college.

- **Live at home and commute:** A family can save several thousand dollars a year by having a student live at home and commute to school.

- **Choose a lower cost school:** State-supported public colleges and universities generally charge a lower tuition for in-state residents. To further save money, some students begin their studies at less expensive community or junior colleges and then transfer to a four-year school to complete their degree.

---

[1] Loans from a cash-value life insurance policy will reduce the available death benefit. If a policy lapses or is surrendered with a loan outstanding, the loan will be treated as taxable income in the current year, to the extent of gain in the policy. Also, policies considered to be modified endowment contracts (MECs) are subject to special rules.

Continu

Paying for College Today

Other Resources

There are a number of published references and guides to paying for college available in bookstores and public libraries, in both print and CD formats. In addition to providing a wide range of reference materials, many high schools and colleges offer free financial aid seminars presented by professional financial aid administrators. The state and federal agencies involved in higher education are also excellent sources of information.

For those linked to the internet, there are a number of websites which can provide information.

- **The College Board** – http://www.collegeboard.com
- **FinAid! The SmartStudent® Guide To Financial Aid** – http://www.finaid.org
- **U.S. Department of Education – student aid website** – http://www.studentaid.ed.gov
- **Free Application For Federal Student Aid (FAFSA)** - http://www.fafsa.ed.gov/
- **CSS/Financial Aid Profile®** - https://profileonline.collegeboard.com/

Begin Early and Seek Professional Advice

The key step in paying for a child's education is to begin the process as early as possible. A great deal of information, as well as counseling, is available from high schools, colleges and the various government agencies involved in higher education, at little or no cost. Questions involving income, gift, or estate taxes should be carefully reviewed with competent professional advisors.

Ways to Pay for College

For many parents, providing a college education for their children is an important family goal. Paying for that education, however, has never been easy. The key step is to begin the planning process as early as possible.

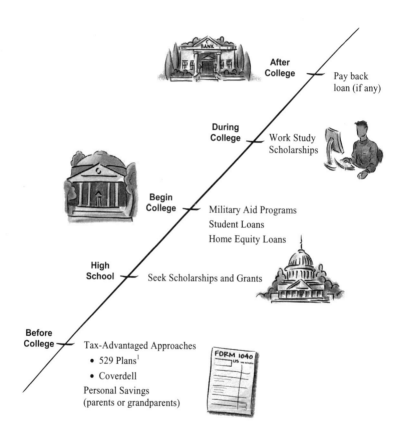

After College — Pay back loan (if any)

During College — Work Study / Scholarships

Begin College — Military Aid Programs / Student Loans / Home Equity Loans

High School — Seek Scholarships and Grants

Before College — Tax-Advantaged Approaches
- 529 Plans[1]
- Coverdell

Personal Savings (parents or grandparents)

FORM 1040

---

[1] Federal law does not allow deductions for contributions to 529 plans, although growth inside a plan is tax-deferred and qualified distributions are tax-exempt. State or local tax law, however, can vary widely. 529 plans involve investment risk, including possible loss of funds, and there is no guarantee a college-funding goal will be met. The fees, expenses, and features of 529 plans vary from state to state.

Choosing a College

With over 4,200[1] colleges, universities and professional schools offering post-high school education in the United States, choosing the right school can be confusing. Although the final choice is an individual one, careful (and early) planning is essential. The following list of key points can help in the decision making process.

Admission

One of the first questions a student faces is whether or not he or she will be accepted for admission to a particular school.

- **Qualifications:** Does the student have the necessary academic and personal qualifications?

- **Ability to pay:** Does the school consider ability to pay as a factor in considering an application? Most colleges evaluate applications on a need-blind basis.

- **Popular schools:** Certain, popular big-name schools may be extremely difficult to enter simply because an overwhelming number of students apply. Less well-known schools may provide an equal education and have admission standards less difficult to meet.

Cost

With the continually rising cost of a college education, paying for school is often a major concern.

- **Affordability:** How affordable is a school? In general, public schools, supported in some part by tax dollars, tend to be less expensive than private institutions.

- **Living expenses:** A family may want to weigh the cost of dormitories or off-campus housing versus the cost of having the student live at home and commute to a local school.

- **Cash flow or savings?** Can the education be paid for from current cash flow? If not, has enough money been saved to pay for the entire education or are additional funds needed?

- **Student debt:** Is the student or family willing and/or able to take on the financial burden of student loans?

- **Financial aid:** How much and what type of financial aid can a school make available? Some forms of aid are based on need; others on merit.

- **Scholarships:** Are there scholarships available for which the student may qualify?

---

[1] Source: Statistical Abstract of the United States: 2007. See Table No. 267 - Higher Education – Summary: 1980 to 2004.

Continued...

Choosing a College

Academics

What type and quality of education does the institution provide?

- **Specific programs:** For those individuals who have a clear idea of what they want to do in life, does the school have the specific type of education and training needed?

- **Breadth:** For students who are less sure of their career goals, does the institution offer the breadth of courses and majors needed for a good liberal arts education? Can a student be undeclared until a major is chosen or must a major and course of study be decided upon immediately?

- **Academic standards:** Are academic standards rigorous or relaxed?

- **Time to complete:** Can a student complete a course of study in four years? Overcrowding may mean that key required courses are not available when needed.

- **Class size:** Are classes large or small? Do the professors do the teaching or is much of the teaching done by graduate students? How much personal contact is there between professors and students?

- **Special programs:** Are there special academic programs available, such as internships or study abroad programs?

Personality

Each college or university has its own personality. Will the student enjoy living and working at a particular school and with a particular student body for four years?

- **Size:** Large institutions can offer greater choice, both academically and in extracurricular activities; however, their large size may be intimidating to some students. Smaller schools can be more personal, with greater opportunities for student involvement.

- **Single sex:** Some students may feel more comfortable and perform better academically at a single-sex, rather than at a co-educational institution.

- **Religious affiliation:** A religious focus to campus life may be an important consideration for a student.

- **Student body diversity:** Is it important that a student body be widely diverse? Or, would a student feel more comfortable at a school where one ethnic or socio-economic group is predominant?

- **Social life:** What is the predominant "flavor" to the social life on campus?

- **Athletics or other extracurricular programs:** Does the student have an interest in a sport or other extracurricular activity that may not be available at certain schools?

Continue

Choosing a College

Location

Very often the geographic location of a college is a major factor in deciding which school to attend.

- **Locale:** Should the student live at home or move out to attend school?

- **Distance:** How far is a school from home? The cost of round-trip transportation between home and school can affect how often a student is able to return home.

- **Housing type:** What type of housing is available? Do most students live in school dorms or is off-campus housing the preferred choice?

- **Community:** Urban, rural, or suburban? Institutions located in large cities offer diversity, while schools located in rural areas can offer a strong sense of community. Institutions located in suburban areas can offer both.

- **Region:** Which part of the Country? A student from one part of the country may simply want a change and choose to attend a college in a different area. For example, a student raised in a large city may want to attend a school located in a rural area; a student from the Northeast may want to study on the West Coast.

- **Safety:** How safe is the school environment? Since 1991, federal law has required colleges to make campus crime statistics available to students and applicants.

Additional Resources

There are a number of excellent college guides and handbooks (in both book and CD format) available in bookstores and public libraries. State and federal agencies involved in higher education are also excellent sources of information. In addition, there are a number of sites on the Internet which can provide information, including:

- **University of Texas:** Maintains a useful website with links to the home pages of many schools in the U. S., at: http://www.utexas.edu/world/univ/alpha/#toc

- **The College Board:** Maintains a searchable database of colleges on their website located at: http://www.collegeboard.com

College and Financial Aid Calendar

As Early as Possible

- Explore college options.
- Research Scholarship opportunities via the Internet.

Junior Year/Summer Prior to Senior Year

- Visit campuses and narrow college choices.
- Learn how to apply for scholarships.
- Find out the priority admission application period for the colleges you wish to attend.

Senior Year In High School

November	December	January
• Admission application period for many colleges begins.	• If needed, complete and mail the CSS Profile. • Attend any financial aid nights offered at your school.	• Apply for financial aid every year at this time. • Mail the completed FAFSA. • Apply for scholarships.
February	**March**	**April/May**
• Student aid report received from processor. Review for accuracy. • Submit required documents to financial aid offices.	• Receive and compare financial aid award letters.	• Make final decision regarding college choice. Submit any required deposits.
June/July	**August/September**	
• Prepare for starting college. • Work extra hours and save money.	• Start college. • Look for on-campus employment.	

Growth in College Costs
1990-2005

Average Annual Costs[1]

School	Tuition & Fees		Room & Board		Total		Average Annual Increase
	1990	2005	1990	2005	1990	2005	
Public 4 Year	$2,035	$5,948	$3,289	$6,657	$5,324	$12,605	$485
Private 4 Year	$10,348	$25,600	$4,750	$9,098	$15,098	$34,698	$1,307
Public 2 Year	$756	$1,847	$2,543	$4,487	$3,299	$6,334	$202
Private 2 Year	$5,196	$12,182	$3,474	$7,718	$8,670	$19,900	$749

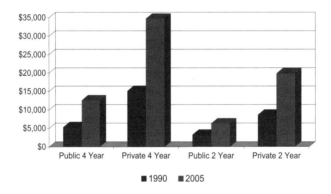

■ 1990 ■ 2005

---

[1] Figures shown are for in-state students. Source: Statistical Abstract of the United States: 2007. See Report no. 282, Institutions of Higher Education - Charges: 1985 to 2005.

Projected Costs of Education

	Luke	Elle	Luker Jr
Name of school	School 1	School 2	School 3
Years until college begins	5	8	11
Years to attend college	6	6	8
Current costs to attend one year	$18,000	$18,000	$22,000
Estimated annual increase in costs	4.00%	4.00%	4.50%
Amount needed at start of college	**$ 125,354**	**$ 141,006**	**$ 271,869**
Amount currently saved	$35,000	$25,000	$10,000
Estimated growth rate	6.00%	6.00%	6.00%
Savings at start of college	**$47,210**	**$40,354**	**$19,316**
Additional amount required	**$78,144**	**$ 100,653**	**$ 252,553**
Monthly deposits for each child	**$1,114**	**$ 815**	**$1,349**

Total monthly deposits for all children
$3,279

Cash Management Tools

There is a wide range of accounts available to a consumer to control his or her monthly cash flow. Such cash management tools are characterized by easy access to funds, as well as providing for safety of principal.[1] They are typically used for transaction purposes, or as a place to store readily available savings.

Transaction-Oriented Accounts

There are several different types of accounts that are used for transactions such as paying bills.

- **Demand deposits (checking accounts):** Demand deposits in banks and savings and loans are accounts which do not earn interest and which are payable to the owner on demand. Checks or electronic debit cards are used to transfer funds to a third party. Most financial institutions offering demand deposits are protected by federal deposit insurance, on account balances up to $100,000.

- **Negotiable order of withdrawal (NOW):** NOW accounts are a type of interest bearing savings account against which checks can be written or electronic debits made. Credit unions offer a similar option in the form of a share-draft account. Most financial institutions offering NOW accounts are protected by federal deposit insurance on account balances up to $100,000.

- **Money market deposit accounts (MMDAs):** Like NOW accounts, MMDAs are a form of savings account against which checks can be written. Unlike NOW accounts, however, MMDAs are limited to six transactions per month, of which only three may be check transfers. Transfers in excess of these limits can be subject to penalties. Minimum balance requirements for MMDA accounts tend to be larger than for NOW accounts, and MMDA accounts usually pay a slightly higher rate of interest. Most financial institutions offering MMDA accounts are protected by federal deposit insurance, on account balances up to $100,000.[2]

Savings Accounts

Savings accounts differ from transaction-oriented accounts in that access to funds in savings accounts may be restricted.

- **Statement savings accounts:** Statement savings accounts, formerly known as "passbook" savings accounts, usually accept small deposits, have no fixed maturity date and pay a relatively low interest rate. Banks and savings and loans that provide this type of account can require a 30-day notice before funds are withdrawn. In practice, however, most institutions do not require advance notice before allowing depositors to withdraw funds. Most financial institutions offering statement savings accounts are protected by federal deposit insurance, on account balances up to $100,000.

---

[1] Most checking and savings accounts in the U.S. are protected by federal deposit insurance, for amounts up to $100,000; certain retirement accounts are protected up to $250,000. Beginning in 2011, the coverage limits on federally insured deposits will be subject to adjustment for inflation, in increments of $10,000.

[2] Some mutual funds offer a money market account with a name similar to money market deposit account. These mutual funds are not protected by federal deposit insurance.

Continued...

Cash Management Tools

- **Certificates of deposit (CDs):** CDs are bank or credit union liabilities which have a fixed maturity date and require certain minimums, for example, $10,000. Some institutions will issue a CD for as little as $500. Interest rates can be either fixed or variable. A substantial penalty[1] generally applies for withdrawals made before the maturity date. Most financial institutions offering these certificates are protected by federal deposit insurance, on account balances up to $100,000.

- **Jumbo CDs:** Jumbo CDs are similar to regular CDs in that they are obligations of the issuing financial institution, have a fixed maturity date, and earn a specified rate of interest. Technically, jumbo CDs are issued only in amounts of $100,000 or more. The interest rate can be either fixed or variable. Penalties apply if funds are withdrawn before the maturity date.[1] Most institutions offering these certificates are protected by federal deposit insurance, on account balances up to $100,000. Amounts in excess of $100,000 are not protected by federal deposit insurance.

Other Options

In addition to the traditional cash management tools available through banks, savings and loans, and credit unions, several other options are available.

- **Money market mutual funds (MMMFs):** Money market mutual funds are a specialized type of mutual fund that invests in short term debt such as CDs, high-grade commercial paper, and U.S. Treasury securities. MMMFs are sold by prospectus[2] and usually have minimum balance and transaction limits. Such funds strive to maintain a constant share price of $1.00 per share. There is no guarantee that a fund will be able to maintain a constant share price, nor is there government insurance for such funds. MMMFs typically pay a slightly higher return than do federally insured accounts.

- **U.S. savings bonds:** U.S. savings bonds are both issued and redeemed by the federal government. As an asset class, they are considered to be very safe from default risk and thus earn a relatively low rate of interest. There are three types of savings bonds:

  - **Series EE bonds:** Series EE bonds sold in paper form are issued at 50% of face value, in face amounts ranging from $50 to $10,000, and earn interest through gradual increases in redemption value. Series EE bonds sold electronically are issued at face amount, in any dollar amount ranging from $25 to $30,000. Series EE bonds issued on or after May 1, 2005 earn a fixed rate of interest; bonds issued before that date earn a variable rate of interest which is adjusted every six months. Series EE bonds issued before February, 2003 could be redeemed after being held six months; bonds issued after that date may be cashed any time after being held 12 months. A bond redeemed within 5 years of issuance is subject to a 3-month interest penalty.

---

[1] For certificates with a maturity of less than one year, the penalty is loss of three months' interest; for certificates longer than one year, the penalty is loss of six months' interest.

[2] The prospectus contains valuable information concerning how an investment works, its goals and risks, and any charges or expenses involved. The prospectus is intended to provide an investor with the facts necessary to make an informed investment decision.

Continued.

Cash Management Tools

- **Series I bonds:** Series I savings bonds strive to provide some protection against inflation. The paper form of Series I bonds is sold at face value in standard denominations ranging from $50 to $10,000; bonds purchased electronically can be bought at face amount in any amount from $25 to $30,000. Series I bonds earn an interest rate that is adjusted periodically for changes in the Consumer Price Index.
- **Series HH bonds:** Series HH bonds were issued at face value, in $500, $1,000, $5,000, and $10,000 denominations, and pay interest every six months. August 2004 was the last month that the U.S. Treasury issued new HH bonds. Before that date, investors could acquire HH bonds by exchanging matured EE/E bonds, or by reinvesting matured series HH/H bonds.

- **Asset management accounts:** Asset management accounts, available through banks, brokerages and insurance companies, combine a number of different financial tools in one package. Such accounts typically include a brokerage account, bank checking account, and a money market mutual fund. The linked accounts enable excess cash to be automatically swept into the money market fund. Other features such as a credit or debit card, or personal line of credit, may also be included. A consolidated monthly statement covers all accounts.

The various elements of an asset management account may or may not be protected by federal deposit insurance. For example, funds kept in a bank checking account are usually protected by federal deposit insurance, on account balances up to $100,000. Dollar amounts kept in a money market fund, however, are not protected by government deposit insurance.

The Personal Budget

The basic purpose of a personal budget is to plan how an individual's money will be spent. Given limited financial resources, a budget is a method of managing personal cash flow, to both meet current obligations as well as provide for future spending.

Reasons to Prepare a Personal Budget

The creation and use of a personal budget serves two key functions.

- **A planning tool:** Correctly used, a personal budget can insure that income and expenditures match, both in amount and timing. It can serve to spotlight potential cash-flow problems, as well as identify opportunities to make better use of current income.

- **A yardstick to measure progress:** By comparing the planned budget against actual results, an individual can see if progress is being made toward meeting specific goals. This measuring process will often highlight areas where changes should be made.

Preparing a Personal Budget

There are a number of steps involved in preparing and using a personal budget.

- **Past income and expenditures:** This initial step is to record information on past cash flow, both income and spending. Ideally, a year's worth of data should be gathered, to even out the effect of seasonal variations[1]. Paycheck stubs, check registers, cancelled checks, copies of paid bills and recent income tax returns are excellent sources of this information. If desired, an individual may want to keep a daily spending diary for a short period of time.

- **Establish goals and designate resources:** Explicit goals should be set, with dollar amounts and a realistic time frame within which each goal is to be accomplished. From the available cash flow, specific dollar amounts are dedicated towards meeting each goal. Goals can be simple and immediate (making ends meet each month) or they can be more complex and long term (funding retirement).

- **Maintain records:** Perhaps the most difficult part of the budgeting process is consistently keeping adequate monthly records of income and expenditures.

- **Periodic review:** A periodic review, comparing the planned budget with actual results, provides a means of measuring progress toward an individual's goals. The review will usually indicate if changes should be made, either in income, expenditures or both.

---

[1] For example, heating bills are usually less in summer than in winter.

Continued..

The Personal Budget

Name: _____

Period covered - From: _____ To: _____

Item	Historical	Current Budget	Current Actual	Difference
Food				
Home consumption	$_____	$_____	$_____	$_____
Outside the home	$_____	$_____	$_____	$_____
Total food:	**$_____**	**$_____**	**$_____**	**$_____**
Clothing				
Clothing and shoes	$_____	$_____	$_____	$_____
Cleaning, laundry	$_____	$_____	$_____	$_____
Jewelry, watches, etc.	$_____	$_____	$_____	$_____
Total clothing:	**$_____**	**$_____**	**$_____**	**$_____**
Housing				
Rent or mortgage	$_____	$_____	$_____	$_____
Real estate taxes	$_____	$_____	$_____	$_____
Insurance	$_____	$_____	$_____	$_____
Furniture and furnishings	$_____	$_____	$_____	$_____
Appliances	$_____	$_____	$_____	$_____
Cleaning, repairs and maint.	$_____	$_____	$_____	$_____
Electricity, gas and heating	$_____	$_____	$_____	$_____
Water and sewer	$_____	$_____	$_____	$_____
Telephone, cable	$_____	$_____	$_____	$_____
Other housing	$_____	$_____	$_____	$_____
Total housing:	**$_____**	**$_____**	**$_____**	**$_____**
Personal and Legal				
Personal care and toiletries	$_____	$_____	$_____	$_____
Child care	$_____	$_____	$_____	$_____
Legal and accounting	$_____	$_____	$_____	$_____
Life and disability insurance	$_____	$_____	$_____	$_____
Other personal and legal	$_____	$_____	$_____	$_____
Total personal and legal:	**$_____**	**$_____**	**$_____**	**$_____**
Medical				
Medicines	$_____	$_____	$_____	$_____
Doctors, dentists and hospitals	$_____	$_____	$_____	$_____
Health insurance	$_____	$_____	$_____	$_____
Other medical	$_____	$_____	$_____	$_____
Total medical:	**$_____**	**$_____**	**$_____**	**$_____**
Totals for this page:	**$_____**	**$_____**	**$_____**	**$_____**

Continued...

The Personal Budget

Worksheet

Name: _____

Period covered - From: _____ To: _____

Item	Historical	Current Budget	Current Actual	Difference
Transportation				
Auto payments	$_____	$_____	$_____	$_____
Repairs and maintenance	$_____	$_____	$_____	$_____
Insurance	$_____	$_____	$_____	$_____
Gas, oil and tires	$_____	$_____	$_____	$_____
Public transportation	$_____	$_____	$_____	$_____
Other transportation	$_____	$_____	$_____	$_____
Total transportation:	**$_____**	**$_____**	**$_____**	**$_____**
Miscellaneous				
Books, magazines and newspapers	$_____	$_____	$_____	$_____
Vacations	$_____	$_____	$_____	$_____
Entertainment and clubs	$_____	$_____	$_____	$_____
Charitable	$_____	$_____	$_____	$_____
Education	$_____	$_____	$_____	$_____
Other miscellaneous	$_____	$_____	$_____	$_____
Total miscellaneous:	**$_____**	**$_____**	**$_____**	**$_____**
Debt, savings and investment				
Credit and charge cards	$_____	$_____	$_____	$_____
Other installment loans	$_____	$_____	$_____	$_____
Education fund	$_____	$_____	$_____	$_____
Retirement	$_____	$_____	$_____	$_____
Other savings goals	$_____	$_____	$_____	$_____
Other	$_____	$_____	$_____	$_____
Total debt, savings and investment:	**$_____**	**$_____**	**$_____**	**$_____**
Totals for this page:	**$_____**	**$_____**	**$_____**	**$_____**
Totals from previous page:	**$_____**	**$_____**	**$_____**	**$_____**
Grand totals:	**$_____**	**$_____**	**$_____**	**$_____**

Personal Cash Flow Statement

Consumption Item	Your Budget		National Spending[1]
Food	$ 250	13.0%	14.9%
Clothing	$75	3.9%	5.4%
Housing	$ 800	41.6%	24.9%
Personal[2]	$ 200	10.4%	8.7%
Medical	$50	2.6%	20.4%
Transportation	$ 150	7.8%	11.9%
Other[3]	$ 400	20.8%	13.8%
Totals	**$1,925**	**100.0%**	100.0%
After-tax income	**$2,250**		
Discretionary income	**$ 325**		

[1] Source: Statistical Abstract of the United States: 2007. Table No. 656 Personal Consumption Expenditures in Current and Real (2000) Dollars, By Type: 1990 to 2004.

[2] Personal includes personal care, legal and financial expenses.

[3] Other includes recreation, education, charitable and net foreign travel expenses.

Sample Family Budget

Compare your spending with these broad national spending patterns.[1]

	National Spending	Your Budget	
Food	14.9%	$_____	____%
Clothing	5.4%	$_____	____%
Housing	24.9%	$_____	____%
Personal	8.7%	$_____	____%
Medical	20.4%	$_____	____%
Transportation	11.9%	$_____	____%
Other	13.8%	$_____	____%
Totals	**100.0%**	**$_____**	**100.0%**

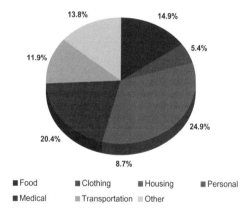

[1] Source: Statistical Abstract of the United States: 2007. Table No. 656 Personal Consumption Expenditures in Current and Real (2000) Dollars, By Type: 1990 to 2004.

Personal Net Worth Statement

A personal net worth statement is a snapshot of an individual's financial health, at one particular point in time. It is a summary of what is owned (assets), less what is owed to others (liabilities).

The formula used is: assets - liabilities = net worth.

If assets are greater than liabilities, the individual has a positive net worth. If assets are less than liabilities the individual has a negative net worth. Many financial advisors regard having a positive net worth as a primary goal.

Reasons to Prepare a Net Worth Statement

There are a number of reasons why an individual or family should prepare a net worth statement, usually on an annual basis.

- **To keep score:** Preparing an annual net worth statement allows an individual to keep track of progress toward meeting long-term financial goals. Ideally, net worth should increase over time.

- **A planning tool:** The net worth statement also serves as a planning tool. For example, a review of the net worth statement may show that an individual has too few liquid assets (for emergencies) or that investments are too heavily concentrated in one area.

- **Lenders may ask:** An individual's net worth is a common question on many loan applications. College financial aid programs will usually require information on the parents' net worth when a child applies.

- **For certain investments:** Certain types of high-risk investments require prospective investors to have a minimum level of net worth before they are allowed to invest money.

Preparing a Personal Net Worth Statement

The personal net worth worksheet on the following page can be used to prepare a net worth statement.

- **Assets:** For all assets categories (except cash or cash equivalents), a realistic valuation of what a willing, knowledgeable buyer would pay for an asset in an arms-length transaction should be used.

- **Liabilities:** It may be necessary to contact the lender or store to get the current balance on a loan or account.

Continued...

Personal Net Worth Statement

Date Prepared: _____

Name: _____

Assets		Liabilities	
Liquid Assets		**Current Liabilities**	
Cash and cash equivalents	$_____	Rent	$_____
Money owed to you	$_____	Utilities	$_____
Life insurance cash value	$_____	Credit and charge cards	$_____
Other liquid assets	$_____	Taxes	$_____
Total liquid assets	$_____	Other current liabilities	$_____
Personal Use Assets		Current portion, LT liabilities	$_____
Personal residence	$_____	**Total current liabilities**	$_____
Home use assets	$_____	**Long-Term Liabilities**	
Autos or other vehicles	$_____	Home mortgage	$_____
Collectibles (art/antiques)	$_____	Auto or other vehicle loans	$_____
Other personal use assets	$_____	Education loans	$_____
Total personal use assets	$_____	Margin account loans	$_____
Investment Assets		Business loan	$_____
Equity assets	$_____	Other long-term loans	$_____
Fixed-income assets	$_____	**Total long-term liabilities**	$_____
Investment real estate	$_____		
Business interests	$_____		
Commodities	$_____	**Net Worth Summary**	
Vested portion - Pension plans	$_____		
IRA or Keogh plans	$_____	**Assets**	$_____
Other investment assets	$_____		
Total investment assets	$_____	**Less liabilities**	$(_____)
Total Assets	$_____	**Equals net worth**	$_____

Continued

Personal Net Worth Statement

Explanatory Notes

- **Liquid assets:** Cash or other assets, which can be easily converted into cash.
  - **Cash and cash equivalents:** These include cash in checking or savings accounts and cash equivalents where there is no concern for any loss of principal if the asset is converted into cash. May include CDs, money market funds and short-term (less than one year) Treasury securities.
  - **Money owed:** Includes those debts owed to you under a written agreement.
  - **Life insurance cash value:** This is the whole life policy cash surrender value.

- **Personal use assets**
  - **Home use assets:** Includes furniture, furnishings, household goods, appliances, and sporting and hobby equipment.
  - **Autos or other vehicles:** Includes motorcycles, boats, airplanes and RVs.
  - **Collectibles (art/antiques):** Includes items that have a potential investment value as well as a personal interest value.

- **Investment use assets:** Includes investments with a maturity or a usual holding period of more than one year.
  - **Equity assets:** These include stocks, stock mutual funds or other investments based on stock market investments.
  - **Fixed-income assets:** Includes bonds, bond-based mutual funds, preferred stock or other investments based on bond or bond-type assets.
  - **Investment real estate:** Refers to real estate purchased for investment rather than shelter.
  - **Business interests:** Includes the equity ownership of any business in which you actively participate.
  - **Commodities:** These are gold, silver or other precious metals. Also gems and commodities contracts.
  - **Vested portion of pension plans:** Refers to the amount to which you are entitled even if you quit today.
  - **IRA or Keogh plans:** Includes the current market value less any taxes payable.

- **Current liabilities:** Refers to bills, which are due today or within thirty days.
  - **Rent and utilities:** Only include those due for the current month.
  - **Credit and charge cards:** Includes the total amount due, even if only minimum payments are made.
  - **Taxes:** Includes income and property taxes due today.[1]
  - **Current portion of long-term liabilities:** Refers to the portion of the total long-term liabilities to be paid within the next 30 days.

- **Long-term liabilities:** These are liabilities, which are typically paid over an extended period of time.

---

[1] Do not include real estate taxes if they are included in the monthly payment.

Personal Net Worth Statement

Assets		Liabilities	
Liquid assets	$50,000	Current liabilities	$26,000
Personal use assets	$25,000	Long-term liabilities	$ 250,000
Investment assets	$ 450,000		
Total assets	**$ 525,000**	**Total liabilities**	**$ 276,000**

Net Worth	
Total assets	$ 525,000
Less: Total liabilities	$ 276,000
Net worth	**$ 249,000**

Lifetime Earnings

Item Description	Client	Spouse
Current age	45	42
Age at retirement	66	68
Current annual income	$48,000	$52,000
Estimated annual increase	6.00%	6.50%
Projected earnings	$1,919,651	$3,313,200
Projected total earnings by retirement	**$5,232,851**	

Managing Your Debt

While earlier generations may have followed a "cash only" spending philosophy, most Americans today cannot imagine living without at least some debt. Relatively few of us are able to pay cash for a home or car. The ability to borrow money, when it's needed and on favorable terms, is a privilege earned by carefully managing your debt obligations.

Why Borrow Money?

Many advisors regard borrowing money as a two-edged sword. It can, for example, be used to finance long-term goals such as a home, a business, or an education. Over time, these "investments" tend to increase in value and return far more than the cost to purchase them. Used to excess, or to constantly pay for short-term consumer items, such as clothing, vacations, or a night on the town, debt can become an overwhelming burden.

Managing Your Credit Record

Most lending decisions are made on the basis of your credit record, also known as your credit report. When lenders size you up to determine how much credit, if any, to grant you, they count on the three Cs:

- **Character:** How responsibly will you handle your credit obligations? Lenders will look at how well (or how poorly) you have repaid previous debts.

- **Capacity:** What is your financial ability to assume a certain amount of debt? Do you have enough money coming in the door each month to pay all of your bills?

- **Capital:** What financial assets are at your disposal to pay off debts? If you don't repay the debt as promised, do you have other financial assets that could be used by the lender to pay off the debt?

How well you manage each of these issues is reflected in your credit report. Because your credit report is constantly changing, you should review it at least once a year to be sure it contains no errors as well as to detect any credit card fraud or identity theft.

What Are My Choices?

A consumer today has many ways to borrow money. You could, for example, use your credit card to finance a college education. However, a better choice might be a government-subsidized student loan which typically carries a lower interest rate and defers payments until after the student has finished school. Similarly, you could use part of your home equity line of credit to pay for a car, but do you really want to be making car payments for the next 10 or 20 years?

Whether you do the homework yourself, or seek the help of an advisor, understanding the loan options available, and then appropriately matching the type of loan to the need, is a key part of effective debt management.

Continue

Managing Your Debt

Managing the Cost of Your Debt

Interest rates constantly move up and down. Thus, the loan that you took out several years ago at what was then a great rate may not be such a good deal today. Lower interest rates may allow you to refinance an existing loan and lower your monthly payment. Or, if you keep the same monthly payments, a lower interest rate may allow you to pay off the loan sooner.

- **Mortgages and other consumer loans:** As a general rule, the interest saved must be greater than the cost (pre-payment penalties and other closing expenses) of acquiring the new loan before it makes sense to re-finance.

- **Credit cards:** The competition between credit card issuers can be intense. You can sometimes "surf" your credit card balance from one issuer to another to take advantage of issuers' low introductory rates. If you do move your balance from one card to another, be sure that you make at least the minimum payment when due; otherwise, the interest rate can permanently jump from the low single digits to the high 20s.

If Needed – Seek Professional Guidance

The advice and guidance of a professional financial advisor can be useful in helping sort out the various options for borrowing money. In addition, a qualified advisor can help you understand the impact of any borrowing upon your personal financial and income tax situation.

Other Resources

The federal government makes a number of resources available to the public:

- The **Federal Trade Commission** has a number of free publications available. On the internet, go to www.ftc/gov/credit.

- The **Federal Consumer Information Center**, at www.pueblo.gsa.gov/, has a number of free and low-cost publications on a number of topics on interest to consumers.

Up to Your Neck in Debt?

Are you afraid to open your bills? Do you juggle bills, paying Paul one month and Peter the next? Do you make only the required minimum payment? Do you have to pay for basic necessities like food, rent, or gasoline on credit because you're out of cash?

If some or all of these apply to you, it's a good bet you've taken on too much debt.

Initial Steps

Many of us have to deal with a financial crisis at some point in our lives. Whatever the cause, there are ways to overcome these financial problems. Often the first step is to recognize that there is a problem. Then you can begin to take action to solve it.

- **Create a budget:** One key step is to create a realistic budget, a cold, hard look at both your income and your necessary living expenses. Are there ways to increase income, as well as reducing expenses?

- **Talk with your creditors:** Contacting your creditors and explaining why you're having trouble paying your bills on time may lead to a reduced payment plan. Setting up an automatic payment plan from your checking or savings account can help establish how serious you are about paying your bills.

- **Check for mistakes:** Your bills or credit report could contain errors that, once corrected, could provide some partial relief.

Lower the Cost of Debt

Lowering the cost of debt is another way to improve the situation:

Method	Description	Comments
Refinance High-Cost Loans	Lower interest rates may allow you to refinance an existing loan and lower your payment.	Mortgages: Generally, the interest saved must be greater than the cost of acquiring the new loan. Credit cards: You may be able to move your balance from one card to another, to take advantage of introductory rates.
Consolidate Loans	Taking a number of high interest rate debts (often credit card debt) and replacing them with a single loan, often secured by the borrower's home or auto.	If payments are not made on the new loan, the lender often can seize the asset securing the loan.
Reposition Assets	Using existing assets such as cash, jewelry, or securities to pay down or pay off debt. Loans with the highest interest rates should be paid off first.	There may be negative tax implications if an asset with long-term appreciation is sold. Be sure you keep adequate liquid reserves to cover any future emergency.

Continued...

Up to Your Neck in Debt?

Outside Help

Many credit counseling agencies are available to help consumers who find themselves in financial trouble. Not all of these agencies work in a consumer's best interest. A reputable credit counseling agency has counselors trained in budgeting, credit, and debt management. A good counselor works closely with you to develop a personalized plan to resolve your individual debt problems.

- **Debt management plan:** A debt management plan, or DMP, may be recommended by a credit counselor. In a DMP, you make monthly payments to the credit counseling agency, which then uses your money to pay your unsecured debts in accordance with an agreement between you and your creditors. DMPs are not for everyone and may have restrictions which are unacceptable to some consumers.

- **Debt negotiation:** For a fee, debt negotiation firms offer to "negotiate" settling a debt with a creditor, often for 10% to 50% of the amount owed. These programs can be highly risky and can have a negative, long-term impact on your credit rating. The IRS may consider any debt forgiven as taxable income.

- **Credit "repair" firms:** Companies or agencies that offer or promise to "repair" your credit record should be regarded as scams. The passage of time and a regular history of repaying your debts are the only way to truly "fix" your credit report.

A Last Resort – Personal Bankruptcy

If your debts are truly overwhelming, personal bankruptcy is a drastic option of last resort. Bankruptcy is a court-supervised process in which a debtor either has his debts eliminated (Chapter 7) or a plan is arranged which allows debt repayment under the supervision of the bankruptcy court (Chapter 13). Certain debts, such as most taxes, child support, and alimony, cannot be "discharged" through bankruptcy. Federal law requires a debtor to undergo credit counseling before filing bankruptcy and to complete debtor education before bankruptcy can be finalized. Competent legal advice is highly recommended.

- **Chapter 7:** Also known as "liquidation", Chapter 7 effectively erases your unsecured debts. With the exception of certain "exempt" property,[1] other assets that you own, such as your home, jewelry, or artwork, may be sold and the proceeds used to pay your debts. Not everyone qualifies for Chapter 7 bankruptcy; if you have a regular income that exceeds certain limits, you may be required to file Chapter 13. A Chapter 7 bankruptcy remains on your credit record for 10 years.

- **Chapter 13:** Also known as "wage earner" bankruptcy, Chapter 13 allows you to propose a plan to repay your debts over a three to five year period. To qualify for Chapter 13, you need a steady source of income and your debts must not exceed certain dollar limits. A Chapter 13 bankruptcy remains on your credit record for 7 years.

- **Online resources:** See the website of the Department of Justice, U.S. Trustee, at www.usdoj.gov/ust.

---

[1] The amount and type of exempt property can vary with state law.

Checking Your Credit Report

Reasons to Check Your Credit Report

Credit information - an individual's financial history - is an integral part of modern life. Although most often used when a consumer applies for a loan, credit reports are also important when an individual applies for life, auto, or home insurance, rents an apartment, or applies for a job[1]. Many financial advisors recommend that a consumer's credit report be reviewed at least once a year, to be sure that all information contained in the report is accurate and complete.

Information Found in a Credit Report

Credit-reporting agencies, commonly known as credit bureaus or consumer reporting agencies, collect information on individuals from a variety of sources. Much of the data comes from a credit bureau's business subscribers, such as banks and other lenders. Other information is obtained from public records. A credit report does not include any statement about whether or not an individual is a good or a poor lending risk. A credit bureau's subscribers evaluate the information in the report using their own criteria.

A typical credit report usually has the following information.

- **Personal data:** Identifying information such as name, Social Security number, birth date, current address and marital status.

- **Credit history:** Including a list of current and past creditors, credit terms and limits, and how well (or poorly) past debts have been repaid.

- **Inquiries:** A list of requests for credit reports on the individual concerned.

- **Public records:** Information such as bankruptcies or lawsuits.

- **Personal statement:** A limited statement where a consumer can explain his or her position in any dispute with a lender.

Free Annual Credit Report

Under federal law, a consumer is entitled to one free credit report every 12 months, from each of the three major credit bureaus: Equifax, Experian, and TransUnion. Under Federal Trade Commission (FTC) rules, these credit bureaus must provide a central access point[2], where a consumer may request a copy of his or her credit report, including:

- **An Internet web site:** www.annualcreditreport.com;

- **A toll-free telephone number:** (877) 322-8228; and

- **A postal mailing address:** Annual Credit Report Request Service, P.O. Box 105283, Atlanta, GA 30348-5281.

---

[1] Federal law prohibits an employer or prospective employer from checking credit records without written permission from the individual involved.

[2] Specialized bureaus (agencies that specialize in areas such as insurance claims, medical records, and tenant or employment histories) are required to maintain only a toll-free telephone number. A consumer may request one free report from these bureaus every 12 months.

Continued..

Checking Your Credit Report

Incorrect Negative Information - Correcting Errors

If a review of a credit report reveals incorrect or incomplete information, a consumer should contact the credit bureau in writing, explaining as fully as possible the information believed to be incorrect. Under the provisions of the Fair Credit-reporting Act, enforced by the Federal Trade Commission (FTC), the credit bureau is required to investigate disputed items, usually within 30 days after receiving a written request.

As a part of the investigation, the credit bureau will contact the lender or other information provider. The law also requires the information provider to investigate the claim and report the results to the credit bureau. When the investigation is complete, the credit bureau must provide to the consumer a written report of the results.

If the disputed data is found to be incorrect, resulting in a change in the credit report, the credit bureau will provide a free copy of the corrected report to the consumer. The information provider is also required to correct its own records and provide the corrected information to all national credit bureaus.

The investigation of a disputed item may not result in a change in the credit report. A consumer can ask the credit bureau to include in his or her file a statement concerning the disputed information.

Correct Negative Information

If negative information in your credit report is correct, generally only the passage of time will remove it from the report. Many items, such as charged-off or collected accounts, delinquencies, and child support judgments, remain in the report for seven years. Other types of information can be retained in the report for longer periods.

- **Criminal convictions:** These may be reported without any time limit.

- **Bankruptcy:** Under Chapters 7, 11, or 12, bankruptcies can be reported for up to 10 years. Under Chapter 13, they remain in the record for seven years.

- **Job application:** Information reported in conjunction with an application for a position with an annual salary of $75,000 or more may be reported with no time limit.

- **Life insurance:** Information reported in conjunction with an application for credit or life insurance in excess of $150,000 may be reported with no time limit.

- **Lawsuit or unpaid judgment:** These can remain on the report for the longer of seven years, or until the statute of limitations expires.

- **Tax liens:** Unpaid liens for federal, state and local taxes can remain in the record for 15 years, while paid liens remain seven years.

Other Useful Resources

- **Fair Credit Reporting Act:** www.ftc.gov/bcp/conline/edcams/credit/index.html

- **Credit repair:** http:www.ftc.gov/bcp/conline/pubs/credit/repair.htm

- **Identity theft:** http://www.consumer.gov/idtheft/

Credit Cards

The use of credit cards has become a widespread and accepted part of modern life. From modest beginnings in the early 1900s, credit card usage has grown to the point where 71.5% of American families have at least one general-purpose credit card, with a median credit balance outstanding of $2,100.[1]

Reasons to Use a Credit Card

There are many reasons individual consumers use a credit card.

- **Safety:** The use of credit cards allows a consumer to purchase goods and services without the need to carry large amounts of cash.

- **Opportunity:** A credit card allows a consumer to deal with short-term situations, such as Christmas or emergency auto repairs, when paying cash might not be possible.

- **Facilitate transactions:** Credit cards allow for payment of goods and services purchased via telephone or the Internet. Some transactions, such as renting a car, purchasing airline tickets or guaranteeing payment for late arrival at a hotel, would be impossible without the use of a credit card.

- **Leverage:** Paying with a credit card can provide a consumer with additional leverage, in case of disputes with merchants over defective or poor quality merchandise.

- **Identity:** In certain types of transactions, such as cashing a check, credit cards have become a means of personal identification.

Types of Credit Cards

Not all credit cards are alike. They will vary widely in terms of issuer, scope of use and contract terms.

- **Bankcards:** Are issued not only by banks, but also by other financial institutions such as savings and loans or credit unions. These general-purpose credit cards can usually be used to purchase a wide range of goods and services. Credit is usually provided on a revolving basis, under which a borrower is granted a specific amount of credit. Typically, minimum monthly payments are required and any unpaid balance is subject to an interest charge. As borrowed amounts are repaid, the amount of available credit increases, up to the credit limit.

- **Charge cards:** Also known as travel and entertainment cards. Unlike bankcards, charge cards typically must be paid in full each month. Balances not paid are subject to heavy penalty fees. Like bankcards, charge cards are usually accepted widely.

---

[1] Taken from The Statistical Abstract of the United States: 2007. See Report No. 1170 - Usage of General purpose Credit Cards by Families: 1992 to 2004. Data is from 2004.

Continued

Credit Cards

- **Retail credit cards:** Retail credit cards are issued by businesses such as department stores, airlines and gasoline companies. Credit is usually provided on a revolving basis and purchases are limited to the goods and services sold by the specific card issuer.

- **Secured credit cards:** Such cards are usually general-purpose bankcards, with a specified (typically lower) credit limit. The card is secured by a deposit in an account with the issuing institution. If a consumer defaults, the card issuer can use the deposited funds to cover the shortage. Such cards are useful for individuals who do not have an established credit history or for those rebuilding their credit rating.

- **Affinity cards:** Affinity cards are issued jointly by a lending institution such as a bank or savings and loan, and some other organization such as an airline, charity or college alumni group. Using an affinity card allows a cardholder to also achieve other goals, such as earning frequent flyer miles or making charitable contributions.

Shopping for a Credit Card

When shopping for a credit card, a consumer should carefully compare the terms under which a card is offered:

- **Interest rate on unpaid balances:** The interest rate on unpaid balances can be either a fixed rate or a variable rate. Card issuers are required to state the interest rate as both an annual percentage rate (APR) and (for each billing cycle) as a periodic interest rate.

- **Unpaid balance computation:** The method by which a card issuer calculates the unpaid balance on an account. The unpaid balance, multiplied by the periodic interest rate, determines the finance charge.

Average Daily Balance	Previous Balance	Adjusted Balance
Each day the issuer subtracts any payments from, and adds new purchases to, the account balance. The daily balances for each day in a billing cycle are added together and then divided by the number of days in that cycle.	The issuer charges interest on the balance outstanding at the end of the previous billing cycle.	The issuer starts with the previous balance, subtracts any payments or credits, and charges interest on any remaining unpaid amount.

- **Fees:** Many card issuers will charge an annual fee, just to have the card. Fees may also be charged for such items as cash advances, late payments, charging over the established credit limit and lost card replacement.

Continued...

Credit Cards

- **Grace period:** The amount of time during which no interest is charged, if the entire amount is paid off.

- **Other benefits:** A card may provide other benefits such as cash advances, flight insurance, or discounts on travel or long-distance telephone charges.

- **Acceptance:** Some merchants may not accept a specific type of card.

Using a Credit Card

Many advisors recommend that consumers develop certain habits when using credit cards.

- Keep the number of open credit card accounts to a minimum.

- Understand the terms under which a card is issued.

- Sign all cards as soon as they are received.

- Pay credit card bills promptly to keep interest charges as low as possible and maintain a good credit rating. Authorizing electronic payment of credit card bills from your checking or savings account can automate this process.

- Keep detailed records of credit card account numbers, expiration dates and the telephone number of card issuers. The easiest way to do this is to photocopy the front and back of each card.

- Protect credit card information to avoid unauthorized use.

- Carefully review credit card statements each month. The customer copy of charge slips should be kept, to allow comparison with the monthly statement.

Lost or Stolen Credit Cards

Under federal law, a cardholder can be held liable for charges of up to $50.00 per card, even though the use was unauthorized. Such unauthorized credit card use is often the result of a card being lost, stolen or even counterfeited. If the loss of a card is reported to the issuer before the card is used, however, the issuer cannot hold the consumer liable for any unauthorized use.

- **Notify issuer:** A consumer should report the loss or theft of a credit card to the issuer as soon as possible. Many card issuers have toll-free, 24-hour telephone numbers for this purpose. Written notification should also be sent to the issuer.

- **Check monthly statement:** Review the monthly card statement to be sure that no unauthorized charges were made before it was noticed that the card was missing.

- **Registration service:** A consumer who carries more than one credit card may want to use a credit card registration service. For an annual fee, such services keep a record of all of a consumer's credit cards. In the event of a loss, the consumer makes one call, to the registration service. The registration service notifies all card issuers of the loss and, in many cases, arranges for replacement cards.

Buying a Home

Owning a home has long been a part of the American dream. It's a goal that many Americans have already achieved. According to recent statistics from the U. S. Census Bureau, 68.9% of all households in the United States live in owner occupied housing.[1]

Although the process of buying a home is often complex and confusing, it can be made more understandable by dividing it into several parts:

Renting vs. Home Ownership

There are advantages and disadvantages to both renting and buying a home:

	Advantages	Disadvantages
Renting	**Mobility** - Renter can move without having to worry about selling the home or the home's market value at time of sale. **Initial cost** - No need for large down payment. **Monthly cost** - Monthly rent usually less than mortgage payment; in some areas rents are controlled; other opportunities may provide greater investment return. **Maintenance** - Few or no maintenance responsibilities.	**Monthly cost** - Rents can increase over time. **Equity** - Renter builds no equity in home. **Space** - Often less floor space. **Personalization** - Less freedom to decorate the home. **Taxes**[2] - No deduction for rent payments.
Buying	**Monthly cost** - With a fixed rate mortgage, monthly payments remain level; with a variable rate mortgage, monthly payments can increase or decrease. **Equity** - Homeowner can build substantial equity over time. **Space** - Typically larger floor space than with a rented home. **Personalization** - Can usually decorate to make home reflect owner's tastes. **Taxes**[2] - Interest and property taxes are usually deductible.	**Mobility** - Ownership limits ability to move; homeowner must be concerned with selling the home as well as the home's market value at time of sale. **Initial cost** - Substantial cash usually needed for down payment and closing costs. **Monthly cost** - Monthly mortgage payment typically higher than monthly rent; other opportunities may provide greater investment return. **Maintenance** - Homeowner is usually responsible for all maintenance and repairs.

---

[1] Taken from the Statistical Abstract of the United States: 2007. See Report No. 957 - Homeownership Rates, by State: 1985 to 2005.

[2] Based on federal law. State law may vary.

Continued...

Buying a Home

Financing a Home

- **Size of mortgage:** One of the key issues a prospective homebuyer confronts is determining what size mortgage can be obtained. As a first step to answering this question, many lenders use two guidelines[1] to determine how much of a monthly payment a borrower can safely manage:

  - The monthly housing payment[2] should be no more than 28% of a consumer's gross monthly income.

  - The monthly housing payment, plus the monthly payments for any other debt, should not exceed more than 36% of a consumer's gross monthly income.

Example: Assume a couple has a total, gross monthly income of $4,000. Under the 28% rule, their total monthly housing payment should be no more than $1,120 ($4,000 x .28). Under the 36% rule, their monthly housing payment plus any other debt should not exceed $1,440 ($4,000 x .36).

Given a specified monthly payment, the next step is to determine what size mortgage that monthly payment will allow. The answer to this depends primarily on the number of years to repay, and the interest rate. The table below illustrates the approximate total monthly payment[3] under various assumptions.

Loan Amount	6.0% Annual Interest Monthly Payment		7.0% Annual Interest Monthly Payment		8.0% Annual Interest Monthly Payment	
	15 Years	30 Years	15 Years	30 Years	15 Years	30 Years
$100,000	$956.36	$712.05	$1,011.33	$777.80	$1,068.15	$846.26
$150,000	$1,434.54	$1,068.08	$1,516.99	$1,166.70	$1,602.23	$1,269.40
$200,000	$1,912.71	$1,424.10	$2,022.66	$1,555.60	$2,136.30	$1,692.53
$250,000	$2,390.89	$1,780.13	$2,528.32	$1,944.51	$2,670.38	$2,115.66

- **Down payment and closing costs:** Lenders ordinarily require a homebuyer to pay a certain portion of the home price in cash. Depending on the lender, this down payment usually ranges from 5% to 20% of the purchase price. With down payments of less than 20%, the lender may require the borrower to apply for private mortgage insurance, which protects the lender in case the buyer defaults. Under some government programs, a buyer may be allowed to purchase a home with no down payment. A buyer will also be required to pay certain "closing costs", fees and charges associated with processing the sale. Closing costs can be 3% to 6% of the purchase price.

---

[1] These guidelines have been developed by the Federal National Mortgage Association (FNMA). Some lending institutions may have different guidelines.

[2] Payment includes principal, interest, property taxes, insurance and any monthly condominium or co-op fees.

[3] Payment includes principal, interest, and estimated taxes and insurance. Monthly repayment figures for principal and interest taken from Barron's Financial Tables for Better Money Management - Mortgage Payments; 2nd Edition, 1992. Property taxes and insurance estimated at 1.35% of loan amount.

Continued

Buying a Home

- **Tax deductibility of interest and property taxes:** Prospective homebuyers will also want to consider the "after-tax" cost of home ownership. Taxpayers who itemize deductions and whose adjusted gross income is less than certain limits can usually deduct mortgage interest and property taxes from taxable income[1]. For example, assuming a taxpayer pays $10,000 in deductible mortgage interest and property taxes during a year, and is in a 28% marginal tax bracket, the after-tax cost of these expenses is $7,200 ($10,000 x .28 = $2,800; $10,000 - $2,800 = $7,200).

Finding a Home

What type of home? There are three basic forms of home ownership:

	Property Owned	Sell or Rent	Maintenance	Owner Payments	Other Issues
Single-Family Home	The structure and the land	Owner can decide to rent or sell home.	Owner responsible for all repairs and maintenance.	Mortgage, insurance, and real estate taxes. Loan secured by home.	Greater freedom to personalize the home. Generally more responsibility.
Condo	Individual living space. Homeowner's association owns building, land and common areas.	Owner can decide to sell. Restrictions on renting will vary.	Homeowner's association pays for most building maintenance and repair.	Mortgage, insurance, and taxes on individual unit; monthly fee to homeowner's association; mortgage secured by individual unit	Can be more restrictive with regard to issues such as children, pets, outside decoration. Fewer maintenance concerns. May have extra amenities such as swimming pools, tennis courts. Owners may be responsible for additional expenses or charges.

---

[1] Based on federal law. State law may vary.

Continued...

71

Buying a Home

	Property Owned	Sell or Rent	Maintenance	Owner Payments	Other Issues
Co-op	Shares in a corporation which owns building. Individual lease with corporation grants exclusive right to use apartment.	Owner can decide to sell. New buyer subject to approval by co-op board. May have restrictions on renting.	Co-op pays for most building maintenance and repair.	Monthly payments to co-op cover insurance, taxes, mortgage on building and operating costs. Loan payments to repay purchase of shares in co-op. Loan secured by shares in co-op.	Can be more restrictive on issues such as children and pets. Fewer maintenance concerns. May have extra amenities (pools, tennis courts, etc.). Owners may be responsible for additional expenses or charges.

Other Factors to Consider

- **Neighborhood:** Real estate agents will often refer to this as "location." In general, the relative attractiveness of an area will usually be reflected in the level of prices in the neighborhood. Personal issues such as good schools, easy access to public transportation, or proximity to features such as shopping, recreation, or work, are important factors in determining what is a "good" location.

- **Home features and characteristics:** Specific home features such as a minimum square footage, number of bedrooms or bathrooms, or a swimming pool. Many shoppers will list the most attractive features in priority order, in case an offered home lacks some of the desirable features. Keeping in mind that the home will one day be sold, many individuals look for features that are attractive and useful both to themselves and to others.

Searching for a Home

- **Real estate agents:** Real estate agents can be quite helpful in locating a home, particularly those who have access to a computerized multiple listings service. A good agent will have extensive real estate experience, as well as detailed knowledge of a specific area or neighborhood.

- **New home developments:** New homes tend to be more expensive than existing homes. New homes also tend to have fewer problems, and often have builder warranties.

- **Classified ads:** Classified ads in newspapers (both in print and via the Internet) can be useful sources of information. Such ads can provide a sense of general price levels. They can also provide leads to homes which are being sold directly by their owners, and not through an agent.

Types of Mortgages

Type	Description	Comments
Fixed-rate mortgage	Fixed interest rate. Borrower makes equal monthly payments of principal and interest until debt is fully paid. Loans can range from 10 - 40 years.	Offers payment stability. Interest rates may be higher than other types of financing. New fixed-rate loans are rarely assumable by later owners.
Home equity loan	A mortgage loan secured by the owner's "equity" (market value of home, less any existing mortgage debt) in the home. The loan may be a lump-sum amount or a line of credit (HELOC). Typically have a shorter term, five to 15 years.	Interest rates are frequently lower than those for traditional second mortgages, and can be either fixed or variable. Many home equity loans are interest-only, with a balloon payment due at the end of the loan term.
Adjustable-rate mortgage (ARM)	Interest rate can vary over the life of the loan, resulting in changes in the monthly payments, loan term, and/or principal balance due. Interest rate is based on an "index," such as the prime rate, with interest rate adjustments being made at specified time intervals.	Starting interest rate is typically slightly below market (a "teaser" rate), but payments can increase sharply if index increases. Some loans have interest rate caps that prevent wide fluctuations in payments, but may result in negative amortization.
Renegotiable rate mortgage (rollover)	Interest rate and monthly payments are constant for several years; possible change thereafter. Long-term mortgage.	Less frequent changes in interest rate offer some payment stability.
Balloon mortgage	Monthly payments based on fixed interest rate; usually short-term; payments may cover interest only with principal due in full at term end.	Offers low monthly payments but possibly no equity until loan is fully paid. When due, loan must be paid off or refinanced. Refinancing poses high risk if rates climb.
Graduated payment mortgage	Monthly payments start low and rise gradually (usually over five to 10 years), then level off for duration of loan term. If the loan has an adjustable interest rate, additional payment changes are possible if the underlying index changes.	Generally easier to qualify for. Buyer's income must be able to keep pace with scheduled payment increases. With an adjustable rate mortgage, payment increases beyond the scheduled graduated payments may result in negative amortization.
Shared appreciation mortgage	Below-market interest rate and lower monthly payments, in exchange for a share of profits when property is sold or on a specified date. Many variations.	If home appreciates greatly, total cost of loan jumps. If home fails to appreciate, projected increase in value may still be due, requiring refinancing at possible higher rates.
Assumable mortgage	Buyer takes over seller's original, below-market rate mortgage.	Lowers monthly payments. May be prohibited if "due on sale" clause is in original mortgage. Not permitted on most new fixed-rate mortgages.

Continued...

Types of Mortgages

Type	Description	Comments
Seller take-back	Seller provides all or part of financing with a first or second mortgage.	May offer a below-market interest rate; may have a balloon payment requiring full payment in a few years or refinancing at market rates, which could sharply increase debt.
Wraparound	Seller keeps original low rate mortgage. Buyer makes payments to seller, who forwards a portion to the lender holding original mortgage. Offers lower effective interest rate on total transaction.	Lender may call in old mortgage and require higher rate. If buyer defaults, seller must take legal action to collect debt.
Growing-equity mortgage (rapid payoff mortgage)	Fixed interest rate but monthly payments may vary according to agreed-upon schedule or index.	Permits rapid payoff of debt because payment increases reduce principal. Buyer's income must be able to keep up with payment increases.
Land contract	Seller retains original mortgage. No transfer of title until loan is fully paid. Equal monthly payments based on below-market interest rate with unpaid principal due at loan end.	May offer no equity until loan is fully paid. Buyer has few protections if conflict arises during loan.
Buy-down	Developer (or another party) provides an interest subsidy which lowers monthly payments during the first few years of the loan. May have a fixed or adjustable interest rate.	Offers a break from higher payments during early years. Enables buyer with lower income to qualify. With adjustable rate mortgage, payments may jump substantially at end of subsidy. Developer may increase selling price to recover loan costs.
Rent with option	Renter pays "option fee" for right to purchase property at specified time and agreed upon price. Rent may or may not be applied to sales price.	Enables renter to buy time to obtain down payment and decide whether to purchase. Locks in price during inflationary times. Failure to take option means loss of option fee and rental payments.
Reverse mortgage	Borrower owns mortgage-free property and needs income. Loan can be a lump-sum or monthly payments to borrower using property as collateral. Generally, borrower must be at least age 62 and live in the home.	No payments are required as long as borrower lives in the home. The outstanding loan balance is due when the last borrower sells the home, permanently leaves, or dies. Borrower can never owe more than the value of the home at the time loan is repaid.
Interest-only mortgage	Borrower pays only the interest due (no repayment of principal) either for an introductory period or for the life of the loan. At the end of the loan term, the loan must either be refinanced or completely paid off.	Interest-only payments generally allow the homeowner to qualify for a larger loan amount. With little or no equity, a homeowner with an interest-only loan faces higher risk if real estate values decline.

The Bi-Weekly Mortgage

By paying one-half of the typical monthly mortgage payment every two weeks rather than one full payment every month, a 30-year mortgage can be paid off in approximately 20 years. The 26 bi-weekly payments are the same as 13 monthly payments during the year; in other words, one "extra monthly payment."

This extra monthly payment, along with the more frequent application of the payments against the loan balance, greatly speeds up the payoff of the loan. Also, since the "extra monthly payment" is spread evenly throughout the year, it generally does not adversely affect the family budget.

Payments on the bi-weekly mortgage are generally made by automatic withdrawal from the homeowner's checking account every two weeks.

Payments on Various Size Loans and Total Interest Saved[1]

Interest Rate / Term in Months[2]	$100,000 Bi-Weekly Payment Amount	$100,000 Total Interest Savings	$150,000 Bi-Weekly Payment Amount	$150,000 Total Interest Savings	$200,000 Bi-Weekly Payment Amount	$200,000 Total Interest Savings
4.5% / 308	$253	$14,019	$380	$21,028	$507	$28,037
5.0% / 303	$268	$17,164	$403	$25,750	$537	$34,328
5.5% / 299	$284	$20,755	$426	$31,128	$568	$41,503
6.0% / 294	$300	$24,808	$450	$37,221	$600	$49,624
6.5% / 290	$316	$29,369	$474	$44,061	$632	$58,746
7.0% / 285	$333	$34,464	$499	$51,700	$665	$68,927
7.5% / 280	$350	$40,096	$524	$60,149	$699	$80,203
8.0% / 274	$367	$46,301	$550	$69,452	$734	$92,602
8.5% / 269	$384	$53,079	$577	$79,600	$769	$106,144

Interest Rate / Term in Months[2]	$250,000 Bi-Weekly Payment Amount	$250,000 Total Interest Savings	$300,000 Bi-Weekly Payment Amount	$300,000 Total Interest Savings	$350,000 Bi-Weekly Payment Amount	$350,000 Total Interest Savings
4.5% / 308	$633	$35,045	$760	$42,050	$887	$49,058
5.0% / 303	$671	$42,907	$805	$51,492	$939	$60,073
5.5% / 299	$710	$51,883	$852	$62,259	$994	$72,632
6.0% / 294	$749	$62,029	$899	$74,440	$1,049	$86,837
6.5% / 290	$790	$73,431	$948	$88,123	$1,106	$102,808
7.0% / 285	$832	$86,155	$998	$103,391	$1,164	$120,619
7.5% / 280	$874	$100,246	$1,049	$120,299	$1,224	$140,352
8.0% / 274	$917	$115,753	$1,101	$138,904	$1,284	$162,042
8.5% / 269	$961	$132,679	$1,153	$159,210	$1,346	$185,743

[1] The interest savings shown illustrate the difference between the interest paid on a 30-year fixed-rate mortgage making monthly payments vs. bi-weekly payments. All figures are approximate.
[2] The number of months required to fully pay off the loan on a bi-weekly payment schedule.

When to Refinance Your Home

There are a number of situations in which refinancing a home mortgage makes sense. For example, you may have purchased a home years ago when interest rates were much higher and now want to take advantage of a decline in mortgage rates. In addition, a homeowner with a volatile variable rate mortgage may want to switch to more predictable fixed-rate loan. Then again, you may even want to shorten the term of your loan.

Is Refinancing Worth the Trouble?

Refinancing can be very beneficial, but it is not always the smart thing to do; the costs associated with refinancing must be balanced against any potential savings.

A general rule of thumb is that refinancing a fixed-mortgage makes sense when the interest rate on the current mortgage is at least 2 percentage points higher than the prevailing market rate.

In some instances, however, following this "rule" may cost the homeowner a lot of money as a very small percentage point spread may justify refinancing if other factors are present.

Other Factors Which Must Be Considered

There are a number of factors which must be considered in this "cost vs. benefits" calculation, including:

- **Closing costs:** Possible pre-payment penalties on the old loan, points and fees on the new loan, and attorney fees generally will total 3% to 4% of the loan amount and must generally be paid when the new loan closes. The borrower must consider the loss of earning power of these funds in future income projections.

- **Projected length of ownership:** The closing costs can be spread over the period of the loan; therefore, the longer the projected period of ownership, the smaller the spread between the old and new mortgages can be.

- **Income tax bracket of the owner:** Higher interest payments mean larger income tax deductions; therefore, the effect on one's taxable income must be considered.

- **Loans in excess of 1987 revenue act limits:** The interest on loan amounts in excess of acquisition debt on a first and second residence (up to $1,000,000) plus $100,000 in home equity loans is not deductible. Acquisition debt refers to loans incurred to buy, construct, or substantially improve a qualified residence.[1]

---

[1] Federal income tax law; state or local law may vary.

Continue

When to Refinance Your Home

The New Mortgage - Variable Rate vs. Fixed Rate

Variable Rate	Fixed Rate
• Initially lower interest rate than with a fixed rate loan, but will increase if interest rates go up or decrease if interest rates go down. • Most variable rate mortgages have a limit or a cap on annual rate increases and on lifetime increases.[1] • Usually preferred for short-term ownership of home; e.g., 2 - 3 yrs.	• Rate does not change if interest rates go up or down. • Best for owners with a fixed income or those who plan to stay in their home for several years. • Rates and monthly payments are higher than with a variable loan, at least in the early years. • Fixed rate loans may not be assumable.

How Many Months Will It Take to Break Even?

The real cost of refinancing is the closing costs. Determine how many months it will take to make up these costs from the savings under the new loan.

$\underline{}$ Minus $\underline{}$ = $\underline{}$
    Old Payment   New Lower   Monthly
                   Payment   Savings

$\underline{}$ Divided by $\underline{}$ = $\underline{}$
    Closing Costs   Monthly   Number of
                   Savings   Months to
                               Break Even

Refinancing an old home loan could mean lower monthly payments and perhaps changing from a variable rate to a fixed rate. If projected time in the house is short, the closing costs may consume any savings.

Also, if one plans to sell in a year or two, a variable rate mortgage with an initially lower rate may be more advantageous. Assuming the refinanced mortgage principal is less than the acquisition debt (up to $1,000,000) and $100,000 in home equity loans, the interest paid will generally be deductible. Consider paying off other consumer debt first on which the interest payments are no longer deductible.

---

[1] Be certain that an annual cap is part of the loan, and carefully examine the index to which the rate is tied.

Financing an Auto

Once a consumer decides to acquire an automobile, the next step is to decide how to pay for it. There are three methods of financing an auto:

- **Pay cash:** Using already accumulated funds.

- **Borrow the funds:** Taking out a loan and paying for the vehicle over time.

- **Lease:** Allows use of an auto for a specified period of time, in return for regular monthly payments.

The decision as to whether to pay cash, take out a loan, or lease a vehicle is usually made after considering a number of personal and financial issues.

Factors to Consider

The table below compares some of the factors to consider when considering how to finance an auto.

	Pay Cash	Borrow the Funds	Lease
Method of financing	Consumer uses cash to completely pay for the vehicle at the time of purchase.	Consumer borrows the funds to purchase the vehicle, and makes monthly payments to repay the loan.	Consumer obtains the right to use the vehicle for a specified period of time, in return for monthly payments.
Out-of-pocket costs	Entire purchase price.	Down payment and/or trade-in. Special offers may allow zero down.	Down payment and/or trade-in. Often less than for an auto loan. Special offers may allow zero down.
Monthly payments	None	Payments cover repayment of loan amount, plus interest.	Payments cover estimated depreciation during the lease period, and other costs. Typically less than for an auto loan.
Vehicle ownership	Consumer is the owner.	Consumer is the owner, subject to a lien held by lender. Once loan is repaid, consumer takes title free and clear. Lender may repossess vehicle if payments not made as scheduled.	Leasing firm retains ownership. Consumer usually has the right to purchase the vehicle at the end of the lease.

Continued..

Financing an Auto

	Pay Cash	Borrow the Funds	Lease
Excess mileage charges	None	None	Typical lease limits consumer to no more than 10,000 – 15,000 miles per year. Miles in excess of lease limits are subject to a per-mile charge.
Excess wear and tear	No additional charges. Excess wear and tear, or high mileage, can reduce a vehicle's resale value.	No additional charges. Excess wear and tear, or high mileage, can reduce a vehicle's resale value.	Additional charges for excess wear and tear usually apply.
Risk of future vehicle resale value	Risk remains with the consumer.	Risk remains with the consumer.	With a closed-end lease, risk of future vehicle resale value remains with leasing firm. With an open-end lease, consumer may be responsible for substantial additional charges.
Early disposal of vehicle	Consumer is free to sell vehicle at any time.	Consumer is free to sell vehicle at any time, subject to repayment of loan balance to lender. Early loan termination fees may apply.	Additional fees for early lease termination normally apply.
Tax issues	Deduction available for business use of vehicle.[1]	Deduction available for business use of vehicle.[1]	Deduction available for business use of vehicle. In certain situations, leasing may provide a larger deduction for business use than an owned vehicle.[1]
Lifestyle issues	Limits consumer to vehicle that he or she can currently afford. Consumer avoids additional debt burden.	Usually allows consumer to purchase more expensive vehicle than if full cash payment is required.	Consumer typically has use of more expensive vehicle than with other financing options. May also allow consumer to drive a new car more frequently. No equity at end of lease.

---

[1] Based on federal law. State law may vary.

Continued...

Financing an Auto

Comparing the Dollar Costs

The following table provides a hypothetical comparison of the costs involved in the three options for financing an auto:

- **Pay cash:** Purchase price of $22,500, sales tax of $1,631, registration and fees of $350. Total purchase price of $24,481.

- **Borrow the funds:** Total purchase price of $24,481, less down payment of $2,250. Financed over a 48-month period at 9.5% annual interest.

- **Lease:** 48-month closed-end lease, with same costs and interest rate as under the "loan" option. $500 down payment, and an assumed resale value at the end of the lease of $12,000.

	Pay Cash	Borrow the Funds	Lease
Up-front cash	$24,481	$2,250	$500
Monthly payment	$0	$554	$388
Total payments over 48 months	$0	$26,592	$18,624
Opportunity costs[1]	$3,117	$286	$64
Total costs after 48 months	$27,598	$29,128	$19,188
Value of vehicle after 48 months	($12,000)	($12,000)	$0
Total	$15,598	$17,128	$19,188

---

[1] The amount of interest the "up-front cash" shown for each option would have earned over the 48 month period, at an assumed 3.0% annual after-tax rate of return.

Loan Amortization Schedule

Assumptions:
Amount of loan: $ 100,000
Annual interest rate: 5.00%
Frequency of payments/compounding periods: Annually
Number of payments: 55
Payment start date: 1/2004
Payment: $5,367
Total payments: $ 295,168
Total interest paid: $ 195,168

Loan Amortization Schedule

The following table shows year-by-year summary of this loan. Note the amount of principal vs. interest paid each year as the loan progresses.

Year	Principal Paid This Year	Interest Paid This Year	Total Paid This Year	Balance Remaining
2004	$ 367	$5,000	$5,367	$99,633
2005	$ 385	$4,982	$5,367	$99,248
2006	$ 404	$4,962	$5,367	$98,844
2007	$ 424	$4,942	$5,367	$98,420
2008	$ 446	$4,921	$5,367	$97,974
2009	$ 468	$4,899	$5,367	$97,506
2010	$ 491	$4,875	$5,367	$97,014
2011	$ 516	$4,851	$5,367	$96,498
2012	$ 542	$4,825	$5,367	$95,957
2013	$ 569	$4,798	$5,367	$95,388
2014	$ 597	$4,769	$5,367	$94,791
2015	$ 627	$4,740	$5,367	$94,163
2016	$ 659	$4,708	$5,367	$93,505
2017	$ 691	$4,675	$5,367	$92,813
2018	$ 726	$4,641	$5,367	$92,087
2019	$ 762	$4,604	$5,367	$91,325
2020	$ 800	$4,566	$5,367	$90,525
2021	$ 840	$4,526	$5,367	$89,684
2022	$ 882	$4,484	$5,367	$88,802
2023	$ 927	$4,440	$5,367	$87,875
2024	$ 973	$4,394	$5,367	$86,902
2025	$1,022	$4,345	$5,367	$85,881
2026	$1,073	$4,294	$5,367	$84,808
2027	$1,126	$4,240	$5,367	$83,682
2028	$1,183	$4,184	$5,367	$82,499
2029	$1,242	$4,125	$5,367	$81,257
2030	$1,304	$4,063	$5,367	$79,954
2031	$1,369	$3,998	$5,367	$78,585
2032	$1,437	$3,929	$5,367	$77,147
2033	$1,509	$3,857	$5,367	$75,638
2034	$1,585	$3,782	$5,367	$74,053

Rate of Interest for a Loan

Item Description	Value
Amount of loan	$ 100,000
Frequency of payments	Annually
Number of Annual payments	360
Payment amount	$1,000
Annual interest rate	**0.969%**

Example

If you have a 360 year loan for $100,000 and your annual payment
is $1,000, then you are paying an annual interest rate of 0.97%.

Payments To Pay Off A Loan

Item Description	Value
Amount of loan	$ 100,000
Annual interest rate	5.00%
Frequency of payments	Annually
Number of Annual payments	55
Annual payment amount to pay off loan	**$5,367**

Example

If you borrow $100,000 for 55 years at an annual interest rate of 5.000%, your annual payment will be $5,367.

The Need for Health Insurance

Most of us would agree that good health is an extremely valuable attribute. Those in poor health generally have a lower quality of life as well as a reduced ability to work and earn an income. Good health is frequently the result of biology (the genes you inherit), the life style choices you make (exercise, diet, smoking), and appropriate medical care.

And even the healthiest among us need some medical care. Regular physician and dental visits are a normal part of maintaining good health. Accidents, illness, and simply growing older are other reasons medical care is necessary.

Paying For Medical Care

Medical care in the United States is, unquestionably, expensive. According to statistics compiled by the federal government, over 20% of personal consumption expenditures are directed to medical care.[1] For those needing medical care, there are three basic choices:

- **Don't go:** Not seeking medical care when it is needed can result in small, treatable health problems becoming much bigger ones, with sometimes fatal consequences.

- **Pay out-of-pocket:** Paying for medical care from your own pocket can quickly exhaust your assets. Huge medical bills are one reason cited as a cause of personal bankruptcy.

- **Health insurance:** Although the premiums can be expensive, for many individuals and families, health insurance is the only practical way to provide needed medical care.

Sources of Health Insurance

There are three broad sources of health insurance in the United States today:

- **Individually owned policies:** The individual or family purchases a health policy directly from an insurance company or health maintenance organization. Individual health policies can be relatively expensive compared to group health insurance.

- **Group health insurance:** Group health insurance is typically provided through an employer or another related group such as a professional association. The premiums for group health policies tend to be less than those for individually owned policies.

- **Government programs:** For those age 65 and older, Medicare provides a base level of health insurance. Medicaid provides health care for the impoverished. The federal government has a number of programs to provide medical care to active duty and former military service members. Some states have individual programs to provide health insurance to low-income individuals and families.

The Choice Is Yours

While health insurance may be expensive, trying to pay medical costs out of your own pocket, or not seeking medical help when needed, can be much more expensive.

---

[1] Source: Statistical Abstract of the United States:2007. Table No. 656 Personal Consumption expenditures in Current and Real (2000) Dollars, by Type: 1990 to 2004.

Health Insurance Issues

The continuing escalation in health care costs makes a well-designed health insurance program essential to your financial security. With semi-private room rates averaging over $500 per day, a few days in the hospital could equal thousands of dollars in expenses.

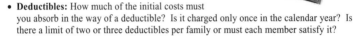

When reviewing your health insurance coverage, consider the following.

- **Deductibles:** How much of the initial costs must you absorb in the way of a deductible? Is it charged only once in the calendar year? Is there a limit of two or three deductibles per family or must each member satisfy it?

- **Coinsurance:** Beyond the deductible, what percentage of the expense must you pay, 10%, 20%? Most important - Is there a stop-loss provision that eliminates all coinsurance and pays 100% of the charges after you reach $1,000 (or some specified dollar amount) in out-of-pocket expense?

- **Family benefit maximums:** These should be unlimited or extremely high; e.g., $1,000,000, due to potential costs of a major surgery, hospitalization, a series of family illnesses, etc.

- **Inside limits:** These limits, like $200 for X-rays, etc., should be avoided in favor of comprehensive coverage; i.e., a flat percentage of the cost incurred.

- **Child age limits:** Determine age limits on child coverage. Full-time students may be covered until 22 or 23.

- **Outpatient benefits:** These benefits should be examined carefully since many procedures are now done on an outpatient basis; e.g., preadmission testing, diagnosis, etc., due to the high costs of hospitalization.

- **Preferred providers:** Some medical plans call for the use of a preferred supplier and provide a list of doctors or hospitals from which you must choose.

- **Health maintenance organizations (HMOs):** These medical plans offer a different approach from traditional health insurance, in which you pick the doctor, pay as you go and receive reimbursement from an insurance company. With an HMO, you or your employer pay an annual fee, for which the plan's own doctors handle almost all of your health needs.

HMOs typically cost less in that there are usually no deductibles and they cover a higher percentage of costs than traditional plans. However, since you are limited to the services of this organization, it is important to ask the following questions.

- Where do I go if I require hospitalization?
- What about emergency treatment out of the local area?
- How substantial is the local staff and are all specialties represented?
- How long must I wait to get an appointment?
- Is the plan facility oversubscribed?

How Employer-Provided Health Insurance Works

Employer and Employee
Each pays a portion
of the premium.

**Employer and
Employee**

Group Health Policy

**Health Insurance
Company**

Medical Event
(e.g., routine care, accident, illness)

Employee
Pays deductible,
co-insurance
amounts and any
balance over
maximum benefit.

**Health Insurance
Company**
Pays benefits under
the terms of the
contract, up to
policy maximums.

Health Care Providers
(e.g., hospitals, doctors)

How Individual Health Insurance Works

Individual
Pays premium.

Individual

Individual Health Policy

Health Insurance Company

Medical Event
(e.g., routine care, accident, illness)

Individual
Pays deductible, co-insurance amounts and any balance over maximum benefit.

Health Insurance Company
Pays benefits under the terms of the contract, up to policy maximums.

Health Care Providers
(e.g., hospitals, doctors)

Critical Illness Insurance

Critical illness insurance is a relatively new type of insurance coverage designed to help meet the extra, unforeseen financial burdens associated with recovering from a serious, life-threatening illness. While comprehensive health and disability insurance plans cover many expenses, they are not designed to pay all of the costs associated with recovering from a critical illness. If you are diagnosed as having a covered illness, a critical illness policy can provide the extra resources to pay for expenses not covered by other insurance:

- Rehabilitation costs
- Co-pays and deductibles
- Experimental and/or alternative medicine
- Out-of-network expenses
- Child care costs
- To supplement or replace lost income
- Travel, for family members or the insured

How Does It work?

Upon being diagnosed with one of the covered illnesses, you will typically receive a lump-sum payment. Some older policies may have a survival period (up to 30 days) that you must live after being diagnosed. Although a policy may cover more than one illness, it will generally only pay benefits on the first one to strike you. With some policies, the payments may be spread out over time.

Types of Illnesses Covered

Coverage will vary from policy to policy and company to company. Typically, however, covered illnesses include: cancer, multiple sclerosis, heart attack, Alzheimer's, stroke, paralysis, renal failure, blindness, deafness, and organ transplant.

Policy Costs

Policy costs vary according to several factors: age; medical condition; and the amount of coverage purchased. If you are a smoker or your family has a history of heart disease, stroke, or cancer, you may be denied coverage – or asked to pay a steep premium. Furthermore, a policy may exclude coverage for a pre-existing condition.

Federal Taxation of Policy Proceeds

The proceeds of a personally owned and paid for critical illness policy are exempt from tax under federal law. In certain situations, the proceeds from an employer-provided policy can be taxable. State and local law can vary. Check with your tax advisor.

As with any insurance purchase, the counsel of a professional advisor is recommended.

Medicare Parts A, B, and D
Consider What Medicare Does and Does Not Cover

Medicare is a health insurance program operated by the federal government. Benefits are available to qualifying individuals age 65 or older and certain disabled individuals under age 65, and those suffering from end-stage renal disease. The traditional Medicare program consists of three parts: Part A, Hospital Insurance, Part B, Medical Insurance, and Part D, Prescription Drug Coverage. There are clearly defined limits as to what Medicare will, and will not, pay.

Medicare (Part A) 2008 Hospital Insurance - Covered Services per Benefit Period

Service	Benefit	Medicare Pays	You Pay
Hospitalization: Semiprivate room and board, general nursing and miscellaneous hospital services and supplies. Includes meals, special care units, drugs, lab tests, diagnostic X-rays, medical supplies, operating and recovery room, anesthesia and rehabilitation services	Medicare pays all covered costs for first 60 days, except the first $1,024. For the 61st through 90th days, it pays all except $256 a day. There are also 60 nonrenewable reserve days that can be used when the 90 days are past. Medicare pays all except the first $512 for each reserve day.		
Post-hospital skilled nursing facility care (in a facility approved by Medicare): You must have been in a hospital for at least three days in a row and enter the facility within 30 days after having been discharged from the hospital.	**First 20 days**	All costs	Nothing
	Next 80 days	All but $128.00	$128.00 per day
	Medicare and private insurance will not pay for most nursing home care, and you pay for custodial care.		
Home health care: Post-institutional care. You must have been in a hospital for at least three days in a row or have been in a skilled nursing facility following a hospital stay.	Pays the cost of 100 home visits, if made under a physician's treatment plan.	Full cost	Nothing for services; 20% of approved amount for durable medical equipment.
Hospice care: May exceed the 210 days of care if recertified as terminally ill.	Two 90-day periods and one 30-day period	All but limited costs for outpatient drugs and inpatient respite care	Limited cost sharing for outpatient drugs and inpatient respite care
Blood	Blood	All but first three pints	For first three pints

Continued...

Medicare Parts A, B, and D

Consider What Medicare Does and Does Not Cover

Medicare (Part B) 2008 Medical Insurance - Covered Services per Calendar Year
Standard Monthly Premium: $96.40

Service	Benefit	Medicare Pays	You Pay[1]
Medical expense: Doctor's services, inpatient and outpatient medical services and supplies, physical and speech therapy, ambulance, etc.	Medicare pays for medical services in or out of hospital. Some insurance policies pay less (or nothing) for hospital outpatient medical services in a doctor's office.	80% of approved amount (after $135.00 deductible). 50% of approved charges for most outpatient mental health services.	$135.00 deductible[2] plus 20% of approved amount and limited charges above approved amount.[3] 50% of approved charges for mental health services.
Home health care[4]	Unlimited, if made under a physician's treatment plan.	Full cost	Nothing for services; 20% of approved amount for durable medical equipment.
Outpatient hospital treatment	Unlimited if medically necessary.	80% of approved amount (after $135.00 deductible).	$135.00 deductible[2] plus 20% of balance of approved amount.
Blood: Any blood deductibles satisfied under Part B will reduce the blood deductible requirements.	Blood	80% of approved amount (after first three pints).	$135.00 deductible[2] plus first three pints plus 20% of balance of approved amount.

Note: If the period of hospitalization covers two calendar years, no new deductible is required for the new year. These figures are for 2008 and are subject to change each year.

---

[1] You pay for charges higher than the amount approved by Medicare unless the doctor or supplier agrees to accept Medicare's approved amount as the total charge for services rendered.

[2] Once you have had $135.00 of expense for covered services in 2008, the Part B deductible does not apply to any further covered services you receive the rest of the year.

[3] Federal law limits charges for physician services.

[4] Home health care is provided under Part B only if not covered under Part A.

Continued

Medicare Parts A, B, and D
Consider What Medicare Does and Does Not Cover

Part B Premium For Higher-Income Beneficiaries

In 2008, Medicare beneficiaries with modified adjusted gross incomes (generally, adjusted gross income plus any tax-free interest income or any excluded foreign earned income) in excess of certain limits will pay an increased Part B premium:

Unmarried Individuals	Married Filing Jointly	Monthly Premium
Less than $82,000	Less Than $164,000	$96.40
$82,000 to $102,000	$164,000 to $204,000	$122.20
$102,000 to $153,000	$204,000 to $306,000	$160.90
$153,000 to $205,000	$306,000 to $410,000	$199.70
More than $205,000	More than $410,000	$238.40

Married Filing Separately	Monthly Premium
Less than $82,000	$96.40
$82,000 to $123,000	$199.70
More than $123,000	$238.40

For 2008, modified-adjusted gross income is measured using the amounts shown on a beneficiary's income tax return for 2006. An appeal process is available in case of a major life change such as the death of a spouse, divorce, or marriage.

Medicare Part D - Prescription Drug Benefit.

Medicare Part D provides coverage for prescription medications. Each eligible Medicare beneficiary must select a drug plan and pay a monthly premium. All drug plans (the choice varies by state) must provide coverage at least as good as the standard coverage specified by Medicare. Some plans may offer extra benefits such as no deductible, higher coverage limits, or cover additional drugs, in exchange for a higher monthly premium. Those with limited income and resources may qualify for help in paying for prescription drug coverage.

Prescription Drug Benefit Standard Coverage

The standard coverage for 2008 as set by Medicare is shown in the following table:

	$275 Deductible	$276 to $2510	$2511 UntilOut of Pocket Totals $4050	Above $4050 in Out of Pocket Costs
Individual Pays	$275.00	25% up to $559	$3,216.25	5%
Plan Pays	$0.00	75% up to $1676	$0.00	95%
Total Drug Expense	$275.00	$2,510.00	$5,726.25	

Medicare Part D - Prescription Drug Coverage

Medicare Part D provides insurance coverage for prescription medications. Under this program, insurance companies and other private firms contract with Medicare (Medicare pays most of the premium) to provide prescription drug benefits to Medicare beneficiaries.

Each eligible Medicare beneficiary must select a drug plan and pay a monthly premium to receive the drug coverage. All drug plans (the choice varies by state) must provide coverage at least as good as the standard coverage specified by Medicare. Some plans may offer extra benefits such as no deductible, higher coverage limits, or cover additional drugs, in exchange for a higher monthly premium. Individuals with limited income and resources may qualify for help in paying for drug coverage.

Making a Choice

There are a number of factors to consider in making a choice about drug plans, including:

- **Initial enrollment:** A new Medicare beneficiary may enroll in a prescription drug plan during the period beginning three months before he or she turns age 65 until three months after reaching age 65. An individual who has lost "creditable coverage" (prescription drug coverage from some other source that is at least as good as the standard Medicare prescription coverage) has 63 days to select and join a Medicare prescription drug plan. An eligible beneficiary who does not enroll in a prescription drug plan within the prescribed time limits faces a penalty for late enrollment.

- **Penalty for late enrollment:** Individuals who delay joining a Medicare prescription drug plan beyond their initial eligibility face a monthly premium that will increase by at least 1% per month for each month of delay. This increased premium applies for as long as the individual is enrolled in a Medicare drug plan.

- **Changing plans:** Each year, from November 15 to December 31, a beneficiary can change to a different prescription drug plan.

- **Current prescription coverage:** Individuals who currently have prescription drug coverage from another source may not wish to enroll in a Medicare prescription drug program. In some cases the benefits provided under these other plans are better than those provided under the standard Medicare prescription drug plan.

- **Medication coverage:** Consider what medications are needed. Compare the needed medications with those covered by each plan. Each plan will have a list (termed a "formulary") showing the drugs (generic and brand-name) the plan will pay for.

- **Out-of-pocket cost:** A prescription drug plan can vary in how much it charges and how much coverage is provided. Issues such as the monthly premium, yearly deductible, any co-insurance or co-payments, and coverage limits must all be considered.

- **Pharmacy convenience:** Not all pharmacies will be contracted with all plans. Some plans will allow a beneficiary to receive prescriptions by mail.

Continued

Medicare Part D - Prescription Drug Coverage

- **Future health changes:** Even though an individual takes few or no medications now, joining a prescription drug plan now means paying the lowest possible monthly premium. Future health changes may require increased use of prescription drugs.

Standard Coverage

The standard coverage for 2008 as set by Medicare is shown in the following table:

	$275 Deductible	$276 to $2510	$2511 Until Out of Pocket Totals $4050	Above $4050 in Out of Pocket Costs
Individual Pays	$275.00	25% up to $559	$3,216.25	5%
Plan Pays	$0.00	75% up to $1676	$0.00	95%
Total Drug Expense	$275.00	$2,510.00	$5,726.25	

For Those Who Currently Have Prescription Drug Coverage

Some retirees may already have prescription drug coverage. For these individuals a key step is to compare the current coverage with that provided through a Medicare plan. The benefits administrator or insurance carrier can provide additional information.

- **Coverage provided by employer or union:** If the drug coverage provided by an employer or union is, on average, at least as good as the standard Medicare coverage, the individual may choose to keep the current plan for as long as it is offered. If the plan is discontinued in the future, the individual can join a Medicare drug plan without penalty within 63 days of the coverage ending.

- **Medicare Advantage or other Medicare health plan:** Some Medicare Advantage or other Medicare health plans cover prescription drugs or have recently added such coverage. If a plan does not offer prescription drug coverage, an individual may wish to switch to another Medicare Advantage or other Medicare health plan that does cover prescription drugs, or change to the original Medicare plan and join a Medicare prescription drug plan.

- **Medigap Supplemental Insurance, with prescription drug coverage:** Medigap policies are supplemental health insurance policies, several of which include some prescription drug coverage. Most prescription drug coverage under these Medigap plans is not, on average, at least as good as the coverage provided under the standard Medicare prescription drug plan.

Continued...

Medicare Part D - Prescription Drug Coverage

- **TRICARE, VA or FEHB coverage:** Generally, the prescription drug benefits provided by TRICARE, the Department of Veteran's Affairs (VA) or Federal Employee's Health Benefits Program (FEHB) are as good as the standard Medicare prescription drug plan. In most cases it will be to the individual's advantage to keep the current plan. If coverage is lost in the future, the individual can join a Medicare drug plan without penalty within 63 days of the coverage ending.

Seek Professional Guidance

The process of making decisions concerning health care insurance can be confusing and complex. The advice and counsel of trained advisers is strongly recommended. Additional information is also available from:

- **On the web:** www.medicare.gov

- **By telephone:** Contact Medicare at 1-(800) 633-4227 (TTY users: 1-(877) 486-2048).

How Medicare Prescription Drug Coverage Works

Individual
Selects policy and
pays premium.

Individual

Prescription Drug Policy

**Health Care
Company**

Physician Prescribes Medication

Individual
Pays deductible,
co-insurance
amounts, and any
balance over
maximum benefit.

**Health Care
Company**
Pays benefits under
the terms of the
contract.

Pharmacy

Medicare Part C – Medicare Advantage

The original Medicare program, created in 1965, consists of Part A (hospital insurance) and Part B (medical insurance) and operates as a "fee-for-service" system. Under this program, a Medicare beneficiary can go to any physician or health facility nationwide which accepts Medicare payments.

An Alternative To Traditional Medicare

In 1997, the federal government created, as Medicare Part C, the Medicare+Choice program. This new program was designed to give Medicare beneficiaries access to a wide array of more cost-effective, private health plan choices, as an alternative to the traditional Parts A and B. In 2003, Medicare+Choice was renamed as "Medicare Advantage", as part of the Medicare Prescription Drug, Improvement, and Modernization Act.

Options Under Medicare Advantage

In general, each Medicare beneficiary is entitled to choose to receive benefits through either the original Medicare fee-for-service program under Parts A and B or through a Medicare Advantage plan. The Medicare Advantage options include:

- Health maintenance organizations (HMOs),
- Point-of-service (POS) plans,
- Preferred provider organizations (PPOs),
- Provider sponsored organizations (PSOs); and
- Private fee-for-service plans.

Benefits Under Medicare Advantage

Medicare Advantage plans are required to provide the same benefits that are covered under the traditional fee-for-service plan, except for hospice care. The plans can offer supplemental benefits not covered by the traditional plan. Medicare Advantage plans are prohibited from denying or limiting coverage based on health-status related factors. The only exception is that Medicare Advantage plans do not have to accept enrollees who have end-stage renal disease.

Continued.

Medicare Part C – Medicare Advantage

Making a Choice

Once a plan has been elected, that choice will remain in effect until the beneficiary changes it or the plan chosen no longer services the area in which the beneficiary resides.[1] If a beneficiary fails to make an election, he or she will remain in the traditional fee-for-service program.

- **Initial Medicare eligibility:** Beneficiaries who enroll in a Medicare Advantage plan when they first become eligible for Medicare benefits can change to the fee-for-service plan at any time during their first 12 months of enrollment. During this period they will have an extended period of guaranteed access to Medigap plans.

- **Annual enrollment:** An annual enrollment period takes place each November. Elections made during this annual enrollment period take effect January 1st of the following year. As a part of the annual enrollment, Medicare beneficiaries will be provided with information about each health plan available to them. The purpose of this information is to allow Medicare beneficiaries to make informed health care choices, based on comparative data regarding quality and performance.

- **Special enrollment periods:** Special enrollment periods are available after the end of the continuous open enrollment if: (1) a plan is discontinued; (2) the Medicare beneficiary moves; (3) the plan violates its contract with Medicare; or (4) the Medicare beneficiary encounters exceptional conditions (to be specified in regulations).

---

[1] Not all Medicare Advantage options are available in all geographical areas.

Medigap Policies

Medigap policies are supplemental health insurance policies sold by private insurers, designed to fill some of the "gaps" in health coverage provided by Medicare. Although Medicare covers many health care costs, you still have to pay certain coinsurance and deductible amounts, as well as paying for services that Medicare does not cover.

Who Can Buy a Medigap Policy?

Generally, you must be enrolled in the original Medicare Parts A and B before you need to purchase a Medigap insurance policy. Other types of health insurance coverage, such as Medicare Advantage, other Medicare health plans, Medicaid, or employer-provided health insurance, do not work with Medigap policies.

Standardized Policies

Under federal regulation, private insurers can only sell "standardized" Medigap policies. From 1992 to 2005 there were 10 standardized Medigap policies, termed plans A, B, C, D, E, F, G, H, I, and J. In 2005, two additional plans, K and L, were added.

These 12 standardized plans are not available to those living in Massachusetts, Minnesota, or Wisconsin; there are separate Medigap policies available for residents of these states.

The standardized policies allow you to compare "apples with apples." For example, a plan F policy will provide the same benefits, no matter which insurance company it is purchased from. However, a plan C policy will provide different coverage than a plan D policy. All Medigap policies must provide certain "core" benefits.

Choosing a Policy

There are two primary factors to consider when choosing a Medigap policy.

- **Needed benefits:** Carefully consider what benefits you are most likely to need; you may not need the most comprehensive plan.
- **Cost:** Once you have decided which benefits you will need, shop for the policy that provides those benefits at the lowest cost.

Policy Costs Can Differ

There can be a wide variation in the cost of a standardized Medigap policy, due to a number of factors:

- **Discounts:** Some insurers may offer discounts to certain classes of people, such as women, non-smokers, or married couples.
- **Medical underwriting:** An insurance company may require you to fill out a detailed questionnaire on your health. The information you provide is used to determine whether or not a policy will be issued, or what premium to charge.

Continued

Medigap Policies

- **Pre-existing conditions:** If you have a "pre-existing condition," a known health problem, before you apply for a Medigap policy, you may have to wait up to six months before that problem is covered.

- **High deductible:** Plans F and J are available in a "high deductible" option, which means that you must pay more of the cost before the policy begins to provide benefits. Premiums for these high deductible policies are typically less.

- **Medicare SELECT:** Medicare SELECT policies are sold in a few states by a few insurers. Except for emergencies, these policies require you to use pre-selected hospitals and physicians.

- **Guaranteed renewable:** Medigap policies issued after 1990 are generally guaranteed renewable. This means that as long as you pay the premiums, are honest about health issues, and the insurance company doesn't go bankrupt, the insurer can't drop your coverage. In some states, policies issued before 1990 may not be guaranteed renewable.

- **Insurer pricing methods:** The table below shows three common methods by which an insurance company will price its Medigap policies:

Pricing Method	Payment	Other Issues
Community (No-Age)	Each insured pays the same premium, regardless of age.	Premiums may increase due to inflation.
Issue-Age	Policy premium is based on your age when you purchase the policy.	Younger buyers pay lower premiums. Premiums may increase due to inflation.
Attained-Age	Premiums are based on your age each year, thus premiums increase annually.	Younger buyers pay lower premiums. Premiums can increase each year. Premiums may also increase due to inflation.

Other Resources

Professional guidance in dealing with any aspect of a Medigap policy is strongly recommended. Other available resources include:

- **Medicare:** The federal government's Centers for Medicare & Medicaid Services (CMS) has a great deal of information available on their website at www.medicare.gov. You can also reach them by phone at (800) 633-4227.

- **State Health Insurance Assistance Programs:** Many states operate health insurance assistance programs designed to provide assistance and information regarding Medicare, Medigap policies, and long-term care policies.

- **State insurance department:** Each state has an insurance department that regulates the sale of all types of insurance within the state. These state agencies can provide information about Medigap policies.

Medigap Policies Compared
Medigap Policies A-L

Medigap policies are designed to fill the "gaps" in health insurance provided under the original Medicare Parts A and B. These policies must provide standardized coverage as specified by the federal government. The table below briefly compares and contrasts the different policies available.

Plan[1]	Core Benefits	Skilled Nursing	Part A Deduct-ible	Part B Deduct-ible	Part B Excess Charges	Emergency Foreign Travel	At Home Recovery	Preven-tive Care
A	Yes							
B	Yes		Yes					
C	Yes	Yes	Yes	Yes		Yes		
D	Yes	Yes	Yes			Yes	Yes	
E	Yes	Yes	Yes			Yes		Yes
F[2]	Yes	Yes	Yes	Yes	100%	Yes		
G	Yes	Yes	Yes		80%	Yes	Yes	
H	Yes	Yes	Yes			Yes		
I	Yes	Yes	Yes		100%	Yes	Yes	
J[2]	Yes	Yes	Yes	Yes	100%	Yes	Yes	Yes
K[3]	Some	50%	50%					
L[3]	Some	75%	75%					

What's Included?

The following paragraphs provide a general description of the various policy benefits available in the standardized Medigap policies.

- **Core benefits:** *Medigap Plans A-J* – Includes all co-pays except that for days 1-60 of hospitalization, plus adding 365 days of hospital coverage after the standard Medicare benefit is exhausted; Medicare B coinsurance amounts after meeting the yearly deductible; the first three pints of blood. Medigap Plans K and L – Includes all co-pays except that for days 1-60 of hospitalization, plus adding 365 days of hospital coverage after the standard Medicare benefit is exhausted; for Part B, Plan K pay 50% of the coinsurance amount after the annual deductible is met; Plan L pays 75% of the coinsurance amounts after the annual deductible is met; Plan K pays 50% of the cost of the first three pints of blood; Plan L pays 75% of the cost of the first three pints of blood.

- **Skilled nursing**: Medigap Plans C-J – Pay the coinsurance amounts under Part A for days 21-100 in a skilled nursing facility. Medigap Plans K and L – Pay the percentage shown of the coinsurance amounts for days 21-100 in a skilled nursing facility.

---

[1] The policies shown in this table are not available to residents of Massachusetts, Minnesota, and Wisconsin. Some policies may not be available in your state.
[2] Medigap Plans F and J also have a high-deductible option available.
[3] The Basic coverage for Medigap Plans K and L also includes some Hospice benefits.

Continued

Medigap Policies Compared
Medigap Policies A-L

- **Part A deductible**: *Medigap Plans B-J* – Pays the Medicare Part A deductible for the first 60 days of hospitalization. Medigap Plans K and L – Pay the percentage shown of the Part A deductible for the first 60 days of hospitalization.

- **Part B deductible**: Medigap Plans C, F, and J – Pays the annual Medicare Part B deductible.

- **Part B excess charges**: Medigap Plans F, I, and J – Pay 100% of the excess charges. *Medigap Plan G* – Pays 80% of the excess charges.

- **Emergency foreign travel**: Medigap Plans C-J – The insured pays a $250 deductible and then 20% of any remaining costs of emergency health care. This benefit is typically limited to a $50,000 lifetime maximum and the first 60 days of each trip.

- **At home recovery**: Medigap Plans D, G, I, or J – If Medicare covered home health benefits are provided, the policy may pay up to $40 per visit for other, non-Medicare covered visits, with a yearly maximum of $1,600.

- **Preventive care**: Medigap Plans E and *J* – For non-Medicare covered preventive services, pay up to $120 per year. The insured pays all costs after the $120 limit has been reached.

Prescription Drug Benefits

A few Medigap policies issued before 2006 included a prescription drug benefit. However, beginning January 1, 2006, Medicare began a separate prescription drug coverage benefit, available to most Medicare beneficiaries. Medigap policies issued January 1, 2006 or later do not include prescription drug benefits.

Seek Professional Guidance

Professional guidance is strongly recommended when choosing a Medigap insurance policy. In addition to consulting you financial advisor, a number of governmental resources are available:

- **Medicare:** On the web at www.medicare.gov, or by phone at (800) 633-4227.

- **State government:** Many states operate a Health Insurance Assistance Program, designed to provide information and assistance. Otherwise, the local state insurance department will often provide information about Medigap policies.

The Impact of Disability

While most Americans insure their lives and physical possessions such as their homes, cars, etc., many overlook the need to protect their most valuable asset – the ability to earn an income.

How likely is it that someone will become disabled? The table below, developed using data collected by the federal government, shows the number of working-age Americans who have a disability that affects their daily lives.

Individuals with Disabilities by Age[1]

Age Range	No Disability	With a Disability
5-15 Years	94%	6%
16-20 Years	93%	7%
21-64 Years	87%	13%
65-74 Years	70%	30%
75 Years and over	48%	52%

Income Down, Expenses Up

The graph below illustrates the problem typically faced by an individual who becomes disabled for an extended period of time – income decreases while expenses increase.

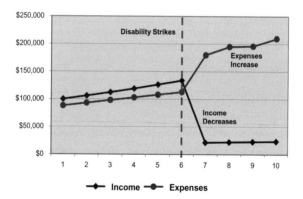

[1] Source: U.S. Census Bureau, 2005 American Community Survey. Table B18002, sex by age by disability status for the civilian noninstitutionalized population 5 years and over, male and female.

The Individual Need for Disability Insurance

Many people believe that their biggest asset is their home. For most of us, our biggest asset is the ability to work and earn an income. Not being able to work – due to a job loss or a disability having taken away the ability to work – is often financially devastating.

Everyone who works for a living is very familiar with what can happen if they are fired. On the other hand, the possibility of becoming seriously disabled is a risk few seem to think much about. How likely is it that you will become disabled? According to one study, 30% of all Americans between the ages of 35 and 65 suffered a disability lasting at least 90 days.[1] The risk of disability is real. The question is, "What to do about it?"

Don't Count on Social Security

A few individuals do manage to qualify for disability benefits from Social Security. However, the Social Security definition of "disability" is so strict that over 60% of initial claims are rejected.[2] Obviously, something else beyond Social Security is needed.

Group Disability Insurance

Many employers will provide – or make available – disability insurance on a group basis. However, even those who are covered by a group policy can still be at substantial risk. Employer-sponsored disability polices seldom provide you with more than 60 % of your monthly salary. Many policies set a monthly maximum benefit that may be far less than what some people earn. Income taxes can also be an issue; if the employer is paying the full cost of the coverage, disability benefits are fully taxable.[3]

Individual Disability Income Insurance

For many, the real solution to the disability problem is individual disability income insurance. Although individual policies may cost you more, as long as you pay the premiums the benefits are not taxable. Plus, an individual policy allows you to tailor its terms to fit your own needs. Factors to consider when shopping for an individual disability policy include:

- **Company strength:** You need to know if the company is financially sound.

- **Definition of disability:** Look for a policy that defines disability in the broadest terms possible. Some policies will permit you to work in a different occupation and still collect disability benefits.

- **Elimination period:** How long must you wait before disability payments begin?

- **Benefit period:** How long will you need coverage? Both short-term and long-term disability benefits are available.

- **Inflation protection**: Try to find a policy that adjusts benefits for inflation.

---

[1] Based upon the 1985 Commissioners' Individual Disability Table.
[2] General Accounting Office, Social Security Administration: More Effort Needed to Assess Consistency of Disability Decisions (Washington, D.C.: GPO, 2004), 7.
[3] This discussion concerns federal income tax law only. State or local law may vary.

The Business Need for Disability Insurance

Self-motivated individuals frequently play a crucial role in the success of a business. This is particularly true of small businesses in which one or two talented people possess highly specialized skills or knowledge that other employees do not have. If such a "key" person were to suffer a long-term disability, not only would the individual face substantial financial risk, but the very survival of the company could be in jeopardy.

Although sole-proprietorships and partnerships are generally the most vulnerable, corporations, particularly corporations built around one or two individuals, are also at significant risk. However the business is organized, when you consider the likelihood that you or one of your key employees may become disabled, there is a clear need to protect both your personal income and the financial well-being of the company.

Options to Consider

There is no single strategy or type of policy to protect your business from the risks posed by a key employee's disability. Like a puzzle, a number of pieces are needed to complete the picture:

- **Adequate cash reserves:** Liquid funds can cover a short-term disability.

- **Key employee disability insurance:** Pays income to a disabled key employee. Generally, if the employer pays the entire premium, disability benefits are taxable income to the employee.

- **Business overhead expense insurance:** This type of insurance covers normal operating expenses such as employee salaries, equipment leases, utilities, rent, advertising, maintenance, etc.

- **Qualified sick pay plan:** The federal tax code prohibits a business owner from paying himself (or herself) a salary while disabled, and then deducting the payments as an allowable business expense. A formal, written qualified sick pay plan (also known as a salary continuation plan), established in advance, can provide for funding the disability benefits as well as maximizing the tax benefits.

- **Disability buy-out:** In the event that you or another owner of the business suffers a permanent disability, disability insurance can be used to fund a buy-sell agreement.

Seek Professional Guidance

The advice and counsel of knowledgeable tax and insurance advisors are essential in preparing for the potential impact of disability on a business.

Sources of Disability Insurance

Disability insurance is designed to replace a portion of the income you can lose if you are too sick or injured to work. There are two main sources of disability insurance: private disability insurance programs and government-sponsored disability insurance programs.

Private Disability Insurance Programs

There are two primary sources of private disability insurance:

The individual purchases the policy directly from an insurance company. The terms and benefits of the policy can vary widely.

Group plans are typically purchased through your employer and generally offer a low-cost alternative to individual coverage. The terms and coverage will vary.

Government-Sponsored Disability Insurance Programs

At the federal level, there are a two primary programs offering disability insurance. Both are administered by the Social Security Administration.

Social Security Disability Insurance (SSDI) pays benefits to qualified individuals under the age of 65 regardless of current income. Benefits are based upon your Social Security earnings history.

Social Security Supplemental Security Income (SSI) pays benefits to qualified individuals who are either over 65, blind or disabled, and with limited income. Benefits are not related to the individual's record of Social Security earnings.

The Department of Defense and Veterans Administration offer military service members and veterans disability compensation for service-related health problems. In addition, federal employees covered under the Federal Employees Retirement System (FERS) are eligible for benefits if they have at least 18 months of service, and are unable to perform their job because of injury or disease.

All states and the District of Columbia have workers' compensation laws that provide disability compensation to employed individuals who get sick, become injured, or who are killed on the job. Although most workers are covered, states laws vary dramatically as to who is excluded and to the amount of benefits paid.

A Word of Caution

Neither of the above programs offered through Social Security covers partial disability and both have a strict definition of what it means to be disabled. In fact, over 60% of initial claims for Social Security disability benefits are denied.[1]

---

[1] General Accounting Office, Social Security Administration: More Effort Needed to Assess Consistency of Disability Decisions (Washington, D.C.: GPO, 2004), 7.

Individual Disability Income Insurance

One approach to the problem of providing income during an extended period of disability is to purchase individual disability income insurance.

What to Look for in a Disability Insurance Policy

- **Definition of disability:** Are education, experience, and past earnings taken into account in determining whether the insured is qualified to resume work? Many policies provide for an initial own occupation[1] definition of disability, for a specified period of time, after which a different definition of disability applies.

- **Partial or residual benefits:** Partial or residual disability benefits may be paid in some policies when the impairment allows the insured to perform only a portion of his or her duties. This provision may also pay benefits in the event the disability reduces the insured's income by a certain amount (e.g. 20% or more) from pre-disability levels.

- **Cost of living adjustment:** Is there a cost of living adjustment (COLA) which would increase benefit payments after a disability occurs?

- **Cancelability and renewability of policy:** Except for nonpayment of premiums, is the policy noncancelable or guaranteed renewable? Noncancelable generally means that the insurance company cannot cancel the policy, change the policy provisions or increase policy premiums after issue, as long as premiums are paid on a timely basis. Guaranteed renewable is similar, but allows the insurance company to increase the premium.

- **Waiting and elimination period:** Is the waiting or elimination period proper for the insured's circumstances? Commonly available periods may include 30, 60, 90, 180 and 360 days. Naturally, the longer the elimination period one selects, the lower his or her premium payments will be. However, a person's needs, cash reserves and income sources should be the deciding factors in selecting a proper elimination/waiting period.

- **Benefit period:** What benefit period should be selected? Since a long-term medical disability can be financially devastating, one should elect a long-term benefit where possible. Some companies offer lifetime benefit periods, but periods as short as 24 months to 60 months are also available.

---

[1] Own occupation generally means the insured's current occupation. The own occupation definition of disability may not be available for all occupations or professions.

Continued

Individual Disability Income Insurance

Types of Disability Contracts

Several other specialized disability contracts are available to the businessperson:

- **Business overhead expense:** Covers expenses such as staff salaries, rent, telephone, utilities, malpractice insurance and other expenses necessary to keep a business open.

- **Key person disability:** Reimburses the business for the loss of a key employee and allows funding of temporary replacement or training of a successor.

- **Disability buyout:** Provides income to fund a buy-sell agreement triggered by the total disability of a shareholder/business owner. Payouts may come in the form of a lump sum, monthly installments or a combination of the two.

Caution: Highly-compensated employees should be aware of payment caps in many group long-term disability policies. While some programs will provide disability income payments at 60% or 66% of salary, many have a relatively low dollar limitation, such as $3,000 per month.

How Individual Disability Income Insurance Works

Individual
Pays premium.

Individual

**Individual Disability
Income Policy**

**Disability Insurance
Company**

Disability Occurs

Employer
Stops paying wages
or salary.

Individual

**Disability Insurance
Company**
Pays disability
income benefits
under the terms of
the contract.

Group Disability Insurance

As the name implies, a "group" disability insurance policy covers a number of people who are linked in some way, such as through an employer, a trade association, or a school. Benefits are paid to replace earnings lost due to accident or sickness. Premiums may be paid for by the individual, the organization, or both.

Generally, the cost of group coverage is less expensive than the cost of individual coverage. Group policy benefits typically are paid for a limited period of time, with the maximum income benefit rarely greater than 50 to 60 % of earnings.

Group policies can vary widely. For example, some policies cover both non-occupational and occupational illnesses and injuries, while others do not. A policy may cover short-term disabilities, long-term disabilities, or both. Additional factors to keep in mind are: eligibility; how long you have to wait before benefits begin (the "elimination" period); the dollar amount that will be paid (benefit level); and for how long benefits will be paid (benefit period).

Short-Term Disability

These policies tend to have short elimination periods (1-14 days) and typically provide benefits for six months to one year. In most cases, maternity is covered the same as any other disability.

Long-Term Disability

There are times when an injury or illness will render an individual unable to perform the essential duties of his or her occupation for an extended period of time. Long-term disability insurance offered through your employer is a start, but group disability benefits often cover only about 50% of your income. Can your family survive on half a paycheck?

Federal Income Tax

As a general rule, premiums paid by an individual for disability insurance are not deductible. The taxability of disability benefits depends primarily upon whether the premiums were paid with pretax or after-tax dollars. If the premium payments are paid with pretax dollars, then benefits are taxable to the individual. On the other hand, if the premiums are paid with after-tax dollars, benefits are nontaxable.

Seek Professional Guidance

The tax issues discussed here reflect federal income tax law. In all situations, you should check with a tax advisor who fully understands your situation. Your tax advisor will understand the taxability of disability benefits under federal, state, or local law.

How Employer-Provided Disability Insurance Works

Employer and Employee
Each pays a portion of the
premium.[1]

**Employer and
Employee**

Group Disability Policy

**Disability Insurance
Company**

— — Disability Occurs — — — — — — — — — — — —

Employer
Stops paying wages
or salary.

Employee

**Disability Insurance
Company**
Pays disability
income benefits
under the terms of
the contract.

---

[1] In some situations, the employer will sponsor a group disability insurance plan, but will not pay any of the premium.

When the Parent Becomes the Child
Providing Care for Older Individuals

It should come as no surprise to anyone that we're living longer.[1] Over the recent past, medical science has defeated numerous diseases that once shortened the lives of many. These extra years are not without their problems; living longer allows people to come down with illnesses that, in years past, they would not have lived long enough to develop.

As a person ages, health problems can gradually become overwhelming, to the point where the individual is no longer capable of living independently or handling his or her personal affairs. Often, a child will then step in to "help out." Gradually, a role reversal takes place in which the child becomes the parent and the parent becomes the child.

Planning Ahead - If Possible

If possible, planning ahead makes the process easier. A child who is taking over a parent's situation will often be handed total responsibility for the parent's well being. To the extent that the parent is able, he or she must be kept involved. Some key areas include:

- **Finances:** Managing the parent's income, assets, and liabilities, paying the bills, and seeing that income tax returns are prepared.

- **Medical:** Understanding the parent's medical situation and history, insuring that needed medical care is provided, and dealing with required medication.

- **Benefits:** Making maximum use of any benefits that might be payable from former employers, Medicare, Medicaid, or the Veteran's Administration.

- **Key Documents:** To carry out the parent's wishes and legally act on the parent's behalf, an adult child will need key documents such as wills, trust documents, a durable power of attorney for health care, a general power of attorney, and a "living will" or advance health care directive.

When to Intervene?

Very few of us want to intrude in our parents' lives. It is only when we begin to notice certain "things" about Mom and Dad that we begin to consider stepping in. Problems such as memory loss, dementia, diminished sight or hearing, incontinence, and falling are signs it's time to intervene. Two initial questions must be answered:

1. **What needs to be done?** What is the appropriate level of care and/or type of living arrangement? Often, this question is answered in consultation with the parent's physician or with the help of a geriatric care manager.
2. **Who will be in charge?** This task frequently falls to the child who is the closest, geographically, to the area where the parent resides. Sometimes, younger family members may decide to share the responsibilities. In other instances, a child with special skills or aptitudes may be chosen.

---

[1] For example, a child born in the year 1900 had an average life expectancy of 47.3 years. However, for a child born in 2004, average life expectancy had increased to 77.8 years. Source: National Center for Health Statistics. Deaths: Final Data for 2004.

Continued...

When the Parent Becomes the Child
Providing Care for Older Individuals

Care and Housing Options

Remaining in the family home is often the first choice of many elderly individuals. However, because the home is either unsafe or ill-suited to their needs, other options must be considered. The chart below lists a few of the alternatives:

Facility Type	Description	Advantages	Disadvantages
Senior Adult Condominiums	Similar to home ownership. Usually age restricted.	Living unit can often be matched to the individual's needs. Few maintenance or security concerns.	Individual must arrange for own healthcare and personal service needs. Rules may be restrictive. Costs may be high.
Senior Apartments	Apartment rental units. Often age restricted.	Individual can select a unit to meet needs. May have common services such as transportation, recreation, or meals.	Individual must be able to live safely and independently; must arrange for own healthcare and personal service needs.
Continuing Care Retirement Community	Provide a range of facilities, including independent living, assisted living, and nursing home care.	Different levels of services and living arrangements are available to meet an individual's needs as those needs change over time.	Usually expensive. Require a large initial entrance fee as well as monthly charges. If care provider is not financially strong, monies paid may be lost.
Assisted Living	Rental of private rooms or apartments, with many services.	A wide range of personal services are provided, including laundry, meals, house keeping, and 24 hour monitoring.	Individual must be able to move about and handle most of their own physical needs.
Nursing Home	Skilled nursing facility	Provide care for individuals who cannot live independently because of physical or mental impairments.	Can be quite expensive. Quality of care can vary.

Preparing for the End

Even longer lives eventually end. The caregiver's responsibilities in this final stage of life are just as important as in any other. One key goal is to honor the terms of the elderly individual's advance health care directive. A "Do Not Resuscitate" order may be required, when even heroic medical efforts serve no real purpose. You may have to arrange for hospice care when death is near. Allowing the elderly the opportunity for a death with dignity is as important as caring for them when they are alive.

Long-Term Care

Long-term care (LTC) is the term used to describe a variety of services in the area of health, personal care, and social needs of persons who are chronically disabled, ill or infirm. Depending on the needs of the individual, long-term care may include services such as nursing home care, assisted living, home health care, or adult day care.

Who Needs Long-Term Care?

The need for long-term care is generally defined by an individual's inability to perform the normal activities of daily living (ADL) such as bathing, dressing, eating, toileting, continence, and moving around. Conditions such as AIDS, spinal cord or head injuries, stroke, mental illness, Alzheimer's disease or other forms of dementia, or physical weakness and frailty due to advancing age can all result in the need for long-term care.

While the need for long-term care can occur at any age, it is typically older individuals who require such care.

Individuals With Disabilities, by Age[1]

Age Range	No Disability	With a Disability
5-15 Years	94%	6%
16-20 Years	93%	7%
21-64 Years	87%	13%
65-74 Years	70%	30%
75 Years and over	48%	52%

What Is The Cost of Long-Term Care?

Apart from the unpaid services of family and friends, long-term care is expensive. The table below contains national average cost data (regional costs can vary widely) for typical long-term care services; it provides an approximate guide to the cost of long-term care:

Service	2004	2005	2006
Assisted living facility[2]	$2,524 per month ($30,288 per year)	$2,905 per month ($34,860 per year)	$2,968 per month ($35,616 per year)
Nursing home[3] (Private room)	$192 per day ($70,080 per year)	$203 per day ($74,095 per year)	$206 per day ($75,190 per year)
Nursing home[3] (Semi-private room)	$169 per day ($61,685 per year)	$176 per day ($64,240 per year)	$183 per day ($66,795 per year)
Home health aide[3]	$19 per hour	$19 per hour	$18 per hour
Homemaker/companion[3]	No data available	$17 per hour	$17 per hour

---

[1] Source: U.S. Census Bureau, 2005 American Community Survey. Table B18002, sex by age by disability status for the civilian noninstitutionalized population 5 years and over, male and female.
[2] Source: The MetLife Market Survey of Assisted Living Costs, October, 2006.
[3] Source: The MetLife Market Survey of Nursing Home and Home Care Costs, September, 2006.

Continued...

Long-Term Care

Paying for Long-Term Care – Personal Resources

Much long-term care is paid for from personal resources:

- **Out-of-Pocket:** Expenses paid from personal savings and investments.

- **Reverse Mortgage:** Certain homeowners may qualify for a reverse mortgage, allowing them to tap the equity in the home while retaining ownership.

- **Accelerated Death Benefits:** Certain life insurance policies provide for "accelerated death benefits" (also known as a living benefit) if the insured becomes terminally ill.

- **Private Health Insurance:** Some private health insurance policies cover a limited period of at-home or nursing home care, usually related to a covered illness or injury.

- **Long-Term Care Insurance:** Private insurance designed to pay for long-term care services, at home or in an institution, either skilled or unskilled. Benefits will vary from policy to policy.

Paying for Long-Term Care – Government Resources

Long-term care that is paid for by government comes from two primary sources:

- **Medicare:** Medicare is a health insurance program operated by the federal government. Benefits are available to qualifying individuals age 65 and older, certain disabled individuals under age 65, and those suffering from end-stage renal disease. A limited amount of nursing home care is available under Medicare Part A, Hospital Insurance. An unlimited amount of home health care is also available, if made under a physician's treatment plan.

- **Medicaid:** Medicaid is a welfare program funded by both federal and state governments, designed to provide health care for the truly impoverished. Eligibility for benefits under Medicaid is typically based on an individual's income and assets; eligibility rules vary by state.

In the past, some individuals have attempted to artificially qualify themselves for Medicaid by gifting or otherwise disposing of assets for less than fair market value. Sometimes known as "Medicaid spend-down", this strategy has been the subject of legislation such as the Omnibus Budget Reconciliation Act of 1993 (OBRA '93). Among other restrictions, OBRA '93 provided that gifts of assets within 36 months (60 months for certain trusts) before applying for Medicaid could delay benefit eligibility.

The Deficit Reduction Act of 2005 (DRA) further tightened the requirements to qualify for Medicaid by extending the "look-back" period for all gifts from 36 to 60 months. Under this law, the beginning of the ineligibility (or penalty) period was generally changed to the later of: (1) the date of the gift; or, (2) the date the individual would otherwise have qualified to receive Medicaid benefits. This legislation also clarified certain "spousal impoverishment" rules as well making it more difficult to use certain types of annuities as a means of transferring assets for less than fair market value.

Choosing a Long-Term Care Policy

Assessing the need for long-term care (LTC) insurance is an
important part of any risk management program. The heavy
economic burden of paying for such care should be measured
against your available resources. If you need LTC for even a short
period of time, what effect will that have on your estate and any
legacy you may wish to leave to your heirs? The decision to
purchase LTC insurance, either individually or under a group plan,
generally must be made while you are still healthy. Once a
disabling condition occurs, it is too late to act.

Common Elements in Long-Term Care Insurance Policies

- **"Qualified" LTC policies**: If a LTC policy meets certain criteria established by the
  federal government, the premiums for the policy are considered "medical care" and thus
  qualify for the medical expense itemized deduction. Federal law limits the amount of
  qualified LTC premiums that may be deducted each year.

- **Amount of the benefit:** Most policies pay a fixed dollar amount for each day you are
  eligible for the benefit; e.g., $200 per day. A survey of nursing homes in the local area
  can help determine the desired amount.

- **Inflation protection:** Since costs inevitably increase, a policy without a provision for
  inflation may be outdated in a few years. Of course, an additional charge is incurred for
  this protection.

- **Guaranteed renewability:** Almost all long-term care policies sold today are guaranteed
  renewable; they cannot be canceled as long as you pay the premiums on time and as
  long as you have told the truth about your health on the application. The fact that a
  policy is guaranteed renewable does not mean that the premiums cannot be increased;
  insurers typically reserve the right to raise premiums for an entire class or group of
  policyholders. Some policies sold in the past were not guaranteed renewable and a few
  of these policies may still be in force.

- **Waiver of premium:** Some policies will waive future premiums after you have been in
  the nursing home for a specified number of days; e.g., 90 days.

- **Prior hospitalization:** This policy provision requires one to be hospitalized (for the
  same condition) prior to entering the nursing home or no benefits will be paid under the
  policy. Although prior hospitalization clauses have been prohibited in all states, some
  older policies still in force may contain this provision. Policies currently sold do not
  contain prior hospitalization clauses.

- **Place of care:** Does the policy require that the nursing home be licensed or otherwise
  certified by the state to provide skilled or intermediate nursing care? Must the facility
  meet certain record keeping requirements?

- **Plan of care:** A plan of care is part of the health care claims process. It is the result of
  an assessment prepared by the insured's physician, and a multi-disciplinary team,
  including practical nurses, social workers, and other health care professionals. The plan
  outlines the appropriate level of care needed to assist the insured in performing the
  activities of daily living.

Continued...

115

Choosing a Long-Term Care Policy

- **Level of care:** There are three generally recognized levels of care in an institutional setting:
    - **Skilled care:** Daily nursing and rehabilitation care under the supervision of skilled medical personnel; e.g., registered nurses and based on a physician's orders.
    - **Intermediate care:** The same as skilled care, except it requires only intermittent or occasional nursing and rehabilitative care.
    - **Custodial care:** Help in one's daily activities including eating, getting up, bathing, dressing, use of toilet, etc. Persons performing the assistance do not need to be medically skilled, but the care is usually based upon the physician's certification that the care is needed.

- **Pre-existing conditions:** Depending on the state, a policy may limit coverage of pre-existing conditions to discourage persons who are already ill from purchasing a policy. Many policies will provide benefits if the pre-existing condition was overcome six months or more prior to applying for the policy. Also, some policies will not pay benefits if the pre-existing condition re-occurs within six months after the effective date of coverage.

- **Deductible or waiting period:** Most LTC policies require you to "pay your own way" for a specified number of days (generally ranging between zero and 120 days) before the insurance company will begin to pay benefits. Of course, the shorter the waiting period, the higher the cost will be. This is usually referred to as an "elimination period."

- **Alzheimer's disease:** Most policies now include coverage for organic brain disorders like Alzheimer's disease.

- **Home health care (home care):** Many long-term care policies can provide coverage in the insured's home. It is most often offered as a rider (requiring an additional premium) to nursing facility coverage, and reimburses the cost of long-term care received at home.

- **Rating the company:** Companies should be financially sound and have a reputation of treating policyholders fairly.

Seek Professional Guidance

A perfect LTC policy does not exist. Many policy features must be compared and weighed. As a general rule, the more benefits included in a policy, the higher the premium will be. Professional guidance is extremely important in this complicated area.

Long-Term Care Tax Issues

Federal law provides generally favorable tax treatment of the expenses connected with long-term care (LTC). However, a number of rules must be carefully followed in order to maximize these tax benefits.[1]

Key Definitions

- **Qualified LTC Services:** The necessary services required by a "chronically ill" individual, provided under a treatment plan prescribed by a licensed health care practitioner.

- **Chronically Ill Individual:** An individual unable to perform at least two of the activities of daily living (ADLs)[2] for at least 90 days, or who requires protective supervision because of severe cognitive impairment. Certification by a licensed health care practitioner within the previous 12 months is required.

- **Qualified LTC Policy:** A LTC policy that meets certain tax-related requirements set by the federal government.

Long-Term Care Expenses

Long-term care expenses are medical expenses: Unreimbursed amounts an individual pays for qualified LTC services, as well as premiums paid for qualified LTC policies, are included in the term "medical care." IRC Sec. 213(d)(1), as amended. For individual taxpayers, such expenses thus qualify for the medical expense itemized deduction. Qualifying medical expenses are deductible as an itemized deduction to the extent they exceed 7.5% of adjusted gross income (AGI).

Current law limits the annual amount of LTC premiums that can be deducted, based on the age of the insured.

Age Before Close of Tax Year	2007 Limitation	2008 Limitation
40 or less	$290	$310
41 to 50	550	580
51 to 60	1,110	1,150
61 to 70	2,950	3,080
Over 70	3,680	3,850

These annual limitation amounts are adjusted for inflation each year.

---

[1] The discussion here concerns federal income tax law; state or local law may vary.
[2] Such as bathing, dressing, eating, toileting, transferring, and continence.

Continued...

Long-Term Care Tax Issues

Long-Term Care Policy Benefits

Benefits excluded from income: Beginning with policies issued in 1997,[1] benefits received under a qualified LTC contract are generally excluded from income as an amount "received for personal injury and sickness." (See IRC Sec. 7702B.) In order for benefits paid under a policy to be excluded from income, the policy must meet strict federal tax requirements to be a qualified contract. Further, benefits must be for services provided to a chronically ill individual. A limited grandfather clause applies to contracts in existence before 1997.

The exclusion from income is limited to the greater of $270 per day (calendar year 2008)[2], or total un-reimbursed LTC expenses actually incurred. The dollar limitation is adjusted for inflation annually.

Other Tax Issues

- **Employees:** Generally, if an employer chooses to purchase tax-qualified long-term care insurance for an employee, neither the coverage provided nor the benefits paid (subject to the limitations described earlier) will be taxable to the employee. If certain requirements are met, self-employed individuals may also include themselves for such coverage.

- **Self-employed individuals:** Self-employed individuals are permitted to deduct qualifying health insurance premiums, including tax-qualified long-term care premiums, as an adjustment to gross income, rather than as an itemized deduction subject to the 7.5% of AGI limitation. This deduction is also generally available to general partners in a partnership, limited partners in a partnership receiving guaranteed payments, and more than 2% owners of subchapter S corporations who receive wages from the corporation.

- **Combination contracts:** A "combination contract" is an annuity or life insurance contract that also provides qualified LTC coverage. Under the Pension Protection Act of 2006 (PPA 2006), withdrawals from the cash value of either the annuity or life portion of a combination contract to pay for the LTC coverage are generally not includable in income and no medical expense deduction is allowed for such charges. The LTC portion of the contract is treated as a separate contract and amounts received are treated for federal income tax purposes as LTC insurance benefits.[3]

Seek Professional Guidance

Federal, state, and local income tax law can be complex and confusing. The guidance and counsel of a qualified tax or other financial professional is highly recommended.

---

[1] The Health Insurance Portability and Accountability Act of 1996, which became law on April 21, 1996, significantly changed the federal income tax treatment of LTC policy premiums and benefits.
[2] This amount was $260 in 2007.
[3] Effective with tax years beginning after December 31, 2009.

How Individual LTC Insurance Works

Individual
Pays premium.

Individual

**Individual
Long-Term Care
Policy**

**Long-Term Care
Insurance
Company**

Long-Term Disability Event
(e.g., stroke, dementia, advancing age)

Individual
Pays any balance
over maximum
benefit.

**Long-Term Care
Insurance Company**
Pays benefits under
the terms of the
contract, up to
policy maximums.

Long-Term Care Providers
(e.g., home care, nursing home)

How Employer-Provided LTC Insurance Works

Employer and Employee
Each pays a portion
of the premium.[1]

Employer and
Employee

Group
Long-Term Care
Policy

Long-Term Care
Insurance
Company

Long-Term Disability Event
(e.g., stroke, dementia, advancing age)

Employee
Pays any balance
over maximum
benefit.

Long-Term Care
Insurance Company
Pays benefits under
the terms of the
contract, up to
policy maximums.

Long-Term Care Providers
(e.g., home care, nursing home)

---

[1] In some situations, the employer will sponsor a group long-term care insurance plan, but will not pay any portion of the premium

The Perfect Investment

Once an individual or family has reached the stage in life where there is enough income to easily pay the monthly bills, there is often a desire to put the excess monthly cash flow to work. For some, an inheritance, a large bonus, or a distribution from a qualified plan can provide an investable, lump sum of money. For most people, the key question is, "How do I put this money to work?" In a perfect world, the answer would be an investment that has certain, ideal characteristics:

- **High rate of return:** A total return high enough to out perform inflation and taxes, and still meet the investment goal.

- **Complete safety:** There would be no concern that any part of the investment could ever be lost.

- **Always liquid:** An investor would be able to redeem the investment, and receive cash, at any time of day or night, every day of the year without any penalty or loss of principal.

- **No income taxes:** There would never be any income taxes due on the investment's yield or growth. The investor keeps everything earned.

- **No skill or knowledge required:** No special skill or knowledge would be required to manage the investment. One could just forget about the investment and enjoy life.

The Real World

Such a "perfect" investment does not exist, of course. In the real world, individual investors must choose from a confusing range of investment tools, each with different characteristics and uses. The process of selecting the best investment for a particular need or situation is made easier by clearly answering the following questions:

- **Why are you investing?** Do you need income for current expenses or are you accumulating money for a future need?

- **When will the money be needed?** At any moment? A year from now? At retirement, 25 years from now?

- **How much risk are you willing to undertake?** Can you afford to lose all or a part of the investment, and not have the loss affect how you live?

- **Are income taxes a concern?** If the investment is currently taxable, to what extent will the additional tax reduce investment growth or push you into a higher tax bracket?

- **What is the economic outlook?** Investment opportunities will vary depending on whether the economy is growing or shrinking.

- **Do you have the skill and knowledge needed to manage your investment?** Is professional investment management needed?

- **How much money is there available to invest?** Are smaller amounts available periodically, or is there currently a larger, lump sum of money?

Key Investment Questions

Many individuals and families have both a need and a desire to accumulate wealth. The inevitable question is, "What do I invest the money in?"

The answer to the question usually depends on the needs, temperament, and available resources of each individual or family. The "best" investment for one person is often not the best for someone else. The process of choosing the most appropriate investment can be made easier by carefully considering, and answering, the following questions:

- **What are your investment goals?** In other words, "What do I want the money to do for me?" For example, an investor might need to have additional income, to meet current living expenses. Other common needs include saving for long term goals such as retirement, a child's education or a dream vacation, or for a quickly available source of emergency funds.

- **How liquid does the investment need to be?** The term "liquidity" refers to how quickly an investment can be turned into cash, without losing any of the invested dollars. The question might also read, "When will the money be needed?" For example, investments meeting longer term goals such as retirement generally do not need to be as liquid as those designed to hold emergency funds.

- **What is your risk tolerance?** Can you afford to risk losing a portion, or even all, of your investment without it affecting how you live? What would be the impact of a loss on your investment goals? In general, risk is related to return: the higher the risk, the higher the potential return; the lower the risk, the lower the potential return.

- **What is the impact of income taxes?** Income taxes can have a significant, negative impact on your investment results. For example, many high-income individuals invest in municipal bonds because the interest from such bonds is generally exempt from federal income tax; in some instances the interest is also exempt from state income tax. Qualified retirement plans, life insurance policies and annuity contracts are used to accumulate funds for retirement because of their tax-deferred nature; generally, no taxes are due until the money is withdrawn.

- **What is the economic outlook?** The state of the economy as a whole can change the mix of desirable investments. For example, during periods of high inflation, tangible assets such as real estate, precious metals, and collectibles such as coins and art, have tended to produce good results. During periods of stable or declining inflation, intangible assets such as stocks and bonds have generally done well. Of course, there is no guarantee that history will repeat itself.

- **Is the skill and knowledge needed to manage the investment available?** An investor may not have the specialized skills and knowledge needed to properly select or manage an investment. In such instances professional investment advice, or investments where such advice is available, should be considered.

- **How much money is available to be invested?** The investment tools open to an investor can vary, depending on the amount of money available. For example, direct investment in the stock market can require a relatively large investment. Many mutual funds, however, will accept smaller contributions on a monthly basis.

Time and Growth of Money

Time is a vital factor in accumulating wealth. The following tables illustrate the effect of time and after-tax interest in accumulating funds.

Growth of a Single Lump-Sum Investment[1]

Years of Growth	$20,000 Compounded at	
	5%	8%
5	$25,526	$29,387
10	$32,578	$43,178
15	$41,579	$63,443
20	$53,066	$93,219
25	$67,727	$136,970
30	$86,439	$201,253
35	$110,320	$295,707
40	$140,800	$434,490

In other words, in a period 8 times longer (40 years rather than 5 years) the investment result at 8% is 15 times greater growth ($434,490 divided by $29,387).

Growth of a Fund to Which $5,000 Is Added[1] at the Beginning of Each Year

$5,000 per Year at 5%	Total Contributed	Will Grow to	Growth	Percent Increase
5	$25,000	$29,010	$4,010	16%
10	$50,000	$66,034	$16,034	32%
15	$75,000	$113,287	$38,287	51%
20	$100,000	$173,596	$73,596	74%
25	$125,000	$250,567	$125,567	100%
30	$150,000	$348,804	$198,804	133%
35	$175,000	$474,182	$299,182	171%
40	$200,000	$634,199	$434,199	217%

These tables assume a 5% rate of return after taxes and that the earnings are reinvested.

---

[1] The rates of return used in this illustration are not indicative of any actual investment and will fluctuate in value. An investment will not provide a consistent rate of return; years with lower (or negative) returns than the hypothetical returns shown may substantially affect the scenario presented.

Future Value of a Single Sum

Item Description	Value
Single sum deposit	$10,000
Annual interest rate[1]	5.00%
How interest is compounded	Annually
Number of Years	55
Amount accumulated at end of period	**$ 146,356**

Example

If you deposit $10,000 into an account earning an annual return
of 5.00%, then in 55 years your account will grow to $146,356.

---

[1] The rates of return used in this illustration are not indicative of any actual investment and will fluctuate in value. An investment will not provide a consistent rate of return; years with lower (or negative) returns than the hypothetical returns shown may substantially affect the scenario presented.

Present Value of a Future Sum

Item Description	Value
Desired future sum	$1,000,000
Annual interest rate[1]	5.00%
How interest is compounded	Annually
Number of Years	55
Present value	**$68,326**

Example

To accumulate $1,000,000 in 55 years earning an annual return of 5.00%, you will need to deposit a current sum of $68,326.

---

[1] The rates of return used in this illustration are not indicative of any actual investment and will fluctuate in value. An investment will not provide a consistent rate of return; years with lower (or negative) returns than the hypothetical returns shown may substantially affect the scenario presented.

Deposits Needed to Accumulate a Future Sum

Item Description	Value
Current sum (if any)	$10,000
Desired future sum	$1,000,000
Annual interest rate[1]	5.00%
Frequency of deposits	Annually
Number of Years	55
Amount of deposits, if made:	
At the end of each Year	**$3,130**
At the beginning of each Year	**$2,981**

Example

To accumulate $1,000,000, with $10,000 to start and earning an
annual return of 5.00%, you will need to deposit $2,981 at the
beginning of each year for 55 years.

---

[1] The rates of return used in this illustration are not indicative of any actual investment and will fluctuate in value. An
investment will not provide a consistent rate of return; years with lower (or negative) returns than the hypothetical
returns shown may substantially affect the scenario presented.

Rate of Return on a Single Sum

Item Description	Value
Value at beginning of period	$ 100,000
Value at end of period	$ 125,000
Holding period	36 Years
Rate of return[1]	**0.62%**

Example

If you paid $100,000 for an asset and sold it for $125,000 after
owning it for 36 years, your annual rate of return was 0.62%.

---

[1] The rates of return used in this illustration are not indicative of any actual investment and will fluctuate in value. An
investment will not provide a consistent rate of return; years with lower (or negative) returns than the hypothetical
returns shown may substantially affect the scenario presented.

Future Value of Periodic Deposits

Item Description	Value
Frequency of periodic deposits	Annually
Annual deposits	$ 555
Annual interest rate[1]	5.00%
Number of deposits to make	55
Amount accumulated at end of period if deposits are made:	
At the end of each Year	**$ 151,356**
At the beginning of each Year	**$ 158,923**

Example

If you deposit $555 at the beginning of each year into an account earning an annual return of 5.00%, then in 55 years your account will grow to $158,923.

---

[1] The rates of return used in this illustration are not indicative of any actual investment and will fluctuate in value. An investment will not provide a consistent rate of return; years with lower (or negative) returns than the hypothetical returns shown may substantially affect the scenario presented.

Future Value of a Single Sum and Periodic Deposits

Item Description	Value
Single sum deposit	$10,000
Frequency of periodic deposits	Annually
Annual deposit	$ 555
Annual interest rate[1]	5.00%
Number of Years to make deposits	55
Future sum, if deposits are made:	
At the end of each Year	**$ 297,712**
At the beginning of each Year	**$ 305,280**

Example

If you place $10,000 into an account earning an annual return of 5.00%, and deposit $555 at the beginning of each year, then in 55 years your account will grow to $305,280.

---

[1] The rates of return used in this illustration are not indicative of any actual investment and will fluctuate in value. An investment will not provide a consistent rate of return; years with lower (or negative) returns than the hypothetical returns shown may substantially affect the scenario presented.

Accumulating One Million Dollars

How long does it take to accumulate $1,000,000?

The answer depends on three things.
1. How many years are available to accumulate the fund,
2. The after-tax rate of return, and
3. The method of contribution: One lump sum, or monthly contributions.

The table below shows how long it takes to accumulate $1,000,000 under varying circumstances. The results shown are hypothetical.[1] The actual growth will depend on a number of factors.

Annual Rate of Return (after taxes)[2]

Years	Annual Rate: 6% Lump Sum	Monthly	Annual Rate: 8%[3] Lump Sum	Monthly	Annual Rate: 10%[3] Lump Sum	Monthly	Annual Rate: 12%[3] Lump Sum	Monthly
5	$741,372	$14,333	$671,210	$13,610	$607,789	$12,914	$550,450	$12,244
10	$549,633	$6,102	$450,523	$5,466	$369,407	$4,882	$302,995	$4,347
15	$407,482	$3,439	$302,396	$2,890	$224,521	$2,413	$166,783	$2,002
20	$302,096	$2,164	$202,971	$1,698	$136,462	$1,317	$91,806	$1,011
25	$223,966	$1,443	$136,237	$1,051	$82,940	$754	$50,534	$532
30	$166,042	$996	$91,443	$671	$50,410	$442	$27,817	$286
35	$123,099	$702	$61,378	$436	$30,639	$263	$15,312	$155
40	$91,262	$502	$41,197	$286	$18,622	$158	$8,428	$85

Example: If you contribute $1,698 per month to an investment which returns 8% after taxes, you should accumulate $1,000,000 in 20 years. Likewise, if you currently have $202,971 invested at 8% (after-tax) for 20 years, it will grow to $1,000,000 without any additional contribution.

---

[1] The calculations shown assume monthly compounding. Monthly contribution amounts are calculated on an end-of-month (ordinary-annuity) basis.

[2] The rates of return used in the illustration are not indicative of any actual investment and will fluctuate in value. An investment will not provide a consistent rate of return; years with lower (or negative) returns than the hypothetical returns shown may substantially affect the scenario presented.

[3] Seeking a higher rate of return generally involves a greater degree of volatility and risk.

Accumulating One Million Dollars

Or Some Other Amount

How long does it take to accumulate $1,000,000?

The answer depends on three things.
1. How many years are available to accumulate the fund,
2. The after-tax rate of return, and
3. The method of contribution: One lump sum or monthly contributions.

The table below shows how long it takes to accumulate $1,000,000 under varying circumstances.[1] The results shown are hypothetical.[2] The actual growth will depend on a number of factors.

Annual Rate of Return (after taxes)

Years	Annual Rate: 4%		Annual Rate: 6%		Annual Rate: 8%	
	Lump Sum	Monthly	Lump Sum	Monthly	Lump Sum	Monthly
5	$ 821,927	$15,083	$ 747,258	$14,333	$ 680,583	$13,610
10	$ 675,564	$6,791	$ 558,395	$6,102	$ 463,193	$5,466
15	$ 555,265	$4,064	$ 417,265	$3,439	$ 315,242	$2,890
20	$ 456,387	$2,726	$ 311,805	$2,164	$ 214,548	$1,698
25	$ 375,117	$1,945	$ 232,999	$1,443	$ 146,018	$1,051
30	$ 308,319	$1,441	$ 174,110	$ 996	$99,377	$ 671
35	$ 253,415	$1,094	$ 130,105	$ 702	$67,635	$ 436
40	$ 208,289	$ 846	$97,222	$ 502	$46,031	$ 286

---

[1] The calculations for lump-sum contributions assume annual compounding; the calculations for monthly contributions assume monthly compounding on an end-of-month (ordinary annuity) basis.

[2] The rates of return used in this illustration are not indicative of any actual investment and will fluctuate in value. An investment will not provide a consistent rate of return; years with lower (or negative) returns than the hypothetical returns shown may substantially affect the scenario presented. Seeking a higher rate of return generally involves a greater degree of volatility and risk.

The Accumulation Process

The three phases of accumulating your retirement nest egg are illustrated below.

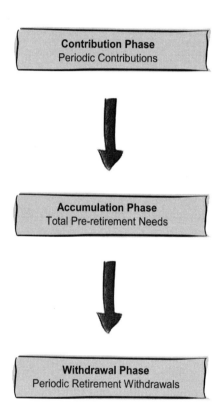

Taxation While Accumulating the Nest Egg

In comparing various types of retirement vehicles, one must consider the question of income taxes. Most retirement vehicles are taxed during one or more of the three phases of building the retirement nest egg.

- **Taxation during the contribution period:** How are contributions made?
  - Pretax dollars
  - After-tax dollars
- **Taxation during the accumulation period:** How are earnings taxed?
  - As income is earned
  - As assets are sold
  - Not taxed during accumulation period
- **Taxation during the withdrawal period:** How are withdrawals taxed?
  - Fully taxable
  - Partially taxable
  - Not taxable

Proper tax deferral or avoidance will result in a larger retirement benefit.

The Rule of 72 and the Rule of 115
How Long Will It Take to Double or Triple Your Investment?

The rule of 72 is a handy mathematical rule that helps in estimating approximately how many years it will take for an investment to **double** in value at a specified rate of return.

Rule of 72: If 72 is divided by an interest rate, the result is the approximate number of years needed to double the investment. For example, at a 1% rate of return, an investment will double in approximately 72 years; at a 10% rate of return it will take only 7.2 years, etc.

The rule of 115 is a similar rule that allows one to estimate how long it will take an investment to **triple** in value.

Rule of 115: If 115 is divided by an interest rate, the result is the approximate number of years needed to triple an investment. For example, at a 1% rate of return, an investment will triple in approximately 115 years; at a 10% rate of return it will take only 11.5 years, etc.

Rate of Return	1%	2%	3%	4%	5%	6%	7%	8%	9%	10%	11%
Years to double	72	36	24	18	14.4	12	10.3	9	8	7.2	6.5
Years to triple	115	57.5	38.3	28.8	23	19.2	16.4	14.4	12.8	11.5	10.5

Rate of Return	12%	13%	14%	15%	16%	17%	18%	19%	20%	21%	22%
Years to double	6	5.5	5.1	4.8	4.5	4.2	4	3.8	3.6	3.4	3.3
Years to triple	9.6	8.8	8.2	7.7	7.2	6.8	6.4	6.1	5.8	5.5	5.2

These rules can also tell you how long before a given item will double or triple in price at an estimated average rate of inflation.

For example, at an estimated average inflation rate of 8%, a loaf of bread will double in price every nine years. $(72 \div 8 = 9)$.

Types of Investment Risk

Whenever an individual takes cash and puts it to work in any form of investment, he or she does so with the anticipation of receiving a return on the money. At some future point in time, the investor expects to get back both the principal amount and something extra as well. The possibility that an investment will return less than expected is known as "investment risk."

Risk vs. Reward

One of the general truths of the investment world is that risk and reward go hand in hand. The greater the risk an investor is willing to undertake, the greater the potential reward. If an investor is willing to assume only a small amount of risk, the potential reward is also low. In an ideal world, there would be no risk to any investment. Unfortunately, such a risk-free investment does not exist.

There is also more than one type of risk. An investor must understand each type of risk, and use that knowledge to create a portfolio of investments that balances the level of risk assumed, with the desired investment return.

Market Risk

In simple terms, market risk can be defined as the possibility that downward changes in the market price of an investment will result in a loss of principal for an investor. For many, market risk is most closely associated with the ups and downs of the stock market.

Market risk exists for other investments as well. For example, the market price of bonds and other debt investments will move up and down in response to changes in the general level of interest rates. If interest rates rise, bond prices generally fall. If interest rates decline, bond prices generally rise. Tangible assets such as real estate and gold, or collectibles such as art or stamps, also face market risk.

Over time, a number of strategies have been developed to help reduce market risk.

- Invest only dollars that are not required to meet current needs. This helps avoid having to sell an asset when the market may be down.

- Develop a long-term approach. A longer time horizon allows an investor to ride out market ups and downs.

- Diversify your investments over a number of asset categories, such as stocks, bonds, or cash, and tangible investments such as real estate. Holding assets in different investment categories reduces the possibility that all investments will be down at the same time.

Continued...

Types of Investment Risk

Inflation Risk

For many individuals, safety of principal is the primary goal when deciding where to place investment funds. Such investors frequently put much of their money in bank savings accounts, CDs or T-Bills. While such investments can provide protection from market risk, they do not provide much protection from inflation risk. An investor may hold the same number of dollars; over time, however, those dollars buy less and less.

For example, consider a hypothetical investor who places $10,000 in a 10-year certificate of deposit, earning 5.0% per year. The table below summarizes the effect of a 3.0% annual inflation rate on the purchasing power of these dollars.

End of Year	CD Value at End of Year[1] (5%)	Purchasing Power at 3% Inflation Rate[2]	"Real" Value of CD	"Loss" Due to Inflation
1	$10,500	97.09%	$10,194	$306
2	$11,025	94.26%	$10,392	$633
3	$11,576	91.51%	$10,594	$982
4	$12,155	88.85%	$10,800	$1,355
5	$12,763	86.26%	$11,009	$1,753
6	$13,401	83.75%	$11,223	$2,178
7	$14,071	81.31%	$11,441	$2,630
8	$14,775	78.94%	$11,663	$3,111
9	$15,513	76.64%	$11,890	$3,624
10	$16,289	74.41%	$12,121	$4,168

Over the 10-year period, inflation reduces the purchasing power of the investor's dollars by more than 25%. The impact of income taxes, ignored in this example, would further decrease the investor's net return.

While there are ways to potentially shield your portfolio from inflation risk, most involve a higher level of market risk:

- Consider placing a portion of your assets in the stock market.

- Historically, tangible assets such as real estate or gold have tended to do well in periods of high inflation.

---

[1] Assumes a 5% annual after-tax return, and that interest is reinvested at the same rate of return.
[2] To calculate, divide previous year's percentage by (1+.03). Example: 1.00 / 1.03 = .9709; .9709 / 1.03 = .9426.

Continued

Types of Investment Risk

Other Common Risk Types

In addition to market and inflation risk, there are a number of other common types of risk that each investor must be aware of:

- **Credit risk:** This is also known as "default risk." The chance that the issuer of a bond or other debt-type instrument will not be able to carry out its contractual obligations. Keeping maturities short, diversifying investments among various companies, and investing in institutions and issues of the highest credit rating are common methods used to help control this type of risk.

- **Liquidity risk:** This risk is the possibility that an investor will not be able to sell or liquidate an asset, without losing a part of the principal, because there is an imbalance between the number of buyers and sellers, or because an asset is not traded very often. Choosing investments traded on an active market, and limiting investments to funds not needed for current expenses are approaches used to help lessen this risk.

- **Interest rate risk:** This is defined as the risk that an increase in the general level of interest rates will cause the market value of existing investments to fall. Generally, this risk applies to bonds and other debt-type instruments, which move opposite to interest rates. As interest rates rise, bond prices tend to fall, and vice versa. One approach to reducing this risk is to stagger or ladder the maturities in the portfolio so that a portion of the portfolio matures periodically, rather than all at the same time. Holding a security until maturity, at which time it is redeemable at full value, is also useful.

- **Tax risk:** This refers to the possibility that a change in tax law, at either the federal, state or local level, will change the tax characteristics of an investment. After such a legislative change, an investment may no longer meet an individual's needs. In some cases, new legislation has included a grandfather clause allowing current investors to continue under the old rules. Making an investment because it's a good investment, rather than focusing on the tax benefits, is an excellent way to help reduce this risk.

Asset Allocation

Asset allocation is an investment strategy that
seeks to reduce investment risk, while
maintaining a desired rate of return, by spreading
an individual's investments over a number of
asset types. It takes advantage of the tendency of
different asset types to move in different cycles,
and thus smooth out the ups and downs of the
entire portfolio. Stocks, bonds, and cash (or cash
equivalents) are the investments normally used. Depending on individual needs or
preferences, tangible assets such as real estate or gold may also be included.

The asset allocation process normally begins with an analysis of the historical levels of
risk and return for each investment type[1] being considered. These historical values are
then used as a guide to structuring a portfolio that matches the investor's individual goals
and overall risk tolerance level.

A Personal Choice

There is no single asset allocation model to fit every investor, or for every stage of a
person's life. The asset allocation decision is a highly individual one, and involves
carefully answering a number of key questions:

- **Investment goals:** Why are you investing? Is the primary need for income, to pay
  current living expenses, or as a source of emergency funds? Or are you accumulating
  money for a future need?

- **Time horizon:** When will the money be needed? At retirement, or sooner, to send a
  child to college, for example?

- **Liquidity needs:** How quickly do you need to be able to recover your investment and
  turn it into cash?

- **Risk tolerance:** How comfortable are you with the inevitable ups and downs of the
  financial markets?

- **Tax impact:** Will the investments add greatly to your income tax burden?

- **Economic conditions:** Inflation, interest rates, and the state of the economy are
  essential factors to consider.

- **International exposure:** How comfortable are you investing in foreign markets?

A Changing Choice

Over time, financial markets and an individual's goals and situation will change.
Periodically, an investor must review his or her situation to ensure that past investment
allocations are still appropriate. If not, adjustments should be made.

---

[1] Historical data, while useful as a general guide, cannot be considered an accurate indicator of future results. There is no
guarantee that past performance is a predictor of future investment performance.

Continued

Asset Allocation

Representative Asset Allocation Models

The charts below illustrate three hypothetical asset allocation models, for three age groups, or types of investor. These models are intended to serve only as representative samples of how asset allocation might work, and are not intended to serve as investment or portfolio recommendations.

Asset Allocation Portfolio #1
Aggressive Investors

■ Large Co. Stocks   ■ Small Co. Stocks   ■ Domestic Bonds

Asset Allocation Portfolio #2
Moderate Investors

■ Large Co. Stocks   ■ Small Co. Stocks   ■ Domestic Bonds

Asset Allocation Portfolio #3
Conservative Investors

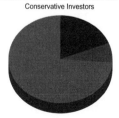

■ Large Co. Stocks   ■ Small Co. Stocks   ■ Domestic Bonds   ■ T-Bills and Cash

Inflation

What Will Inflation Do to Your Estate?

The consumer price index is the government's statistical measure of the changes in prices of goods and services. It is commonly used to measure the rate of inflation.

Year	Index	Percent Increase	Purchasing Power of the Dollar[1]
1967 (Base)	100.0	n/a	$1.00
1970	116.3	5.9%	.86
1971	121.3	4.3%	.82
1972	125.3	· 3.3%	.80
1973	133.1	6.2%	.75
1974	147.7	11.0%	.68
1975	161.2	9.1%	.62
1976	170.5	5.8%	.59
1977	181.5	6.5%	.55
1978	195.4	7.7%	.51
1979	217.4	11.3%	.46
1980	246.8	13.5%	.41
1981	272.4	10.4%	.37
1982	290.6	6.7%	.34
1983	301.5	3.8%	.33
1984	312.2	3.5%	.32
1985	323.4	3.6%	.31
1986	325.7	0.7%	.31
1987	340.2	4.4%	.29
1988	357.9	5.2%	.28
1989	371.1	3.7%	.27
1990	399.4	7.6%	.25
1991	404.7	1.3%	.25
1992	416.3	2.9%	.24
1993	423.1	1.6%	.24
1994	438.6	3.7%	.23
1995	449.5	2.5%	.22
1996	464.3	3.3%	.22
1997	471.3	1.5%	.21
1998	478.6	1.6%	.21
1999	491.8	2.8%	.20
2000	508.5	3.4%	.20
2001	515.0	1.3%	.19
2002	527.2	2.4%	.19
2003	535.6	1.6%	.19
2004	554.2	3.5%	.18
2005	573.3	2.4%	.17
2006	587.3	2.4%	.17
2007	604.0[2]	2.8%	.17

Source: U.S. Bureau of Labor Statistics, Consumer Price Index for Urban Wage Earners and Clerical Workers (CPI-W): U.S. City Average, by expenditure category and commodity and service group. Purchasing power of the dollar is rounded off to the nearest cent.

---

[1] Base year index of 100 is divided by the index for the year in question.
[2] If the 1982-1984 base year is used, the December 2007 index is 202.77 and the percentage increase is 2.82%.

Inflation

Inflation is the annual increase in the price of goods and services as measured by the federal government. The graph[1] below illustrates the annual percentage change every other year since the base year of 1967. Over the last 40 years, the average annual inflation rate in the U.S. has been 4.64%.

Annual Inflation Rates

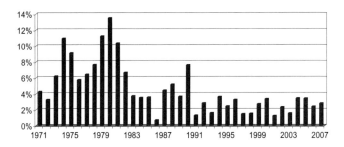

---

[1] Source: U.S. Bureau of Labor Statistics (CPI-W) (1967 - 2007).

Effect of Inflation
Past

Over the last 40 years, the average annual inflation rate in the U.S. has been 4.64%.[1]

Item Description	Value
Average annual inflation rate	2.50%
Number of years ago	20
Current item cost	$ 100
Past item cost	**$61**

Example

Assuming an average annual inflation rate of 2.50%, an item which costs $ 100 today cost $61 20 year(s) ago.

---

[1] Source: U.S. Bureau of Labor Statistics, Consumer Price Index for Urban Wage Earners and Clerical Workers (CPI-W); U.S. City Average, by expenditure category and commodity and service group. 1967-2007.

Rate of Inflation
Past

Over the last 40 years, the average annual inflation rate in the U.S. has been 4.64%.[1]

Item Description	Value
Past item cost	$ 125
Current item cost	$ 100
Number of years ago	20
Annual inflation rate	**-1.11%**

Example

If an item costs $ 125 20 year(s) ago and currently costs $ 100, it has experienced an average annual inflation rate of -1.11%.

---

[1] Source: U.S. Bureau of Labor Statistics, Consumer Price Index for Urban Wage Earners and Clerical Workers (CPI-W); U.S. City Average, by expenditure category and commodity and service group. 1967-2007.

Consumer Price Index

The Consumer Price Index is the government's method of measuring the price of goods and services bought by urban wage earners and clerical workers. The graph[1] below illustrates the overall increase in the cost of living since 1967. Over the last 40 years, the average annual inflation rate in the U.S. has been 4.64%.

1901 = $.03
TODAY = $1.02

Consumer Price Index

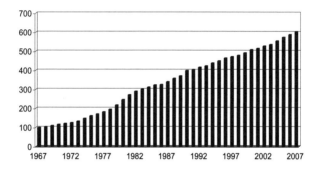

---

[1] Source: U.S. Bureau of Labor Statistics (CPI-W) (1967 – 2007).

Purchasing Power of One Dollar

The Consumer Price Index is the government's method of measuring the price of goods and services bought by urban wage earners and clerical workers. The graph[1] below illustrates the decline in the purchasing power of one dollar since 1967, as a result of inflation. Over the last 40 years, the average annual inflation rate in the U.S. has been 4.64%.

Annual Purchasing Power of One Dollar

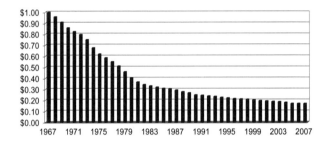

---

[1] Source: U.S. Bureau of Labor Statistics (CPI-W) (1967 – 2007).

The Effect of Inflation and Taxes on Investment Returns

To determine the true return on an investment, one must consider the effect of inflation and taxes on the gross return.

Worksheet for 2008

Taxable Income	Single	Married Filing Jointly	Married Filing Separate	Head of Household	Estate or Trust
$6,000	10.00%	10.00%	10.00%	10.00%	28.00%
$10,000	15.00%	10.00%	15.00%	10.00%	33.00%
$25,000	15.00%	15.00%	15.00%	15.00%	35.00%
$50,000	25.00%	15.00%	25.00%	25.00%	35.00%
$75,000	25.00%	25.00%	28.00%	25.00%	35.00%
$100,000	28.00%	25.00%	33.00%	25.00%	35.00%
$125,000	28.00%	25.00%	33.00%	28.00%	35.00%
$175,000	33.00%	28.00%	33.00%	28.00%	35.00%
$200,000	33.00%	28.00%	35.00%	33.00%	35.00%
$275,000	33.00%	33.00%	35.00%	33.00%	35.00%
$375,000	35.00%	35.00%	35.00%	35.00%	35.00%

1. In a perfect world you would be able to keep 100% of your investment return.   1.000

2. Determine your marginal tax bracket from the table above. Enter your marginal bracket as a decimal, e.g., 28.00% = .280.   _____

3. Subtract line 2 from line 1. This is the percentage left after taxes are paid.   _____

4. Enter the before-tax return on the investment as a decimal, e.g., 10% = .10.   _____

5. **After-tax return** - Multiply line 3 times line 4.   _____

6. Enter an estimated average annual inflation rate, as a decimal, e.g., 5.0% = .05.[1]   _____

7. **Inflation-adjusted return** - Subtract line 6 from line 5.[2]   _____

---

[1] If line 6 is larger than line 5, there is a negative rate of return on the investment.
[2] To express line 7 as a percent, multiply line 7 by 100.

The Effect of Inflation and Taxes on Investment Returns

How much must you earn on an investment (the gross return) to obtain your desired net return (after taxes and inflation)? The examples shown below are hypothetical.[1]

Assuming 2.5% Inflation

Approx. Tax Bracket	Break Even	Desired Net Return						
		5.00%	6.00%	8.00%	10.00%	12.00%	15.00%	20.00%
0.00%	2.5%	7.5%	8.5%	10.5%	12.5%	14.5%	17.5%	22.5%
10.00%	2.8%	8.3%	9.4%	11.7%	13.9%	16.1%	19.4%	25.0%
15.00%	2.9%	8.8%	10.0%	12.4%	14.7%	17.1%	20.6%	26.5%
25.00%	3.3%	10.0%	11.3%	14.0%	16.7%	19.3%	23.3%	30.0%
28.00%	3.5%	10.4%	11.8%	14.6%	17.4%	20.1%	24.3%	31.3%
33.00%	3.7%	11.2%	12.7%	15.7%	18.7%	21.6%	26.1%	33.6%
35.00%	3.8%	11.5%	13.1%	16.2%	19.2%	22.3%	26.9%	34.6%
50.00%	5.0%	15.0%	17.0%	21.0%	25.0%	29.0%	35.0%	45.0%

Assuming 4.0% Inflation

Approx. Tax Bracket	Break Even	Desired Net Return						
		5.00%	6.00%	8.00%	10.00%	12.00%	15.00%	20.00%
0.00%	4.0%	9.0%	10.0%	12.0%	14.0%	16.0%	19.0%	24.0%
10.00%	4.4%	10.0%	11.1%	13.3%	15.6%	17.8%	21.1%	26.7%
15.00%	4.7%	10.6%	11.8%	14.1%	16.5%	18.8%	22.4%	28.2%
25.00%	5.3%	12.0%	13.3%	16.0%	18.7%	21.3%	25.3%	32.0%
28.00%	5.6%	12.5%	13.9%	16.7%	19.4%	22.2%	26.4%	33.3%
33.00%	6.0%	13.4%	14.9%	17.9%	20.9%	23.9%	28.4%	35.8%
35.00%	6.2%	13.8%	15.4%	18.5%	21.5%	24.6%	29.2%	36.9%
50.00%	8.0%	18.0%	20.0%	24.0%	28.0%	32.0%	38.0%	48.0%

Assuming 6.0% Inflation

Approx. Tax Bracket	Break Even	Desired Net Return						
		5.00%	6.00%	8.00%	10.00%	12.00%	15.00%	20.00%
0.00%	6.0%	11.0%	12.0%	14.0%	16.0%	18.0%	21.0%	26.0%
10.00%	6.7%	12.2%	13.3%	15.6%	17.8%	20.0%	23.3%	28.9%
15.00%	7.1%	12.9%	14.1%	16.5%	18.8%	21.2%	24.7%	30.6%
25.00%	8.0%	14.7%	16.0%	18.7%	21.3%	24.0%	28.0%	34.7%
28.00%	8.3%	15.3%	16.7%	19.4%	22.2%	25.0%	29.2%	36.1%
33.00%	9.0%	16.4%	17.9%	20.9%	23.9%	26.9%	31.3%	38.8%
35.00%	9.2%	16.9%	18.5%	21.5%	24.6%	27.7%	32.3%	40.0%
50.00%	12.0%	22.0%	24.0%	28.0%	32.0%	36.0%	42.0%	52.0%

Example: Assume 2.5% inflation, 28.00% tax bracket and 8.0% desired net rate of return. You would need to earn 14.6% before tax to achieve an 8.0% after-tax and after-inflation net return.

---

[1] The rates of return used in the illustration are not indicative of any actual investment and will fluctuate over time.

The Effect of Inflation and Taxes on Investment Returns

To determine the true return on an investment, one must consider the effect of inflation and taxes on the overall return.

Assumptions:
Tax year: 2008
Taxable income: $48,000
Filing status: Single
Marginal income tax bracket: 25.00%
Estimated average inflation rate: 2.50%

Item Description	Value
Before-tax investment return[1]	8.00%
Percentage left after taxes at 25.00%	75.00%
After-tax return[1]	6.00%
Inflation-adjusted return at 2.50% inflation rate	**3.50%**

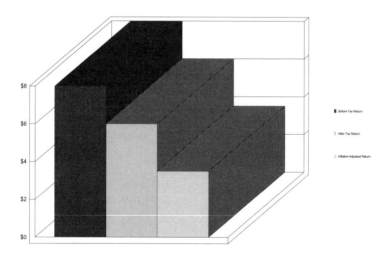

---

[1] The rates of return used in this illustration are not indicative of any actual investment and will fluctuate in value.

Tax-Exempt vs. Taxable Income

The following charts allow you to compare the returns on tax-exempt investments to those that are taxable. After determining your marginal federal income tax bracket on the top chart, locate the taxable or tax-exempt return of interest in the lower tables.

Filing Status	Taxable Income[1] up to:					
	10.00%	15.00%	25.00%	28.00%	33.00%	35.00%
Single	$8,025	$32,550	$78,850	$164,550	$357,700	$357,700+
Married filing joint	$16,050	$65,100	$131,450	$200,300	$357,700	$357,700+
Married filing separate	$8,025	$32,550	$65,725	$100,150	$178,850	$178,850+
Head of household	$11,450	$43,650	$112,650	$182,400	$357,700	$357,700+
Estates and trusts	N/A	$2,200	$5,150	$7,850	$10,700	$10,700+

Tax-Exempt Return[2]	Taxable Return Required to Equal a Tax-Exempt Return at Various Top Tax Brackets					
	10.00%	15.00%	25.00%	28.00%	33.00%	35.00%
3%	3.33%	3.53%	4.00%	4.17%	4.48%	4.62%
4%	4.44%	4.71%	5.33%	5.56%	5.97%	6.15%
5%	5.56%	5.88%	6.67%	6.94%	7.46%	7.69%
6%	6.67%	7.06%	8.00%	8.33%	8.96%	9.23%
7%	7.78%	8.24%	9.33%	9.72%	10.45%	10.77%
8%	8.89%	9.41%	10.67%	11.11%	11.94%	12.31%
9%	10.00%	10.59%	12.00%	12.50%	13.43%	13.85%
10%	11.11%	11.76%	13.33%	13.89%	14.93%	15.38%
11%	12.22%	12.94%	14.67%	15.28%	16.42%	16.92%
12%	13.33%	14.12%	16.00%	16.67%	17.91%	18.46%
13%	14.44%	15.29%	17.33%	18.06%	19.40%	20.00%

Taxable Return[2]	Tax-Exempt Return Required to Equal a Taxable Return at Various Top Tax Brackets					
	10.00%	15.00%	25.00%	28.00%	33.00%	35.00%
3%	2.70%	2.55%	2.25%	2.16%	2.01%	1.95%
4%	3.60%	3.40%	3.00%	2.88%	2.68%	2.60%
5%	4.50%	4.25%	3.75%	3.60%	3.35%	3.25%
6%	5.40%	5.10%	4.50%	4.32%	4.02%	3.90%
7%	6.30%	5.95%	5.25%	5.04%	4.69%	4.55%
8%	7.20%	6.80%	6.00%	5.76%	5.36%	5.20%
9%	8.10%	7.65%	6.75%	6.48%	6.03%	5.85%
10%	9.00%	8.50%	7.50%	7.20%	6.70%	6.50%
11%	9.90%	9.35%	8.25%	7.92%	7.37%	7.15%
12%	10.80%	10.20%	9.00%	8.64%	8.04%	7.80%
13%	11.70%	11.05%	9.75%	9.36%	8.71%	8.45%
14%	12.60%	11.90%	10.50%	10.08%	9.38%	9.10%

---

[1] Taxable income is gross income, less adjustments, exemptions and itemized deductions. 2008 federal income tax rates are shown.

[2] The rates of return used in this illustration are hypothetical, are not indicative of any actual investment, and will fluctuate in value.

Tax-Exempt vs. Taxable Income

Item Description	Value
Combined federal and state marginal income tax bracket	45.00%
Rate of return on taxable investment	8.00%
Required rate of return on tax-free to match taxable	4.40%
Rate of return on tax-free investment	6.00%
Required rate of return on taxable to match tax-free	10.91%

Pyramid of Investments

An investment program should be built like a pyramid - with a strong, broad base. The diagram below illustrates a typical investment pyramid.

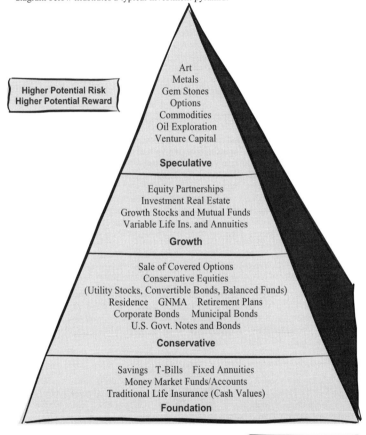

Higher Potential Risk
Higher Potential Reward

Art
Metals
Gem Stones
Options
Commodities
Oil Exploration
Venture Capital

Speculative

Equity Partnerships
Investment Real Estate
Growth Stocks and Mutual Funds
Variable Life Ins. and Annuities

Growth

Sale of Covered Options
Conservative Equities
(Utility Stocks, Convertible Bonds, Balanced Funds)
Residence   GNMA   Retirement Plans
Corporate Bonds   Municipal Bonds
U.S. Govt. Notes and Bonds

Conservative

Savings   T-Bills   Fixed Annuities
Money Market Funds/Accounts
Traditional Life Insurance (Cash Values)

Foundation

Lower Potential Risk
Lower Potential Reward

Note: This pyramid is intended solely to illustrate a concept; it is not a promise of investment performance. Investors may differ on the risk level to which a particular asset is assigned. Before making any investment in mutual funds or variable annuities, you should be sure to read the appropriate prospectus or offering documents for a complete discussion of the fees and risks involved.

Basic Investment Tools

Individuals with investable funds often have a desire to put those "extra" dollars to work to meet a specific purpose. For some, there may be a desire to accumulate funds for a future purchase, or a need to generate more income to pay current expenses. For others, it may be to put money aside for a "rainy day," or simply to "get rich." Whatever the investment goal, an investor should clearly understand both the role and the potential risks and rewards of each type of investment tool.

Stocks

The terms "stock" and "share" both refer to a fractional ownership interest in a corporation. As "owners," stockholders vote for the company's Board of Directors, and receive information on the firm's activities and business results. Stockholders may share in current profits through "dividends" declared by the firm's Board.

When a corporate business is first organized, investors contribute money to fund the enterprise, and in return receive shares of stock representing their ownership in the company. If the business is successful, it will grow and have increasing profits, and the shares generally become more valuable. If the business is not successful, the value of the shares usually declines.

- **Uses:** Investors typically buy and hold stock for its long-term growth potential. Stocks with a history of regular dividends are often held for both income and growth.

- **Risks:** As the long-term growth of a company cannot be predicted, the short-term market value of the company's stock will fluctuate up and down. If need or fear cause an investor to sell when the market is "down," a capital loss will result. If the market is "up," the investor will realize a capital gain.

Bonds

While stocks represent ownership in a business, bonds are debt. Issued by institutions such as the federal government, corporations, and state and local governments, a bond is evidence of money borrowed by the bond issuer. In return, bondholders receive interest and, at "maturity," the principal amount of the bond.

When first issued, a bond will have a specified rate of return, or "yield." For example, a 6.0% bond will pay $60.00 per year for each $1,000 invested. If a bond is traded on a public exchange, the market price will fluctuate, generally with changes in interest rates. Later investors will receive a yield that may be more, or less, than 6.0%, depending on the price paid for the bond in the open market.

Continued

Basic Investment Tools

- **Uses:** Bonds are typically bought by investors seeking current income. In some instances, bonds are also used for capital growth.

- **Risks:** Like stocks, the market price of bonds will fluctuate up and down. If an investor sells a bond before it matures, a capital gain or loss may result. Unless the issuer defaults, bonds held to maturity will recover the principal amount. Since a bond pays a fixed return, inflation risk can be a problem; over time, the dollars received will buy less and less. Also, the interest income received may be subject to current income taxation.

Savings Accounts

Most investors are familiar with a savings account at a bank, savings and loan, or credit union. For many, the generic term "savings account" includes both the traditional savings account (allowing for deposits and withdrawals of small amounts), as well as fixed-term certificates of deposit (CDs), for larger sums. Savings accounts are usually prized by investors for two primary characteristics: safety of principal, and liquidity. Such accounts are insured (against a failure of the savings institution) by agencies of the Federal government, such as the Federal Deposit Insurance Corporation (FDIC) or the National Credit Union Administration (NCUA), for up to $100,000 per account.[1]

- **Uses:** Savings accounts are often used as a reservoir for emergency funds, or as a "warehouse" for dollars ultimately earmarked for some other purpose. Some investors also use such accounts to generate current income.

- **Risks:** Because there is little risk of principal loss, savings accounts typically have a lower yield than other investments. One "risk" to such accounts is the potential additional interest income foregone in exchange for safety of principal. The relatively low yield can also be heavily impacted by inflation and current income taxes.

Life Insurance

In the last several decades, the life insurance industry has developed a number of products that combine the protection of life insurance death benefits, with a significant cash value element. Policies such as universal life, variable life, and universal-variable life allow an individual to purchase a single financial instrument providing for both life insurance and long-term accumulation goals.[2] Such policies may serve as a form of "forced investment" for those who find it difficult to put funds aside on a regular basis, but who routinely pay their bills.

---

[1] Certain retirement accounts are protected up to $250,000. Beginning in 2011, the coverage limit on federally insured deposits will be subject to adjustment for inflation, in increments of $10,000.

[2] The Securities and Exchange Commission requires that all policies labeled "variable" be accompanied by a prospectus as such policies involve marketable securities. The prospectus contains detailed information about a policy, including fees and expenses, and should be read carefully.

Continued...

Basic Investment Tools

Additionally, life insurance company "annuities," with either a fixed or variable return, offer a tax-deferred method of accumulating additional retirement funds[1].

- **Uses:** While life insurance products are primarily used for death benefit protection, they are commonly used for long-term accumulation goals. Available cash values may also serve as an "emergency reserve," if needed, or a source of loans, since life policies frequently include features permitting borrowing against these cash values.[2]

- **Risks:** Fixed contracts rely on the financial strength of the issuing life insurance company. Inflation may negatively impact a fixed return contract. Variable contracts share the risks of the underlying investments. Loans and withdrawals must be carefully structured to avoid negative income tax results.[2]

Real Estate

Real estate has long been a favored investment for those seeking tax benefits and a hedge against inflation. "Improved" real estate refers to land with apartments, a home, office, store, or other rentable enhancement. Rental income in excess of expenses may provide a "positive" cash flow. Additionally, depreciation may shelter a portion of the cash flow from current income tax. If all goes well, inflation will gradually increase rental income, thus raising the market value of the property.

Real estate investors may also choose to invest in "unimproved" or "raw" land. Typically such land generates no current cash flow, unless rented for agricultural purposes such as animal grazing or farming. Investors in raw land usually try to buy property in the path of expected, long-term growth, with the hope of selling the property at a gain when future demand pushes market prices up.

- **Uses:** Investors in improved real estate typically seek tax-sheltered, current income along with long-term capital growth. Investors in unimproved real estate primarily seek long-term capital gains. Real estate serves as a hedge against inflation.

- **Risks:** A real estate investor may find it difficult to keep a property rented, and thus not receive the expected cash flow. Deflation may decrease both rents and property values. Expected long-term growth in a geographical area may not occur. Real estate can be very illiquid; a quick sale may require a substantial reduction in price. Changes in tax law may reduce or eliminate anticipated tax benefits.

---

[1] Variable annuity products must also be accompanied by a prospectus.
[2] A policy loan or withdrawal will generally reduce cash values and death benefits. If a policy lapses or is surrendered with a loan outstanding, the loan will be treated as taxable income in the current year, to the extent of gain in the policy. Policies considered to be modified endowment contracts (MECs) are subject to special rules.

Continued

Basic Investment Tools

Gold

For centuries gold has served as an enduring store of value during periods of political and social turmoil. It has also functioned to preserve purchasing power during times of high inflation. Demand for gold, for jewelry and industrial purposes, also impacts the price of gold.

There are a number of different ways for an individual to invest in gold. For example, an investor can purchase bars of gold bullion (gold refined to a high level of purity). Gold bullion coins, such as the South African Kruggerand or U.S. Eagle offer a more portable way to own the metal. Risk-oriented speculators can participate in gold markets indirectly via gold futures on commodities exchanges. More conservative individuals may choose to invest in mutual funds which specialize in the stocks of companies mining gold.

- **Uses:** Gold serves as a permanent store of value during periods of economic and political anxiety. It also acts as a hedge against inflation.

- **Risks:** The market value of gold can fluctuate widely. Selling gold when the market is down can result in a capital loss. It can be difficult to own and protect. Direct ownership provides no current income.

Stocks

The terms "stock" and "share of stock" both refer to ownership of a business corporation. When a corporation is first founded, investors provide the capital (money) to get the business going. Those who provide this financing become part owners of the company. A "stock certificate" is then issued, showing the number of "shares" that each investor holds, as evidence of this ownership status.

Common Stock

The most prevalent form of stock is termed "common" stock. As owners of a company, common stockholders have certain rights and privileges:

- **To vote for the board of directors:** The members of the board of directors of a corporation are responsible for the overall direction of the business, and are elected by the stockholders.

- **To receive information about the firm:** Most corporations will hold an "annual meeting" of the stockholders, to conduct necessary corporate business and to publicize the results of the most recent business year. A stockholder unable to attend the meeting may vote by mail or select a "proxy" to act in his or her place. Most corporations publish an "annual report" reviewing the firm's business results.

- **To share in the profits:** Common stockholders may share in the profits of the firm, through payments known as "dividends."[1] Dividends are not guaranteed. Before a dividend is paid, the board of directors must first "declare" a dividend, and decide how large a dividend to pay, and when to pay it. If a firm has no profits, or if the profits are needed by the company for business purposes, the board may decide not to pay a dividend.

Preferred Stock

"Preferred" stock is a hybrid, mixing characteristics of both common stock and bonds. The term "preferred" comes from its status within the financial structure of the firm.

- **Dividend preference:** A company which has issued both common and preferred stock generally must first pay a dividend to the preferred stockholders before it can pay a dividend to the common stockholders. Unlike the variable dividend of common stock, preferred stock typically has a fixed dividend amount. Only in dire situations will a firm reduce or eliminate a preferred dividend payment.

- **Preferred position in liquidation:** If a company gets into serious financial trouble, and is forced to sell its assets to pay creditors, there may not be enough money to pay all bills, and also return something to the stockholders. Preferred stockholders have priority over common stockholders in liquidation.

- **Lack of voting control:** Unlike common stockholders, holders of preferred stock generally do not have a right to vote for the members of the board of directors.

---

[1] Under current legislation, during 2003-2010, federal law taxes qualifying stock dividends at marginal rates lower than those generally applicable to ordinary income. State and local income tax treatment of such dividends may differ.

Continued

Stocks

Investment Uses

Investors typically buy and hold stocks for long-term capital growth. If a business is successful, over time the value of the business, and the market price of the firm's shares, generally increase. Shareholders who purchased the stock at a lower price can then sell their shares at a profit. If a business is not successful, the value of a firm's shares can fall, sometimes to zero, resulting in an investor loss.

In some instances, investors will purchase stock in companies with a history of paying regular dividends, as a way of generating additional current income. If a firm continues to grow, dividends and stock price can increase, potentially providing both capital gain and increasing current income.

How to Invest

- **Direct ownership:** Working with a stockbroker or other securities licensed professional, investors can own stock by direct purchase, with the shares registered in their own names.

- **Indirect ownership:** Open-end investment companies known as "mutual funds" are an indirect method of stock ownership. Mutual funds pool the resources of many individuals, and offer an investor access to a diversified portfolio of professionally managed securities. Exchange-traded funds, or ETFs, are a variation of the standard mutual fund, and are another way of investing in stocks. Certain life insurance products such as variable life, universal-variable life, and variable annuities, provide another indirect means of stock market participation.[1]

Possible Risks

- **Market risk:** A key risk involved in stock ownership is that of "market risk," the fluctuation of share prices up and down. Stockowners have invested in a business enterprise, and the price of the company's stock will generally follow the firm's business results. Stock prices will also fluctuate in response to general economic and market factors.

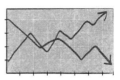

---

[1] The Securities and Exchange Commission requires that all prospective ETF and mutual fund investors be given a "prospectus." The prospectus contains valuable information concerning how a fund works, its goals and risks, and any expenses and charges involved. All "variable" life insurance and annuity products also require a prospectus.

Stock Market Indexes and Averages

News reports about the stock market that you see or hear every day on television, on the radio, and in newspapers track the movement of groups of stocks, not individual issues. Citing a specific "index" or "average," these reports give you a general sense of the direction of stock prices. They will not, however, tell you whether the stocks in your own portfolio are up or down. Understanding what these reports mean is important because they are commonly used as benchmarks to measure the performance of individual stocks.

What are Indexes and Averages?

At their most basic, stock indexes and averages are simply ways to measure changes in the market value of certain groups of stocks.

An "average," as the name implies, is the arithmetic average price of a group of stocks. The Dow Jones Industrial Average (DJIA) is such an average. Made up of 30 large industrial stocks, the DJIA was originally calculated by adding up the price of the stocks included in the average and then dividing by 30. This divisor has since been adjusted a number of times to account for mergers, additions, deletions, and other technical factors.

An index, on the other hand, is an average value expressed in relation to a previously determined base number. The Standard & Poors 500 Index (S&P 500), for example, uses a base value of 10, determined during 1941-1943.[1]

These measuring tools can be associated with specific exchanges or industry groups. More specialized indexes are geared toward tracking the performance of specific market sectors, such as high technology, energy, health care, finance, or transportation.

Price-Weighted vs. Market-Value Weighted

An index or average may also be classified according to the method used to determine its price. In a price-weighted index (e.g., the DJIA), the price of each component stock is the only consideration when determining the value of the index. Thus, the price movement of higher-priced stocks influences the average more than that of lower-priced stocks.

In contrast, a market-value weighted index (e.g., the S&P 500) factors in a stock's total market value, equal to the share price times the number of shares outstanding. Therefore, a relatively small shift in the price of a large company can significantly influence the value of the index.

Commonly Encountered Indexes and Averages

Standard & Poor's 500 Index: The S&P 500 is the benchmark against which many portfolio managers compare themselves. The "S&P" (as it is commonly referred to) is composed of 500 "blue chip" stocks, separated by industry, so that almost all key industries are represented.

---

[1] It is not possible to directly invest in an index.

Stock Market Indexes and Averages

Dow Jones Industrial Average (DJIA): This commonly quoted average tracks the movement of 30 of the largest blue chip stocks traded on the New York Stock Exchange (NYSE). When people ask, "How did the market do today?" they are usually referring to this index.

Component Stocks of the Dow Jones Industrial Average[1]			
3M	Citigroup	Honeywell Int'l	Pfizer
Alcoa	Coca-Cola	Intel	Procter & Gamble
Altria Group	E.I. DuPont	IBM	United Technologies
American Express	Exxon Mobil	Johnson & Johnson	Verizon
American Int'l Group	General Electric	JPMorgan Chase	Wal-Mart
AT&T	General Motors	McDonald's	Walt Disney
Boeing	Hewlett-Packard	Merck	
Caterpillar	Home Depot	Microsoft	

Dow Jones and Co., which maintains the DJIA, also tracks utilities (electric and gas) in the Dow Jones Utilities Average and transportation stocks (airlines, railroads, and trucking firms) in the Dow Jones Transportation Average. The combined industrial, utilities, and transportation averages are called the Dow Jones Composite Average.

NASDAQ Composite Index: This index tracks the movement of all companies traded on the NASDAQ National Market System (NMS), which tend to be smaller and more volatile than those in the Dow Jones Industrial Average or the S&P 500. The NASDAQ Composite is market-value weighted, which gives more influence to larger and higher priced stocks.

NYSE Composite Index: This is the index for the trading of all New York Stock Exchange stocks. It is market-value weighted and expressed in dollars and cents. When commentators say, "The average share lost 15 cents on the New York Exchange today," this is the index to which they are usually referring.

AMEX Composite Index: This index tracks the average of stocks traded on the American Stock Exchange (AMEX), which tend to be medium and small-sized growth stocks. The index is weighted by the market capitalization of its components, meaning that stocks with a larger number of shares outstanding and with higher stock prices affect the index more than smaller companies with lower prices.

Wilshire 5,000 Equity Index: The broadest measure of all indexes, the market-value-weighted Wilshire includes all major NYSE, AMEX, and NASDAQ stocks and gives a good indication of the overall direction of all stocks, large and small.

Foreign Indexes: A number of indexes follow markets in foreign countries, such as the British FTSE 100, the French CAC 40, the German DAX, and the Japanese Nikkei 225.

---

[1] As of January 11, 2008.

Growth vs. Value Investing: Which is Best?

There are two schools of thought within the investment community as to whether higher returns can be achieved by investing for "growth" or by investing for "value."

Value Investing

Those who espouse value investing favor purchasing stocks with higher than average dividend yields and relatively low market value indicators, such as price-to-earnings, price-to-book, and price-to-sales ratios. Value investors rely heavily on their analytical judgment as to whether or not a stock is mispriced in the marketplace; if a stock is underpriced, it's a good buy; if the stock is overpriced, it's time to sell.

Value investors typically buy stocks that have been beaten down in price because the companies they represent, although basically sound, are going through a period of adversity. This strategy then calls for selling these shares after they have risen in price as a result of the underlying company having recovered from its difficulties.

Growth Investing

By comparison, growth-style investors are more apt to subscribe to the "efficient market" hypothesis, which maintains that the current market price of a stock reflects all the "knowable" information about a company and inherently represents the most reasonable price at that given point in time. In other words, it could be said that "growth investors look for good companies – not good stocks."

Thus, those in the growth camp seek optimum investment performance by investing in quality companies with higher than average earnings growth rates, regardless of the current market valuation of the company's stock.

Which Approach Is Best?

For several years now, common stock funds have been routinely divided according to whether or not their investment styles are predominantly "growth" oriented, "value" oriented, or a "blend" of the two. This data has provided an opportunity to study, compare, and contrast the performance records of large numbers of mutual funds using "growth" and "value" stock approaches as their primary investment strategies.

As for which strategy achieves the highest returns, most studies show that this largely depends upon the specific period over which the two styles are compared. For example, throughout the 1990s the public was deluged with studies extolling the virtues of growth investing over value. However, since the dot.com bubble burst in the early 2000s, the reverse has been true.

An individual investor must understand the strengths and weaknesses of each investment approach and choose that with which he or she is most comfortable. The advice and guidance of professional financial advisors can be of great help in making this decision.

Bonds

When an individual borrows money to purchase a home, a type of debt called a "mortgage" is created. A single organization such as a bank or credit union will loan money to the homeowner, who, in return, makes monthly payments to pay off the loan. Each monthly mortgage payment is part interest and part principal.

When an institution such as a government, a government agency, or a corporation wants to borrow money, it can do so by creating a form of debt called a "bond." Rather than going to a single source for the money, institutional borrowers will sell bonds to many separate investors. In return, investors receive periodic, interest-only payments, with the principal amount of the bond being repaid in a lump sum, no later than a specified future date.

Types of Bonds

There are two basic ways to classify bonds:

- **Bond issuer:** The federal government, state and local governments and agencies, and corporations all issue bonds.

- **Maturity:** Refers to the date when the money borrowed must be repaid. Bond maturities can range from one to 30 years.

The Language of Bonds

There are a number of terms investors use when discussing bonds:

- **Form:** Bonds are issued in many different forms. If a bond is "registered," a bond certificate is issued, listing the name of the owner. The bond issuer sends the interest payment to the owner when due. Some bonds are "bearer" bonds; whoever bears (has possession of) the bond is presumed to be the owner. The "book-entry" form is usually used for very short-term bonds. No certificate is issued; the bond issuer keeps a list of the owners, and sends an informal statement to each investor to confirm ownership.

- **Denomination:** Refers to the amount to be repaid when the bond matures. The terms "face value," "par," and "par value" are also used. Bonds are most commonly issued in $1,000 denominations.

- **Yield:** The annual return on a bond. For example, an investor who pays $1,000 for a bond paying $60.00 per year has a 6.0% yield. The term "coupon" is also used. Early bonds were issued with a sheet of coupons attached. To receive his interest payment, an investor would clip one of the coupons and return it to the issuer. Zero coupon bonds do not pay interest currently. Instead, such bonds are issued at a discount from face value. The investor receives both principal and interest in a lump sum at maturity. Floating rate bonds have a yield that can change under specified circumstances.

Continued...

Bonds

- **Credit rating:** Before a bank makes a mortgage loan, it does a credit check to gauge the prospective borrower's ability to repay both principal and interest. The risk that a debt will not be repaid is termed "default" risk. Investors can estimate the probability of default in a particular bond by checking an issuer's credit rating. Moody's Investors Service and Standard and Poor's are two well-known bond-rating agencies. In general, the higher the credit rating, the lower the default risk. A bond issuer's credit rating can change over time.

Bond Prices and Interest Rates

If an investor buys a bond, and holds it to maturity, the issuer is obligated to repay the full face amount. If a bond is sold before it matures, however, the investor may receive more, or less, than originally paid. Bond prices can move up and down, usually in response to changes in the general level of interest rates. If rates rise, the price of existing bonds usually falls; if interest rates decline, the market value of existing bonds generally increases. Other factors may also affect bond prices.

Bonds and Income Taxes

The income tax treatment of bond interest depends primarily on who issued the bond:

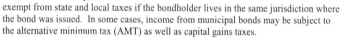

- **U.S. government bonds:** Interest from direct obligations of the U.S. government is taxable by the federal government, but is generally exempt from tax at the state and local level.

- **Municipal bonds:** Income from municipal bonds is generally exempt from federal tax. Normally, the interest is also exempt from state and local taxes if the bondholder lives in the same jurisdiction where the bond was issued. In some cases, income from municipal bonds may be subject to the alternative minimum tax (AMT) as well as capital gains taxes.

- **Corporate bonds:** Interest income from corporate bonds is generally taxable by the federal government and state and local governments.

Investment Uses

Bonds are most frequently used as a stable, predictable source of current income. The favorable tax treatment of U.S. government and municipal bond interest is a plus.

How to Invest

- **Direct ownership:** Working with a stockbroker or other securities-licensed professional, investors can buy bonds directly, holding the securities in their own names.

Continued.

Bonds

- **Indirect ownership:** Open-end investment companies known as mutual funds are an indirect method of bond ownership. Mutual funds pool the resources of many individuals, and offer an investor access to a diversified, professionally managed portfolio. Exchange-traded funds, or ETFs, are a variation of the standard mutual fund, and are another way of investing in bonds. Unit Investment Trusts (UITs) are a third form of indirect bond ownership. The bond portfolio in a UIT is fixed and not actively managed.[1]

Possible Risks

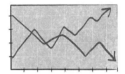

- **Market risk:** If a bond is sold before maturity, an investor may receive more or less than originally paid.

- **Default risk:** An issuer may default on payment of the principal or interest of a bond.

- **Inflation risk:** As fixed return investments, bonds are subject to inflation risk; over time, the dollars received have less purchasing power.

---

[1] The Securities and Exchange Commission requires that all prospective UIT, ETF, and mutual fund investors be given a prospectus. The prospectus contains valuable information concerning how an investment works, its goals and risks, and any expenses and charges involved.

Corporate Bonds

Corporate bonds are debt instruments issued by large corporations. The proceeds of corporate bond issues are often used to purchase new plant and equipment, or to fund research for future company growth.

Corporate bonds issued today are usually registered in form, and pay interest on a semi-annual basis. Maturities typically range from one to 30 years. By way of contrast, bonds issued in the 19th century were often "bearer" bonds with detachable coupons. The owner of the bond had to clip a coupon every six months and return it to the bond issuer for payment. Maturities could reach up to 100 years.

Types of Corporate Bonds

There are a number of different types of corporate bonds:

- **Mortgage bonds:** Bonds that are secured by identifiable assets such as real estate or equipment.

- **Debentures:** Bonds that are secured only by the faith and credit of the issuer.

- **Convertible bonds:** Bonds that can be converted into a specified number of shares of the common stock of the issuing corporation. An investor who buys a convertible bond usually expects the price of the underlying common stock to rise over time.

- **Commercial paper:** Commercial paper is used to meet very short-term (30-90 days) corporate financing needs. It is essentially an unsecured corporate IOU.

Other Corporate Bond Features

Occasionally, corporate bonds will have additional features.

- **Sinking fund:** Some bonds require the issuing corporation to make regular payments into a special, dedicated fund, designed to ensure that interest and principal payments are made when due.

- **Call feature:** Bonds issued during periods of high interest rates may have a feature which allows the issuer to redeem or "call" the bond prior to maturity. If a bond issue is called, the issuer will normally redeem the bond for full face value, or with a slight premium. Such bonds usually have an initial period of time during which the call feature cannot be used.

- **Put feature:** If a bond has this feature, it allows the investor to force the corporation to redeem the bond and "put" the bond back where it came from, usually at face value.

Continued.

Corporate Bonds

Bond Prices and Interest Rates

If a corporate bond is held to maturity, the issuer is obligated to repay the full face amount. If the bond is sold before it matures, however, the investor may receive more, or less, than originally paid. Bond prices can fluctuate, most often in response to changes in the general level of interest rates. If rates rise, the price of existing bonds usually falls; if interest rates decline, the market value of existing bonds generally increases. Corporate bond prices may also be affected by general business and economic factors.

Income Tax Treatment

Interest income and capital gain from corporate bonds are fully taxable at the federal, state and local levels.

Investment Uses

Corporate bonds are most frequently used as a stable, predictable source of current income. They typically have a higher yield than either municipal or government bonds due to the tax treatment of the interest income and a generally higher level of default risk. High-quality corporate bonds can be very useful inside a tax-deferred framework such as an IRA or other qualified retirement plan.

How to Invest

- **Direct ownership:** Working with a stockbroker or other securities-licensed professional, investors can buy corporate bonds directly, holding the securities in their own names.

- **Indirect ownership:** Mutual funds (open-end investment companies) are an indirect method of corporate bond ownership. Mutual funds pool the resources of many individuals and offer an investor access to a diversified portfolio of professionally managed securities. Exchange-traded funds, or ETFs, are a variation of the standard mutual fund and are another way of investing in corporate bonds. Unit investment trusts (UITs) are a third form of indirect ownership. The corporate bond portfolio in a UIT is fixed and not actively managed[1].

Possible Risks

- **Market risk:** If a corporate bond is sold before maturity, an investor may receive more or less than originally paid.

- **Default risk:** An issuer may default on payment of a bond's principal or interest.

- **Inflation risk:** As fixed return investments, corporate bonds are subject to inflation risk. Over time, the dollars received have less purchasing power.

---

[1] The Securities and Exchange Commission requires that all prospective UIT, ETF, and mutual fund investors be given a prospectus. The prospectus contains valuable information concerning how an investment works, its goals and risks, and any expenses and charges involved.

U.S. Government Securities

The federal government of the United States issues a wide array of debt securities. Securities which are direct obligations of the federal government are backed by the "full faith and credit" of the government. In terms of default risk, these bonds are widely considered to be the safest debt investment available. Interest income from U.S. government bonds is generally not taxable at the state or local level.

Savings Bonds

The federal government's savings bond program was started in 1935 to provide a refuge for individual savings that would be free from market fluctuation. Unlike marketable Treasury securities, savings bonds are not traded on any exchange. The U.S. government is both the issuer and ultimate purchaser of all savings bonds. There are several types of savings bonds currently available:

- **Series EE bonds:** Series EE bonds can be purchased at banks and other financial institutions, as well as on the internet. A paper EE bond is purchased at 50% of its face value, in denominations ranging from $50 to $10,000.[1] Interest is earned by a gradual increase in the value of the bonds, with interest being credited every six months. Bonds purchased electronically are issued at face value, in any dollar amount. Bonds issued on or after May 1, 2005 earn a fixed rate of interest.[2] The bonds may be cashed any time after 12 months.[3] Current EE bonds earn interest up to 30 years. EE bond holders can choose to be taxed each year on the increase in value, or to defer taxation until the bonds are cashed or they mature.

- **Series I bonds:** Series I bonds are a type of government security whose purpose is to provide some protection against loss of purchasing power due to inflation. Paper I bonds are issued at face value, in seven denominations.[4] Electronically issued I bonds may be purchased in any dollar amount. I bonds have a return composed of two parts: (1) a fixed interest rate, and (2) an inflation-adjusted interest rate. Each May and November the Treasury announces the fixed rate of return (which will never change) that will apply to all I bonds sold during the following six months. Every six months, the Treasury also determines an inflation-adjusted rate, based on changes in the consumer price index.[5] The total return for the following six months is the sum of the fixed and inflation adjusted rates. Interest is credited monthly and compounded on a semiannual basis. I bonds may be redeemed any time after 12 months. I bonds earn interest for a maximum period of 30 years. I bond holders can choose to be taxed each year on the interest income, or to defer taxation until the bonds are cashed or they mature.

---

[1] For example, the purchaser of a $50 savings bond will pay $25. The denominations (face value) are $50, $75, $100, $200, $500, $1,000, $5,000, and $10,000.

[2] Series EE bonds issued before May 1, 2005 earned a variable rate of interest which was adjusted every six months.

[3] Series EE bonds issued before February, 2003 could be redeemed after being held six months. An EE or I bond redeemed within five years of issuance is subject to a 3-month interest penalty.

[4] The denominations are $50, $75, $100, $200, $500, $1,000, and $5,000..

[5] The CPI-U is used for this purpose, the consumer price index for all consumers.

U.S. Government Securities

- **Purchase limits:** Beginning January 1, 2008, specific limits apply to the dollar amount of the various types of savings bonds that may be purchased by a single individual in any one calendar year, for a total not to exceed $20,000:
  - Paper EE bonds - $5,000 ($10,000 face value)
  - Electronic EE bonds - $5,000
  - Paper I bonds - $5,000
  - Electronic I bonds - $5,000

- **Series HH bonds:** Unlike series I or EE bonds, HH bonds pay interest to the bondholder every six months. Yields are fixed, but can change after 10 years. The interest from HH bonds is taxable each year. These bonds were issued in four denominations: $500, $1,000, $5,000, and $10,000, and have a 20-year maturity. August, 2004 was the last month that the Treasury issued new series HH bonds. Before that date, investors could acquire HH bonds by exchanging matured EE/E bonds, or by reinvesting matured series HH/H bonds.[1]

Marketable U.S. Government Securities

There are several types of marketable government debt securities. These bonds are termed "marketable" because they are widely traded in public markets. New issues are in book-entry form. Existing and new marketable U.S. government bonds can be purchased through government securities dealers, usually for a small commission. New issues may be purchased directly from the government without paying commission through the Bureau of Public Debt's Treasury Direct program, at www.treasurydirect.gov.

- **Treasury bills** (T-Bills): T-Bills are short-term debt obligations, with maturities of 13, 26, or 52 weeks. They are sold at a discount from face value; the difference between the purchase price and the face value (or the sales price if sold) is the "interest." The interest is not taxable until the bill is sold, or at maturity. The minimum initial investment is $1,000.

- **Treasury notes:** Treasury notes are medium term debt obligations, with maturities ranging from one to 10 years. Notes have a fixed interest rate and pay interest on a semi-annual basis. The minimum initial investment is $1,000.

- **Treasury bonds:** Treasury bonds have maturities greater than 10 years. Like Treasury notes, T-bonds have a fixed interest rate and pay interest on a semi-annual basis. The minimum initial investment is $1,000.

---

[1] Series E bonds were issued from 1941 to 1980. Series H bonds were issued from 1952 to 1979.

U.S. Government Securities

- **Treasury inflation-protected securities:** Treasury inflation-protected securities (TIPS) are a relatively new type of government debt. With a fixed percentage yield, and paying interest every six months, TIPS are intended to provide protection from loss of purchasing power due to inflation. At issue, TIPS have a par value or principal amount; the value of the principal amount is adjusted for changes, up or down, in the Consumer Price Index, CPI-U. Each interest payment is calculated by multiplying the adjusted principal amount by the fixed percentage rate. At maturity, the investor receives the greater of the inflation-adjusted principal amount or the face value at original issue. TIPS are issued with maturities of 5, 10, and 20 years.

Other Government Securities

There are a number of debt securities available that are widely thought of as being "government" bonds. These debt instruments are normally issued under authority of an act of Congress and usually involve some form of government guarantee or sponsorship. Most are freely traded in public markets. These securities come in different forms and are issued by entities such as the Government National Mortgage Association (GNMA), the Federal National Mortgage Association (FNMA), or the Federal Financing Bank (FFB).

Not all of these securities are backed by the "full faith and credit" of the U.S. government. Further, interest income from these securities may not be exempt from state and local income tax. Investors should check the underlying security for such bonds, as well as the taxability of the interest income.

Marketable Government Bonds and Interest Rates

If an investor buys a marketable government bond and holds it to maturity, the issuer is obligated to repay the full face amount. If such a bond is sold before it matures, however, the investor may receive more, or less, than originally paid. Bond prices can move up and down, most often in response to changes in the general level of interest rates. If rates rise, the price of existing bonds usually falls; if interest rates decline, the market value of existing bonds generally increases. Marketable government bond prices may also be affected by general business and economic factors.

U.S. savings bonds are not subject to fluctuating market values; they are not traded on any market. The U.S. government is both the issuer and ultimate purchaser of savings bonds.

Investment Uses

U.S. government bonds that pay interest currently are frequently used as a stable source of income. Treasury bonds of all types, backed by the full faith and credit of the federal government, are considered highly safe from the risk of default. In a tax-deferred framework such as an IRA or other qualified plan, U.S. government securities are useful investments for retirement purposes. If certain requirements are met, series I or EE Savings Bonds can be a tax-free method of accumulating funds for a child's college education.

Continued

U.S. Government Securities

How to Invest

- **Direct ownership**
  - **Savings bonds:** Can only be owned directly, and may be purchased at banks and other local financial institutions, and on the Internet at www.treasurydirect.gov.
  - **Marketable U.S. government securities:** At original issue, can be purchased directly from the Treasury on the Internet at www.treasurydirect.gov. May also be purchased through stockbrokers or other securities-licensed professionals.

- **Indirect ownership**
  - **Marketable U.S. government securities:** Open-end investment companies known as "mutual funds" are an indirect method of owning marketable U.S. government securities. Mutual funds pool the resources of many individuals and allow an investor to share in a diversified, professionally managed portfolio. Exchange-traded funds, or ETFs, are a variation of the standard mutual fund, and are another way of investing in marketable U.S. government securities. Unit Investment Trusts (UITs) are a third form of indirect ownership. The portfolio in a UIT is fixed and not actively managed.[1]

Possible Risks

- **Savings bonds**
  - **Inflation risk:** Although yields can vary somewhat, savings bonds are subject to inflation risk; over time, the dollars received have less purchasing power. Series I savings bonds are structured to avoid inflation risk.

- **Marketable U.S. government securities**
  - **Market risk:** If a bond is sold before maturity, an investor may receive more or less than originally paid.
  - **Inflation risk:** As fixed return investments, marketable government securities are subject to inflation risk; over time, the dollars received have less purchasing power. Treasury inflation-protected securities are structured to avoid inflation risk.
  - **Default risk:** Some government bonds are not backed by the full faith and credit of the federal government; owners of such bonds face the possibility that interest or principal may not be repaid.

---

[1] The Securities and Exchange Commission requires that all prospective UIT, ETF, and mutual fund investors be given a prospectus. The prospectus contains valuable information concerning how an investment works, its goals and risks, and any expenses and charges involved.

Treasury Inflation-Protected Securities

All bond investors face the risk of inflation. Long-term bond investors in particular can lose a substantial portion of the purchasing power of their invested funds due to a gradual increase in prices. Treasury inflation-protected securities (TIPS) are one answer to the inflation risk problem.

How It Works

TIPS are marketable, book-entry debt securities issued by the U.S. Treasury. TIPS are sold by the government at a quarterly auction, in minimum amounts of $1,000. They carry a fixed annual interest rate, and pay interest twice a year. The inflation protection is provided by adjusting the principal amount of the security according to changes in the inflation rate.[1] The semiannual interest payment is then calculated based on the adjusted principal amount. The inflation-adjusted principal amount is paid at maturity. TIPS are issued with maturities of 5, 10, and 20 years.

Example: An investor purchases a $1,000 TIPS bond, paying 3.0% annual interest, in January. By July, when the first interest payment is due, inflation has increased 1.0%. The adjusted principal amount of the bond is now $1,010. The interest payable at that time is $15.15, calculated as ($1,010 x 3.0%) ÷ 2. If by January of the following year, when the second interest payment becomes due, inflation had run at a 3.0% level for the whole year, the principal amount of the bond would be $1,030. The second interest payment would be $15.45, calculated as ($1,030 x 3.0%) ÷ 2.

In a deflationary environment, the principal amount is adjusted downward, resulting in an interest payment that may be less than the stated "coupon" payment. If the adjusted principal amount of the bond at maturity is less than the principal amount at issue, an additional sum will be paid to return to the investor at least the original principal amount.

Income Tax Issues[2]

Interest income from treasury inflation-protected securities is treated in the same manner as interest income from other "direct obligations" of the federal government. The interest is taxable by the federal government, but is generally exempt from state and local tax.

A unique characteristic of TIPS is that any adjustment of the principal amount is considered to be currently taxable "interest" income. Thus, in our example above, the investor would have $25.15 of taxable interest income from the bond for the first year; $15.15 of interest actually received as cash, and $10.00 in the form of inflation adjustment to the principal amount.

---

[1] As measured by the change in the inflation rate between the date the bond is issued and the current interest payment date. The index used is the non-seasonally adjusted, U.S. City Average All Items Consumer Price Index for Urban Consumers, the CPI-U. The CPI-U is published every month by the Bureau of Labor Statistics.

[2] See Treasury Decision 8830, IRB 1999 – 38, and Treasury Decision 8709, IRB 1997 – 9, for a more detailed discussion of the tax treatment of Treasury Inflation-Protection Securities.

Continued

Treasury Inflation-Protected Securities

TIPS - Market Prices and Interest Rates

Although Treasury inflation-protected securities are guaranteed against default by the U.S. government, they are also marketable securities, which means they can be bought and sold in the open market. If an investor buys a TIPS and holds it to maturity, the government is obligated to repay at least the original principal amount. If a bond is sold before it matures, however, the investor may receive more, or less, than originally paid, due to fluctuations in market value. TIPS prices in the open market can move up and down, most often in response to changes in the general level of interest rates. In general, if rates rise, the price of existing bonds will fall; if interest rates decline, the market value of existing bonds will increase.

Investment Uses

Treasury inflation-protected securities can serve as a source of periodic income, for investors seeking to meet current expenses. The inflation adjustment feature of these bonds is expected to be a prime attraction for many fixed-income investors. The currently taxable nature of the inflation adjusted principal amount may be a drawback for some. TIPS can be a useful investment in a tax-deferred IRA or other qualified retirement plan.

How to Invest

- **Direct ownership:** Investors can own TIPS directly, in their own names, either through an account with a securities brokerage firm or through an online account with the Treasury Department at www.treasurydirect.gov.

- **Indirect ownership:** Open-end investment companies, known as mutual funds, are an indirect method of owning treasury inflation-protected securities.[1] Mutual funds pool the resources of many individuals, and offer an investor access to a diversified, professionally managed portfolio.

Possible Risks

- **Market risk:** If a bond is sold before maturity, an investor may receive more or less than originally paid.

---

[1] The Securities and Exchange Commission requires that all prospective mutual fund investors be given a prospectus. The prospectus contains valuable information concerning how an investment works, its goals and risks, and any expenses and charges involved.

Municipal Bonds

Municipal bonds are debt instruments issued by states, counties, cities and local government authorities such as a school or water district. The proceeds of municipal bond issues are used for a wide range of public purposes, including building schools, highways or airports, or to fund general government operations.

Perhaps the most notable feature of municipal bonds is the tax treatment of the interest income received. With a few limited exceptions, interest income from municipal bonds is exempt from federal income tax.[1] See IRC Sec. 103(a). Generally, municipal bond interest is also exempt from state and local income tax if the bondholder resides in the same jurisdiction where the bond was issued.

Municipal bonds typically pay interest on a semi-annual basis. On the open market, they normally trade in multiples of $5,000 (par value).

Types of Municipal Bonds

There are two primary categories of municipal bonds.

- **General obligation:** Also known as G.O. bonds, these bonds are secured by the full faith and credit of the issuer. In effect, this means the full taxing power of the issuing government or agency.

- **Revenue bonds:** Revenue bonds are bonds issued by agencies such as a port authority, highway commission or water and sewer district, to build specific public works projects. Such bonds are backed by the revenues generated by these projects for payment of principal and interest.

Other Municipal Bond Concepts

- **Private activity bonds:** Private Activity bonds are municipal bonds which serve mixed public and private purposes. Unless such bonds meet certain requirements (IRC Sec. 103(b)), the interest income from them is not exempt from federal income tax. State and local taxability will vary. Interest income on private activity bonds which do meet the requirements is federally tax-exempt; in certain cases, interest income from tax-exempt private activity bonds is a preference item for the alternative minimum tax (AMT). See IRC Sec. 57(a)(5).

- **Serial and term bonds:** These terms refer to the manner in which a municipal bond issue is redeemed at maturity. A serial bond issue matures over a number of years, with a portion of the issue retired each year. With term bonds, the entire bond issue is retired at one time.

---

[1] To qualify for the federal income tax exemption, bonds issued after 1982 generally must be in registered form. See IRC Sec. 149(a)(1).

Continued

Municipal Bonds

- **Insured municipal bonds:** Municipal bonds described as being "insured" carry an additional protection against the risk of default. A private corporation agrees to pay principal and interest if the issuer of the bond defaults. Investors should check the credit rating of both the bond issuer and the corporation insuring the bond. Such insurance protects only against the risk of default, not the market value of a bond.

Bond Prices and Interest Rates

If an investor buys a municipal bond and holds it to maturity, the issuer is obligated to repay the full face amount. If the bond is sold before it matures, however, the investor may receive more or less, than originally paid. Bond prices can move up and down, most often in response to changes in the general level of interest rates. If rates rise, the price of existing bonds usually falls; if interest rates decline, the market value of existing bonds generally increases. Municipal bond prices may also be affected by general business and economic factors.

Income Tax Treatment

The income from municipal bonds is generally exempt from federal income tax and state and local income tax (if the bondholder resides in the same jurisdiction where the bond was issued.) In some cases, income from municipal bonds may be subject to the alternative minimum tax (AMT) as well as capital gains taxes. No federal deduction is allowed for interest or investment expenses attributable to tax-exempt interest. See IRC Secs. 265(a)(1) and (2). Tax-exempt income is added back to a taxpayer's income to determine taxable Social Security. See IRC Sec. 86(b)(2)(B).

Investment Uses

Municipal bonds are attractive to high-tax-bracket individuals seeking a stable source of tax-advantaged income. They can supplement IRAs and other qualified retirement plans when a taxpayer has already made the maximum allowable plan contribution.

How to Invest

- **Direct ownership:** Working with a stockbroker or other securities-licensed professional, investors can buy bonds directly, holding the bonds in their own names.

- **Indirect ownership:** Open-end investment companies known as mutual funds are an indirect method of municipal bond ownership. Mutual funds pool the resources of many individuals and offer access to a diversified, professionally-managed portfolio. Exchange-traded funds, or ETFs, a variation of the standard mutual fund, are another way of investing in municipal bonds. Unit Investment Trusts (UITs) are a third form of indirect ownership. The municipal bond portfolio in a UIT is fixed and not actively managed.[1]

---

[1] The Securities and Exchange Commission (SEC) requires that all prospective UIT, ETF, and mutual fund investors be given a prospectus. The prospectus contains valuable information concerning how an investment works, its goals and risks, and any expenses and charges involved.

Continued...

Municipal Bonds

Possible Risks

- **Market risk:** If a municipal bond is sold before maturity, an investor may receive more or less than originally paid.

- **Default risk:** An issuer may default on payment of the principal or interest of a bond.

- **Inflation risk:** As fixed return investments, municipal bonds are subject to inflation risk; over time, the dollars received have less purchasing power.

- **Tax risk:** Federal or local government law concerning the taxability of municipal bond interest income could change.

Mutual Funds

Individuals with excess dollars to put to work in some form of investment have an often-bewildering range of choices. An investor may decide to tackle the financial markets alone, and buy and sell investments directly, in his or her own name. A second option is to invest indirectly, using an investment medium known as a mutual fund.

What Is a Mutual Fund?

A mutual fund is an organization designed to pool the assets of many investors, to achieve a common purpose. The money raised is then invested in accordance with pre-defined goals. This mutual effort of a number of investors provides benefits that an individual, working alone, might not be able to receive.

- **Professional management:** Trained, experienced investment professionals provide the research, selection and monitoring skills needed to manage an investment portfolio.

- **Diversification:** Owning shares in a mutual fund allows an investor to participate in a diversified portfolio. Instead of placing all the eggs in one basket, diversification spreads the risk over many different securities.

- **Convenience:** Mutual funds offer many conveniences. Investment programs can be started with relatively small amounts of money. Dividends and other gains can be automatically reinvested. Many funds offer features to automate both contributions and withdrawals. Regular fund statements ease bookkeeping by tracking an investor's purchases, withdrawals and reinvestments, as well as providing tax information.

Types of Mutual Funds

Mutual funds are classified according to their structure and investment objectives:

- **Open-end mutual funds:** Mutual funds that issue as many shares as the public wishes to buy are called open-end mutual funds. When a shareholder wants to sell, open-end funds redeem all shares tendered.

- **Closed-end mutual funds:** Closed-end mutual funds are funds that have a fixed number of shares. Unlike shares in an open-end fund, where the fund itself sells and redeems all shares, the shares in a closed-end fund are traded on public exchanges.

- **Investment objective:** Mutual funds are also classified according to the investment objective of the fund. Examples of mutual fund investment goals include:
  - **Money market funds:** These funds invest in a variety of short-term, money market debt, such as Treasury bills or commercial paper.
  - **Growth funds:** Have an emphasis on long-term capital growth, usually through investment in common stock.
  - **Income funds:** Focus on providing high, current income, using bonds and other income producing securities.
  - **Balanced funds:** Strive to provide income and long-term capital gain. Both stocks and bonds are used.

Continued...

Mutual Funds

Key Mutual Fund Concepts

- **Prospectus:** The Securities and Exchange Commission (SEC) requires that every prospective investor in an open-end mutual fund be provided a document called a prospectus. The prospectus contains valuable information concerning how the fund works, the fund's goals and risks, its history, and any expenses or charges involved. The prospectus is intended to provide the facts necessary for an investor to make an informed investment decision and should be reviewed carefully. For closed-end mutual funds, a prospectus is issued only when shares are first offered to the public.

- **Net asset value:** At the end of each business day, the managers of a fund will add up the market value of all securities held by the fund. The total market value is then divided by the number of outstanding shares in the fund. The result is the Net Asset Value (NAV) per share. For open-end funds, NAV is used to calculate the price per share for both purchases and sales. For closed-end funds, NAV measures only the value of the securities in the fund; the market price of shares in the fund can be higher or lower than NAV.

- **Load vs. no-load:** The term "load" traditionally refers to a commission paid to purchase shares in an open-end mutual fund. Funds which are no load do not charge a commission to purchase their shares. Even though a fund is no load, other fees or expenses may apply. Investors are encouraged to consult a fund's prospectus for a discussion of the fees and expenses charged by a fund.

- **Offering price:** This is the price charged to purchase shares in an open-end fund. For a load fund, it is the net asset value (NAV) plus the commission charged. For a no-load fund, offering price and NAV are the same.

Possible Risks

The risks involved in owning shares in a mutual fund are the same as those involved in directly owning the underlying securities. However, these risks are generally "spread" by the fund manager over a range of securities, to help minimize the impact of any one risk on the fund's performance as a whole.

- **Mutual funds holding stock investments**
  - **Market risk:** The value of stock can fluctuate up and down. If stock purchased at a higher price is sold when the market is down, a loss will result.

- **Mutual funds holding bonds or other debt instruments**
  - **Market risk:** The value of a bond will fluctuate, usually in response to changes in interest rates. If a bond is sold before it matures, the investor may receive more or less than originally paid.
  - **Default risk:** The possibility that the issuer of a bond or other debt will not pay either principal or interest.
  - **Inflation risk:** As fixed-return investments, bonds are subject to inflation risk; over time, the dollars received have less purchasing power.

Mutual Fund Share Classes – A, B, and C

Mutual funds can be divided into two broad groups, based upon the method by which they are marketed. When you pay a commission to a financial adviser or stock broker to buy mutual fund shares, that charge is called a "load" and the type of fund involved is called a "load fund." With a "no-load" fund, however, there is no commission charged to purchase fund shares. Shares in a no-load fund are purchased directly from the fund itself.

Load or No-Load?

Both load and no-load funds have their role in the marketplace and you must decide which is best for your needs:

- **No-load funds:** The advantage of a no-load fund is that you have all of your money working for you the moment you make your investment. The disadvantage is the lack of professional guidance with regard to your investment; you take direct responsibility for what to buy, when to buy or sell, or when to make changes to your portfolio.

- **Load funds:** The advantage of a load fund is that the broker or adviser can provide professional investment guidance. Your adviser monitors market conditions and can help you select the appropriate fund as well as recommend when to make other portfolio changes. The disadvantage of a load fund is that the commission or fees paid reduce your investment return.

Load Fund Share Classes

Over time the brokerage industry has developed various share "classes," to allow investors a choice as to how to pay the sales charges and service fees associated with load funds. Although the specifics vary from mutual fund to mutual fund, there are three common share classes that generally can be described as follows:

- **Class A Shares:** With the exception of very large purchases, these shares impose a "front-end" sales charge. This means that a sales charge is deducted from your investment each time you purchase shares. For example, if you invest $1,000 with a 4% sales charge, your commission will be $40 and you will receive shares valued at $960. These shares typically have a lower "expense ratio" (total annual operating expenses as a percentage of the fund's assets) compared with other share classes. Most companies will offer discounts for large purchases of Class A shares, termed "breakpoints."

- **Class B shares:** Instead of imposing a sales charge up-front, as with Class A shares, Class B shares levy a "back-end" or "contingent deferred sales charge" (CDSC), which is a sales charge you pay when you redeem your shares. For example, if your mutual fund has a CDSC of 3% and you redeem $1,000 worth of shares, you will receive $970 in cash. $30 is deducted for the CDSC. The percentage amount of the CDSC normally declines over time until it eventually reaches zero. The period of time over which the CDSC is phased out varies, but can range from five to eight years. Once the CDSC is eliminated, Class B shares usually convert to Class A, with the conversion occurring some time (generally one year) after the CDSC reaches zero. Class B shares typically have a higher operating expense ratio than Class A shares.

Continued...

Mutual Fund Share Classes – A, B, and C

- **Class C shares:** Class C shares are similar to Class B shares in that they share the same higher operating expenses and both have a CDSC. The CDSC for Class C shares; however, is often lower than that for Class B share and frequently disappears after a relatively short period of time, generally two years or less. Unlike Class B shares, Class C shares generally do not convert to Class A shares once the CDSC is eliminated.

Factors To Consider

There are a number of factors to consider when deciding which share class to use:

- **How much you plan to invest:** If you plan to invest a large amount of money, Class A shares, with their breakpoint discounts and lower operating expenses, may be preferable to Class B or Class C shares.

- **How long you plan to hold your funds:** The length of time you plan to hold your funds is an important factor in deciding whether an up-front sales charge or a back-end sales charge would be more advantageous.

- **Class annual operating expenses:** Annual operating expenses have a direct impact on your investment return. Funds with lower operating expenses are highly desirable.

Do Your Homework

Each fund makes available a "prospectus" which explains the investment objective of the fund and details all of the expenses and fees the fund charges. Read the prospectus carefully before investing.

Crunch The Numbers

The Financial Industry Regulatory Authority (FINRA) makes available on its website a Mutual Fund Expense Analyzer which allows you to compare the costs of different mutual funds or share classes and estimate the impact that the various expenses and fees can have over time. This calculator automatically provides the fee and expense data for you. The calculator can be found on the internet at:

http://apps.finra.org/investor_Information/ea/1/mfetf.aspx

Seek Professional Advice

Your broker or other financial adviser is a key source of information and guidance in selecting and managing your investment portfolio.

Mutual Funds – Glossary of Terms

12b-1 Fees: "12b-1" refers to the Securities and Exchange Commission (SEC) rule which permits money to be taken out of a fund's assets to pay the expenses of distributing and marketing the fund. 12b-1 fees (similar to sales charges) may be used to compensate a broker or other financial advisor.

Account Fee: Fee charged by some funds to their shareholders in connection with the maintenance of their accounts.

Account Minimum: Some funds require an investor to make an initial minimum investment, often between $1,000 and $10,000.

Asset-Based Sales Charge: Fees taken out of a mutual fund's assets to pay for marketing and distribution expenses. Asset-based sales charges also include "12b-1" fees.

Average Price Per Share: One of three methods used to determine the cost basis of mutual fund shares. Average price per share is calculated by adding up the total cost of all shares owned and then dividing by the total number of shares owned. (See also "First-In, First-Out (FIFO)" and "Specific Identification.") Also known as "Average Cost."

Back-End Sales Charge: A sales commission paid by mutual fund investors when they redeem shares. These charges typically decline after a certain time period has expired between the purchase and sale of shares and are usually charged in one of two ways: 1) as a percentage of the value of the shareholder's initial investment; or 2) as a percentage of the shareholder's investment upon redemption.

Breakpoint: A mutual fund may offer you a discount ("breakpoint") on the front-end sales charge if any one of the following conditions is met: 1) you make a large purchase; 2) you already hold other mutual funds in the same "fund family"; or 3) you commit to purchasing shares on a regular basis.

Closed-End Fund: A mutual fund with a fixed number of shares. Shares in a closed-end fund are traded on public exchanges.

Contingent Deferred Sales Charge (CDSC): (See "Back-End Sales Charge.")

Dollar Cost Averaging: An investment strategy of buying, at regular intervals, equal dollar amounts of a security such as a mutual fund. When the share price drops, more shares are purchased; when the share price rises, fewer shares are purchased.

Exchange Fee: Fee that some funds impose upon their shareholders if they exchange (transfer) to another fund within the same fund group or "fund family."

Continued...

Mutual Funds – Glossary of Terms

Exchange-Traded Fund (ETF): An investment vehicle that is similar in concept to a mutual fund in that it pools the resources of many investors to achieve a pre-determined investment goal. A primary difference is that shares of an ETF are traded on an exchange, rather than being purchased from, or redeemed by, the fund itself.

Expense Ratio: Percentage of assets used to cover all expenses associated with the operation of a mutual fund.

Family Discount: Allows an investor to combine purchases made by related individuals or in related accounts, to reach a higher breakpoint discount.

First In-First Out (FIFO): One of three methods used to determine the cost basis of fund shares. Under FIFO, the shares sold are assumed to be the oldest shares owned. (See also "Average Price Per Share" and "Specific Identification.")

Front-End Sales Charge: A sales commission mutual fund investors pay immediately upon the purchase of shares.

Fund Family: A group of mutual funds offered by the same mutual fund manager. Generally, exchanges are permitted within the fund family for a modest fee.

Investment Advisor: Refers to the company in charge of the person or organization employed by a mutual fund to manage the fund's investment portfolio. The investment advisor is responsible for hiring and monitoring the firm's portfolio manager(s).

Load Fund: A mutual fund which has a sales charge or commission.

Letter of Intent (LOI): A statement signed by an investor that he or she intends to make additional future fund purchases, sufficient to reach a certain discount breakpoint. The LOI allows the investor to obtain a reduced sales charge on all purchases made. If the investor does not invest the amount listed in the LOI, the mutual fund may retroactively levy the higher sales charge.

Management Fees: Fees paid out of the fund's assets to provide compensation to the fund's investment advisor and its affiliates for managing the fund's investment portfolio.

Mutual Fund: An investment vehicle operated by an investment company which pools the assets of many individuals. The money raised is then invested in accordance with pre-defined goals.

Net Asset Value (NAV): The total market value of the securities held by a mutual fund, divided by the number of outstanding fund shares.

Continued...

Mutual Funds – Glossary of Terms

No-Load: A fund that does not charge any type of sales charge ("load").

Open-End Fund: A mutual fund that issues as many shares as the public wishes to buy. When an individual wants to sell, an open-end fund redeems all shares tendered.

Operating Expenses: These are the total expenses paid annually by a mutual fund, generally expressed as a percentage of net assets.

Prospectus: A document which explains a mutual fund's goals, risks, history, and any expenses or charges involved in owning shares of the fund. The prospectus is intended to provide the facts necessary for an investor to make an informed investment decision.

Purchase Fee: A type of fee charged by some funds when shareholders purchase their shares. Purchase fees are not considered sales charges ("loads") because they are paid directly to the fund and are not used to compensate outside brokers.

Rebalancing: An investment strategy which requires a periodic adjustment in the investment mix, to maintain a specific asset allocation or risk tolerance.

Redemption Fee: A type of fee that some funds charge their shareholders upon the redemption of shares. Although similar to a back-end or contingent deferred sales charge, redemption fees are not considered sales charges ("loads") because they are paid directly to the fund and not used to compensate outside brokers.

Right of Accumulation (ROA): The right to receive a discounted sales charge on current fund purchases by combining both earlier and current purchases to reach a specific discount breakpoint.

Sales Charge: A sales charge is a commission paid by investors who have purchased shares in a mutual fund. These charges vary from fund to fund and are generally used to provide compensation to outside brokers that distribute fund shares.

Share Class: A mutual fund with one investment advisor may offer more than one share "class" to investors. Each class represents a similar interest in the fund's portfolio. The principal difference between the various share classes is that different fees and expenses apply to each class. The most common share classes are Class A, Class B, and Class C.

Specific Identification: One of three methods used to calculate the cost basis of mutual funds. When you sell or redeem shares, you specifically identify the shares (quantities and dates purchased) to be sold or redeemed. Example: "Sell 300 of the shares of XYZ fund that I purchased on July 5, 1998." (See also "First-In, First Out (FIFO)" and "Average Price Per Share.")

Continued...

Mutual Funds – Glossary of Terms

Statement of Additional Information (SAI): A highly detailed version of the prospectus. A SAI is usually written in technical, legal language and can be obtained either from the fund or from the Securities and Exchange Commission (SEC).

Turnover: A measure of the length of time a fund holds the securities it purchases. When a fund purchases or sells securities, it incurs both trading expenses and potential capital gains or losses. Funds with lower turnover typically have lower operating expenses; funds with higher turnover generally have higher operating expenses.

Index Funds

An index fund is a type of mutual fund, exchange-traded fund, or unit investment trust whose primary investment objective is to mimic the performance of a specified market index, such as the S&P 500 Index or the Wilshire 5000 Index. To achieve this, an index fund will hold all (or a representative sample) of the securities in the chosen index, in the same proportions as those securities making up the index.

Investing in an index fund is often referred to as "passive" investing, since changes in the portfolio are generally made only when there is a change in the underlying index. Index funds owners generally believe that it is impossible to "beat" the market; the primary goal is to come as close as possible to a "market" return. Mutual funds that are "actively" managed seek to beat the market, often by frequently trading individual stocks or bonds.

Advantages of Index Funds

For many investors, index funds have several distinct advantages:

- **Lower management costs:** Without the need for expenses such as investment research and the costs of buying and selling, index funds typically have lower management costs.

- **Lower portfolio turnover:** With a passive investment strategy, there is less portfolio turnover in index funds than with actively managed funds. Such trading activity can generate taxable capital gains.

Disadvantages of Index Funds

By their nature and design, index funds will never "beat" the market.

Possible Risks

Shares in an index fund involve the same risks as owning the underlying securities:

- Funds holding stock investments: The value of a stock can fluctuate up and down. If shares purchased at a higher price is sold when the market is down, a loss will result.

- Funds holding bonds or other debt instruments: Market Risk – the value of a bond will fluctuate, usually in response to changes in interest rates. If a bond is sold before it matures, an investor may receive more or less than originally paid; Default Risk – the issuer of a bond may not pay principal or interest when due; Inflation Risk – as fixed-return investments, bonds are subject to inflation risk – over time the dollars received have less purchasing power.

Before investing in an index fund, you should carefully read all of the fund's information, including its prospectus and most recent shareholder report.

Exchange-Traded Funds

Many investors use open-end mutual funds as an important part of their investment tool kit. One limitation to such funds is that they can only be bought from or sold to the issuing mutual fund and only at the net asset value (NAV) as calculated at the end of the trading day. Shares in an exchange-traded fund (ETF); however, can be bought and sold through a brokerage firm at the current market price any time the exchange is open.

How Are Exchange-Traded Funds Structured?

In a regular, open-end mutual fund, individual investors buy shares in the fund directly from the mutual fund itself. The money is then put to work according to the fund's investment goals. When an investor wishes to sell his or her fund shares, the mutual fund will redeem the shares. If many shareholders redeem their shares at one time, the fund may have to sell some of its portfolio to be able to repay the departing investors.

An ETF, however, does not deal directly with individual investors. Rather, "creation units" (usually representing 50,000 shares) are "sold" to institutional investors, such as a brokerage firm, in exchange for a portfolio of securities that match the ETF's investment goals. The institutional investor, in turn, can then sell the ETF shares to individual investors in the open market. If an individual wishes to sell ETF shares, he or she can do so by selling to other individual investors in the open market. An institutional investor can "sell" a creation unit's worth of ETF shares back to the fund. To complete the redemption, the fund does not have to sell anything, but simply distributes the underlying securities to the institutional investor and then "destroys" the creation unit.

Most ETFs use an indexing approach. Some ETFs are designed to track a certain market index, such as the S&P 500. Other ETFs follow market segments (for example mid-cap stocks), individual countries, selected industries, or even commodities such as gold or oil.

Advantages Of Exchange-Traded Funds

ETFs can have several significant advantages:

- **Generally lower operating costs:** Not having to deal with a large number of individual investors allows many ETFs to have very low annual expense ratios. In a mutual fund, the need to provide shareholder services is an additional expense.

- **Tax efficiency:** The low-turnover, buy-and hold approach of many ETFs typically leads to a high degree of tax efficiency. Individual investors will generally realize a gain or loss only when they sell their own ETF shares.

- **Trading flexibility:** Because ETF shares are bought and sold in the open market, an investor can use trading tools such as limit or stop-loss orders, "sell short" the ETF shares, or even trade the shares on margin, using borrowed money.

- **No required minimum purchases:** There are no minimum purchase requirements to buy shares in an ETF. Many mutual funds have minimum purchase requirements.

Continued

Exchange-Traded Funds

Disadvantages of Exchange-Traded Funds

ETFs also have several disadvantages:

- **Commission charges:** To buy or sell shares in an ETF, an individual investor must pay a commission for each transaction. Many mutual funds are no-load and do not charge a fee for purchases or redemptions.

- **Client services:** Most mutual funds provide client services such as automatic dividend reinvestment or keeping track of average cost basis for tax purposes. For investors in ETFs, these services may be available from the broker, sometimes for an extra fee.

Exchange Traded Funds vs. Index Mutual Funds

ETFs are often seen as an alternative to index mutual funds. Both types of investment typically use a passive, indexing investment approach. ETFs can provide trading flexibility, but at the cost of paying commission charges. Index mutual funds provide many investor services, but have a more limited ability to be bought or sold.

Consider ETFs For....	Consider Index Mutual Funds For....
Investors who buy and hold for long periods of time. ETFs often have very low annual operating expenses.	Those who buy or sell frequently. Investors using dollar cost averaging or who make periodic purchases or sales will incur commission costs with each transaction if ETFs are used.
Those with a single, large, lump-sum to invest. Over time, the lower operating costs of ETFs can outweigh the initial cost to purchase the shares.	Those with a small amount to invest. Regardless of the amount of money invested, a commission must be paid to buy or sell ETF shares.
Those seeking trading flexibility. ETFs can usually be traded with the same ease as can other exchange-listed securities.	Investors who re-balance their portfolios regularly. Commission charges can significantly reduce the benefit of low ETF expense ratios.

Another way to approach this question is to compare the total cost of owning an ETF with the total cost of owning a mutual fund. The Financial Industry Regulatory Authority (FINRA) makes available on its website a Mutual Fund and ETF Expense Analyzer which allows you to compare the costs of different funds or share classes and estimate the impact that the various expenses and fees can have over time. This calculator automatically provides the fee and expense data for you. The calculator can be found on the internet at:

http://apps.finra.org/investor_Information/ea/1/mfetf.aspx

Seek Professional Guidance

The advice and counsel of trained professionals can be helpful both in selecting the right investment and in monitoring the investment for any needed changes.

Exchange-Traded Funds vs. Index Mutual Funds

Exchange traded funds and index mutual funds have similarities and differences:

Issue	Exchange-Traded Funds	Index Mutual Funds
How structured?	Creation units (typically 50,000 shares) are "sold" to institutional investors in exchange for a basket of securities matching the ETF's investment goals. The institutional investor can then sell the ETF shares to individual investors in the open market. An individual investor wanting to sell shares can do so by selling to other individual investors in the open market. An institutional investor can "sell" a creation unit's worth of ETF shares back to the fund. To complete the transaction, the fund distributes the underlying securities to the institutional investor and then "destroys" the creation unit.	Individual investors buy shares in the fund directly from the mutual fund itself. The money is then invested in accordance with the fund's goals. If many shareholders redeem their shares at one time, the fund may have to sell some of its portfolio to be able to repay the departing investors.
How purchased or sold?	Through a stock broker	Directly with the fund or through a stock broker
Any cost to purchase or sell shares?	Yes. A commission is paid to the broker. There is usually a "spread" between the bid and ask price	For no-load funds, none. A load fund will levy a sales charge.
Trading options?	Trades are executed on the open market. An investor can use a limit or stop order, "sell short," or use a margin account.	Purchases or redemptions are made directly with the fund itself.
What determines the share price?	Supply and demand on the exchange. Prices will typically stay near the Net Asst Value (NAV) but may be slightly lower or higher than NAV.	Net Asset Value based upon securities prices at the market close.
Average annual operating expenses	Typically (but not always) lower than that of an index mutual fund.	Low, but generally slightly higher than for an ETF.
Tax efficiency	Low portfolio turnover can provide high tax efficiency.	Usually slightly less tax efficient than ETFs.
Automatic dividend reinvestment or average cost statement?	May be available from the broker, sometimes for a fee	Typically provided free of charge by the mutual fund.
Investors who should consider this are:	• Investors who buy and hold for long periods of time. • Those with a single, large, lump-sum to invest. • Those seeking trading flexibility.	• Those who buy or sell frequently. • Those with a small amount of money to invest. • Investors who rebalance their portfolio regularly.

How a Mutual Fund Works

A large number of people with a common goal purchase shares in a mutual fund

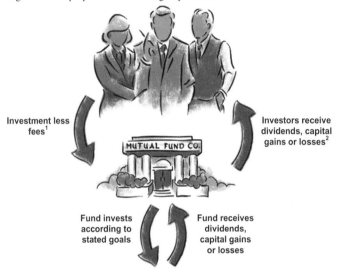

Investment less fees[1]

Investors receive dividends, capital gains or losses[2]

MUTUAL FUND CO.

Fund invests according to stated goals

Fund receives dividends, capital gains or losses

Money Market Funds	Growth Funds	Income Funds	Balanced Funds
Invest in a variety of short-term debt (Treasury Bills, commercial paper, etc.).	Emphasize long-term capital growth. Usually invest in common stock.	Focus on current income using bonds and other income producing securities.	Strive for both income and long-term gain, using both stocks and bonds.

Advantages

- **Professional management:** Experienced professionals manage the portfolio.

- **Diversification:** Owning shares in a mutual fund allows an investor to participate in a diversified portfolio, spreading the investment risk over several securities.

- **Convenience:** Many funds offer convenient features, such as consolidated statements, automatic reinvestment of gains and dividends, tax information, etc.

---

[1] Depending on the fund, sales charges may be deducted at the time an investor purchases shares in the fund, or at a later date. Some mutual funds do not have a sales charge. The Securities and Exchange Commission requires that all prospective mutual fund investors be given a booklet (the prospectus) clearly explaining how a fund works, its goals and risks, and all expenses or charges.

[2] Mutual fund shares will fluctuate in value and investors will receive more or less than their original investment when the shares are redeemed. Investors must include dividends and capital gains in current taxable income even if reinvested in the mutual fund.

Mutual Fund Families

Mutual funds offer the investor immediate diversification into carefully selected and managed securities. An investment program can be started for a small amount of money (typically $500-$1,000), and subsequent purchases can be as small as $50. Automatic reinvestment of capital gains and dividends[1] is a convenient way to purchase additional shares.

Family of Funds

Many mutual fund families have a broad spectrum of funds to meet the needs and temperaments of various investors. A typical family of funds might include:

Money Market Funds[2]	Sector Funds
• Invest in short-term money market (debt) instruments. • Yields fluctuate daily. • Taxation of dividends received depends on underlying investments. • Often used as a liquid, short-term storehouse for funds.	• Generally invest in stocks and bonds of companies focusing on a particular sector of the economy. • Typical areas might include technology, health, energy, utilities, precious metals, etc. • Income and capital gains generally taxable. • Usually appeal to investors with a concern or interest in a particular area of the economy.

Municipal Bond Funds	Aggressive Growth Funds
• Invest primarily in municipal bonds, or other short-term municipal debt. • Federally tax-free dividends. • Dividends may also be state tax exempt. • Dividend income may be subject to alternative minimum tax. • Typically used by high tax-bracket investors seeking current income.	• Typically invest in stocks of companies with high potential earnings growth. • Generally seek capital appreciation. • Relatively high risk/reward potential; market value can be volatile.

Bond Funds	Growth Funds
• Invest in bonds and debt-type instruments. • Taxability of dividends received depends on underlying investments. • Commonly used as source of current income.	• Commonly invest in stocks of companies with relatively stable potential earnings growth. • Generally seek capital appreciation. • Typically follow a more conservative investment strategy than aggressive growth funds.

---

[1] Under current legislation, during 2003-2010, federal law taxes qualifying stock dividends at marginal rates lower than those generally applicable to ordinary income. State and local income tax treatment of such dividends may differ.

[2] Money market mutual funds (MMMFs) are neither insured nor guaranteed by any government agency. There is no assurance that a MMMF will be able to maintain a fixed, net-asset value of $1.00 per share. Such funds should be clearly distinguished from money market deposit accounts (MMDAs) in banks and savings and loans. Most financial institutions offering MMDAs are protected by government deposit insurance.

Continue

Mutual Fund Families

Income Funds
• Invest in bonds and other debt-type instruments such as preferred or high-yield stocks.
• Usually seek maximum current income.
• Taxation of dividends received depends on underlying investments.
• Appeals to investors seeking a relatively high level of current income.

Growth and Income Funds
• Often invest in both stocks and bonds or other debt-type instruments.
• Commonly seek both capital appreciation and current income.
• Taxation of dividends received depends on underlying investments.
• Also called balanced funds.

Possible Risks

The risks involved in owning shares in a mutual fund are the same as those involved in directly owning the underlying securities. However, these risks are generally spread by the fund manager over a range of securities, to help minimize the impact of any one risk on a fund's performance as a whole.

- **Mutual funds holding stock investments**
  - **Market risk:** The value of a stock can fluctuate up and down.
- **Mutual funds holding bonds or other debt instruments**
  - **Market risk:** The value of a bond will fluctuate, up and down, usually in response to changes in interest rates.
  - **Default risk:** The possibility that the issuer of a bond or other debt will not pay either interest or principal.
  - **Inflation risk:** As fixed-return investments, bonds are subject to inflation risk; over time, the dollars received may have less purchasing power.

Exchange Privilege

Exchange from one fund to another may be allowed at any time for a nominal fee and no commission charge. There will be tax consequences at the time of exchange if there is a profit or a loss. Purchasing mutual funds from different mutual fund companies may result in paying additional sales loads.

Timing Services

For a fee, these organizations manage funds, typically shifting in and out of the market by switching from growth funds to money market funds through the exchange privilege.

Seek Professional Guidance

All investment decisions should be made only after consultation with a professional advisor and a complete review of the appropriate prospectuses. Investors in mutual funds are subject to a variety of risks; both investment return and market value can fluctuate. When redeemed, an investor's shares may be worth more or less than their original cost.

Dollar Cost Averaging

Many investors look to the stock market for capital growth, investing in individual stocks or mutual funds. Historically, the stock market has charted a long-term upward trend. In the short run, however, daily fluctuations in market prices can make it difficult to decide when to buy.

Rather than trying to time the market, and making a single purchase, many investors use a method called dollar cost averaging. Using dollar cost averaging, an investor buys the same stock or mutual fund at regular intervals; e.g., monthly or quarterly, and with a fixed amount of investment dollars; e.g., $100 per month.

When the selected stock or mutual fund declines in value, the investor's $100 will buy a greater number of shares. When the market price increases, the investor's $100 will buy fewer shares. Over a period of time, as market prices fluctuate, the average cost per share to the investor will be less than the average price per share.

For example, assume that a person invests $100 per month for 12 months in XYZ mutual fund.

Month	Dollars Invested	Price per Share	Number of Shares Purchased
Jan	$100	$11.00	9.09
Feb	$100	$13.00	7.69
Mar	$100	$9.00	11.11
Apr	$100	$11.00	9.09
May	$100	$12.00	8.33
Jun	$100	$8.00	12.50
July	$100	$9.00	11.11
Aug	$100	$10.00	10.00
Sept	$100	$12.00	8.33
Oct	$100	$11.00	9.09
Nov	$100	$8.00	12.50
Dec	$100	$11.00	9.09
Total	$1,200	$125.00	117.94

The average price per share: ($125.00 / 12) = $10.42

The average cost per share: ($1,200 / 117.94) = $10.17

Continued...

Dollar Cost Averaging

Graphically, the results of dollar cost averaging in our example would look like this.

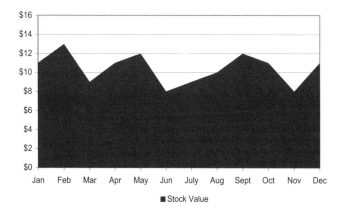

Stock Value

Notes:
1. Investments must be regular and the same amount each time. If the investor discontinues the plan when the market value is less than the cost of the shares he or she will obviously lose money.
2. The investor must be willing and able to invest during the low price levels.
3. Dollar cost averaging cannot assure a profit and does not protect the investor in a steadily declining market.

Reverse Mortgages

Many retired individuals find themselves living on a fixed income. Many also own a home which is either paid for, or which has a very small mortgage, a situation often described as "house-rich-and-cash-poor." In the past, there have been few acceptable ways to take advantage of this home equity, apart from selling the home. Recently, however, a new financial tool has been developed – the reverse mortgage – which provides qualified individuals access to the equity in their homes, and still permits them to retain ownership of the home.

What Is a Reverse Mortgage?

Most homeowners are familiar with the traditional home mortgage. An individual buys a home, and, over time, as the monthly payments are made, the balance due on the mortgage is gradually reduced. A homeowner's equity – the difference between what is owed and the market value – is also increased if a home's market value increases. In the traditional, forward mortgage, as debt decreases, equity increases.

A reverse mortgage, as the name implies, works in the other direction. With a reverse mortgage, cash flows from a lender to a borrower. Over time, the balance due increases. In a reverse mortgage, as debt increases, equity decreases.

- **Eligibility:** Reverse mortgage programs generally require that all borrowers be at least 62 years of age. The home must be owner-occupied, and be the borrower's principal residence. Not all types of homes qualify; all programs accept single-family detached homes, and some allow 2-4 unit owner-occupied homes, condominiums and manufactured homes. Only first mortgages are permitted. Any other debt secured by the home must either be first paid off, or paid off with proceeds from the reverse mortgage.

- **Ownership:** During the term of the mortgage, the borrower remains the owner of the home, and is responsible for payment of property taxes, maintenance and repair, and keeping the home insured.

- **Repayment:** No payments are required as long as the borrower lives in the home. The outstanding loan balance, including accrued interest and any loan costs, is due when the last borrower sells the home, permanently leaves or dies. In a few instances, the loan is due at the end of a fixed term. Typically, the loan is repaid by either selling or refinancing the home. Any remaining equity is paid to the borrower, the borrower's estate or heirs.

- **Maximum loan balance:** A borrower can never owe more than the value of the home at the time the loan is repaid. Reverse mortgages are generally nonrecourse loans, which means the lender can only look to the value of the home for repayment.

Continued...

Reverse Mortgages

The Pros and Cons of Reverse Mortgages

There are a number of reasons why a reverse mortgage may not be appropriate:

- **Not needed:** Some retired individuals will not want to consider a reverse mortgage simply because it is not needed; their financial needs during retirement are already adequately met.

- **Security:** Reflecting long-held attitudes toward savings and debt, some individuals may not be comfortable with the idea of placing any type of mortgage on the home, once it is paid for.

- **Legacy for heirs:** Rather than using the equity in the home for current needs, a homeowner may want the equity to pass to family members or other beneficiaries, such as a charity.

There are also a number of situations where a reverse mortgage can help:

- **Enjoy life:** For some, the extra dollars provided by a reverse mortgage may make it easier to pay routine monthly expenses. For others, it may allow an occasional splurge.

- **Pay off debt:** Funds from a reverse mortgage can be used to pay off other types of personal debt that require monthly payments, such as credit card balances.

- **Maintain independence:** Some may wish to make improvements to the home, or pay for in-home care, to allow them to remain independent as long as possible

- **Provide for the future:** Even though the present financial situation is stable, a reverse mortgage can provide a way to meet unforeseen future circumstances.

Choosing a Reverse Mortgage

Unlike just a few years ago, a wide range of reverse mortgage programs is available today. Further, the specific details of each program can vary greatly. A standard series of questions can be used to compare and contrast each program:

- **How much cash?** In general, the amount of cash which can be borrowed will depend on the lender's policies, the age of the borrowers, the value of the home, the home's condition and location, and the interest rate. The amount of available cash can vary greatly from one lender to the next.

- **How will the cash be paid?** Depending on the lender, the cash from a reverse mortgage is typically available to the borrower in one of three ways. In some cases a combination of payment methods may be available:
  - **Lump sum:** The loan proceeds can be paid with one check, usually at the time the loan is closed.

Continued...

Reverse Mortgages

- **Periodic advances:** Cash payments of a fixed amount are usually made monthly. Term advances are made for a specified period of time; tenure advances continue as long as the borrower lives in the home; lifetime advances are paid as long as the borrower lives.
- **Credit line:** This is a line of credit the borrower can use when needed, up to the loan limit. Some credit lines are flat, i.e., the total amount of available credit is fixed. Other credit lines grow and provide an amount of credit which increases over time.

- **Cost of the loan:** Federal law requires reverse mortgage lenders to provide prospective borrowers with a loan cost analysis. The total annual loan cost (TALC) analysis looks at the cost of a loan under a specified set of circumstances, over the entire length of the loan. The standardized nature of the TALC makes it easy to compare the cost of loans from different lenders.

- **Remaining equity:** If a borrower decides to sell the home after only a few years, how much equity would be left?

Major Reverse Mortgage Programs

While there are a number of lenders in the private sector who make reverse mortgage loans, the two most widely available programs are operated under the auspices of the federal government:

- **Federal Housing Administration (FHA):** The Federal Housing Administration, part of the U.S. Department of Housing and Urban Development, insures reverse mortgage loans made by private lenders under its Home Equity Conversion Mortgage (HECM) program. If a lender fails to make the promised payments, the FHA takes over responsibility for fulfilling the lender's obligations. The HECM program has specific loan limits and is targeted at moderate-income families.

- **Federal National Mortgage Association (FNMA):** The Federal National Mortgage Association, also know as Fannie Mae is a government created private corporation. FNMA operates the Home Keeper reverse mortgage program, with many features similar to the FHA's HECM program.

Additional Resources

The federal government entities directly involved with reverse mortgages, the FHA and FNMA, have freely available information on the details of each reverse mortgage program. Further, these agencies require consumer education as a part of the lending process. There are also several independent, third-party sources of information on reverse mortgages:

Continued..

Reverse Mortgages

- **American Association of Retired Persons (AARP):** The AARP provides publications on reverse mortgages. On the Internet, the AARP maintains a website at: http://www.aarp.org

- **National Center for Home Equity Conversion (NCHEC):** The NCHEC is an independent, not-for-profit organization whose goal is to provide consumer education about home equity conversion options. On the Internet their website is: http://www.reverse.org/

- **U.S. Department of Housing and Urban Development (HUD):** Information on reverse mortgages is available from the U. S. Department of Housing and Urban Development at their website at: http://www.hud.gov

Seek Professional Advice

Because they are relatively new, reverse mortgages are unfamiliar to many. Also, those most likely to consider a reverse mortgage are usually at a point in life where long-term commitments must be very carefully considered. Individuals considering a reverse mortgage are strongly advised to seek professional advice before entering into a loan contract.

How a Reverse Mortgage Works

Loan Amount (typically as a series of payments)

Mortgage Lender

Repayment at sale of home or death of last owner

Home Owner/Borrower

Must keep as primary residence

Permanent Residence

Borrowing

- Must own home free-and clear or pay-off any existing loan balances with proceeds from reverse mortgage.

- The amount of cash available can vary widely from lender to lender.

- Borrower receives loan as lump sum, line of credit, or periodic payments. Some programs allow for a combination of payment methods.

- Borrower remains owner of home and must continue payments for property taxes, insurance, and repairs.

Repayment

- No repayment required as long as home is borrower's primary residence[1].

- Repayment is due when last borrower sells home, permanently[2] moves away or dies.

- Loan is typically repaid by either selling the home or refinancing the loan.

- A borrower can never owe more than value of home, at the time loan is repaid.

- If proceeds from sale of home exceed loan amount due, borrower or heirs receive the difference.

---

[1] Primary residence is typically defined as where an individual resides at least six months of the year.
[2] Permanently moving away generally means not residing in the home for at least 12 months or more at one time.

Limited Partnerships

A limited partnership is a form of business partnership similar to a general partnership, except that in addition to one or more general partners (GPs), there are one or more limited partners (LPs).[1] The general partners have management control and share in the profits of the firm in predefined proportions. In addition, the general partners are subject to joint and several liability with regard to the debts of the partnership.

Limited partners have a role similar to that of shareholders in a corporation. Typically, limited partners share in the profits of the firm in a predetermined fashion, but have no management authority and are generally only liable for debts incurred by the partnership to the extent of their investment.

The limited partnership has been a popular method of structuring investments having two or more investors. Common limited partnership programs include real estate (residential, commercial, and raw land), oil and gas (exploration and producing properties), equipment leasing, and participating mortgage pools.

Topics	Limited Partners	General Partners
Contribution	Cash or assets	Expertise and time (sometimes money)
Risks	Liability is limited to amount of investment and agreed upon future investments.[2]	Liability is unlimited - creditors can reach the general partner's entire estate.
Management responsibility	None	Provide full management.
Benefits flow through the partnership to the limited partners	Depreciation/depletion, interest deductions, capital growth and periodic distributions.[3]	A percentage of the profits and losses, often after limited partners receive original investment and a specified return.

Use Caution with Limited Partnerships

Since limited partnership investments are highly illiquid and traditionally long term, they should be examined carefully. Also, your attorney, accountant or other tax professional should be consulted.

- **Considerations**
  - Performance record and demonstrated integrity of the general partner.
  - Tax opinion - The IRS is retroactively disallowing abusive tax shelters and charging interest on the disallowed deductions.
  - What cash flow is anticipated? When?

---

[1] Definition is taken from the Uniform Limited Partnership Act.
[2] In some instances, you may be personally liable for partnership loans.
[3] A combination of the benefits may produce tax write-offs in excess of the contribution. However, there are limitations on the use of these excess losses.

Continued...

Limited Partnerships

- When will the partnership sell or liquidate? These investments can be difficult to get out of.
- Will tax preference items or recapture be generated by the partnership ultimately?
- Will additional investment be required beyond the initial deposit? Are recourse notes involved?

- **Most important:** Forgetting the tax benefits, does the investment make economic sense?

- **Caution:** Current prospectus or offering statement must be read carefully.

Real Estate Investment Trusts

Many individuals are attracted to the benefits of investing in real estate, such as current income or the potential for capital gain. Direct investment in real estate, however, can require large amounts of capital, as well as the time and expertise to properly manage real estate properties. At times, the cyclical nature of real estate can make such investments difficult to sell.

One alternative to direct real estate investment is the real estate investment trust (REIT). REITs allow small investors to share in both the risks and rewards of real estate investing.

What Is a Real Estate Investment Trust?

First authorized by Congress in the 1960s, REITs bring together capital from many individuals specifically to invest in a diversified portfolio of income real estate, or in real estate-related debt (mortgages). A REIT can take the form of a trust, association or corporation. Individuals invest in a REIT by purchasing shares, similar to shares of common stock. The shares of many REITS are publicly traded on major stock exchanges and over-the-counter markets.

Full-time managers conduct the day-to-day operations of a REIT. If a REIT is successful, shareholders can receive dividend income (from rental income and mortgage interest) and capital gain from the profitable sale of real estate assets. Some REITs specialize in a single type of commercial property or region of the country. Other REITs diversify their investments over various types of property or in different geographical areas.

Types of Real Estate Investment Trusts

REITs are usually classified according to their investment focus.

- **Equity REIT:** Equity REITs directly own and operate income properties such as apartment buildings, discount outlet centers, mobile home parks, office buildings, industrial parks, or hotels. Income is generated from property rents. Capital gain income is also possible if properties are sold at a profit.

- **Mortgage REIT:** Mortgage REITs invest their money in various types of mortgages, usually for existing properties. In some cases REIT funds will back mortgages on new construction. Income is generated from the interest received on the mortgages.

- **Hybrid REIT:** As the name suggests, hybrid REITs invest in both direct ownership of real estate as well as mortgage loans.

- **Finite life real estate investment trust (FREIT):** FREITs are a type of equity REIT which have a stated goal of liquidating the real estate portfolio by a specific date. The primary investment goal of a FREIT is to maximize potential capital gain.

Continued...

Real Estate Investment Trusts

Income Tax Issues

The Internal Revenue Code (IRC) contains a number of conditions which a trust must meet to qualify as a Real Estate Investment Trust, including the requirement that a REIT pay out at least 90% of its taxable income.[1] If a REIT meets these conditions, the income paid to the shareholders is not taxed twice (as it would be in a regular corporation), but is taxed only once, in the hands of the shareholders.

- **Ordinary income distributions:** Income from sources such as rents and mortgage interest received is fully taxed to the shareholder as ordinary income.[2]

- **Capital gain distributions:** Capital gain from the profitable sale of real estate investments is long-term gain, regardless of the length of time an individual has owned his or her shares in the REIT.[3]

If a shareholder sells his or her shares in a REIT, the gain or loss for federal income tax purposes generally depends on how long the shares were owned.[4]

Investment Uses

Many investors are attracted to mortgage REITs because of the relatively high level of current income; REITs in general tend to provide a current yield greater than long-term U.S. Treasury bonds. Equity REITs are often sought for their long-term appreciation potential and as a hedge against inflation. Many investors view real estate as a separate asset class – distinct from other financial assets such as stocks or bonds – and thus value REITs for their diversification benefits.

How to Invest

- **Direct ownership:** Individuals can invest in a publicly traded REIT by purchasing shares through a stockbroker or other securities-licensed professional, holding the shares in their own names.

- **Indirect ownership:** Open-end investment companies, known as mutual funds, are an indirect method of REIT ownership. Mutual funds pool the resources of many individuals and offer an investor access to a diversified portfolio of professionally managed securities. There are many mutual funds that specialize in REITs,[5] including those with a global orientation.

---

[1] See IRC Sec. 857(a)(1).
[2] Under current legislation, during 2003-2010, federal law taxes qualifying stock dividends at marginal rates lower than those generally applicable to ordinary income. Unless certain narrow conditions are met, ordinary income distributions from a REIT will not qualify for the lower dividend tax rates.
[3] See IRC Sec. 857(b)(3)(B). For 2003 - 2010, capital gain distributions from a REIT will generally be taxable at the favorable capital gains rates available to a taxpayer under JGTRRA of 2003 and TIPRA of 2005.
[4] State or local law may provide for different tax treatment of income received from a REIT.
[5] The Securities and Exchange Commission requires that all prospective mutual fund investors be given a prospectus. The prospectus contains valuable information concerning how an investment works, its goals and risks, and any expenses and charges involved.

Continued..

Real Estate Investment Trusts

Possible Risks

- **Market risk:** As with all stocks, the value of shares in publicly-traded REITs can fluctuate. An investor who sells shares in a REIT could receive more, or less, than the original purchase price. Factors that can influence market risk include the general level of real estate property values, REIT dividend payouts, management skill, and broad stock market trends.

- **Interest rate risk:** Shares of REITs, especially mortgage REITs, are sensitive to changes in the general level of interest rates. Mortgage REITs respond much like bonds, generally increasing in value as interest rates fall and decreasing in value if interest rates rise.

Hedge Funds

Because they can vary considerably, there is no single definition of a "Hedge Fund." In general terms, a hedge fund is a private investment corporation or partnership that provides investors the opportunity to participate in specialized, flexible, and often risky trading strategies, to take advantage of perceived opportunities in the stock, bond, currency, and commodities markets.

Unlike traditional equity fund managers, hedge fund managers typically have far greater flexibility with regard to employing sophisticated investment strategies. In many cases the overall performance of the hedge fund is driven by the unique skill of the portfolio manager(s), rather than general market movements. Also in contrast to most mutual funds, hedge funds are usually set up by principals who typically invest a significant amount of their personal assets in the fund. Most hedge funds have an incentive management fee structure; the higher the investment return, the higher the fee paid to the fund managers.

What Kinds Of Strategies Do Hedge Funds Use?

The investment strategies used will vary from fund to fund. Some hedge funds only invest in a specific asset class (e.g., stocks, bonds, currencies, etc.) or in a combination of asset classes. Others are highly leveraged (meaning they use borrowed money), while some do not use leverage at all. There are hedge funds with the ability to "sell short," and some that trade only on the "long side" of the market. Relatively few are fully "hedged." In fact, a great many hedge funds are far more speculative than traditional funds.

Who Typically Invests In Hedge Funds?

There is no specific profile of a "typical" hedge fund investor. There are "suitability" requirements before a hedge fund will accept an investor, expressed in terms of income and net worth. For example, a fund may require that new investors have a minimum net worth of $1,000,000 and annual income of $200,000. There are also requirements for a minimum investment amount. For example, some hedge funds require a $10,000,000 initial minimum investment, limiting their availability to institutions and the super wealthy. There are other hedge funds that allow one to invest as little as $10,000. In most cases, investors in hedge funds (known as "accredited" investors) tend to be aggressive and willing to sacrifice safety to achieve higher returns.

What Is A "Lock-up" Period?

This is the period of time that a hedge fund requires an accredited investor to hold assets within the fund before they can be removed.

Continued

Hedge Funds

What Should I Know Before Investing?

A hedge fund is a complex investment. Before investing any money, you should be fully aware of the objectives of the fund and the risks involved. When you consider investing in a hedge fund, make sure that you are familiar with the following:

- The track record and investment style of the portfolio manager(s) of the fund.

- The fund's investment strategy and whether or not it is based upon fundamental or technical analysis.

- The fund's decision-making process during the implementation of a strategy.

- The risk-controls and stop-losses employed by the fund.

- The amount of leverage employed by the fund; the greater the leverage the greater the potential for loss.

- The amount and method of calculation for management/performance-based fees.

- The frequency and transparency of the fund's reporting and valuation methods.

- The types of underlying assets the fund invests in and any liquidity constraints (e.g., lock-up periods) imposed by the fund.

- The experience and reputation of all those involved with the management and operation of the fund (brokers, lawyers, custodians, administrators, and portfolio managers).

Seek Professional Guidance

Because hedge funds are complex, risky investments, the advice and counsel of experienced investment advisors is highly recommended.

Income Taxes Generally

Earned Income	Portfolio Income	Passive Income[1]
• Salary, bonus	• Dividends	• Limited partnership Income
• Commissions	• Interest	• Rental income
• Business income	• Royalties	• Capital gains on passive activities
• Up to 85% of social security	• Capital gains or losses on portfolio assets	

Adjustments

• Contributions to MSAs	• Student loan interest	• Alimony
• Contributions to IRAs, Keoghs, self-employed SEP/SIMPLE plans	• One-half of SE tax	• Early withdrawal penalty
	• SE health insurance	• Moving expense
	• Tuition and fees	• Educator expenses

Adjusted Gross Income

$ _____

Itemized Deductions[2]
(Subtract from AGI)

$ _____

• Medical expenses over 7.5% of AGI

• State and local property taxes (real and personal)

• State income **or** sales taxes

• Mortgage interest on 1st and 2nd residences, investment interest.

• Charitable contributions

• Miscellaneous deductions (most must exceed 2% of AGI)

• Or, use the standard deduction

Minus

Equals

Personal Exemptions
$ _____

Taxable Income
$ _____

Tax determined from schedules $ _____

Less: Available credits $ _____

Tax due $ _____

---

[1] Passive activity losses and credits (carried forward if not used) cannot be used to offset nonpassive income, except certain real estate losses.

[2] For higher-income taxpayers, the deductibility of both itemized deductions and personal exemptions is generally reduced, as adjusted gross income rises. Under EGTRRA of 2001, this reduction in deductibility is gradually phased-out, by one-third in 2006-2007, and by two-thirds in 2008-2009. In 2010 there is no reduction to either of these items, regardless of the level of income. However, unless the law is changed, in 2011 the prior rules will apply.

Federal Income Tax Approximator
Tax Years 2007 and 2008

Item Description	2007		2008	
Filing status	Married filing joint		Married filing joint	
Personal exemptions		2		2
Adjusted gross income (AGI)		$60,000		$55,000
Standard deduction, or	-	$10,700	-	$10,900
Itemized deductions, if more	-	$11,000	-	$10,000
AGI minus deduction(s)		**$49,000**		**$44,100**
Exemptions (with phase outs)	-	$6,800	-	$7,000
Taxable income		**$42,200**		**$37,100**
Federal income tax		**$5,548**		**$4,763**
Credits	-	$ 300	-	$ 250
Other taxes[1]		$1,100		$1,000
Estimated total federal income tax		**$6,348**		**$5,513**

---

[1] Other taxes might include AMT, self-employment tax, etc.

Federal Income Tax Tables - 2008

Filing Status	If Taxable Income Is Between			Pay	Plus	Percent on Excess Over 1st Column
Single tax payers	$0	-	$8,025	$0.00		10.0%
	8,025	-	32,550	802.50		15.0%
	32,550	-	78,850	4,481.25		25.0%
	78,850	-	164,550	16,056.25		28.0%
	164,550	-	357,700	40,052.25		33.0%
	357,700	-	Up	103,791.75		35.0%
Married filing jointly	$0	-	$16,050	$0.00		10.0%
	16,050	-	65,100	1,605.00		15.0%
	65,100	-	131,450	8,962.50		25.0%
	131,450	-	200,300	25,550.00		28.0%
	200,300	-	357,700	44,828.00		33.0%
	357,700	-	Up	96,770.00		35.0%
Married filing separately	$0	-	$8,025	$0.00		10.0%
	8,025	-	32,550	802.50		15.0%
	32,550	-	65,725	4,481.25		25.0%
	65,725	-	100,150	12,775.00		28.0%
	100,150	-	178,850	22,414.00		33.0%
	178,850	-	Up	48,385.00		35.0%
Head of household	$0	-	$11,450	$0.00		10.0%
	11,450	-	43,650	1,145.00		15.0%
	43,650	-	112,650	5,975.00		25.0%
	112,650	-	182,400	23,225.00		28.0%
	182,400	-	357,700	42,755.00		33.0%
	357,700	-	Up	100,604.00		35.0%

Example

Married Filing Jointly			
Taxable income	$70,000		
Tax on the 1st	65,100	is	$8,962.50
Tax on the remaining	4,900	x 25.0% is	1,225.00
Total Tax			$10,187.50

Continued...

Federal Income Tax Tables - 2008

Personal and Dependent Exemptions

Year	Amount of Exemption for Each		
	Taxpayer	Spouse	Dependent Child
2005	3,200	$3,200	$3,200
2006	3,300	3,300	3,300
2007	3,400	3,400	3,400
2008	3,500	3,500	3,500
2009	Adjusted for Inflation		

There is a phase-out of the personal and dependency exemptions for taxpayers with adjusted gross incomes in excess of the following threshold amounts: married filing jointly - $239,950; head of household - $199,950; single taxpayer - $159,950; and married filing separately - $119,975. Each allowable exemption is reduced by 2% for each $2,500 of adjusted gross income ($1,250 for married persons filing separate returns) in excess of the threshold amount.[1]

Standard Deduction - Persons Who Do Not Itemize Deductions

Year	Amount of Deduction			
	Married Jointly	Married Separate	Heads of Household	Single
2005	10,000	5,000	7,300	5,000
2006	10,300	5,150	7,550	5,150
2007	10,700	5,350	7,850	5,350
2008	10,900	5,450	8,000	5,450
2009	Adjusted for Inflation			

Year	Additional Standard Deductions (Each Spouse)			
	65 or Older		Blind	
	Married	Single	Married	Single
2005	1,000	1,250	1,000	1,250
2006	1,000	1,250	1,000	1,250
2007	1,050	1,300	1,050	1,300
2008	1,050	1,350	1,050	1,350
2009	Adjusted for Inflation			

Children: Children with income who can be claimed as dependents on a parent's return (even if the exemption has no benefit due to the phase-out) cannot take their own personal exemption. A child's standard deduction is up to $900 for unearned income or up to $5,450 for earned income.

---

[1] For higher-income taxpayers, the deductibility of personal exemptions is generally reduced, as adjusted gross income rises. Under EGTRRA of 2001, this reduction in deductibility is gradually phased-out, by 1/3 in 2006-2007, and by 2/3 in 2008-2009. In 2010 there is no reduction in personal exemptions, regardless of the level of income. However, unless the law is changed, in 2011 the prior rules will again apply.

Federal Income Tax Tables - 2007

Filing Status	If Taxable Income Is Between		Pay	Plus	Percent on Excess Over 1st Column
	$0	-	$7,825	$0.00		10.0%
	7,825	-	31,850	782.50		15.0%
Single tax	31,850	-	77,100	4,386.25		25.0%
payers	77,100	-	160,850	15,698.75		28.0%
	160,850	-	349,700	39,148.75		33.0%
	349,700	-	Up	101,469.25		35.0%
	$0	-	$15,650	$0.00		10.0%
	15,650	-	63,700	1,565.00		15.0%
Married	63,700	-	128,500	8,772.50		25.0%
filing jointly	128,500	-	195,850	24,972.50		28.0%
	195,850	-	349,700	43,830.50		33.0%
	349,700	-	Up	94,601.00		35.0%
	$0	-	$7,825	$0.00		10.0%
	7,825	-	31,850	782.50		15.0%
Married	31,850	-	64,250	4,386.25		25.0%
filing	64,250	-	97,925	12,486.25		28.0%
separately	97,925	-	174,850	21,915.25		33.0%
	174,850	-	Up	47,300.50		35.0%
	$0	-	$11,200	$0.00		10.0%
	11,200	-	42,650	1,120.00		15.0%
Head of	42,650	-	110,100	5,837.50		25.0%
household	110,100	-	178,350	22,700.00		28.0%
	178,350	-	349,700	41,810.00		33.0%
	349,700	-	Up	98,355.50		35.0%

Example

Married Filing Jointly			
Taxable Income	$70,000		
Tax on the 1st	63,700	is	$8,772.50
Tax on the remaining	6,300	x 25.0% is	1,575.00
Total tax			$10,347.50

Income Taxes Payable

$80,000 Adjusted Gross Income[1]

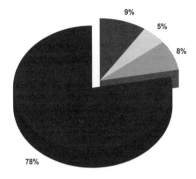

9%

5%

8%

78%

■ Fed Tax ■ State Tax ■ FICA ■ After Tax Income

$150,000 Adjusted Gross Income[1]

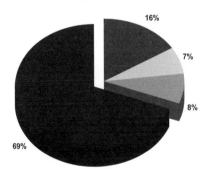

16%

7%

8%

69%

■ Fed Tax ■ State Tax ■ FICA ■ After Tax Income

[1] Assumes married filing jointly, two children, both spouses employed and using the standard deduction. Results based on 2008 federal income tax rates. Percentages may not exactly equal 100% due to rounding.

Income Tax Tables for
Estates – Trusts – Corporations

Estates and Trusts - 2008[1]

If Taxable Income Is Between...			Pay	Plus	Percent on Excess Over 1st Column
$0	-	$2,200	$0.00		15.00%
2,200	-	5,150	$330.00		25.00%
5,150	-	7,850	$1,067.50		28.00%
7,850	-	10,700	$1,823.50		33.00%
10,700	-	and higher	$2,764.00		35.00%

Corporations

If Taxable Income Is Between...			Pay	Plus	% on Excess Over 1st Column
$0	-	$50,000	$0		15.00%
50,000	-	75,000	7,500		25.00%
75,000	-	100,000	13,750		34.00%
100,000	-	335,000	22,250		39.00%
335,000	-	10,000,000	113,900		34.00%
10,000,000	-	15,000,000	3,400,000		35.00%
15,000,000	-	18,333,333	5,150,000		38.00%[2]
18,333,333	-	and higher	6,416,667		35.00%

Note: Personal service corporations pay a flat 35% [IRC Sec. 11(b)(2)] of taxable income and the lower brackets are not available.

---

[1] Rates are linked to changes in inflation.

[2] An additional 3% tax is imposed on income between $15,000,000 and $18,333,333. This in effect makes the corporate tax a flat 35% for corporations with taxable income in excess of $18,333,333. The corporate tax rate brackets are not linked to changes in inflation, as are the individual rates.

Sources of Government Revenues

For the fiscal year ending September 30, 2006, the federal government collected over 2.407 trillion dollars in revenues from the following sources.[1]

Individual income tax	$938,730,000,000	39.0%
Corporate income tax	$312,910,000,000	13.0%
Social insurance tax	$770,240,000,000	32.0%
Miscellaneous Taxes and Receipts[2]	$168,490,000,000	7.0%
Borrowing to Cover Deficit	$216,630,000,000	9.0%
Totals	**$2,407,000,000,000**	**100.0%**

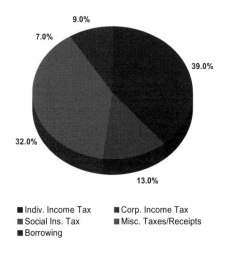

- ■ Indiv. Income Tax
- ■ Corp. Income Tax
- ■ Social Ins. Tax
- ■ Misc. Taxes/Receipts
- ■ Borrowing

[1] Source: 2007 IRS 1040 Package.
[2] Includes excise, customs, estate and gift taxes.

Federal Government Expenditures

Total federal expenditures[1] for the fiscal year ending September 30, 2006 were 2.655 trillion dollars, allocated as follows:

Social Security, Medicare, Other Retirement	$955,800,000,000	36.0%
National Defense, Veterans, Foreign Affairs	$610,650,000,000	23.0%
Net Interest on Public Debt	$212,400,000,000	8.0%
Physical, Human and Community Development	$318,600,000,000	12.0%
Social Welfare Programs	$504,450,000,000	19.0%
Law Enforcement and General Government	$53,100,000,000	2.0%
Total	**$2,655,000,000,000**	**100.0%**

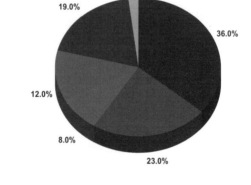

■ Soc. Sec., Medicare ■ Nat'l Def., Vets, Foreign ■ Interest on Debt
■ Development ■ Social Welfare ■ Law and General Gov't

[1] Source: 2007 IRS 1040 Package.

Personal Income Tax History
Top Marginal Rates 1913 to Present

The chart[1] traces the highest federal personal income tax rates from 1913 to today. The amount of income subject to these varying rates has also changed. In 1965-67, a rate of 70% applied to taxable incomes over $200,000, equal to approximately $1,194,903 in current dollars.

Top Federal Income Tax Rate

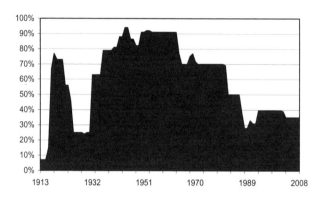

[1] Source: Joseph A. Pechman, "Federal Tax Policy" Fifth Edition.

Capital Gains and Losses

Individuals, Estates, and Trusts[1]

The Internal Revenue Code has long distinguished between income paid due to a person's individual effort (such as wages or self-employment earnings), and income received from the profitable sale of assets known as "capital" assets. Wages and salaries are classified as "ordinary" income. Gain from the sale of a capital asset is termed a "capital" gain. Gains from the sale of capital assets that meet certain requirements are generally accorded more favorable tax treatment than ordinary income.

Basic Terminology

There are several concepts essential to understanding capital gains and losses.

- **Capital asset:** The law defines the term "capital" asset in a negative sense by first declaring that all types of property are capital assets, and then listing certain exceptions. (See IRC Sec. 1221.) Assets such as stocks, bonds and other securities held by individuals are capital assets. In general terms, assets that are held for investment purposes are capital assets. Some assets are not capital assets by definition, but may be treated as such if used in a trade or business, and sold or exchanged at a gain.

- **Holding period:** This is the length of time an asset is owned, beginning on the day after it is acquired and ending on the day it is disposed of. The amount of time an asset has been held impacts the tax treatment of any gain or loss when the asset is sold. The law currently provides for two holding periods: short-term and long-term. Short-term assets are those held exactly 12 months or less. Long-term assets are those held more than 12 months.

Capital Losses

At the end of a tax year, a taxpayer's capital gains and losses are totaled and compared. If losses exceed gains, a taxpayer may use up to $3,000 of losses to offset other ordinary income ($1,500 if married filing separately). (See IRC Sec. 1211(b).) Losses that exceed the $3,000 limit may be carried to future tax years until used up. If a taxpayer dies during the year, any un-used capital loss is gone forever; it may not be carried over to future tax years.

Capital Gains

Ordinary income such as wages and salaries can be taxed at marginal federal income tax rates as high as 35.0%. Short-term capital gains are treated as ordinary income, taxable at the taxpayer's highest rate. Long-term capital gains are taxed at rates which are capped, and which may be less than a taxpayer's regular rate.

---

[1] Corporate taxpayers are subject to different rules regarding capital gains.

Continued

Capital Gains and Losses
Individuals, Estates, and Trusts

Capital Gains – Prior Law vs. JGTRRA of 2003

The recent past has seen many changes in the federal income tax treatment[1] of capital gains, beginning with the Taxpayer Relief Act of 1997 (TRA '97). Among other things, this Act lowered tax rates on long-term capital gains and completely rewrote the rules on taxation of gain from the sale of a personal residence. The changes made by TRA '97 were further modified by the IRS Restructuring and Reform Act of 1998.

The Jobs and Growth Tax Relief Reconciliation Act of 2003 (JGTRRA)[2] lowered even more the marginal rates applicable to many capital gains transactions and extended these lower rates through the end of 2008. The Tax Increase Prevention and Reconciliation Act of 2005 (TIPRRA) further extended these lower rates to the end of 2010. The table below provides a brief summary of the capital gains rates under both prior law and JGTRRA.

Item	Holding Period	Type of Gain	Prior Law	JGTRRA
Property sold at any time	Exactly 12 months or less	Short-term	Ordinary income - taxed at taxpayer's regular marginal rate	Ordinary income - taxed at taxpayer's regular marginal rate
Property sold after 12/31/97 - Tax bracket greater than 15%	More than 12 months	Long-term	20%	15%
Property sold after 12/31/97 - Tax bracket 15% or less	More than 12 months	Long-term	10%	5% through 2007. A 0% rate applies in 2008.
Real estate depreciation treated as capital gain [3]	More than 12 months	Long-term	25%	25%
Sale of collectibles [4]	More than 12 months	Long-term	28%	28%
Sales of property acquired after 12/31/2000 - Tax bracket greater than 15%	More than 5 years	Long-term	18%	Repealed
Sales of property - Tax bracket 15% or less	More than 5 years	Long-term	8%	Repealed

---

[1] The discussion here concerns federal income tax law; state or local law may differ.
[2] The capital gains provisions of JGTRRA were effective May 6, 2003.
[3] Gain in excess of recaptured depreciation is taxed at a maximum rate of 20% (prior law) or 15% (JGTRRA).
[4] This is defined in IRC Sec. 408(m). Some exceptions apply.

Continued...

Capital Gains and Losses
Individuals, Estates, and Trusts

Special Rules for Personal Residence

Under current law, a taxpayer may exclude from income up to $250,000 of gain from the sale of a principal residence, if the taxpayer has owned and used the property as his or her principal residence for at least two years of the five-year period ending on the date of the sale or exchange. Only one such exclusion is permitted every two years.

For married couples filing a joint return, the maximum exclusion amount is increased to $500,000 if (a) either spouse meets the ownership requirement; (b) both spouses meet the use requirements, and (c) neither spouse is ineligible because of the one sale every two years rule. If a married couple does not meet the requirements for the $500,000 exclusion, the amount of gain eligible for exclusion is the sum of the amounts to which each spouse would be entitled if they had not been married.

Beginning January 1, 2008, the surviving spouse of a couple who had jointly owned and occupied a residence and who met the general requirements discussed above immediately before the deceased spouse's death, may exclude up to $500,000 of gain as long as the sale of the residence takes place within two years of the date of the deceased spouse's death. Under prior law, the $500,000 exclusion would generally have been available to the surviving spouse only in the year of the deceased spouse's death.

The law also provides for a reduced maximum exclusion for taxpayers who do not meet the requirements to qualify for the full $250,000 ($500,000 if married) exclusion, and who sell or exchange a principal residence because of changes in place of employment, health, or unforeseen circumstances.

A member of the U.S. armed forces, U.S. Foreign Service, or specified members of the intelligence community serving on qualified extended duty may choose to suspend the five-year period of use and ownership for up to 10 years.

An individual who acquires his or her principal residence in an IRC Sec. 1031 "like-kind-exchange" must own the property for five years before the exclusion applies.

Timing of Capital Gains Transactions

Note that a taxpayer generally controls when a capital asset will be sold and can, therefore, choose the year in which a gain or loss is to be included in his or her taxable income.

Seek Professional Guidance

The income tax treatment of capital gains and losses is complex and often confusing. Individuals facing decisions concerning the tax implications of the sale or exchange of a capital asset are strongly advised to first consult with a CPA, IRS enrolled agent, or other competent professional.

Utilizing Passive Losses

Since the Tax Reform Act of 1986, losses flowing through limited partnership investment interests to individuals are generally classified as passive activity losses. The law states that such losses cannot be used to offset or reduce earned or portfolio (dividends, interest, etc.) income. Thus, persons with existing limited partnership interests, many in multiple-year funding commitments, may be unable to fully utilize these tax losses.

The Solution—Passive Income

Passive activity losses may be used to offset income from passive sources. Many investors are therefore acquiring limited partnership programs producing substantial taxable income in order to utilize existing losses. Typical partnerships producing high taxable income include oil and gas income programs, unleveraged equipment leasing and unleveraged rental real estate.

Passive losses in excess of passive income are not lost. Any suspended losses from a passive activity are carried forward until the year in which the investor disposes of his or her interest in the passive activity. For example, unused passive losses may be used when a limited partnership terminates or is dissolved.

Limited Exceptions to the Rule

The following are exceptions to the passive loss limitation rules.

- **Rental real estate**
  - Taxpayers considered to be real estate "professionals" are allowed to deduct their passive losses against income. Real estate professions include brokerage, construction, rental, development, management, or leasing. To qualify for this exception, a taxpayer must "materially participate" in such real estate activities, spend over 750 hours per year working in them, and devote more than one-half of his or her personal services to such businesses. The "material participation" standard requires an individual to participate on a regular, continuous, and substantial basis. Service as an employee is not considered part of a real estate profession, unless the individual is a more than 5% owner. See IRC Sec. 469(c)(7).
  - Taxpayers who actively participate in rental real estate activities may deduct up to $25,000 from nonpassive income.[1] This exception is phased out by 50% of the amount by which their adjusted gross income exceeds $100,000 (no deduction at $150,000 of AGI or above). The "active participation" exception may be easier to qualify for than the "material participation" exception for real estate professionals. Active participation could include approving leases, tenants, capital improvements, etc. See IRC Sec. 469(i).
  However, a merely formal or nominal participation in management, without a genuine exercise of independent discretion and judgment, is insufficient.

---

[1] This amount is reduced to $12,500 for married persons filing separately and who lived apart for the entire year. The amount is reduced to zero for married persons not living apart.

Continued...

Utilizing Passive Losses

- **Low-income and historic rehabilitation credits**
  - Credits from low-income housing or historic rehabilitation may be applied against the tax on up to $25,000 of nonpassive income even if taxpayer was not personally active[1].
  - Low-income credits range from 4% to 9% annually depending on the type of building and whether or not it is federally subsidized. IRC Sec. 42.
  - Historic rehabilitation credits are 20% for costs on certified historic structures and 10% on other pre-1936 buildings. See IRC Sec. 47(a). The rehabilitation credit is phased out by 50% of the amount by which AGI exceeds $200,000 (no deduction for AGI of $250,000 or greater). There is no phase-out for low-income housing credits on property placed in service after 1989.
  - Suspended credits are not allowed when a passive activity is disposed of.

---

[1] Active participation is not required for these credits.

Personal Alternative Minimum Tax

The alternative minimum tax (AMT) is designed to prevent taxpayers with substantial income from avoiding or deferring all tax liability through the use of deductions, exemptions and credits. The rules add substantial complexity to the tax system. (See IRC Sec. 55 and IRS Form 6251 and its instructions.)

Adjusted gross income is adjusted to reflect different treatment of certain items by the AMT rules.

Steps in Computing the AMT

1. Adjusted Gross Income (AGI)[1] $ _____

2. Plus or Minus: Certain adjustments $ _____

3. Plus: AMT preferences   _____

4. Equals: AMT income   _____

5. Less: Exemptions (see last page)   (_____)

6. Equals: Net AMT income   _____

7. Times: Tax rate
    (26% of 1st $175,000 and 28% of amounts over $175,000.
    For married filing separate, the breakpoint is $87,500.)[2]
    ($ _____ x 0.26) + ($ _____ x 0.28) =   _____

8. Tentative AMT before credits   _____

9. Less: AMT foreign tax credit [3]   (_____)

10. Equals: Tentative minimum tax   _____

11. Less: Regular tax   (_____)

12. Alternative minimum tax due[4] $ _____

---

[1] If the return includes Schedule A, use AGI less the allowable itemized deductions from Schedule A.
[2] Under JGTRRA of 2003, the AMT attributable to capital asset sales is determined using the 5% (0% after 2007) or 15% rates (unrecaptured IRC Sec 1250 gain).
[3] Any part of the AMT foreign tax credit that is not used in a tax year may be carried back one year and forward 10 years.
[4] The AMT only applies to the extent it is larger than the regular tax liability. Once a taxpayer is subject to the AMT, he or she may be entitled to a credit that can reduce future tax liability. The Tax Act of 2001 made permanent the use of the child credit, the adoption credit and the IRA credit to offset both regular tax liability and AMT liability. The Tax Increase Prevention Act of 2007 extended the use of the dependent care credit, the credit for the elderly and disabled, the credit for interest on certain mortgages, the HOPE Scholarship and Lifetime Learning credits, and the D.C. homebuyer's credit against both the regular tax and the AMT to 2007. Any part of these credits that is not used in a tax year is lost; i.e., it may not be carried backward or forward to other tax years.

Continued...

Personal Alternative Minimum Tax

Adjustments

Certain items are treated differently for AMT
purposes than for the regular tax and must
therefore be adjusted. A partial list includes
the following:

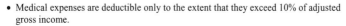

- Generally, no deduction is allowed for state
  and local taxes or for miscellaneous
  itemized deductions.

- Medical expenses are deductible only to the extent that they exceed 10% of adjusted
  gross income.

- Accelerated depreciation under the cost-recovery rules of the AMT will more closely
  approximate the investment's useful life.[1]

- Passive investments that offset taxable income generally will not reduce AMTI
  (alternative minimum taxable income). Therefore, deductions for passive losses may be
  claimed only against passive income.

- Certain interest on a home mortgage not used to build, buy, or improve a house, is not
  deductible for AMT purposes.

- Investment interest is deductible for AMT purposes only to the extent of net investment
  income.

- Incentive stock options: The excess of the fair market value of the stock at the time of
  exercise, over the price paid for the stock, including any amount paid for the option.

Preferences

Taxable income for AMT purposes must be increased by the following preferences:

- Tax-exempt interest from certain private purpose bonds issued by state and local
  governments.

- The excess of the deduction for depletion over the adjusted basis of the property at the
  end of the taxable year.

- Certain expensing of intangible drilling costs to the extent they exceed 65% of net oil
  and gas income.

Note: The untaxed appreciation on gifts of appreciated property to charities is no longer a preference item.

---

[1] For property placed in service after 1998, AMT depreciation is computed using 150% DB; for real property, straight-line
depreciation is used. The recovery period is the same for both AMT and regular tax.

Continued.

Personal Alternative Minimum Tax

Exemption Amounts - 2007

Varies with filing status and is phased out for persons with high income. The exemption amounts for 2007 are:

Filing Status	Exemption Amount	Less 25% of AMTI Over	No Exemption if AMTI is Over
Married joint/Surviving Spouse	$66,250	$150,000	$415,000
Married separately	33,125	75,000	207,500
Single or heads of household	44,350	112,500	289,900

Exemption Amounts - 2008

Under current law, the AMT exemption amounts for 2008 are scheduled to return to their pre-2001 levels, as follows:

Filing Status	Exemption Amount	Less 25% of AMTI Over	No Exemption if AMTI is Over
Married joint/Surviving Spouse	$45,000	$150,000	$330,000
Married separately	22,500	75,000	165,000
Single or heads of household	33,750	112,500	247,500

Standard Deduction

Neither the personal exemptions nor the standard deduction are deductible in this calculation.

Note: This summary is not intended to cover all of the details of the alternative minimum tax. It is a very complicated set of rules and will require careful planning to avoid or reduce its negative effect on taxation of income.

Corporate Alternative Minimum Tax

The corporate alternative minimum tax (AMT) is a second tax system which is parallel to the regular corporate income tax. It is designed to make certain that all corporations pay a tax in their profitable years. Small corporations[1] are exempt from the AMT. This exemption continues to apply as long as a corporation has under $7.5 million of average gross receipts.

The corporation must compute its tax liability under both the regular tax and the AMT and then pay the higher tax.[2] See IRS Form 4626 and its instructions.

Steps in Computing the Corporate AMT

1. Regular taxable income	$ _____	
2. Plus or minus: Certain adjustments	_____	
3. Plus: AMT preferences	_____	
4. Equals: AMT income	_____	
5. Less: Exemptions	(_____)	
6. Equals: Net AMT income	_____	
7. Times: Tax rate (20%)	x .20	
8. Tentative AMT before credits	_____	
9. Less: AMT foreign tax credit	(_____)	
10. Equals: Tentative minimum tax	_____	
11. Less: Regular tax	(_____)	
12. Alternative minimum tax due	$ _____	

---

[1] Small corporations are those with average gross receipts for the three previous tax years of $5,000,000 or less.
[2] The AMT is available as a credit to offset future years regular tax liability for years in which the regular tax exceeds AMT liability.

Continued...

Corporate Alternative Minimum Tax

Adjustments

Certain items are treated differently for AMT purposes than for the regular tax and must therefore be adjusted. Some of these adjustments are listed below.

- **Alternative depreciation**
  - **Real property:** 1987 and prior to 1999 - Excess of accelerated over 40-year straight line.[1]
  - **Personal property:** 1987 and prior to 1999 - Excess of accelerated over 150% declining balance method switching to straight line.[2]

- **Amortization of circulation costs:** (Applies only to personal holding companies.) Excess of expensed costs over 3-year amortization.

- **Amortization of mining exploration and development costs:** Excess of expensed costs over 10-year amortization.

- **Percentage of completion method for long-term contracts:** Generally, a corporation must use the percentage of completion method for any long-term contracts.

- **Full reporting of certain installment sales:** Any disposition of dealer property must be reported fully in year of sale for AMT.

- **Amortization of certified pollution control facilities:** The AMT adjustment is computed using the MACRS ADS method. For property placed in service after 1998, the adjustment is computed using the MACRS straight-line method.

- **Capital construction funds for shipping companies:** Shipbuilders permitted to deduct these contributions must include them in Alternative Minimum Taxable Income (AMTI).

- **Untaxed book income/profits:** 75% of the excess of adjusted current earnings (ACE)[3] over AMTI.

- **Net operating loss (NOL):** There is an adjustment for AMT purposes under which the NOL deduction is not allowed and, instead, an alternative NOL tax deduction is allowed.

---

[1] The AMT is available as a credit to offset future years regular tax liability for years in which the regular tax exceeds AMT liability.

[2] Under TRA '97, for property placed in service after 1998, no AMT adjustment will be required for IRC Sec. 1250 property, or for other MACRS property depreciated for regular taxes using either the straight-line or 150% DB methods.

[3] Annual increases in policy cash value and life insurance proceeds paid to a corporation in excess of the policy's' cash value are included in ACE.

Continued...

Corporate Alternative Minimum Tax

Preferences

Taxable income for AMT purposes must be increased by the following.

- **Excess of percentage depletion:** Over adjusted basis of property at the end of the year

- **Excess of expensed intangible drilling costs:** Over 10-year amortization to the extent it exceeds 65% of net oil and gas income

- **Tax-exempt interest:** On nongovernmental purpose bonds issued after August 7, 1986, subject to certain exceptions

Note: The untaxed appreciation on gifts of appreciated property to charities is no longer a preference item.

Exemption

The exemption varies with corporate AMTI.

Exemption Amount	Less 25% of AMTI Over	No Exemption if AMTI is at Least
$40,000	$150,000	$310,000

Note: This is only a summary of a very detailed set of rules.

Social Security and Medicare Taxes

FICA (Federal Insurance Contributions Act) taxes are deducted from an employee's paycheck each pay period. Commonly referred to as Social Security taxes, there are actually two separate taxes: the Old-Age, Survivors and Disability Insurance (OASDI) tax and the Medicare Hospital Insurance (HI) tax. For calendar year 2008, OASDI is 6.2% of the first $102,000 of wages. HI is 1.45% of all wages.[1]

Social Security Taxes for Employees The Employer Must Pay an Equal Amount				
Year	OASDI Wage Base	OASDI Rate	Maximum OASDI Tax	Hospital Insurance Rate
2005	90,000	6.2%	$5,580	1.45%
2006	94,200	6.2%	5,840	1.45%
2007	97,500	6.2%	6,045	1.45%
2008	102,000	6.2%	6,324	1.45%

Social Security Taxes for the Self-Employed				
Year	OASDI Wage Base	OASDI Rate	Maximum OASDI Tax	Hospital Insurance Rate
2005	90,000	12.4%	$11,160	2.90%
2006	94,200	12.4%	11,681	2.90%
2007	97,500	12.4%	12,090	2.90%
2008	102,000	12.4%	12,648	2.90%

Note: Individuals with $400 or more per year in net earnings from self-employment must file IRS schedule SE with his or her income tax return.

Calculating the Social Security Tax (2008)			
Employee Portion		Self-Employed	
Covered wages	$	Covered wages	$
6.2% of 1st $102,000	$	12.4% of 1st $102,000	$
1.45% of covered wages	$	2.9% of covered wages	$
Total tax	$	Total tax	$

---

[1] Source: Social Security Administration, Social Security Administration news release, 10-17-07. The dollar amount of wages subject to OASDI is termed the wage base. The wage base is adjusted each year for changes in the national average wage.

Taxation of Social Security Benefits

A portion of Social Security benefits may be subject to income taxation. The following worksheet will assist in determining that tax.

1. Social Security benefits for the year $ _____
2. 50% of line 1   _____
3. Modified adjusted gross income:
   a. AGI less net Social Security benefits received   _____
   b. Tax-exempt interest and dividends received or accrued   _____
   c. Line 3a plus line 3b   _____
4. Provisional income (line 2 plus line 3c)   _____
5. Applicable "first-tier" threshold[1]   _____
6. Line 4 less line 5 (not less than zero)   _____
7. 50% of line 6   _____
8. Amount of benefits subject to tax (smaller of line 2 or line 7)   _____

If the provisional income (line 4, above) does not exceed the corresponding first-tier threshold (line 5, above), no amount is taxable. However, if provisional income exceeds the corresponding threshold, continue with the worksheet below.

9. Applicable second-tier threshold[1] $ _____
10. Line 4 minus line 9 (if less than zero then enter zero)   _____
11. 85% of line 10   _____
12. Amount taxable under first-tier (from line 8, above)   _____
13. Applicable dollar amount[1]   _____
14. Smaller of line 12 or line 13   _____
15. Line 11 plus line 14   _____
16. 85% of line 1   _____
17. Amount of benefits subject to tax (smaller of line 15 or line 16)   _____

Filing Status	First Tier Threshold (for line 5)	Second Tier Threshold (for line 9)	Applicable Dollar Amount (for line 13)
Married filing jointly	$32,000	$44,000	$6,000
Married filing separately (but lived together part of the year)	$0	$0	$0
All others	$25,000	$34,000	$4,500

Note: This is not an official IRS worksheet.

Caution: Any increase in income, such as from the sale of stock or a retirement plan distribution, may subject one to an unexpected tax on the Social Security benefits.

---

[1] See applicable column in table.

Taxable Portion of Social Security Benefits

Status: Married Filing Joint	
Social Security benefits received	$10,000
One-half of Social Security benefits received	$5,000
Income (taxable income)	$25,000
Tax exempt income	$ 555
Excluded income	$ 555
Subtotal	**$31,110**
Adjustments to gross income	- $ 555
Modified AGI	**$30,555**
1st tier base amount	-$32,000
Excess[1]	**$0**

If "Excess" is zero, none of your benefits are taxable. If "Excess" is greater than zero, the calculation continues below.

2nd tier base amount	$12,000
"Excess" minus "2nd tier base amount"[1]	$0
The smaller of "Excess" or "2nd tier base amount"	$0
One-half of amount on previous line	$0
The smaller of "One-half of Social Security benefits received" and previous line	$0
85% of "Excess minus 2nd tier base amount"	$0
Sum of previous two lines	$0
85% of "Social Security benefits received"	$8,500
Taxable benefits (lesser of previous two lines)	**$0**

---

[1] This amount cannot be less than zero.

Types of Trusts and Their Tax Treatment

Type of Trust	Income Tax	Estate Tax[1]	Gift Tax[2]
Testamentary trust: Created in the trustor's will and takes effect only at his death. Can be used to avoid tax on a portion of the first spouse's share of the estate; e.g., the credit shelter trust.	Income which is distributed is taxed to the beneficiary; if income is accumulated, it is taxed to the trust until later distributed to the beneficiary.	Trust assets are included in decedent's estate.	No gift tax.
Revocable living trust: Created while the trustor is still living but can be revoked or amended during his or her lifetime. Assets in the trust will avoid probate expenses, delay and publicity.	No income tax savings while trustor lives. After death, same as testamentary trust for income tax purposes.	Trust assets are included in decedent's gross estate.	No gift tax. Trust is revocable.
Irrevocable life insurance trust: Created while the trustor is still living and cannot be revoked by the trustor. Used to reduce the size of the estate. Works best for removing insurance from the estates of both spouses. Some are "funded," and others are "unfunded" or just own a life insurance policy.[3]	Same as testamentary trust above, except if income from a funded trust is accumulated, it is taxable to the trustor.	Usually excluded unless gift of policy was within three years prior to insured's death.	There may be a gift tax liability, but gifts to the trust can usually be made to qualify for the $12,000[4] annual gift tax exclusion.
Sec. 2503(c) minor's trust: A type of irrevocable trust for minors which qualifies for the annual gift tax exclusion even though the gifts to it are "future interest."[5]	Same as testamentary trust above.	Usually excluded unless transfer was within three years prior to death.	There may be a gift tax liability, but gifts to the trust can usually be made to qualify for the $12,000[4] annual gift tax exclusion.

Note: The Small Business and Work Opportunity Tax Act of 2007 expanded the "kiddie tax" to include a child up to age 18, or a child who is a full-time student age 19 to 23. Children who are age 18 or who are full-time students age 19 to 23, and whose earned income exceeds one-half of the amount of their support, are exempt from the tax. This legislation was effective for tax years beginning after May 25, 2007. If a child subject to the kiddie tax has unearned income in excess of $1,800 for 2008 (adjusted annually for inflation), the excess will be taxed at the parents' top marginal income tax bracket. State or local law may vary.

---

[1] The Tax Act of 2001 has increased the estate tax exemption to $3.5 million by 2009 and repeals the tax for one year in 2010. In 2011, the rates (55% top rate) and exemptions ($1 million) in force in 2001 will return. Beginning in 2002, the top estate tax rates begin a slow decline from 50% in 2002 to 45% in 2009.

[2] Effective in 2010, Tax Act of 2001 imposes a tax on gifts in excess of a lifetime $1 million. The tax will be at the top individual income tax rate at that time.

[3] Cash contributions may be made to the trust, to be used by the trustee to make premium payments on the life insurance policy. Careful drafting of the trust document is required to qualify the cash gifts for the annual gift tax exclusion.

[4] The annual gift tax exclusion ($12,000 in 2008) is indexed for inflation in increments of $1,000.

[5] Under federal law, the minor must become the owner of the assets no later than age 21.

Accumulation of Trust Income for Minors

Often, trusts for children grant the trustee the discretion of either accumulating income or distributing it as the trustee determines to meet the needs of the beneficiaries. Under current federal law,[1] however, income accumulated inside a trust is taxed at relatively high marginal income tax rates.

Potential Problem

In 2008, estates and trusts with taxable income in excess of $10,700 are subject to the highest federal marginal income tax rate of 35.0%. A married couple, however, does not reach this 35.0% marginal bracket until their taxable income reaches $357,700.

As an example, a trust containing $250,000 of assets invested at 5.0% would earn $12,500 per year. Any amount in excess of $10,700 would need to be distributed to avoid taxation at the top 35.0% federal income tax rate. Even if the trustee wants to distribute all or part of the earnings, how can he or she do so if the beneficiaries are minors?

Possible Solutions

If the trust document allows the trustee to make distributions "to or for the benefit of" the beneficiary, the trustee might consider making transfers to the beneficiary under the Uniform Transfer to Minors Act. The person named as custodian can invest these funds and use them for the minor's benefit until he or she is an adult. The advantage of the custodial arrangement is that all of its earnings are taxed at the beneficiary's rate even though they are not distributed. A single person does not reach the 35.0% bracket until his or her taxable income reaches $357,700.[2] For certain children, unearned income in excess of $1,800[2] is subject to taxation at the parent's top marginal income tax bracket.[3]

If it is not desirable (or permitted by trust language) to use the custodial arrangement, the trustee should look for other methods of reducing taxable income. One approach would be to switch from income producing assets to more growth-oriented investments.

Tax-exempt investments are another possible alternative. The yield on a tax-exempt investment can be lower than that of a taxable investment and still enjoy the same net return. For example, to match a tax-free return of 5.00%, an investor in the 35.0% marginal bracket would have to earn a taxable return of 7.69%.

The high marginal income tax rates applicable to trusts apply also to estates. Caution should be used in choosing the executor of one's estate. An unwise executor may allow the income tax burden to be higher than necessary.

---

[1] The issues discussed here concern federal income tax law; state and local law may vary.
[2] This value applies to 2008 and is subject to adjustment for inflation in future years.
[3] The Small Business and Work Opportunity Tax Act of 2007 expanded the "kiddie tax" to include a child up to age 18, or a child who is a full-time student age 19 to 23. Children who are age 18 or who are full-time students age 19-23, and whose earned income exceeds one-half of the amount of their support, are exempt from the tax. This legislation was effective for tax years beginning after May 25, 2007.

Income Tax Basis

Basis is a value used to determine the amount of gain or loss on the sale of an asset and will vary, depending upon how it was acquired:

Cost Basis	=	The amount paid for an asset
Adjusted Basis	=	Cost basis plus improvements less depreciation
Capital Gain	=	Sales price is higher than adjusted basis
Capital Loss	=	Sales price is less than adjusted basis
FMV	=	Fair market value

Basic Rules as They Apply to Various Transfers

Assume owner paid $5,000 for a lot (his cost basis).

Method of Transfer	Basis in Hands of New Owner	Assume at Time of Transfer Lot Had		
		Declined in Value to $3,000	Retained Same Value of $5,000	Increased in Value to $8,000
Sale	Purchaser receives a new basis (the amount he pays for the asset).	$3,000	$5,000	$8,000
Lifetime gift	**For computing gain:** Donee takes donor's basis.	–	$5,000	$5,000[1]
	For computing loss: Donee's basis is FMV at time of gift, or the donor's basis, whichever is lower.	$3,000	–	–
Transfer at death	Beneficiary's basis is equal to value at decedent's death or six months thereafter.[2]	$3,000	$5,000	$8,000
Like kind exchange IRC Sec. 1031	Basis in newly acquired property will be the same as basis in the transferred property, plus any recognized gain and less any cash received.	$5,000	$5,000	$5,000

Note: Transfers of appreciated property to a spouse or former spouse who is a non-resident alien will trigger tax on the gain. See IRC Sec. 1041(d).

---

[1] This amount plus gift tax paid, if any, at time of gift attributable to the appreciation.
[2] IRC 1014(b), unless the beneficiary or his or her spouse had transferred the specific piece of property to the decedent within one year prior to his demise, in which case the beneficiary must carry over the decedent's basis. See IRC Sec. 1014(e).

Taxation of Disability Insurance Premiums and Benefits

Personally-Owned Policies

Premiums for a non-medical benefit such as disability insurance are not deductible when purchased by an individual. See IRC Sec. 213(d)(1).

The benefits from a personally owned disability insurance policy are exempt from income taxation. See IRC Sec. 104(a)(3). State disability compensation is nontaxable if the benefits paid are in the nature of workmen's compensation. However, unemployment compensation from federal and state programs is fully includable in gross income.[1]

Business-Owned Policies

If the premium is paid by the employer for its employee, the results are different.

- The premium is deductible by the employer whether the insurance is a group policy or individual policies, so long as the benefits are payable to the employees or their beneficiaries. See Reg. Sec. 1.162-10(a).

- The amount paid by the employer for disability insurance premiums is not taxable to the employee. See IRC Sec. 106, Reg. Sec. 1.106-1 and Reg. Sec. 1.79-3(f)(3).

- When a benefit is collected, it is fully includable in gross income of the employee. If the employee paid part of the premium, that portion of the benefit will be tax-free.[2] See Reg. Sec. 1.105-1(c).

- If the policy pays for accidental death, the proceeds are generally tax-exempt to the beneficiary under IRC Secs. 106 and 101(a). (Policies issued after 12/31/84 must meet the statutory definition of life insurance under IRC Sec. 7702.)

Key Person Disability Insurance

If the policy is payable to the business to protect it from the loss of services of a key employee, the premium is not tax deductible. See IRC Sec. 265(a)(1), and Rev. Rul. 66-262 and 1966-2 CB 105.

On the other hand, benefits collected by the company are received income tax free. See IRC Sec. 104(a)(3) and Rev. Rul. 66-262.

---

[1] Based on federal law. State law may vary.

[2] In Revenue Ruling 2004-55, IRB 2004-26, 6/9/04, the IRS reviewed an employer-sponsored disability plan in which an employee could choose to have the employer-paid premium included in current wages, thus treating the premiums as having been made by the employee on an after-tax basis. Any disability benefits received under this arrangement would be excluded from the employee's gross income.

Deductibility of Interest

Under the current income tax law, not all interest is deductible on your tax return.

Nondeductible Interest

Personal interest is not deductible and includes all interest, except those types listed below. Examples of nondeductible personal interest would include interest on credit card purchases, auto loans, unpaid income taxes and deferral of federal estate taxes made at the government's discretion for "reasonable cause" under IRC Sec. 6161.

Deductible[1] Interest

A partial list of types of deductible interest includes:

- **Interest on loans used to purchase investment properties:** This interest is deductible to the extent there is net investment income. Interest paid on money borrowed to purchase or carry tax-exempt securities is not deductible. Any unused deduction is carried over to future years until used.[2]

- **Interest incurred in the conduct of your trade or business** (IRC Sec. 163)

- **Qualified residence interest:** This is one type of loan for which the interest paid is deductible without regard to the use of the borrowed funds.
  A "qualified residence" is your principal residence and one other property, such as a vacation home, a boat you live on, etc., which you use more than 14 days during the year (or 10% of the number of days it is rented, if that is larger), or any number of days if you use it as a residence but do not rent it. See IRC Secs. 163(h)(5)(A) and 280A(d)(1).

There are two types of deductible qualified residence interest.

- **Acquisition indebtedness:** Mortgage debt which you incur when you purchase, build or substantially improve a qualified residence. There is a limit on acquisition indebtedness incurred after October 13, 1987 of $1,000,000 ($500,000 for married persons filing separately). See IRC Sec. 163(h)(3)(B)(ii).[3]

- **Home Equity indebtedness:** Loans against the equity of the home (over and above the acquisition indebtedness); for example, a second mortgage to purchase an automobile. The limit is the lesser of: (a) the fair market value (FMV) of the home less any acquisition indebtedness; or, (b) $100,000 ($50,000 for married filing separate). See IRC Sec. 163(h)(3).

---

[1] Individuals with an adjusted gross income (AGI) in excess of certain limits face a phase out of otherwise allowable itemized deductions. Itemized deductions not phased out include medical expenses, net investment interest expense, casualty and theft losses, and net gambling losses. (See IRC Sec. 68.) Under the Tax Act of 2001, the limitation will be phased out (1/3rd in 2006 – 2007, by 2/3rd in 2008 – 2009 and completely eliminated starting in 2010).

[2] Net capital gain included in net investment income is ineligible for capital gains treatment. See IRC Sec 163(d)(4)(B)(iii).

[3] Under the provisions of the Tax Relief and Health Care Act of 2006, premiums paid for qualified mortgage insurance in connection with acquisition indebtedness on a taxpayer's qualified residence are treated as deductible mortgage interest. This provision applies only to mortgage insurance contracts issued after December 31, 2006 and only for premium amounts paid, accrued, or allocable to calendar 2007.

Continued

Deductibility of Interest

- **Interest on educational loans:** Taxpayers may deduct interest paid on "qualified" education loans. The deduction is taken as an "above-the-line adjustment," directly reducing adjusted gross income (AGI). For 2001 and later tax years, the deduction is limited to $2,500.

  The deduction is phased out for taxpayers with a modified AGI in excess of certain limits.

Filing Status	2007	2008	2009
Married Filing Jointly	$110,000 - $140,000	$115,000 - $145,000	Adjusted for inflation
Single, Head of Household, Widow	$55,000 - $70,000	$55,000 - $70,000	Adjusted for inflation

Highlights of the Pension Protection Act of 2006

The Pension Protection Act of 2006 (PPA 2006) was signed into law by President George W. Bush on August 17, 2006. During the signing ceremony, President Bush described the act as the "most sweeping reform of America's pension laws in over 30 years."

Over 900 pages in length, the new legislation reflects the move by many employers away from traditional defined benefit (DB) pension plans and toward defined contribution (DC) plans. Its provisions also highlight governmental concern over the shaky financial condition of many DB plans and the potential adverse effect that any future defaults by plan sponsors may have on the federal government and the American taxpayer.

Defined contribution plans are also affected, in a myriad of ways. The act makes permanent many of the provisions of EGTRRA 2001, which encouraged individuals to establish and contribute to both IRAs and employer-sponsored DC plans. PPA 2006 also impacts distributions from qualified plans, with both temporary and permanent changes.

Further, PPA 2006 includes many "miscellaneous" provisions, including those affecting employer-owned life insurance, charitable giving, IRC Sec. 529 plans, and long-term care.

The following is a brief summary of a few notable provisions of this new legislation. Individual taxpayers are strongly encouraged to consult with their own financial and tax advisors to review in detail how the act may impact their own personal situations.

Traditional Defined Benefit (DB) Pension Plans

Much of PPA 2006 is devoted to bolstering traditional DB plans, as well as strengthening the government's "safety net," the Pension Benefit Guaranty Corporation (PBGC).

Item	Prior Law	2006 Legislation
Minimum plan funding	Employer generally required to fund up to 90% of plan's liabilities. Current law applies in 2006 and 2007.	Generally requires employers to fund 100% of plan's liabilities. Underfunded plans have seven years to reach 100%. Minimum annual contribution must cover the value of benefits earned during the years. Effective for plan years beginning in 2008.
Employer deduction limits	Contributions deductible up to 100% of current plan liability.	For new plans, in 2006 and 2007, maximum deduction limited to 150% of current liabilities. In 2008 and later, the maximum deduction will generally be the amount necessary to bring the plan assets up to 150% of the applicable funding target. Some restrictions on this 50% "cushion" apply for small plans recently amended to increase benefits.

Continued

Highlights of the Pension Protection Act of 2006

Traditional Defined Benefit (DB) Pension Plans (continued)

Item	Prior Law	2006 Legislation
"At risk" plans	Lump-sum distributions limited for certain highly compensated employees if less than 110% of current liability funded.	Employer generally subject to funding requirements greater than the normal 100%. Restrictions on certain benefits may apply. Extremely underfunded plans would be automatically frozen. Notices are required to participants in certain events. For plan years beginning in 2008 and later.
Valuing plan liabilities	Valued using investment grade corporate bonds. Prior law applies in 2006 and 2007.	Beginning in 2008, a three-segmented yield curve will be used. May include updated mortality tables or tables based on a plan's experience and trends.
Maximum plan benefit	EGTRRA 2001 increased the maximum annual dollar limit to the lesser of $160,000 (indexed for inflation) or 100% of compensation (maximum of $200,000). Benefits were reduced if begun before age 62 and increased if begun after age 65. The provision was originally set to "sunset" on 12/31/2010.	Makes permanent the increased benefit allowed under EGTRRA 2001.[1]
Cash balance plans	Prior legislation left employers who switched to a "cash balance" hybrid plan open to lawsuits over age discrimination.	If a plan meets certain requirements, new cash balance plans are not considered discriminatory. Conversions of existing DB plans to cash balance plans will be permissible, subject to certain requirements.[2]
Fully insured DB plans	Currently described in IRC Sec. 412(i).	Moved to new IRC Sec. 412(e)(3).[1]

---

[1] Effective August 17, 2006, the date of enactment.
[2] Generally effective for periods beginning after June 29, 2005.

Continued...

Highlights of the Pension Protection Act of 2006

IRAs and Defined Contribution (DC) Plans

PPA 2006 includes many provisions designed to encourage individuals to participate in IRAs and employer-sponsored DC plans. The law makes permanent[1] a number of EGTRRA 2001 provisions that originally were to "sunset" after 2010, including:

- **Increased IRA contribution limits:** In 2006 and 2007, $4,000; in 2008, $5,000; adjusted for inflation in later years.

- **Increased limits for defined contribution plans:** In 2006, a total maximum contribution of $44,000; elective deferrals limited to $15,000 (401(k) and 457 plans) and $10,000 for SIMPLE plans; compensation that may be taken into account ($220,000); all adjusted for inflation in later years.

- **"Catch-up" contributions for workers age 50 and older:** For IRAs, in 2006, $1,000. In 2006 for 401(k) plans, $5,000; for SIMPLE plans, $2,500; adjusted for inflation in later years.

- **Vesting of employer contributions:** 100% vesting under either a three-year cliff or six-year graded schedule.

- **Increased employer deduction for qualified plan contributions:** EGTRRA generally increased the deduction limit from 15% to 25% of compensation and modified the definition of compensation for certain types of plans.

- **Roth 401(k) and 403(b) contributions:** Under EGTRRA 2001, Roth contributions to 401(k) and 403(b) plans were allowed only during 2006-2010.

- **"Deemed" IRAs:** Established under an employer plan which provided for separate employee contributions.

- **"Solo" 401(k) plans:** Elective deferrals are not taken into account for purposes of the limit on deductible plan contributions.

PPA 2006 also included a number of notable new items:

Item	Prior Law	2006 Legislation
Automatic 401(k) plan enrollment	Permitted by IRS and DOL regulations, but restricted by law in many states.	Beginning with enactment, preempts state laws prohibiting automatic enrollment and withholding of employee wages. Employees must opt-out if they do not wish to participate.
Automatic enrollment safe harbor 401(k) plan	No comparable provision.	Beginning in 2008, allows a new safe harbor 401(k) plan with automatic enrollment features. Must meet special employee notice, matching contribution, and vesting requirements.

---

[1] Effective August 17, 2006, the date of enactment.

Continued

Highlights of the Pension Protection Act of 2006

IRAs and Defined Contribution (DC) Plans (continued)

Item	Prior Law	2006 Legislation
Custom investment advice for employee-participants	Considered a "prohibited transaction" under prior law.	Beginning in 2007, allows for an "eligible investment advice arrangement." Any fees or commissions must not vary with the investment option chosen or else a computer model meeting certain requirement must be used.
Direct deposit of federal income tax refunds into an IRA	Allows refunds of federal income taxes to be directly deposited into a checking or savings account.	Beginning in 2007, allows refunds of federal income taxes to also be directly deposited into an IRA.

Distributions from IRAs and Qualified Retirement Plans

Item	Prior Law	2006 Legislation
Qualified reservist distribution	No comparable provision. IRC Sec. 72(t) generally applies a 10% tax penalty to withdrawals from IRAs and other qualified retirement plans made by owners or participants under age 59½, unless certain exceptions apply.	Waives the 10% early withdrawal penalty for withdrawals from an IRA or other retirement plan by qualifying military reservists called to active duty between 09/11/2001 and 12/31/2007. Allows for re-contribution of withdrawn amounts during the two years after active duty ends.
Public safety employees – distributions from defined benefit plans after age 50	No comparable provision. IRC Sec. 72(t) generally applies a 10% tax penalty to withdrawals from IRAs and other qualified retirement plans made by owners and participants under age 59½, unless certain exceptions apply. One exception applies to employees who separate from service after age 55.	The 10% tax penalty for early withdrawals does not apply to distributions from a qualified governmental defined benefit plan to a qualified public safety employee who separates from service after age 50.[1]

---

[1] Effective for distributions made after the date of enactment, August 17, 2006.

Continued...

Highlights of the Pension Protection Act of 2006

Distributions from IRAs and Qualified Retirement Plans (continued)

Item	Prior Law	2006 Legislation
Public safety employees – tax-free distributions to pay for health and long-term care insurance	No comparable provision. Distributions from IRAs and qualified retirement plans are generally taxable to the extent the distribution represent a return of before-tax contributions. A 10% penalty tax may also apply to distributions made before the participant reaches age 59½, unless certain exceptions apply.	Beginning in 2007, provides an exclusion from income of up to $3,000 for distributions from qualifying retirement plans for retired public safety officers to pay for qualified accident, health, or long-term care insurance. Premium payments must be made directly from the retirement plan to the insurer.
Rollovers by nonspouse beneficiaries	No comparable provision. Only a surviving spouse could roll over a distribution from a deceased spouse's qualified plan to his or her own IRA.	Beginning in 2007, beneficiaries other than a surviving spouse may roll over benefits received from a qualified retirement plan, a 457 plan, or a tax sheltered annuity to an inherited IRA.
Direct rollover from a qualified plan to a Roth IRA	No comparable provision. Under prior law, a distribution from a qualified retirement plan, 457 plan, or tax-sheltered annuity had to first be rolled over to a traditional IRA before it could be transferred to a Roth IRA.	Beginning in 2008, distributions from qualified retirement plans, 457 plans, and tax-sheltered annuities may be rolled directly into a Roth IRA. These distributions are subject to the same requirements as a Roth conversion.
Phased retirement	No comparable provision. Prior law generally prohibited a qualified plan from making retirement distributions to a participant who had not reached normal retirement age and who had not separated from service. Proposed regulations would permit plans to pay a portion of benefits to employees who are at least age 59½ and reduce their work time by at least 20%.	Beginning in 2007, allows retirement distributions to employees who are at least age 62 even if they have not separated from employment at the time of the distribution.

Continued...

Highlights of the Pension Protection Act of 2006

Charitable Giving

Although the vast majority of the act concerns pensions and retirement plans, there are a number of provisions affecting charitable giving. Among these are:

Item	Prior Law	2006 Legislation
Qualified charitable distributions from IRAs	No comparable provision. Withdrawals from IRAs are generally subject to tax, to the extent that they represent a return of before-tax contributions. Contributions to charitable organizations are subject to a number of limitations on the deductibility of such contributions.	For 2006 and 2007, provides an exclusion from gross income of up to $100,000 for distributions made from a Roth or Traditional IRA directly to a qualified charitable organization. The IRA owner must be at least age 70½ when the distribution is made. No charitable deduction is allowed for such qualified charitable distributions.
Charitable contributions of clothing and household items	Generally, taxpayers are permitted to deduct the fair market value of tangible personal property donated to charity. Certain substantiation requirements apply.	Prohibits a charitable deduction for contributions of used clothing or household items unless the items donated are in good used condition or better. A deduction may be allowed for donations of property that is not in good used condition or better if the value exceeds $500 and a qualified appraisal accompanies the taxpayer's return.[1]
Cash contributions to charities	Generally requires a donor to substantiate a charitable donation of cash through written records such as a cancelled check, a receipt, or a letter of acknowledgement from the charitable donee showing the donee's name, the amount and date of the contribution, or other reliable written records.	Requires the donor to substantiate a charitable donation of cash through either a bank record or a written communication from the charitable donee showing the donee's name and the amount, and date of the contribution.[2]
Charitable contributions of food inventory and book inventory	Under the Katrina Emergency Tax Relief Act of 2005 (KETRA), allowed an expanded business charitable deduction for donations of food items from inventory or donations of books to a public school. Applicable to donations made on or after 08/25/05 and before 01/01/06.	Extends the effective date of these provisions for one year to donations made after 12/31/05 and before 01/01/08.

---

[1] Effective for contributions made after August 17, 2006.
[2] Effective for contributions made in tax years beginning after August 17, 2006.

Continued...

Highlights of the Pension Protection Act of 2006

Charitable Giving (continued)

Item	Prior Law	2006 Legislation
Qualified conservation easement	Generally allows an income tax deduction for the value of a qualified conservation easement. The deduction is limited to 30% of the donor's adjusted gross income in the year the contribution is made; any excess may be carried forward and deducted for up to five years.	For 2006 and 2007, generally increases the allowable deduction to 50% of the donor's adjusted gross income, with any excess being carried forward for up to 15 years. For qualified farmers and ranchers, the allowable deduction is 100% of the donor's adjusted gross income.

Miscellaneous Provisions

As with many major legislative acts, there are always a few "miscellaneous" provisions:

Item	Prior Law	2006 Legislation
IRC Sec. 529 plans	Many of the key provisions concerning qualified tuition plans came into being with the EGTRRA 2001. Under that act, these provisions were originally set to "sunset" on 12/31/10.	Makes the "temporary" provisions of EGTRRA that apply to qualified tuition plans permanent.[1]
Saver's credit	Provides for a nonrefundable tax credit for lower-income taxpayers for contributions to IRAs and certain qualified retirement plans. The credit amount varies with the adjusted gross income of the taxpayer. The provision was originally set to "sunset" on 12/31/06.	Makes the credit permanent. Beginning in 2007, indexes for inflation the income limits applicable to the credit, in multiples of $500.[1]
Start-Up tax credit for small employer-sponsored plans	Allowed small employers a credit of up to $500 per year for the costs of establishing a new qualified retirement plan. The provision was originally set to "sunset" on 12/31/10.	Makes the credit permanent.[1]
1035 exchanges and LTC	No comparable provisions.	Expands the scope of IRC Sec. 1035 to include tax-free exchanges of qualified long-term care (LTC) contracts. The provision also covers LTC provided as a part of, or a rider to, a life or annuity contract.[2]

---

[1] Effective August 17, 2006, the date of enactment.
[2] Applicable to exchanges occurring after December 31, 2009.

Continued..

Highlights of the Pension Protection Act of 2006

Miscellaneous Provisions (continued)

Item	Prior Law	2006 Legislation
Tax treatment of LTC as a rider to life or annuity contracts	Some provision for LTC coverage as a part of a life insurance contract.	Establishes new, complex tax rules for long-term care insurance (LTC) which is provided by a rider on, or a part of, either a life insurance or annuity contract. A withdrawal from the life or annuity contract used to pay for LTC is generally not includable in income.[1] No itemized medical expense deduction is allowed for charges against the life or annuity contract for LTC coverage.
Employer-owned life insurance	Generally, amounts received under a life insurance contract paid by reason of the death of the insured are excluded from gross income for federal income tax purposes.	Generally provides that in the case of an employer-owned life insurance contract, the amount excluded from the policyholder's income cannot exceed the premiums and other amounts paid for the contract.[2] Death benefit above these payment amounts is included in income. The new law adds certain notice and consent requirements and provides for specified exceptions to the income inclusion rules.
Restrictions on executive deferred compensation	No comparable provisions.	Generally provides that during periods in which a qualified retirement plan is "at-risk," any funds set aside in a nonqualified deferred compensation plan for high-level executives will become taxable in the year of transfer. An underpayment interest penalty and a 20% penalty tax also apply. Further, the employer is denied a deduction for such transfers.[3]

[1] Generally effective for contracts issued after December 31, 1996, but only with respect to taxable years beginning after December 31, 2009.
[2] Effective for contracts issued after August 17, 2006 (the date of enactment) except for contracts acquired under an IRC Sec. 1035 exchange.
[3] Effective for funds transferred or set aside after August 17, 2006, the date of enactment.

Highlights of Hurricane Tax Relief
A Brief Summary of Selected Provisions

In the wake of the destruction left by Hurricane Katrina, Congress and President Bush moved quickly to provide legislative relief to those affected by that storm. The Katrina Emergency Tax Relief Act of 2005 (KETRA) was passed unanimously by Congress on September 21, 2005 and signed into law by the President on September 23, 2005.

In response to Hurricanes Rita and Wilma, KETRA was soon followed by the Gulf Opportunity Zone Act of 2005, (GOZA), passed by Congress on December 16, 2005, and signed into law on December 21, 2005. This second relief act established a Gulf Opportunity (GO) Zone, for Hurricane Katrina victims, a Rita GO Zone, for victims of Hurricane Rita, and a Wilma GO Zone, for victims of Hurricane Wilma. GOZA provided additional tax relief to those impacted by Hurricane Katrina, and extended a number of the KETRA provisions to those living in areas affected by Hurricanes Rita and Wilma.

Although much of this legislation[1] aids those directly affected by the storms, taxpayers living outside the impacted geographical areas also benefit.

Provisions Applicable to Hurricanes Katrina, Rita, and Wilma

A number of relief provisions apply to individuals affected by any of the storms:

- **Withdrawals from IRAs and qualified plans:** The legislation generally allows an individual living in one of the three disaster zones, and who suffered an economic loss as a result of the hurricanes, to withdraw up to $100,000 in "qualified hurricane distributions" penalty-free (the 10% early withdrawal penalty) from an IRA or other qualified retirement plan. While such withdrawals are subject to normal income tax, they are not subject to the 20% mandatory withholding requirements.[2] These distributions must be made before January 1, 2007, and on or after August 25, 2005 (to a Hurricane Katrina individual), on or after September 23, 2005 (to a Hurricane Rita individual), or on or after October, 23, 2005 (to a Hurricane Wilma individual).

- **Three-year income inclusion:** Amounts withdrawn from an IRA or qualified plan that must be included in gross income can be recognized ratably over three years, unless the taxpayer elects otherwise.

- **Repaying IRA and qualified plan withdrawals:** If a taxpayer repays a qualified distribution from an IRA or qualified plan within three years, the initial distribution is treated as a non-taxable rollover. The taxpayer should file an amended return to claim a refund of tax paid on amounts previously included in income.

- **Loans from qualified plans:** The legislation expands from $50,000 to $100,000 the maximum amount that a qualifying hurricane victim may borrow from his or her pension plan to purchase a principal residence. Such loans must be made before January 1, 2007, and on or after September 24, 2005 (to a Hurricane Katrina individual), or on or after December 21, 2005 (to a Hurricane Rita or Hurricane Wilma individual).

---

[1] The discussion here concerns federal income tax law. State or local law may differ.
[2] Separately, the IRS, in Announcement 2005-70, liberalized the rules for hardship distributions from qualified plans for victims of the hurricane as well as for family members who may be living in other parts of the country.

Continued.

Highlights of Hurricane Tax Relief
A Brief Summary of Selected Provisions

- **Expanded charitable deduction for cash donations:** The legislation generally expands the deduction available to both individuals and corporations for donations of cash made between August 28, 2005 and December 31, 2005 to qualifying organizations. For corporations, donations must be for relief efforts related to Hurricane Katrina, Hurricane Rita, or Hurricane Wilma.

- **Casualty losses:** Individuals generally may deduct personal casualty or theft losses only to the extent that they exceed $100 per casualty or theft, and to the extent they exceed 10% of the taxpayer's adjusted gross income. For personal losses from Hurricane Katrina on or after August 25, 2005, these casualty loss limitations do not apply. GOZA extended this relief to losses arising from Hurricane Rita on or after September 23, 2005, and to losses arising from Hurricane Wilma on or after October 23, 2005.

- **Earned income and child credits:** The legislation permits qualified low-income taxpayers displaced by the hurricanes to use their 2004 earned income to calculate for 2005 any allowable earned income credit (EIC) or refundable child credit.

- **Employee Retention Credit:** Provides for a credit of 40% of qualified wages (up to $6,000 in qualified wages per employee) paid to an eligible employee by an eligible employer in one of the disaster areas. For employers in the Katrina core disaster area, the wages must have been paid between August 28, 2005 and January 1, 2006. For Hurricanes Rita and Wilma, respectively, these dates are September 23, 2005 - January 1, 2006, and October 23, 2005 - January 1, 2006.

- **Mortgage revenue bonds:** These bonds are commonly used by state and local governments to fund low-interest rate mortgages for low-income, first-time homebuyers. The legislation expands eligibility to receive such loans by eliminating the "first-time homebuyer" requirement for residences located in the GO Zone, the Rita GO Zone, or the Wilma GO Zone. The new laws also expand to $150,000 from $15,000 the permitted amount for a home improvement loan used to repair damage caused by the hurricanes. The rules apply to loans made before January 1, 2011.

Provisions Applicable Only to Hurricane Katrina

Certain provisions of the legislation target those affected by Hurricane Katrina, or those working or living in the Gulf Opportunity Zone:

- **Sheltering evacuees:** A special personal exemption deduction is allowed for a taxpayer (anywhere in the country) who uses his or her principal residence to provide free housing to Katrina evacuees (up to four) for at least 60 consecutive days. The deduction, limited to $2,000, may be claimed, for both 2005 or 2006.

- **Discharge of indebtedness:** Cancellation of a debt generally results in taxable income to the taxpayer whose debt was cancelled. If certain requirements are met, KETRA provides an exclusion from income for victims of Katrina for the cancellation of non-business debt on or after August 25, 2005 and before January 1, 2007.

Continued...

Highlights of Hurricane Tax Relief
A Brief Summary of Selected Provisions

- **Charitable mileage for Hurricane Katrina relief:** KETRA increased the standard charitable mileage rate from its 2005 value of 14 cents per mile to 70% of the standard business mileage rate, rounded to the next highest cent.[1] If a volunteer is reimbursed for charitable use of a passenger automobile, the legislation generally allows the reimbursement to be excluded from income. Both provisions apply for miles driven from August 25, 2005 through December 31, 2006.

- **Charitable contributions of food and books from inventory:** KETRA expanded the deduction allowed to a business for donations of food items from inventory. For C corporations, the Act also expanded the deduction for donations of books to a public school. Both provisions apply to contributions made on or after August 28, 2005 and before January 1, 2006.[2]

- **Hope Scholarship and Lifetime Learning Credits:** For 2005 and 2006, students attending eligible institutions within the Gulf Opportunity Zone may claim a Hope Scholarship Credit or Lifetime Learning Credit of up to twice the normally applicable dollar limits. Thus, for 2006, a qualified individual may claim a Hope Scholarship Credit of up to $3,300 or a Lifetime Learning Credit of up to $4,000.[3] Additionally, the definition of "qualified tuition and related expenses" has been expanded to match the much broader definition used for IRC Sec. 529 qualified tuition plans.

- **Work Opportunity Tax Credit:** Expands eligibility for the Work Opportunity Tax Credit by including a "Hurricane Katrina employee" as a member of a "targeted group" for purposes of the credit.

Seek Professional Guidance

Many of the provisions of both KETRA and GOZA are complex. As with all tax-related matters, the advice and guidance of an experienced tax professional is highly recommended.

---

[1] For the period August 25, 2005 through August 31, 2005, the Hurricane Katrina standard charitable mileage rate is 29 cents per mile. For the period September 1, 2005 though December 31, 2005, this rate is 34 cents per mile. For 2006, this rate is 32 cents per mile. These provisions apply solely for charitable mileage related to Hurricane Katrina relief efforts.

[2] The Pension Protection Act of 2006 extended the effective date of these provisions for one year, to include donations made after 12/31/05 and before 01/01/08.

[3] For 2005, a qualified individual may claim a Hope Scholarship Credit of up to $3,000 or a Lifetime Learning Credit of up to $4,000.

Highlights of 2003 Tax Legislation
As Amended

The Jobs and Growth Tax Relief Reconciliation Act (JGTRRA) of 2003 became law on May 28, 2003. Many sections of this act coordinated with portions of an earlier tax bill, EGTRRA of 2001. The Working Families Tax Relief Act (WFTRA) of 2004 modified parts of both previous acts. The table below summarizes selected provisions of these tax bills.

Item	Prior Law	2003 Legislation	Effective Date	Sunset Date
Individual Marginal Income Tax Rates	For 2003, brackets are 10, 15, 27,30, 35, and 38.6%. EGTRRA of 2001 gradually reduced brackets over time, reaching lowest level in 2006.	Immediately reduces marginal brackets to 2006 levels projected under EGTRRA: 10, 15, 25, 28, 33 and 35%.	Retroactive to 01/01/03	12/31/05[1]
10% Bracket	For single taxpayers, up to $6,000 of taxable income. For MFJ, up to $12,000 of taxable income.	For single taxpayers, up to $7,000[2] of taxable income. For MFJ, up to $14,000[2] of taxable income.	Retroactive to 01/01/03	12/31/10[3]
Long-Term Capital Gains	Long-term gains taxed at 8-28% depending on type of asset, taxpayer's marginal bracket, and holding period. Five years generally required for lowest rate.	For taxpayers in 10% or 15% tax brackets, LT gain taxed at 5% through 2007; 0% in 2008. For all others, LT gain taxed at 15% through 2008. Repeals five-year holding requirement. Retains existing law for certain types of transactions.	05/06/03	12/31/10[4]
Dividends	Taxed as ordinary income, with marginal rates from 10-38.6%.	For taxpayers in 10% or 15% tax brackets, dividends taxed at 5% through 2007; 0% in 2008. For all others, dividends taxed at 15% through 2008.	Retroactive to 01/01/03	12/31/10[4]

---

[1] This portion of the 2003 Act dovetails with EGTRRA in that the lower rates of EGTRRA will begin in 2006 as scheduled.
[2] Subject to adjustment for inflation
[3] As modified by WFTRA of 2004.
[4] As modified by TIPRA of 2005.

Continued...

Highlights of 2003 Tax Legislation

As Amended

Item	Prior Law	2003 Legislation	Effective Date	Sunset Date
AMT Exemption	Single/HoH: $35,750 MFJ or QW: $49,000 MFS: $24,500	Single/HoH: $40,250 MFJ or QW: $58,000 MFS: $29,000.	Retroactive to 01/01/03	12/31/05[1]
Child Tax Credit	For 2003, $600 per qualifying child. Under EGTRRA, credit would be increased periodically, reaching $1,000 per qualifying child in 2010.	$1,000 per qualifying child.	Retroactive to 01/01/03	12/31/10[1]
Married Filing Separately	Under EGTRRA, beginning in 2005, gradually increases both the standard deduction and the 15% tax bracket for MFS filers until they reach the same amounts allowed single taxpayers.	Immediately increases the standard deduction and 15% tax bracket for MFS filers to the same amounts allowed single taxpayers.	Retroactive to 01/01/03	12/31/10[1]
Marriage Penalty Relief	Beginning in 2005, EGTRRA gradually increases both the standard deduction and the 15% tax bracket for MFJ filers until they reach 200% of the amounts allowed single taxpayers.	Immediately increases the standard deduction and 15% tax bracket for MFJ filers to 200% of the amounts allowed single taxpayers.	Retroactive to 01/01/03	12/31/10[1]
IRC. Sec.179 Expensing	Allows small business to "expense" (rather than depreciating over time) up to $25,000 of assets annually. Deduction phased-out for qualifying property over $200,000.	Increases expensing limit to $100,000. Deduction phased-out for qualifying property over $400,000. Indexes both values for inflation in 2004 and 2005.	Retroactive to 01/01/03	12/31/09[2]
Bonus Depreciation	Allows additional 30% depreciation on certain business use assets.	Increases allowable bonus depreciation to 50%.	05/06/03	12/31/04

Seek Professional Advice

Given a constantly changing tax environment, individual taxpayers are strongly advised to consult with their own financial and tax advisors.

---

[1] As modified by WFTRA of 2004.
[2] As modified by AJCA of 2004 and TIPRA of 2005

Tax Act of 2003 Phase-In Timeline
As Amended

The Jobs and Growth Tax Relief Reconciliation Act (JGTRRA) of 2003 became law on May 28, 2003. Many sections of this act coordinated with portions of an earlier tax bill, EGTRRA of 2001. The Working Families Tax Relief Act (WFTRA) of 2004 and the Tax Increase Prevention and Reconciliation Act (TIPRA) of 2005 modified parts of both acts. The table below shows the effective dates for selected provisions.

Income Tax Provisions	2003 Prior Law	2003	2004	2005	2006	2007	2008	2009	2010	2011
For Individuals										
Marginal rates	38.6%	35%								39.6%
	35.0%	33%								36.0%
	30.0%	28%								31.0%
	27.0%	25%								28.0%
	15.0%	15%								15.0%
	10.0%	10%								None[1]
10% bracket top[2]										
Single	$6,000	$7,000	$7,000[3]							n/a[1]
Married - Joint	$12,000	$14,000	$14,000[3]							n/a[1]
LT Capital Gains										
Tax rate >15%	20%	15%[4]								20%
Tax rate <=15%	10%			5%[4]				0%[4]		10%
Qualified Dividends										
Tax rate >15%	n/a[5]	15%[4]								n/a[5]
Tax rate <=15%	n/a[5]			5%[4]				0%[4]		n/a[5]
AMT Exemption[2]										
Single	$35,750		$40,250		$42,500			$33,750		
Married – Joint	$49,000		$58,000		$62,550			$45,000		
Married – Sep.	$24,500		$29,000		$31,275			$22,500		
Child Tax Credit[2]	$600	$1,000								$500
Married – Separate[2]										
Top of 15% bracket (vs. single)	n/a[1]	100%								n/a[1]
Standard Deduction (vs. single)	n/a[1]	100%								n/a[1]
Marriage Penalty Relief (MFJ)[2]										
Top of 15% bracket (vs. single)	n/a[1]	200%								n/a[1]
Standard Deduction (vs. single)	n/a[1]	200%								n/a[1]
For Businesses										
IRC Sec. 179[6]										
Deduction	$25,000	$100,000	$100,000[3]						$25,000[4]	
Phase-out limit	$200,000	$400,000	$400,000[3]						$200,000[4]	
Bonus Depreciation	30%	50%[4]		n/a[1]						

[1] Not applicable in year shown.
[2] As modified by WFTRA of 2004 and TIPRA of 2005.
[3] The amount shown is subject to adjustment for inflation.
[4] As modified by TIPRA of 2005.
[5] Dividends taxed as ordinary income at taxpayer's regular rates.
[6] As modified by AJCA of 2004

Highlights of 2001 Tax Legislation

On June 7, 2001, President Bush signed into law H.R. 1836, The Economic Growth and Tax Relief Reconciliation Act of 2001, (EGTRRA). It is an enormous and complex piece of legislation, targeted primarily at individual taxpayers. In addition to granting general income tax relief, the law impacts education funding, creates new retirement planning opportunities, gradually reduces the federal estate tax and, for one year, repeals the federal estate tax entirely. If fully implemented as passed, the Act will reduce federal taxes by an estimated $1.35 trillion over a 10-year period.

While some provisions of the Act are retroactive, many sections of the new law take effect in future years. Most of the tax reduction, an estimated $875 billion, is scheduled to occur in the last five years of the 10-year transition. As an additional complication, the entire Act "sunsets" after 2010. This means that without further legislative action, all provisions of the bill disappear and the prior law will be reinstated.

The following is a partial and summary description of a few of the provisions in the Act. Individual taxpayers are strongly advised to consult with their own financial and tax advisors to review in detail how this new legislation affects their personal situations.

General Income Tax Provisions

Item	Prior Law	2001 Legislation
Individual income tax rates	Five marginal tax brackets, 15%, 28%, 31%, 36% and 39.6%.	A new 10% income tax bracket is carved from the existing 15% bracket. All other tax brackets – except the 15% bracket – will be gradually reduced over six years. Effective for tax years beginning after 12/31/2000.

Individual Tax Rate Reduction Schedule

Year	10%	15%	28%	31%	36%	39.6%
2001	Credit/Refund	15.0%	27.5%[1]	30.5%[1]	35.5%[1]	39.1%[1]
2002-2003	10.0%	15.0%	27.0%	30.0%	35.0%	38.6%
2004-2005	10.0%	15.0%	26.0%	29.0%	34.0%	37.6%
2006 – later	10.0%	15.0%	25.0%	28.0%	33.0%	35.0%

For 2001, most taxpayers will receive the benefit of the new 10% bracket through a rate reduction credit or a refund check from the Treasury. Based on the 2000 income tax returns, single filers could receive refund checks up to $300, MFJ filers could receive up to $600, and HoH filers could receive up to $500.

---

[1] Averaged rates for entire year. Marginal rate reductions are effective July 1, 2001. For 2001-2007, the 10% rate applies to the first $6,000 of taxable income (Single, MFS), $12,000 (MFJ), and $10,000 (HoH). For 2008 these amounts increase to $7,000 (Single, MFS), $14,000 (MFJ), and $10,000 (HoH). For tax years after 2008, the 10% bracket will be adjusted for inflation.

Continued

Highlights of 2001 Tax Legislation

Item	Prior Law	2001 Legislation
Phaseout of itemized deductions for high-income taxpayers	Allowable itemized deductions of taxpayers with adjusted gross income in excess of certain limits[1] are reduced by 3% of adjusted gross income (AGI) in excess of those limits.	Phases out the limitation on itemized deductions by 1/3 in 2006 and 2007, and by 2/3 in 2008 and 2009. Limitation entirely repealed for tax years beginning after 12/31/09.
Phaseout of personal exemptions for high-income taxpayers	Deduction from taxable income for personal exemptions is ratably reduced for taxpayers with an AGI in excess of certain limits.[2]	Personal exemption phase-out is reduced by 1/3 in 2006 and 2007, and by 2/3 in 2008 and 2009. Limitation is entirely repealed for tax years beginning after 12/31/09.
Child tax credit	Taxpayer is allowed a credit of $500 for each qualifying child under age 17. In limited circumstances, a portion of the credit is refundable.	Increases annual credit amount per child to $600 in 2001 – 2004, $700 in 2005 – 2008, $800 in 2009, and $1,000 in 2010 and later. Also expands refundability of credit.
Adoption tax credit	Allows tax credit of up to $5,000 for qualified adoption expenses (scheduled to expire after 2001) and $6,000 for a special needs child. Also allows an exclusion from income up to $5,000 ($6,000 for a special needs child) for employer-paid/reimbursed adoption expenses.	Increases maximum dollar limitation for adoption credit and income exclusion to $10,000 per child, including special needs children. The tax credit and income exclusion are made permanent. Effective for tax years beginning after 12/31/01.
Dependent care tax credit	Allows a credit of up to 30% of qualifying expenses, limited to $2,400 for one qualifying individual or $4,800 for two. 30% rate reduced (not below 20%) for taxpayers with AGI in excess of $10,000.	Increases maximum credit to 35% of qualifying expenses and credit phase-out applies to taxpayers with AGI in excess of $15,000. Effective for tax years beginning after 12/31/02.

---

[1] For 2001 these limitations are either $132,950, or $66,475 for married couples filing separate returns.
[2] For 2001 these limitations are either $199,450, or $99,725 for married couples filing separate returns.

Continued...

Highlights of 2001 Tax Legislation

Item	Prior Law	2001 Legislation
Marriage penalty relief Standard deduction	The standard deduction amount for couples filing MFJ is set at approximately 167% of the value for single filers.	Beginning in 2005, annually increases the standard deduction amount for MFJ filers (as a % of the amount allowed single filers) until it reaches 200% in 2009.
15% tax bracket breakpoint	The top of the 15% tax bracket for couples filing MFJ is set at approximately 167% of the dollar amount for single filers.	Beginning in 2005, annually increases the top of the 15% tax bracket for MFJ filers (as a % of the dollar amount for single filers) until it reaches 200% in 2008.
Individual alternative minimum tax (AMT)	AMT exemption amounts: $45,000 for couples filing MFJ and surviving spouses; $33,750 for other unmarried persons; $22,500 for married couples filing MFS and estates and trusts.	For calendar years 2001 – 2004 *only, increases the AMT* exemption amounts as follows: $49,000, MFJ and surviving spouses; $35,750 for other unmarried persons; $24,500 for couples filing MFS and estates and trusts. After 2004, the AMT exemption amounts revert to those in the prior law.

Education Provisions

Item	Prior Law	2001 Legislation
Education IRAs[1]	Allows a maximum annual contribution per beneficiary of $500. Qualified expenses are limited to college level studies. Contributions are phased out for contributors with modified AGI in excess of certain limits. Contribution must be made by 12/31 of a particular tax year.	Maximum annual contribution per beneficiary increased to $2,000. Qualified expenses now include both elementary and secondary education costs. Increased phase-out range for contributions from MFJ taxpayers. Contributions may be made up to due date of return (generally April 15th). Provisions effective for tax years beginning after 12/31/01.

---

[1] Subsequent legislation changed the name of education IRAs to Coverdell education savings accounts.

Continued.

Highlights of 2001 Tax Legislation

Item	Prior Law	2001 Legislation
Qualified tuition programs (QTPs)	Grants tax-exempt status to state-run prepaid tuition programs or higher education savings accounts. Distributions from such plans used to pay qualified higher education expenses are taxed under the annuity rules found in IRC Sec. 72.	Extends tax-exempt status to QTPs run by private institutions. Qualifying distributions from QTPs are now excluded from gross income (they are tax-free). Generally effective for tax years beginning after 12/31/01. Distributions from QTPs sponsored by private institutions are excluded from gross income if made on or after 01/01/04.
Student loan interest deduction	Allows a maximum deduction from AGI of $2,500 for interest paid on qualified student loans. Deduction allowed only for interest during first 60 months payments are required. Deduction phased out for taxpayers with modified AGI in excess of specified limits[1].	Repeals the 60-month limitation. Applies to loan interest paid after 12/31/01. Increases the modified AGI phase-out ranges to $50,000 - $65,000 for single taxpayers and $100,000 - $130,000 for MFJ taxpayers. Effective for tax years ending after 12/31/01.
Deduction for qualified higher-education expenses	Did not exist under prior law.	Allows a deduction from AGI for qualified higher education tuition and related expenses. Maximum deduction is $3,000 for 2002 and 2003, and $4,000 for 2004 and 2005. Maximum deduction subject to reduction if taxpayer's AGI exceeds certain limits. Deduction limits coordinated with other federal education tax provisions. Deduction ceases to exist for tax years after 12/31/05.

---

[1] $40,000-$55,000 for single taxpayers; $60,000 - $75,000 for married taxpayers filing jointly.

Continued...

Highlights of 2001 Tax Legislation

Retirement Planning Provisions

Item	Prior Law	2001 Legislation
IRAs - Increased contribution limits, including "catch-up" contributions.	Maximum annual contribution to an IRA is limited to $2,000 per year. No catch-up contributions for older taxpayers.	Increases maximum annual contribution to an IRA until it reaches $5,000 for 2008 and later. Allows taxpayers 50 and over to make additional catch-up contributions.

Maximum IRA Dollar Contribution Limits

Tax Years Beginning In	Taxpayers Under Age 50	Taxpayers Age 50 or Over
2002-2004	$3,000	$3,500
2005	$4,000	$4,500
2006	$4,000	$5,000
2007	$4,000	$5,000
2008 and later	$5,000	$6,000

Item	Prior Law	2001 Legislation
Defined contribution plans Contribution limits	Generally, for 2001, the maximum annual addition per participant limited to the lesser of $35,000 or 25% of compensation (maximum of $170,000).	Maximum annual addition per participant limited to the lesser of $40,000 or 100% of compensation (maximum of $200,000). Effective for 2002 tax year and indexed for inflation thereafter.
Elective deferral limitations	For 2001, the maximum annual elective deferral to an IRC Sec. 401(k) plan or 403(b) annuity is $10,500. The maximum annual elective deferral to an IRC Sec. 408(p) SIMPLE plan is $6,500. No age 50 and over catch-up contributions permitted.	Increases the maximum elective deferral amounts as shown in the table below. Maximum deferral amounts indexed for inflation in years after 2006 (2005 for SIMPLE plans). Participants 50 and older permitted to make catch-up contributions.
Tax-exempt or state/local government (IRC Sec. 457) plans	Generally, the maximum annual deferral is the lesser of $8,500 or 1/3 of participant's compensation (limited to $170,000). No age 50 and over catch-up contributions permitted.	Increases the maximum elective deferral amounts as shown in the table below. Deferral amounts indexed for inflation in years after 2006. Participants 50 and older permitted to make catch-up contributions.

Continued..

Highlights of 2001 Tax Legislation

Maximum Elective Deferral Limitations

Year	401(k), 403(b), 457 Plans		408(p) SIMPLE Plans	
	General Limit	Catch-Up Limit	General Limit	Catch-Up Limit
2002	$11,000	$12,000	$7,000	$7,500
2003	$12,000	$14,000	$8,000	$9,000
2004	$13,000	$16,000	$9,000	$10,500
2005	$14,000	$18,000	$10,000	$12,000
2006	$15,000	$20,000	$10,000[1]	$12,500

Item	Prior Law	2001 Legislation
Defined benefit plans – Maximum benefit	Generally, the lesser of $140,000 or 100% of average compensation (maximum of $170,000 considered). Limit is reduced if benefits begin prior to Social Security retirement age and limitation increased if benefits begin after Social Security retirement age.[2]	Increases the annual dollar limit to the lesser of $160,000 or 100% of compensation (maximum of $200,000 considered). Dollar limitation reduced if benefits begin before age 62 and increased if begun after age 65.
Credit for IRA contributions and elective deferrals	Did not exist under prior law.	Provides a nonrefundable income tax credit for lower income taxpayers who make qualified contributions to IRAs or deferrals to retirement savings plans. Effective for tax years beginning after 12/31/01 through 12/31/06.

---

[1] Indexed for inflation in $500 increments in this and later years.
[2] The Social Security normal retirement age is scheduled to increase until it reaches age 67 for individuals born in 1960 and later.

Continued...

Highlights of 2001 Tax Legislation

Estate and Gift Tax Provisions

Item	Prior Law	2001 Legislation
Estate and generation-skipping transfer (GST) tax	The federal estate tax imposes a levy on the transfer assets at death. The GST tax is an additional tax on the transfer of assets at death, specifically on transfers to distant generations.	Repeals both the federal estate tax and the GST tax for decedents dying after 12/31/09. The repeal is effective for only one year (2010). Current law is reinstated for decedents dying after 12/31/10.
Estate and gift tax rates	Transfers during life and at death are taxed under a Unified Transfer Tax Schedule, with marginal rates ranging from 18% to 55%. Cumulative transfers in excess of $10,000,000 have an additional 5% surcharge added until the benefits of the lower, graduated rates are recaptured.	For the estates of decedents dying, and gifts made, after 12/31/01, the 5% surcharge is repealed. The top marginal rate applicable to both estate and gift taxes is reduced, as shown in the following "Estate Tax Changes" table. In 2010, the highest marginal gift tax rate will be 35%.
Estate and GST at-death transfer exemption	Allows a specified dollar amount of assets transferred during life and at death to be exempt from tax. For 2001, this "applicable exclusion amount" is equal to $675,000 of assets.	Gradually increases the applicable exclusion amount for assets transferred at death (estate taxes) for decedents dying after 12/31/01 and before 01/01/10, as shown in the following "Estate Tax Changes" table. For assets transferred during life (gift taxes), increases the applicable exclusion amount to $1,000,000, for gifts made after 12/31/01.

Federal Estate Tax Changes (FET)

Calendar Year	FET and GST At-Death Exemption	Highest FET Rate	Gift Tax Exemption	Highest Gift Tax Rate
2002	$1,000,000	50%	$1,000,000	50%
2003	$1,000,000	49%	$1,000,000	49%
2004	$1,500,000	48%	$1,000,000	48%
2005	$1,500,000	47%	$1,000,000	47%
2006	$2,000,000	46%	$1,000,000	46%
2007	$2,000,000	45%	$1,000,000	45%
2008	$2,000,000	45%	$1,000,000	45%
2009	$3,500,000	45%	$1,000,000	45%
2010	Tax Repealed	Tax Repealed	$1,000,000	35%
2011	$1,000,000	55%	$1,000,000	55%

Continued...

Highlights of 2001 Tax Legislation

Item	Prior Law	2001 Legislation
Basis of inherited assets	The tax basis of property acquired from a decedent at death was generally adjusted to its fair market value on the date of death (or on the alternative valuation date, if selected). Assets that had appreciated in value received a "stepped-up" basis while assets that had declined in value received a "stepped-down" basis.	Effective for decedents dying after 12/31/09, a "carry-over" basis rule applies. The tax basis of inherited property will generally be the lesser of the adjusted basis in the hands of the decedent or the fair market value on the date of death. Executors will be able to increase the basis of inherited assets up to $1,300,000 (additional $3,000,000 for property passing to a surviving spouse). The carry-over basis rules expire in 2011.
Credit for state death taxes	A credit against the federal estate tax for death taxes paid to states was allowed.	Reduces the allowable state death tax credit as follows by 25% in 2002, 50% in 2003 and 75% in 2004. In 2005, the credit is repealed entirely and is replaced with a deduction.
Qualified family-owned business interest (QFOBI) exclusion	An exclusion from the gross estate for the value of certain family-owned business interests was allowed.	QFOBI exclusion repealed for estates of decedents dying after 12/31/03.

Tax Act of 2001 Phase-in Timeline

Due to the dependence of The Economic Growth and Tax Relief Reconciliation Act of 2001 (hereafter tax act) on future budget surpluses, many of the provisions are phased in over a significant period of time. The table below illustrates some of the key aspects of the tax act and the timeline during which full implementation will take place. Some experts feel that such a long timetable almost guarantees that certain provisions will be changed prior to full implementation.

In addition to the long phase-in period, the act contains a "sunset provision" that returns the pre-tax act law in 2011. This means that it will require another act of Congress to continue the provisions of this act beyond 2010.

Provision	Pre-Tax Act	2001	2002	2003	2004	2005	2006	2007	2008	2009	2010
Estate Tax											
Top rate	55%	55%	50%	49%	48%	47%	46%	45%			Repealed
Exemption	$675,000		$1M		$1.5M		$2M			$3.5M	Repealed
Income Tax											
Marginal rates	39.6%	39.1%	38.6%		37.6%		35.0%				
	36.0%	35.5%	35.0%		34.0%		33.0%				
	31.0%	30.5%	30.0%		29.0%		28.0%				
	28.0%	27.5%	27.0%		26.0%		25.0%				
	15.0%	First $6,000 for single and $12,000 for married moved to 10% bracket							Increase to $7,000 and $14,000	$7,000 and $14,000 threshold amounts indexed for inflation	
	10.0% rate did not exist	10.0% rate introduced on first $6,000 for single and $12,000 for married							Increase to $7,000 and $14,000	$7,000 and $14,000 threshold amounts indexed for inflation	
Standard deduction for married filing joint (MFJ)	Less than twice single level						Gradually increases			Twice single level	
15% bracket for MFJ	Less than twice single level						Less than twice single level		Twice single level		
Child credit	$500	$600				$700				$800	$1,000
Personal exemption limit	Current level						Phase-in of repeal				Repealed
IRA contributions limit	$2,000		$3,000			$4,000			$5,000	$5,000 indexed for inflation	
Alternative minimum tax exemption	$33,750 for single $45,000 for married	$35,750 for single $49,000 for married				$33,750 for single $45,000 for married					

Personal Property and Casualty Insurance

Protecting What You Own

Property and casualty (P&C) is the term commonly used to describe insurance designed to protect an individual from loss or damage to the physical assets he or she owns. For example, a fire may seriously damage or completely destroy a home. Without adequate homeowner's insurance to provide the funds to repair or rebuild, such a loss could be a  financial disaster. Homeowner's policies can also provide protection for the home's contents, such as furniture, appliances, and other personal belongings.

Many P&C policies also provide liability protection. For example, the owner of an automobile who causes an accident may be required by a court (be found "liable") to pay others for repair of property damage, medical expenses, lost wages, or pain and suffering. The dollar amounts of such court decisions can be enormous.

Types of Policies

There is a wide variety of property and casualty policies. A number of additional coverages (endorsements) can be added to a basic policy to provide protection against risks found only in certain geographical areas, to protect specific types of property, or to cover a temporary situation. Some of the most common types of policies and endorsements include:

- **Automobile insurance:** Auto policies typically cover repair of physical damage, payments for medical expenses, and liability protection. A separate policy is often used to cover recreational vehicles such as motor homes, golf carts, snowmobiles, trailers, ATVs, or campers.

- **Homeowner's insurance:** A homeowner's policy can provide protection for both the home and its contents, against a wide range of perils, as well as provide very broad personal liability coverage.

- **Condo unit owner's insurance:** Similar to the homeowner's policy, the condo unit owner's policy differs primarily in that coverage is provided primarily for the contents.

- **Renter's insurance:** Renter's policies provide coverage for the personal property of an individual renting a home, condo, or apartment. A renter's policy can also include personal liability coverage similar to that found in a homeowner's or condo unit owner's policy.

- **Earthquake insurance:** Earthquake insurance is normally offered as an endorsement to a homeowner's, condo unit owner's policy, or renter's policy to provide protection against loss caused by earthquake. It can also be a stand-alone policy.

- **Flood insurance:** Flood insurance is provided through a separate policy. The federal government stands as the ultimate guarantor for flood policies.

Continued...

Personal Property and Casualty Insurance

- **Watercraft insurance:** Watercraft policies cover loss and liability for the personal use of small watercraft such as boats or jet skis or for larger craft such as ocean-going yachts.

- **Umbrella liability:** Acts as excess or catastrophic protection to the basic liability protection offered with most other P&C policies. The liability coverage offered by an "umbrella" policy begins where the coverage in a basic policy ends and, in some instances, offers broader protection.

Uniform Policy Forms

The Insurance Service Office (ISO) and the American Association of Insurance Services (AAIS) are industry service organizations that provide actuarial and loss information to P&C insurers. These service organizations also provide standardized, uniform policy agreements, called "forms," which are used by many insurers[1]. Such standardized policy forms make it easier for a consumer to understand the terms of the policy and to compare policies offered by different insurance firms.

Understand the Contract

An insurance policy is a written contract between the insured and the insurance company. The protection provided by P&C policies of all types typically represents a significant part of an individual's overall risk management program. Thus, it's important for an insured individual to read and understand key policy provisions, such as:

- **What perils (or risks) are covered in the policy?** Two basic approaches are involved. In the "named-peril" form, the policy will specify only those perils that are covered. In the "all-risk" form, the policy will list only those perils that are not covered and provide protection for all others.

- **What perils are not covered?** In many cases, perils that are excluded can be covered by endorsement and payment of an additional premium.

- **What are the policy limits?** What is the maximum benefit/coverage payable by the insurance company in the event of a loss? Is a home that would cost $200,000 to rebuild insured for $100,000?

- **What are the deductible amounts?** A policy deductible is the self-insurance element in an insurance policy; the term refers to the part of the loss the policy buyer must pay before the insurance company pays its portion. The deductible can be a flat amount or a percentage of the insured value at the time of a loss.

---

[1] Some insurers have their own forms, which may differ from the standard contracts developed by ISO or AAIS.

Continued.

Personal Property and Casualty Insurance

- **Impact of inflation:** A home built 20 years ago can be rebuilt, but at a much higher cost. Most policy forms provide for replacement cost of a home and contents, along with an annual inflation guard of between 2% and 6%.

- **In the event of a loss, what are the duties of the insured?** Each policy will specify certain actions that an insured must take in the event of a loss.

Seek Professional Guidance

Insurance agents and brokers, insurance counselors, and other trained financial advisors can help provide detailed answers to questions about a particular policy. These professionals are also helpful in selecting the right policy and the appropriate amount of coverage.

Automobile Insurance

Why Automobile Insurance?

For most Americans, the automobile is a beneficial and
essential part of modern life. Owning or operating a
car, however, can also be a source of serious financial
risk. Personal liability arising from losses suffered by
others, or the cost of repairing or replacing a damaged
or stolen vehicle, can be very high.

Also, most states have compulsory auto liability insurance laws, requiring auto owners to
maintain liability insurance as a condition of licensing or use on public roadways. Other
states require auto owners to show proof of financial responsibility before and after an
accident.

Coverage Under the Policy

Automobile insurance usually covers a number of risks in one package policy. The most
frequently used policy is the personal automobile policy (PAP).[1] The PAP is designed
primarily for private passenger automobiles, but protection can be extended to cover other
types of vehicles. Typical coverage includes the following:

- **Liability insurance:** This coverage protects the owner against losses from legal liability
  arising from bodily injury or property damage caused by an automobile accident. The
  coverage can be a single limit ($100,000 for each accident) or split limits such as
  $50,000 / $100,000 / $25,000 (per person / per accident for bodily injury / property
  damage).

- **Medical payments coverage:** This provision pays medical or funeral expenses because
  of bodily injury. The coverage is generally in increments of $1,000 to $5,000 up to
  $25,000 per person per accident.

- **Physical damage coverage:** This section of the policy is designed to cover physical
  damage to the insured auto. Collision covers, as the name implies, collision losses.
  Comprehensive (also known as other-than-collision) insurance covers losses from non-
  collision incidents, such as theft, fire, or storm damage. Losses for physical damage are
  generally based on the cost to repair or replace the damaged or stolen vehicle.

- **Uninsured/underinsured motorist:** Even though many states have enacted financial
  responsibility laws, not all automobile owners comply. Uninsured motorist coverage
  pays for injuries[2] sustained in an accident with an uninsured (or a hit-and-run) driver.
  Underinsured motorist insurance covers the difference between actual losses sustained,
  and what an insured individual can collect from an at-fault uninsured or underinsured
  driver, up to policy limits.

---

[1] The specific coverage and terms of a policy may vary from company to company, and from state to state.
[2] In some states, uninsured motorist property damage is also included.

Continued..

Automobile Insurance

Adding Additional Coverage

There are a number of additional coverages that can be added (by endorsement) to a basic policy to provide insurance for unusual situations or to protect other types of vehicles. Two of the most common endorsements include:

- **Extended liability:** Used to cover automobiles that are not legally owned by the insured, such as an auto furnished by an employer for the regular use of the insured and/or the family. Extends the policy coverage to situations involving non-owned vehicles, which standard policy provisions would otherwise exclude.

- **Miscellaneous type vehicle endorsements:** Allows the insured to cover vehicles such as snowmobiles, motorcycles, motor scooters, go-carts, golf carts, antique and classic cars, motorhomes, and campers. In some states, a separate policy is used to cover these vehicles.

Understand the Policy

An insurance policy is a written contract between the insured and the insurance company. The protection provided by the policy typically represents a significant part of an individual's overall risk management program. Thus, it is important for an insured individual to read and understand key policy provisions such as:

- **What perils are covered in the policy?** A basic policy may not provide as much protection as is necessary.

- **What perils are not covered?** For an additional premium, coverage for excluded perils or situations can often be added to a policy.

- **What are the limits of coverage?** The maximum dollar amount the insurance company will pay in the event of a covered loss.

- **What are the deductible amounts?** A deductible is a dollar amount the insured must pay before the insurance company pays its portion.

- **In the event of a loss, what are the duties of the insured?** A policy will usually list the steps that must be taken in the event of a loss.

Seek Professional Guidance

Insurance agents and brokers, insurance counselors, and other trained financial advisors can help provide answers to detailed questions about a particular policy. These professionals are also helpful in selecting the right policy and the appropriate amount of coverage.

Homeowner's Insurance

Why Homeowner's Insurance?

A home is the single biggest investment most
individuals will ever make; it is typically the largest
asset on the family "balance sheet." Also, the contents
of a typical home, in the form of furniture, appliances,
clothing, family heirlooms, and other movable
personal belongings, represent a substantial additional
investment. The unprotected loss (or partial loss) of a home and its contents to theft, fire,
windstorm, or some other disaster, could be financially devastating.[1]

Further, everyone faces the risk of personal liability. For example, a visitor to the
residence could slip and fall. Such accidents can result in court decisions awarding large
sums to the injured party for medical expenses, and "pain and suffering."

Coverage Under the Policy

Originally, a standard homeowner's policy covered only the risk of fire. Today's
homeowner's policies provide protection against a number of the "perils" of modern life,
in one "package" policy. A typical[2] homeowner's policy can provide insurance protection
for the following:

- **Home:** The physical dwelling structure and other structures attached to it.

- **Other structures:** For example, a detached garage, pool house, guesthouse, green
house, or tool shed.

- **Personal property:** This covers the contents of the home, such as furniture, appliances
or clothing. Certain types of property[3] may have specific dollar limits.

- **Loss of use or additional living expense:** If a home is damaged by a covered peril,
loss-of-use coverage helps meet the costs of hotel bills, apartment or rental home, eating
out, and other living expenses while the home is being repaired. This policy section can
also reimburse a homeowner for lost income if a room in the home were rented out.
This is sometimes insured on an actual-loss-sustained basis.

- **Personal liability:** Provides protection against legal liability for bodily injury or
property damage if a third party is accidentally injured.

- **Medical payments:** Also known as guest-medical payments, this section provides
coverage if a third party is accidentally injured and needs medical treatment.

---

[1] Many mortgage lenders require homeowner's insurance, to protect the dwelling, as a condition of granting the mortgage.
[2] The specific coverage and terms of a policy will vary from company to company, and from state to state.
[3] Jewelry, silverware, securities, cash, and collectibles are examples of personal property subject to these "internal" policy
limits.

Continu

Homeowner's Insurance

Policy Forms

There are several organizations that work with insurance companies to provide standardized homeowner's policies. While the details of a particular policy can vary, these standardized policies, or "forms" are generally very similar.[1] Some of the most commonly found homeowner's insurance forms include:

- **Broad form package policy (HO 02):** This contract covers liability exposures and property damage on a named-peril basis. There are 16 named perils, and only these named perils are covered.

- **Special form package policy (HO 03):** The principal difference between the HO 02 and the HO 03 is that the HO 03 is written on an "all-risk" basis. This means that damage from any peril is covered, unless specifically excluded. This is the most widely used policy form for most insurance companies.

- **Modified form coverage (HO 08):** This policy is designed to cover homes where the cost to rebuild exceeds the market value of the property. If a home is destroyed, the insurance will restore the home on a "functionally equivalent" basis using modern construction techniques.

Policy Exclusions

The standard homeowner's policies specifically exclude a number of perils from coverage. Policy coverage of these excluded perils can generally be added through an endorsement and payment of an additional premium. Typical policy exclusions might include the following:

- **Ordinance or law:** Many homeowner's policies do not cover losses, or have limitations, due to a law or ordinance of the community in which the home is located. For example, if a home is damaged or destroyed, changes in building codes could result in additional, uncovered expense when the home is repaired or rebuilt. Ordinance or law coverage is included in some package policies, often as a percentage of the dwelling coverage (10%, 25%, 50%, etc.). This coverage is required in some states.

- **Earth movement:** Excludes loss caused by events such as earthquake, volcanic eruption, or landslide.

- **Water damage:** Refers to damage from water that backs up from sewers or drains, or water seeping through walls. Many policies contain dollar limits for water damage due to such things as a broken pipe.

- **Flood damage:** Refers to damage from rising water, mudslide, or wave action.

- **Mold Exclusion:** Due to high claims activity for losses caused by mold, many insurance companies are excluding coverage for mold damage.

- **Other exclusions:** Other specific exclusions include war, nuclear hazard, neglect, and intentional loss.

---

[1] The specific coverage and terms of a policy will vary from company to company and from state to state.

Continued...

Homeowner's Insurance

Other Issues

- **Replacement cost condition - Dwelling and other structures:** If a home is damaged or totally destroyed, a homeowner's policy will generally pay (within policy limits) to rebuild or repair on an "actual-cash-value" basis. In simple terms, actual cash value means replacement cost, less a deduction for depreciation or for wear and tear. Reimbursement on this basis could leave a homeowner short of the total funds needed to restore the home.

  Through an endorsement and payment of an additional premium, reimbursement can be on a "replacement-cost" basis. Replacement cost means, simply, restoring the home to its previous condition, using materials and workmanship of similar quality. In some policies, the availability of this feature requires the homeowner to maintain coverage on the home equal to at least 80% of the cost to rebuild or repair. If insurance coverage were not maintained at the 80% level, any loss would be reimbursed at a lesser amount, or on an actual-cash-value or depreciated basis.

- **Replacement cost - Personal property (contents):** Coverage is normally on an actual-cash-value basis. For an additional premium, the policy can usually be endorsed to protect covered personal property on a replacement-cost basis (the cost to buy the item new today) without considering depreciation.

- **Inflation guard rider:** The standard policy forms can usually be endorsed to provide for automatic, periodic increases in policy limits. These increases in policy coverage generally apply to both the dwelling and contents, and help avoid being underinsured due to inflation. Such an endorsement also helps meet the 80%-of-replacement-cost condition to qualify for replacement cost on the home.

Understand the Policy

An insurance policy is a written contract between the insured and the insurance company. The protection provided by the policy typically represents a significant part of an individual's overall risk management program. Thus, it's important for an insured individual to read and understand key policy provisions such as the following.

- **What perils are covered in the policy?** A basic policy may not provide as much protection as is necessary.

- **What perils are not covered?** For an additional premium, perils or situations not covered can often be added to a policy.

- **What are the limits of coverage?** This refers to the maximum dollar amount the insurance company will pay, in the event of a covered loss.

- **What are the deductible amounts?** A deductible is a dollar amount or percentage the insured must pay before the insurance company pays its portion of the loss.

- **In the event of a loss, what are the duties of the insured?** A policy will usually list the steps that must be taken in the event of a loss.

Continue

Homeowner's Insurance

Seek Professional Guidance

Insurance agents and brokers, insurance counselors, and other trained financial advisors can help provide answers to detailed questions about a particular policy. These professionals are also helpful in selecting the right policy and the appropriate amount of coverage.

Renter's Insurance

Why Renter's Insurance?

Many people who rent their home do not consider insurance, usually because they are not making an investment in real property. However, the contents of a home, in the form of furniture, appliances, clothing, family heirlooms and other movable personal belongings, often represent a substantial investment. The unprotected loss (or partial loss) of a renter's personal property to theft, fire, windstorm or some other incident could be financially devastating.

Further, each individual, whether a renter or homeowner, faces the risk of personal liability. For example, a visitor to the residence could slip and fall. Such accidents can result in court decisions awarding large sums to the injured party for medical expenses and "pain and suffering."

Coverage Under the Policy

Most renter's policies available today are closely related in design to policies created for homeowners, and combine protection against a number of the perils of modern life in a single package policy. The primary difference is that a renter's policy does not provide protection for the building structure. A typical[1] renter's policy can provide insurance protection for the following.

- **Personal property:** Covers the contents of the home, such as furniture, appliances, or clothing. Coverage is generally provided on a named-peril basis. Perils that are not named are excluded from coverage. Certain types of property[2] may have specific dollar limits.

- **Loss of use or additional living expenses:** If a rented home is damaged by a covered peril, loss-of-use coverage helps meet the costs of hotel bills, apartment or rental home, eating out, and other living expenses, while the home is being repaired.

- **Personal liability:** Provides protection against legal liability for bodily injury or property damage if a third party is accidentally injured.

- **Medical payments:** Also known as guest medical payments, this section provides coverage if a third party is accidentally injured and needs medical treatment.

- **Building additions and alterations:** Covers improvements, fixtures or alterations made by a tenant, such as paint, wallpaper, carpets, drapes, and blinds.

---

[1] The specific coverage and terms of a policy will vary from company to company, and from state to state.
[2] Jewelry, silverware, securities, cash, and collectibles are examples of personal property subject to these "internal" policy limits.

Continue

Renter's Insurance

Policy Exclusions

A standard renter's policy specifically excludes a number of perils from coverage. Policy coverage of these excluded perils can generally be added through an endorsement and payment of an additional premium. Typical policy exclusions include the following:

- **Earth movement:** Losses caused by earthquake, volcanic eruption, or landslide.

- **Water damage:** Refers to damage from water that backs up from sewers or drains, or water seeping through walls. Many policies contain dollar limits for water damage due to such things as a broken pipe.

- **Flood damage:** Refers to damage from rising water, mudslide, or wave action.

- **Mold exclusion:** Due to high claims activity for losses caused by mold, many insurance companies are excluding coverage for mold damage.

- **Other exclusions:** Such as wear and tear, war, nuclear hazard, neglect, and intentional loss.

Other Issues

- **Personal property (contents):** A standard renter's policy will insure a home's contents for actual cash value; e.g., replacement cost less an allowance for depreciation or wear and tear. For an additional premium, the policy can usually be endorsed to protect covered personal property on a replacement-cost basis (the cost to buy the item new today), without considering depreciation.

- **Inflation guard rider:** The standard policy can usually be endorsed to provide for automatic, periodic increases in policy limits. These automatic increases in policy coverage help avoid being underinsured because items cost more due to inflation.

Understand the Policy

An insurance policy is a written contract between the insured and the insurance company. The protection provided by the policy typically represents a significant part of an individual's overall risk-management program. Thus, it's important for an insured individual to read and understand key policy provisions such as the following:

- **What perils are covered in the policy?** A basic policy may not provide as much protection as is necessary.

- **What perils are not covered?** For an additional premium, excluded perils or situations can often be added to a policy.

- **What are the limits of coverage?** This refers to the maximum dollar amount the insurance company will pay in the event of a covered loss.

- **What are the deductible amounts?** A deductible is a dollar amount or percentage the insured must pay before the insurance company pays its portion of the loss.

- **In the event of a loss, what are the duties of the insured?** A policy will usually list the steps that must be taken in the event of a loss.

Continued...

Renter's Insurance

Seek Professional Guidance

Insurance agents and brokers, insurance counselors, and other trained financial advisors can help provide answers to detailed questions about a particular policy. These professionals are also helpful in selecting the right policy and the appropriate amount of coverage.

Condominium Unit Owner's Insurance

Why Condo Unit Owner's Insurance?

A home, be it a single-family dwelling or a condominium unit, is usually the biggest investment that most individuals will ever make; it is typically the largest asset on the family balance sheet. Also, the contents of a typical home, in the form of furniture, appliances, clothing, family heirlooms, and other movable personal belongings, represent a substantial additional investment. The unprotected loss (or partial loss) of a home and its contents, to theft, fire, windstorm, or some other disaster, could be financially devastating.

Further, everyone faces the risk of personal liability. For example, a visitor to the residence could slip and fall. Such accidents can result in court decisions awarding large sums to the injured party for medical expenses, and "pain and suffering."

Condominium Ownership

A condominium is a building divided into separate living spaces (units), owned by individuals, and the common areas, owned jointly by all of the individual unit owners. Overall management of the complex is carried out by a homeowner's or condo unit owner's association. This association makes policy decisions for the community and is responsible for maintaining and insuring the building structure and common areas of the condominium complex. The individual condo unit owner is responsible for the interior of his or her own unit.

Coverage Under the Policy

Most condo unit owner's policies available today are closely related in design to policies created for single-family homeowners, and provide protection against a number of the perils of modern life in a single package policy. The protection available under a condo unit owner's policy differs from a typical homeowner's policy primarily in the type of coverage provided for the dwelling. A typical[1] condo unit owner's policy can provide coverage for the following:

- **Condo unit:** This section provides protection for the unit owner's real property, also known as "unit owner's additions and alterations."[2] The items included here will vary with state law, but can include such interior furnishings as wallpaper, paneling, kitchen and bathroom cabinets, carpeting or wet bar. Coverage is generally provided on a named-peril basis. Perils that are not named are excluded. This can be endorsed on an all-risk basis for an additional premium.

---

[1] The specific coverage and terms of a policy will vary from company to company and from state to state.
[2] In common practice, this has also been described as "from the bare wall in."

Continued...

Condominium Unit Owner's Insurance

- **Other structures:** These might include a detached garage or tool shed, if owned solely by the insured.

- **Personal property:** Covers the contents of the unit, such as furniture, appliances or clothing. Certain types of property[1] may have specific dollar limits.

- **Loss of use or additional living expenses:** If a condo unit is damaged by a covered peril, loss-of-use coverage helps meet the costs of hotel bills, apartment or rental home, eating out, and other living expenses while the home is being repaired.

- **Personal liability:** Provides protection against legal liability for bodily injury or property damage if a third party is accidentally injured.

- **Medical payments:** Also known as guest medical payments, this section provides coverage if a third party is accidentally injured and needs medical treatment.

- **Loss assessment:** If the homeowner's association suffers a loss[2], it may assess each owner to pay a portion of the loss. If the loss were the result of a covered peril, this policy provision would pay the insured's portion of the assessment, up to the limit specified in the endorsement.

Policy Exclusions

A standard policy specifically excludes a number of perils from coverage. Policy coverage of these excluded perils can generally be added through an endorsement and payment of an additional premium. Typical policy exclusions include the following:

- **Earth movement:** Losses caused by earthquake, volcanic eruption, or landslide.

- **Water damage:** Refers to damage from water that backs up from sewers or drains, or water seeping through walls. Many policies contain dollar limits for water damage due to such things as a broken pipe.

- **Flood damage:** Refers to damage from rising water, mudslide or wave action.

- **Mold exclusion:** Due to high claims activity for losses caused by mold, many insurance companies are excluding coverage for mold damage.

- **Other exclusions:** Such as wear and tear, war, nuclear hazard, neglect and intentional loss.

Other Issues

- **Personal property** (contents): A standard policy will insure a condominium unit for actual cash value; e.g., replacement cost less an allowance for depreciation or wear and tear. For an additional premium, the policy can usually be endorsed to protect covered property on a replacement cost basis (the cost to buy the item new today), without considering depreciation.

---

[1] Jewelry, silverware, securities, cash, and collectibles are examples of personal property subject to these internal policy limits.

[2] For example, from deductible liability or major, uncovered property damage.

Continued...

Condominium Unit Owner's Insurance

- **Inflation guard rider:** The standard policy can usually be endorsed to provide for automatic, periodic increases in policy limits. These increases in policy coverage generally apply to both the dwelling and contents, and help avoid being underinsured due to inflation.

Understand the Policy

An insurance policy is a written contract between the insured and the insurance company. The protection provided by the policy typically represents a significant part of an individual's overall risk-management program. Thus, it's important for an insured individual to read and understand key policy provisions such as the following.

- **What perils are covered in the policy?** A basic policy may not provide as much protection as is necessary.

- **What perils are not covered?** For an additional premium, excluded perils or situations can often be added to a policy.

- **What are the limits of coverage?** This refers to the maximum dollar amount the insurance company will pay in the event of a covered loss.

- **What are the deductible amounts?** A deductible is a dollar amount or percentage the insured must pay before the insurance company pays its portion of the loss.

- **In the event of a loss, what are the duties of the insured?** A policy will usually list the steps that must be taken in the event of a loss.

Seek Professional Guidance

Insurance agents and brokers, insurance counselors, and other trained financial advisors can help provide answers to detailed questions about a particular policy. These professionals are also helpful in selecting the right policy and the appropriate amount of coverage.

Earthquake Insurance

Why Earthquake Insurance?

Earthquakes can do a great deal of damage to a home and the personal possessions in it. A severe earthquake can completely destroy a home and its contents. Such a loss, if uninsured, could devastate most individuals and their families.

Excluded from Standard Policies

In most homeowner's, renter's, and condominium unit owner's policies there is a specific exclusion for loss caused by "earth movement," a term that includes earthquakes. To cover this, a basic policy must be endorsed to include earth movement, for which the insured pays an additional premium. As an alternative, a separate earthquake policy may be purchased.

Earth movement is generally defined as "earthquake, including land shockwaves or tremors before, during or after a volcanic eruption; landslide; mine subsidence, mudflow, earth sinking, rising or shifting." The term earthquake generally means a "vibration generating rupture event caused by displacement within the earth's crust through release of strain associated with tectonic processes and includes effects such as ground shaking, liquefaction, seismically-induced land sliding and damaging amplification of ground motion."

Adding Other Coverage

In many locations, an insured can add an earth movement endorsement to a basic policy. The endorsement usually covers only structures and/or personal property, and does not cover damage to the land itself. It usually excludes flood or tidal waves generated by earth movement.

The earth movement endorsement is subject to a percentage deductible (generally 10% to 25% of the value of the property insured), compared with the usual flat dollar deductible amount. To understand this different type of deductible, suppose a person's home is insured for $200,000 and its contents insured for $60,000. If there is a total loss from an earthquake and the policy has a 10% deductible, the individual would face a deductible of $20,000 on the value of the home and $6,000 on the value of the contents.

Seek Professional Guidance

Insurance agents and brokers, insurance counselors, and other trained financial advisors can help provide answers to detailed questions about a particular policy. These professionals are also helpful in selecting the right policy and the appropriate amount of coverage.

Flood Insurance

Why Flood Insurance?

A moderate flood can do a great deal of
damage to a home and its personal belongings.
A severe flood can completely destroy a home
and its contents. Such a loss, if uninsured,
could financially devastate most individuals
and their families.

In addition to the risk of severe financial loss, individuals purchasing or constructing
property in areas subject to severe flooding (a special flood hazard area) may be required
to obtain flood insurance as a condition of obtaining a mortgage. Further, the owner of
property in a special flood hazard area may be denied federal disaster relief after a flood,
unless the owner had previously purchased flood insurance.

Excluded from Standard Policies

In virtually all homeowner's, renter's and condominium unit owner's policies, there is a
specific exclusion for loss caused by flood. To cover this peril, a separate flood insurance
policy must be purchased.

The term "flood" is generally defined as, "A general and temporary condition of partial or
complete inundation of two or more acres of normally dry land area or of two or more
properties (at least one of which is your property) from: overflow of inland or tidal waters;
or the unusual and rapid accumulation or runoff of surface waters from any source;
mudflow; or the collapse or subsidence of land along the shore of a lake or similar body of
water as a result of erosion or undermining caused by waves or currents of water
exceeding anticipated cyclical levels that result in a flood as defined above."

The National Flood Insurance Program

Because of the catastrophic nature of property losses suffered in floods, flood insurance
was, for many years, generally unavailable. In response to this need, the federal
government, in 1968, established the National Flood Insurance Program (NFIP). Under
this program, managed by the Federal Emergency Management Agency (FEMA), the
federal government stands as an insurer of last resort for flood insurance. In exchange for
this guarantee, the government requires participating communities to adopt and enforce
land use measures that direct future development away from flood prone areas.

The availability of flood insurance under the NFIP is conditioned on a community
agreeing to follow federal flood planning requirements. The amount of insurance
available and the type of structures covered, will vary depending on how far along a
community is in meeting all federal conditions.

Continued...

Flood Insurance

- **Emergency program:** Basic coverage under the emergency program (EP) is available when a community agrees to adopt federal standards. For example, coverage under the EP for a single-family residence would be limited to $50,000 on the dwelling and $15,000 on personal property.

- **Regular program:** When a community has completed certain federal requirements, it enters the regular program (RP). Under the RP, additional coverage becomes available. For example, coverage under the RP for a single-family residence can be as much as $250,000 on the dwelling and $100,000 for personal property. Excess flood insurance for higher limits outside the program is available.

Purchasing Flood Insurance

Flood insurance can be purchased from either the federal government or private insurers and is sold by insurance agents and brokers. The insurance agents receive a commission for policies sold.

With limited exceptions, there is a 30-day waiting period between the time an insured applies for coverage and pays the premium, before the coverage is in effect.

Coverage Under the Policy

A typical residential flood policy provides coverage for "direct physical loss by or from flood," for the following:

- **Dwelling:** Covers damage or loss to the building.

- **Personal property:** Refers to the contents of a home, such as furniture, appliances or clothing. Certain types of property may be excluded or have a specific dollar limit.[1]

- **Debris removal:** Covers debris removal of or on an insured property after a flood.

Policy Exclusions

The standard flood policy specifically excludes a number of perils from coverage. Policy coverage of these excluded perils can generally be added through an endorsement and payment of an additional premium. Typical policy exclusions include the following.

- **Ordinance or law:** Many flood policies do not cover losses due to a law or ordinance of the community in which a building is located. For example, if a home is damaged or destroyed, changes in building codes could result in additional, uncovered expense when the home is repaired or rebuilt. Ordinance or law coverage is included in some package policies, often as a percentage of the dwelling coverage (10%, 25%, 50%, etc.).

- **Earth movement:** Excludes loss caused by events such as earthquake, volcanic eruption or landslide.

---

[1] Money, securities, and animals are examples of property usually excluded. Specific dollar limits may apply to items such as paintings, jewelry or furs.

Continued...

Flood Insurance

- **Other exclusions:** Other specific exclusions include war, nuclear hazard, neglect, intentional loss, fire, windstorm and explosion.

Other Issues

- **Replacement cost condition - Dwelling:** If a home is damaged or totally destroyed, a flood policy will generally pay (within policy limits) to rebuild or repair on an actual-cash-value basis. In simple terms, actual cash value means replacement cost, less a deduction for depreciation or wear and tear. Reimbursement on this basis could leave a homeowner short of the total funds needed to restore the home.
  If coverage under the policy is high enough, however, reimbursement can be on a replacement-cost basis. Replacement cost means, simply, restoring the home to its previous condition using materials and workmanship of similar quality. To receive the benefit of replacement cost coverage, the insured must carry either the maximum amount of insurance available under the program or 80% of the replacement cost of the dwelling at the time of loss.

Understand the Policy

An insurance policy is a written contract between the insured and the insurance company. The protection provided by the policy typically represents a significant part of an individual's overall risk management program. Thus, it is important for an insured individual to read and understand key policy provisions such as the following:

- **What perils are covered in the policy?** A basic policy may not provide as much protection as is necessary.

- **What perils are not covered?** For an additional premium, perils or situations not covered can often be added to a policy.

- **What are the limits of coverage?** This refers to the maximum dollar amount the insurance company will pay, in the event of a covered loss.

- **What are the deductible amounts?** A deductible is a dollar amount or percentage the insured must pay before the insurance company pays its portion of the loss.

- **In the event of a loss, what are the duties of the insured?** A policy will usually list the steps that must be taken in the event of a loss.

Seek Professional Guidance

Insurance agents and brokers, insurance counselors, and other trained financial advisors can help provide answers to detailed questions about a particular policy. These professionals are also helpful in selecting the right policy and the appropriate amount of coverage.

Watercraft Insurance

Why Watercraft Insurance?

A large and increasing number of individuals enjoy
the benefits of owning and using a personal
watercraft such as a sailboat or motorboat. Owning
or operating such watercraft, however, can also be a
potential source of serious financial risk. Personal
liability arising from losses suffered by others, or the
cost of repairing or replacing a damaged, destroyed,
or stolen watercraft can be very high.

Further, some states, yacht clubs, marinas, and lake associations have mandatory
watercraft liability requirements, compelling owners to maintain liability insurance as a
condition of licensing or use of facilities and recreation areas.

Sources of Watercraft Insurance

There are a number of sources of insurance coverage for watercraft owners.

- **Homeowner's insurance:** A limited amount of liability coverage for certain types of
small watercraft is provided in many homeowner's[1] policies.

- **Endorsement of a homeowner's policy:** Some homeowner's policies may provide for
coverage for watercraft through endorsement and payment of an additional premium.

- **Comprehensive watercraft insurance:** Such policies can provide a boat owner with
higher levels of coverage, as well as protection against a broader spectrum of perils,
than does a homeowner's policy. Coverage can also be provided for situations unique
to watercraft ownership and use.

Watercraft Insurance - Coverage Under the Policy

In many respects, the protection provided by a comprehensive watercraft insurance policy
(also known as a boat owner's policy) is similar to the coverage offered in many
automobile insurance policies; protection is provided against a number of perils in one
package. Typical coverage[2] includes the following:

- **Physical damage:** Also known as hull coverage, this coverage protects the insured
against damage or loss to a covered watercraft, including trailers[3], outboard motors,
equipment and furnishings. Insurance is typically provided on an all-risk basis, subject
to certain standard exclusions. Reimbursement is generally based on actual cash value,
although some insurers may offer policies using either an agreed value (face amount of
insurance) or a replacement cost option.

---

[1] Policy forms for renter's and condo owners may also provide such coverage.
[2] The specific coverage and terms of a policy may vary from company to company and from state to state.
[3] In some policies, coverage on the trailer is optional.

Continued...

Watercraft Insurance

- **Liability coverage:** This coverage is sometimes called protection and indemnity (P&I) coverage. It protects the owner against losses from legal liability arising from bodily injury or property damage caused by a watercraft accident. Coverage is normally provided up to a specific dollar amount.

- **Medical payments:** This policy provision pays medical expenses because of an injury sustained during an accident involving the insured watercraft. Coverage is usually provided up to a specific dollar amount.

- **Uninsured boater:** This coverage pays for bodily injury sustained in an incident caused by an uninsured boater. The provision usually pays up to a specified dollar limit and is normally offered as an optional coverage.

Common Policy Exclusions

A standard, comprehensive watercraft policy will specifically exclude a number of perils from coverage. In some situations, policy coverage for these excluded perils can be added through an endorsement and the payment of an additional premium. In other situations, a separate policy may be required to provide coverage. Typical policy exclusions might include the following:

- **High-risk watercraft:** Many policies exclude certain types of high-risk watercraft such as waverunners and jet skis. Special policies are available to cover such craft.

- **Nonstandard watercraft:** These include submersible or air-propelled (hovercraft) watercraft.

- **Yachts:** Generally refers to larger vessels capable of navigating on the high seas. Such craft are normally covered under yacht policies.

- **Watercraft used for charter:** The term "charter" refers to using the insured watercraft for hire, rent, or lease.

- **High-risk activities:** Excluded high-risk activities include powerboat racing in an official race or speed contest, as well as towing individuals paragliding or parasailing. Some policies exclude water skiers towed by the insured craft from medical payments coverage.

Other Issues

While property damage and liability are coverages common to many types of property insurance, the ownership and use of watercraft present some unique situations, some of which may be covered in a comprehensive watercraft policy.

- **Wreck removal:** Coverage to pay for the removal of a wreck. For example, the Coast Guard or Army Corps of Engineers may deem a partially sunken vessel to be a hazard to navigation and order it to be removed or destroyed.

- **Salvage charges:** Refers to reasonable and necessary expenses incurred to protect a covered watercraft from a dangerous situation where loss or destruction is possible. May also cover a reward to the salvor.

Continued...

Watercraft Insurance

- **Towing:** Some policies may provide coverage for towing a watercraft (on land or in the water) to the nearest repair site, if the craft is damaged by a covered peril.

- **Longshoremen's and harbor workers' compensation:** Provides coverage for an insured's liability, under the Federal Longshoremen's and Harbor Workers' Compensation Act, for injury to dockside workers. Coverage is statutory, with the terms of coverage prescribed by federal law. It is usually included as a part of the liability coverage in those states that require it.

- **Jones Act:** Protects the owner of the vessel from liability arising from the death of, or injury to, the captain or crew while on the water.

Understand the Policy

An insurance policy is a written contract between the insured and the insurance company. The protection provided by the policy typically represents a significant part of an individual's overall risk management program. Thus, it's important for an insured individual to read and understand key policy provisions such as the following:

- **What perils are covered in the policy?** A basic policy may not provide as much protection as is necessary.

- **What perils are not covered?** For an additional premium, coverage for excluded perils can often be added to a policy.

- **What are the limits of coverage?** The maximum dollar amount the insurance company will pay in the event of a covered loss.

- **What are the deductible amounts?** A deductible is a dollar amount or percentage the insured must pay before the insurance company pays its portion of the loss.

- **In the event of a loss, what are the duties of the insured?** A policy will usually list the steps that must be taken in the event of a loss.

Seek Professional Guidance

Insurance agents and brokers, insurance counselors, and other trained financial advisors can help provide answers to detailed questions about a particular policy. These professionals are also helpful in selecting the right policy and the appropriate amount of coverage.

Individual Liability Insurance

Why Individual Liability Insurance?

The risk of legal liability is a fact of modern life. It is perhaps the largest financial risk most individuals face. Common incidents, such as an automobile accident, or a neighbor's child slipping on a kitchen floor, can result in lawsuits, with damage awards of enormous size. Without liability insurance, most individuals and families could be faced with a financial disaster of enormous proportions.

Further, state law may require liability insurance. For example, some states have compulsory auto liability insurance laws, requiring auto owners to maintain automobile liability insurance as a condition of licensing or use on public roadways. Other states require auto owners to show financial responsibility after an accident.

Sources of Individual Liability Insurance

Liability insurance is designed to cover an insured for acts of negligence that create a legal obligation to a third party. Such liability can have its source in any part of an individual's life. For many individuals, liability insurance is acquired as part of the package policies purchased to protect major assets such as a home, automobile, or watercraft. Typical[1] policies provide the following liability coverage.

- **Homeowner's[2] insurance:** Liability coverage under a homeowner's policy is provided in one of three sections:
  - **Personal liability** – These are payments the insured is legally obligated to make because of bodily injury or property damage.
  - **Medical payments to others** – These are medical expenses of injured third parties.
  - **Additional coverages** – These cover certain expenses incurred by the insured in the event of bodily injury or property damage.
- **Automobile insurance:** Liability coverage under an automobile policy is provided in one of two sections:
  - **Automobile liability** – These are payments the insured is legally obligated to make because of bodily injury or property damage due to an auto accident.
  - **Medical payments** – These are medical or funeral expenses payable because of bodily injury.

---

[1] The specific coverage and terms of a policy will vary from company to company and from state to state.
[2] The liability coverage usually provided under a renter's or a condominium unit owner's policy is similar to that provided in a homeowner's policy.

Continued...

Individual Liability Insurance

- **Watercraft liability insurance:** Liability protection under a watercraft policy is typically provided in the protection and indemnity (P&I) section. P&I includes coverage for the following.
  - **Bodily injury** – These are payments the insured is required to make for pain and suffering, disfigurement, loss of mobility, or actual medical costs.
  - **Property damage** – Covers damage or destruction of someone else's property, including loss of use. Depending on the policy, additional coverage may be available for excess medical payments, longshoremen's and harbor worker's compensation, Jones Act and damage to wharfs and piers.

A standalone, comprehensive personal liability (CPL) policy can be purchased by individuals who do not have homeowner's insurance. Liability coverage under the CPL parallels that provided in a typical homeowner's package.

Policy Exclusions

Standard policies specifically exclude liability arising from a number of activities or situations. Such exclusions limit the range of risks covered in a standard policy, allowing an insurer to provide the protection most commonly needed, at a reasonable cost. Policy coverage for these excluded risks can generally be added through an endorsement and payment of an additional premium or the purchase of a separate policy. Typical liability policy exclusions include the following:

- **Business and professional activities:** Coverage can be added for certain occupations.
- **Watercraft:** There are certain exceptions. A separate watercraft policy should be considered.
- **Aircraft:** A separate aircraft policy should be considered.
- **Other:** Excludes, among others, liability for bodily injury or property damage arising from war, communicable disease, sexual molestation or abuse, controlled substances, and workers compensation.

Personal Umbrella Excess Liability Insurance

Personal umbrella excess liability insurance is designed to provide liability coverage for situations where potential liability could exceed the limits of the protection provided in a typical homeowner's, automobile, or watercraft policy. Those who have acquired wealth, and individuals practicing certain professions, often face such risks, simply because they are seen as having the ability to pay. To meet such needs, an individual may want to consider an umbrella excess liability policy.

Continued

Individual Liability Insurance

The term "umbrella" derives from the fact that such policies require an insured to have a base amount of liability coverage, often in the form of specified policies. In the event of a covered loss, reimbursement comes first from the base policies. Liability in excess of the limits of the base policies is then covered by the umbrella or excess policy, up to its policy limits.

Coverage under an umbrella excess liability policy has two primary goals:

1. To provide larger amounts of protection than are available under other policies.

2. To broaden the protection, filling in coverage gaps that may exist. Umbrella liability policies generally have fewer exclusions than other policies.

Understand the Policy

An insurance policy is a written contract between the insured and the insurance company. The protection provided by the policy typically represents a significant part of an individual's overall risk management program. Thus, it is important for an insured individual to read and understand key policy provisions such as the following.

- **What losses are covered in the policy?** A basic policy may not provide as much protection as is necessary.

- **What losses are not covered?** For an additional premium, perils or situations not covered can often be added to a policy.

- **What are the limits of coverage?** This refers to the maximum dollar amount the insurance company will pay in the event of a covered loss.

- **What are the retention amounts?** A retention is a dollar amount or percentage the insured must pay before the insurance company pays its portion of the loss.

- **In the event of a loss, what are the duties of the insured?** A policy will usually list the steps that must be taken in the event of a loss.

Seek Professional Guidance

Insurance agents and brokers, insurance counselors, and other trained financial advisors can help provide answers to detailed questions about a particular policy. These professionals are also helpful in selecting the right policy and the appropriate amount of coverage.

General Purposes of Life Insurance

Life insurance is a unique asset. Because of its potential high yield and its tax-favored benefits, it can be used to solve some of life's perplexing financial problems.

Death Benefit Uses for Life Insurance

- **Create an estate:** Where time or other circumstances have kept the estate owner from accumulating sufficient assets to care for his or her loved ones, life insurance can create an instant estate.

- **Pay death taxes and other estate settlement costs:** These costs can vary from a low of three to four percent to over 50 percent of the estate. Federal Estate Taxes are due nine months after death.

- **Fund a business transfer:** Business owners often agree to buy a deceased owner's share from his or her estate after death. Life insurance provides the ready cash to finance the transaction.

- **Pay off a home mortgage:** Many people would like to pass the family residence to their spouse or children free of any mortgage. Often a decreasing term policy is used, which decreases in face amount as the mortgage balance is paid down.

- **Protect a business from the loss of a key employee:** Key employees are difficult to attract and retain. Their untimely death may cause a severe financial strain on the business.

- **Replace a charitable gift:** Gifts of appreciated assets to Charitable Remainder Trusts can provide income and estate tax benefits. Life insurance can be used to replace the value of the donated assets. Proceeds from life insurance policies can also be paid directly to a charity.

- **Pay off loans:** Personal or business loans can be paid off with insurance proceeds.

- **Equalize inheritances:** When the family business passes to children who are active in it, life insurance can give an equal amount to the other children.

- **Accelerated death benefits:** Federal tax law allows a "terminally ill" individual to receive the death benefits of a life insurance policy on his or her life income tax free. Such "living benefits", received prior to death, can allow a person to pay medical bills or other expenses and maintain his or her dignity by not dying destitute. If certain conditions are met, a "chronically ill" person may also receive accelerated death benefits free of federal income tax.[1]

Existing life insurance policies should be reviewed to verify that policy provisions allow for payment of such "accelerated death" benefits.

---

[1] The discussion here concerns federal income tax law; state or local tax law may vary.

Continue

General Purposes of Life Insurance

Other Uses for Life Insurance

While life insurance products are primarily used for death benefit protection, they are also commonly used for long-term accumulation goals.

- **College fund for children or grandchildren:** Cash value increases in a policy on a minor's life (or the parent's life) can be used to fund college expenses.

- **Supplement retirement funds:** Current insurance products provide competitive returns and are a prudent way of accumulating additional funds for retirement.

Available cash values may also serve as an "emergency reserve," if needed, or a source of loans, since life policies frequently include features permitting borrowing against these cash values[1].

---

[1] A policy loan or withdrawal will generally reduce cash values and death benefits. If a policy lapses or is surrendered with a loan outstanding, the loan will be treated as taxable income in the current year, to the extent of gain in the policy. Policies considered to be modified endowment contracts (MECs) are subject to special rules.

Life Insurance: Glossary of Terms

Accumulation Value: Term used in Universal Life policies to describe the total of all premiums and earnings credited to the account before deductions for any expenses, loans, and surrenders.

Adjustable Life: Form of life insurance allowing the owner to change the face amount, premium amount, period of protection, or the length of the premium payment period.

Attained Age: The age of the insured on a given date.

Automatic Premium Loan: Provision in a life insurance policy authorizing the insurer to use the loan value to pay any premiums still due at the end of the grace period.

Beneficiary: Individual or entity (e.g., trust, corporation) designated to receive the proceeds of a life insurance policy upon the death of the insured.

Cash Value: Generally, the amount of cash due an owner upon surrendering a policy.

Contingent Beneficiary: Individual or legal entity designated to receive the proceeds of a life insurance policy if the primary beneficiary is deceased at the time the benefits become payable.

Contributory: Term used to describe a plan of employee coverage in which the employee pays at least part of the premium.

Cost-of-Living Rider: Designed to adjust benefits in relation to changes in the cost of living. The majority of such riders are tied to changes in the Consumer Price Index (CPI). Generally, the amount of insurance is automatically increased, without evidence of insurability, at predetermined periods for a maximum amount.

Credit Life Insurance: Group life insurance contract whereby a creditor is protected in the event of death of the insured prior to the indebtedness being paid in full.

Death Benefit: Amount stated in a policy contract as payable upon the death of the person whose life is being insured.

Decreasing Term: Form of life insurance that provides a death benefit which declines throughout the term of the contract, reaching zero at the end of the term.

Dependent Coverage: Coverage on the head of a family which is extended to his or her dependents, including only the lawful spouse and unmarried children who are not yet employed on a full-time basis. "Children" may be step, foster, adopted, or natural.

Dependent Life Insurance: Benefit that is part of a group life insurance contract, providing death protection to the eligible dependents of a covered employee.

Continue

Life Insurance: Glossary of Terms

Dividend Accumulation: Option in a life insurance policy allowing the policyholder to leave any premium dividends with the insurer to accumulate at compound interest.

Dividend Additions: Option whereby the owner can leave policy dividends with the insurer, and each dividend is used to buy a single premium life insurance policy for whatever amount it will purchase. Also called paid-up additions.

Dividend Option: Alternative ways in which an insured under a participating life insurance policy may elect to receive policy dividends.

Extended Term Insurance: Provision found in most policies which provides the option of continuing the existing amount of insurance as term insurance for as long a period of time as the contract's cash value will purchase. This is one of the nonforfeiture options available to the insured in case a premium is not paid within the grace period.

Face Amount: Amount that will be paid in the case of death or maturity of a policy.

Family Income Policy: Policy that pays an income up to a future date designated in the policy to the beneficiary after the death of the insured. The period of payment is measured from the date of the inception of the contract, and at the end of the income period the face amount of the policy is paid to the beneficiary. If the insured lives beyond the income period, only the face amount is payable in the event of his death.

Flexible Premium: Policy allowing the owner to vary the amount or timing of premiums.

Free Look: Period of time (usually 10, 20 or 30 days) during which a policyholder may examine a newly issued individual policy and surrender it in exchange for a full refund of premium if not satisfied for any reason.

Grace Period: Prescribed period, usually 30 to 31 days after the premium due date, during which an insurance contract remains in force and the premium may be paid.

Group Life Insurance: Life Insurance provided for members of a group. It is most often issued to a group of employees but may be issued to any group provided it is not formed for the purpose of buying insurance. The cost is typically lower than for individual policies because administrative expenses per life are decreased, there are certain tax advantages, and measures taken against adverse selection are effective.

Guaranteed Renewable: Contract in which the insured has the right to keep a policy in force by the timely payment of premiums for a period of time as set forth in the contract. During that period of time, the insurer has no right to make any change in any provision of the contract other than a change in the premium rate for all insureds in the same class.

Continued..

Life Insurance: Glossary of Terms

Incidents of Ownership: Various rights which may be exercised under the policy contract by the policy owner. These include: (1) the right to cash in the policy; (2) to receive a loan on the cash value of the policy; and (3) to change the beneficiary.

Incontestable Clause: Clause in a policy providing that after a policy has been in effect for a given length of time (typically two or three years), the insurer shall not be able to contest the statements contained in the application.

Irrevocable Beneficiary: Beneficiary that cannot be changed without his or her consent.

Loan Value: The amount of money a policy owner can borrow using the cash value of the life insurance policy as security.

Maturity Date: Date at which the face amount of a life insurance policy becomes payable by reason of endowment.

Net Surrender Value: Amount of cash due an owner upon surrendering a policy.

Noncontributory: Plan or program of insurance, usually a group program, for which the employer or sponsor pays the entire premium.

Nonforfeiture Values: Values in a life insurance policy that by law the policy owner cannot forfeit, even if ceasing to pay the premiums. Depending on state law, these benefits may include the cash surrender value, the loan value, the paid-up insurance value, and the extended term insurance value.

Ordinary Life Policy: Life insurance policy for which premiums are paid continuously as long as the insured lives.

Permanent Life Insurance: One of three basic types of life insurance (whole life, universal life, and endowment) that remains in force until the policy matures, unless the owner fails to pay the premium and the cash value is insufficient to cover policy charges and expenses. The policy cannot be cancelled by the insurer for any reason except fraud in the application; that cancellation must occur within a period of time defined by law (usually two years). Over time, permanent insurance builds cash values which the owner can borrow against.

Policy Loan: Loan made by an insurer to a policy owner of part of or all of the cash value of the policy assigned as security for the loan.

Policy Proceeds: Amount paid on a life insurance policy at death or when the owner receives payment at surrender or maturity. This includes any dividends left on deposit and the value of any additional insurance purchased with dividends; it excludes any loans not repaid, plus unpaid interest on those loans.

Primary Beneficiary: First to receive proceeds or benefits from a policy when due.

Continued...

Life Insurance: Glossary of Terms

Proceeds: (See Policy Proceeds)

Rated: Policies issued at a higher rate than standard due to impairment of the insured.

Ratings: Refers to the financial strength of an insurance company. AM Best, Standard and Poor's, and Moody's are three well-known rating services.

Renewable Term: Term insurance that may be renewed for another term without evidence of insurability.

Return of Cash Value: Provision in a life insurance policy that states that if death occurs during a certain period of years (often 20), the policy will pay an amount, in addition to the face amount, equal to the cash value of the policy as of the date of death.

Return of Premium: Rider on a life insurance policy providing that, in the event of the death of the insured within a specified period of time, the policy will pay, in addition to the face amount, an amount equal to the sum of all premiums paid.

Revocable Beneficiary: Beneficiary in a life insurance policy in which the owner reserves the right to revoke or change the beneficiary.

Secondary Beneficiary: Individual or legal entity designated to receive the proceeds of a life insurance policy if the primary beneficiary is deceased at the time the benefits become payable. (See Contingent Beneficiary)

Settlement Options: Various methods for the payment of the proceeds of a life insurance policy that may be selected in lieu of a lump sum.

Surrender: Termination of a policy.

Term Insurance: Provides life insurance coverage for a specified term of years for a specified premium. Term policies do not accumulate cash value.

Universal Life: Combination flexible premium and adjustable life policy in which the owner may modify premium payments in response to changing needs and circumstances.

Variable Life: Policy featuring level premiums allowing the owner to allocate the cash value of the policy to a wide variety of investment accounts.

Variable Universal Life: Policy combining the features of variable life insurance and universal life insurance under the same contract. Benefits are variable based upon the value of variable sub accounts; premiums and benefits are adjustable by the owner.

Waiver of Premium: Provision of a life insurance policy that continues coverage without further premium payments due to the total disability of the insured.

War Clause: Provision excluding liability of an insurer if a loss is caused by war.

Spouse Insurance

The death of a spouse is perhaps the most emotionally traumatic event which humans experience. What would you do if your spouse died unexpectedly?

In over 58% of married-couple families today, both marriage partners work outside the home at least part time.[1] Often the financial requirements to run the household substantially exceed the income of either spouse alone.

If an untimely death were to occur, the inability to meet financial obligations with the single remaining spouse's income might require the hasty sale of assets or, even worse, a bank foreclosure on the family residence.

Life insurance is an excellent means of providing money when it is needed in these traumatic moments.

Some families are fortunate enough to allow either the mother or father to stay home with small children while the other earns sufficient cash to meet household and living expenses.

It is obvious that the loss of a breadwinner would create a financial calamity. Couples should consider the potential cost of replacing the services of the spouse who stays at home to care for the children.

Without the deceased spouse, a surviving spouse working outside the home would face new expenditures for:

- Child care, either in the home or at a baby-sitter or day care center;

- Someone to take the children to the doctor, dentist, piano lessons; etc.

Perhaps the surviving parent could take time off work to fulfill these obligations, but this time off work would also amount to a financial loss.

Most families can help effectively remove this potential financial emergency by acquiring a life insurance policy on each spouse.

---

[1] Source: Statistical Abstract of the United States: 2007, Table 681 Married-Couple Families; data from 2003.

Considerations in the Purchase of Life Insurance

Who Will Be the Owner of the Policy?

Life insurance proceeds are included in the estate of a deceased if he or she has any incidents of ownership in the policy. Ownership by adult children or an irrevocable life insurance trust should be considered if there is an estate tax problem.[1]

How Much Life Insurance?

This will depend on the need it is fulfilling. Amounts needed to fund a business transfer or to pay death taxes may be readily determined.

Calculating the value of a human life to a family is more difficult. Consider these projected total earnings up to age 65 assuming a 5% annual increase including inflation.

Projected Total Earnings to Age 65

Current Age	Current Monthly Income		
	$2,000	**$4,000**	**$8,000**
25	$3,044,154	$6,088,309	$12,176,618
35	1,674,259	3,348,518	6,697,036
45	833,262	1,666,524	3,333,048
55	316,963	633,926	1,267,852

What Type of Policy Should Be Purchased?

A person trained in life insurance can explain the many different policies available and assist in selecting the one which best fits your needs.

How Should the Premium Be Paid?

Sometimes the amount of the premium can be paid from current income, while other times it may be prudent to reposition other assets so as to be able to acquire sufficient insurance protection.

If the insured is a business owner or executive, a corporation may assist in paying premiums. Other times it may be better to have the corporation own the policy and use the proceeds to purchase part or all of the owner's interest at death.

Insurance can also be purchased in certain qualified retirement plans.

---

[1] Under the Tax Act of 2001, the federal estate tax is gradually phased out until its final repeal in the year 2010. If Congress does not act at that time to repeal it for the years following, it will automatically revert back to the rates in effect during the year 2001, with an exemption for the first $1,000,000 of assets.

First-to-Die Life Insurance Policies
Joint Life

As the name implies, first-to-die or joint-life insurance policies pay out the face amount when the first named insured dies. This reduces the cost of paying premiums on two separate policies, when the insurance proceeds are most needed when only the first insured dies.

The following examples illustrate how this type of policy can be effectively used.

Buy-Sell Funding

A corporation or partnership with two or more owners often experiences problems of transferring ownership to the surviving owner or owners and paying a fair cash price to the deceased owner's heirs.

This problem is usually remedied with a properly structured buy-sell agreement, which assures a fair price for the decedent's share of the business and allows the surviving business partner to retain control and ownership of the business.

Life insurance is well established as the ideal method of funding buy-sell agreements. By using a joint-life policy, the company may be able to reduce the amount of cash flow required to pay the premiums, while still guaranteeing that the funds will be available for the buy-out no matter which partner or shareholder dies first.[1]

Key Person Protection

The loss of a key employee or executive can have a devastating effect on the future of a business. The use of joint-life policies can reduce the required cash flow to insure against the loss of any one person from a selected group of key persons. Insurance proceeds can be used to find, recruit, and train replacement employees and sustain or strengthen the company's credit position.[1]

Working Couples

With the growing percentage of families today relying on two incomes, it is prudent to insure against the loss of either spouse. The joint-life policy should be considered as part of the solution to the loss of income from the prior death of either spouse.

---

[1] Both buy-sell arrangements and key person protection plans are frequently funded with life insurance. Under the provisions of IRC Sec. 101(j), added by the Pension Protection Act of 2006, death proceeds from a life insurance policy owned by an employer on the life of an employee are generally includable in income, unless certain requirements are met. Until the full scope of this new law is clarified by the IRS, caution is advised. State or local law may vary.

Survivorship Life Insurance
Second-to-Die

The Problem: Deferred Estate Tax Build-Up

The Economic Recovery Tax Act of 1981 allowed postponement of estate taxes - through the unlimited marital deduction - until after the death of both husband and wife. While this provides couples with increased flexibility during lifetime, in many cases it places a substantial tax burden on the combined estate when the surviving spouse dies.[1]

The Survivorship Life Solution

Unlike traditional life insurance, which provides protection on the life of a single insured, survivorship life covers two lives with proceeds payable at the second death. As such, it is perfectly suited to deal with the problem discussed above.

Advantages Over Individual Coverage
• Lower premiums – can be more cost effective than two policies.
• Medical underwriting standards may be eased with respect to one of the insureds due to second death payouts.

Ownership Arrangements

Third party ownership (adult children or an irrevocable life insurance trust) is often desirable for persons with potential estate tax problems. The policy may sometimes be transferred out of the estate after the first insured dies. If the survivor lives three years after the gift, the full face amount should be out of his or her estate. Questions of ownership should be discussed with an attorney.

Other Uses for Survivorship Life
• **Key person insurance:** Useful when the employer can self insure or absorb the loss of one key individual but not two.
• **Business buyout:** Facilitates purchase of family business from aging parents. Child working in the business owns policy on parents.
• **Charitable gift asset replacement:** Provides heirs with replacement cash when assets are used to fund a charitable remainder trust.

---

[1] Under the Tax Act of 2001, the federal estate tax is gradually phased out until its final repeal in the year 2010. If Congress does not act at that time to repeal it for the years following, it will automatically revert back to the rates in effect during the year 2001, with an exemption for the first $1,000,000 of assets.

Tax-Free Policy Exchanges
IRC Sec. 1035

Due to a number of factors, some newer life insurance policies may be a better buy than older, smaller policies. A tax-free exchange allows one to defer the gain on any old policies at the time they are exchanged for the new policies.

Policy Values

Policies Which Can Be Exchanged Tax-Free

From This ↓ To This →	To Life Insurance	To an Endowment Contract	To an Annuity	To a Variable Annuity
		Type of New Contract		
Life insurance	Yes	Yes	Yes	Yes
Endowment contract	No	Yes[1]	Yes	Yes
Annuity contract	No	No	Yes[2]	Yes[2]

Key Points

- Life policies must be on the life of same person.[3]

- Annuity contracts must be payable to the same person(s).

- When contracts are assignable, there should be a direct transfer of funds between insurance companies.[4]

- The cost basis of the old policy (including certain riders and/or rating) is carried over to the new policy.

- If cash or other property is part of the exchange, any gain will be recognized up to that amount.

- A permanent policy with an outstanding loan can be exchanged for another similar policy with the same indebtedness. If the indebtedness is reduced in the exchange, there will be income tax consequences.

- If there is a gain, it is ordinary income.

---

[1] Provided payments begin no later than under the old contract. Endowment Contracts must meet definition of life insurance.

[2] In Notice 2003-51, IRB 2003-33, 7/9/2003, the IRS published interim guidance on the tax treatment of partial exchanges of annuity contracts.

[3] A single policy may not be exchanged for one on multiple lives, (e.g., a second-to-die policy.)

[4] Some exceptions for troubled insurers. Rev. Proc. 92-44 and 92-44A

Continued...

Tax-Free Policy Exchanges
IRC Sec. 1035

Potential Problems

The early surrender of certain life insurance policies or annuity contracts may have significant, negative consequences. For example, a policy or contract owner may be required to pay a surrender charge, there may be tax penalties due, or the owner may receive less than he or she originally invested or paid into the contract.

Questions to Consider

- Determine whether the incontestability period and suicide provisions are based on the issue date of the new policy or the old one.

- Consider the rating of the new company.

- Determine whether the old policy has favorable tax status which would not transfer to the new policy.

- Determine whether the premium on the new policy will be more expensive. This may happen, for example, because of changes in health.

An experienced life agent is an important guide through this process. Make certain you are medically insurable before the old policy is terminated and that there is not a period during the exchange when you have no coverage.

Long-Term Care Insurance

Beginning in 2010, the Pension Protection Act of 2006 allows for the following tax-free policy exchanges involving long-term care (LTC) insurance, including combination policies in which the LTC coverage is provided as a rider to, or a part of, an annuity or life insurance contract:

- A qualified long-term care contract exchanged for a qualified long-term care contract;

- A life insurance contract exchanged for a qualified long-term care contract;

- An annuity contract exchanged for a qualified long-term care contract; and

- An endowment insurance contract exchanged for a qualified long-term care contract.

Modified Endowment Contracts

Life insurance policies issued on or after June 21, 1988 may be
defined as "modified endowment contracts" (MECs) if the cumulative
premiums paid during the first seven years (7-pay test) at any time
exceed the total of the net level premiums for the same period.

As an example, assume that the net level premium for a policy is
$1,000 per year and the following payments are made by two different
policy owners.

Year	7-Pay Test Cumulative Net Level Premiums	Policy Owner A		Policy Owner B	
		Annual Premium	Cumulative Premiums	Annual Premium	Cumulative Premiums
1	$1,000	$1,000	$1,000	$1,000	$1,000
2	2,000	500	1,500	1,000	2,000
3	3,000	1,000	2,500	1,000	3,000
4	4,000	1,500	4,000	1,500	4,500
5	5,000	1,000	5,000	500	5,000
6	6,000	1,000	6,000	1,000	6,000
7	7,000	1,000	7,000	1,000	7,000

In the policy owner A example above, even though the premium paid during the fourth
year exceeds the annual net level premium of $1,000, the cumulative premiums do not
exceed four times (for the four years) the net level premium; and, therefore, this is not a
modified endowment contract.

In the policy owner B example above, however, the premiums paid in the fourth year
cause the cumulative premiums paid to exceed the cumulative net level premiums allowed
and thus cause this contract to become a modified endowment contract.

Additional 7-pay test periods will be required if the policy is materially changed.

Taxation of Modified Endowment Contracts

Withdrawals from modified endowment contracts (including loans) will be taxed as
current income until all of the policy earnings have been taxed. There is also a 10%
penalty tax if the owner is under age 59½ unless payments are due to disability or are
annuity type payments.

Well-designed premium payment schedules can avoid the modified endowment contract
treatment and retain the benefits which are unique to the life insurance contract.

The Need for Responsible Planning
What If You Were to Die Today?

Many individuals recognize the benefits of planning for the future. Such efforts often uncover problems and frequently provide the motivation to make needed changes. For the most part, the issues involved are positive and enjoyable (e.g., retirement, well-educated children).

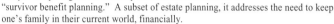

However, planning for the unexpected – known as risk management – can be less pleasant. A key part of risk management is answering the question, "What if I were to die today?" Preparing for an untimely death is often referred to as "survivor benefit planning." A subset of estate planning, it addresses the need to keep one's family in their current world, financially.

Understandably, no one likes to contemplate his or her own demise. For some, death seems a distant, future event. Others are simply too "busy." Whatever the reason, delaying this part of planning can result in expensive, unintended, even tragic consequences.

Survivor Benefit Needs

The ultimate purpose of survivor benefit planning is twofold: (1) to ensure that the ongoing income needs of the survivor(s) are met, and (2) to provide for immediate lump-sum cash needs.

- **Income needs:** How much income will the survivors need, now and in the future, to cover the following:
  - **Household living expenses:** Will the family stay in the same house? Can they afford to? Do they want to? Will they have the option?
  - **Additional childcare:** Will there be a need for more help with young children?
  - **Educational expenses:** Will there be enough money for the children to go to college?
- **Lump-sum needs:** How much will the survivors need immediately and in cash? Consider the following:
  - **Final expenses:** More than the funeral, this includes unpaid medical bills, which, after a long illness, can be substantial.
  - **Estate settlement costs:** Probate expenses, attorney's fees, death taxes, etc.
  - **Mortgage payoff and debt reduction:** Will it be important to provide a paid-off house? Are there debts that should be retired?

One Final Question

If you died today, would your plan be ready?

How Much Life Insurance?

1. Annual living expenses of survivors[1] (spouse, children, etc.)
   a. After-tax living expenses $_____
   b. Average tax rate[2] (as decimal value)   _____
   c. Tax factor (one minus line 1b)   _____
   Pre-tax annual living expenses of survivors $_____
   (Line 1a divided by line 1c)

2. Less: Expected pre-tax annual income
   a. Social Security benefits $_____
   b. Survivor's pension benefits $_____
   c. Survivor's earned income $_____
   d. Other income $_____
   Total expected pre-tax annual income $_____

3. Equals: Annual net living expense shortage, if any.[3] $_____
   (Line 1 minus line 2)

4. Capital required to produce income to meet the annual living expense shortage
   a. Pre-tax annual rate of return   _____ %
   b. Annual inflation rate   _____ %
   c. Years of income required   _____ yrs
   d. Multiplication factor[4]   _____
   Capital required due to shortage $_____
   (Line 3 times factor on line 4d)

5. Plus: Lump-sum expenses
   a. Final expenses and/or estate costs $_____
   b. Mortgage cancellation $_____
   c. Emergency fund $_____
   d. Other fund (education, etc.) $_____
   Total lump-sum expenses $_____

6. Total capital required $_____
   (Line 4 plus line 5)

7. Less: Existing capital
   a. Income producing assets $_____
   b. Life insurance $_____
   Total Present Capital $_____

8. Amount of capital to be added, if any (Line 6 minus line 7) $_____

---

[1] Consider using 70% of current family living expenses.
[2] This value should be based on the total income and payroll taxes divided by total gross income.
[3] If Line 2 is greater than Line 1, enter a zero value for Lines 3 and 4, then skip to Line 5.
[4] See tables on following pages.

Continued

296

How Much Life Insurance?

Multiplication Factors (for line 4d)

Years of Income	1% Pre-Tax Annual Return			2% Pre-Tax Annual Return		
	Inflation at 3.00%	Inflation at 4.00%	Inflation at 5.00%	Inflation at 3.00%	Inflation at 4.00%	Inflation at 5.00%
5	5.20	5.31	5.41	5.10	5.20	5.30
10	10.94	11.45	11.98	10.45	10.93	11.43
15	17.27	18.56	19.96	16.07	17.24	18.52
20	24.25	26.79	29.66	21.98	24.20	26.71
25	31.95	36.32	41.42	28.17	31.87	36.18
30	40.44	47.35	55.72	34.68	40.32	47.12
35	49.81	60.12	73.07	41.51	49.63	59.78
40	60.14	74.90	94.14	48.69	59.89	74.40
45	71.54	92.01	119.73	56.22	71.20	91.31
50	84.11	111.81	150.81	64.13	83.66	110.86

Years of Income	3% Pre-Tax Annual Return			4% Pre-Tax Annual Return		
	Inflation at 3.00%	Inflation at 4.00%	Inflation at 5.00%	Inflation at 3.00%	Inflation at 4.00%	Inflation at 5.00%
5	5.00	5.10	5.20	4.90	5.00	5.10
10	10.00	10.45	10.92	9.58	10.00	10.44
15	15.00	16.06	17.22	14.03	15.00	16.05
20	20.00	21.96	24.16	18.27	20.00	21.94
25	25.00	28.14	31.79	22.32	25.00	28.11
30	30.00	34.63	40.20	26.17	30.00	34.58
35	35.00	41.44	49.46	29.84	35.00	41.38
40	40.00	48.59	59.65	33.34	40.00	48.50
45	45.00	56.10	70.86	36.67	45.00	55.97
50	50.00	63.97	83.21	39.85	50.00	63.82

Years of Income	5% Pre-Tax Annual Return			6% Pre-Tax Annual Return		
	Inflation at 3.00%	Inflation at 4.00%	Inflation at 5.00%	Inflation at 3.00%	Inflation at 4.00%	Inflation at 5.00%
5	4.81	4.91	5.00	4.72	4.81	4.91
10	9.18	9.58	10.00	8.82	9.19	9.59
15	13.16	14.04	15.00	12.36	13.17	14.05
20	16.76	18.29	20.00	15.44	16.79	18.31
25	20.04	22.34	25.00	18.10	20.08	22.36
30	23.02	26.20	30.00	20.40	23.07	26.24
35	25.72	29.88	35.00	22.40	25.79	29.93
40	28.17	33.39	40.00	24.13	28.26	33.45
45	30.40	36.74	45.00	25.63	30.51	36.81
50	32.43	39.93	50.00	26.92	32.55	40.01

Continued...

How Much Life Insurance?

Multiplication Factors (for line 4d)

Years of Income	7% Pre-Tax Annual Return			8% Pre-Tax Annual Return		
	Inflation at 3.00%	Inflation at 4.00%	Inflation at 5.00%	Inflation at 3.00%	Inflation at 4.00%	Inflation at 5.00%
5	4.64	4.73	4.82	4.56	4.64	4.73
10	8.47	8.83	9.20	8.15	8.49	8.84
15	11.64	12.39	13.19	10.99	11.67	12.41
20	14.26	15.47	16.82	13.23	14.31	15.51
25	16.43	18.15	20.12	15.00	16.49	18.20
30	18.22	20.47	23.12	16.39	18.30	20.54
35	19.70	22.48	25.86	17.49	19.79	22.57
40	20.92	24.23	28.35	18.36	21.03	24.33
45	21.93	25.75	30.61	19.04	22.06	25.87
50	22.77	27.06	32.67	19.58	22.91	27.20

Years of Income	9% Pre-Tax Annual Return			10% Pre-Tax Annual Return		
	Inflation at 3.00%	Inflation at 4.00%	Inflation at 5.00%	Inflation at 3.00%	Inflation at 4.00%	Inflation at 5.00%
5	4.48	4.56	4.65	4.40	4.48	4.57
10	7.85	8.17	8.50	7.57	7.87	8.18
15	10.40	11.02	11.70	9.85	10.43	11.05
20	12.31	13.28	14.35	11.50	12.36	13.32
25	13.76	15.06	16.55	12.68	13.82	15.12
30	14.84	16.47	18.37	13.53	14.93	16.55
35	15.66	17.59	19.89	14.14	15.76	17.68
40	16.28	18.47	21.14	14.58	16.39	18.58
45	16.75	19.17	22.18	14.90	16.86	19.29
50	17.10	19.72	23.05	15.13	17.22	19.85

Years of Income	11% Pre-Tax Annual Return			12% Pre-Tax Annual Return		
	Inflation at 3.00%	Inflation at 4.00%	Inflation at 5.00%	Inflation at 3.00%	Inflation at 4.00%	Inflation at 5.00%
5	4.33	4.41	4.49	4.26	4.33	4.41
10	7.31	7.59	7.89	7.06	7.33	7.61
15	9.36	9.89	10.46	8.90	9.39	9.92
20	10.77	11.55	12.41	10.11	10.82	11.60
25	11.74	12.75	13.89	10.91	11.80	12.81
30	12.40	13.61	15.01	11.44	12.48	13.69
35	12.86	14.24	15.85	11.78	12.95	14.33
40	13.18	14.69	16.50	12.01	13.28	14.79
45	13.40	15.01	16.98	12.16	13.50	15.12
50	13.55	15.25	17.35	12.26	13.66	15.37

How Much Life Insurance?

1. Annual living expenses of survivors (spouse, children, etc.)
   a. After-tax living expenses $75,000
   b. Average tax rate   45.00 %
       Pre-tax annual living expenses of survivors $ 136,364

2. Less: Expected pre-tax annual income
   a. Social Security benefits $25,000
   b. Survivor's pension benefits $10,000
   c. Survivor's earned income $15,000
   d. Other income $1,500
       Total expected pre-tax annual income $51,500

3. Equals: Annual net living expense shortage, if any $84,864

4. Capital required to produce annual living expense shortage
   a. Pre-tax annual rate of return   8.00 %
   b. Annual inflation rate   4.00 %
   c. Years of income required   25 yrs
       Capital required due to shortage $1,399,400

5. Plus: Lump-sum expenses
   a. Final expenses and/or estate costs $25,000
   b. Mortgage cancellation $ 250,000
   c. Emergency fund $50,000
   d. Other fund (education, etc.) $ 150,000
       Total lump-sum expenses $ 475,000

6. Total capital required $1,874,400

7. Less: Existing capital
   a. Income producing assets $ 250,000
   b. Life insurance $ 100,000
       Total Present Capital $ 350,000

8. Amount of capital to be added, if any $1,524,400

How Much Life Insurance?

Item	Value
Annual living expenses of survivors	$ 136,364
Expected pre-tax annual income	-$51,500
Annual net living expense shortage, if any	**$84,864**
Capital required to produce shortage	$1,399,400
Lump-sum expenses	$ 475,000
Total capital required	**$1,874,400**
Existing capital	- $ 350,000
Amount of capital to be added, if any	**$1,524,400**

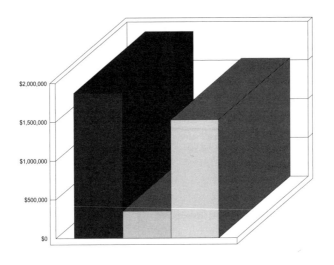

■ Total Capital Required

▨ Present Capital

▨ New Capital Needed

Types of Life Insurance Policies

In choosing the type of life insurance policy you purchase, consideration must be given to the need which is being filled; e.g., creation of an estate, payment of estate settlement costs (federal and state death taxes,[1] last illness and burial costs, probate fees, etc.), business buy-out, key-man coverage, etc.

Decreasing Term

Level premium, decreasing coverage, no cash value: Suitable for financial obligations which reduce with time; e.g., mortgages or other amortized loans.

Annual Renewable Term

Increasing premium, level coverage, no cash value: Suitable for financial obligations which remain constant for a short or intermediate period; e.g., income during a minor's dependency.

Long-Term Level Premium Term

Level premium, level coverage, no cash value: The annual premiums are fixed for a period of time, typically 5, 10, 15 or 20 years. Suitable for financial obligations which remain constant for a short or intermediate period; e.g., income during a minor's dependency.

Whole Life

Level premium, level coverage, cash values: Cash value typically increases based on insurance company's general asset account portfolio performance. Suitable for long-term obligations; e.g., surviving spouse lifetime income needs, estate liquidity, death taxes, funding retirement needs, etc.

Universal Life

Level or adjustable premium and coverage, cash values: Cash values may increase, based on the performance of certain assets held in the company's general account. Suitable for long-term obligations or sinking-fund needs: estate growth, estate liquidity, death taxes, funding retirement needs, etc.

---

[1] Under the Tax Act of 2001, the federal estate tax is gradually phased out until its final repeal in the year 2010. If Congress does not act at that time to repeal it for the years following, it will automatically revert back to the rates in effect during the year 2001, with an exemption for the first $1,000,000 of assets.

Continued...

Types of Life Insurance Policies

Variable Life and Variable Universal Life

Level/adjustable premium, level coverage,[1] cash value: Suitable for long-term obligations and those who are more active investors and for estate growth and death tax liquidity.

Single Premium Whole Life

Entire premium is paid at purchase, cash values, level coverage: Provides protection as well as serving as an asset accumulation vehicle.

Note: Withdrawals and loans may be available from permanent policies. Withdrawals and policy loans will have the effect of reducing the death benefit. There are different income tax consequences if they are modified endowment contracts.

---

[1] Can be increased by positive investment performance. The policy owner directs cash values to a choice of investment accounts (bond, stock, money market, etc.). However, cash values are not guaranteed.

Term Life Insurance

What Is Term Life Insurance?

Term life insurance, as the name suggests, provides life insurance only for a limited period of time, or term. Other types of policies, such as whole life, universal life, or variable life, are considered to be permanent insurance, and are designed to provide protection for the entire life of the insured.

Term insurance might be compared to an automobile insurance policy. While the auto policy is in force, the insured enjoys protection against loss from an auto accident. If no accident happens, no benefits are paid under the policy. At the end of the period covered by the policy, there is no refund of premiums paid. Term life insurance works in much the same way.

Term insurance thus provides only pure insurance protection and does not have the cash value feature typically found in most permanent life insurance policies. Unlike most permanent policies, in which premiums usually remain level over the life of the policy, the periodic cost of term life insurance increases as the insured becomes older. The cash-value feature found in permanent policies provides a cash build-up within the policy which allows for the level periodic premium. In later years, the premiums for a typical term life policy will far exceed those of the typical permanent policy.

Policy Variations

There are a number of different types of term insurance:

- **Annual renewable term:** Term insurance characterized by a level death benefit, a premium that increases at each annual policy renewal, and no cash-value accumulation.

Example of Annual Renewable Term

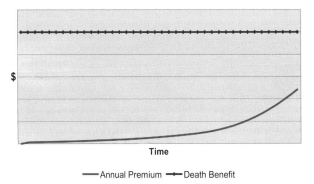

Annual Premium ━━━ Death Benefit

Continued...

Term Life Insurance

- **Long-term level premium term:** The annual premiums are fixed for a specified period of time, typically 5, 10, 15, or 20 years. The death benefit remains constant, and there are no accumulated cash values.

Example of Long-Term Level Term

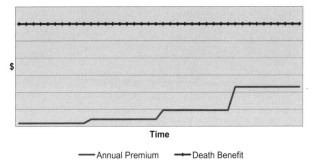

- **Decreasing term:** A policy that has a level premium, a decreasing death benefit, and no accumulation of cash values.
- **Combination policies:** In some cases, term life insurance is teamed with a permanent policy to provide the benefits of both types of policies. In both the family income policy, and the family maintenance policy, for example, a term policy with a decreasing death benefit is combined with a permanent, level benefit policy.

Common Uses of Term Insurance

Term life insurance is most useful when an insured is relatively young and the need is for temporary or short-term coverage. Some common use of term insurance include:

- **Family protection:** To provide the funds to support a surviving spouse and/or minor children or to provide the cash for a child's college education or pay for other capital needs; to pay final bills such as medical or other estate expenses.
- **Declining needs:** In some instances, a debt, such as a mortgage, is matched with a decreasing term policy. As the debt is paid off, the policy's death benefit is reduced.
- **Business planning:** A business may use term insurance to insure a key employee, or to recruit or retain key employees through a salary continuation plan. Term insurance is also useful as a way to fund a cross-purchase buy-sell agreement, particularly where one owner is significantly younger than another.
- **Charitable gifts:** To provide funds for a gift to charity.

Continued...

Term Life Insurance

Optional Policy Provisions

A number of optional policy provisions, commonly referred to as riders, can be added to a basic term life policy, through payment of an additional premium:

- **Renewable:** This provision allows the policy to be renewed at the end of the term without the insured having to show that he or she is still insurable.

- **Convertible:** Provides the insured the option to convert a term policy to a permanent policy, usually without having to prove good health.

- **Accidental death:** Pays the beneficiaries double (in some situations triple) the face amount of the policy if the insured dies in an accident.

- **Waiver of premium:** Allows an insured to stop paying premiums if he or she becomes disabled and is unable to work.

- **Accelerated death benefits:** An accelerated death benefits provision allows for payment of part of a policy's death benefit while an insured is still alive. Such benefits are typically payable when the insured develops a medical condition expected to lead to death within a short period of time.

Whole Life Insurance

What Is Whole Life Insurance?

Whole life insurance, sometimes called permanent insurance, or ordinary life, is designed to stay in force throughout one's lifetime. As long as the policy owner meets his or her obligations under the policy, the policy remains in force, regardless of any changes in health that may occur.

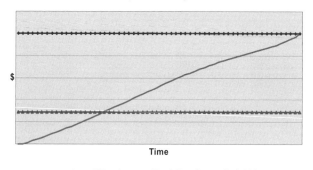

Unlike term insurance, where premium payments generally increase, as the insured gets older (the chance of death increases with age), premiums for most whole life policies remain level. A portion of each premium payment is set aside to earn interest. Over time, a whole life policy will develop cash values. The accumulated cash values form a reserve which enable the insurer to pay a policy's full death benefit, while keeping premiums level.

During life, many whole life policies have provisions to borrow a portion of the accumulated cash value. If a policy is terminated without the insured dying, there are various surrender options for the cash value available to a policy owner.

Policy Variations

There are two primary types of whole life insurance, based on the period over which the premium payments are made:

- **Ordinary life:** An ordinary life policy assumes that premiums will be paid until the insured dies. Premiums are based on the assumption that the insured will die at a certain age, typically age 100. If an insured lives to this age, the policy pays the face amount of the death benefit.

Example of Ordinary Life

$

Time

——Annual Premium ——Death Benefit ——Cash Value

Continued..

Whole Life Insurance

- **Limited-payment life:** This type of whole life policy assumes that all premium payments are made over a specified, limited period, typically ranging from one to 30 years. Premiums for a limited-payment life policy are generally higher than for an ordinary life policy, because the payment period is shorter.

Example of Limited-Payment Life

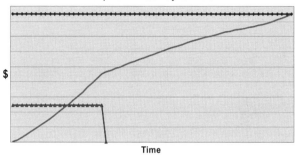

—•—Annual Premium —•—Death Benefit ——Cash Value

Common Uses of Whole Life Insurance

Whole life policies are well suited for needs that do not diminish over time. Some commonly found uses for whole life are:

- **Family protection:** To provide funds to support a surviving spouse and/or minor children, particularly for individuals who start a family later in life; to pay final bills, such as medical or other estate expenses and federal[1] and state death taxes.

- **Business planning:** Whole life insurance is often used for many different business purposes, such as insuring key employees, in split-dollar insurance arrangements, and funding nonqualified deferred compensation plans. Business continuation planning often involves using whole life insurance as a source of funds for buy-sell agreements.

- **Accumulation needs:** Some individuals will use the cash value feature of whole life as a way of accumulating funds for specific purposes, such as funding college education, or as a supplemental source of retirement income.

- **Charitable gifts:** To provide funds for a gift to charity.

---

[1] Under the Tax Act of 2001, the federal estate tax is gradually phased out until its final repeal in the year 2010. If Congress does not act at that time to repeal it for the years following, it will automatically revert back to the rates in effect during the year 2001, with an exemption for the first $1,000,000 of assets.

Continued...

Whole Life Insurance

Modified Endowment Contracts (MECs)

A life insurance policy issued on or after June 21, 1988[1] may be classified as a modified endowment contract (MEC) if the cumulative premiums paid during the first seven years (7-pay test) at any time exceed the total of the net level premiums for the same period.

If a policy is classified as a MEC, all withdrawals (including loans) will be taxed as current income, until all of the policy earnings have been taxed. There is an additional 10% penalty tax if the owner is under age 59½ at the time of withdrawal, unless the payments are due to disability or are annuity type payments.

A whole life policy can avoid treatment as a MEC through a well-designed premium payment schedule.

Additional Policy Elements

Whole life policies often have additional, useful features:

- **Policy loans:** Almost all whole policies permit the policy owner to borrow a portion of the accumulated cash value, with the insurance company charging interest on the loan. The rate charged to borrow the funds is often lower than current open market rates. A policy loan will reduce the death benefit payable if the insured dies before the loan and any interest due is repaid. A policy loan will also reduce the cash surrender value if a policy is terminated. If a policy lapses or is surrendered with a loan outstanding, the loan will be treated as taxable income for the current year, to the extent of gain in the policy.

- **Policy dividends:** Whole life contracts classified as "participating" offer the possibility of policy "dividends." Such policy dividends are not guaranteed, and represent a return to the policy owner of part of the premium paid. A dividend may be taken as cash or a policy may offer a number of other ways the dividend might be used:
  - To reduce current premium payments;
  - To buy additional, completely paid-up insurance (known as paid-up additions);
  - To be retained by the insurer, earning interest for the policyholder;
  - To purchase one-year term insurance;
  - To be added to the policy's cash value;
  - To "pay up" the policy earlier than originally scheduled.

---

[1] Including a policy issued before that date, but later materially changed.

Continued..

Whole Life Insurance

Policy Dividends Used To Purchase Paid-Up Additions

Although policy dividends are not guaranteed, using available dividends to purchase paid-up additions can, over time, have a significant, positive impact on both the death benefit and cash value of whole life policy. The diagram below illustrates how this might work, in a hypothetical life insurance policy.

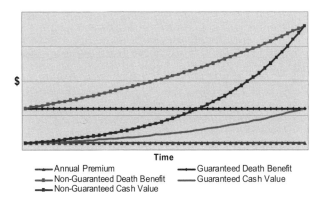

Time

— Annual Premium   — Guaranteed Death Benefit
— Non-Guaranteed Death Benefit   — Guaranteed Cash Value
— Non-Guaranteed Cash Value

Optional Policy Provisions

A number of optional provisions, commonly referred to as riders, can be added to a basic whole life policy, through payment of an additional premium:

- **Waiver of premium:** Allows an insured to stop paying premiums if he or she becomes disabled and is unable to work.

- **Accidental death:** Pays the beneficiaries double (in some situations triple) the face amount of the policy if the insured dies in an accident.

- **Spousal or family term insurance:** Allows a policy owner to purchase term insurance on a spouse or children.

- **Accelerated death benefits:** An accelerated death benefits provision allows for payment of part of a policy's death benefit while an insured is still alive. Such benefits are typically payable when the insured develops a medical condition expected to lead to death within a short period of time.

Universal Life Insurance

What Is Universal Life Insurance?

Universal life insurance contracts differ from traditional whole life policies by specifically separating and identifying the mortality, expense, and cash value parts of a policy. Dividing the policy into these three components allows the insurance company to build a higher degree of flexibility into the contract. This flexibility allows (within certain limits) the policy owner to modify the policy face amount or premium, in response to changing needs and circumstances.

A monthly charge for both the mortality element and the expense element is deducted from a policy's account balance. The remainder of the premium is allocated to the cash value element, where the funds earn interest. Unlike traditional whole life policies, complete disclosure of these internal charges against the cash value element is made to the policy owner in the form of an annual statement.

Many universal life policies have several different provisions by which the accumulated cash value can be made available to a policy owner during life, without causing the policy to lapse. If a policy is terminated without the insured dying, there are various surrender options for the cash value.

Policy Variations

There are two primary types of universal life, based on the level of death benefits:

- **Type I universal life:** Also known as option A, type I universal policies pay a fixed, level death benefit, generally the face amount of the policy.

Example of Type I Universal Life

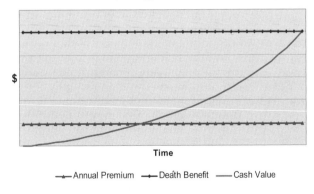

—•—Annual Premium   —•—Death Benefit   ——Cash Value

Continue

Universal Life Insurance

- **Type II universal life:** Also known as option B, type II universal policies generally pay the face amount of the policy plus the accumulated cash values. As the cash values grow, so does the potential death benefit.

Example of Type II Universal Life

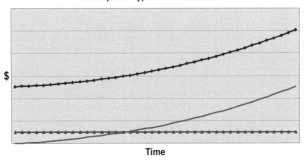

—◆—Annual Premium —◆—Death Benefit ——Cash Value

Common Uses of Universal Life

Universal life policies are useful for policy owners who expect their needs to change over time. Within certain guidelines, a universal life policy can be modified by changing the death benefit or premium payments. Some common uses are:

- **Family protection:** To provide the funds to support a surviving spouse and/or minor children, or to pay final bills such as medical or other estate expenses, as well as federal[1] and state death taxes.

- **Business planning:** Because of its flexibility, universal life insurance is often used for many different business purposes, such as insuring key employees, in split-dollar insurance arrangements, and funding nonqualified deferred compensation plans. Business continuation planning often involves using universal life as a source of funds for buy-sell agreements.

- **Accumulation needs:** Some individuals will use the cash value feature of universal life as means of accumulating funds for specific purposes, such as funding college education, or as a supplemental source of retirement income.

- **Charitable gifts:** To provide funds for a gift to charity.

---

[1] Under the Tax Act of 2001, the federal estate tax is gradually phased out until its final repeal in the year 2010. If Congress does not act at that time to repeal it for the years following, it will automatically revert back to the rates in effect during the year 2001, with an exemption for the first $1,000,000 of assets.

Continued...

Universal Life Insurance

Modified Endowment Contracts (MECs)

A life insurance policy issued on or after June 21, 1988[1] may be classified as a modified endowment contract (MEC) if the cumulative premiums paid during the first seven years (7-pay test) at any time exceed the total of the net level premiums for the same period.

If a policy is classified as a MEC, all withdrawals (including loans) will be taxed as current income, until all of the policy earnings have been taxed. There is an additional 10% penalty tax if the owner is under age 59½ at the time of withdrawal, unless the payments are due to disability or are annuity type payments.

A universal life policy can avoid treatment as a MEC through a well-designed premium payment schedule. Caution must be exercised when changes in policy premium payments or death benefits are made, or when making partial withdrawals, to avoid having the policy inadvertently classified as a MEC.

Additional Policy Elements

Universal life policies have a number of additional elements to consider:

- **Surrender charges:** Most universal life policies have substantial surrender charges, if a policy is terminated. These surrender charges are generally highest in the early years of a policy, and decline over a period of time, usually from seven to 15 years.

- **Policy loans:** Universal life policies typically permit the policy owner to borrow at interest a portion of the accumulated cash value. The rate charged on the borrowed funds is often lower than current open market rates. A policy loan will reduce the death benefit payable if the insured dies before the loan is repaid; a policy loan will also reduce the cash surrender value if a policy is terminated. If the policy lapses or is surrendered with a loan outstanding, the loan will be treated as taxable income in the current year, to the extent of gain in the policy.

- **Partial withdrawals:** Most universal life policies allow a policy owner to withdraw a portion of the cash value, without terminating the policy. Such withdrawals reduce the amount of death benefit payable, and may be subject to current income tax, if the policy is classified as a MEC, or if the withdrawal exceeds cost basis for a non-MEC policy. Some contracts allow a policy owner to put the withdrawn funds back into the policy, but the insured may have to provide evidence of insurability to restore the original death benefit.

- **Surrender options:** If a policy owner surrenders a policy, there are generally three ways in which the accumulated cash value may be received, including: (1) taking the accumulated cash value, less any surrender charges; (2) receiving a reduced amount of paid-up insurance; or (3) taking paid-up term insurance in an amount equal to the original face amount of the policy.

---

[1] Including a policy issued before that date, but later materially changed.

Continue

Universal Life Insurance

Optional Policy Provisions

A number of optional provisions, commonly referred to as riders, can be added to a basic universal life policy, through payment of an additional premium:

- **Waiver of premium:** Suspends the monthly deduction for the mortality element of the policy, if the insured becomes disabled and is unable to work.

- **Accidental death:** Pays the beneficiaries double (in some situations triple) the face amount of the policy if the insured dies in an accident.

- **Spousal or family term insurance:** Allows a policy owner to purchase term insurance on a spouse or children.

- **Accelerated death benefits:** An accelerated death benefits provision allows for payment of part of a policy's death benefit while an insured is still alive. Such benefits are typically payable when the insured develops a medical condition expected to lead to death within a short period of time.

Variable Life Insurance

What Is Variable Life Insurance?

Variable life insurance is similar to whole life in that the premium payments are level, and there is generally a minimum guaranteed death benefit. Unlike whole life policies however, variable life insurance permits the policyowner to allocate a portion of each premium payment to one or more investment options, in separate subaccounts after a deduction for expense and mortality charges.

The death benefit and cash value of a variable life policy will increase or decrease based on the performance of the investment options chosen. The death benefit, however, will not drop below an initial guaranteed amount, unless policy premiums are not paid or if loans or other withdrawals are taken from the policy. The ultimate death benefit is subject to the claims paying ability of the insurer.

Because the investment options available inside a variable life policy usually involve securities (e.g., stocks and bonds), the Securities and Exchange Commission (SEC) requires this type of policy to be accompanied by a prospectus. The prospectus provides detailed information on how the policy works, its risks, and all expenses or charges involved. The SEC also requires individuals selling variable life policies to be licensed to sell securities.

Policy Variations

There are two primary variations of variable life insurance, based on the formula used to link the amount of death benefit to the performance of the investments chosen by the policyowner. In general, if investment performance is positive, the amount of the death benefit increases; if investment performance is negative, the death benefit amount will decrease.

Example of Variable Life

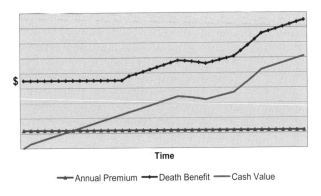

Time

—◆—Annual Premium —•—Death Benefit ——Cash Value

Continued..

Variable Life Insurance

- **Corridor percentage:** Under this method, also know as the constant ratio method, the amount of the death benefit is periodically changed to equal a certain percentage of the cash value. Under current tax law, this percentage is 250% up to the insured's age 40, gradually decreasing to 100%, usually at age 95.

- **Level additions:** Also known as the net single premium approach, this method uses excess investment earnings to purchase an additional amount of single premium, paid-up insurance.

Common Uses of Variable Life

Variable life policies are well suited for use by policyowners who are comfortable with the risks and rewards of investments, and who need life insurance with the potential to provide an increasing death benefit. Some common uses are:

- **Supplement existing family protection:** As a supplement to an existing, basic life insurance plan. If the market is down when an insured dies, the variable death benefit of a variable life policy may not provide adequate funds to support a surviving spouse and/or minor children, or to pay final estate expenses.

- **Business planning:** Variable life insurance is often used for many different business purposes, such as insuring key employees, in split-dollar insurance arrangements, and funding nonqualified deferred compensation plans. Business continuation planning often involves using variable life insurance as a source of funds for buy-sell agreements.

- **Accumulation needs:** Some individuals will use the cash value feature of variable life as a way of accumulating funds for specific purposes, such as funding college education, or as a supplemental source of retirement income.

- **Charitable gifts:** To provide funds for a gift to charity.

Modified Endowment Contracts (MECs)

A life insurance policy issued on or after June 21, 1988[1] may be classified as a modified endowment contract (MEC) if the cumulative premiums paid during the first seven years (7-pay test) at any time exceed the total of the net level premiums for the same period. If a policy is classified as a MEC, all withdrawals (including loans) will be taxed as current income, until all of the policy earnings have been taxed. There is an additional 10% penalty tax if the owner is under age 59½ at the time of withdrawal, unless the payments are due to disability or are annuity type payments.

A variable life policy can avoid treatment as a MEC through a well-designed premium payment schedule.

---

[1] Including a policy issued before that date, but later materially changed.

Continued...

Variable Life Insurance

Additional Policy Elements

Variable life policies have a number of additional elements to consider:

- **Investment options:** Most variable life policies offer a policyowner a wide range of investment options, including basic stock, bond and money market funds. Depending on the policy and insurer, other options, such as index funds, real estate funds, foreign stock funds, or zero coupon bond funds may also be offered. A policy may also include a fixed account option, in which the insurer guarantees a fixed rate of return.

- **Portfolio changes:** Many variable life policies allow a policyowner to change their investment allocation at least once a year (sometimes more frequently), usually at no charge.

- **Policy loans:** Almost all variable life policies permit the policyowner to borrow a portion of the accumulated cash value, with the insurance company charging interest on the loan. The rate charged to borrow the funds is often lower than current open market rates. A policy loan will reduce the death benefit payable if the insured dies before the loan and any interest due is repaid. A policy loan will also reduce the cash surrender value if a policy is terminated. If a policy lapses or is surrendered with a loan outstanding, the loan will be treated as taxable income in the current year, to the extent of gain in the policy.

- **Partial withdrawals:** Many variable life policies allow a policyowner to withdraw a portion of the cash value, without terminating the policy. Withdrawals may be subject to certain restrictions and/or withdrawal charges. Such withdrawals reduce the amount of death benefit payable, and may be subject to current income tax, if the policy is classified as a MEC, or if the withdrawal exceeds cost basis for a policy not classified as a MEC.

- **Policy dividends:** Variable life policies classified as participating offer the possibility of policy dividends. Dividends from a participating variable life policy are not guaranteed, and represent a return to the policyowner of a portion of the premium paid. Most participating policies offer a number of options as to how the dividends may be used.

- **Surrender charges:** Most variable life policies have substantial surrender charges, if a policy is terminated. These surrender charges are generally highest in the early years of a policy, and decline over a period of time, usually from seven to 15 years.

- **Surrender options:** If a policyowner surrenders a policy, there are generally three ways in which the accumulated cash value may be received, including: (1) taking the accumulated cash value, less any surrender charges; (2) receiving a reduced amount of paid-up insurance; or (3) taking paid-up term insurance in an amount equal to the original face amount of the policy.

Continued...

Variable Life Insurance

Optional Policy Provisions

A number of optional provisions, commonly referred to as riders, can be added to a variable life policy, through payment of an additional premium:

- **Waiver of premium:** Allows an insured to stop paying premiums if he or she becomes disabled and is unable to work.

- **Accidental death:** Pays the beneficiaries double (in some situations triple) the face amount of the policy if the insured dies in an accident.

- **Spousal or family term insurance:** Allows a policy owner to purchase term insurance on a spouse or children.

- **Accelerated death benefit:** An accelerated death benefit provision allows for payment of part of a policy's death benefit while an insured is still alive. Such benefits are typically payable when the insured develops a medical condition expected to lead to death within a short period of time.

Variable Universal Life Insurance

What Is Variable Universal Life Insurance?

A variable universal life insurance policy combines features found in both universal life policies, and variable life policies.

As with a variable life policy, a variable universal contract permits a policyowner to allocate a portion of each premium payment to one or more investment options, in separate accounts, after a deduction for expense and mortality charges. An annual statement detailing the expenses, charges, and credits allows a policyowner to track performance over time.

Following universal life policies, a variable universal contract permits the owner of a policy, within certain guidelines, to modify the policy death benefit, and change the amount and timing of premium payments, to meet changing circumstances. The ultimate death benefit is subject to the claims paying ability of the insurer.

Because the investment options available inside a variable universal life policy usually involve securities (e.g., stocks and bonds), the Securities and Exchange Commission (SEC) requires this type of policy to be accompanied by a prospectus. The prospectus provides detailed information on how the policy works, its risks, and all expenses or charges involved. The SEC also requires individuals selling variable universal life policies to be licensed to sell securities.

Policy Variations

There are two primary types of variable universal life, based on the level of death benefits:

- **Type I variable universal life:** Also known as option A, type I variable universal policies pay a fixed, level death benefit, generally the face amount of the policy.

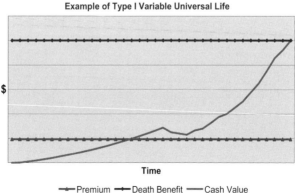

Example of Type I Variable Universal Life

Continued

Variable Universal Life Insurance

- **Type II variable universal life:** Also known as option B, type II variable universal policies generally pay the face amount of the policy plus the accumulated cash values. As the cash values grow, so does the potential death benefit.

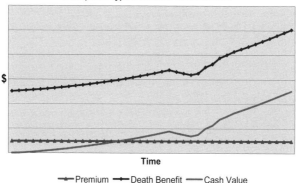

Example of Type II Variable Universal Life

—◆—Premium —◆—Death Benefit ——Cash Value

Common Uses of Variable Universal Life

Variable universal life policies are useful for policyowners who expect their needs to change over time. Within certain guidelines, the policy can be modified by changing the death benefit or premium payments. They are also well suited for use by policyowners who are comfortable with the risks and rewards of investments, or who need life insurance with the potential to provide an increasing death benefit. Some common uses are:

- **Supplement existing family protection:** As a supplement to an existing, basic life insurance plan. If the market is down when an insured dies, the variable death benefit of a variable universal life policy may not provide adequate funds to support a surviving spouse and/or minor children, or to pay final estate expenses.

- **Business planning:** Because of its flexibility, variable universal life insurance is often used for many different business purposes, such as insuring key employees, in split-dollar insurance arrangements, and funding nonqualified deferred compensation plans. Business continuation planning often involves using variable universal life as a source of funds for buy-sell agreements.

- **Accumulation needs:** Some individuals will use the investment features of variable universal life as means of accumulating funds for specific purposes, such as funding college education, or as a supplemental source of retirement income.

- **Charitable gifts:** To provide funds for a gift to charity.

Continued...

Variable Universal Life Insurance

Modified Endowment Contracts (MECs)

A life insurance policy issued on or after June 21, 1988[1] may be classified as a modified endowment contract if the cumulative premiums paid during the first seven years (7-pay test) at any time exceed the total of the net level premiums for the same period.

If a policy is classified as a MEC, all withdrawals (including loans) will be taxed as current income, until all of the policy earnings have been taxed. There is an additional 10% penalty tax if the owner is under age 59½ at the time of withdrawal, unless the payments are due to disability or are annuity type payments.

A variable universal life policy can avoid treatment as a MEC through a well-designed premium payment schedule. Caution must be exercised when changes in policy premium payments or death benefits are made, or when making partial withdrawals, to avoid having the policy inadvertently classified as a MEC.

Additional Policy Elements

Variable universal life policies have a number of additional elements to consider:

- **Investment options:** Most variable universal life policies offer a policyowner a wide range of investment options, including basic stock, bond and money market funds. Depending on the policy and insurer, other options, such as index funds, real estate funds, foreign stock funds, or zero coupon bond funds may also be offered. A policy may also include a fixed account option, in which the insurer guarantees a fixed rate of return.

- **Surrender charges:** Most variable universal life policies have substantial surrender charges, if a policy is terminated. These surrender charges are generally highest in the early years of a policy, and decline over a period of time, usually from seven to 15 years.

- **Policy loans:** Variable universal life policies typically permit the policyowner to borrow at interest a portion of the accumulated cash value. The rate charged on the borrowed funds is often lower than current open market rates. A policy loan will reduce the death benefit payable if the insured dies before the loan is repaid; a policy loan will also reduce the cash surrender value if a policy is terminated. If a policy lapses or is surrendered with a loan outstanding, the loan will be treated as taxable income in the current year, to the extent of gain in the policy.

- **Partial withdrawals:** Most variable universal life policies allow a policyowner to withdraw a portion of the cash value, without terminating the policy. Such withdrawals reduce the amount of death benefit payable, and may be subject to current income tax, if the policy is classified as a MEC, or if the withdrawal exceeds cost basis for a non-MEC policy. Some contracts allow a policy owner to put the withdrawn funds back into the policy, but the insured may have to provide evidence of insurability to restore the original death benefit.

---

[1] Including a policy issued before that date, but later materially changed.

Continue

Variable Universal Life Insurance

- **Surrender options:** If a policyowner surrenders a policy, there are generally three ways in which the accumulated cash value may be received, including: (1) taking the accumulated cash value, less any surrender charges; (2) receiving a reduced amount of paid-up insurance, or (3) taking paid-up term insurance in an amount equal to the original face amount of the policy.

Optional Policy Provisions

A number of optional provisions, commonly referred to as riders, can be added to a basic variable universal life policy, through payment of an additional premium:

- **Waiver of premium:** Suspends the monthly deduction for the protection element of the policy, if the insured becomes disabled and is unable to work.

- **Accidental death:** Pays the beneficiaries double (in some situations triple) the face amount of the policy if the insured dies in an accident.

- **Spousal or family term insurance:** Allows a policy owner to purchase term insurance on a spouse or children.

- **Accelerated death benefit:** An accelerated death benefit provision allows for payment of part of a policy's death benefit while an insured is still alive. Such benefits are typically payable when the insured develops a medical condition expected to lead to death within a short period of time.

Immediate Annuities

Immediate annuities are long-term contracts issued by a life insurance company. Typically purchased with a single, lump-sum investment, an immediate annuity can provide an income stream for a set period of time or for the rest of your life.

How Much Income Can I Receive?

The amount of income will vary, generally depending upon the following factors:

- **Amount of your purchase payment:** Generally, the larger the payment, the larger the income stream.

- **Your age:** Older individuals typically receive larger periodic payments.

- **Length of payout period selected:** A shorter payout period will usually result in a larger payment.

- **The underlying investment medium**, usually either a fixed or variable annuity.

Funding the Annuity – Fixed or Variable

As the name implies, a "fixed" annuity pays a fixed rate of return. The insurance company invests in a portfolio of mortgages and bonds and pays out a specified rate of return. Generally, this rate is only guaranteed for a certain period of time, after which a new rate is calculated based upon then prevailing market conditions. However, most insurance companies offer a guaranteed minimum rate throughout the life of the contract.

Bear in mind that annuities are not insured by the FDIC or any other government agency. All guarantees are based upon the credit worthiness of the life insurance company.

The other primary alternative is the variable annuity, which offers the potential for higher returns in exchange for your willingness to assume a greater level of risk. A typical variable annuity contract will give you a choice among several types of investment portfolios, such as stocks or bonds, or a combination. As the markets move up and down, your annuity's value will also rise and fall. Consequently, the amount of each annuity payment will fluctuate depending upon the performance of the underlying investments.

Variable annuities are sold by prospectus only. The prospectus contains more complete information including investment objectives, risk factors, fees, surrender charges, and any other applicable costs. Study the information in the prospectus carefully before investing.

Federal Income Taxation of Annuity Income

Because immediate annuities are purchased with after-tax dollars, the income received is pro-rated between ordinary income, which is taxable, and a return of principal, which is not taxable. This calculation takes into account your life expectancy and the amount of each payout. Please remember that state and local income tax law can vary. See your tax advisor for guidance.

Deferred Annuities

What Is a Deferred Annuity?

Life insurance is used to create an estate for an individual if he or she dies too soon. A deferred annuity, however, can provide protection against the possibility that an individual will live too long and outlive his or her accumulated assets.

The term "annuity" derives from a Latin term meaning "annual" and generally refers to any circumstance where principal and interest are liquidated through a series of regular payments made over a period of time. A "deferred" annuity is an annuity in which both the income, and any taxes due on growth inside the contract, are pushed into the future, until they are actually received by the owner.[1]

A commercial[2] deferred annuity is a special type of policy issued by an insurance company. In a typical situation, the policyowner contributes funds to the annuity. The money put into the policy is then allowed to grow for a period of time. At a future date, the policy may be "annuitized" and the accumulated funds paid out, generally through periodic payments made over either a specified period of time, or the life of an individual, or the joint lives of a couple.

Parties to an Annuity

There are four parties involved in a typical annuity.

1. **Insurance company:** This is the issuer of the annuity.
2. **Policyowner:** This is the individual or entity that contributes the funds. The policyowner typically has the right to terminate the annuity, to gift it to someone else, to withdraw funds from it, and to change the annuitant or beneficiary. Depending on the type of annuity, a policyowner may have other rights as well.
3. **Annuitant:** This is the individual whose life is used to determine the payments during annuitization. An annuity will remain in force unless terminated by the owner, or as a result of the death of the owner, or the annuitant dies.
4. **Beneficiary:** This is the individual or entity that receives any proceeds payable on the death of the annuitant or the policy owner, depending on whether the annuity is "annuitant driven" or "owner driven."

A single individual may be the policyowner, annuitant, and the beneficiary. In other situations, these roles may be held by different individuals or entities.

---

[1] Under federal law, the deferral of income tax on growth inside the policy is available only to natural persons; the tax-deferral is generally not permitted if the annuity owner is a non-natural person such as a trust or corporation.

[2] A private annuity is an agreement between individuals, usually exchanging a valuable asset (such as a business) for a lifetime income. The party promising to pay the annuity is someone who is not in the business of issuing annuities.

Continued...

Deferred Annuities

Types of Deferred Annuities

There are many different ways to classify deferred annuities.

- **Method of purchase:** Annuities can be purchased with a single lump-sum of cash; such annuities are often referred to as single premium annuities. They may also be purchased with installment payments over time, either of a fixed dollar amount on a regular basis or with flexible payments.

- **When annuity payments begin:** Payments under a deferred annuity typically begin at some future time. One variation, an "immediate" annuity, is purchased with a single premium, with annuity payments beginning one payment period (monthly, annual, etc.) later.

- **Investment options:** During the period before a policy is annuitized or completely liquidated, the funds invested by the policyowner are put to work. Depending on the type of annuity, the underlying investment vehicle will vary.

  - **Fixed annuity:** In a fixed annuity, the issuing life insurance company will guarantee a certain rate of interest, for a specified period of time, typically 1-10 years. Such annuities are useful for conservative, risk averse individuals. The investment risk rests on the insurance company and any annuity payments are relatively predictable.

  - **Variable annuity:** A buyer of a variable annuity has the option of placing the funds in the policy in a variety of investment options. The investment risk rests largely on the policyowner. Annuity payments are linked to the value of the underlying investments, which can fluctuate up or down.

  - **Equity-index annuity:** An equity-index annuity is a type of fixed-rate annuity which combines a guaranteed minimum interest rate with a potential for greater growth, with returns being based on a formula related to a specific equities market index such as the Standard & Poor's 500 index. If the chosen index rises sufficiently during a specific period, a greater rate is credited to the policyowner's account for that period. Unlike variable annuities, where poor market performance can lead to decreased policy values, equity-indexed annuities are structured to not lose value due to a declining stock market. However, because of surrender charges, an investor may lose principal value if an equity index annuity is surrendered early.

Continued.

Deferred Annuities

Payments from an Annuity

There are a number of ways that money may be withdrawn or received from a deferred annuity.

- **Lump-sum withdrawal:** A policyowner can withdraw all of the funds in an annuity in a single lump sum. Such a withdrawal is considered a surrender of the policy and the annuity ends. Depending on the policy and the length of time it has been in force, the insurance company may impose surrender charges, generally expressed as a percentage of the balance.

- **Partial withdrawal:** Many annuity policies allow an owner to withdraw a certain portion of the balance each year (usually 10% - 15%), without a surrender charge.

- **Life only annuity:** Regular payments are made for as long as the annuitant lives. When the annuitant dies, payments cease and no refund is made, even if the policyowner has not recovered the initial investment.

- **Life with term certain:** Regular payments are made for the life of the annuitant, or a specified number of years. If the annuitant dies before the specified term has passed, annuity payments continue to a beneficiary for the remainder of the term.

- **Joint and survivor:** Regular payments are made over the lives of two individuals. When one dies, annuity payments (or a specified portion) continue to the survivor.

- **Refund options:** Regular payments are made over the life of the annuitant. However, if the annuitant dies before the policyowner's investment has been recovered, the balance is refunded to a named beneficiary through either a lump-sump payment or continued annuity payments.

- **Specified period:** Regular payments are made for a pre-selected number of years. If the annuitant dies before the specified period has expired, payments are continued to a named beneficiary for the remaining term.

- **Specified amount:** Payments of a set amount are paid out regularly as long as there is money in the account.

Continued...

Deferred Annuities

The Value of Tax Deferral

Funds contributed to a deferred annuity have the potential to grow without current taxation. Assume the following facts in a hypothetical example.[1]

Assumptions:
Initial sum: $20,000
Growth of taxable investment: 6%
Growth deferred annuity: 6%
Current marginal tax bracket: 35%
Tax bracket at retirement: 28%
Current Year: 2008

Number of Years	Taxable Investment at 6%	Growth of Annuity at 6% Tax Deferred	Before Tax Additional Accumulation With Annuity	Taxes Paid at Time Withdrawn from Annuity at 28%[1]	Net Savings with Annuity
5	$25,065[2]	$26,765	$1,699	$1,894	-$195
10	30,349	35,817	5,468	4,429	1,039
15	36,747	47,931	11,184	7,821	3,363
20	44,494	64,143	19,649	12,360	7,289
25	53,874	85,837	31,963	18,434	13,529
30	65,232	114,870	49,638	26,564	23,075

Taxation of Annuity Payments

The tax treatment of payments made from an annuity will vary, depending on where in the life cycle of the annuity the payments are made. In general, the following rules apply.[3]

- **Before annuitization:** Funds withdrawn from an annuity prior to annuitization are considered to be made first from interest or other growth.[4] These earnings are taxable as ordinary income. If the annuity owner is under age 59½ at the time a withdrawal is made, the earnings are also subject to a 10% IRS penalty.[5] If earnings are completely withdrawn and payments are then made from the owner's initial investment, the payment is treated as a tax-free recovery of basis.

- **After annuitization:** Regular annuity payments are treated as being composed of part earnings and part return of investment. The earnings portion is taxable as ordinary income. Once the owner has completely recovered his or her investment, all remaining payments are fully taxable as ordinary income. In some situations, if the owner is under age 59½ when payments are received, a 10% penalty tax may apply.

---

[1] This hypothetical example is designed to illustrate the effects of tax deferral and is not intended to predict the results of an actual investment. Deferred annuities are subject to a number of fees and charges. A policy may include charges for investment management, administrative and mortality risk, cost of guaranteed death benefit, and surrender charges. If these expenses, charges, and fees had been included in this example, the tax-deferred performance would have been less.

[2] For years 2007 through 2010, the table assumes that the taxable investment is subject to a maximum federal tax rate of 15% (applicable to capital gains and interest) for an effective growth rate of 5.10%. For years after 2010, the table assumes that the taxable investment is subject to the full marginal rate of 35%, for an effective growth rate of 3.90%.

[3] This information is based on federal law. State law may vary.

[4] Withdrawals from annuity policies entered into before August 14, 1982 were treated as first coming from principal.

[5] Two exceptions to the 10% penalty involve the death or disability of the policy owner.

Continue

Deferred Annuities

- **Estate taxes:** Any amount payable to a beneficiary under an annuity by reason of an owner's death is includible in the owner's gross estate. If an annuitant/owner receiving payments under a life-only annuity dies, no further payments are due and nothing is includible in his or her estate.

Other Common Annuity Provisions

There are several standard provisions commonly found in annuity policies:

- **Bailout provision:** The bailout provision applies only to fixed annuity policies. In a fixed annuity, an insurer will typically offer a guaranteed rate of interest for a specified period of time. For any subsequent time periods, a different rate of interest will usually be offered. Under the bailout provision, generally, if a renewal interest rate is more than 1% less than that offered in the previous period, the policy owner has the option of terminating the policy without paying any insurance company surrender charges. Interest or other growth withdrawn will generally be subject to current income tax and may also be subject to the 10% penalty tax if taken before age 59½.

- **Surrender charges:** Most commercial annuities do not charge a commission when an annuity is purchased. Many, however, impose a surrender charge if withdrawals in excess of a certain amount are made, or if the policy is surrendered completely. Surrender charges can range from 0% to 10% and typically decline over time.

- **Prospectus:** Variable annuities are considered by the Securities and Exchange Commission (SEC) to be a security. The SEC requires that the purchaser of a variable annuity be given a prospectus, which provides detailed information on how the annuity works, the investment options available, the risks involved, and any expenses or charges. The SEC also requires individuals selling variable annuities to be licensed to sell securities.

Certain optional provisions may be available by paying an additional charge:

- **Guaranteed death benefit:** The guaranteed death benefit provision applies only to variable annuities. If an annuitant or owner in some contracts dies before annuity payments begin, the policy will pay the named beneficiary the greater of the investment in the policy (less any withdrawals) or the policy value on the date of death.

- **Enhanced death benefit:** Some variable annuities offer an enhanced death benefit option. This feature provides that upon the death of the annuitant or owner in some contracts, the beneficiary will receive the greater of the policy's value on the date of death, or the original principal (plus any additions) compounded at 5% per year. Other enhanced death benefits include percentage increases and highest anniversary valuation.

Seek Professional Guidance

Deferred annuities are primarily intended to be long-term investments. Because of this, and because of the complexity of many annuity policies, an individual considering the purchase of a deferred annuity should carefully consider all aspects. The advice and counsel of appropriate tax, legal, and other advisors is highly recommended.

Variable Annuities

The term "annuity" derives from a Latin term meaning "annual" and generally refers to any circumstance where principal and interest are liquidated through a series of regular payments made over a period of time. A "deferred" annuity is an annuity in which both the income, and any taxes due on growth inside the contract, are pushed into the future, until they are actually received by the owner.[1]

A commercial,[2] tax-deferred annuity is a contract between an insurance company and a contract owner. In a typical situation, the contract owner contributes funds to the annuity. The money put into the contract is then allowed to grow for a period of time. At a future date, the contract may be annuitized and the accumulated funds paid out, generally through periodic payments made over either a specified period of time, or the life of an individual or the joint lives of a couple.

A variable annuity is a type of annuity in which the contract owner directs the overall investment strategy for the funds placed in the contract.

Fixed vs. Variable Annuities

Two primary annuity types are fixed and variable annuities. Although these annuities share many features in common, the key differences between them arise from the means used to grow the funds contributed by the contract owner.

- **Fixed annuities:** Fixed annuities are characterized by a minimum interest rate guaranteed by the issuing insurance company. Typically, a minimum annuity benefit is also guaranteed. The funds contributed to the contract by the annuity owner are placed in the insurance company's general account, and the investment risk involved rests entirely on the insurance company. With a fixed annuity, the focus is on safety of principal and stable investment returns.

- **Variable annuities:** In contrast, a variable annuity contract generally has no guarantees as to investment return or annuity benefits[3]. The funds contributed by the contract owner are placed in special, variable annuity subaccounts. Within these subaccounts, the annuity owner may choose to invest the funds in a wide variety of investment options. Annuity benefits depend upon the investment results achieved, and the investment risk rests entirely on the contract owner. With a variable annuity, the goal is to provide benefits that keep pace with inflation.

---

[1] Under federal law, the deferral of income tax on growth inside the contract is available only to natural persons; the tax-deferral is generally not permitted if the annuity owner is a non-natural person such as a trust or corporation.

[2] A private annuity is an agreement between individuals, usually exchanging a valuable asset (such as a business) for a lifetime income. The party promising to pay the annuity is someone who is not in the business of issuing annuities.

[3] Unless the contract owner selects the "Fixed Account" option.

Continue

Variable Annuities

How a Variable Annuity Works

There are two distinct phases involved in the typical deferred variable annuity:

- **Accumulation:** During the accumulation phase, the contract owner contributes funds to the contract through either a single lump sum, or a series of payments. Each payment is used to purchase accumulation units in the investment subaccounts selected by the contract owner.[1] The cost of each accumulation unit is based on the market value of the investments underlying the subaccount, and the number of units outstanding. The number of accumulation units can vary, up or down, through additional contributions to the contract, or because of withdrawals from the contract. Any increase, or decrease, in the market price of the underlying investments is always reflected in the value of each accumulation unit. Expenses are deducted daily and are reflected in the value of each underlying unit.

- **Annuitization:** When a contract owner decides to annuitize the contract, the accumulation units are exchanged for annuity units. The number of annuity units received will depend on the price per unit, and certain insurance company assumptions regarding income, mortality and expenses. Once determined, the number of annuity units remains constant. The amount of periodic income payable is determined by multiplying the current value of each annuity unit, by the number of units. As the value of each annuity unit increases or decreases, so does the periodic income.

Common Investment Options

Depending on the insurance company and the contract, a wide variety of investment options are often available to the buyer of a variable annuity:

- **Stock:** The subaccount options which may be available can include aggressive growth, focusing on high risk/high return stocks; global and international stock, with equity investments from around the world; and specialty, emphasizing a particular industry or segment of the economy.

- **Bonds:** May include subaccounts focusing on corporate bonds; government bonds; and global or international bonds from around the world.

- **Balanced:** Includes a blend of stocks and bonds.

- **Precious metals:** Some variable contracts will offer subaccount options involving precious metals, such as gold or silver, investing either directly in the metals themselves, or through equity or debt investments in mining companies.

- **Money market:** Includes extremely high-quality short-term debt investments with an average maturity ranging from 30 – 120 days.

---

[1] Some variable annuity contracts will deduct a portion of each payment for charges and expenses, with the remainder used to purchase accumulation units.

Continued...

Variable Annuities

- **Fixed account:** In this option, the insurer guarantees a specific rate of return, for a particular period of time. Within a variable annuity contract, this is the only investment option where the investment risk rests on the insurer and not the contract owner.

Other Variable Annuity Contract Provisions

There are a number of key contract provisions that a buyer of a variable annuity contract should be aware of. Among these are:

- **How the contract is driven:** Some contracts are owner-driven while others are annuitant-driven. The word "driven" refers to what happens when a specific party dies or becomes disabled. With an owner-driven contract, the death of the annuitant will not terminate the contract. With an annuitant-driven contract, the death or disability of the contract owner will not result in death benefit payment, but IRC Sec. 72(s) requires payment within five years of death, unless the beneficiary is the spouse.

- **Guaranteed death benefit:** If an annuitant dies before annuity payments begin, the contract will pay the named beneficiary the greater of the investment in the contract (less any withdrawals) or the contract value on the date of death.

- **Enhanced death benefit:** Some variable annuities offer an enhanced death benefit option. This feature provides that upon the death of the annuitant, the beneficiary will receive the greater of the account's value on the date of death, or the original principal (plus any additions) compounded at 5% per year. The ultimate death benefit is subject to the claims paying ability of the insurer.

- **Exchange privilege:** Allows the contract owner to periodically change the allocation of funds among the subaccounts. Such exchanges are usually allowed, often without a charge, several times a year.

- **Prospectus:** Variable annuities are considered by the Securities and Exchange Commission (SEC) to be a security. The SEC requires that the purchaser of a variable annuity be given a prospectus, which provides detailed information on how the annuity contract works, the subaccounts available, the risks, and all expenses or charges involved. The SEC also requires individuals selling variable annuities to be licensed to sell securities.

- **Contract fees and charges:** Although there is typically no commission paid when a variable annuity is purchased, variable contracts are subject to a number of fees and charges. A contract may include charges for investment management, paid to the manager of the investment subaccounts; administrative and mortality risk charges to cover the insurer's basic expenses, as well as the cost of the guaranteed death benefit provision; and surrender charges, fees imposed if withdrawals in excess of a certain amount are made, or if the contract is surrendered completely. Surrender charges can range from 0 to 10%, and typically decline over time.

Continued.

Variable Annuities

Taxation of Annuity Payments

The tax treatment of payments made from an annuity will vary, depending on where in the life cycle of the annuity the payments are made. In general, the following rules apply:[1]

- **Before annuitization:** Funds withdrawn from an annuity contract prior to annuitization are considered to be made first from interest or other growth.[2] These earnings are taxable as ordinary income. If the annuity owner is under age 59½ at the time a withdrawal is made, the earnings are also generally subject to a 10% IRS penalty.[3] If earnings are completely withdrawn, and payments are then made from the owner's initial investment, the withdrawal is treated as a tax-free recovery of capital.

- **After annuitization:** Regular annuity payments are treated as being composed of part earnings, and part return of capital. The earnings portion is taxable as ordinary income. Once the owner has completely recovered his or her investment in the contract, all remaining payments are fully taxable as ordinary income.

- **Estate taxes:** Any amount payable to a beneficiary under an annuity contract by reason of an owner's death is includable in the owner's gross estate. If an annuitant/owner receiving payments under a Life Only annuity contract dies, no further payments are due, and nothing is includable in his or her estate.

Seek Professional Guidance

Tax-deferred annuities are primarily intended to be long-term investments. Because of this, and because of the complexity of many annuity contracts, an individual considering the purchase of a tax-deferred annuity should carefully consider all aspects before entering into the contract. The advice and counsel of appropriate tax, legal, and other advisors is highly recommended.

---

[1] This information is based on federal law. State law may vary.

[2] For annuity contracts entered into prior to August 14, 1982, withdrawals are treated as first coming from principal.

[3] Two exceptions to the 10% penalty involve the death or disability of the contract owner or annuitant, depending on the wording of the contract.

Equity-Indexed Annuities

The term "annuity" derives from a Latin term meaning "annual" and generally refers to any circumstance where principal and interest are liquidated through a series of regular payments made over a period of time. A tax-deferred annuity is an annuity in which taxation of interest or other growth is deferred until it is actually paid.[1]

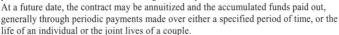

A commercial[2] tax-deferred annuity is a contract between an insurance company and a contract owner. In a typical situation, the contract owner contributes funds to the annuity. The money put into the contract is then allowed to grow for a period of time. At a future date, the contract may be annuitized and the accumulated funds paid out, generally through periodic payments made over either a specified period of time, or the life of an individual or the joint lives of a couple.

An equity-indexed annuity is a type of annuity that grows at the greater of an annual, guaranteed minimum rate or the return based on a formula related to a specific stock market index.

Fixed vs. Equity-Indexed Annuities

Two primary annuity types are the fixed and variable annuities. (An equity-indexed annuity is a type of fixed-rated annuity.) Although these annuities share many features in common, the primary difference between them is in the mechanism used to credit earnings to the annuity.

- **Fixed annuities:** Fixed annuities are characterized by a minimum interest rate guaranteed by the issuing insurance company. Typically, a minimum annuity benefit is also guaranteed. With a fixed annuity, the focus is on safety of principal and stable investment returns.

- **Equity-indexed annuities:** In contrast, equity-indexed annuities (EIA) are characterized by a contract return that is the greater of an annual minimum rate (typically 3%) or the return based on a formula related to a specific stock market index, such as the Standard & Poor's 500 index, reduced by certain expenses. If the chosen index rises sufficiently during a specific period, a greater return is credited to the contract owner's account for that period. If the stock market index does not rise sufficiently, or even declines, the lower minimum rate is credited. An owner is guaranteed to receive back at least all principal, if an EIA contract is held for a minimum period of time, known as the penalty period.[3]

---

[1] Under federal law, the deferral of income tax on growth inside the contract is available only to natural persons; the tax deferral is generally not permitted if the annuity owner is a non-natural person such as a trust or corporation.

[2] A private annuity is an agreement between individuals, usually exchanging a valuable asset (such as a business) for a lifetime income. The party promising to pay the annuity is someone who is not in the business of issuing annuities.

[3] The penalty period for some equity-indexed annuity contracts can be quite lengthy.

Continued...

Equity-Indexed Annuities

Understanding Equity-Indexed Annuities

Although all equity-indexed annuities share the same objective, contracts can vary greatly. The specific structure of a contract will affect the amount and timing of growth in the contract, as well as its liquidity. Below are definitions of some common terminology.

- **Term:** This is the length of time the penalty period lasts and/or the time when the investor has the option to renew. The period is commonly three to seven years.

- **Participation rate:** This is also known as the index rate. The percentage increase in the index by which a contract will grow. For example, "75% of the S&P's increase for the calendar year" means that if the S&P 500 index increases 10% for the year, the contract would be credited with 7.5%. This rate is usually less than 100%. The participation rate is subject to change by the insurance company.

- **Administrative fee:** This is also known as an annual fee, spread yield or expense load. It is a fixed charge subtracted annually by the insurer. This fee ranges from 1.0% to 2.25%.

- **Cap rate:** This is the annual maximum percentage increase allowed. For example, if the chosen market index increases 35%, a contract with a 14% cap rate will limit the client's increase to 14%. The cap rate is subject to change by the insurance company. Some contracts do not have a cap rate.

- **Floor:** This is the minimum guaranteed amount credited to the contract. It is typically in the three to four percent range.

- **Reference (contract) value:** This is the amount the investor is entitled to; i.e., the greater of the current account value less any remaining surrender charges.

- **Anniversary date:** This is the beginning of the term used to measure the growth in a contract.

- **Index credit period:** Amounts are credited to a contract at specific points in time. The three most common period methodologies used to determine the credited amount are as follows.
  - Annual reset – This measures the change in the market index over a one year period
  - Point-to-point – While similar to annual reset, the period used is usually five years
  - Annual high watermark with look back – While similar to point-to point, the highest annual anniversary value[1] is used to determine the gain instead; (i.e., the largest number at the end of any of the five years).

- **Averaging:** Some equity index annuities will determine any increased contract value based on an average of the monthly changes in the market index, measured over a specified period.

---

[1] For example, the credited amount might be the largest number at the end of any of the five years.

Continued...

Equity-Indexed Annuities

A Hypothetical Example

The following example will illustrate how the various methods of computing the amount credited to a contract might operate.[1]

Assumptions:
Initial Investment: $50,000
Date of Investment: May 30th, Year 0
Market Index, May 30th, Year 0: 1,422
Market Index, May 30th, Year 1: 1,600
Market Index, May 30th, Year 2: 1,300
Market Index, May 30th, Year 3: 1,590
Market Index, May 30th, Year 4: 1,785
Market Index, May 30th, Year 5: 1,700

Annual Reset – 100 % Participation and 16% Cap Rate

End Of	Computation	Contract Value
Year 1	1,600-1,422 = 178; 178/1,422 = 12.5% gain	$50,000 x 1.125 = $56,250
Year 2	1,300-1,600 = negative number = market loss	$56,250 (no drop in value)
Year 3	1,590-1,300 = 290; 290/1,300 = 22.3% gain	$56,250 x 1.16^2 = $65,250
Year 4	1,785-1,590 = 195; 195/1,590 = 12.3% gain	$65,250 x 1.123 = $73,276
Year 5	1,700-1,785 = negative number = market loss	$73,276 (no drop in value)

Point-To-Point – 90% Participation Rate and No Cap Rate

End Of	Computation	Contract Value
Year 5	1,700 (end) – (1,422 (beginning) = 278 278/1,422 = 19.5% gain	$50,000 + $8,775 = $58,775 (19.5% x 90% x $50,000 = $8,775)

Annual High-Water Mark With Look-Back – 100% Participation and No Cap Rate

End Of	Computation	Contract Value
Year 5	1,785 (peak) – (1,422 (beginning) = 363 363/1,422 = 25.5%	$50,000 x 1.255% = $62,750

Summary

Method	Contract Value after 5 Years
Annual reset, 100% participation, 16% cap rate	$73,276
Point-to-point, 90% participation, no cap rate	$58,775
Annual high-water mark, 100% participation, no cap rate	$62,750

---

[1] The results shown exclude any deductions for expenses.
[2] Despite a 22.3% gain, the contract is subject to a 16% cap.

Continued

Equity-Indexed Annuities

Other Issues

Other issues to keep in mind when considering an equity-indexed annuity include the following.

- **Guaranteed death benefit:** Some contracts offer, as an optional feature, a guaranteed death benefit. If an annuitant dies before annuity payments begin, the contract will pay the named beneficiary the greater of the investment in the contract (less any withdrawals) or the contract value on the date of death.

- **Regulation:** Although equity-indexed annuities have a connection to the stock market, their sale is typically not regulated by the Securities and Exchange Commission (SEC) as are other types of securities-related investments. An insurance company may register an equity-indexed annuity product with the SEC, if desired, and must do so under certain circumstances. If an equity-indexed annuity is SEC registered, a prospectus[1] must be provided to the buyer and only those individuals with both securities and insurance licenses may sell it.

- **Contract fees and charges:** Although there is typically no commission charged when an equity-indexed annuity is purchased, these contracts are subject to a number of fees and charges. These include administrative and mortality risk charges to cover the insurer's basic expenses as well as the cost of any guaranteed death benefit provisions. Surrender charges may also be imposed if withdrawals in excess of a certain amount are made or if the contract is surrendered completely. Surrender charges can range from 0 to 15% and typically decline over time. Payment of a surrender charge will result in a redemption less than the principal amount invested.

Taxation of Annuity Payments

The tax treatment of payments made from an annuity will vary, depending on where in the life cycle of the annuity the payments are made. In general, the following rules apply.[2]

- **Before annuitization:** Funds withdrawn from an annuity contract prior to annuitization (i.e., the beginning of regular payments) are considered to be made first from interest or other growth.[3] These earnings are taxable as ordinary income. If the annuity owner is under age 59½ at the time a withdrawal is made, the earnings are also generally subject to a 10% IRS penalty.[4] If earnings are completely withdrawn and payments are then made from the owner's initial investment, the withdrawal is treated as a tax-free recovery of capital.

Changes to the annuity contract, including loans, collateral assignments, and ownership changes may also result in income tax consequences.

---

[1] A prospectus provides detailed information on how an annuity contract works, the risks involved and all expenses or charges involved.
[2] Based on federal law. State law may vary.
[3] Withdrawals from annuity contracts entered into before August 14, 1982 were treated as first coming from principal.
[4] Two exceptions to the 10% penalty involve the death or disability of the contract owner.

Continued...

Equity-Indexed Annuities

- **After annuitization:** Regular annuity payments are treated as being composed of part earnings and part return of capital. The earnings portion is taxable as ordinary income. Once the owner has completely recovered his or her investment in the contract, all remaining payments are fully taxable as ordinary income.

- **Estate taxes:** Any amount payable to a beneficiary under an annuity contract by reason of an owner's death is includable in the owner's gross estate. If an annuitant/owner receiving payments under a life-only annuity contract dies, no further payments are due and nothing is includable in his or her estate.

- **Income in respect of a decedent:** Payments are still subject to income tax when received by the beneficiary. However, the beneficiary may also be eligible for a federal income tax deduction for a portion of the estate tax paid.

Seek Professional Guidance

Tax-deferred annuities are primarily intended to be long-term investments. Because of this and the complexity of many annuity contracts, an individual considering the purchase of a tax-deferred annuity should carefully consider all aspects before entering into the contract. The advice and counsel of appropriate tax, legal, and other advisors is highly recommended.

Combination Annuities

Combination annuities include two separate annuities:

- **Fixed immediate annuity:** Begins to return monthly payments currently; and
- **Fixed deferred annuity:** Accumulates the interest payments (tax deferred) until a future time; e.g. in 5 years.

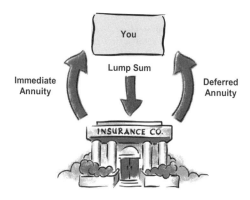

Note: Under IRC Sec. 72 (e)(11)(A)(ii), if two annuity contracts are issued to the same person within the same calendar year, they will be treated as one contract. There is some uncertainty as to whether or not this aggregation rule applies to immediate annuities. To avoid this issue, consider two policy holders; e.g. husband and wife, or two different calendar years.

The following hypothetical example compares the combination annuity technique using a fixed rate immediate annuity and a fixed rate deferred annuity with a certificate of deposit (CD). The comparison assumes the taxpayer is in the 28% marginal income tax bracket.[1]

Interest Rates Shown Are Hypothetical	Plan One	Plan Two	
	$150,000 in a 3.50% CD	$27,795 in a 3.50% Immediate Annuity for 6 Years	$122,025 in a 3.50% Deferred Annuity Begins in 6 Years
Annual return for 6 years	$5,250	$5,168	$0
Taxes on income portion	$1,470	$141[2] (90% tax free)	$0
Net return after taxes	$3,780	$5,026	$0
Monthly return after taxes	$315	$419	$0
Amount left after 6 years	$150,000[3]	Fully paid out	$150,000[3]

---

[1] CDs are generally protected against a failure of the savings institution by federal deposit insurance. A fixed annuity is guaranteed by the insurance company.

[2] 90%of the annual payment is a return of principal. The balance is taxable at 28%.

[3] At the end of six years, the $150,000 in the CD may be withdrawn income tax free as a return of the investor's principal. The $150,000 in the deferred annuity will be composed of $122,025 of principal, and $27,795 of taxable earnings. Withdrawals from an annuity prior to age 59½ may be subject to a 10% penalty tax.

Life Insurance Options for the Terminally Ill

The emotional stress of dealing with one's impending death due to a terminal illness like cancer, AIDS, etc., is further compounded by the customary increase in medical bills and a likely reduction in earning capacity.

A person owning life insurance policies may have several options for reducing some of his or her financial concerns.

Methods of Reducing Financial Concerns

- **Borrow against cash values:** Permanent type policies such as whole life, variable life, universal life, etc., build up cash values over the years. The owner of the policy is usually able to borrow money from the cash value, often at favorable interest rates. When death occurs, the policy loans and any interest will be subtracted from the face amount of the policy before payment is made to the beneficiary.
If there is also a "waiver of premium" provision the insured may be relieved of the monthly premium payments, in certain circumstances.

- **Surrender the policy:** Policies with accumulated cash values can be surrendered to the life insurance company. However, this would generally not be desirable, since the face amount of the policy is usually much higher than the surrender value and the time of death is close.

- **Borrow funds from a third party:** Other friends, family members, and possibly the beneficiary of the policy may be willing to lend money to the person who is terminally ill and then receive repayment from the insurance proceeds.

- **Accelerated death benefits:** Some life policies provide for payment of a portion of the face amount if the insured becomes terminally ill. This is generally called a "living benefit" or an "accelerated death benefit." Even if it is not mentioned in the policy the company may have extended the right to the policy owner; the availability of such benefits should be investigated.
Some companies require the owner to have a life expectancy of from six to nine months or less.
Terminally ill persons (diagnosed by a physician as expected to die within 24 months) may receive accelerated death benefits free of federal income taxes. IRC Sec. 101(g). Chronically ill individuals (as defined in new IRC Sec. 7702B (c)(2)) may also exclude from income-accelerated death benefits which are used to pay the actual costs of qualified, long-term care. See IRC Sec. 101(g) for more detail.

Continued

Life Insurance Options for the Terminally Ill

- **Viatical settlements:** Another option is to sell one's life policy to a third party in exchange for a percentage of the face amount. This is called a viatical settlement. It comes from the Latin word "viaticum" which means "supplies for a difficult journey." These settlements may also be available with contracts that have no cash value such as individual or group term life insurance policies. Factors which will determine the amount of the settlement include:

  - The insured's life expectancy is a factor. In general, the shorter the period, the more a viatical settlement company will pay. Some companies will accept up to a five-year life expectancy, but many prefer a shorter term of years.

  - The period in which the company can contest the existence of a valid contract must have passed, as well as the "suicide provision" (typically two years after issue). This period may begin again for policies that have been reinstated after a lapse for non-payment of premium.

  - The financial rating of the company that issued the policy is important. A lower rating can result in a smaller settlement.

  - The dollar amount of the premiums is a factor. The buyer of the policy is likely to be required to continue making the payments for the remainder of the insured's lifetime.

  - The size of the policy is a factor. Most settlement companies have upper and lower limits; for example, a top limit of $1,000,000 down to a low-end limit of $10,000.

  - The current prime interest rate is important, since the buyer will compare the settlement agreement to other types of investments.

After examining the above factors, a settlement company will generally offer the owner of the policy between 25% and 85% of the policy's face amount. The settlement amount may be received free of federal income tax under conditions similar to those described above under "accelerated death benefits."

Other Considerations

- If the terminally ill person is presently receiving benefits that are dependent upon his or her "means" (income or assets), like Medicaid, food stamps, etc., he or she must weigh the affect of a viatical settlement on these benefits. Benefits may be terminated or reduced until the settlement amount is "spent down."

- If the policy also has an accidental death or dismemberment rider, those rights should be specifically retained by the insured in the viatical settlement agreement.

- The time between applying for a viatical settlement and having the cash is generally three to eight weeks. However, this will depend on how quickly the medical information and beneficiary release forms are in the hands of the settlement company.

Continued...

Life Insurance Options for the Terminally Ill

- Most viatical settlement companies stress the confidential nature of the transaction but they require the named beneficiary to release any possible claim to the proceeds. If the insured does not want the beneficiary to know of the illness, he or she may change beneficiaries just prior to completing the settlement. If the estate were named as beneficiary, the insured (owner) would be the only one who would need to sign the release forms.
  If death occurs before the viatical settlement is completed, with the insured's estate as the beneficiary, the life insurance proceeds would be paid to the estate and would, therefore, be subject to probate administration.

- Viatical settlement of group insurance policies will usually require that one's employer be notified.

- Confidentiality may also be lost if the policy is sold by the settlement company in the "secondary market" to individual investors, since a new investor would want to know the health status of the insured.

- An escrow account is generally used to make certain that the payment of the agreed upon amount is made to the insured shortly after the insurance company notifies the escrow company that the ownership of the policy has been transferred to the viatical settlement company.

- Several viatical settlement companies should be investigated in order to negotiate the best offer.

Typical Uses for the Cash Received Include

- Cover out of pocket medical expenses.

- Finance alternative treatments not covered by existing medical insurance.

- Purchase of a new car or finance a dream vacation.

- To be able to personally distribute cash to loved ones.

- Ease financial stress to perhaps further extend life expectancy.

- Maintain one's dignity by not dying destitute.

- Pay off loans.

The sale of one's life insurance policies can have far reaching effects and should be done only after consulting with one's attorney, certified public accountant or other advisors.

1980 Commissioners Standard Ordinary Mortality Table

Life Expectancy in Years

Age	Male	Female	Age	Male	Female	Age	Male	Female
0	70.83	75.83	34	39.54	43.91	68	12.14	15.10
1	70.13	75.04	35	38.61	42.98	69	11.54	14.38
2	69.20	74.11	36	37.69	42.05	70	10.96	13.67
3	68.27	73.17	37	36.78	41.12	71	10.39	12.97
4	67.34	72.23	38	35.87	40.20	72	9.84	12.26
5	66.40	71.28	39	34.96	39.28	73	9.30	11.60
6	65.46	70.34	40	34.05	38.36	74	8.79	10.95
7	64.52	69.39	41	33.16	37.46	75	8.31	10.32
8	63.57	68.44	42	32.26	36.55	76	7.84	9.71
9	62.62	67.48	43	31.38	35.66	77	7.40	9.12
10	61.66	66.53	44	30.50	34.77	78	6.97	8.55
11	60.71	65.58	45	29.62	33.88	79	6.57	8.01
12	59.75	64.62	46	28.76	33.00	80	6.18	7.48
13	58.80	63.67	47	27.90	32.12	81	5.80	6.98
14	57.86	62.71	48	27.04	31.25	82	5.44	6.49
15	56.93	61.76	49	26.20	30.39	83	5.09	6.03
16	56.00	60.82	50	25.36	29.53	84	4.77	5.59
17	55.09	59.87	51	24.52	28.67	85	4.46	5.18
18	54.18	58.93	52	23.70	27.82	86	4.18	4.80
19	53.27	57.98	53	22.89	26.98	87	3.91	4.43
20	52.37	57.04	54	22.08	26.14	88	3.66	4.09
21	51.47	56.10	55	21.29	25.31	89	3.41	3.77
22	50.57	55.16	56	20.51	24.49	90	3.18	3.45
23	49.66	54.22	57	19.74	23.67	91	2.94	3.15
24	48.75	53.28	58	18.99	22.86	92	2.70	2.85
25	47.84	52.34	59	18.24	22.05	93	2.44	2.55
26	46.93	51.40	60	17.51	21.25	94	2.17	2.24
27	46.01	50.46	61	16.79	20.44	95	1.87	1.91
28	45.09	49.52	62	16.08	19.65	96	1.54	1.56
29	44.16	48.59	63	15.38	18.86	97	1.20	1.21
30	43.24	47.65	64	14.70	18.08	98	0.84	0.84
31	42.31	46.71	65	14.04	17.32	99	0.50	0.50
32	41.38	45.78	66	13.39	16.57			
33	40.46	44.84	67	12.76	15.83			

Deaths per Thousand at Various Ages
1980 Commissioners Standard Ordinary Mortality Table

Number Expected to Die Each Year

Age	Males Per 1,000	Females Per 1,000	Age	Males Per 1,000	Females Per 1,000	Age	Males Per 1,000	Females Per 1,000
0	4.18	2.89	34	2.00	1.58	68	33.19	18.84
1	1.07	.87	35	2.11	1.65	69	36.17	20.36
2	.99	.81	36	2.24	1.76	70	39.51	22.11
3	.98	.79	37	2.40	1.89	71	43.30	24.23
4	.95	.77	38	2.58	2.04	72	47.65	26.87
5	.90	.76	39	2.79	2.22	73	52.64	30.11
6	.85	.73	40	3.02	2.42	74	58.19	33.93
7	.80	.72	41	3.29	2.64	75	64.19	38.24
8	.76	.70	42	3.56	2.87	76	70.53	42.97
9	.74	.69	43	3.87	3.09	77	77.12	48.04
10	.73	.68	44	4.19	3.32	78	83.90	53.45
11	.77	.69	45	4.55	3.56	79	91.05	59.35
12	.85	.72	46	4.92	3.80	80	98.84	65.99
13	.99	.75	47	5.32	4.05	81	107.48	73.60
14	1.15	.80	48	5.74	4.33	82	117.25	82.40
15	1.33	.85	49	6.21	4.63	83	128.26	92.53
16	1.51	.90	50	6.71	4.96	84	140.25	103.81
17	1.67	.95	51	7.30	5.31	85	152.95	116.10
18	1.78	.98	52	7.96	5.70	86	166.09	129.29
19	1.86	1.02	53	8.71	6.15	87	179.55	143.32
20	1.90	1.05	54	9.56	6.61	88	193.27	158.18
21	1.91	1.07	55	10.47	7.09	89	207.29	173.94
22	1.89	1.09	56	11.46	7.57	90	221.77	190.75
23	1.86	1.11	57	12.49	8.03	91	236.98	208.87
24	1.82	1.14	58	13.59	8.47	92	253.45	228.81
25	1.77	1.16	59	14.77	8.94	93	272.11	251.51
26	1.73	1.19	60	16.08	9.47	94	295.90	279.31
27	1.71	1.22	61	17.54	10.13	95	329.96	317.32
28	1.70	1.26	62	19.19	10.96	96	384.55	375.74
29	1.71	1.30	63	21.06	12.02	97	480.20	474.97
30	1.73	1.35	64	23.14	13.25	98	657.98	655.85
31	1.78	1.40	65	25.42	14.59	99	1,000.00	1,000.00
32	1.83	1.45	66	27.85	16.00			
33	1.91	1.50	67	30.44	17.43			

The Chance of Dying Before Age 65[1]

From a group of 1,000 persons your age, the chart below illustrates the number who will still be alive at age 65. The third column indicates the probability that you will not be alive at age 65.

From 1,000 Males			From 1,000 Females		
Age at Last Birthday	Number Still Alive at 65	Chance of Not Being Alive	Age at Last Birthday	Number Still Alive at 65	Chance of Not Being Alive
30	755	25%	30	832	17%
31	757	24%	31	833	17%
32	759	24%	32	834	17%
33	761	24%	33	835	17%
34	763	24%	34	836	16%
35	764	24%	35	837	16%
36	766	23%	36	839	16%
37	767	23%	37	841	16%
38	769	23%	38	843	16%
39	772	23%	39	845	16%
40	773	23%	40	847	15%
41	775	23%	41	850	15%
42	778	22%	42	853	15%
43	780	22%	43	855	15%
44	784	22%	44	858	14%
45	787	21%	45	860	14%
46	791	21%	46	863	14%
47	795	21%	47	867	13%
48	800	20%	48	871	13%
49	805	20%	49	875	13%
50	810	19%	50	879	12%
51	816	18%	51	882	12%
52	823	18%	52	886	11%
53	829	17%	53	892	11%
54	835	17%	54	898	10%
55	843	16%	55	904	10%
56	854	15%	56	911	9%
57	864	14%	57	918	8%
58	876	12%	58	926	7%
59	888	11%	59	935	7%
60	903	10%	60	944	6%
61	918	8%	61	953	5%
62	935	7%	62	963	4%
63	954	5%	63	973	3%
64	976	2%	64	986	1%

---

[1] Based on Commissioners 1980 Standard Ordinary Mortality Table.

2001 Commissioners' Standard Ordinary Mortality Table

Average Life Expectancy in Years

Age	Male	Female	Age	Male	Female	Age	Male	Female
0	76.62	80.84	41	37.39	41.05	82	6.57	8.81
1	75.69	79.88	42	36.46	40.11	83	6.14	8.29
2	74.74	78.91	43	35.53	39.17	84	5.74	7.79
3	73.76	77.93	44	34.61	38.23	85	5.36	7.32
4	72.78	76.95	45	33.69	37.29	86	5.00	6.87
5	71.80	75.96	46	32.78	36.36	87	4.66	6.43
6	70.81	74.97	47	31.87	35.43	88	4.35	6.02
7	69.83	73.99	48	30.97	34.51	89	4.07	5.64
8	68.84	73.00	49	30.07	33.60	90	3.81	5.29
9	67.86	72.02	50	29.18	32.69	91	3.57	4.96
10	66.88	71.03	51	28.28	31.79	92	3.35	4.61
11	65.89	70.05	52	27.40	30.90	93	3.15	4.26
12	64.91	69.07	53	26.52	30.01	94	2.96	3.93
13	63.93	68.08	54	25.65	29.14	95	2.78	3.63
14	62.95	67.10	55	24.79	28.27	96	2.62	3.38
15	61.98	66.13	56	23.94	27.41	97	2.47	3.18
16	61.02	65.15	57	23.10	26.57	98	2.32	3.02
17	60.07	64.17	58	22.27	25.73	99	2.19	2.82
18	59.12	63.20	59	21.45	24.90	100	2.07	2.61
19	58.17	62.23	60	20.64	24.08	101	1.96	2.42
20	57.23	61.26	61	19.85	23.27	102	1.86	2.23
21	56.29	60.28	62	19.06	22.47	103	1.76	2.06
22	55.34	59.31	63	18.29	21.68	104	1.66	1.89
23	54.40	58.34	64	17.54	20.90	105	1.57	1.74
24	53.45	57.37	65	16.80	20.12	106	1.48	1.60
25	52.51	56.40	66	16.08	19.36	107	1.39	1.47
26	51.57	55.43	67	15.37	18.60	108	1.30	1.36
27	50.62	54.46	68	14.68	17.86	109	1.22	1.25
28	49.68	53.49	69	13.99	17.12	110	1.14	1.16
29	48.74	52.53	70	13.32	16.40	111	1.07	1.08
30	47.79	51.56	71	12.66	15.69	112	0.99	1.00
31	46.85	50.60	72	12.01	14.99	113	0.92	0.93
32	45.90	49.63	73	11.39	14.31	114	0.85	0.86
33	44.95	48.67	74	10.78	13.64	115	0.79	0.79
34	44.00	47.71	75	10.18	12.98	116	0.72	0.73
35	43.05	46.75	76	9.61	12.34	117	0.66	0.67
36	42.11	45.80	77	9.05	11.71	118	0.61	0.61
37	41.16	44.84	78	8.50	11.10	119	0.55	0.56
38	40.21	43.89	79	7.98	10.50	120	0.50	0.50
39	39.27	42.94	80	7.49	9.92			
40	38.33	42.00	81	7.01	9.35			

Note: Table based on composite (not smoker distinct) data.

Deaths per Thousand at Various Ages

2001 Commissioners' Standard Ordinary Mortality Table

Number Expected to Die Each Year

Age	Males per 1000	Females Per 1000	Age	Males Per 1000	Females Per 1000	Age	Males Per 1000	Females Per 1000
0	0.97	0.48	41	1.79	1.38	82	86.54	54.95
1	0.56	0.35	42	1.96	1.48	83	95.51	60.81
2	0.39	0.26	43	2.15	1.59	84	105.43	67.27
3	0.27	0.20	44	2.39	1.72	85	116.57	74.45
4	0.21	0.19	45	2.65	1.87	86	128.91	80.99
5	0.21	0.18	46	2.90	2.05	87	142.35	90.79
6	0.22	0.18	47	3.17	2.27	88	156.73	101.07
7	0.22	0.21	48	3.33	2.50	89	171.88	112.02
8	0.22	0.21	49	3.52	2.78	90	187.66	121.92
9	0.23	0.21	50	3.76	3.08	91	202.44	126.85
10	0.23	0.22	51	4.06	3.41	92	217.83	136.88
11	0.27	0.23	52	4.47	3.79	93	234.04	151.64
12	0.33	0.27	53	4.93	4.20	94	251.14	170.31
13	0.39	0.30	54	5.50	4.63	95	269.17	193.66
14	0.47	0.33	55	6.17	5.10	96	285.64	215.66
15	0.61	0.35	56	6.88	5.63	97	303.18	238.48
16	0.74	0.39	57	7.64	6.19	98	321.88	242.16
17	0.87	0.41	58	8.27	6.80	99	341.85	255.23
18	0.94	0.43	59	8.99	7.39	100	363.19	275.73
19	0.98	0.46	60	9.86	8.01	101	380.08	297.84
20	1.00	0.47	61	10.94	8.68	102	398.06	322.21
21	1.00	0.48	62	12.25	9.39	103	417.20	349.06
22	1.02	0.50	63	13.71	10.14	104	437.56	378.61
23	1.03	0.50	64	15.24	10.96	105	459.21	410.57
24	1.05	0.52	65	16.85	11.85	106	482.22	443.33
25	1.07	0.54	66	18.47	12.82	107	506.69	476.89
26	1.12	0.56	67	20.09	13.89	108	532.69	510.65
27	1.17	0.60	68	21.85	15.07	109	560.31	545.81
28	1.17	0.63	69	23.64	16.36	110	589.64	581.77
29	1.15	0.66	70	25.77	17.81	111	620.79	616.33
30	1.14	0.68	71	28.15	19.47	112	653.84	649.85
31	1.13	0.73	72	31.32	21.30	113	688.94	680.37
32	1.13	0.77	73	34.62	23.30	114	726.18	723.39
33	1.15	0.82	74	38.08	25.50	115	765.70	763.41
34	1.18	0.88	75	41.91	27.90	116	807.61	804.93
35	1.21	0.97	76	46.08	30.53	117	852.07	850.44
36	1.28	1.03	77	50.92	33.41	118	899.23	892.44
37	1.34	1.11	78	56.56	36.58	119	949.22	935.11
38	1.44	1.17	79	63.06	40.05	120	1000.00	1000.00
39	1.54	1.23	80	70.14	43.86			
40	1.65	1.30	81	78.19	49.11			

Note: Table based on composite (not smoker distinct) data.

The Chance of Dying Before Age 65

Commissioners' 2001 Standard Ordinary Mortality Table

From a group of 1,000 persons your age, the chart below illustrates the number who will still be alive at age 65. The third column indicates the probability that you will not be alive at age 65.

From 1,000 Males			From 1,000 Females		
Age at Last Birthday	Number Still Alive at Age 65	Chance of Not Being Alive at Age 65	Age at Last Birthday	Number Still Alive at Age 65	Chance of Not Being Alive at Age 65
30	850	15%	30	881	12%
31	851	15%	31	882	12%
32	852	15%	32	882	12%
33	853	15%	33	883	12%
34	854	15%	34	884	12%
35	855	15%	35	884	12%
36	856	14%	36	885	12%
37	858	14%	37	886	11%
38	859	14%	38	887	11%
39	860	14%	39	888	11%
40	861	14%	40	889	11%
41	863	14%	41	890	11%
42	864	14%	42	892	11%
43	866	13%	43	893	11%
44	868	13%	44	894	11%
45	870	13%	45	896	10%
46	872	13%	46	898	10%
47	875	13%	47	900	10%
48	877	12%	48	902	10%
49	880	12%	49	904	10%
50	884	12%	50	906	9%
51	887	11%	51	909	9%
52	890	11%	52	912	9%
53	894	11%	53	916	8%
54	899	10%	54	920	8%
55	904	10%	55	924	8%
56	910	9%	56	929	7%
57	916	8%	57	934	7%
58	923	8%	58	940	6%
59	931	7%	59	946	5%
60	939	6%	60	953	5%
61	948	5%	61	961	4%
62	959	4%	62	969	3%
63	971	3%	63	979	2%
64	984	2%	64	989	1%

Note: Table based on composite (not smoker distinct) data.

1986 Life Expectancy Table

Life Expectancy in Years[1]

Age	Male	Female	Age	Male	Female	Age	Male	Female
0	71.3	78.3	29	44.6	50.7	58	19.5	24.1
1	71.1	78.0	30	43.7	49.7	59	18.8	23.3
2	70.2	77.0	31	42.7	48.8	60	18.0	22.5
3	69.2	76.1	32	41.8	47.8	61	17.3	21.7
4	68.2	75.1	33	40.9	46.8	62	16.7	20.9
5	67.3	74.1	34	40.0	45.9	63	16.0	20.1
6	66.3	73.1	35	39.1	44.9	64	15.3	19.4
7	65.3	72.2	36	38.2	44.0	65	14.7	18.6
8	64.3	71.2	37	37.3	43.0	66	14.1	17.9
9	63.3	70.2	38	36.4	42.1	67	13.4	17.1
10	62.4	69.2	39	35.5	41.1	68	12.8	16.4
11	61.4	68.2	40	34.5	40.2	69	12.2	15.7
12	60.4	67.2	41	33.6	39.2	70	11.7	15.0
13	59.4	66.2	42	32.8	38.3	71	11.1	14.3
14	59.4	65.2	43	31.9	37.3	72	10.6	13.7
15	57.5	64.3	44	31.0	36.4	73	10.1	13.0
16	56.5	63.3	45	30.1	35.5	74	9.6	12.4
17	55.6	62.3	46	29.2	34.6	75	9.1	11.7
18	54.6	61.3	47	28.4	33.7	76	8.6	11.1
19	53.7	60.4	48	27.5	32.8	77	8.2	10.5
20	52.8	59.4	49	26.6	31.8	78	7.7	9.9
21	51.9	58.4	50	25.8	31.0	79	7.3	9.4
22	51.0	57.5	51	25.0	30.1	80	6.9	8.8
23	50.1	56.5	52	24.1	29.2	81	6.5	8.3
24	49.2	55.5	53	23.3	28.3	82	6.1	7.8
25	48.2	54.6	54	22.5	27.5	83	5.8	7.3
26	47.3	53.6	55	21.8	26.6	84	5.5	6.8
27	46.4	52.6	56	21.0	25.8	85	5.2	6.4
28	45.5	51.7	57	20.2	24.9			

[1] Latest table available in 1990 from the Department of Health and Human Services. Based on expectancies during 1986.

Insurance Company Rating Systems

A.M. Best

Grade	Interpretation
A++/A+	Superior. Very strong ability to meet obligations.
A/A-	Excellent. Strong ability to meet obligations.
B++/B+	Very good. Strong ability to meet obligations.
B/B-	Fair. Adequate ability to meet obligations.
C++/C+	Marginal. Reasonable ability to meet obligations.
C/C-	Weak. Currently has the ability to meet obligations.
D	Poor. Below minimum standards.
E	Under state supervision.
F	In liquidation.
S	Rating Suspended – usually due to insufficient information.

Standard and Poor's

Grade	Interpretation
AAA	Extremely strong financial security. Highest safety.
AA	Very strong financial security. Highly safe.
A	Strong financial security. More susceptible to economic change than highly rated companies.
BBB	Good financial security. More vulnerable to economic changes than highly rated companies.
BB	Marginal financial security. Ability to meet obligations may not be adequate for long-term policies.
CCC	Very weak. Currently able to meet obligations. Highly vulnerable to adverse economic conditions.
CC	Extremely weak. Questionable ability to meet obligations.
R	Regulatory action. Under supervision of insurance negotiators.

Moody's

Grade	Interpretation
Aaa	Exceptional security. Unlikely to be affected by change.
Aa 1-3	Excellent security. Lower than Aaa because long-term risks appear somewhat larger.
A 1-3	Good security. Possibly susceptible to future impairment.
Baa 1-3	Adequate security. Certain protective elements may be lacking.
Ba 1-3	Questionable security. Ability to meet obligations may be moderate.
B 1-3	Poor security. Assurance of punctual payment of obligations is small over the long run.
Caa	Very poor security. There may be elements of danger regarding the payment of obligations.
Ca	Extremely poor security. Companies are often in default.
C	Lowest security. Extremely poor prospects of offering financial security.

Insurance Company Rating Systems

Fitch

Grade	Interpretation
AAA	Exceptionally strong. Unlikely to be affected by change.
AA+/AA/AA-	Very strong. Moderate risk factors. Very strong ability to meet obligations
A+/A/A-	Strong. Moderate risk factors. Strong ability to meet obligations.
BBB+/BBB/BBB-	Good. Risk factors may be somewhat high. Good ability to meet obligations.
BB+/BB/BB-	Moderately weak. Uncertain ability to meet obligations.
B+/B/B-	Weak. Poor ability to meet obligations.
CCC+/CCC/CCC- CC+/C/C-	Very weak. Insurers in any of these ratings viewed as having poor ability to meet obligations.
DDD/DD/D	Distressed. Insurers have either failed to meet obligations or are under regulatory supervision/intervention.
NR	Not rated

Weiss Research, Inc.

Grade	Interpretation
A+/A/A-	Excellent financial security. Strong ability to deal with economic adversity.
B+/B/B-	Good financial security. Severe economic conditions may affect this company.
C+/C/C-	Fair financial security. Susceptible to downturns in the economy.
D+/D/D-	Weak financial security. Could impact policyholders.
E+/E	Very weak financial security. Significant risk, even in a stable economy.
F	Failed. Under supervision of state insurance commissioners.

Note: Some of the classifications of the above rating companies are broken down into more levels than illustrated. The financial strength of an insurance company is a very important factor to consider in purchasing life insurance or annuities.

Group Term Life Insurance

An employee is not taxed on premiums paid by an employer under a group term plan meeting the requirements of IRC Sec. 79, unless the amount of coverage exceeds $50,000. If the coverage exceeds $50,000, the employer must compute the cost of the additional protection, and notify the employee of the amount to include in his or her gross income. The government's Table I is used to determine the tax-reportable cost of the excess insurance protection. See Reg. Sec. 1.79-3(d)(2).

Age	Cost per Thousand per Month
Under Age 25	$0.05
25 through 29	0.06
30 through 34	0.08
35 through 39	0.09
40 through 44	0.10
45 through 49	0.15
50 through 54	0.23
55 through 59	0.43
60 through 64	0.66
65 through 69	1.27
70 and over	2.06

Example: A 44-year-old employee has $150,000 of employer-paid group term:

Total Insurance	$150,000
Less: 1st $50,000	- 50,000 (not reportable)
Taxable Amount	$100,000 X $.10 per thousand

Result: The employee must report as income an extra $10 per month, or $120 per year.

The premiums are tax deductible by the corporation under IRC Sec. 162(a)(1).

If a group term plan is discriminatory with regard to benefits or eligibility to participate, the $50,000 income tax exclusion will not be available to key employees. For discriminatory plans, the amount of imputed income is the greater of actual cost or the IRS Table I cost. See IRC Sec. 79(d). Payments for group term insurance which are included in the employee's income are also subject to FICA taxes. See IRC Sec. 3121(a).

Should an employer not be able to meet these rules, consideration should be given to personally-owned insurance as a supplement or substitute for existing employer plans.

Table I Rates for Group Term Insurance

Item Description	Value
Age of employee	45
Face amount of group term	$ 250,000
Tax-free portion (up to $50,000)	$50,000
Taxable portion of face amount	$ 200,000
Table I rate per $1,000 of face amount[1]	0.15
Income reportable each month	**$30**

An employee is not taxed on the premiums paid by the employer under a group term plan which meets the requirements of Sec. 79, unless the amount of the coverage exceeds $50,000.

If the face amount exceeds $50,000, the employer must compute the cost of the additional protection and notify the employee of the amount to include in his or her taxable income.

---

[1] Based on rates in effect on July 1, 1999 and later.

Group Health Insurance

Employer-paid premiums for employee medical insurance are deductible by the company whether the coverage is under a group policy or individual policies. See Reg. Sec. 1.162-10(a).

The employee need not report the amount paid by the employer as current income. See IRC Sec. 106.

When an employee pays the premium and is then reimbursed by the employer, the amount received is not included in the employee's gross income. See Reg. Sec. 1.106-1.

Benefits paid under the insurance plan, which reimburse the employee for payments made for hospital, surgical or other medical expenses, are not included in the employee's gross income.

Group medical plans are an attractive fringe benefit because personally paid medical insurance premiums and medical expenses are only deductible in excess of 7.5% of the taxpayer's adjusted gross income. See IRC Sec. 213.

Self-insured medical reimbursement plans which favor employees who are officers, shareholders or highly-paid employees may not qualify for the above tax benefits.

The Code sets certain eligibility requirements for self-insured plans, similar to those applied in qualified retirement plans, which are designed to discourage discrimination. See IRC Sec. 105(h).

The Health Insurance Portability and Accountability Act of 1996, signed into law on August 21, 1996, expanded the availability of coverage under group health plans. Effective with plan years beginning after June 30, 1997, the Act:

- Limits exclusions for pre-existing conditions;

- Prohibits discrimination in eligibility or premiums solely on the basis of an individual's health situation;

- Guarantees renewability for those employers with group health plans; and

- Provides penalties for employers who do not comply with the law.

Health Care Portability

During the summer of 1996, Congress passed the Health Insurance Portability and Accountability Act of 1996. This legislation made it easier for people with existing health insurance to change jobs, and still maintain health insurance coverage. The legislation does nothing to cover those who are currently uninsured, nor does it address the cost of individually owned health policies. Among other points, the Act:

- Restricts exclusions for pre-existing conditions.

- Requires special open enrollment periods.

- Prohibits plans from dropping or denying coverage for employees with medical conditions.

- Guarantees the availability of health insurance to small employers and individuals losing group health coverage, and guarantees renewability for all groups.

Pre-Existing Conditions

The legislation provides that group health plans must reduce any pre-existing conditions exclusion period by the length of time a person had prior coverage. Such prior coverage does not count if there has been a break in coverage longer than 62 days, not counting waiting periods. For example, if someone who had already satisfied a pre-existing condition exclusion, lost his or her group health coverage on June 30, and got a new job September 1, they would not have to satisfy a new pre-existing condition exclusion.

Certain individuals may qualify under federal law to elect COBRA continuation coverage during a special second election period. For these individuals, any days between the initial loss of group health coverage and the first day of the special second election period will not count as a break in coverage.

In order to allow individuals to present evidence of prior creditable coverage, the law requires group health plans to issue a certificate describing the previous coverage, which can include short-term coverage. Employers or insurers must provide this certificate when an individual loses coverage under the plan, or upon request at any time within the following two years.

Continued...

Health Care Portability

Under certain circumstances, the law does permit a group health plan to impose a pre-existing condition exclusion. An exclusion is allowed only if related to a condition for which the individual received medical care (or for which medical care was recommended) within the 6-month period ending on the enrollment date. This exclusion period cannot extend more than 12 months after the enrollment date (18 months for a late enrollee), and is reduced by any creditable prior coverage.

Waiting periods must run concurrently with any pre-existing conditions exclusion. Pre-existing conditions exclusions cannot apply to newborn children or children placed for adoption if they are enrolled within 30 days of birth or placement. Pre-existing conditions exclusions cannot apply to pregnancies.

Special Enrollment Periods

The law requires special open enrollment periods for people who lose other coverage, subject to certain conditions. Group health plans offering dependent coverage must allow at least 30 days in which to enroll new dependents following marriage, birth, adoption, or placement for adoption. If the employee is eligible but not enrolled, he or she must also be allowed to enroll at the same time. Plans must now allow eligible spouses to enroll within 30 days of the birth or adoption of a child.

Medical Conditions

Group health plans cannot establish any rules for benefits, premiums, eligibility or continued eligibility based on health-related factors. Insurers can no longer require employees or dependents to complete medical questionnaires in order to prove insurability, although they can require questionnaires as part of the rate–setting process.

This new rule also means that groups cannot single out an individual, based on health status, for denial of a benefit otherwise provided. For example, the plan may not deny prescription drug coverage to a particular person if prescription coverage is available to similarly situated individuals. However, a plan could exclude prescription drug coverage for all beneficiaries. An entire group can be charged higher premiums based on health experience, but a plan cannot single out an individual for higher premiums.

Guaranteed Availability and Renewability

Insurers cannot refuse to cover small groups (2 to 50 employees) based on the health of group members. Larger groups are not guaranteed the availability of coverage, but once they have coverage they are guaranteed renewability. Renewability may be denied for groups that fail to pay premiums, commit fraud, or fail to meet participation or contribution requirements. Employees who lose group coverage can purchase individual health insurance policies without providing evidence of insurability.

Caution

This law is filled with complexities and ambiguities. A complete understanding of the law's impact may require the assistance of a qualified group insurance representative.

COBRA Coverage Continuation

An employer who has 20 full-time-equivalent employees or more on at least 50% of its working days during the prior year must meet the requirements of IRC Sec. 4980B, also known as COBRA.

Failure to comply with COBRA requirements may result in serious penalties.

Under COBRA, an employer must give his covered employees (including spouses and dependent children who are covered) the opportunity to elect continuation coverage under an employer maintained group health plan (including plans to which the employer does not contribute financially) after any of the following events that would otherwise result in loss of coverage:

- The death of the covered employee

- The divorce or legal separation of the covered employee

- The termination of the employee's employment, unless for gross misconduct, or a reduction in hours that results in a loss of coverage

- The covered employee becomes entitled to Medicare

- A dependent child ceases to be covered by the plan due to his or her attained age

- For retired employees, the filing by the employer for Chapter 11 bankruptcy

Continuation Coverage

The coverage which is offered must be identical to the coverage offered prior to the event causing the continuation.

The plan may require the covered employee (spouse or dependents) to pay a premium, but it generally cannot exceed 102% of the cost to the plan for a person in a similar situation.

Terminated employees and employees with reduced hours must be provided coverage for up to 18 months (up to 29 months if disabled [by Social Security definition] during the first 60 days of COBRA coverage). Widows, divorced spouses, spouses of employees or retirees who lose coverage due to Medicare eligibility and dependent children who become ineligible are given up to 36 months of coverage.

Each health plan must give written notice to each covered employee of his or her continuation coverage rights.

Continued...

COBRA Coverage Continuation

Notice and Election Requirements

COBRA contains detailed rules and timelines specifying when employers, covered employees, and health plans/plan administrators must provide notices of certain events or take certain actions. The most important of these is the notice of an individual's right to elect continuation coverage. An individual normally has only 60 days from the date of the COBRA election notice (triggered by a loss of group health coverage due to one of the events discussed earlier) in which to elect continuation coverage. If they do not elect continuation coverage during this period, they normally give up their rights under COBRA to choose continuation coverage.

However, the Trade Act of 2002 created a special second 60-day election period for certain individuals who do not elect COBRA coverage during the initial 60-day period. The rules regarding this special second election period are complex. Employers whose employees may be entitled to assistance under the Trade Act of 2002 should check with their insurers or COBRA administrators to make sure that individuals who are qualified to receive trade adjustment assistance under the Trade Act of 2002 receive an appropriate notice of this special second COBRA election period.

Failure to Comply

Employers who fail to comply with the COBRA Rules can incur an excise tax of $100 per qualified beneficiary for each day of noncompliance (with a maximum of $200 per day per covered family). COBRA Administrators who fail to provide the initial COBRA notice or the COBRA election notice when a qualifying event occurs are subject to a penalty of up to $110 per affected beneficiary per day under the Employee Retirement Income Security Act. If the failure to comply is not intentional, but due to reasonable cause, the maximum excise tax is limited to 10% of the prior year's group health plan costs (with a maximum of $500,000).

Regulations

In February 1999 and again in January 2001, the IRS issued final regulations under COBRA, plus new proposed regulations. The regulations include dozens of changes and clarifications regarding the details of COBRA. In May 2004, the Department of Labor issued additional regulations (effective the first day of the first plan year that occurs on or after November 26, 2004) that make significant changes to the notice requirements. The regulations include model notices that should be customized for each plan.

Cafeteria Plans
IRC Sec. 125

Also called flexible benefit plans, cafeteria plans allow participating employees to choose among two or more benefits consisting of cash and qualified benefits. See IRC Sec. 125(d)(1)(B).

There is no need to change current benefit programs. If the employer is unable to pay for fringe benefits, the employee can enter into a salary-reduction agreement with the employer. The employer then uses these funds to pay for the employee's benefits. This allows the employee to pay for his or her own benefits with pre-tax dollars.

Employee Benefits

Some of the benefits that can be enjoyed by employees include the following.

- Lower FICA and income tax withholding due to lower gross pay

- Ability to select those benefits most needed

- Opportunity to refuse benefits already provided by a spouse's employer

- Option of redirecting tax savings to meet retirement needs; i.e., 401(k) plan.

- Potential qualification for the earned-income credit due to lower gross income

Employer Benefits

Some of the benefits that can be enjoyed by employers include the following.

- Lower payroll taxes (FICA, FUTA and sometimes worker's compensation insurance) due to lower gross pay

- Sharing cost of benefits with employee, if desired

- Help in retaining key employees

- Improved employee morale due to show of employer concern

- Potential reduction in fringe benefit costs

Continued...

Cafeteria Plans
IRC Sec. 125

Qualified Benefits May Include

- Accident and health insurance
- Health Savings Account (HSAs)
- Group term life insurance
- Dependent care assistance
- Flexible-spending accounts
- Cash-or-deferred arrangements (401(k) plans)
- Adoption assistance

Excluded Benefits

- Scholarships or fellowships described in IRC Sec. 117
- Educational assistance programs described in IRC Sec. 127
- Miscellaneous fringe benefits (including transportation and parking) described in IRC Sec. 132[1]
- Nonqualified deferred compensation plans
- Qualified retirement plans, except cash or deferred arrangements under IRC Sec. 401(k)
- Long-term care benefits, including long-term care insurance or services
- Contributions to medical savings accounts described in IRC Sec. 220
- Health reimbursement arrangements described in Revenue Ruling 2002-41

Plan Requirements

The plan must be written and include only employees.[2] The plan should include the following items.

- Description of benefits and coverage periods
- Eligibility rules for participation
- How benefit elections are to be made
- How employer contributions are to be made; i.e., employer funds or salary reduction
- Maximum amount of employer contributions
- Plan year[3]

---

[1] The Transportation Equity Act of 1998 allows pretax contributions for qualifying transit vouchers or parking, but these cannot be part of a cafeteria plan.
[2] Sole proprietors and partners (or attributed partners) or subchapter S shareholders who own (or who are attributed to own) 2% or more of the business may not participate.
[3] See proposed Regulation Sec. 1.125-(d)

Continue

Cafeteria Plans
IRC Sec. 125

Discrimination

The plan must be available to employees who qualify under a classification established by the employer and cannot discriminate in favor of highly-compensated or key employees.

One discrimination test that greatly impacts smaller employers is the 25% rule. The statutory, non-taxable benefits provided to key employees may not exceed 25% of the statutory, non-taxable benefits provided to all employees. If nondiscrimination rules are violated, key employees lose the benefit of the cafeteria plan and are taxed on the maximum amount of cash or taxable benefits. There is no effect on rank and file workers.

Key participants are any participants and participants' beneficiaries who, during the determination year,[1]

- are or were an officer of the sponsoring employer and earning more than $150,000[2];

- owned more than 5%[3] of the employer; or

- owned more than 1%[3] of the employer and received more than $150,000 of compensation from the employer.

2007 Proposed Regulations

On August 6, 2007, the IRS issued proposed regulations (NPRM REG-142695-05) on a number of issues related to cafeteria plans, including nondiscrimination rules. This suggest that the IRS will be paying more attention to this area in the future. These proposed regulations are generally applicable to plan years beginning on or after January 1, 2009.

---

[1] In-service distributions are subject to a five-year look-back period.
[2] This value applies to 2008.
[3] The family attribution rules of IRC Sec. 318 apply. Any participant is deemed to have the same ownership share as his or her spouse, children, parents and grandparents.

Flexible Spending Accounts

Flexible spending accounts (FSA) are a type of cafeteria plan commonly used by many employers. In an FSA, participating employees generally elect to have their salary reduced each month. The employer then uses these funds to pay for certain benefits with pretax dollars. There are three types of FSAs.

1. Medical expenses not otherwise covered

2. Dependent care expenses for both children and parents

3. Adoption Expenses

Tax Benefits

The payment of the benefit is tax deductible for the employer and is not considered additional income to the employee. As these dollars are not considered to be wages, they are not subject to either FICA or FUTA tax.

Health Benefits

If an FSA provides health benefits (like medical or dental expenses) to participants, it must be ready to pay the full year's benefits to an employee who qualifies for the benefit.

For example, if the employee has contributed for only one or two months at the time of the claim, the employer must pay for the entire expense up to the amount projected for the full year of contributions by the employee.

If the employee then terminates employment before the amounts are deducted from his or her paycheck, the employer must suffer the loss.

"Use-Or-Lose" Rule

Any unused funds remaining in an FSA at the end of the year will be forfeited by the employee. At the beginning of the year, a careful estimate of future expenses is helpful in avoiding this "use it or lose it" problem. However, employers may (but are not required to) establish a grace period of 2 ½ months after the end of a plan year. During this grace period, any unused funds may be paid or reimbursed to the employee for qualified expenses incurred during the grace period.[1]

Transfers of FSA Funds to Health Savings Accounts (HSAs)

The Tax Relief and Health Care Act of 2006 included a provision which allows for a one-time, direct transfer of certain amounts in a health FSA to an HSA; a number of restrictions and conditions apply. The provision is effective for distributions on or after the date of enactment and before January 1, 2012.

---

[1] See proposed regulation Sec. 1-125-1 (e)

Medical Reimbursement Plans

A plan set up by an employer to reimburse employees for their medical expenses that are not covered by their regular medical insurance is called a medical expense reimbursement plan. Reimbursable expenses might include dental expenses, expenses in excess of policy limits, etc.

Either reimbursement payments to the employee or insurance premiums paid to an insurance company (under an insured plan) are deductible by the corporation.

Payments are generally received by the employee free of income tax, unless he or she is a highly-compensated employee and the plan does not meet the nondiscrimination requirements.

Nondiscrimination Rules

Self-insured plans that discriminate in favor of highly compensated employees will cause the excess reimbursement benefit[1] to be included in the highly-compensated employee's taxable income. To avoid being discriminatory as to who may participate, a plan must meet one of the following tests:

- Benefit 70% or more of all employees

- Cover 80% of eligible employees where 70% or more of them are eligible

- Cover a special classification of employees which the IRS determines not to be discriminatory

To avoid being discriminatory in actual operation, highly-compensated employees must not have greater benefits than the other employees. For example, benefits should not be a percentage of salary.

Highly-Compensated Employees

Those persons who would be classified as highly-compensated employees include:

- The five highest-paid officers

- Shareholders owning more than 10% of stock

- The highest paid 25% of all employees[2]

Uninsured or Insured

Payment from the general funds of the business to reimburse the employee for his or her medical expenses is called an uninsured or self-insured plan. When the corporation pays premiums to an insurance company and thereby shifts the risk to an unrelated third party, it is called an insured plan. The nondiscrimination rules do not apply to insured plans. See Treasury Regs. 1.105-11(b)(1)(ii).

---

[1] Reimbursement for benefits not available to other plan participants.
[2] See IRC Sec. 105(h)(5).

Health Reimbursement Arrangements

A Health Reimbursement Arrangement (HRA) is an arrangement in which an employer reimburses an employee for certain medical expenses. The employee first pays for the medical expense out of his or her own pocket and is then reimbursed by the employer. If IRS requirements[1] are met, HRA payments are excluded from the employee's income (i.e. they are received income tax-free) and are a deductible business expense for the employer.

At the beginning of the year, the employer will specify the maximum amount that each employee can "spend" under the HRA. Unused HRA balances may be held over to increase the amount available for medical expenses in future years. An employee has no right to any "cash-out," nor is the arrangement portable, upon termination of employment.

In General

Sometimes known as "defined contribution health plans," HRAs can vary in their details, but are designed to provide a financial incentive for employees to make cost-conscious decisions regarding health care. Certain basic requirements apply to all HRAs:

- **Funding:** Only the employer may contribute to an HRA. No employee contributions are permitted, through a salary reduction plan or otherwise. An HRA is typically set up as an unfunded employee benefit program, with reimbursement payments being made from the employer's general assets as medical expenses are incurred.

- **Use of funds:** Generally, HRA funds may only be used to reimburse an employee for qualified, substantiated "medical expenses[2]," as that term is defined in IRC Sec. 213(d).

- **Maximum amount:** There is no IRS limit on the dollar amount that an employer may contribute to an HRA. The employer determines the maximum amount that will be reimbursed during the year.

Other Key Points

In some instances, an HRA will be combined with an employer-provided health plan, often a high-deductible health plan. In others, HRA reimbursements allow an employee to pay the premiums for the health insurance plan of his or her choice.

- **Eligible individuals:** Include current employees[3], their spouses and dependents, and the spouses and dependents of deceased employees. An HRA may reimburse the medical expenses of retired or terminated employees up to the amount of unused reimbursement left at the time the employee leaves the employer.

- **Non-discrimination:** An HRA may not discriminate in favor of highly compensated employees.

- **COBRA and HIPAA:** An HRA must comply with the requirements of both COBRA and HIPAA.

---

[1] The rules discussed here concern federal income tax law. State or local law may differ.
[2] Including premiums for health or long-term care insurance. See IRS Publication 502, "Medical and Dental Expenses" for a general guide as to what qualifies as a deductible medical expense. Some exceptions apply.
[3] Self-employed individuals, including partners in a partnership and more than 2% owners in a S corporation, may not participate in an HRA.

Continued

Health Reimbursement Arrangements

Transfers of HRA Funds to Health Savings Accounts (HSAs)

The Tax Relief and Health Care Act of 2006 included a provision which allows for a one-time, direct transfer of certain amounts in an HRA to an HSA; a number of restrictions and conditions apply. The provision is effective for distributions on or after the date of enactment and before January 1, 2012.

How a Health Reimbursement Arrangement Works

A Health Reimbursement Arrangement (HRA) is an arrangement in which an employer reimburses an employee for qualifying medical expenses. If IRS requirements are met, the reimbursements are income tax-free to the employee and a deductible expense for the employer.

Employer

Establishes
HRA

Makes Tax
Deductible
Payments as
Claims Occur

HRA

- Specifies maximum amount of yearly reimbursements

- May be funded or unfunded

Qualified Medical Expense Incurred

Employee

Pays
Medical
Expense

Submits
Claim

Receives Tax-Free
Reimbursement

Hospital

HRA

- Pays reimbursement (up to maximum amount)

- Unused balance carried forward for future medical expenses

Health Savings Account

A Health Savings Account (HSA) is a tax-favored[1] account set up exclusively to pay certain medical expenses of the account owner, spouse, and dependents. Health insurance coverage must be provided under a high-deductible health plan. Qualified contributions by the account owner are deductible from gross income and growth inside the account is not taxed. Distributions to pay for qualified medical expenses are received income tax-free. Funds not used during one year can be held over and used to pay qualified medical expenses in a later year even if no further contributions are permitted.

Similar in nature to an Individual Retirement Account (IRA) or Archer Medical Savings Account (Archer MSA), an HSA is owned by an individual and is thus portable. If an individual changes employers, the HSA moves with the individual and does not stay with the former employer even though that employer may have contributed to the HSA.

Key Concepts

There are a number of key concepts involved in understanding HSAs:

- **Eligible individual:** Only an "eligible individual" may establish, and then contribute to, an HSA. This is someone who on the first day of any month: (1) is covered by a high-deductible health plan (HDHP); (2) is not also covered by another health plan that is not a HDHP[2]; (3) is not enrolled in Medicare (generally, under age 65); and (4) may not be claimed as a dependent on someone else's tax return.

- **High-deductible health plan:** A health plan that meets certain requirements (adjusted annually for inflation) regarding deductibles and out-of-pocket expenses:

Coverage Type	2008 Minimum Deductible	2008 Maximum Out-of-Pocket
Self-Only	$1,100	$5,600
Family	2,200	11,200

As a general rule, the HDHP may not provide benefits (except for certain preventive care) until the minimum deductible for the year has been met.

- **Permitted insurance:** An individual is considered to be "eligible" without regard to any coverage he or she may have under certain "permitted" insurance such as worker's compensation, tort liability, or liability arising from the use or ownership of property (e.g. auto insurance). Also disregarded is insurance for a specific illness or disease or that pays a fixed amount (per day or other period) for hospitalization. Coverage for accidents, disability, dental care, vision care, and long-term care is also disregarded. Flexible Spending accounts are permitted only if they cover dental or vision care and/or meet the minimum deductible requirement.

---

[1] The rules discussed here concern federal income tax law. State or local law may differ.
[2] Certain limited exceptions apply.

Continued...

Health Savings Account

- **A trust or custodial account:** An HSA must be in the form of a trust or custodial account, established with a qualified trustee or custodian, such as an insurance company, bank, or similar financial institution.

Contributions To An HSA

Contributions to an HSA generally must be in cash:

- **2007 and 2008 annual contribution limit:** For 2007 and 2008, the maximum deductible contribution to an HSA is as follows:

Coverage Type	2007 Specified Maximum	2008 Specified Maximum
Self-Only	$2,850	$2,900
Family	5,650	5,800

Federal law allows an individual who becomes covered under a high-deductible plan in a month other than January to make a full, deductible HSA contribution for the year; certain restrictions and limitations apply. Individuals over age 55 may also make "catch-up" contributions of $800 per year in 2007, $900 per year in 2008, and $1,000 per year thereafter.

- **Individuals who may contribute:** Contributions may be made by an eligible individual, either directly or through a cafeteria plan, or by the individual's employer. Any person, including family members, may also contribute on behalf of an eligible individual.

- **Deadline for making contributions:** Contributions may be made in one or more payments and must be made no later than the due date for filing the eligible individual's federal income tax return for the year, generally April 15 of the following year. Contributions may not be made before the first day of the year to which they apply.

- **Income tax treatment of contributions:** Qualified contributions (including contributions by family members) to the HSA by an eligible individual are deductible from the eligible individual's gross income. Employer contributions to an HSA are excludable from an employee's income and are not subject to withholding for federal income taxes or for federal payroll taxes.[1] Growth or earnings on the contributions are not taxable while held inside the account. Excess contributions may be subject to a 6% excise tax.

- **Other:** Rollover contributions from an Archer MSA (or another HSA) to a HSA are permitted and need not be made in cash.

---

[1] Such as the Federal Insurance Contributions Act (FICA), the Federal Unemployment Tax (FUTA), or the Railroad Retirement Act (RRA).

Continued

Health Savings Account

Distributions From a HSA

Distributions from an HSA may be made at any time. Distributions used solely to pay for qualified medical expenses for the account owner, spouse, and dependents, are excludable from gross income (i.e. tax-free).

- **Qualified medical expenses:** Qualified medical expenses are expenses (incurred after the HSA has been established) for "medical care" as that term is used in IRC Sec. 213(d). Generally, this includes amounts spent for the diagnosis, cure, mitigation, treatment, or prevention of disease, or for the purpose of affecting any structure or function of the body, to the extent not reimbursed by insurance. Qualified medical expenses do not generally include health insurance premiums.[1]

- **Taxation of amounts not used for qualified medical expenses taxed:** Any distribution from an HSA that is not used for qualified medical expenses is included in the income of the account owner and a 10% penalty is added. The 10% penalty does not apply if a distribution is made because of an account owner's death, disability, or reaching age 65.

- **No longer an eligible individual:** If an account owner is no longer an "eligible individual" (for example, becoming enrolled in Medicare or no longer being covered by a HDHP), the HSA account may continue to be used. Distributions used solely to pay for qualified medical expenses continue to be received income tax-free.

- **Death of the account owner:** At death, funds in an HSA pass to a named beneficiary. If the beneficiary is a surviving spouse, the account becomes the HSA of the surviving spouse, subject to the normal rules that apply to all HSAs. If the funds in an HSA pass to a non-spousal beneficiary, the account ceases to be an HSA as of the date of death, and the non-spousal beneficiary must include in taxable income the value of HSA assets as of the date of death.[2]

Tax Relief and Health Care Act of 2006

The Tax Relief and Health Care Act of 2006 (TRHCA 2006) contained a number of provisions designed to promote the use of HSAs. Among these new provisions are:

- **Rollovers from Health FSAs and HRAs into HSAs:** This provision allows certain amounts in a health Flexible Spending Account (FSA) or Health Reimbursement Arrangement (HRA), to be contributed to an HSA in a direct transfer. The amount that may be transferred cannot exceed the lesser of (i) the balance in the FSA or HRA as of September 21, 2006, or (ii) the amount in the FSA or HRA as of the date of transfer. The amount transferred is not deductible, is not taken into account in applying the maximum deduction limitation for other HSA contributions, and is excludable from income. An individual may make only one such distribution from each FSA or HRA.

---

[1] Certain exceptions apply to qualified long-term care insurance, COBRA health continuation coverage, and health insurance premiums paid by an individual while receiving unemployment compensation. For those over age 65, premiums paid for Medicare Part A, Part B, Part D, a Medicare HMO, or premiums paid under an employer-sponsored health insurance plan also qualify.

[2] Less any qualified medical expenses of the deceased account owner, paid within one year after death.

Continued...

Health Savings Account

An individual who makes such a transfer must remain an eligible individual during a 12 month "testing" period, beginning with the month of the contribution and ending on the last day of the 12th month following that month. If the individual does not remain an eligible individual during this testing period, any amounts transferred are included in income and a 10% penalty tax applies.[1] This provision is effective for distributions on or after the date of enactment and before January 1, 2012.

- **Full contribution for months preceding becoming an "eligible" individual:**
  An individual who becomes an "eligible" individual during a month other than January is allowed to make contributions for the months in the year preceding the month he or she enrolls in a HDHP. If an individual makes contributions under this provision, he or she must remain an eligible individual for a "testing period." The testing period is the period beginning with the last month of the taxable year and ending on the 12th month following such month. If an individual makes deductible contributions under this provision and does not remain an eligible individual during the testing period,[1] the amount of contributions made for the months preceding the month the individual became eligible are included in income and a 10% additional tax applies.

- **One time rollovers from IRAs:** This provision allows for a once-in-a-lifetime distribution of amounts from an IRA (either a Traditional IRA or a Roth IRA), in a direct trustee-to-trustee transfer. Amounts distributed under this provision are not includible in income to the extent that they would otherwise be includible in income, and they are not subject to the 10% penalty tax on early distributions. The maximum amount that may be distributed from the IRA and contributed to the HSA is limited to the otherwise maximum deductible contribution amount to the HSA. No deduction is allowed for amount contributed from an IRA to an HSA.

An individual who makes such a transfer must remain an eligible individual during a 12 month "testing" period, beginning with the month of the contribution and ending on the last day of the 12th month following that month. If the individual does not remain an eligible individual during this testing period, any amounts transferred are included in income and a 10% additional tax applies.[1] This provision is effective for taxable years beginning after December 31, 2006.

Seek Professional Guidance

Heath Savings Accounts provide a tax favored means to accumulate funds to pay for qualified health care expenses. Because of the complexity of such accounts, the advice and guidance of trained tax and financial professionals is strongly recommended.

---

[1] An exception applies for death or disability.

How a Health Savings Account Works

A Health Savings Account (HSA) is a tax-favored account established exclusively to pay certain medical expenses of the account owner, spouse, and dependents. Health insurance coverage must be provided under a qualifying high-deductible health plan.

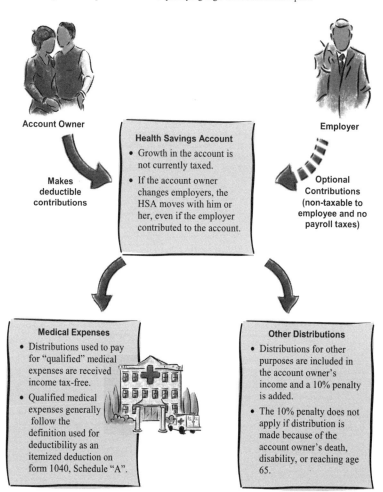

Account Owner

Makes deductible contributions

Employer

Optional Contributions (non-taxable to employee and no payroll taxes)

Health Savings Account
- Growth in the account is not currently taxed.
- If the account owner changes employers, the HSA moves with him or her, even if the employer contributed to the account.

Medical Expenses
- Distributions used to pay for "qualified" medical expenses are received income tax-free.
- Qualified medical expenses generally follow the definition used for deductibility as an itemized deduction on form 1040, Schedule "A".

Other Distributions
- Distributions for other purposes are included in the account owner's income and a 10% penalty is added.
- The 10% penalty does not apply if distribution is made because of the account owner's death, disability, or reaching age 65.

Medical Savings Accounts

The Health Insurance Portability and Accountability Act of 1996 created a new type of savings account designed to help individual taxpayers meet unreimbursed medical expenses on a tax-favored basis. This saving account, called a medical savings account (MSA), was available only to employees of small businesses and self-employed individuals, and only in conjunction with a high deductible health insurance policy.

MSAs were initially available, on a test basis, for 1997 through 2000.[1] The Job Creation and Worker Assistance Act of 2002 extended this trial period to December 31, 2003. The Working Families Tax Relief Act of 2004 further extended the period to open an MSA account to December 31, 2005. The Tax Relief and Health Care Act of 2006 extended the period to open an MSA for a third time, to December 31, 2007.

Key Points

- **Contributions:** Employee contributions to an MSA are deductible from gross income in calculating adjusted gross income (AGI). Employer contributions to an MSA are not taxable to the employee but must be reported on the employee's W-2 form. Contributions may be made at any time, up to the due date of the return (not counting filing extensions). Earnings on funds in an MSA are not currently taxable. MSAs cannot be part of an IRC Sec. 125 cafeteria plan, but a high-deductible policy can be.

- **Limit on contributions:** Contributions to an MSA are limited, based on the dollar amount of the health policy's deductible. For single coverage, the annual contribution limit is 65% of the deductible amount. For family coverage, the annual limit is 75% of the deductible amount. The Act sets limits for minimum and maximum deductibles, as well as the maximum out-of-pocket expense. These limits are indexed for inflation annually.[2]

Coverage Type	2008 Minimum Deductible	2008 Maximum Deductible	2008 Maximum Out-of-Pocket
Single	$1,950	$2,900	$3,850
Family	$3,850	$5,800	$7,050

- **Distributions from an MSA:** Funds distributed from an MSA to pay for qualified medical expenses (unreimbursed expenses that would otherwise qualify for the medical expense itemized deduction) are generally tax free. No itemized deduction is allowed for medical expenses paid from an MSA. Funds distributed for other purposes are taxed as ordinary income. A 15% penalty tax would also apply, unless a distribution is made because of death, disability or an MSA owner reaches age 65.

- **Tax savings:** The tax benefits of paying medical expenses through an MSA are significant. The ability to deduct contributions to an MSA above-the-line amounts to a dollar-for-dollar reduction in taxable income. Otherwise, unreimbursed medical expenses are deductible as an itemized deduction only to the extent that they exceed 7.5% of AGI, an amount that many taxpayers never reach.

---

[1] The Community Renewal Tax Relief Bill of 2000 (HR 5662) renamed MSAs as Archer MSAs.
[2] See Revenue Procedure 2007-66.

The Need for Retirement Planning

For much of the 20th century, retirement in America was
traditionally defined in terms of its relationship to participation in
the active work force. An individual would work full-time until a
certain age, and then leave employment to spend a few years
quietly rocking on the front porch. Declining health often made
retirement short and unpleasant. Retirement planning, as such,
typically focused on saving enough to guarantee minimal survival
for a relatively brief period of time.

More recently, however, many individuals are beginning to recognize that for a number of
reasons, this traditional view of retirement is no longer accurate. Some individuals, for
example, are voluntarily choosing to retire early, in their 40s or 50s. Others, because they
enjoy working, choose to remain employed well past the traditional retirement age of 65.
And, many retirees do more than just rock on the front porch. Retirement is now often
defined by activities such as travel, returning to school, volunteer work, or the pursuit of
favorite hobbies or sports.

This changed face of retirement, however, with all of its possibilities, does not happen
automatically. Many of the issues associated with retirement, such as ill health, and the
need to provide income, still exist. With proper planning, however, these needs can be
met.

Longer Lives

The single most important factor in this changed retirement picture is the fact that we now
live much longer than before. A child born in 1900, for example, had an average life
expectancy of 47.3 years. For a child born in 2004, however, average life expectancy had
increased to 77.8 years.[1] The graph below illustrates this change.

Average U.S. Life Expectancy (1900 - 2004)

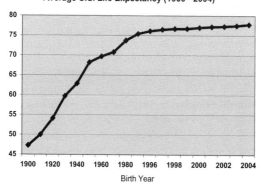

Birth Year

---

[1] Source: National Center for Health Statistics. Deaths: Final data for 2004.

Continued...

The Need for Retirement Planning

Common Retirement Planning Issues

Planning for a much longer life span involves addressing problems not faced by earlier generations. Some of the key issues include the following.

- **Paying for retirement:** Providing a steady income is often the key problem involved in retirement planning. Longer life spans raise the issue of the impact of inflation on fixed dollar payments, as well as the possibility of outliving accumulated personal savings. Social Security retirement benefits, and income from employer-sponsored retirement plans typically provide only a portion of the total income required. If income is insufficient, a retiree may be forced to either continue working, or face a reduced standard of living.

- **Health care:** The health benefits provided through the federal government's Medicare program are generally considered to be only a foundation. Often a supplemental Medigap policy is needed, as is a long-term care policy, to provide needed benefits not available through Medicare. Health care planning should also consider a health care proxy, allowing someone else to make medical decisions when an individual is temporarily incapacitated, as well as a living will that expresses an individual's wishes when no hope of recovery is possible.

- **Estate planning:** Retirement planning inevitably must consider what happens to an individual's assets after retirement is over. Estate planning should ensure not only that assets are transferred to the individuals or organizations chosen by the owner, but also that the transfer is done with the least amount of tax.

- **Housing:** This question involves not only the size and type of home (condo, house, shared housing, assisted living), but also its location. Such factors as climate and proximity to close family members and medical care are often important. Completely paying off a home loan can reduce monthly income needs. A reverse mortgage may provide additional monthly income.

- **Lifestyle:** Some individuals, accustomed to a busy work life, find it difficult to enjoy the freedom offered by retirement. Planning ahead can make this transition easier.

Seek Professional Advice

Developing a successful retirement plan involves carefully considering a wide range of issues and potential problems. Finding solutions to these questions often requires both personal education and the guidance of knowledgeable advisors, from many professional disciplines. The key is to begin planning as early as possible.

Sources of Retirement Income

Most retirees derive their retirement income from three primary sources: Social Security retirement benefits, qualified retirement plans, and individual savings/investments.

Social Security Retirement Benefits

Social Security retirement benefits are intended to provide only a portion of an individual's retirement income. Traditionally, retirement benefits began at age 65. For those born after 1937, however, normal retirement age, when full retirement benefits begin, will increase gradually, until it reaches age 67 for those born in 1960 and later. A reduced benefit is available, beginning at age 62. The monthly benefit amount is based on an individual's past earnings record. A worker can earn a larger retirement benefit by continuing to work past normal retirement age. Up to 85 percent of a retiree's Social Security retirement benefits may be taxable as ordinary income. Retirement benefits are adjusted for inflation on an annual basis.

Qualified Retirement Plans

A retirement plan is considered to be "qualified" if it meets certain requirements set by the federal government. In general, employer or employee contributions to a qualified plan are currently deductible and the earnings are tax deferred until paid out of the plan. Mandatory distribution rules typically apply and withdrawals before age 59½ may be subject to an additional 10% penalty tax.[1]

- **Employer-sponsored qualified plans:** Employer-sponsored plans can generally be classified as either defined benefit or defined contribution. Defined benefit plans specify the benefit amount a participant will receive at retirement; an actuary estimates how much must be contributed each year to fund the anticipated benefit. The investment risk rests on the employer. Benefits are generally taxable.
  Defined contribution plans, such as 401(k), 403(b) or SEP plans, typically put a percentage of current salaries into the plan each year. The retirement benefit will depend on the amount contributed, the investment return and the number of years until a participant retires. The investment risk rests on the participant. Benefits are generally taxable.

- **Individual qualified plans:** Include the traditional individual retirement account (IRA) and the Roth IRA. Contributions to a traditional IRA may be deductible and earnings grow tax deferred. Distributions from a traditional IRA are taxable to the extent of deductible contributions and growth. Contributions to a Roth IRA are never deductible and earnings grow tax deferred. If certain requirements are met, retirement distributions from a Roth IRA are tax free.

- **Nonqualified retirement plans:** An employer may set up a plan, often in the form of a deferred compensation plan, which does not meet federal requirements to be considered "qualified." Benefits are generally taxable when received. Such plans are often used as a supplement to qualified retirement plans.

---

[1] The rules and regulations surrounding qualified plans are complex. This discussion is intended to be only a brief, general description. State or local law may vary.

Continued...

Sources of Retirement Income

Individual Savings

Individual savings and investments are the third primary source of retirement income. An individual can choose to accumulate funds using a wide range of investment vehicles. The appropriate type of investment will depend on a number of factors such as an individual's investment skill and experience, risk tolerance, tax bracket, and the number of years until retirement. Below are listed some of the more commonly used choices.

- **Savings accounts:** Including regular savings accounts, money market funds and certificates of deposit (CDs) at banks, savings and loans and credit unions.

- **Common stock:** May also include other forms of equity ownership such as preferred stock or convertible bonds. Stock can be owned directly, in a personal portfolio or indirectly through a mutual fund.

- **Bonds:** Includes corporate, government or municipal bonds. Bonds can be owned directly, in a personal portfolio or indirectly, through either a mutual fund or unit investment trust.

- **Real estate:** Individually owned investment real estate or indirect investment through a real estate investment trust or limited partnership.

- **Precious metals:** Such as gold or silver, in the form of coins, bullion or in the common stock of mining companies.

- **Commercial deferred annuities:** Commercial, deferred annuities are purchased from a life insurance company and can provide tax-deferred growth through a variety of investment choices.

Other Income Sources

Other retirement income sources include the following.

- **Continued employment:** On either a full or part-time basis. Wage and salary income is usually taxable and before-normal-retirement-age[1] earnings above a certain level may affect the amount of Social Security retirement benefits received.

- **Home equity:** If a home is completely paid for, a reverse mortgage may provide additional income, without giving up home ownership.

---

[1] "Normal retirement age" is the age at which an individual is entitled to "full" Social Security retirement benefits – 100% of an individual's Primary Insurance Amount. Under current law, this age will vary from 65 to 67, depending on an individual's year of birth.

When Will Your "Nest Egg" Run Out?

A Hypothetical Look at Retirement

Assumptions:
Inflation rate: 2.50%
Annual pre-tax investment rate: 8.00%

Current Scenario	Amount	Inflate?
Annual pre-tax income desired (in today's dollars)	$ 100,000	Yes
Years until retirement begins	20	
Desired income in first year of retirement	**$ 163,862**	
Anticipated annual pension income	- $35,000	Yes
Annual social security estimate	- $25,000	Yes
Other anticipated annual retirement income	- $10,000	Yes
Amount needed from nest egg in first year of retirement	**$93,862**	
Amount currently in nest egg	$ 100,000	
Annual contribution to nest egg	$10,000	Yes
Amount in nest egg in first year of retirement	**$1,015,612**	

Full years until nest egg runs out:	**15**

For most, the primary objective of their working lives is to fund a comfortable and secure retirement. The feeling of security comes from the knowledge that their nest egg – accumulated to fund that retirement – is sufficient.

How to Make the Nest Egg Last Longer

Advance planning is the key to ensuring that there will be enough set aside for a worry-free retirement. If a retirement plan analysis shows that the funds are insufficient, one may change that outcome by several methods. Consider the following:

- **Increase the potential rate of return by reallocating investment assets:** Being sure to get the biggest bang for the buck, while managing investment risk, can have the most dramatic affect on the size of the nest egg;

- **Increase the annual contribution:** Putting more away will certainly help and may require reprioritizing today's spending decisions;

- **Retire later:** Delaying retirement allows more years to accumulate funds while requiring less from the nest egg.

- **Reduce the objective:** Requiring less retirement income, by either living on less or continuing to work after retirement, can help solve the problem.

It is important to understand that the amounts represented on this page, although calculated with a high degree of accuracy, are merely hypothetical, broad-brush indications of a potential problem. The only conclusions that should be drawn from this page are that additional action may be appropriate and that professional advice can help identify the size of a retirement funding problem as well as the solutions that make the most sense.

Evaluating Early Retirement Offers

In recent years cost-cutting and restructuring measures have forced a number of companies to offer many of their employees early retirement packages. Although initially attractive, these packages require careful analysis. In deciding to either accept or reject an early retirement offer, several key questions must be answered:

1. Do you want to retire?
2. If you don't want to retire, what happens if you reject the offer?
3. If you do want to retire, can you realistically afford retirement?

Common Elements in Early Retirement Packages

Early retirement offers are carefully structured and may include "sweeteners" such as:

- **Cash:** A cash bonus, either as a lump-sum or periodic payments, may be included. Consider your cash-flow and income tax situation before deciding which to take.

- **Defined benefit pensions:** For companies with defined benefit retirement plans, retirement income is often based on years of service, age at retirement, and a percentage of the highest three years earnings. Any or all of these factors can be adjusted to give an employee a higher pension benefit.

- **Defined contribution pensions:** Employers who sponsor defined contribution plans such as 401(k) or 403(b) plans may allow employees who take early retirement to keep their funds in the company plan.

- **Other fringe benefits:** Some early retirement offers will include valuable benefits such as group health or life insurance, counseling by professional financial advisors, and education or job placement assistance, if the employee wishes to continue working.

Do You Want to Retire?

Before the offer was made, what were your plans for the future? Were you already considering early retirement or were you planning on working for a few more years? For some, continuing to work is not only enjoyable, but it also helps in reaching goals such as putting a child or grandchild through college or paying off a mortgage. For others, the freedom retirement offers to pursue more personal goals is a life-long dream.

What Happens if You Decide to Reject the Offer?

Sometimes remaining with your current employer is a realistic option, sometimes it isn't. Refusing an early retirement offer may lead to promotions or salary increases that, in the long run, could result in a higher retirement benefit. Also, working longer allows you to save more and reduces the number of retirement years. Alternatively, rejecting an offer may result in being demoted or simply let go when your position is eliminated. Often, you have only a very brief period of time to make this critical decision, typically 60 to 90 days.

Continued.

Evaluating Early Retirement Offers

Can You Afford to Retire?

For most of us the key question frequently comes down to whether or not we can financially afford to retire. There are a number of issues to consider when answering this question, focusing on how much income you need and where it will come from:

- **A longer retirement:** Early retirement effectively means that your retirement will last longer. With people living longer, some of us may spend as much as 1/3 of our lives in retirement.

- **Taxes and inflation:** When planning your income needs, be sure to keep the impact of both taxes and inflation in mind. What will your marginal tax rate be in retirement? To offset inflation, your income goal cannot remain level, but must increase each year.

- **Lower pension and Social Security income:** Early retirement often results in lower pension income as well as reduced Social Security retirement benefits.

- **Less time to plan and save:** Early retirement leaves you less time to plan for the psychological adjustment needed when you retire. It also leaves less time to save for what will likely be a longer period of retirement.

- **Health care:** Medical care is expensive and as we age we typically need more of it. During our working years, employer provided health insurance is an extremely valuable benefit. After retirement, however, we are much more on our own. Medicare is generally available once you reach age 65, but Medicare has specific limits. Often, additional medical insurance is necessary, but the individual typically has to personally pay for this extra coverage.

- **Continue working:** Some of us, either because we enjoy working, or because we need the income, will want to consider continued employment.

Seek Professional Guidance

Evaluating an early retirement offer from your employer can be a complex and confusing task. The advice and counsel of trained professional advisors are strongly recommended.

Making the Most of Your Retirement Plan
Defined Contribution Retirement Plans

Many employers offer some form of defined contribution retirement plan. Although the name may vary (401(k), 403(b), 457(b))[1], on a basic level they all function in much the same way. During your working years money is automatically deducted from your paycheck and contributed to the plan. The accumulated funds are ultimately used to help pay for your retirement.

Why Participate?

The answer to this is simple: you'll likely need the money. With people living longer, more money is needed to pay for retirement. And two of the traditional financial pillars of retirement, defined benefit pension plans (providing a known benefit) and Social Security are playing a smaller role in meeting this increased need for retirement income.

Over the past several decades many employers have changed from defined benefit to defined contribution plans. From 1985 to 2000, for example, the rate of participation in defined benefit plans by full-time employees of medium and large private firms dropped from 80% to 36%.[2] Social Security also faces problems. As the baby boom generation enters retirement (the so-called "silver tsunami"), the number of individuals remaining in the workforce to support these retirees grows smaller. Although politically unpleasant, harsh fiscal realities may force increased payroll taxes, reductions in benefits, or both.

What to Do?

Today, to a greater extent than ever before, you're on your own. One starting point is to take a more active role in your employer's defined contribution plan:

- **Investment options:** Or, where do I invest my money? This will depend on a number of factors, including the plan's available options, the amount of your retirement income goal, the number of years until retirement begins, and your tolerance for risk.

- **Contribution rate:** A 3% rate may be the default, but is that enough to meet your needs? Another factor to consider is whether there is an employer match for part of your contributions. At the least you should contribute to the level which will maximize the employer match. Otherwise, you're walking away from "free money."

- **Annual checkup:** Everyone's situation changes over time. Make sure that you conduct a thorough review of your retirement plan at least once a year. Are you saving enough? Are your investments still appropriate?

Seek Professional Guidance

Successful long-term investing requires discipline and patience. The advice and guidance of professional financial advisors is also strongly recommended.

---

[1] These refer to the sections of the Internal Revenue Code which authorize the different types of retirement plans.
[2] See, "Employee Participation in Defined Benefit and Defined Contribution Plans, 1985-2000." U.S. Bureau of Labor Statistics, updated June 16, 2004.

Length of Time a Sum Will Last

Item Description	Value
Current sum	$ 100,000
Annual interest rate[1]	5.00%
Frequency of withdrawals	Annually
Withdrawal amount each Year	$2,500
Number of Years sum will last	**2999**

Example

If you have $100,000 in an account earning an annual return of 5.00% and you withdraw $2,500 per year, the account will not be depleted.

---

[1] The rates of return used in this illustration are not indicative of any actual investment and will fluctuate in value. An investment will not provide a consistent rate of return; years with lower (or negative) returns than the hypothetical returns shown may substantially affect the scenario presented.

Present Value of Future Annuity Payments

Item Description	Value
Frequency of annuity payments	Annually
Annual payment	$1,000
Annual interest rate[1]	5.00%
Number of Years to receive payments	55
Total annuity payments received	**$55,000**
Amount of annuity, if payments are:	
At the end of each Year	**$18,633**
At the beginning of each Year	**$19,565**

Example

An annuity of $19,565 earning an annual return of 5.00%, would
pay you $1,000 at the beginning of each year for the next 55
years, at which time your account would be depleted.

---

[1] The rates of return used in this illustration are not indicative of any actual investment and will fluctuate in value. An
investment will not provide a consistent rate of return; years with lower (or negative) returns than the hypothetical
returns shown may substantially affect the scenario presented.

Net Present Value

Net Present Value Defined

Net present value (NPV) is a mathematical tool used to analyze financial situations involving variable cash flows (money going out and coming in) occurring at regular intervals. The calculation is done as if the cash flows shown here were placed in an account earning a rate of return equivalent to the discount rate.

A Positive NPV means that the illustrated investment performs better.

A Negative NPV means that the account earning the discount rate may be the better choice.

Assumptions:
Discount rate: 5.00%
Cash flows:

Cash Flow	Amount	Duration in Years
Initial	$10,000	1
1	$7,500	2
2	$5,000	2
3	$2,500	2
4	$1,000	2
5	$ 120,000	1
6	$16,500	2
7	$ 500	1
8	$7,000	1
9	$2,500	1
10	$1,250	1

Net present value for the assumed cash flows: $ 140,575

Internal Rate of Return

Internal Rate of Return Defined

The internal rate of return (IRR) is the interest rate at which the present value of expected cash flows equals the value of the initial outlay. Simply put, if all the negative cash flows listed below were placed into an interest-bearing account (in the timeframes indicated) and all the positive cash flows were withdrawn from that same account (in the timeframes indicated), the account would have to earn the rate represented by the IRR in order to have a zero balance after the last cash flow. It can be used to help evaluate the anticipated cash flows of a purchase or investment. If the IRR is positive, then the present value of the positive cash flows outweigh the negative and vice versa.

Assumptions:
  Cash flows:

Cash Flow	Amount	Duration in Years
Initial	- $ 100,000	1
1	$1,000	1
2	$5,000	2
3	$10,000	3
4	$25,000	5
5	$ 234,234	1
6	$ 234	1
7	$ 243	1
8	$24	1
9	$ 234	1
10	$4	1

Internal Rate of Return for the assumed cash flows: 15.38%

Annuities In Retirement Income Planning

For much of the recent past, individuals entering retirement could look to a number of potential sources for the steady income needed to maintain a decent standard of living:

- **Defined benefit (DB) employer pensions:** In these plans the employer promises to pay a specified monthly amount for the life of the retiree and/or spouse.

- **Social Security:** Designed to replace only a part of an individual's working income, Social Security provides a known benefit for the life of a retiree and his or her spouse

- **Defined contribution (DC) plans:** Such as 401(k), 403(b), or 457[1] plans, which allow for contributions from the employee (in some cases from the employer as well) to a retirement account. The funds in the account, whatever they amount to at retirement, are used to provide retirement income.

- **Individual retirement plans:** Such as Traditional IRAs or Roth IRAs. These are "individual" versions of employer-sponsored DC plans. The funds in the IRA at retirement, whatever the amount, are used to provide retirement income.

The Changing Face Of Retirement

The saying that "life is what happens when you're making other plans" is particularly true when it comes to retirement income planning, for several key reasons:

- **Fewer employer pensions:** Over the past several decades, many employers have changed from defined benefit to defined contribution plans. From 1985 to 2000, for example, the rate of participation in defined benefit plans by full-time employees of medium and large private firms dropped from 80% to 36%.[2]

- **Social Security:** Social Security is a "pay-as-you-go" system, with current workers supporting those already receiving benefits. As the baby boom generation begins to retire, the number of individuals remaining in the workforce to support them grows smaller. Although politically unpleasant, fiscal reality may force higher payroll taxes, reductions in benefits, or both.

- **We're living longer:** A child born in 1900 had an average life expectancy of 47.3 years. For a child born in 2004, however, average life expectancy had increased to 77.8 years.[3]

With the stable, lifetime income stream from employer pensions and Social Security playing an ever shrinking role, retirement income planning demands that each individual accept a higher degree of personal responsibility for both accumulating and managing the assets needed to pay for retirement. And managing these assets has to be done in a world where fluctuating interest rates and sometimes volatile financial markets are a fact of life.

Extended life spans mean that the money has to last longer, although exactly how long is unknown. Rampant inflation, a bad investment, major health problems, or an extended period of "down" markets could lead to outliving your assets.

---

[1] These refer to the sections of the Internal Revenue Code which authorize these different types of retirement plans.
[2] See, "Employee Participation in Defined Benefit and Defined Contribution Plans, 1985-2000." U.S. Bureau of Labor Statistics, updated June 16, 2004.
[3] Source: National Center for Health Statistics: Deaths: Final data for 2004.

Continued...

Annuities In Retirement Income Planning

One Possible Answer – Immediate Annuities

Life insurance is designed to help solve the problems created when someone dies prematurely. An annuity, on the other hand, is designed to protect against the possibility of living too long. An "immediate" annuity is a contract between an individual and an insurance company. In exchange for a single, lump-sum premium, the insurance company agrees to begin paying a regular income to the purchaser for a period of years or for life.

The payment amount depends on a number of factors:

- **Premium paid:** Generally the larger the payment, the larger the income stream.

- **Age:** Older individuals typically receive larger periodic payments.

- **Payout period selected:** A shorter payout period usually results in a larger payment.

- **Underlying investment medium:** Generally, either a fixed or a variable annuity.

Fixed Annuity	Variable Annuity
A fixed annuity pays a fixed rate of return. The insurance company invests in a portfolio of debt securities such as mortgages or bonds and pays out a fixed rate of return. Generally, this rate of return is guaranteed for a certain period of time after which a new rate is calculated. Most insurance companies offer a guaranteed minimum rate throughout the life of the contract.[1]	A variable annuity offers the potential for higher returns in exchange for assuming a higher level of risk. You can choose from among several types of investment portfolios, such as stocks or bonds. The amount of each annuity payment will fluctuate depending on the performance of the underlying investments. Variable annuities are sold by prospectus only.[2]

Annuities are not insured by the FDIC or any government agency. Since an annuity may be payable for decades into the future, dealing with a financially solid insurer is essential. Credit rating companies such as A.M. Best, Standard and Poor's, or Moody's can provide an objective measure of a firm's financial stability.

Seek Professional Guidance

For many individuals, an immediate annuity can form an important part of their retirement income planning. Because an immediate annuity is a complex product, the advice and guidance of a trained financial professional is highly recommended.

---

[1] Such guarantees are based upon the claims-paying ability of the issuing insurance company.
[2] The prospectus for a variable annuity contains complete information including investment objectives, risk factors, fees, surrender charges, and any other applicable costs.

Pension Income Alternative

The Problem

At retirement, married pension plan participants typically must make a choice. They can choose to take:

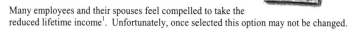

- The maximum monthly income for the life of the retiring employee only (e.g., $1,000 per month); or

- A substantially reduced pension for the lifetime of both the retiring employee and his/her spouse (e.g., $800 per month).

Many employees and their spouses feel compelled to take the reduced lifetime income[1]. Unfortunately, once selected this option may not be changed.

Consider the Potential Costs

- If spouse lives but a short time, the surviving retiree faces a lifetime of reduced pension benefits.

- If both live a full life and die within a year or so of each other, little benefit is ever realized after 20 years or more of reduced pension.

- In no case do children or other heirs inherit any benefits.

The following examples illustrate the potential lifetime cost of the survivorship benefit:

Example 1 - Full Survivorship Benefit on Pension Plan

	With No Survivorship	With 100% Survivorship
Anticipated monthly income at retirement (age 65)	$1,000	$800
Cost of survivorship election	$200 per month for both spouses' remaining lifetimes	
Joint life expectancy[2] at 65	25 years x $2,400 = $60,000 total potential cost	

Example 2 - 50% Survivorship Benefit on Pension Plan

	With No Survivorship	With 50% Survivorship	
		Retiree	Spouse
Anticipated monthly income at retirement (age 65)	$1,000	$900	$450
Cost of survivorship election	$100 per month for both spouses' remaining lifetimes		
Joint life expectancy[2] at 65	25 years x $1,200 = $30,000 total potential cost		

---

[1] **Caution:** In some cases, eligibility for continuing the surviving spouse's group health care is dependent on choosing the survivor option.
[2] Based on IRS Annuity Table VI - Ordinary Joint and Last Survivor. Assumes both spouses are the same age.

Continued...

Pension Income Alternative

Conclusion

Pension survivorship options equate to very expensive term life insurance that may never pay a benefit.

A Solution – Alternative Funding

Purchase permanent life insurance prior to retirement in an amount that would provide the survivor or other heirs with a similar monthly income benefit. Then still take the maximum monthly pension benefit.

For example, to provide $800 per month for 25 years (assuming a 5% growth rate on the remaining balance) would require an initial lump sum or life insurance death benefit of approximately $137,000. Of course, the 5% return is not guaranteed, so, if desired, a guaranteed lifetime payout available from the insurance company could be used.

Advantages to Alternative Funding

- Premiums can be paid when income is higher, before retirement, from discretionary income.

- The monthly premium may be more or less than the difference between the Life Only and the Joint & Survivor, depending on the insured's age and health at the time a life insurance policy is issued. However, in general, the overall cost of the life insurance will be less than the total potential cost of lower pension benefits if the insured lives to normal life expectancy.

- A large part of the death benefit proceeds payable in monthly installments will be income tax free. Normally, pension income is fully taxable.

- If the retiree and spouse die simultaneously or if the spouse dies first, their children or other heirs may receive the insurance death benefits. Typically, no additional benefits would be payable from the pension plan. If the spouse dies first and the retiree does not have any other beneficiaries deserving of the proceeds, the retiree can surrender the policy for its cash surrender value.

Social Security Retirement Benefits

Social Security retirement benefits usually begin at "normal retirement age" (NRA).[1] For those born in 1937 or earlier, NRA is age 65. For those born after 1937, NRA gradually increases until it reaches age 67 for those born in 1960 and later. A worker can earn a larger benefit by continuing to work past NRA.

If a person is willing to accept a reduced payment, retirement benefits may begin as early as age 62. If a worker's NRA is age 65, retirement at age 62 will reduce the monthly benefit by approximately 20%.[2] For each month (up to 36 months) that a worker is under NRA, benefits are reduced by 5/9 of 1% (1/180 or 0.555556%). For each month in excess of 36, benefits are reduced an additional 5/12 of 1% (1/240 or .416667%). Persons in poor health or with a short life expectancy may benefit from an early retirement.

Social Security also provides some disability benefits for those unable to work because of illness or other disability. Also, if death occurs, benefits may be available to one's spouse and children. Medicare benefits are available at age 65 even though a person continues to work; under certain circumstances, Medicare benefits may be limited.

Annual Social Security Statement

Because Social Security benefits are based on a worker's earning record, it is important to ensure that all earnings are accurately recorded on a worker's Social Security records. The Social Security Administration (SSA) sends an annual Social Security Statement to each worker age 25 and older and not currently receiving Social Security benefits. The annual statement is automatically mailed approximately one month before a worker's birthday. An individual's earnings record may also be checked by completing Form SSA-7004, "Request for Social Security Statement."[3] Once completed, Form SSA-7004 should be mailed to the Social Security Administration, P.O. Box 7004, Wilkes-Barre, PA 18767-7004.

Retirement Benefit Estimates

For general planning purposes, retirement benefit estimates are shown on the following pages. The monthly retirement benefit used (at ages 62, 65, or 70) is the maximum benefit payable to a worker who retires in 2008 and who has had steady earnings at the maximum level since age 22.[4] Average benefits are calculated at 75% of maximum; low benefits are calculated at 60% of maximum. The first table increases the 2008 benefit at a conservative 2.5% annual rate; the second table increases the benefit at a more aggressive 4.0% annual rate. It may be prudent to use the more conservative table in estimating the potential Social Security benefits available at one's retirement. Increases in Social Security benefits are not guaranteed; they are based on changes in the Consumer Price Index.

---

[1] "Normal" retirement age is also commonly referred to as "full" retirement age.
[2] If a worker's NRA is age 67, retirement at age 62 will reduce the monthly benefit by approximately 30%.
[3] Available on the SSA website at www.ssa.gov or by calling (800) 772-1213.
[4] Source: SSA website, www.ssa.gov/OACT/COLA/examplemax.html, accessed 12/04/07.

Continued...

Social Security Retirement Benefits

Conservative 2.5% Annual Increase Benefit Projections

Age 62

Year	Monthly Benefit			Annual Benefit		
	Low	Average	Max[1]	Low	Average	Max
2008	$1,009	$1,262	$1,682	$12,110	$15,138	$20,184
2009	1,034	1,293	1,724	12,413	15,516	20,689
2010	1,060	1,325	1,767	12,723	15,904	21,206
2011	1,087	1,358	1,811	13,042	16,302	21,736
2012	1,114	1,392	1,857	13,368	16,710	22,279
2013	1,142	1,427	1,903	13,702	17,127	22,836
2014	1,170	1,463	1,951	14,044	17,555	23,407
2015	1,200	1,500	1,999	14,395	17,994	23,992
2016	1,230	1,537	2,049	14,755	18,444	24,592
2017	1,260	1,575	2,101	15,124	18,905	25,207
2018	1,292	1,615	2,153	15,502	19,378	25,837
2019	1,324	1,655	2,207	15,890	19,862	26,483
2020	1,357	1,697	2,262	16,287	20,359	27,145
2021	1,391	1,739	2,319	16,694	20,868	27,824

Age 65

Year	Monthly Benefit			Annual Benefit		
	Low	Average	Max[2]	Low	Average	Max
2008	$1,218	$1,523	$2,030	$14,616	$18,276	$24,360
2009	1,248	1,561	2,081	14,981	18,733	24,969
2010	1,280	1,600	2,133	15,356	19,201	25,593
2011	1,312	1,640	2,186	15,740	19,681	26,233
2012	1,344	1,681	2,241	16,133	20,173	26,889
2013	1,378	1,723	2,297	16,537	20,678	27,561
2014	1,413	1,766	2,354	16,950	21,195	28,250
2015	1,448	1,810	2,413	17,374	21,724	28,956
2016	1,484	1,856	2,473	17,808	22,268	29,680
2017	1,521	1,902	2,535	18,253	22,824	30,422
2018	1,559	1,950	2,599	18,710	23,395	31,183
2019	1,598	1,998	2,664	19,177	23,980	31,962
2020	1,638	2,048	2,730	19,657	24,579	32,761
2021	1,679	2,099	2,798	20,148	25,194	33,581

---

[1] Assumes a reduced benefit, with retirement at age 62 years, one month.
[2] Retirement is assumed to be at age 65 and zero months. For those born before 1938, age 65 is the normal retirement age (NRA). For years after 2002, the monthly benefit shown is reduced for early retirement as NRA gradually increases, until it reaches age 67 for those born in 1960 and later.

Continue

Social Security Retirement Benefits

Conservative 2.5% Annual Increase Benefit Projections (Continued)

Age 70

Year	Monthly Benefit			Annual Benefit		
	Low	Average	Max[1]	Low	Average	Max
2008	$1,676	$2,096	$2,794	$20,117	$25,152	$33,528
2009	1,718	2,148	2,864	20,620	25,781	34,366
2010	1,761	2,202	2,935	21,135	26,425	35,225
2011	1,805	2,257	3,009	21,664	27,086	36,106
2012	1,850	2,314	3,084	22,205	27,763	37,009
2013	1,897	2,371	3,161	22,760	28,457	37,934
2014	1,944	2,431	3,240	23,329	29,169	38,882
2015	1,993	2,491	3,321	23,913	29,898	39,854
2016	2,043	2,554	3,404	24,510	30,645	40,851
2017	2,094	2,618	3,489	25,123	31,411	41,872
2018	2,146	2,683	3,577	25,751	32,197	42,919
2019	2,200	2,750	3,666	26,395	33,002	43,992
2020	2,255	2,819	3,758	27,055	33,827	45,091
2021	2,311	2,889	3,852	27,731	34,672	46,219

[1] This table illustrates the affect of delayed retirement credits.

Continued...

Social Security Retirement Benefits

Aggressive 4% Annual Increase Benefit Projections

Age 62

Year	Monthly Benefit			Annual Benefit		
	Low	Average	Max[1]	Low	Average	Max
2008	$1,009	$1,262	$1,682	$12,110	$15,138	$20,184
2009	1,050	1,312	1,749	12,595	15,744	20,991
2010	1,092	1,364	1,819	13,099	16,373	21,831
2011	1,135	1,419	1,892	13,623	17,028	22,704
2012	1,181	1,476	1,968	14,167	17,709	23,612
2013	1,228	1,535	2,046	14,734	18,418	24,557
2014	1,277	1,596	2,128	15,324	19,154	25,539
2015	1,328	1,660	2,213	15,936	19,921	26,561
2016	1,381	1,726	2,302	16,574	20,717	27,623
2017	1,436	1,796	2,394	17,237	21,546	28,728
2018	1,494	1,867	2,490	17,926	22,408	29,877
2019	1,554	1,942	2,589	18,643	23,304	31,072
2020	1,616	2,020	2,693	19,389	24,236	32,315
2021	1,680	2,100	2,801	20,165	25,206	33,608

Age 65

Year	Monthly Benefit			Annual Benefit		
	Low	Average	Max[2]	Low	Average	Max
2008	$1,218	$1,523	$2,030	$14,616	$18,276	$24,360
2009	1,267	1,584	2,111	15,201	19,007	25,334
2010	1,317	1,647	2,196	15,809	19,767	26,348
2011	1,370	1,713	2,283	16,441	20,558	27,402
2012	1,425	1,782	2,375	17,099	21,380	28,498
2013	1,482	1,853	2,470	17,783	22,236	29,638
2014	1,541	1,927	2,569	18,494	23,125	30,823
2015	1,603	2,004	2,671	19,234	24,050	32,056
2016	1,667	2,084	2,778	20,003	25,012	33,338
2017	1,734	2,168	2,889	20,803	26,012	34,672
2018	1,803	2,254	3,005	21,635	27,053	36,059
2019	1,875	2,345	3,125	22,501	28,135	37,501
2020	1,950	2,438	3,250	23,401	29,260	39,001
2021	2,028	2,536	3,380	24,337	30,431	40,561

---

[1] Assumes a reduced benefit, with retirement at age 62 years, one month.
[2] Retirement is assumed to be at age 65 and zero months. For those born before 1938, age 65 is the normal retirement age (NRA). For years after 2002, the monthly benefit shown is reduced for early retirement as NRA gradually increases, until it reaches age 67 for those born in 1960 and later.

Continued

Social Security Retirement Benefits

Aggressive 4% Annual Increase Benefit Projections (Continued)

Age 70

Year	Monthly Benefit			Annual Benefit		
	Low	Average	Max[1]	Low	Average	Max
2008	$1,676	$2,096	$2,794	$20,117	$25,152	$33,528
2009	1,743	2,180	2,906	20,921	26,158	34,869
2010	1,813	2,267	3,022	21,758	27,204	36,264
2011	1,886	2,358	3,143	22,629	28,293	37,714
2012	1,961	2,452	3,269	23,534	29,424	39,223
2013	2,040	2,550	3,399	24,475	30,601	40,792
2014	2,121	2,652	3,535	25,454	31,825	42,424
2015	2,206	2,758	3,677	26,472	33,098	44,121
2016	2,294	2,869	3,824	27,531	34,422	45,885
2017	2,386	2,983	3,977	28,632	35,799	47,721
2018	2,481	3,103	4,136	29,778	37,231	49,630
2019	2,581	3,227	4,301	30,969	38,720	51,615
2020	2,684	3,356	4,473	32,208	40,269	53,679
2021	2,791	3,490	4,652	33,496	41,880	55,827

---

[1] This table illustrates the affect of delayed retirement credits.

When to Take Social Security Retirement Benefits

Research by the Federal government indicates that Social Security retirement benefits make up almost 38%[1] of the income of Americans age 65 or older. Thus, the decision as to when to begin to take Social Security retirement benefits is an important one. It's also an irrevocable decision. Once you decide to begin receiving Social Security retirement benefits you cannot change your mind. The initial benefit will serve as the "base" amount for the rest of your life, subject only to adjustment for increases in the cost of living.

The question is made a little easier to answer if you separate when you want to retire from when you want to begin receiving Social Security retirement benefits; these two events don't necessarily have to occur at the same time. An understanding of how your benefits are calculated, how they are taxed, and what happens if you continue to work after beginning to receive benefits, is also important.

"Normal" Retirement Age – "Full" Benefits

For many years, normal retirement age (NRA), the age at which "full" benefits – 100% of an individual's Primary Insurance Amount[2] (PIA) – are available was set at age 65. This is still true for those born in 1937 or earlier. However, for those born in 1938 or later, NRA gradually increases until it reaches age 67 for those born in 1960 or later.

Early Retirement – Reduced Benefits

Age 62 is generally the earliest age that someone can begin to receive Social Security retirement benefits. However, if retirement benefits begin before the "normal" retirement age, the benefit paid is reduced to reflect the income that will be paid over a longer period of time. The amount of the reduction varies with the year of birth. For example, an individual born in 1937 (NRA = age 65) who began receiving benefits at age 62 had his or her retirement benefit reduced to 80% of what it would have been had they chosen to wait until normal retirement age. However, for a worker born in 1962, for whom NRA is age 67, choosing to receive retirement benefits at age 62 results in an initial benefit reduced to 70% of what it would have been had the individual waited to age 67.

Delay Retirement – A Bigger Benefit

What happens if you decide to wait and take your retirement benefits later than your NRA? You get paid for waiting, in the form of a larger retirement benefit. For each year beyond your NRA that you delay receiving retirement benefits, up to age 70, your benefit is increased by a specified percentage of the PIA. The amount of the credit for each year of delay beyond NRA will vary depending on the year of birth. For example, an individual born in 1935 who delayed receiving benefits until age 70 had his or her benefit increased by 6% for each year (five years in this case) beyond the NRA of age 65. For those born in 1943 and later, delaying retirement increases their benefit by 8% per year for each year they wait beyond their NRA.

---

[1] William J. Wiatrowski, "Changing retirement age: ups and downs," Monthly Labor Review, published by the Bureau of Labor Statistics, April 2001.
[2] The PIA is calculated by the Social Security Administration based on a person's lifetime earnings record.

Continued.

When to Take Social Security Retirement Benefits

Which Is Better? – Early or Late?

One way to answer this question is to perform a "break-even" analysis which estimates the age at which the total value of higher benefits (from delaying retirement) is greater than the total value of lower benefits (from starting retirement early). The Social Security Administration (SSA) has a break-even calculator available on its web site at: http://www.ssa.gov/OACT/quickcalc/when2retire.html. You'll need to have the estimated retirement benefits from your annual statement available.[1]

If you expect to live longer than this break-even age you would likely benefit from delaying the start of Social Security retirement benefits. If you are in poor health, or if members of your family tend to die at relatively young ages, you will likely receive a greater benefit by beginning your benefits early.

Federal Income Taxation of Social Security Benefits

Under federal law, Social Security benefits may be subject to income tax. If one-half of your Social Security benefits plus your "modified adjusted gross income" (often the same as adjusted gross income) exceed certain limits, then a portion (up to 85%) of your benefits is taxable. For married couples filing jointly this threshold is $32,000; for all others it is $25,000. State or local tax treatment of Social Security benefits can vary.

If You Continue Working

If you begin taking Social Security retirement benefits early and also continue working, your retirement payments will be temporarily reduced if your earnings exceed certain limits. For this purpose, "earnings" generally include wages received as an employee or the net income received from self-employment. The amount of the reduction will vary:

- **Under NRA:** One dollar of benefits is lost for every two dollars you earn over $13,560.[2]

- **The year you reach NRA:** One dollar of benefits is lost for every three dollars you earn over $36,120.[2]

Once you reach NRA there is no reduction in your retirement benefits, regardless of how much you earn.

Seek Professional Guidance

The decision as to when to take Social Security retirement benefits is an important one. A wrong decision can cost a retiree literally thousands of dollars. The advice and guidance of financial professionals, to insure that all relevant issues are considered, is highly recommended.

---

[1] As with all numerical projections, the "break-even" analysis on the Social Security web page is neither a guarantee nor a projection and your actual results may differ significantly.

[2] 2008 value. These "exempt amounts" are subject to adjustment for inflation each calendar year.

The Effect of Early or Delayed Retirement on Social Security Retirement Benefits

Normal retirement age (NRA) is the age at which "full" Social Security retirement benefits – 100% of an individual's Primary Insurance Amount (PIA)[1] – are available. For many years, NRA was set at age 65. Beginning with individuals born in 1938, NRA gradually increases until it reaches age 67 for those born in 1960 or later.

If an individual chooses to receive retirement benefits before his or her NRA, the benefit paid is reduced to reflect the fact that income will be paid over a longer period of time. Similarly, if an individual chooses to delay retirement benefits, the benefit is increased for each year of delay (up to age 70) beyond NRA. The table below shows the effect of early or delayed retirement on an individual's retirement benefit, depending on the year of birth.

Retirement Benefit as a Percentage of the Primary Insurance Amount at Various Ages[2]									
Year of Birth	Normal Retirement Age (NRA)	Credit for each year of delayed retirement after NRA (Percent)	Benefit as a % of PIA at Age						
			62	63	64	65	66	67	70
1924	65	3	80	$86^2/_3$	$93^1/_3$	100	103	106	115
1925-1926	65	3½	80	$86^2/_3$	$93^1/_3$	100	103½	107	117½
1927-1928	65	4	80	$86^2/_3$	$93^1/_3$	100	104	108	120
1929-1930	65	4½	80	$86^2/_3$	$93^1/_3$	100	104½	109	122½
1931-1932	65	5	80	$86^2/_3$	$93^1/_3$	100	105	110	125
1933-1934	65	5½	80	$86^2/_3$	$93^1/_3$	100	105½	111	127½
1935-1936	65	6	80	$86^2/_3$	$93^1/_3$	100	106	112	130
1937	65	6½	80	$86^2/_3$	$93^1/_3$	100	106½	113	132½
1938	65, 2 mos	6½	$79^1/_6$	$85^5/_9$	$92^2/_9$	$98^8/_9$	$105^5/_{12}$	$111^{11}/_{12}$	$131^5/_{12}$
1939	65, 4 mos	7	$78^1/_3$	$84^4/_9$	$91^1/_9$	$97^7/_9$	$104^2/_3$	$111^2/_3$	$132^2/_3$
1940	65, 6 mos	7	77½	$83^1/_3$	90	$96^2/_3$	103½	110½	131½
1941	65, 8 mos	7½	$76^2/_3$	$82^2/_9$	$88^8/_9$	$95^5/_9$	102½	110	132½
1942	65, 10 mos	7½	$75^5/_6$	$81^1/_9$	$87^7/_9$	$94^4/_9$	101¼	108¾	131¼
1943-1954	66	8	75	80	$86^2/_3$	$93^1/_3$	100	108	132
1955	66, 2 mos	8	$74^1/_6$	$79^1/_6$	$85^5/_9$	$92^2/_9$	$98^8/_9$	$106^2/_3$	$130^2/_3$
1956	66, 4 mos	8	$73^1/_3$	$78^1/_3$	$84^4/_9$	$91^1/_9$	$97^7/_9$	$105^1/_3$	$129^1/_3$
1957	66, 6 mos	8	72½	77½	$83^1/_3$	90	$96^2/_3$	104	128
1958	66, 8 mos	8	$71^2/_3$	$76^2/_3$	$82^2/_9$	$88^8/_9$	$95^5/_9$	$102^2/_3$	$126^2/_3$
1959	66, 10 mos	8	$70^5/_6$	$75^5/_6$	$81^1/_9$	$87^7/_9$	$94^4/_9$	$101^1/_3$	$125^1/_3$
1960 and later	67	8	70	75	80	$86^2/_3$	$93^1/_3$	100	124

[1] The PIA is calculated by the Social Security Administration based on a person's lifetime earnings record.
[2] Source: Social Security Administration.

How Work Affects
Social Security Retirement Benefits

On April 12, 2000, President Clinton signed into law P.L. 106-182, the Senior Citizens' Freedom To Work Act of 2000. This legislation, which was retroactive to January 1, 2000, repealed an earnings limitation on Social Security benefits for individuals ages 65 to 69.

Earnings Test: Under this legislation, generally you can receive full Social Security benefits, regardless of earnings, starting with the month you reach normal retirement age (NRA).

For workers born before 1938, NRA (also known as full retirement age) is age 65. For those born after 1937, NRA will gradually increase until it reaches age 67 for those born in 1960 and later.

Age of Social Security Benefits Recipient	Annual Exempt Amount		One Dollar of Benefits Is Lost for Every Two or Three Dollars You Earn Over the Exempt Amount
	2007	2008	
Under NRA	$12,960	$13,560	Every Two Dollars
Year NRA Reached	$34,440	$36,120	Every Three Dollars
Month NRA Reached	No Limit	No Limit	No Loss of Benefits

Example (1): An individual begins receiving Social Security benefits at age 63 in January 2008, with an entitlement of $500 per month. If the retiree works and earns $23,560 during the year, he or she would have to give up $5,000 of Social Security benefits ($1 for every $2 over the $13,560 limit), but would still receive $1,000.

Example (2): Assume an individual is age 65 at the beginning of the year, but reaches NRA in November 2008. Also assume the individual earns $46,944 during the year, with $39,120 of this amount being received in the first 10 months of the year. The individual would give up $1,000 in benefits, $1 for every $3 earned above the $36,120 limit. Assuming a Social Security retirement benefit of $500 per month, the individual would still receive $4,000 out of $5,000 for the first 10 months of the year. Full benefits of $1,000 ($500 per month) would be received for November and December, after NRA was reached.

What Counts as Earnings?

Any wages earned after retirement from work as an employee and any net earnings from self-employment count as earnings. Wages include bonuses, commissions, fees, vacation pay, pay in lieu of vacation and cash tips of $20 or more in a month.

Continued...

How Work Affects
Social Security Retirement Benefits

What Doesn't Count as Earnings?

- Investment income, including stock dividends, interest from savings accounts, income from annuities, limited partnership income and rental income from real estate you own (unless you are a real estate dealer).

- Income from Social Security, pensions, other retirement pay and Veterans Administration Benefits.

- Gifts or inheritances.

- Royalties received after age 65 from patents or copyrights obtained before that year.

- If you are a retired partner, retirement payments from partnerships don't count if:
  - The payments continue for life under a written agreement which provides for payments to all partners or a class of them; and
  - You rendered no services to the partnership during the taxable year the retirement payments were received; and
  - Your share of the partnership capital was paid to you in full before the end of the partnership's taxable year and there is no obligation to you other than retirement payments.

- Income from self-employment received in a year after the year a person becomes entitled to benefits. This refers to income which is not attributable to services performed after the month of entitlement.

IRAs Compared

There are substantial differences between a traditional (nondeductible) IRA, a traditional (deductible) IRA and a Roth IRA.

Item	Traditional IRA (Nondeductible)	Traditional IRA (Deductible)	Roth IRA
Basic eligibility requirements	Any person under age 70½ who has compensation	Any person under age 70½ who has compensation	Any person of any age who has compensation[1]
Maximum contribution	Generally, the lesser of $5,000[2] ($10,000[3] for a married couple) or 100% of compensation.[4]		
Is the contribution deductible?	No	Yes, if neither participant nor spouse is covered by a qualified plan (QP). If single and covered by a QP, contribution is deductible if adjusted gross income (AGI) is less than $53,000. Deduction phased out for AGI between $53,000 and $63,000. If MFJ and one spouse is covered by a QP, the nonparticipant spouse may make a deductible contribution if AGI is $159,000 or less. This deduction is phased out for AGI between $159,000 and $169,000. The participant spouse may make a deductible contribution if AGI is $85,000 or less. This deduction is phased out for AGI between $85,000 and $105,000.[5]	No
Are earnings currently taxed?	No	No	No

---

[1] For 2008, the maximum contribution to a Roth IRA is phased out for single taxpayers with adjusted gross income (AGI) between $101,000 and $116,000. For married couples filing jointly, the phaseout range is an AGI of $159,000 to $169,000. For married individuals filing separately, the phaseout range is an AGI of $0 to $10,000.
[2] This amount applies to 2008. For 2007, the maximum allowable contribution was $4,000.
[3] This amount applies to 2008. For 2007, the maximum allowable contribution was $8,000.
[4] If an IRA owner is age 50 or older, he or she may contribute an additional $1,000 ($2,000 if spouse is also over 50).
[5] These are 2008 limits. For 2007 the phase-out ranges were (1) MFJ - AGI of $83,000 - $103,000; (2) Single - $52,000 - $62,000. For taxpayers using the MFS filing status, the phase-out range is $0 - $10,000, which does not change.

Continued...

IRAs Compared

Item	Traditional IRA (Nondeductible)	Traditional IRA (Deductible)	Roth IRA
Taxation of withdrawals at death and disability[1]	Contributions are received tax-free and earnings are taxable.	All distributions are taxable.	No taxation of qualified distributions.
Taxation of $10,000 withdrawn for first-time home purchase[1]	Proportionate part attributable to earnings is taxable	All $10,000 subject to income tax	No taxation of qualified distributions.
Taxation on withdrawals to pay for medical expenses[1]	Proportionate part attributable to earnings taxed as ordinary income. For those under age 59½, 10% penalty does not apply to amounts that qualify as deductible medical expenses; e.g., amounts in excess of 7.5% of AGI.	Entire withdrawal taxable as ordinary income. For those under age 59½, 10% penalty does not apply to amounts that qualify as deductible medical expenses; e.g., amounts in excess of 7.5% of AGI.	Earnings are taxable at ordinary rates unless IRA owner is age 59½ or older and established Roth IRA five or more years prior.
Taxation on withdrawal to pay for educational expenses[1]	Proportionate part attributable to earnings is taxable.	Entire withdrawal is subject to income tax.	Earnings are taxable at ordinary rates unless IRA owner is age 59½ or older and established Roth IRA five or more years prior.
Taxation of distributions not covered above[2]	Nondeductible contributions received tax-free. Earnings are taxed at ordinary rate.	All distributions are taxable at ordinary rates.	Earnings are taxable at ordinary rates unless IRA owner is age 59½ or older and established Roth IRA five or more years prior.
Are there required, minimum distributions?	Distributions must start at age 70½.	Distributions must start at age 70½.	No minimum distribution is required during the life of owner.
Are direct transfers of funds in an IRA to an Health Savings Account allowed?	Yes	Yes	Yes
By when must an IRA be set up and funded?	By the due date for filing the IRA owner's federal income tax return for the year of the contribution, generally April 15 of the following year.		
Federal bankruptcy protection	Federal bankruptcy law protects assets in all IRAs, up to $1,000,000. In the future, the $1,000,000 limit will be indexed for inflation. Funds rolled over from qualified plans are protected without limit.		

[1] For individuals under age 59½, the 10% penalty tax does not apply in these situations.
[2] All taxable amounts are subject to penalty tax of 10% if received prior to age 59½, unless the above exceptions apply. For traditional IRAs, the penalty is waived if the distribution is annuitized over the participant's life or life expectancy.

Continue

398

IRAs Compared

Item	Traditional IRA (Nondeductible)	Traditional IRA (Deductible)	Roth IRA
May federal income tax refunds be directly deposited into the IRA?[1]	Yes	Yes	Yes
Are tax-free direct transfers of up to $100,000 to a qualified charity by an owner at least age 70½ allowed?[2]	Yes	Yes	Yes

Comparison of Returns from Various Types of IRAs

The table below is a hypothetical illustration of the impact of time and income taxes on the various types of IRAs.[3] The calculations assume that any tax savings from deductible contributions are invested in a separate, annually-taxable fund and that all funds are withdrawn in a lump sum at retirement.

Assumptions:
Desired net annual contribution: $5,000
Marginal income tax bracket – pre-retirement: 28.00%
Marginal income tax bracket – post-retirement: 25.00%
Tax-deferred growth rate: 8.00%
After-tax growth rate: 5.76%
Number of years until retirement: 20

Item	Traditional Nondeductible IRA	Traditional Deductible IRA	Roth IRA
A. Pre-Retirement			
1. Contributions are made	After-tax	Before-tax	After-tax
2. Gross amount	$6,944	$5,000	$6,944
3. Income taxes payable	1,944	0	1,944
4. Net annual contribution to IRA	5,000	5,000	5,000
5. Annual tax savings to taxable account	0	1,400	0
Total net annual savings	**$5,000**	**$6,400**	**$5,000**
B. At Retirement			
1. Net accumulation in the IRA[4]	$247,115	$247,115	$247,115
2. Future value of tax savings	0	53,082	0
3. Total available before taxes	$247,115	$300,196	$247,115
4. Income taxes payable	-36,779	-61,779	0
Net after income taxes	**$210,336**	**$238,418**	**$247,115**

---

[1] Beginning in 2007.
[2] Applicable to 2006 and 2007 only. No charitable deduction is allowed for such transfers.
[3] Based on federal law. State or local law may differ.
[4] Assumes annual contributions are made at the beginning of each year.

IRAs Compared

The calculator below provides a hypothetical illustration of the impact of time and income taxes on various types of IRAs.[1] The calculations assume that any tax savings from deductible contributions are invested in a separate, annually-taxable fund and that all funds are withdrawn in a lump sum at retirement.

Assumptions:
Desired net annual contribution: $2,000
Marginal tax bracket (pre-retirement): 45.00%
Marginal tax bracket (post-retirement): 35.00%
Tax-deferred growth rate: 8.00%
After-tax growth rate: 4.40%
Number of years until retirement: 20

Item	Traditional Nondeductible IRA	Traditional Deductible IRA	Roth IRA
A. Pre-Retirement			
1. Contributions are made	After-tax	Before-tax	After-tax
2. Gross amount	$3,636	$2,000	$3,636
3. Income taxes payable	- $1,636	$0	- $1,636
4. Net annual contribution to IRA	$2,000	$2,000	$2,000
5. Annual tax savings to taxable account	$0	$ 900	$0
Total net annual savings	**$2,000**	**$2,900**	**$2,000**
B. At Retirement			
1. Net accumulation in the IRA[2]	$98,846	$98,846	$98,846
2. Future value of tax savings	$0	$29,170	$0
3. Total available before taxes	$98,846	$ 128,016	$98,846
4. Income taxes payable	-$20,596	-$34,596	$0
Net after income taxes	**$78,250**	**$93,420**	**$98,846**

---

[1] Based on federal law. State or local law may differ.
[2] Assumes annual contributions are made at the beginning of each year.

Traditional IRAs

Deadline to Establish and Fund an IRA

An IRA can be established and funded at any time from January 1 of the current year and up to and including the date an individual's income tax return is due (generally, April 15 of the following year), not including extensions.

Can Deduction Be Taken Prior to Investment of the Funds?

Yes! This, in effect, permits an individual to file his return early in the year (e.g., January) and use his or her tax refund to make the actual contribution prior to April 15. If desired, refunds of federal income taxes may be directly deposited into an IRA.

Types of Arrangements Permitted

There are currently two types of IRAs.

- **Individual retirement accounts:** These are trusts or custodial accounts with a corporate trustee or custodian.

- **Individual retirement annuities:** These are special annuities issued by an insurance company.

Contribution and Deduction Limits

A wage earner may contribute the lesser of $5,000[1] or 100% of compensation for the year. If the wage earner is married, an additional $5,000 may be contributed on behalf of a lesser earning (or nonworking) spouse, using a spousal IRA. This means the family unit may contribute up to a total of $10,000[2] as long as family compensation is at least that amount. If certain requirements are met, the amount contributed may also be deducted from gross income on the federal income tax return.

Other Retirement Plans May Reduce or Eliminate Deductions

Taxpayers who participate in an employer's plan may make fully-deductible IRA contributions only if their adjusted gross income (AGI) is below $85,000 if married filing jointly, $53,000 if single and $0 if married filing separately. If AGI exceeds these amounts, the $10,000 family or $5,000 individual maximum is reduced by a formula that eventually permits no deduction. No IRA deduction is allowed for married couples filing jointly with AGI over $105,000, single individuals with an AGI over $63,000 and married couples filing separately with an individual AGI over $10,000[3].

---

[1]This amount applies to 2008. For 2007, the maximum allowable contribution was $4,000. If an IRA owner is age 50 or older, he or she may contribute an additional $1,000 ($2,000 if spouse is also over 50).
[2]This amount applies to 2008. For 2007, the maximum allowable contribution was $8,000.
[3]These are 2008 limits. For 2007 the phase-out ranges were (1) MFJ - AGI of $83,000 - $103,000; (2) Single - $52,000 - $62,000. For taxpayers using the MFS filing status, the phase-out range is $0 - $10,000, which does not change.

Continued...

Traditional IRAs

For 2008, a taxpayer who is not an active participant in an employer plan, but whose spouse is, the maximum deductible IRA contribution is phased out if their combined AGI is between $159,000 and $169,000.

Employer plans include: regular qualified plans; Keogh plans; Sec. 403(b) tax-sheltered annuity plans; simplified employee pension (SEP) plans; SIMPLE plans; and state, federal and local government plans (except Sec. 457 tax-exempt employer sponsored nonqualified deferred compensation plans).

Individuals with income in excess of the above limits may wish to make contributions to a Roth IRA on a nondeductible basis. Income limits also apply to Roth IRA contributions.

Distributions, Withdrawals and Taxation

- **Typical distribution plans**
  - **Single-sum distribution:** Becomes part of taxable income for that year (less any nondeductible contributions).
  - **Life expectancy:** Each year, participant calculates payout based upon the attained-age life expectancy, using life expectancy tables issued by the federal government.
  - **Life annuity:** For individual retirement annuities only, participant/annuitant may elect guaranteed income for life (and the life of a joint annuitant, if desired).

- **Premature distributions:** Withdrawals and distributions prior to age 59½ are subject to a 10% penalty tax, in addition to current income tax, unless one or more of the following apply.[1]
  - A distribution is made because of the death or disability of the participant.
  - A distribution is paid as substantially equal periodic payments over the life of the participant, or the joint lives of the participant and a designated beneficiary. The 10% penalty is triggered if the distribution schedule is modified within five years or before attainment of age 59½, if later.
  - The distribution is rolled over into another IRA.
  - The distribution is used to pay for medical expenses in excess of 7.5% of AGI.
  - An IRA distribution is used by an unemployed individual to pay health insurance premiums. (Only applies to certain situations.)
  - The IRA distribution is used to pay for qualified, higher education expenses for the individual, a spouse, a child or a grandchild.
  - For a first-time homebuyer, there is a lifetime exception of $10,000 from the 10% penalty tax.[2] The purchaser of the home may be the individual, a spouse, a child, a grandchild, or an ancestor. A first-time homebuyer is someone (or his or her spouse) who had no ownership in a principal residence during the preceding two years prior to the purchase of the new home.
  - A distribution is rolled over to a Health Savings Account (HSA).

---

[1] Note that not all exceptions to the 10% penalty are listed.
[2] Based on federal law. State law may vary.

Continue

Traditional IRAs

- **Required distributions:** Minimum distributions must begin by April 1 of the calendar year following the year in which the participant reaches age 70½. However, if the distribution is received in the year following attainment of age 70½, two distributions are required in that specific year. Thereafter, the minimum distribution must be made by the end of each calendar year. The minimum distributions may be paid using one of two methods.

  - **Over the life expectancy of the participant:** In general, the required minimum distribution is calculated using the IRA participant's attained age and a minimum distribution factor table prescribed by the IRS.[1]

  - **Spouse more than 10 years younger:** If the participant's spouse is more than 10 years younger than the participant and the spouse is the IRA's sole designated beneficiary for the entire calendar year, the minimum distribution factor used in calculating the required distribution amount is determined in accordance with the Joint and Last Survivor Table specified in Treas. Reg. 1.401(a)(9)-9, Q&A3. The participant's marital status is determined on January 1 of the calendar year. A 50% excise tax is levied[2] on amounts that should have been distributed, but were not.

- **Taxation of distributions**

  - **During life:** Distributions are taxable as ordinary income.[3]

  - **At death:** At the participant's demise, the distributions received by a beneficiary are taxed as ordinary income.[3] If the participant dies before payments have begun, distributions must generally be paid out over a five-year period or less, or over the life expectancy of a designated beneficiary, if payments begin by December 31 of the year following the year of the participant's death. If the distributions are paid solely to the surviving spouse, they may be paid out over the life expectancy of the spouse and must begin by the end of the year in which the participant would have attained age 70½.[4] If the surviving spouse elects to treat the IRA as his or her own, distributions must begin by April 1 of the year following the year in which the surviving spouse attains age 70½. Caution is required in making a QTIP trust the beneficiary of an IRA. For federal estate tax purposes, the value of the IRA is included in the gross taxable estate of the participant. Proper planning is necessary to avoid losing the benefit of the marital deduction.

- **Charitable distribution:** For 2006 and 2007 federal law provides an exclusion from gross income of up to $100,000 for distributions made from a Roth or Traditional IRA directly to a qualified charitable organization. The IRA owner must be at least age 70½ when the distribution is made. No charitable deduction is allowed for such qualified charitable distribution.

- **Transfers to Health Savings Accounts (HSAs):** Federal law allows for a limited, one-time, direct transfer of funds from an IRA to an HSA. If certain requirements are met, any otherwise taxable portion of the distribution is excluded from income and the 10% early distribution penalty will not apply.

---

[1] See Treas. Reg. Sec. 1.401(a)(9)-5, Q&A4(a).
[2] Based on federal law. State law will vary.
[3] Taxes and penalties do not apply to nondeductible contributions.
[4] Or, if later, by the end of the calendar year following the year the participant died.

Continued...

Traditional IRAs

Investment Alternatives

- **Banks, savings and loans, credit unions:** Certificates of deposit in Traditional IRAs are generally protected by either the FDIC or the NCUA for amounts up to $250,000. Fixed and variable rates are available. There may be penalties for early withdrawal.

- **Annuities:** Traditional individual retirement annuities issued by insurance companies can guarantee a fixed monthly income at retirement. Variable annuities do not guarantee a fixed monthly income at retirement.

- **Money market:** Yield fluctuates with the economy. Investor cannot lock in the higher interest rates. It is easy to switch to other investments.

- **Mutual funds:** Capital gains, interest and dividends are tax-deferred in an IRA but are taxed as ordinary income at withdrawal.

- **Zero coupon:** Bonds are bought at deep discount originally. There are no interest payments to worry about reinvesting. Zero coupon bonds are subject to inflation risk and interest rate risk.

- **Stocks and bonds:** A wide variety of investments and risk is possible. Capital gains are taxed as ordinary income at withdrawal. Losses are generally not deductible.

- **Limited partnerships:** Some limited partnerships are especially designed for qualified plans, specifically in the areas of real estate and mortgage pools.

Prohibited Investments or Transactions for IRAs

- **Life insurance:** IRAs cannot include life insurance contracts.

- **Loans to IRA taxpayer:** Self-borrowing disqualifies the IRA and triggers constructive distribution of the entire amount deemed distributed. It becomes currently taxable plus a 10% penalty if the account owner is under age 59½.

- **Collectibles:** Purchases of art works, antiques, metals, gems, stamps, etc., will be treated as a taxable distribution. Coins issued under state law and certain U.S. gold, silver and platinum coins are exceptions. Some kinds of bullion may be purchased.

- **IRA as collateral:** Using the IRA as security for a loan, e.g. buying stock on margin, will trigger a distribution tax.

Other Factors to Consider

- Is the interest rate fixed or variable? If interest rates drop, a fixed rate is better, especially if you can make future contributions at the same fixed rate. If interest rates go up, you may be able to roll the current IRA over to another IRA.

- What is the yield? More frequent compounding will produce a higher return.

- How often can you change investments? What is the charge?

- Federal bankruptcy law protects assets in traditional IRA accounts, up to $1,000,000. In future years, the $1,000,000 limit will be indexed for inflation. Funds rolled over from qualified plans are protected without limit.

How a Traditional IRA Works

Account Owner

- Contribution may be tax deductible.[1]
- Total annual contribution is limited.[2]
- Annual contribution limits are coordinated with any Roth IRA.

IRA Account

- May be opened anytime between January 1 of current year until due date of tax return.
- Earnings accumulate tax deferred.
- Account is usually self-directed (owner controls investments).
- A separate spousal IRA may be established for a spouse with little or no earned income.

Early Withdrawal

- A 10% penalty applies if withdrawals are made before age 59½.
- Some exceptions to 10% penalty are available.
- Earnings + deductible contributions are taxed as ordinary income in year received.

Retirement

- Distributions must begin by April 1 of year following year owner reaches age 70½.
- Required minimum distribution rules apply.
- Earnings + deductible contributions are taxed as ordinary income in year received.

Death

- Value of IRA is included in owner's gross estate.
- Proceeds can pass to surviving spouse, with payments made over survivor's lifetime.
- Income and estate taxes can severely reduce IRA funds left to non-spousal beneficiaries.

---

[1] If an IRA owner (or spouse) is a participant in an employer-sponsored qualified plan, the deductibility of traditional IRA contributions may be limited, based on income level and filing status.

[2] The maximum annual contribution is the lesser of $5,000 ($10,000 for a married couple) or 100% of compensation. For married couples, no more than $5,000 may be contributed for either spouse. If an IRA owner is age 50 or older, he or she may contribute an additional $1,000 ($2,000 if spouse is also over 50).

Roth IRAs

The Roth IRA differs from the traditional IRA in that contributions are never deductible and, if certain requirements are met, account distributions are free of federal income tax.[1]

Funding a Roth IRA

Annual contributions: A Roth IRA may be established and funded at any time between January 1 of the current year, up to and including the date an individual's federal income tax return is due, (generally April 15 of the following year), not including extensions. The account must be designated as a Roth IRA at the time it is established.[2]

Conversion of existing IRA account: An existing, traditional IRA (either an annual contribution IRA or a rollover IRA) may be converted to a Roth IRA. The conversion from the traditional IRA to the Roth IRA is a taxable event. Previously deducted IRA contributions and all earnings are added to the taxpayer's gross income for the year of conversion. Any 10% penalty tax for withdrawals before age 59½ which might apply to converted amounts is waived. However, if a taxpayer withdraws amounts from the Roth IRA within five years of the year of conversion, the 10% penalty tax will apply to those amounts deemed to be part of the conversion.[3]

To qualify for a conversion, a taxpayer must have an adjusted gross income (AGI) of $100,000 or less in the year of conversion. The law also prohibits conversion if a taxpayer is using the married filing separate status.[4] A taxpayer who converts amounts from a traditional IRA to a Roth IRA may reverse the transaction and recharacterize the converted funds. Only one such conversion and recharacterization is permitted during a tax year. If, for example, a taxpayer converts and then unconverts a Roth IRA in 2008, he or she must wait until tax year 2009 before again converting amounts from a traditional IRA to a Roth IRA. The recharacterization of converted amounts must generally be made by the due date for the taxpayer's return, plus any extensions.

Direct rollover from a designated Roth account: Funds may be rolled into a regular Roth IRA from a designated Roth account that is part of a 401(k) or 403(b) plan. Such a rollover is not a taxable event and the filing status and AGI limitations normally applicable to regular Roth IRA contributions do not apply.

Direct rollover from a qualified plan: Beginning in 2008, distributions from qualified retirement plans, IRC Sec. 457 plans, and IRC Sec. 403(b) plans may be rolled directly into a Roth IRA. These rollovers will be taxable events, subject to the same requirements as a Roth conversion, e.g. filing status limitations and AGI of $100,000 or less.

---

[1] Income tax treatment of Roth IRAs at the state or local level may differ.

[2] Federal law allows a 401(k) or 403(b) plan sponsor to modify plan provisions to allow participants the option to contribute to a Roth account. Contributions to a Roth 401(k) or Roth 403(b) account are made with after-tax dollars and are subject to the same employee elective deferral limits as the 401(k) or 403(b) plan.

[3] The 10% penalty will apply to the extent that converted amounts would have been included in income because of the conversion. See IRC Sec. 408A(d)(3)(F).

[4] Converted amounts are not included in determining if AGI is $100,000 or less. The converted amounts are, however, taken into account for all other income tax purposes. Beginning in 2010, the $100,000 and filing status limitations will no longer apply.

Continue

Roth IRAs

Type of Arrangements Permitted

There are currently two types of Roth IRAs.

- **Individual retirement accounts:** trusts with a corporate trustee
- **Individual retirement annuities:** special annuities issued by a life insurance company

Contribution Limits

Limits: For 2008, an individual may contribute (but not deduct) the lesser of $5,000 or 100% of compensation for the year. For a married couple, an additional $5,000 may be contributed on behalf of a lesser earning (or nonworking) spouse, using a spousal account. A husband and wife may contribute up to a total of $10,000, as long as their combined compensation is at least that amount.[1] If an IRA owner is age 50 or older, he or she may contribute an additional $1,000 ($2,000 if the spouse is also over 50).

Contribution phase out: For 2008, the maximum contribution to a Roth IRA is phased out for single taxpayers with adjusted gross income between $101,000 and $116,000. For married couples filing jointly, the phase-out range is an AGI of $159,000 to $169,000. For married individuals filing separately, the phase-out range is an AGI of $0 to $10,000.

Other IRAs: The contribution limits for a Roth IRA are coordinated with those of the traditional IRA; a taxpayer may not contribute more than $5,000 ($10,000 for a married couple) per year into a single IRA or a combination of traditional and Roth IRAs[1]. Excess contributions to a Roth IRA are subject to a 6% excise tax.

Federal refunds: Refunds of federal income taxes may be directly deposited into an IRA.

Taxation of Distributions

A distribution from a Roth IRA that is a "qualified" distribution is excluded from gross income and is not subject to federal income tax. A distribution is qualified if it is made after a five-year waiting period[2] and at least one of the following requirements is met:

- after the taxpayer reaches age 59½; or
- due to the taxpayer's death; or
- because the taxpayer becomes disabled; or
- to pay for first-time-home-buyer expenses.[3]

---

[1] These amounts apply to 2008. For 2007, the maximum allowable contribution was $4,000 for a single individual and $8,000 for a married couple.

[2] Five years after a contribution is first made, or amounts are converted to, a Roth IRA. Subsequent contributions or conversions do not start a new five-year waiting period. See IRC Sec. 408A(d)(2) (B), as amended by the Internal Revenue Restructuring and Reform Acts of 1998.

[3] Limited to $10,000, which must be used within 120 days of withdrawal. Distribution must be used to acquire or rebuild a first home of the taxpayer, spouse, or any descendent or ancestor of the taxpayer or his or her spouse.

Continued...

Roth IRAs

The **earnings** portion of a "non-qualified" distribution is subject to tax. To determine any taxable distribution, the funds are considered to be withdrawn in a specified order:

- Any withdrawal is considered to come first from nondeductible **contributions**, which are not subject to tax.

- After all contributions have been withdrawn, any **conversion** amounts are considered next. A distribution of converted funds is not included in gross income, but may be subject to the 10% premature distribution penalty if the funds are withdrawn within five years of being converted.

- Once all contributions and conversions have been withdrawn, any remaining funds are deemed to be **earnings**, and, when distributed, are included in gross income.

Premature Distributions

If a **taxable** distribution is received prior to age 59½, a 10% penalty tax is added to the regular income tax due, unless one or more of the following exceptions apply:

- A distribution is made because of the death or disability of the account owner.

- A withdrawal is part of a scheduled series of substantially equal periodic payments.

- A withdrawal is used to pay deductible medical expenses, or is made pursuant to a qualified domestic relations order, e.g., a divorce decree.

- The distribution is used to pay for qualified higher education expenses of the account owner, spouse, child, or grandchild.

- Amounts are withdrawn to pay for first-time homebuyer expenses of up to $10,000.

- In certain situations, to pay health insurance premiums for unemployed individuals.

- A distribution is transferred to a Health Savings Account (HSA).

- Withdrawals by military reservists called to active duty for more than 179 days, or indefinitely, between September 11, 2001 and December 31, 2007.

- In case of an IRS levy on the account.

Other Differences

There are several other significant differences between the traditional and Roth IRAs:

- **Contributions after age 70½:** Contributions to a Roth IRA may be made even after the taxpayer has reached age 70½, as long as the taxpayer has compensation at least equal to the contribution, subject to the phase out rules.

- **Distribution requirements:** Roth IRAs are not subject to the mandatory distribution rules during the life of the owner (triggered at age 70½), applicable to traditional IRAs.

Continued

Roth IRAs

Charitable Distributions

For 2006 and 2007 federal law provides an exclusion from gross income of up to $100,000 for distributions made from a Roth or Traditional IRA directly to a qualified charitable organization. The IRA owner must be at least age 70½ when the distribution is made. No charitable deduction is allowed for such qualified charitable distribution.

Transfers to Health Savings Accounts (HSAs)

Federal law allows for a limited, one-time, direct transfer of funds from an IRA to an HSA. If certain requirements are met, any otherwise taxable portion of the distribution is excluded from income and the 10% early distribution penalty will not apply.

Factors Favoring Conversion to a Roth IRA

Factors that favor converting an existing traditional IRA to a Roth IRA include:

- The dollar amount in an existing IRA is relatively small.

- The majority of contributions in an existing IRA consist of nondeductible contributions.

- A taxpayer has at least five years before withdrawals are planned.

- A taxpayer anticipates that the funds in an IRA will not be needed at retirement and would like to continue tax-free growth for as long as possible.

- Sufficient non-IRA funds are available to pay the additional income tax due as a result of the conversion from a traditional IRA to a Roth IRA.

- It is anticipated that a taxpayer's marginal tax bracket during retirement will be the same as, or higher than, the current marginal bracket.

Investment Alternatives

- **Banks, savings and loans, credit unions:** Certificates of deposit in Roth IRAs are generally insured by either the FDIC or the NCUA for amounts up to $250,000. Fixed and variable rates are available. There may be stiff penalties for early withdrawal.

- **Annuities:** Traditional, fixed individual retirement annuities issued by life insurance companies can guarantee fixed monthly income at retirement and may include a disability-waiver-of-premium provision. Variable annuities do not guarantee a fixed monthly income at retirement.

- **Money market:** Yield fluctuates with the economy. Investor cannot lock in higher interest rates. It is easy to switch to other investments.

- **Mutual funds:** A wide variety of mutual funds with many investment objectives are available.

- **Zero coupon bonds:** Bonds are issued at a deep discount from face value. There are no worries about reinvesting interest payments. Zero coupon bonds are subject to inflation risk and interest rate risk.

Continued...

Roth IRAs

- **Stocks:** A wide variety of investments (and risk) is possible. Losses are generally not deductible.
- **Limited partnerships:** Some limited partnerships are especially designed for qualified plans, specifically in the areas of real estate and mortgage pools.

Prohibited Investments or Transactions

- **Life insurance:** Roth IRAs cannot include life insurance contracts.
- **Loans to IRA taxpayer:** Self-borrowing triggers a constructive distribution of the entire amount in an IRA.
- **Collectibles:** Purchase of art works, antiques, metals, gems, stamps, etc., will be treated as a taxable distribution. Coins issued under state law and certain U.S. gold, silver and platinum coins are exceptions. Certain kinds of bullion may be purchased.

Other Factors to Consider

- Is the interest rate fixed or variable? If interest rates drop, a fixed rate may be better, especially if you can make future contributions at the same fixed rate. If interest rates go up, you may be able to roll the account to another Roth IRA.
- What is the yield? More frequent compounding will produce a higher return.
- How often can you change investments? Is there a charge?
- Federal bankruptcy law protects assets in Roth IRA accounts, up to $1,000,000. In future years, the $1,000,000 limit will be indexed for inflation. Funds rolled over from qualified plans are protected without limit.

How a Roth IRA Works

Account Owner

- Contributions are not tax deductible.
- Total annual contribution is limited.[1]
- Annual contribution limits are coordinated with any traditional IRA.

Roth IRA Account

- May be opened anytime between January 1 of the current year and the due date of the tax return.
- Traditional IRA can be converted to a Roth IRA[2].
- Earnings accumulate tax-deferred.
- Account is usually self-directed (owner controls investments).
- A separate spousal Roth IRA may be established for a spouse with little or no earnings.

Qualified Distributions

- Qualified distributions are tax-free if a five-year holding period is met and one of the following applies - The owner is over 59½, dies, becomes disabled or the distribution is for up to $10,000 of qualified first-time homebuyer expenses.

Retirement

- Assuming compensation, contributions may continue to any age.
- No mandatory age for starting withdrawals.
- No minimum distributions required while owner is alive.
- Qualified distributions are received free of federal income tax.

Death

- Value of Roth IRA is included in owner's federal gross estate.
- If five-year holding period is met, beneficiaries receive funds free of federal income tax.
- A surviving spouse may choose to treat an inherited Roth IRA as his or her own.

---

[1] The maximum annual contribution is the lesser of $5,000 ($10,000 for a married couple) or 100% of compensation. For married couples, no more than $5,000 may be contributed for either spouse. For a Roth IRA owner age 50 or older, an additional $1,000 may be contributed ($2,000 if the spouse is also age 50). The maximum annual contribution to a Roth IRA is phased out for individuals with incomes in excess of certain limits.

[2] The conversion is a taxable event. Previously deducted contributions and all earnings are added to the taxpayer's gross income in the year of conversion. Taxpayers with a modified AGI greater than $100,000 may not convert. Beginning in 2010, the $100,000 income limit will no longer apply.

Roth 401(k) and Roth 403(b)

Qualified Roth Contribution Program

The Economic Growth and Tax Relief Reconciliation Act of 2001 (EGTRRA) contained a new code section, IRC Sec. 402A, effective January 1, 2006, which allows an employer to add a "qualified Roth contribution program" to a regular 401(k) or 403(b) qualified retirement plan.[1] These plans are popularly known as a "Roth 401(k)" plans.

Qualified Roth Contribution Program

Under a regular 401(k) or 403(b) plan, a participant chooses to defer a portion of his or her compensation into the retirement plan. Such "elective deferrals" are made on a **pre-tax** basis, any account growth is tax-deferred, and withdrawals are taxed as ordinary income.

In a qualified Roth contribution program, a participant can choose to have all or part of his elective deferrals made to a separate, designated Roth account. Such "designated Roth contributions" are made on an **after-tax** basis. Growth in the designated Roth account is tax-deferred and qualified distributions are excluded from gross income. Other points:

- Separate accounting and recordkeeping are required for the deferrals under the 401(k) or 403(b) portions of the plan and for those made to the designated Roth account. Assets may not be transferred between a regular 401(k) or 403(b) plan and a designated Roth account.

- Individuals whose adjusted gross income exceeds certain limits may not contribute to a regular Roth IRA. There are no income limits applicable to a designated Roth account.

- For 401(k) plans, contributions to a designated Roth account are elective deferrals for purposes of the Actual Deferral Percentage (ADP) test.

Contributions

A number of rules apply to contributions to a qualified Roth contribution program:

- **Dollar limitation:** For 2008, a maximum of $15,500 may be contributed. Those who are age 50 and older may make additional contributions of $5,000. A participant may choose to place all of his or her contributions in the regular 401(k) or 403(b) portion of the plan, all in the designated Roth account, or split the deferrals between the two.

- **Employer contributions:** Employer contributions will be credited to the regular 401(k) or 403(b) portion of the plan; they may not be designated as Roth contributions.

- **Excess contributions:** Excess deferrals to a qualified Roth contribution program must be distributed to the participant no later than April 15 of the year following the year in which the excess deferral was made. Otherwise, the excess deferral will be taxed twice, once in the year of deferral and a second time the year a corrective distribution is made.

---

[1] The discussion here concerns federal income tax law. State or local income tax law may differ.

Continued

Roth 401(k) and Roth 403(b)
Qualified Roth Contribution Program

Distributions

A distribution from a designated Roth account will be excluded from income if it is made at least five years after a contribution to such an account was first made and at least one of the following applies:

1. The participant reaches age 59½;
2. The participant dies;
3. The participant becomes disabled.

Such distributions are known as "qualified" distributions. Other points:

- **Nonqualified distributions:** If a distribution does not meet the above requirements, it is termed a "nonqualified" distribution. Such distributions are subject to federal income tax, including a 10% premature distribution penalty if the distribuee is under age 59½, in the year distributed. Such distributions are taxed under the annuity rules of IRC Sec. 72; any part of a distribution that is attributable to earnings is includable in income; any portion attributable to the original investment (basis) is recovered tax-free. This contrasts sharply with the taxation of nonqualified distributions from a regular Roth IRA account. Nonqualified distributions from a regular Roth IRA are taxed following pre-defined ordering rules under which basis is recovered first, followed by earnings.

- **First-time homebuyer expenses:** In a regular Roth IRA, a qualified distribution may be made to pay for first-time homebuyer expenses. This provision **does not apply** to distributions from a designated Roth account.

- **Rollovers:** A distribution from a designated Roth account may be rolled over into either a Roth IRA or another designated Roth account.

- **Required minimum distributions:** Generally, amounts in a designated Roth account are subject to the required minimum distribution rules applicable to plan participants when they reach age 70½. However, a participant can avoid the mandated distributions by rolling over amounts in the designated Roth account into a regular Roth IRA.

Which Account To Choose?

The decision as to which type of account should be used will generally be made on factors such as the length of time until retirement (or until the funds are needed), the amount of money available to contribute each year, the participant's current tax situation, and the anticipated marginal tax rate in retirement. An important issue to keep in mind is the overall, lifetime tax burden.

- **Regular 401(k) or 403(b):** Generally, individuals with a relatively short period of time until retirement, or who expect that their marginal tax rate will be lower in retirement, will benefit more from the regular 401(k) or 403(b) plan.

Continued...

Roth 401(k) and Roth 403(b)

Qualified Roth Contribution Program

- **Designated Roth account:** Younger individuals with more years until retirement and those who anticipate that their marginal tax rate will rise in retirement will generally benefit more from a designated Roth account. The fact that contributions to a designated Roth account are after-tax may cause current cash-flow problems for some individuals. Higher income participants may find that taxable income will be higher with a designated Roth account than with a regular 401(k) or 403(b) plan, potentially reducing tax breaks such as the child tax credit or AMT exemption.

- **Both:** Some individuals may choose to contribute to both types of plan, to provide flexibility in retirement.

Seek Professional Guidance

Because of the complexities involved, the advice and counsel of tax and financial professionals is strongly recommended.

Deductible IRA Contributions for Traditional IRAs

The annual amount that an individual can contribute to a traditional IRA and then deduct on his or her income tax return cannot exceed the lesser of $5,000[1] or total compensation for that year. For a married couple filing a joint return, where only one spouse is employed (or where one spouse earns less than $5,000), the annual contribution is limited to the lesser of $10,000[2] (a maximum of $5,000 each to separate accounts) or their combined annual compensation. The contributions on behalf of the non-employed (or lesser earning) spouse are made to an arrangement called a spousal IRA.[3]

The $5,000/$10,000 limits assume no contributions to a Roth IRA. The contribution limits for both a traditional IRA and a Roth IRA are coordinated: a taxpayer may not contribute more than $5,000 ($10,000 spousal) per year into a single IRA or combination of IRAs. Excess contributions are subject to a 6% excise tax.

The maximum limit on the amount that may be deducted is restricted, however, if the individual (or spouse) is a participant in an employer-sponsored retirement plan. If this is the case, and depending on the level of modified adjusted gross income (MAGI), a deduction may be allowed for all, none or only a portion of an IRA contribution.

The chart below shows the traditional IRA contribution phase-out ranges for tax year 2008.

Status	No Participation in a Company Retirement Plan	If Covered by a Company Retirement Plan[4]	
Single	Up to $5,000 is deductible.	**MAGI**	**IRA Deduction**
		Up to $53,000	$5,000
		$53,000 - $63,000	Phased out
		Over $63,000	None
Married filing joint	Up to $5,000 for each is deductible, including spousal IRAs.	**MAGI**	**IRA Deduction**
		Up to $85,000	$5,000 ($10,000 spousal)
		$85,000 - $105,000	
		Over $105,000	Phased out
			None
Married filing separate	Up to $5,000 for each is deductible, if both spouses are employed.	**MAGI**	**IRA Deduction**
		Up to $10,000	Phased out
		Over $10,000	None

---

[1] This amount applies to 2008. For 2007, the maximum allowable contribution was $4,000.
[2] This amount applies to 2008. For 2007, the maximum allowable contribution was $8,000.
[3] If an IRA owner is age 50 or older, he or she may contribute an additional $1,000 ($2,000 if spouse is also over 50).
[4] A taxpayer will not be considered an active participant in an employer-sponsored retirement plan merely because the taxpayer's spouse is an active participant. However, in this situation, the taxpayer's deductible IRA contribution will be phased out for couples with an AGI of $159,000 -$169,000.

Continued...

Deductible IRA Contributions for Traditional IRAs

Other Considerations

- Company retirement plans include pension plans, profit sharing plans, 401(k), 403(b) plans, SEP-IRAs, Keogh plans, and SIMPLE plans.

- Generally, compensation includes wages, salaries, professional fees, net self-employment income and other amounts received for performing personal services.

- Compensation also includes alimony received by a divorced spouse.

Calculating the Maximum Deductible Amount – Single Or MFS

For 2008, the following steps may be used to calculate the deductible portion of a contribution to a traditional IRA for a single individual or a married individual using the married filing separately filing status:[1]

1. Modified adjusted gross income (MAGI):[2] $ _____

2. Applicable dollar amount:[3]   (_____)

3. Line 1 minus Line 2:   _____

4. Deduction: _____
    a. If line 3 is greater than $10,000, no deduction allowed.
    b. If line 3 is between $0 and $10,000, subtract line 3 from $10,000.

5. Multiplication factor: .40 (.50 if age 50 or greater)   _____

6. Multiply line 4 x line 5   _____

7. Round line 6 to next highest $10   _____

8. Your compensation for the year: _____

9. Contributions you plan to make   _____
    (Do not enter more than $5,000 [$6,000 if age 50 or older])

10. Maximum deductible IRA amount:[4]   _____
    (Compare the amounts on Lines 7, 8, and 9, and enter the smallest amount.)

---

[1] Married couples where both spouses contribute to an IRA should compute each deduction separately. If an individual receives social security benefits in the same year that a contribution is made to a traditional IRA, a different calculation is involved. See IRS Publication 590, Individual Retirement Arrangements (IRAs) for details.

[2] MAGI = adjusted gross income increased by: (1) student loan interest deduction; (2) tuition and fees deduction; (3) foreign earned income or housing exclusion; (4) foreign housing deduction; (5) excluded qualified savings bond interest; and (6) excluded employer-paid adoption expenses.

[3] The applicable dollar amount varies with filing status. For 2008 these amounts are: Single and Head of Household - $53,000; MFS - $0.

[4] If the deductible portion of the IRA is between $1 and $200, round up to $200. IRC Sec. 219(g)

Continued...

Deductible IRA Contributions for Traditional IRAs

Calculating the Maximum Deductible Amount – Married Filing Jointly

For 2008, the following steps may be used to calculate the deductible portion of a contribution to a traditional IRA for a married individual using the married filing jointly filing status:[1]

1. Modified adjusted gross income (MAGI):[2] $ _____

2. Applicable dollar amount:[3]   ($85,000)

3. Line 1 minus Line 2:   _____

4. Deduction: _____
   a. If line 3 is greater than $20,000, no deduction allowed.
   b. If line 3 is between $0 and $20,000, subtract line 3 from $20,000.

5. Multiplication factor: .20 (.25 if age 50 or greater)   _____

6. Multiply line 4 x line 5   _____

7. Round line 6 to next highest $10   _____

8. Your compensation for the year: _____

9. Contributions you plan to make   _____
   (Do not enter more than $5,000 [$6,000 if age 50 or older])

10. Maximum deductible IRA amount:[4]   _____
    (Compare the amounts on Lines 7, 8, and 9, and enter the smallest amount.)

---

[1] Married couples where both spouses contribute to an IRA should compute each deduction separately. If an individual receives social security benefits in the same year that a contribution is made to a traditional IRA, a different calculation is involved. See IRS Publication 590, Individual Retirement Arrangements (IRAs) for details.

[2] MAGI = adjusted gross income increased by: (1) student loan interest deduction; (2) tuition and fees deduction; (3) foreign earned income or housing exclusion; (4) foreign housing deduction; (5) excluded qualified savings bond interest; and (6) excluded employer-paid adoption expenses.

[3] The value for 2008. This amount varies with filing status and will change each year.

[4] If the deductible portion of the IRA is between $1 and $200, round up to $200. IRC Sec. 219(g)

Tax-Deferred Growth in an IRA
Traditional IRA

The chart below illustrates the advantage of tax-deferred growth in a fully-deductible IRA, compared with an alternative in which both the annual contribution and annual growth are taxable each year. The results shown in the chart are hypothetical and simplified to facilitate understanding.

Assumptions:
Annual[1] contribution: $5,000[2]
Annual return: 6%[3]
Combined state and federal marginal income tax bracket: 30%

	Tax-Deferred		Currently Taxable	
Years Until Withdrawal of Funds	IRA Balance Assuming a $5,000 Annual Deductible Contribution	After-Tax Amount[4] If Withdrawn from the IRA at a 30% Tax Rate	$3,500 Annual Contribution Invested at an Equivalent After-Tax Rate of 4.20%	Benefit Due to Tax-Deferral
5	$28,185	$19,730	$19,033	$697
10	65,904	46,133	42,413	3,720
15	116,380	81,466	71,133	10,333
20	183,928	128,750	106,413	22,337
25	274,323	192,026	149,750	42,276
30	395,291	276,704	202,986	73,718
35	557,174	390,022	268,380	121,642
40	773,810	541,667	348,710	192,957

Note: If the tax bracket at retirement is lower, the tax savings would be even greater.

There is a 10% penalty tax on withdrawals from an IRA before age 59½, unless for disability or death, or if the distribution is paid as an annuity over the life of the IRA owner or the joint lives of the IRA owner and a designated beneficiary, or the distribution is rolled over to another IRA.[5]

---

[1] Assumes contributions are made at the end of each year.
[2] This amount applies to 2008. If an IRA owner is age 50 or older, he or she may contribute an additional $1,000 ($2,000 if spouse is also over 50).
[3] The rates of return used in this illustration are not indicative of any actual investment and will fluctuate in value. An investment will not provide a consistent rate of return; years with lower (or negative) returns than the hypothetical returns shown may substantially affect the scenario presented.
[4] Taxes are due when the funds are distributed from the IRA.
[5] The 10% penalty will not be imposed if distributions are used to pay medical expenses in excess of 7.5% of adjusted gross income, or, in certain cases, to pay for health insurance premiums for unemployed individuals. Further, the 10% penalty will not be imposed if distributions are used to pay for qualified higher education expenses, or for first time homebuyer expenses. Certain withdrawals by qualified military reservists and qualified public safety officials also avoid the pentalty.

Tax-Deferred Growth in an IRA
Traditional IRA

The chart below illustrates the advantage of tax-deferred growth in a fully-deductible IRA, compared with an alternative in which both the annual contribution and annual growth are taxable each year. The results shown in the chart are hypothetical and simplified to facilitate understanding.

Assumptions:
Annual contribution:[1] $2,000
Annual return:[2] 5.00%
Combined state and federal marginal income tax bracket: 45.00%

Years Until Withdrawal of Funds	Tax Deferred		Currently Taxable	Benefit Due To Tax Deferral
	IRA Balance Assuming a $2,000 Annual Deductible Contribution	After-tax Amount[3] if Withdrawn from the IRA at a 45.00% Tax Rate	$1,100 Annual Contribution Invested at an Equivalent After-tax Rate of 2.75%	
5	$11,051	$6,078	$5,811	$ 267
10	$25,156	$13,836	$12,466	$1,370
15	$43,157	$23,736	$20,088	$3,648
20	$66,132	$36,373	$28,817	$7,555
25	$95,454	$52,500	$38,814	$13,685
30	$ 132,878	$73,083	$50,264	$22,819
35	$ 180,641	$99,352	$63,377	$35,975
40	$ 241,600	$ 132,880	$78,395	$54,485

Note: If the tax bracket at retirement is lower, the tax savings would be even greater.

There is a 10% penalty tax on withdrawals from an IRA before age 59½, unless for disability or death, or if the distribution is paid as an annuity over the life of the IRA owner or the joint lives of the IRA owner and a designated beneficiary, or the distribution is rolled over to another IRA.[4]

---

[1] Assumes contributions are made at the end of each year.
[2] The rates of return used in this illustration are not indicative of any actual investment and will fluctuate in value. An investment will not provide a consistent rate of return; years with lower (or negative) returns than the hypothetical returns shown may substantially affect the scenario presented.
[3] Taxes are due when the funds are distributed from the IRA.
[4] The 10% penalty will not be imposed if distributions are used to pay medical expenses in excess of 7.5% of adjusted gross income, or, in certain cases, to pay for health insurance premiums for unemployed individuals. Further, the 10% penalty will not be imposed if distributions are used to pay for qualified higher education expenses, or for first time homebuyer expenses. Certain withdrawals by qualified military reservists and qualified public safety officials also avoid the penalty.

Tax-Deferred Growth in an IRA
Traditional IRA

Assumptions:
Annual contribution:[1] $2,000
Annual return:[2] 5.00%
Combined state and federal marginal income tax bracket: 45.00%

| Years until Withdrawal of Funds | Tax Deferred | | Currently Taxable | |
	IRA Balance Assuming a $2,000 Annual Deductible Contribution	After-tax Amount[3] if Withdrawn from the IRA at a 45.00% Tax Rate	$1,100 Annual Contribution Invested at an Equivalent After-tax Rate of 2.75%	Benefit Due to Tax Deferral
5	$11,051	$6,078	$5,811	$ 267
10	$25,156	$13,836	$12,466	$1,370
15	$43,157	$23,736	$20,088	$3,648
20	$66,132	$36,373	$28,817	$7,555
25	$95,454	$52,500	$38,814	$13,685
30	$ 132,878	$73,083	$50,264	$22,819
35	$ 180,641	$99,352	$63,377	$35,975
40	$ 241,600	$ 132,880	$78,395	$54,485

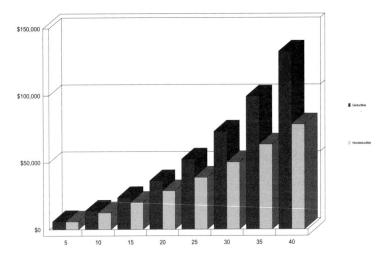

[1] Assumes contributions are made at the end of each year.
[2] The rates of return used in this illustration are not indicative of any actual investment and will fluctuate in value. An investment will not provide a consistent rate of return; years with lower (or negative) returns than the hypothetical returns shown may substantially affect the scenario presented.
[3] Taxes are due when the funds are distributed from the IRA.

Does It Matter When You Contribute to an IRA?

When contributions to an IRA are consistently made at the beginning of the year rather than at the end, the funds have an extra 12 months in which to grow.

Over a period of years there is a substantial difference in the amount accumulated.

$5,000[1] per Year Accumulated at Various Rates of Return[2]

Number of Years from the Beginning of the First Year	5% Return		
	Contribution Made Jan. 1	Contribution Made Dec. 31	Increase in Amount Accumulated
5	$29,010	$27,628	$1,381
10	66,034	62,889	3,144
15	113,287	107,893	5,395
20	173,596	165,330	8,266
25	250,567	238,635	11,932
30	348,804	332,194	16,610
35	474,182	451,602	22,580
40	634,199	603,999	30,200

Number of Years from the Beginning of the First Year	8% Return		
	Contribution Made Jan. 1	Contribution Made Dec. 31	Increase in Amount Accumulated
5	$31,680	$29,333	$2,347
10	78,227	72,433	5,795
15	146,621	135,761	10,861
20	247,115	228,810	18,305
25	394,772	365,530	29,242
30	611,729	566,416	45,313
35	930,511	861,584	68,927
40	1,398,905	1,295,283	103,623

The overall effect is that you have one full extra year of growth when you make the contribution at the beginning of the tax year.

---

[1] This amount applies to 2008. If an IRA owner is age 50 or older, he or she may contribute an additional $1,000 ($2,000 if spouse is also over 50).

[2] Assumes compounding annually. The rates of return used in this illustration are not indicative of any actual investment and will fluctuate in value. An investment will not provide a consistent rate of return; years with lower (or negative) returns than the hypothetical returns shown may substantially affect the scenario presented.

Does It Matter When You Contribute to an IRA?[1]

When contributions to an IRA are consistently made at the beginning of the year rather than at the end, the funds have an extra 12 months in which to grow. Over a period of years there is a substantial difference in the amount accumulated.

Assumptions:
  Annual contribution: 2,000
  Annual growth rate:[2] 5.00%

Number of Years from the Beginning of the First Year	Contribution Made Jan. 1	Contribution Made Dec. 31	Increase in Amount Accumulated
5	$11,604	$11,051	$ 553
10	$26,414	$25,156	$1,258
15	$45,315	$43,157	$2,158
20	$69,439	$66,132	$3,307
25	$ 100,227	$95,454	$4,773
30	$ 139,522	$ 132,878	$6,644
35	$ 189,673	$ 180,641	$9,032
40	$ 253,680	$ 241,600	$12,080

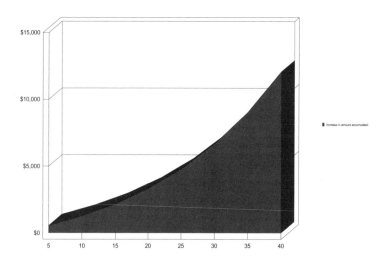

---

[1] Results shown are hypothetical and simplified to facilitate understanding.
[2] Growth is compounded annually. The rates of return used in this illustration are not indicative of any actual investment and will fluctuate in value. An investment will not provide a consistent rate of return; years with lower (or negative) returns than the hypothetical returns shown may substantially affect the scenario presented.

Qualified Retirement Plans

Qualified retirement plans are Congressionally approved retirement plans which have several major tax benefits.

- The employer's contributions can be deducted for income tax purposes.

- The earnings on the plan's investments accumulate on a tax-deferred basis.

- When the funds are distributed at retirement age, they may be eligible for favorable tax treatment.[1]

- Taxpayers may be in a lower income tax bracket after retirement.

Two Principal Types of Plans

Qualified retirement plans can generally be classified as either defined benefit or defined contribution plans.[2]

Defined benefit plans define the benefit amount each participant will receive at retirement age and then estimate how much must be contributed each year to accumulate the necessary future fund. Interest rates, ages of participants, etc., will have an effect on the calculation. The amount of the contribution is generally determined by an actuary. The investment risk rests on the employer.

Defined contribution plans generally put a percentage of current salaries into the plan each year. The amount at retirement will depend on the investment return and number of years until a participant retires. The investment risk rests on the participant.

Plan Type	Contributions	Retirement Benefits	Investment Risk
Defined benefit	Vary	Fixed	Employer
Defined contribution	Pension – Fixed Profit sharing – Vary	Vary	Employee

What Is the Best Type of Plan?

There is no best type of plan. The choice of what type of plan to use is an individual one. The answer depends on factors such as employer goals and available cash flow.

---

[1] Those born before 1936 may be able to elect 10-year averaging or capital gains treatment; these strategies are not available to those born after 1935.

[2] Note that some plans have features of both types.

Continued...

Qualified Retirement Plans

Defined Benefit Plans

The employer contributes an actuarially-determined amount sufficient to pay each participant a fixed or defined benefit at his or her retirement. Methods of defining the benefit may be based on a flat percentage of compensation, a percentage which increases with years of service, a percentage which changes at certain compensation levels, etc.

This type of plan generally favors older employees, because more of the employer's contributions must go into his or her account to make certain that there will be enough to pay the promised (or defined) benefit at retirement age.

Defined Contribution Plans

There are several variations of defined contribution plans. Some of the more common ones include the following.

- **Money purchase pension:** The employer contributes a specified percentage of the participating employee's salary each year. Whatever that fund grows to is what the retiring employee receives.

- **Target benefit pension plan:** The target benefit plan has elements of both the defined benefit and defined contribution plans. The benefits are determined as if the plan were a defined benefit plan, while the defined contribution plan annual contribution percentage and dollar amount limitations apply to the actual contributions.

- **Traditional profit sharing plan:** Similar to the money purchase pension, except that contributions do not need to be a specific percentage and they do not need to be made every year, as long as they are substantial and recurring.

- **Age-weighted money purchase and profit sharing plans:** Money purchase and profit sharing plans in which employer contributions are allocated to provide an assumed equivalent retirement benefit at normal retirement age.

- **Cross-tested or super-integrated money purchase and profit sharing plans:** These plans establish groups of participants to which are allocated specified allocation percentages. They must satisfy very complicated discriminatory requirements under Reg. 1.401(a)(4).

- **Stock bonus plan:** Similar to the traditional profit sharing plan. The plan may, but is not required to, invest primarily in the employer's stock.

- **ESOP - Employee stock ownership plan:** Like a stock bonus plan, to which the employer can contribute company stock instead of cash. The plan must be primarily invested in company stock.

Continued

Qualified Retirement Plans

- **IRC Sec. 401(k) plan:** Also called a cash or deferred plan, this plan is any stock bonus plan or profit sharing plan which meets certain participation requirements of IRC Sec. 401(k). An employee can agree to a salary reduction or to defer a bonus which he or she has coming.

- **SIMPLE plans:** SIMPLE stands for Savings Incentive Match Plan for Employees. SIMPLE plans can be in either an IRA format or a 401(k) format.

- **SEP:** This stands for Simplified Employee Plan. A SEP is a group of individual IRAs established for employees to which the employer and employees may contribute more than an individual employee could contribute to a traditional IRA or Roth IRA.

Life Insurance in Qualified Plans
Legal Limitations

Personal Plans

- **IRAs:** IRAs, IRA rollovers, Roth IRAs, SEPs, and SIMPLE IRA arrangements may not pay the premium for life insurance policies.

- **Tax sheltered annuities:** 403(b) plans may invest in contracts that provide incidental life insurance protection. See Reg. Sec. 1.403(b)-1(c)(3).[1]

Business Plans

- **Defined contribution plans:** The percentage of the total annual employer contribution that can be allocated to life insurance premiums varies with the type of policy. There is no limit on the face amount.
  - **Term, variable, and universal life insurance:** Less than 25% of the annual allocation.
  - **Ordinary whole life insurance:** Less than 50% of annual allocation.
  - **Combination:** One-half of the ordinary life premium and all of the term, variable, and/or universal life premium must be less than 25% of the total.

  Special rule for profit sharing plans: Allocations that are more than two years old may, in some cases, be totally invested in life insurance.[2] See Rev. Ruls. 61-164 1961-2 CB 99.

- **Defined benefit plans**
  - **Basic rule:** The face amount of the insurance may not exceed 100 times the anticipated monthly retirement benefit. For example, if a $5,000 per month retirement benefit were anticipated, the maximum amount of life insurance would be $500,000.
  - **Alternative rule:** Total premiums for ordinary life must be less than 66 2/3% (or 33 1/3% for term, variable, and universal life insurance) of the assumed aggregate contributions[3] that have been made for the participant from the beginning of his or her participation in the plan. See IRS Rev. Rul. 74-307.
  - **Fully Insured Plan:** Some plans are funded exclusively with annuities or a combination of annuities and life insurance. Special rules apply to these types of plans.

- **Other general rule:** Insurance must be made available or purchased on a uniform and non-discriminatory basis.

---

[1] Under proposed regulations issued by the Treasury Department on 11/15/04, annuity contracts issued prior to 2/14/05 may provide incidental life insurance protection; contracts issued on or after that date may not provide any life insurance. See proposed reg. 1.403(b) – 8(c)(2) and proposed Reg. 1.403(b)-11(d).

[2] The IRS has never formally ruled on the taxability of using aged contributions, in excess of the incidental insurance rules, to purchase life insurance. See also Rev. Ruling 60-83 and Rev. Ruling 68-24.

[3] The assumed aggregate contribution is a special calculation separate from the funding calculations.

Continued

426

Life Insurance in Qualified Plans
Legal Limitations

Advantages to the Employee

- Because income and estate taxes on the death benefit may be very substantial, the non-income-taxable insurance proceeds may be used to pay the income taxes and/or estate taxes due on the other plan assets or estate assets. Life insurance protects the other non-insurance assets.

- It is an easy way to provide additional protection for one's family if death occurs prior to retirement age.

- It frees up other personal dollars now being spent for life insurance outside the plan.

- The majority of the premium for ordinary, variable, and universal life insurance is not taxable to the employee. Taxable income to the employee is calculated using IRS Table 2001.

- The policy can be moved to another plan if the employee changes employment, providing the new plan will accept it.

- At retirement age, the employee may be able to take a fully paid up policy, rather than face the expense of converting his or her group insurance.

- The pure insurance portion (the face amount less the accumulated cash values) of the death benefit passes to the beneficiaries income tax free, but may be subject to estate tax.

- A waiver of premium may be added which will continue to pay the life insurance premiums should the employee become disabled.

- Uninsurable participants may be able to purchase a limited amount of guaranteed-issue insurance. In larger plans it may be a substantial amount.

- When a participant in a defined benefit plan is rated for insurance risk purposes (usually for poor health or occupational hazards), the plan can pay the higher premium without increasing the cost to the participant.

- Net investment returns over time can be competitive with other types of investments.

- Table I costs for group insurance reported as income under group coverage in excess of $50,000 are not recoverable. Economic benefit costs incurred for the pure insurance portion of policies in qualified plans may be recovered at the time of distribution.

- Ordinary, variable, or universal life policies can be used as an annuity at retirement age. The insurer will give the participant the higher of either the rate guaranteed in the contract or the then current rates.

- Traditional financial and estate planning seeks a balanced approach to investment portfolios. Ordinary and universal life insurance policies can represent the fixed side of the program. Variable life and variable universal life policies also offer an equity or stock market option for the cash value portion of the policy.

Continued...

Life Insurance in Qualified Plans
Legal Limitations

Advantages to the Employer

- The premiums are deductible as a part of the plan contribution.

- If the employee has a paid-up policy under the qualified plan at retirement age, he or she may not need to convert group insurance to permanent. With larger, experience-rated group life contracts, there is typically a charge (sometimes substantial) to the experience when a policy is converted.

- Under a defined benefit plan, if the insurance proceeds equal the entire preretirement death benefit and a participant dies, all of the other equity assets for that participant can be used to reduce future employer contributions to the plan.

- If participating whole life contracts are used and dividends are used to reduce the premium, the long-term cost in a defined benefit plan may be very favorable.

- In defined benefit plans the employer may be able to make a larger contribution and deduction by including ordinary life insurance in the plan. This is often helpful because of the restrictions on retirement plan benefits and contributions.

- Corporate retained earnings problems may be lessened by increasing the contribution to a defined benefit plan that provides for life insurance. Pension plan assets do not appear on the corporation's balance sheet.

- Younger employees may look at the protection as a current benefit, whereas retirement age may seem to be a long way off.

Disadvantages to the Employee

- If there is an estate tax problem, the life insurance proceeds will increase the size of the gross taxable estate. If the surviving spouse is the beneficiary, there will be no immediate death tax payable, due to the unlimited marital deduction. However, the surviving spouse's estate will be increased, thus increasing the potential estate tax at his or her subsequent death.
  As an alternative, consider having any additional life insurance owned by an irrevocable life insurance trust, designed to keep the proceeds out of the estates of both spouses.

- It is a tax shelter within a tax shelter. Under current law, the buildup of cash values in a life insurance contract are tax deferred and do not need to be in a qualified plan to get this tax advantage.

- If the employee did not recognize the annual imputed income for the insured death benefit per IRS Table 2001, the death benefits paid from the policy are taxable.

Keogh Plans
H.R. 10

Keogh plans are retirement plans for self-employed individuals, e.g. sole proprietors, partners in a partnership,[1] and employees of either. The differences between Keogh plans and corporate sponsored plans are small and are limited to different tax treatment of life insurance.

The Basics of Keogh Plans

- **Plan type:** A Keogh plan may be either a defined contribution plan or a defined benefit plan.

- **Defined contribution plans:** Contributions for individual participants may not exceed the lesser of 100% of includable compensation[2] or $46,000 per year. At the employer level, no more than 25% of the covered compensation of all participants may be deducted. Thus, if the Keogh plan covers only one participant, the effective contribution limit becomes 25% of the includable compensation[2] of the business owner,[3] not to exceed $46,000.

- **Defined benefit plans:** For defined benefit plans, the plan actuary determines the contributions. The deduction for contributions to a defined benefit plan may not exceed net self-employment income. In unusual circumstances, the required contribution may exceed the allowable deduction, which will trigger an excise tax.

- **Benefit limits:** Defined benefit Keogh plans are subject to the same percentage of average compensation and dollar limits that apply to all defined benefit plans. For 2008, these figures are 100% and $185,000.

- **Framework:** May use a trust, a custodial account or an insurance company annuity.

- **Evidence of plan:** The plan must be in writing and meet certain coverage and non-discrimination requirements for present and future employees.

- **Distributions:** Distributions prior to age 59½ (other than for disability or death) are subject to both a 10% penalty and current income tax. However, if a participant terminates service on or after age 55,[4] or receives a series of substantially-equal periodic payments based on his or her life expectancy (or joint life expectancy with a designated beneficiary), the penalty is avoided. For more than 5% owners, distributions must begin when the participant reaches age 70½.

- **Phased retirement:** Federal law allows retirement distributions to employees who are at least age 62 even if they have not separated from employment at the time distributions begin.

---

[1] A partner who owns more than 10% of the capital or profits of the partnership is considered to be an owner-employee. See Reg. Sec. 1.401-10(d).

[2] The "net" self-employment income of the owner or partner, less the contribution and the deduction allowed for one-half of the self-employment tax. For 2008, $230,000 is the maximum income that may be considered.

[3] This is the same as 20% of the gross pre-contribution net income.

[4] Owner-employees may find it difficult to separate from employment.

Continued...

Keogh Plans
H.R. 10

- **Available payment plans**
  - Lump-sum distribution
  - Lifetime of the participant (and spouse if desired)
  - Fixed period of years not to exceed the participant's life expectancy or the joint life expectancy of the participant and a designated beneficiary (see IRC Sec. 401(a)(9))

- **Other plans:** A participant in a Keogh plan may also have a traditional, deductible IRA (subject to certain income level limitations based on filing status), a traditional, nondeductible IRA, or a Roth IRA.

- **Taxation:** Distributions are generally taxed as ordinary income. Special 10-year income averaging may be available for certain individuals.[1]

- **401(k) feature:** A 401(k) feature may be added, if desired, to a profit sharing plan.

- **Allocation methods:** The same kinds of allocation methods that are available under a corporate-sponsored defined contribution plan are also available under a Keogh plan. These can be age-weighted, tiered, or integrated with Social Security.

- **Participant loans:** Participant loans are permitted without any adverse consequences, provided they follow the regular rules for participant loans.

- **Top-heavy defined contribution plans:** If more than 60% of plan assets are allocated to key employees[2], non-key employees must receive the same percentage contribution as that received by the key employee with the highest contribution percentage. This requirement applies only to a contribution of up to the first 3% of includable compensation; a higher contribution may be required in some instances, such as when the plan is combined with a defined benefit plan.

- **Top-heavy defined benefit plans:** If more than 60% of the accrued benefits are attributable to key employees[2], the plan must provide a minimum level of retirement benefits. This is 2% of compensation at retirement for each year of participation, not to exceed 10 years (20%).

- **Federal bankruptcy law:** Effective 10/17/05, federal bankruptcy law provides significant protection from creditors to participant accounts or accrued benefits in tax-exempt retirement plans.

---

[1] Those born before 1936 may be able to elect 10-year averaging or capital gain treatment; these strategies are not available to those born after 1935.

[2] A "key" employee is someone who, at any time during the plan year was: (1) an officer of the employer whose compensation from the employer exceeded $150,000; or (2) a more than 5% owner; or (3) a 1% owner whose compensation from the employer exceeded $150,000.

Traditional Profit Sharing Plan

The basics: Employer contributions to the plan need not be a specific percentage and they need not be made every year, as long as they are "recurring and substantial."[1] Profits are not required in order to make a contribution.

How It Works

- Employer contributions are tax deductible.

- Contributions are not taxed currently to the employee.

- Earnings accumulate income tax-deferred.

- Distributions are generally taxed as ordinary income. Distributions may be eligible for 10-year income averaging[2], or, at retirement from the current employer, rolled over to a Traditional or a Roth IRA[3], or to another employer plan if that plan will accept such a rollover.

Additional Considerations

- **Maximum annual deduction:** Up to 25% of covered payroll can be contributed and deducted by the employer.

- **Contribution base:** Plan contributions are normally based on total compensation; e.g., base salary, bonuses, overtime, etc. The maximum compensation recognized in 2008 is $230,000.

- **Individual limits:** The allocation of contributions to a participant's account may not exceed the lesser of 100% of includable compensation[4] or $46,000 per year.

- **Employer contributions**
  - Most plans are discretionary as to the amount that the employer contributes.
  - If there are profits, the employer is expected to make "recurring and substantial[1]" contributions.[1]

- **Excluding persons:** Certain persons can be eliminated on the basis of months of service, age or coverage in a union plan; for example, persons under age 21 can be excluded from the plan.

---

[1] See IRS Reg. 1.401-1 (b)(2).
[2] Those born before 1936 may be able to elect 10-year averaging or capital gain treatment; these strategies are not available to those born after 1935.
[3] Beginning in 2008, distributions from qualified retirement plans, IRC Sec. 457 plans, and tax-sheltered annuities may be rolled directly into a Roth IRA. These rollover distributions are taxable events, subject to the same requirements as a Roth conversion.
[4] For those self employed, this rate applies to "net" self-employment income of the owner or partner, less the contribution and the deduction allowed for one-half of the self-employment tax.

Continued...

Traditional Profit Sharing Plan

- **Investment of plan assets:** Investments must be diversified and prudent. Subject to plan provisions, plan assets may be invested in equity products like mutual funds, stocks and debt-free real estate; or debt instruments like T-Bills and CD's. Insurance products like life insurance and annuity policies may also be used.

- **Social Security integration:** Since the employer already contributes to the employee's Social Security retirement benefit, these contributions can be integrated into the allocation formula of the plan.

- **Forfeitures:** As participants leave the company and separate from the plan, those less than 100% vested forfeit that part of the account in which they are not vested. The nonvested forfeitures may then be allocated to the remaining participants. Those participants who remain in the plan the longest will share in the most forfeitures, or forfeitures may be used to reduce future employer contributions.

- **Parties which are favored:** Typically younger participants are favored because they have a longer time for their fund to grow and share in forfeitures.

How Much Will There Be at Retirement?

This will depend upon three factors.
1. The frequency and amount of contributions,
2. The number of years until retirement, and
3. The investment return.

The risk of poor investment returns rests upon the employee. However, if investment results are favorable, the participant will have a larger fund at retirement age.

An Example of What $10,000 Per Year Will Grow to Over Several Years at Various Rates of Growth Without Tax[1]				
Years	4.00%	6.00%	8.00%	10.00%
5	$54,163	$56,371	$58,666	$61,051
10	$120,061	$131,808	$144,866	$159,374
15	$200,236	$232,760	$271,521	$317,725
20	$297,781	$367,856	$457,620	$572,750
25	$416,459	$548,645	$731,059	$983,471
30	$560,849	$790,582	$1,132,832	$1,644,940
35	$736,522	$1,114,348	$1,723,168	$2,710,244

---

[1] The rates of return used in this illustration are not indicative of any actual investment and will fluctuate in value. An investment will not provide a consistent rate of return; years with lower (or negative) returns than the hypothetical returns shown may substantially affect the scenario presented.

Continued.

Traditional Profit Sharing Plan

Top-Heavy Plans

If more than 60% of the plan assets are allocated to "key" employees[1], then the employer must contribute at least as much for "non-key" participants as it does for key employees. This requirement applies only to a contribution of up to the first 3% of includable compensation (higher in some instances).

Advantages to Employer

A. Contributions are tax deductible.

B. Contributions and costs are totally flexible.

C. The plan is easy to understand by the employees.

D. Forfeitures of terminating employees may reduce future costs or be reallocated among the accounts of those in the plan.

E. It can provide employees with permanent life insurance benefits that need not expire or require costly conversion at retirement age.

F. The employer can direct investments.

G. Coordination with Social Security will reduce contributions for rank and file employees.

H. If former participants do not provide the plan with distribution instructions, the plan may automatically distribute accounts less than $5,000. In the case of a plan that provides for such mandatory distributions, the plan must automatically roll an eligible distribution amount that exceeds $1,000 to a Rollover IRA in the former participant's name. A plan may allow direct rollovers of less than $1,000.

Advantages to Employees

A. Annual employer contributions are not taxed to the participant.

B. Earnings on the account are not currently taxed.

C. Federal bankruptcy law provides significant protection from creditors to participant accounts or accrued benefits in tax-exempt retirement plans.

D. Participants can have the right to direct investments.

---

[1] A "key" employee is someone who, at any time during the plan year was: (1) an officer of the employer whose compensation from the employer exceeded $150,000; or (2) a more than 5% owner; or (3) a 1% owner whose compensation from the employer exceeded $150,000.

Continued...

Traditional Profit Sharing Plan

E. Federal law allows a qualified plan to establish an "eligible investment advice arrangement" under which individually tailored investment advice is provided to plan participants. Any fees or commissions charged must not vary with the investment options chosen, or else a computer model meeting certain requirements must be used.

F. Participants may also have a traditional, deductible IRA (subject to certain income limitations based on filing status), a traditional, nondeductible IRA, or a Roth IRA.

G. If the plan allows, there is the ability to purchase significant permanent life insurance under the plan. Purchase of life insurance will create taxable income to the employee.

H. Younger employees can accumulate a larger fund than with a defined benefit plan.

I. The forfeited, unvested portion of accounts of former participants may be reallocated to the active participants' accounts; this can have a major impact on future benefits.

J. If the plan so provides, vested balances may be withdrawn if the participant has a "financial hardship." Under IRS regulations, this is defined as "immediate and heavy financial need where funds are not reasonably available from other sources." There are safe harbor rules listing the conditions and requirements for hardship distributions.

K. Participants may borrow from the plan within certain guidelines if provided for in the plan documents.

Disadvantages to Employer

A. The profit sharing plan will generally not produce as large a contribution and deduction for older employees as will a defined benefit plan.

B. Deductible contribution limits are set at 25% of covered payroll.

Disadvantages to Employees

A. There is no guarantee as to future benefits.

B. Investment risks rest on the participant.

C. Older participants may not receive as large a benefit as with a defined benefit plan.

D. There is no assurance as to the frequency and amount of employer contributions.

How a Traditional Profit Sharing Plan Works

Employer

- Employer contributions are discretionary and flexible.
- Employer contributions need not be a specified percentage of compensation, nor made each year, as long as they are recurring and substantial.
- Contributions are tax deductible to the business.[1]

Traditional Profit Sharing Plan

- Employer contributions are not currently taxable to employee and account growth is tax deferred.
- Investment risk remains on employee.
- The forfeited, unvested portion of former employee's accounts may be reallocated to current participants.

Employee

- The allocation of contributions to an employee's account may not exceed the lesser of 100%[2] of compensation or $46,000[2] per year.
- The maximum compensation recognized in 2008 is $230,000.[3]
- Employee may be given right to direct investments.

Early Withdrawal

- A 10% penalty generally applies if withdrawals are made before age 59½.
- Some exceptions to 10% penalty are available.
- Employee may borrow from plan within certain guidelines if provided for in plan documents.

Retirement

- Distributions must begin by specified date.[4]
- Funds may be distributed as lump sum or periodic payments.
- Distributions are generally taxed as ordinary income; may be eligible for 10-year income averaging or rolled over into an IRA.

Death

- Value of account is included in owner's gross estate.
- Proceeds can pass to surviving spouse with payments made over survivor's lifetime.
- Income and estate taxes can severely reduce funds left to nonspousal heirs.

---

[1] Up to 25% of covered payroll can be contributed and deducted by the employer.
[2] These are 2008 limits.
[3] For those self-employed, compensation is limited to net self-employment income; e.g. gross income less the contribution and the deduction allowed for one-half of the self-employment tax.
[4] Except for more than 5% owners, distributions must begin by the later of (1) April 1 of the year following the year in which the participant reaches age 70½, or (2) the year following the year in which the participant retires.

Traditional Money Purchase Plan

The basics: The employer contributes a defined or fixed percentage of the participating employee's compensation each year. The amount to which the fund grows is the amount the retiring employee receives.

How It Works

- Employer contributes a fixed percentage of the participant's compensation each year to the plan.

- The total employer contribution is then allocated on that basis or on a separately defined basis, such as tiered or integrated with Social Security.

- Employer contributions are tax deductible.

- Contributions are not taxed currently to the employee.

- Earnings accumulate income tax-deferred.

- Distributions are generally taxed as ordinary income. Distributions may be eligible for 10-year income averaging[1], or, at retirement from the current employer, rolled over to a Traditional or a Roth IRA[2] or to another employer plan if that plan will accept such a rollover. Federal law allows retirement distributions to employees who are at least age 62 even if they have not separated from employment at the time distributions begin.

Additional Considerations

- **Maximum annual contribution:** Up to 25% of covered payroll can be contributed and deducted by the employer.

- **Contribution base:** Plan contributions are normally based on total compensation; e.g., base salary, bonuses, overtime, etc. The maximum compensation recognized in 2008 is $230,000.

- **Individual limits:** The allocation of contributions to a participant's account may not exceed the lesser of 100% of compensation[3] or $46,000 per year.

- **Excluding persons:** Certain persons can be eliminated on the basis of months of service, age or coverage in a union plan; for example, persons under age 21 can be excluded from the plan.

- **Investment of plan assets:** Investments must be diversified and prudent. Subject to plan provisions, plan assets may be invested in equity products like mutual funds, stocks and debt-free real estate; or debt instruments like T-Bills and CDs. Insurance products like life insurance and annuity policies may also be used.

---

[1] Those born before 1936 may be able to elect 10-year averaging or capital gain treatment; these strategies are not available to those born after 1935.

[2] Beginning in 2008, distributions from qualified retirement plans, IRC Sec. 457 plans, and tax-sheltered annuities may be rolled directly into a Roth IRA. These rollover distributions are taxable events, subject to the same requirements as a Roth conversion.

[3] For those self employed, this rate applies to "net" self-employment income of the owner or partner, less the contribution and the deduction allowed for one-half of the self-employment tax.

Continued

Traditional Money Purchase Plan

- **Social Security integration:** Since the employer already contributes to the employee's Social Security retirement benefit, these contributions can be integrated into the contribution and/or allocation formulas of the plan.

- **Parties which are favored:** Typically, younger participants are favored because their fund may grow for a longer period and, in some instances, they share in forfeitures that other participants do not.

- **Forfeitures:** As participants leave the company and separate from the plan, those less than 100% vested forfeit that part of the account in which they are not vested. The nonvested forfeitures may then be allocated to the remaining participants. Those participants who remain in the plan the longest will share in the most forfeitures, or forfeitures may be used to reduce future employer contributions.

How Much Will There Be at Retirement?

This will depend upon three factors.
1. The amount of contributions
2. The number of years until retirement
3. The investment return

The risk of poor investment returns rests upon the employee; however, if investment results are favorable, the participant will have a larger fund at retirement age.

An Example of What $10,000 Per Year Will Grow to Over Several Years at Various Rates of Growth Without Tax[1]				
Years	**4.00%**	**6.00%**	**8.00%**	**10.00%**
5	$54,163	$56,371	$58,666	$61,051
10	$120,061	$131,808	$144,866	$159,374
15	$200,236	$232,760	$271,521	$317,725
20	$297,781	$367,856	$457,620	$572,750
25	$416,459	$548,645	$731,059	$983,471
30	$560,849	$790,582	$1,132,832	$1,644,940
35	$736,522	$1,114,348	$1,723,168	$2,710,244

Future Contributions

An employer must make annual contributions to the plan; but to the extent that the future payroll can be forecast, so can the approximate amount of future contributions. Changes may be made prospectively in the level of employer contributions by plan amendment, with advance notice to plan participants.

---

[1] The rates of return used in this illustration are not indicative of any actual investment and will fluctuate in value. An investment will not provide a consistent rate of return; years with lower (or negative) returns than the hypothetical returns shown may substantially affect the scenario presented.

Continued...

Traditional Money Purchase Plan

Zero Percent Plans

In some special situations an employer may maintain a money purchase plan that requires no contributions. Creditor protection and self-trusteed asset management are the most common reasons for this.

Top-Heavy Plans

If more than 60% of the plan assets are allocated to "key" employees[1], the employer must contribute at least as much for "non-key" participants as it does for key employees. This requirement applies only to a contribution of up to the first 3% of includable compensation (higher in some instances).

Advantages to Employer

A. Contributions are tax deductible.

B. Contributions and costs are known in advance.

C. Contributions will rise as compensation rises, but they are controllable both by formula and absolute dollar amounts.

D. Forfeitures of terminating employees may reduce future costs or be reallocated among the accounts of those still in the plan.

E. The plan is easier to understand by the employees than is a defined benefit plan.

F. It can provide employees with permanent life insurance benefits that need not expire nor require costly conversion at retirement age.

G. The employer can direct investments.

H. If former participants do not provide the plan with distribution instructions, the plan may automatically distribute accounts less than $5,000. In the case of a plan that provides for such mandatory distributions, the plan must automatically roll an eligible distribution amount that exceeds $1,000 to a Rollover IRA in the former participant's name. A plan may allow direct rollovers of less than $1,000.

Advantages to Employees

A. Annual employer contributions are not taxed to the participant.

B. Earnings on the account are not currently taxed.

---

[1] A "key" employee is someone who, at any time during the plan year was: (1) an officer of the employer whose compensation from the employer exceeded $150,000; or (2) a more than 5% owner; or (3) a 1% owner whose compensation from the employer exceeded $150,000.

Continued

Traditional Money Purchase Plan

C. Participants can be given the right to direct investments.

D. Federal law allows a qualified plan to establish an "eligible investment advice arrangement" under which individually tailored investment advice is provided to plan participants. Any fees or commissions charged must not vary with the investment options chosen, or else a computer model meeting certain requirements must be used.

E. Participants may also have a traditional, deductible IRA (subject to certain income limitations based on filing status), a traditional, nondeductible IRA, or a Roth IRA.

F. If the plan allows, there is the ability to purchase significant permanent life insurance under the plan. Purchasing life insurance will create taxable income to the employee.

G. Younger employees can accumulate a larger fund than with a defined benefit plan.

H. Participant may borrow from the plan within certain guidelines if provided for in the plan documents.

I. The forfeited, unvested portion of accounts of former participants may be reallocated to the active participants' accounts. This can have a substantial impact on future benefits. Forfeitures may also be used to reduce employer contributions.

J. Federal bankruptcy law provides significant protection from creditors to participant accounts or accrued benefits in tax-exempt retirement plans.

Disadvantages to Employer

A. In low profit years, the employer is still obligated to make contributions pursuant to the plan's contribution formula.

B. While the plan may be amended to change contribution levels from time to time, this should not be done annually.[1]

C. The money purchase plan will generally not produce as large of a contribution and deduction for employees in their late 30's and older, as will a defined benefit plan.

Disadvantages to Employees

A. There is no guarantee as to future benefits.

B. Investment risks rest on the participant.

C. Older participants may not receive as great of a benefit as with a defined benefit plan.

---

[1] In 2002, the overall profit sharing plan contribution limit increased to 25% of covered compensation with much greater employer flexibility. However, there are still instances where the employer will want to have a money purchase plan.

How a Traditional Money Purchase Plan Works

Employer

- Contributes a fixed percentage of each participant's compensation.
- Total employer contribution is then allocated on that basis or on a separately defined basis.
- Contributions are tax deductible to the business.[1]
- Nondiscrimination rules apply.

Money Purchase Plan

- Employer contributions are not currently taxable to employee and account growth is tax deferred.
- Investment risk remains on employee.
- The forfeited, unvested portion of former employee's accounts may be reallocated to current participants.

Employee

- The allocation of contributions to an employee's account may not exceed the lesser of 100%[2] of compensation or $46,000[2] per year.
- The maximum compensation recognized in 2008 is $230,000.[3]
- Employee may be given right to direct investments.

Early Withdrawal

- A 10% penalty generally applies if withdrawals are made before age 59½.
- Some exceptions to 10% penalty are available.
- Employee may borrow from plan within certain guidelines if provided for in plan documents.

Retirement

- Distributions must begin by specified date.[4]
- Funds may be distributed as lump sum or periodic payments.
- Distributions are generally taxed as ordinary income and may be eligible for 10-year income averaging or rolled over into an IRA.

Death

- Value of account is included in owner's gross estate.
- Proceeds can pass to surviving spouse with payments made over survivor's lifetime.
- Income and estate taxes can severely reduce funds left to nonspousal heirs.

[1] Up to 25% of covered payroll can be contributed and deducted by the employer.
[2] These are 2008 limits.
[3] For those self-employed, compensation is limited to net self-employment income, e.g. gross income less the contribution and the deduction allowed for one-half of the self-employment tax.
[4] Except for more than 5% owners, distributions must begin by the later of (1) April 1 of the year following the year in which the participant reaches age 70½, or (2) the year following the year in which the participant retires.

Nontraditional Defined Contribution Plan

The basics: These plans are different from traditional money purchase pension and profit sharing plans in that they define different participant groups who will receive different levels of employer contributions. They must comply with very detailed and complicated regulations under IRC Sec. 401(a)(4). They are typically called either cross-tested, tiered or super-integrated money purchase pension or profit sharing plans.

How It Works

- Employer contributions are tax deductible.

- Contributions are not taxed currently to the employee.

- Earnings accumulate income tax-deferred.

- Distributions are generally taxed as ordinary income. Distributions may be eligible for 10-year income averaging[1], or, at retirement from the current employer, rolled over to a Traditional or a Roth IRA[2] or to another employer plan if that plan will accept such a rollover. Federal law allows pension plans to make retirement distributions to employees who are at least age 62 even if they have not separated from employment at the time distributions begin.

Additional Considerations

- **Maximum annual deduction:** Up to 25% of covered payroll may be contributed and deducted by the employer.

- **Compensation base:** Plan contributions are normally based on total compensation; e.g., base salary, bonuses, overtime, etc. The maximum compensation recognized in 2008 is $230,000.

- **Employer contributions**
    - For money purchase pension plans, the employer contribution for the specified participant groups is determined by the plan formula and will be fixed unless amended at some future date.
    - Profit sharing plans have a discretionary employer contribution on behalf of the specified participant groups. If there are profits, the employer is expected to make "substantial and recurring" contributions.[3]

- **Individual limits:** The allocation of contributions to a participant's account may not exceed the lesser of 100% of compensation[4] or $46,000 per year.

---

[1] Those born before 1936 may be able to elect 10-year averaging or capital gain treatment; these strategies are not available to those born after 1935.

[2] Beginning in 2008, distributions from qualified retirement plans, IRC Sec. 457 plans, and tax-sheltered annuities may be rolled directly into a Roth IRA. These rollover distributions are taxable events, subject to the same requirements as a Roth conversion.

[3] See IRS Reg. 1.401-(b)(2).

[4] For those self-employed, compensation is limited to "net" self-employment income, e.g., gross income less the contribution and the deduction allowed for one-half of the self-employment tax.

Continued...

Nontraditional Defined Contribution Plan

- **Excluding persons:** Certain persons can be eliminated on the basis of months of service, age or coverage in a union plan. For example, persons under age 21 can be excluded from the plan.

- **Investment of plan assets:** Investments must be diversified and prudent. Subject to plan provisions, plan assets can be invested in equity products like mutual funds, stocks and debt-free real estate; debt instruments like T-Bills and CDs. Insurance products like life insurance and annuity policies may also be used.

- **Social Security integration:** While these plans may recognize the impact of Social Security, the differential realized by integrating with Social Security may be minimal.

- **Forfeitures:** As participants leave the company and separate from the plan, those less than 100% vested forfeit that part of the account in which they are not vested. The nonvested forfeitures may then be allocated to the remaining participants. Those participants who remain in the plan the longest will share in the most forfeitures, or forfeitures may be used to reduce future employer contributions.

- **Parties which are favored:** Cross-tested and super-integrated plans are typically designed to favor the most highly compensated participants in the plan. While these participants will often be the older employees, such is not necessarily the case. In fact, the use of these types of plans is one way in which equity can be achieved between an older owner/professional and a younger owner/professional. At the same time, other participants often receive allocations that are greater than the 3% top-heavy contributions minimum. These types of plans also may aid in allowing owner(s) to reach the maximum $46,000 allocation permitted without having to use a second plan.

How Much Will There Be at Retirement?

This will depend on three factors.
1. The frequency and amount of contributions,
2. The number of years until retirement, and
3. The investment return.

The risk of poor investment returns rests upon the employee. However, if investment results are favorable, the participant will have a larger fund at retirement age.

An Example of What $10,000 Per Year Will Grow to Over Several Years at Various Rates of Growth Without Tax[1]				
Years	4.00%	6.00%	8.00%	10.00%
5	$54,163	$56,371	$58,666	$61,051
10	$120,061	$131,808	$144,866	$159,374
15	$200,236	$232,760	$271,521	$317,725
20	$297,781	$367,856	$457,620	$572,750
25	$416,459	$548,645	$731,059	$983,471
30	$560,849	$790,582	$1,132,832	$1,644,940
35	$736,522	$1,114,348	$1,723,168	$2,710,244

---

[1] The rates of return used in this illustration are not indicative of any actual investment and will fluctuate in value.

Continued...

Nontraditional Defined Contribution Plan

Top-heavy Plans

If more than 60% of the plan assets are allocated to "key" employees[1], the employer must contribute at least as much for "non-key" participants as it does for key employees up to the first 3% of includable compensation (higher in some instances). The plan is typically structured to provide top-heavy benefits for all participants before providing additional allocations to any specified group.

Gateway Contributions

Beginning in 2002 an additional contribution was required on behalf of the nonhighly-compensated participants.[2] The nonhighly-compensated participants must receive a contribution that is the lesser of 5% of compensation or one third the highest allocation percentage of the highly-compensated participants. Any top-heavy contribution is applied to satisfying this requirement.

Advantages to Employer

A. Contributions are tax deductible.

B. For profit sharing plans, contributions and costs are totally flexible. For money purchase pension plans, the employer contribution is known in advance.

C. The plan is easily understood by employees.

D. Forfeitures of terminating employees may reduce future costs or be reallocated among the accounts of those still in the plan.

E. It can provide employees with permanent life insurance benefits that need not expire or require costly conversion at retirement age.

F. The employer can direct investments.

G. If former participants do not provide the plan with distribution instructions, the plan may automatically distribute accounts less than $5,000. In the case of a plan that provides for such mandatory distributions, the plan must automatically roll an eligible distribution amount that exceeds $1,000 to a Rollover IRA in the former participant's name. A plan may allow direct rollovers of less than $1,000.

---

[1] A "key" employee is someone who, at any time during the plan year was: (1) an officer of the employer whose compensation from the employer exceeded $150,000; or (2) a more than 5% owner; or (3) a 1% owner whose compensation from the employer exceeded $150,000.

[2] Highly-compensated employees generally include 5% or more owners and those earning more than $100,000 in the prior year.

Continued...

Nontraditional Defined Contribution Plan

Allocation of Employer Contributions[1]			
Participant	Age	Annual Compensation	Cross-Tested Allocation
Owner A	55	$230,000	$46,000[2]
Owner B	50	150,000	$46,000[2]
Employee 1	40	55,000	$2,750[3]
Employee 2	35	30,000	$1,500[3]
Employee 3	30	30,000	$1,500[3]
Employee 4	25	30,000	$1,500[3]
Totals		$525,000	$99,250

The cross-tested plan maximizes the contribution for both owners.

Advantages to Employees

A. Annual employer contributions are not taxed to the participant.

B. Earnings on the account are not currently taxed.

C. Participants can have the right to direct investments.

D. Federal law allows a qualified plan to establish an "eligible investment advice arrangement" under which individually tailored investment advice is provided to plan participants. Any fees or commissions charged must not vary with the investment options chosen, or else a computer model meeting certain requirements must be used.

E. Participants may also have a traditional, deductible IRA (subject to certain income level limitations based on filing status), a traditional, nondeductible IRA, or a Roth IRA.

F. If the plan allows, there is the ability to purchase significant permanent life insurance under the plan. Purchase of life insurance will create taxable income to the employee.

G. The forfeited, unvested portion of accounts of former participants may be reallocated to the accounts of active participants. This can have a substantial impact on future benefits.

H. Participant may borrow from the plan within certain guidelines if provided for in the plan documents.

I. Federal bankruptcy law provides significant protection from creditors to participant accounts or accrued benefits in tax-exempt retirement plans.

---

[1] Assumes a profit sharing plan.
[2] Specified allocation to maximum limits.
[3] Specified allocation of 5.0% of compensation.

Continued..

Nontraditional Defined Contribution Plan

Disadvantages to Employer

A. Money purchase pension plans
1. In low profit years, the employer is still obligated to make contributions.
2. While the plan may be amended to change contribution levels from time to time, this should not be done annually.

B. Profit sharing plans: Deductible contributions are limited to 25% of covered payroll.

Disadvantages to Employees

A. There is no guarantee as to future benefits.

B. Investment risk rests on the participant.

How a Nontraditional Defined Contribution Plan Works

Employer

- Allows definition of different participant groups who can receive different levels of employer contributions.

- Typically called cross-tested, tiered or super-integrated plans.

- Must comply with detailed and complex regulations under IRC Sec. 401(a)(4).

Nontraditional Defined Contribution Plan

- Employer contributions[1] are not currently taxable to employee and account growth is tax deferred.

- Investment risk remains on employee.

- The forfeited, unvested portion of former employee's accounts may be reallocated to current participants.

Employee

- The allocation of contributions to an employee's account may not exceed the lesser of 100%[2] of compensation or $46,000[2] per year.

- The maximum compensation recognized in 2008 is $230,000.[3]

- Employee may direct investments.

Early Withdrawal

- 10% penalty generally applies if withdrawals made before age 59½.

- Some exceptions to 10% penalty are available.

- Employee may borrow from plan within certain guidelines if provided for in plan documents.

Retirement

- Distributions must begin by specified date.[4]

- Funds may be distributed as lump sum or periodic payments.

- Distributions generally taxed as ordinary income and may be eligible for 10-year income averaging or rolled over into an IRA.

Death

- Value of account is included in owner's gross estate.

- Proceeds can pass to surviving spouse with payments made over survivor's lifetime.

- Income and estate taxes can severely reduce funds left to nonspousal heirs.

---

[1] Up to 25% of covered payroll may be contributed and deducted by the employer.
[2] These are 2008 limits.
[3] For those self-employed, compensation is limited to net self-employment income; e.g. gross income less the contribution and the deduction allowed for one-half of the self-employment tax.
[4] Except for more than 5% owners, distributions must begin by the later of (1) April 1 of the year following the year in which the participant reaches age 70½, or (2) the year following the year in which the participant retires.

Traditional Defined Benefit Plan

The basics: Employer contributes an actuarially determined amount sufficient to pay each participant a fixed or defined benefit at his or her retirement.

How It Works

- Employer contributes an actuarially determined amount each year to the plan.

- Employer contributions are tax deductible.

- Contributions are not taxed currently to the employee.

- Earnings accumulate income tax-deferred.

- Distributions are generally taxed as ordinary income. Distributions may be eligible for 10-year income averaging[1], or, at retirement from the current employer, rolled over to a Traditional or a Roth IRA[2] or to another employer plan if that plan will accept such a rollover. Federal law allows retirement distributions to employees who are at least age 62 even if they have not separated from employment at the time distributions begin.

Methods of Defining the Benefit

- **Level percentage plan:** Example - The benefit is equal to 50% of compensation[3], reduced by 1/25 for each year of participation less than 25 years.

- **Step rate service weighted for prior service:** Example - The benefit is equal to 8% of compensation[3] for the first ten years of service plus 5.2% of compensation[3] for all other years, but not to exceed a total of 33 years.

- **Service plan:** Example - The benefit is 2.5% of compensation[3] for each year of service. Younger participants – with a potentially longer working career – may also be favored if the benefit formula is service related.

- **Plan participation:** Example - The benefit is 5% of compensation per year of participation with a maximum of 20 years.

- **Top-heavy plans:** If the present value of the accrued benefits of "key" employees[4] is 60% or more of the total value of all accrued benefits, the plan is top heavy. In that instance, the plan must provide for a minimum level of benefits for "non-key" participants.

---

[1] Those born before 1936 may be able to elect 10-year averaging or capital gain treatment; these strategies are not available to those born after 1935.

[2] Beginning in 2008, distributions from qualified retirement plans, IRC Sec. 457 plans, and tax-sheltered annuities may be rolled directly into a Roth IRA. These rollover distributions are taxable events, subject to the same requirements as a Roth conversion.

[3] For those self-employed, compensation is limited to "net" self-employment income, e.g., gross income less the contribution and the deduction allowed for one-half of the self-employment tax. In 2008, $230,000 is the maximum income that may be considered. In unusual circumstances, the required contribution may exceed the allowable deduction, which can trigger an excise tax.

[4] A "key" employee is someone who, at any time during the plan year was: (1) an officer of the employer whose compensation from the employer exceeded $150,000; or (2) a more than 5% owner; or (3) a 1% owner whose compensation from the employer exceeded $150,000.

Continued...

Traditional Defined Benefit Plan

Additional Considerations

- **Investment of plan assets:** Investments must be diversified and prudent. Subject to plan provisions, plan assets can be invested in equity products like mutual funds, stocks and debt-free real estate; or in debt instruments like T-Bills and CDs. Insurance products like life insurance and annuity policies may also be used.

- **Social Security integration:** Since the employer already contributes to the employee's Social Security retirement benefit, these benefits can be integrated into the benefit formula of the plan.

- **Parties which are favored:** Usually favors older employees.

Maximum Benefit

Maximum benefit under a defined benefit plan is measured in two ways:

- **Percentage:** The retirement benefit cannot exceed 100% of the average compensation[1] for the highest three consecutive years of employment. This is reduced by 10% for each year of service less than 10.

- **Dollar amount:** The maximum annual dollar benefit is indexed at $185,000 per year (2008) for retirement at age 62. For retirement prior to age 62, this amount is actuarially reduced. Retirement at age 55 would typically produce a maximum annual benefit of approximately $100,000, depending on the number of years of participation. The dollar amount will also be increased for retirement after age 65, subject to the percentage and dollar limitations. Lastly, if the individual has fewer than 10 years of participation at normal retirement age, the dollar amount is reduced proportionately.

Contributions

The table below illustrates hypothetical first-year contributions for an employee retiring at age 62 with at least 5 years of plan participation. In all instances, the employee's compensation is $185,000 or more. The benefit is 10% of compensation per year of plan participation, which provides the IRS maximum annual benefit per year.[2]

Current Age	1st Year Contributions
30	$48,066
35	61,557
40	78,873
45	101,094
50	129,626
55	140,351
60	179,506

---

[1] For those self-employed, compensation is limited to "net" self-employment income, e.g., gross income less the contribution and one-half of the deduction allowed for the self-employment tax.

[2] The Pension Protection Act of 2006 permits a plan sponsor to contribute and deduct an additional amount, generally 50% of the plan's funding target, as advance funding for future plan years.

Continued.

Traditional Defined Benefit Plan

First-Year Contributions

A number of assumptions must be made in determining the amount of current contributions necessary to accumulate the future retirement benefit. The list below includes some of these assumptions.

- Death benefits
- Retirement age
- Form of annuity
- IRS Requirements
- Various government interest rates
- Interest rate on earnings
- Annuity rates at retirement
- Statutory requirements and limits
- Participants' current ages
- Compensation

Annual Contributions

Year-to-year contributions will fluctuate based on the following items.

- Earnings on previous contributions
- Gains and losses on investments (realized and unrealized)
- Participants' actual compensation
- Death of participants before retirement
- Disability retirements
- Age mix of participants
- Turnover in participants
- Cost of annuities at retirement
- Rate of vesting
- Timing of contributions
- Assumptions mandated by IRS
- Funding limits and requirements of the Internal Revenue Code
- Legal/actuarial requirements
- The Pension Protection Act of 2006 mandates a new uniform method of calculating minimum required contributions effective in 2008.

Continued...

Traditional Defined Benefit Plan

Annual funding is done on the assumption that each participant will retire. Accrued benefits are earned each year, and if the participant does not work until scheduled retirement, he or she will not be entitled to the entire benefit.

Advantages to Employer

A. Contributions are tax deductible.

B. Can reward long-term employees with a substantial retirement benefit even though they are close to retirement age.

C. Larger contributions for older employees may reduce corporate tax problem; e.g., excess accumulated earnings, high tax bracket current earnings, etc.

D. Forfeitures of terminating employees will reduce future costs.

E. It can provide employees with permanent life insurance benefits that need not expire or require costly conversion at retirement age.

F. The employer directs investments.

G. If former participants do not provide the plan with distribution instructions, the plan may automatically distribute accounts less than $5,000. In the case of a plan that provides for such mandatory distributions, the plan must automatically roll an eligible distribution amount that exceeds $1,000 to a Rollover IRA in the former participant's name. A plan may allow direct rollovers of less than $1,000.

Advantages to Employees

A. Annual employer contributions are not taxed to the participant.

B. Earnings are not currently taxed.

C. Participants may also have a traditional, deductible IRA (subject to certain income level limitations), a traditional, nondeductible IRA, or a Roth IRA.

D. There is the ability to purchase significant permanent life insurance, which is not contingent upon the company group insurance program. Purchase of life insurance will generate taxable income to the employee.

E. Employee is guaranteed a known retirement benefit.

F. Participant may borrow from the plan within certain guidelines if provided for in the plan documents.

Continued

Traditional Defined Benefit Plan

    G. Federal bankruptcy law provides significant protection from creditors to participant accounts or accrued benefits in tax-exempt retirement plans.

Disadvantages to Employer

    A. In low profit years, the employer is often still obligated to make contributions.

    B. Even if profits are low, there is less flexibility with the level of contribution than with some other types of plans.

    C. Investment risks are on the employer.

    D. Administration costs are usually higher because an actuary must certify as to the reasonableness of the contribution and deduction (unless it is a fully insured plan).

    E. Participants often do not understand the defined benefit plan as easily as they do other types of plans.

    F. If there are rank and file employees and the plan terminates, there may be insufficient assets to pay all accrued benefits. The shortfall must be made up by either the business making a contribution, or by the assets being reallocated from owner-participants to nonhighly compensated participants.

    G. When a plan terminates, it may find that there are surplus assets which may not be distributed to participants. Any such surplus returned to the employer is subject to a 50% (20% in some instances) excise tax.

    H. An employer with an older work force may find the cost of a defined benefit plan to be prohibitively expensive.

    I. If a small defined benefit plan terminates with insufficient assets, the rank and file participants receive the full value of their benefits, while the business owners receive the remaining balance. If there are insufficient assets, the pension benefit guarantee corporation (PBGC) will guarantee some benefits

Disadvantages to Employees

    A. Younger employees will generally not receive as great of a benefit as they would under other types of plans.

    B. The plan concept is more difficult to understand.

How a Traditional Defined Benefit Plan Works

Employer

- Employer contributes an actuarially-determined amount sufficient to pay each participant a fixed or defined benefit at retirement.

- Employer contributions are tax deductible.

Traditional Defined Benefit Plan

- Employer contributions are not currently taxable to employee and earnings accumulate tax deferred.

- Investment risk remains on employer. Investments must be diversified and prudent. Both equity and debt investments may be used.

- Retirement benefit is typically defined as a percentage of compensation for each year of service or participation.

Employee

- Employee has a known retirement benefit.

- Maximum retirement benefit is the lesser of $185,000 per year[1] or 100% of the individual's average compensation for the three highest consecutive years.[2]

Early Withdrawal

- A 10% penalty generally applies if withdrawals are made before age 59½.

- Some exceptions to 10% penalty are available.

- Employee may borrow from plan within certain guidelines if provided for in plan documents.

Retirement

- Distributions must begin by specified date.[3]

- Funds may be distributed as lump sum or periodic payments.

- Distributions are generally taxed as ordinary income and may be eligible for 10-year income averaging or rolled over into an IRA.

Death

- The PV of the accrued retirement benefit is usually included in owner's gross estate.

- Proceeds can pass to surviving spouse with payments made over survivor's lifetime.

- Income/estate taxes can severely reduce funds left to nonspousal heirs.

---

[1] These are 2008 limits. This amount is subject to indexing for inflation. Applies when retirement occurs at age 65 or the Social Security normal retirement age, if later.
[2] The 100% is reduced by 10% for each year of service less than 10.
[3] Except for more than 5% owners, distributions must begin by the later of (1) April 1 of the year following the year in which the participant reaches age 70½, or (2) the year following the year in which the participant retires.

Target Benefit Plan

The basics: The target benefit plan has elements of both the defined benefit and defined contribution plans. The contributions are determined as if the plan were a defined benefit plan, while the defined contribution plan annual contribution percentage and dollar amount limitations apply to the actual contributions made on behalf of each participant. Target benefit plans are very rare.

How It Works

- Employer contributes an actuarially determined amount each year subject to percentage and dollar limitations to the plan.

- Employer contributions are tax deductible.

- Contributions not taxed currently to the employee.

- Earnings accumulate income tax-deferred.

- Distributions are generally taxed as ordinary income. Distributions may be eligible for 10-year income averaging[1], or, at retirement from the current employer, rolled over to a Traditional or a Roth IRA[2] or to another employer plan if that plan will accept such a rollover. Federal law allows retirement distributions to employees who are at least age 62 even if they have not separated from employment at the time distributions begin.

Methods of Defining the Benefit

- **Level percentage plan:** Example: The benefit is equal to 50% of compensation[3], reduced by 1/25 for each year of participation less than 25.

- **Yearly accrual:** Example: The benefit is equal to 5.0% of compensation[3] for each year of participation.

- **Top-heavy plan:** If more than 60% of the plan assets are allocated to key employees[4], the employer must contribute at least as much for non-key participants as it does for key employees. This requirement applies only to a contribution of up to the first 3% of includable compensation (higher in some instances).

Additional Considerations

- **Contribution limitations:** The employer contributes an amount actuarially determined but not more than the lesser of 100% of includable compensation or $46,000 annually for each participant.[3] If the plan is top heavy, minimum contributions are required.

---

[1] Those born before 1936 may be able to elect 10-year averaging or capital gain treatment; these strategies are not available to those born after 1935.

[2] Beginning in 2008, distributions from qualified retirement plans, IRC Sec. 457 plans, and tax-sheltered annuities may be rolled directly into a Roth IRA. These rollover distributions are taxable events, subject to the same requirements as a Roth conversion.

[3] 2008 values. For those self-employed, compensation is limited to net self-employment income, e.g., gross income less the contribution and the deduction allowed for one-half of the self-employment tax. For 2008, $230,000 is the maximum income that may be considered

[4] A "key" employee is someone who, at any time during the plan year was: (1) an officer of the employer whose compensation from the employer exceeded $150,000; or (2) a more than 5% owner; or (3) a 1% owner whose compensation from the employer exceeded $150,000.

Continued...

Target Benefit Plan

- **Deduction limits:** Not withstanding the individual allocation limits, the maximum employer deduction is limited to 25% of covered compensation.

- **Parties which are favored:** Older employees are favored. A company with principals and key workers older than the rank and file should consider a target plan.

- **Investment of plan assets:** Investments must be diversified and prudent. Subject to plan provisions, plan assets can be invested in equity products like mutual funds, stocks and debt free real estate; or in debt instruments like T-Bills and CDs. Insurance products like life insurance and annuity policies may also be used.

- **Social Security integration:** Since the employer already contributes to the employee's Social Security retirement benefit, these contributions can be integrated into the benefit formula of the plan.

How Much Will There Be at Retirement?

This will depend upon three factors.
1. The amount of contributions,
2. The number of years until retirement, and
3. The investment return.

The risk of poor investment returns rests upon the employee. However, if the investment results are favorable, the participant will have a larger fund at retirement age.

An Example of What $10,000 Per Year Will Grow to Over Several Years at Various Rates of Growth Without Tax[1]				
Years	4.00%	6.00%	8.00%	10.00%
5	$54,163	$56,371	$58,666	$61,051
10	$120,061	$131,808	$144,866	$159,374
15	$200,236	$232,760	$271,521	$317,725
20	$297,781	$367,856	$457,620	$572,750
25	$416,459	$548,645	$731,059	$983,471
30	$560,849	$790,582	$1,132,832	$1,644,940
35	$736,522	$1,114,348	$1,723,168	$2,710,244

Advantages to Employer

A. Contributions are tax deductible.

B. Contributions will rise as compensation rises, but they are controllable both by formula and absolute dollar amounts.

C. Forfeitures of terminating employees may reduce future costs.

---

[1] The rates of return used in this illustration are not indicative of any actual investment and will fluctuate in value. An investment will not provide a consistent rate of return; years with lower (or negative) returns than the hypothetical returns shown may substantially affect the scenario presented.

Continued

Target Benefit Plan

D. It can provide employees with permanent life insurance benefits that need not expire or require costly conversion at retirement age.

E. The employer usually directs investments.

F. Often the advantages of a defined benefit plan can be obtained without its problems.

G. If former participants do not provide the plan with distribution instructions, the plan may automatically distribute accounts less than $5,000. In the case of a plan that provides for such mandatory distributions, the plan must automatically roll an eligible distribution amount that exceeds $1,000 to a Rollover IRA in the former participant's name. A plan may allow direct rollovers of less than $1,000.

Advantages to Employees

A. Annual contributions are not taxed to the participant.

B. Earnings on the account are not currently taxed.

C. Participants may be given the right to direct investments..

D. Federal law allows a qualified plan to establish an "eligible investment advice arrangement" under which individually tailored investment advice is provided to plan participants. Any fees or commissions charged must not vary with the investment options chosen, or else a computer model meeting certain requirements must be used.

E. Participants may also have a traditional, deductible IRA (subject to certain income limitations based on filing status), a traditional, nondeductible IRA, or a Roth IRA.

F. If the plan allows, there is the ability to purchase significant permanent life insurance under the plan. Purchase of life insurance will generate taxable income to the employee.

G. Participant may borrow from the plan within certain guidelines if provided for in the plan documents.

H. Federal bankruptcy law provides significant protection from creditors to participant accounts or accrued benefits in tax-exempt retirement plans.

Disadvantages to Employer

A. In low profit years, the employer is still obligated to make contributions.

B. There is no flexibility with the level of contributions.

C. In some cases, the target benefit plan may not produce as large of a contribution and deduction for older employees as a defined benefit plan might.

Continued...

Target Benefit Plan

D. Since these plans are so rare, it may be difficult to find a plan administrator.

Disadvantages to Employees

A. There is no guarantee as to future benefits.

B. Investment risks rest on the participant.

C. Older participants may not receive as great of a benefit as with a defined benefit plan.

D. Plan is not easily understood by participants.

Employee Stock Ownership Plan (ESOP)

The basics: The ESOP is essentially a stock bonus plan in which employer stock may be used for contributions.

How It Works

- Employer contributes company stock or cash to the plan.

- Employer contributions are tax deductible.

- Contributions are not taxed currently to the employee.

- Earnings accumulate income tax-deferred.

- Distributions are generally taxed as ordinary income. Distributions may be eligible for 10-year income averaging[1], or, at retirement from the current employer, rolled over to a Traditional or a Roth IRA[2] or to another employer plan if that plan will accept such a rollover.

- A "KSOP" is an ESOP that allows for employee deferrals and employer matching contributions.

Additional Considerations

- **Maximum annual deduction:** Up to 25% of covered payroll (up to 25% for a leveraged ESOP) can be contributed and deducted by the firm.

- **Individual limits:** For 2008, the annual allocation of contributions to a participant's account may not exceed the lesser of 100% of includable compensation or $46,000 per year. If the plan is a KSOP permitting participant deferrals, participants age 50 and older may also make a $5,000 "catch-up" contribution.

- **Employer contributions**
    - Most plans are discretionary as to the amount that the employer contributes. If there are profits, the employer is expected to make substantial and recurring contributions.[3]
    - For a "C" corporation, up to an additional 25% of covered compensation may be contributed and deducted if this contribution is used to repay the principal of a loan used by to the plan to acquire employer stock. Contributions used to pay interest on loans used to acquire stock are deductible without limit.

- **Excluding persons:** Certain persons can be eliminated on the basis of months of service, age and coverage in a union plan; for example, persons under age 21 can be excluded from the plan.

- **Investment of plan assets:** Plan assets are required to be invested in employer stock with some exceptions for those participants nearing retirement. In addition, assets may be used to purchase life insurance in some circumstances.

---

[1] Those born before 1936 may be able to elect 10-year averaging or capital gain treatment; these strategies are not available to those born after 1935.

[2] Beginning in 2008, distributions from qualified retirement plans, IRC Sec. 457 plans, and tax-sheltered annuities may be rolled directly into a Roth IRA. These rollover distributions are taxable events, subject to the same requirements as a Roth conversion.

[3] See IRS Reg. 1.401-1(b)(2).

Employee Stock Ownership Plan (ESOP)

- **Forfeitures:** As participants leave the company and separate from the plan, those less than 100% vested forfeit that part of the account in which they are not vested. The nonvested forfeitures may then be allocated to the remaining participants. Those participants who remain in the plan the longest will share in the most forfeitures.

- **Parties which are favored:** Typically, younger participants are favored because they have a longer time for their fund to grow. Also, there may be some special advantages to the major shareholders.

How Much Will There Be at Retirement

This will depend upon three factors.
1. The frequency and amount of contributions,
2. The number of years until retirement, and
3. The investment return.

The risk of poor investment returns rests upon the employee. However, if the investment results are favorable, the participant will have a larger fund at retirement age.

An Example of What $10,000 Per Year Will Grow to Over Several Years at Various Rates of Growth Without Tax[1]				
Years	4.00%	6.00%	8.00%	10.00%
5	$54,163	$56,371	$58,666	$61,051
10	$120,061	$131,808	$144,866	$159,374
15	$200,236	$232,760	$271,521	$317,725
20	$297,781	$367,856	$457,620	$572,750
25	$416,459	$548,645	$731,059	$983,471
30	$560,849	$790,582	$1,132,832	$1,644,940
35	$736,522	$1,114,348	$1,723,168	$2,710,244

Top-Heavy Plans

If more than 60% of the plan assets are allocated to key employees[2], the employer must contribute at least as much for non-key participants as it does for key employees. This requirement applies only to a contribution of up to the first 3% of includable compensation (higher in some instances).

How ESOPs Differ from Stock Bonus Plans

- Under an ESOP the participants have the absolute right to demand distribution of company stock.

- The plan may repurchase the distributed shares of stock but is not required to do so; only the employer is so required.

---

[1] The rates of return used in this illustration are not indicative of any actual investment and will fluctuate in value.
[2] A "key" employee is someone who, at any time during the plan year was: (1) an officer of the employer whose compensation from the employer exceeded $150,000; or (2) a more than 5% owner; or (3) a 1% owner whose compensation from the employer exceeded $150,000.

Continued.

Employee Stock Ownership Plan (ESOP)

- The plan must pass certain voting rights through to the participants.

- If the stock is not publicly traded or is restricted, the participant or his or her heirs must have the right to offer the stock for sale to the employer.

- The plan may borrow money from a bank to purchase stock, with the employer guaranteeing such loan, without it being considered a prohibited transaction.

- The plan may borrow money from a prohibited person without incurring any penalty.

- The plan may not be integrated with Social Security.

- Whereas a stock bonus plan is not required to invest in employer securities, an ESOP must invest primarily in employer securities, to the extent that employer stock is available.

- The employer can contribute company stock directly to the plan.[1]

- The plan may purchase the securities on the open market for public companies, from the company itself or from the shareholders.

- The employer can contribute and deduct up to 25% of compensation for a leveraged ESOP, which is repaying loan principal. In addition, it can make deductible contributions to pay interest on the loan used to purchase securities.

Advantages to Employer

A. Contributions are tax deductible.

B. Contributions and costs are totally flexible.

C. The plan is easy to understand by the employees.

D. It can provide employees with permanent life insurance benefits that need not expire or require costly conversion at retirement age.

E. Since all or substantially all of the assets may be invested in employer's stock, this is a good method for raising additional capital without going to the market place.

F. In effect, the corporation can raise capital with deductible contributions to its plan.

G. Stock, rather than cash, can be contributed to the plan.[1]

H. An ESOP may be used to facilitate the buyout of a stockholder.

I. Dividends paid on stock owned by the ESOP may be deducted if, in accordance with plan language, several requirements are met.

---

[1] However, it may be better to contribute cash and then have the plan purchase stock from the employer. The valuation of stock directly contributed to the plan may be challenged by the IRS. Contributing cash clearly establishes the value of the contribution.

Continued...

Employee Stock Ownership Plan (ESOP)

J. In effect, both the interest and principal of loans are made on a deductible basis.

K. If former participants do not provide the plan with distribution instructions, the plan may automatically distribute accounts less than $5,000. In the case of a plan that provides for such mandatory distributions, the plan must automatically roll an eligible distribution amount that exceeds $1,000 to a Rollover IRA in the former participant's name. A plan may allow direct rollovers of less than $1,000.

Advantages to Employees

A. Annual employer contributions are not taxed to the participant.

B. Earnings on the account are not currently taxed.

C. Special treatment of unrealized gains upon the distribution of stock permits significant tax deferral.

D. Participants may also have a traditional, deductible IRA (subject to certain income limitations based on filing status), a traditional, nondeductible IRA or a Roth IRA.

E. There is the ability to purchase significant permanent life insurance, which is not contingent upon the company group insurance program. Purchase of life insurance will generate taxable income to the employee.

F. Younger employees can accumulate a larger fund than with a defined benefit plan.

G. The forfeited, unvested portion of accounts of former participants is allocated to the active participants' accounts. This can have a major impact on the future benefits.

H. Employee participates in employer's growth.

I. A potential market is created for deceased owner's stock.

J. At distribution, the gain on the stock is not taxed until it is sold.

K. The ESOP can provide significant estate planning benefits for shareholders

L. The gain on the sale of employer securities to the ESOP can be deferred under certain situations.

M. Participant may borrow from the plan within certain guidelines if provided for in the plan documents.

N. Federal bankruptcy law provides significant protection from creditors to participant accounts or accrued benefits in tax-exempt retirement plans.

Continued.

Employee Stock Ownership Plan (ESOP)

Disadvantages to Employer

A. The ESOP will generally not produce as large of a contribution and deduction for older employees as will a defined benefit plan.

B. Deductible contribution limits are set at 25% of covered compensation.

C. Certain voting rights must be passed through to the participants.

D. An ESOP can be costly to set up. Ongoing administration can also be expensive because of the need to have the stock value appraised each year.

E. Future repurchases may not come at a convenient time and must be made with after-tax dollars. This could place a financial strain on the employer.

Disadvantages to Employees

A. There is no guarantee as to future benefits.

B. Investment risks rest on the participant.

C. There is no assurance as to the frequency and amount of employer contributions.

D. Older participants may not receive as great of a benefit as with a defined benefit plan.

E. The value of closely held stock may be difficult to determine at retirement age.

F. If the founder or key people die, retire or terminate employment, the company stock may be worth very little.

G. The company may not be financially able to repurchase the stock, even though required to do so.

H. If the employer's stock is depressed in value at retirement time, there could be a significant loss in the retirement account.

I. Both the participant's current livelihood and retirement savings are dependent on the employer's ongoing viability.

Cash or Deferred – IRC Sec. 401(k) Plan

The Basics

Any profit sharing or stock bonus plan that meets certain participation requirements of IRC Sec. 401(k) can be a cash or deferred plan. An employee can agree to a salary reduction or to defer a bonus which he or she has coming. Tax-exempt entities may also adopt a 401(k) plan.

How It Works

- Employee has the option of taking cash or having it paid to the trust for retirement. This is equivalent to an employee tax-deductible contribution. However, employee deferrals are subject to FICA and FUTA payroll taxes, with applicable payments from both the employer and employee.

- Any additional employer contributions are tax deductible.

- Employer contributions, if any, are not taxed currently to the employee.

- Earnings accumulate income tax-deferred.

- Distributions are generally taxed as ordinary income. Distributions may be eligible for 10-year income averaging[1], or, at retirement from the current employer, rolled over to a Traditional or a Roth IRA[2] or to another employer plan if that plan will accept such a rollover.

Two Types of Plans

- **Salary reduction:** An employee can agree to a salary reduction; e.g., 10% of compensation, which the employer then pays to the retirement plan trust. It is deductible to the employer but is not included in the employee's gross income.

- **Cash or deferred:** The employer can decide to pay a bonus and give the employees the following choices.
  - Take it as cash.
  - Defer it to the trust.
  - Take part and defer the rest.

---

[1] Those born before 1936 may be able to elect 10-year averaging or capital gain treatment.
[2] Beginning in 2008, distributions from qualified retirement plans, IRC Sec. 457 plans, and tax-sheltered annuities may be rolled directly into a Roth IRA. These rollover distributions are taxable events, subject to the same requirements as a Roth conversion.

Continued

Cash or Deferred – IRC Sec. 401(k) Plan

Deposit of 401(k) Salary Deferrals

The Department of Labor (DOL) has conducted many 401(k) plan audits. The deposit rule originally issued by the DOL was that "The employer must deposit the funds as soon as practical, but not later than 15 business days following the close of the calendar month during which the deferrals were made." It is now clear that the DOL is enforcing the "as soon as practical" portion of this rule and not the "15 business days" part. For a small employer, "as soon as practical" is the day the payroll is paid. If this is not done, the employer will be required to make up lost earnings and possibly be subject to other sanctions.

How Much Will There Be at Retirement?

This will depend upon three factors.
1. The frequency and amount of contributions
2. The number of years until retirement
3. The investment return

The risk of good or bad investment returns rests upon the employee.

An Example of What $10,000 Per Year Will Grow to Over Several Years at Various Rates of Growth Without Tax[1]				
Years	4.00%	6.00%	8.00%	10.00%
5	$54,163	$56,371	$58,666	$61,051
10	$120,061	$131,808	$144,866	$159,374
15	$200,236	$232,760	$271,521	$317,725
20	$297,781	$367,856	$457,620	$572,750
25	$416,459	$548,645	$731,059	$983,471
30	$560,849	$790,582	$1,132,832	$1,644,940
35	$736,522	$1,114,348	$1,723,168	$2,710,244

Additional Considerations

- **Maximum annual allocation:** Employers may deduct contributions of up to 25% of covered payroll. This amount includes employer contributions and account forfeitures.

- **Individual limits:** The allocation total of employer contributions and employee deferrals to a participant's account may not exceed the lesser of 100% of compensation or $46,000 per year. An employee's elective contributions to the plan are limited to $15,500 on a calendar year basis. For those age 50 and older, additional "catch-up" contributions of $5,000 may be made.[2]

- **Roth 401(k):** Federal law allows a 401(k) plan sponsor to modify plan provisions to allow participants the option to contribute to a Roth account. Contributions to a Roth 401(k) account are made with after-tax dollars and are subject to the same employee elective deferral limits as the 401(k) plan.

---

[1] The rates of return used in this illustration are not indicative of any actual investment and will fluctuate in value.
[2] These values apply to 2008.

Continued...

Cash or Deferred – IRC Sec. 401(k) Plan

- **Investment of plan assets:** Plan investments must be diversified and prudent. Subject to plan provisions, plan assets can be invested in equity products like mutual funds, stocks and debt free real estate; or in debt instruments like T-Bills and CDs. Insurance products such as life insurance and annuity policies may also be used. If the plan mandates that employee deferrals must be invested in employer stock, or the trustee can direct such an investment, then the maximum that can be invested in employer stock is generally 1%.

- **Typically, participants direct the investment of their own deferrals:** They may also direct the investment of employer contributions.

- **Parties which are favored:** Since funds are typically employee dollars, the higher paid younger employee is favored because he or she has a longer time for funds to accumulate tax-deferred.

- **Matching programs:** Some employers choose to match each dollar put in by the employee with some multiple; e.g., 50%, 75%, etc. If the employee does not defer, the employer does not make a match.

- **Qualification contributions:** If the non-highly compensated employees have not deferred enough, relative to what the highly compensated employees would like to defer, the Treasury Regulations permit the employer to make a contribution which is sufficient to bring the non-highly compensated employees up to the level necessary to support the highly compensated employee's deferral percentage. This type of contribution must always be fully vested.

Highly compensated employees include 5%-or-more owners and those earning more than $105,000[1] in the prior year. If the employer so chooses, the plan may include only those earning more than $105,000 who are also among the top-paid 20% of employees.

- **Salary reductions:** Participants must enter into or be deemed to have entered into a salary-reduction agreement permitting a payroll deduction. This must be done prior to being eligible to receive the compensation.

- **Withdrawal of funds:** As with other profit sharing plans, the funds can generally be withdrawn in the event of (a) termination of employment, (b) death or disability, (c) attainment of age 59½.

- **Financial hardship:** Under a Sec. 401(k) plan, elective contributions can be withdrawn if the participant has a "financial hardship." Under the Treasury Regulations, this is defined as "immediate and heavy financial need where funds are not reasonably available from other sources." There are safe harbor rules that spell out the conditions and requirements for hardship distributions.

- **Forfeitures:** As participants leave the company and separate from the plan, those less than 100% vested in the employer contribution account forfeit that part of the account in which they are not vested. The nonvested forfeitures may then be allocated to the remaining participants. Those participants who remain in the plan the longest will share in the most forfeitures, or forfeitures may reduce future employer contributions.

---

[1] This limit applies to 2008. This limit was $100,000 for 2007.

Continued

Cash or Deferred – IRC Sec. 401(k) Plan

- **Top-heavy plans:** If 60% or more of plan assets are allocated to key employees,[1] the employer will be required to contribute up to 3% of compensation to all non-key participants if any key participant defers, and/or receives an employer contribution, up to 3% of his or her compensation. In order to meet top-heavy minimum allocation requirements, employee contributions are not recognized.[2]

- **Discretionary contributions:** In addition to any matching and/or top-heavy contributions, an employer may make discretionary contributions from year to year so long as the allocation among the participants is on a non-discriminatory basis. These contributions may be allocated in several different ways. These contributions can be made to the plan up to the due date of the return plus any extension granted to the employer. Any employer contributions made on a discretionary basis that are not required to maintain the plan qualification may have gradual vesting.

- **Automatic enrollment arrangement:** An employer may adopt an arrangement under which a specified percentage of salary will automatically be contributed to the 401(k) plan for each employee unless an employee chooses to "opt-out" of the system.

Nondiscrimination Rules

A mathematical test is used to determine whether a plan is discriminatory. First, all employees eligible to participate are divided into two groups according to their compensation and ownership in the employer. The highly compensated[3] may defer up to two times what the non-highly compensated can for the first 2%. If the non-highly compensated on average defer between 2% and 8%, the highly compensated may contribute an additional 2%. (If more than 8%, then up to 125% of the rate.)

In the first year of a 401(k) plan, a 3% deferral rate for non-highly compensated employees may be used if greater than the actual deferral rate.

The amounts contributed by the non-highly compensated employees will set the limit on how much the highly compensated can defer. The deferral percentages must be satisfied for the entire year. An excise tax is assessed if excess deferral amounts are not returned within 2½ months after the close of the plan year. Or, instead of returning deferrals, the employer may make a contribution to the non-highly compensated participants.

If the Nonhighly Compensated Employees Defer (on average)						
.75%	2%	4%	6%	8%	10%	12%
Then the Highly Compensated Employees Can Defer (on average)						
1.5%	4%	6%	8%	10%	12.5%	15%

Average percentages: Highly compensated = 8%; Nonhighly compensated employees = 6%—The test is satisfied.

---

[1] A "key" employee is someone who, at any time during the plan year was: (1) an officer of the employer whose compensation from the employer exceeded $150,000; or (2) a more than 5% owner; or (3) a 1% owner whose compensation from the employer exceeded $150,000.

[2] Employer-matching contributions, if any, count toward satisfying the top-heavy requirement. However, if a non-key person does not defer and, hence, not receive a match, the employer would have to make the top-heavy contribution.

[3] In general, a highly compensated participant is one who owns 5% or more of the employer or was paid $105,000 or more (year 2008 limit) in the prior year.

Continued...

Cash or Deferred – IRC Sec. 401(k) Plan

	Example		Percentage of Compensation		
Employee	Salary and Bonus	Contribution to 401(k) Plan	Individual	Group	Average
HC1	$230,000	$15,500	6.74%		
HC2	150,000	15,500	10.33%	17.07%	8.54%
NHC3	55,000	12,000	21.82%		
NHC4	30,000	1,500	5.00%		
NHC5	30,000	1,200	4.00%		
NHC6	30,000	900	3.00%		
NHC7	25,000	0	0.00%	33.82%	6.76%

IRA vs. 401(k)

Since most 40l(k) plans are funded with employee money, the chart below compares the 401(k) plan to an individual retirement arrangement.

Concern	IRA	Sec. 401(k)
Limitations on contributions/ allocations	$5,000 or $10,000 (if nonworking spouse is included)[1]	Lesser of 100% or $46,000 of net compensation. Maximum employee elective deferral is $15,500[2] in 2008
Mandatory withdrawal at age 70½	Yes, if traditional IRA No, if Roth IRA	Maybe[3]
Subject to Social Security tax (FICA) and federal unemployment tax (FUTA)	Yes	Yes
Can life insurance be purchased?	No	Yes
Do distributions qualify for 10-year income averaging?	No	Maybe[4]
Can funds be borrowed?	No	Yes, within limits
Anti-discrimination test?	None	Yes - highly compensated/nonhighly compensated employees
Access to funds for financial hardship before age 59½	10% penalty applies, with limited exceptions[5]	Yes, as to elective contributions, but subject to 10% penalty[6]

---

[1] For those aged 50 and older, additional "catch-up" contributions of $1,000 may be made.
[2] For those age 50 and older, additional "catch-up" contributions of $5,000 may be made.
[3] Except for more-than-5% owners, payments must begin by the later of (1) April 1 of the year following the year in which the participant reaches age 70½, or (2) the year following the year in which the participant retires. If the employee is a 5%-or-more owner, withdrawals may not be delayed beyond April 1 of the year he or she reaches age 70½.
[4] Those born before 1936 may be able to elect 10-year averaging or capital gain treatment.
[5] Distributions made because of disability or to pay medical expenses in excess of 7.5% of adjusted gross income are not subject to the 10% penalty. In certain situations, withdrawals by unemployed individuals to pay health insurance premiums, or withdrawals made to pay certain first-time homebuyer or educational expenses, may also avoid the 10% penalty.
[6] Unless covered by penalty exception.

Continue

Cash or Deferred – IRC Sec. 401(k) Plan

Advantages to Employer

A. Employers are not required to make discretionary contributions.

B. If the employer does make a discretionary contribution, it is deductible.

C. Any employer discretionary contribution is flexible.

D. The plan is easily understood by employees.

E. An employer matching contribution is a very popular benefit to employees and can be provided at a modest cost.

E. The plan can provide employees with permanent life insurance benefits that need not expire nor require costly conversion at retirement age.

F. The employer can direct employer investments.

G. Of all the allocation techniques that can be used for employer discretionary contributions, the one best fitting the employer's objectives can be utilized.

H. If former participants do not provide the plan with distribution instructions, the plan may automatically distribute accounts less than $5,000. In the case of a plan that provides for such mandatory distributions, the plan must automatically roll an eligible distribution amount that exceeds $1,000 to a Rollover IRA in the former participant's name. A plan may allow direct rollovers of less than $1,000.

Advantages to Employees

A. Participant deferrals are with pre-tax dollars.

B. Any employer contributions are not taxable to participant.

C. Participants may have the right to direct investments.

D. Federal law allows a qualified plan to establish an "eligible investment advice arrangement" under which individually tailored investment advice is provided to plan participants. Any fees or commissions charged must not vary with the investment options chosen, or else a computer model meeting certain requirements must be used.

E. Participants may also have a traditional, deductible IRA (subject to certain income limitations based on filing status), a traditional, nondeductible IRA, or a Roth IRA.

F. There is the ability to purchase significant permanent life insurance that is not contingent upon the company group insurance program. Purchase of life insurance will generate taxable income to the employee.

Continued...

Cash or Deferred – IRC Sec. 401(k) Plan

G. Younger employees can accumulate a larger fund than with a defined benefit plan.

H. The forfeited, unvested portion of any employer-generated accounts may be reallocated to the active participants' accounts.

I. Participant may borrow from the plan within certain guidelines if provided for in the plan documents.

J. If the plan permits, participants can make hardship withdrawals within the requirements of the plan;[1] these may not be rolled over to any IRA.

K. The employer may make matching contributions of some amount.

L. The employer may be required to make additional contributions to satisfy top heavy and/or discrimination tests.

M. Federal bankruptcy law provides significant protection from creditors to participant accounts or accrued benefits in tax-exempt retirement plans.

Disadvantages to Employer

A. Employers may be required to make a variety of mandated contributions to satisfy top-heavy requirements and/or discrimination requirements.

B. The more highly paid participants may not be able to make sufficient contributions to build an adequate retirement. This may bring pressure on the employer to provide additional retirement benefits.

C. Since a 401(k) plan can be the most complicated type of plan to have, the administration costs will be greater than with other types of plans.

D. If the plan fails the discrimination tests, it may have to make refunds to the highly compensated participants, or make a contribution on behalf of non-highly compensated individuals.

E. Because there are employee contributions made through payroll, a 401(k) plan increases the workload of company staff who handle payroll.

Disadvantages to Employees

A. There is no guarantee as to future benefits.

B. The investment risk rests on the participant.

C. The employer may or may not make discretionary contributions.

---

[1] See IRC Sec. 402(c)(4) as amended by the IRS Restructuring and Reform Act of 1998.

Safe Harbor 401(k) Plan

Introduction

In general, the Internal Revenue Code (IRC) requires all qualified employer plans to meet certain nondiscrimination requirements. Employer plans established under IRC Sec. 401(k) are subject to one or two additional tests. The first test, applicable to employee deferrals only, is known as the "actual deferral

percentage" (ADP) test. The second possible test is the "actual contribution percentage" (ACP) test and is applied only when there are employer-matching contributions.

The Small Business Job Protection Act of 1996 provided 401(k) plans with alternative, simplified methods of meeting these additional nondiscrimination requirements. 401(k) plans that adopt one of these alternative methods are referred to as "safe harbor" 401(k) plans. A safe harbor plan is very similar to a non-safe harbor plan. The primary difference is how a safe harbor plan satisfies the IRC's additional nondiscrimination requirements.

Beginning in 2008, the Pension Protection Act of 2006 added a separate safe harbor 401(k) plan for plans that use automatic enrollment.

Requirements for a Safe Harbor 401(k) Plan[1]

Effective January 1, 1999, a 401(k) plan which operates as a safe harbor plan must meet one of two employer contribution formulas, as well as a written notice requirement:

- **Employer contributions:** One of two formulas must be followed.
  - **100% vested of 3% of compensation:** The employer may make a 100% vested contribution of 3% of compensation to all non-highly compensated participants. This contribution formula will also satisfy any "top-heavy" requirements, and may be used in the testing for a non-traditional profit sharing plan.[2]
  - **100% vested matching:** As an alternative, the employer may choose to make a 100% vested matching contribution to all non-highly compensated participants who defer under the plan. The match must be 100% of the first 3% of compensation deferred, plus 50% of the next 2% of compensation deferred. The match may also be at the rate of 100% of the first 4% of compensation deferred. This formula is considered to satisfy the deferral discrimination tests, and can also be used towards satisfying the top-heavy requirements.[3] If the employer is making the matching contributions during the year, the safe harbor rules permit the plan to compute the safe harbor match on a "per pay period" basis, or on an annual basis. If computed annually, the employer may have to true up the match after the plan year end for participants who changed their rate of deferral during the year.

---

[1] See IRS Notices 98-52, 2000-3 and IRS 401(k) regulations effective 1/1/06 for additional detail.
[2] This contribution formula serves triple duty for discrimination, top-heavy and nontraditional profit sharing testing.
[3] The match will also satisfy the top-heavy requirements. But the discrimination tests on the employer discretionary contributions must still be met. Hence, it will satisfy two tests but not the third.

Continued...

Safe Harbor 401(k) Plan

The plan may not have any restrictions on receiving the employer contribution, except the minimum age and service requirements needed for plan participation. Neither a 1,000-hour work requirement, nor a requirement that a participant be employed at the end of the plan year, is permitted.

- **Written notice:** To qualify as a safe harbor plan, a 401(k) plan must also provide for written notice to the employees, with both content and timing elements.
  - **Content:** The notice must describe the various conditions concerning the employer's contribution(s), the conditions and methods for employee deferrals, and the employee vesting and withdrawal provisions of the plan.
  - **Timing:** The employer must give notice at least 30 (but not more than 90) days prior to the beginning of the plan year.

If a plan fails to make the required contribution, or fails to meet any other requirement, it is not a safe harbor plan and is treated like a regular 401(k) plan, subject to the usual discrimination testing requirements.

Stacked Matches

In addition to the basic match or the 3% of compensation employer contribution, the plan may provide for two additional types of matches. The plan may have a mandatory employer match, which is based on the first 6% of compensation. There may also be a discretionary match limited to 4% of compensation. Here are two examples:

Item Description	Value
Maximum compensation for 2008	$230,000
Maximum deferral	15,500
Maximum total allocation	46,000
Matching Approach	
Participant deferral	$15,500
Basic match (4% x $230,000)	9,200
Mandatory match (87.68% x 6.00% x $230,000)	12,100
Discretionary match (4% x $230,000)[1]	$9,200
Total	**$46,000**
3.0% Flat Approach	
Participant deferral	$15,500
Flat contribution (3% x $230,000)	6,900
Mandatory match (104.35% x 6.00% x $230,000)[2]	14,400
Discretionary match (4% x $230,000)	$9,200
Total	**$46,000**

---

[1] The actual percentage calculated to satisfy the $46,000 limit.
[2] The actual result rounded down to satisfy the $46,000 limit.

Continue

Safe Harbor 401(k) Plan

Top Heavy Plans

Safe harbor 401(k) plans that consist solely of employee 401(k) deferrals and employer contributions that meet the Code Sec. 401(k)(12) safe harbor requirements are exempt from top heavy rules.[1]

Catch-Ups

If a plan participant attains age 50 at any time during 2008 he or she may defer an additional $5,000 to the Safe Harbor 401(k) Plan. This means in the illustrated examples the participant could defer an additional $5,000 for a total allocation of $51,000. The Catch-up would not be subject to any of the matches.

Automatic Enrollment Safe Harbor 401(k) Plan

Beginning in 2008, a 401(k) plan with automatic enrollment will qualify as a safe harbor 401(k) plan if it provides for:

- Automatic enrollment of newly eligible employees, at a contribution rate of at least 3% of compensation, but no more than 10% of compensation.

- Automatic annual increases of 1% per year, such that the employee's 401(k) deferral is at least 6% by their fourth year in the plan.

- Employer matching contributions of 100% on the first 1% of compensation deferred and 50% on the next 5% deferred, or, alternatively, a 3% non-elective employer contribution to all participants.

The plan may provide that employer contributions vest 100% after two years of service.

This automatic enrollment safe harbor 401(k) plan is in addition to other safe harbor 401(k) plans available.

---

[1] If more than 60% of the plan assets or accrued benefits are allocated to key employees, the plan is top heavy. A "Key" employee is someone who, at any time during the plan year was (1) an officer of the employer whose compensation from the employer exceeded $150,000; or (2) a more than 5% owner; or (3) a 1% owner whose compensation from the employer exceeded $150,000

How a 401(k) Cash or Deferred Plan Works

Employer

- May provide a voluntary matching fund.
- Contributions are tax deductible to the business.[1]
- May make discretionary contributions any year, so long as allocation is nondiscriminatory.
- Special rules apply for nondiscrimination.

Sec. 401(k) Plan

- Employer contributions are not currently taxable to employee and earnings accumulate tax deferred.
- Most plans are self-directed (employee controls investments).
- Investment risk remains on employee.

Employee

- Employee elects to defer a portion of salary or bonus.
- Amounts deferred are subject to FICA and FUTA taxes but not current income tax.
- Employee's elective contributions are limited to $15,500[2] per year (2008).[3]

Early Withdrawal

- A 10% penalty generally applies if withdrawals are made before age 59½.
- Some exceptions to the 10% penalty are available.
- Employee elective contributions can be withdrawn for financial hardship.[4]

Retirement

- Distributions must begin by specified date.[5]
- Funds may be distributed as a lump sum or periodic payments.
- Earnings + deductible contributions taxed as ordinary income in the year received.

Death

- Value of account is included in owner's gross estate.
- Proceeds can pass to surviving spouse with payments over the survivor's lifetime.
- Income and estate taxes can severely reduce funds left to nonspousal heirs.

---

[1] The total deductible employer contribution may not exceed 25% of covered payroll, including employer contributions and account forefeitures.

[2] For those age 50 and older, additional "catch-up" contributions of $5,000 may be made.

[3] For 2008, the allocation total of employer contributions and employee deferrals to a participant's account may not exceed the lesser of 100% of compensation or $46,000 per year.

[4] If provided for by the plan. Under Treasury regulations, financial hardship is defined as "immediate and heavy financial need where funds are not reasonably available from other sources."

[5] Except for more than 5% owners, distributions must begin by the later of April 1 of (a) the year following the year in which the participant reaches age 70½, or (b) the year following the year in which the participant retires.

Solo 401(k)

A "Solo 401(k)" is a regular 401(k) plan that covers only
a business owner, or the business owner and his or her
spouse. In such a plan, the business owner plays two
roles, that of employee and that of employer.

How It Works

- As an "employee," the business owner can choose to either receive cash (salary or
  bonus) or defer the funds into the 401(k) plan. If the 401(k) plan is chosen, these
  "elective deferrals" are not subject to current income tax, but are subject to FICA and
  FUTA payroll taxes.[1] For 2008, employee deferrals are limited to $15,500. Additional
  deferrals of $5,000 may be made if the individual is age 50 or over.

- As the "employer," the business owner may also contribute to the plan. For 2008, the
  employer's deductible contribution is limited to 25% of the employee's compensation.[2]
  Employer contributions are not currently taxed to the employee.

- In 2008, total 401(k) contributions (from both employer and employee) are limited to
  the lesser of 100% of the employee's compensation or $46,000. Assets in the plan grow
  on a tax-deferred basis. Distributions are generally taxed as ordinary income.

- All 401(k) plans must meet prescribed nondiscrimination tests. Plans in which the
  business owner, or the business owner and spouse, are the only employees, effectively
  avoid this issue. Just one additional eligible employee, however, can trigger these
  nondiscrimination requirements, increasing the administrative complexity and cost.

How Much Can Be Contributed?

A key attraction of a 401(k) plan is the significant amount of money that can be
contributed to the plan, as well as being deducted from taxable income. This amount will
vary with the level of income and the form of business ownership.

2008 Maximum Deductible Contributions – Incorporated Business

Wages & Salary (W-2)	$75,000	$150,000	$200,000	$300,000
401(k)				
Employee Contribution	$15,500	$15,500	$15,500	$15,500
Employer Contribution[3]	18,750	30,500	30,500	30,500
TOTAL	$34,250	$46,000	$46,000	$46,000
SEP IRA, Profit Sharing or Money Purchase				
Employer-only Contribution	$18,750	$37,500	$46,000	$46,000
SIMPLE IRA				
Employee Contribution	$10,500	$10,500	$10,500	$10,500
Employer Match at 3.0%	2,250	4,500	6,000	9,000
TOTAL	$12,750	$15,000	$16,500	$19,500

---

[1] The discussion here concerns federal income tax law. State and/or local tax law may differ.
[2] In 2008, a maximum of $230,000 of compensation may be considered in this calculation.
[3] Equals 25% of the employee's W-2 income, subject to the overall $46,000 limitation.

Continued...

Solo 401(k)

2008 Maximum Deductible Contributions – Unincorporated Business

Self-Employment Income	$75,000	$150,000	$200,000	$300,000
401(k)				
Employee Contribution	$15,500	$15,500	$15,500	$15,500
Employer Contribution[1]	13,940	28,333	30,500	30,500
TOTAL	**$29,440**	**$43,833**	**$46,000**	**$46,000**
SEP IRA, Profit Sharing, or Money Purchase				
Employer Only Contribution	**$13,940**	**$28,333**	**$38,200**	**$46,000**
SIMPLE IRA				
Employee Contribution	$10,500	$10,500	$10,500	$10,500
Employer Match at 3.0%	2,030	4,126	5,563	6,900
TOTAL	**$12,530**	**$14,626**	**$16,063**	**$17,400**

Other Points to Consider – Pros and Cons

- **Pros**
  - **Flexible contributions:** Contribution amounts may vary from year to year.
  - **Loan provisions:** A 401(k) plan may allow for participant loans.
- **Cons**
  - **Co-ordination with other plans:** If a business owner is also a participant in another 401(k) plan,[2] the overall elective deferral limits apply to deferrals made to both plans.

Seek Professional Guidance

Setting up a qualified plan involves a number of complex issues. The guidance of qualified financial professionals is highly recommended.

---

[1] Equals 25% of "net" self-employment income, i.e., gross income less the contribution and one-half the self-employment tax, subject to the overall $46,000 limitation.
[2] For example, this would include someone who works full-time for one employer, but who also has a side business from which he or she earns self-employment income.

How a Solo 401(k) Plan Works

Individual as Employer

- Makes contributions up to allowable limits.[1]
- Contributions are tax deductible to the business.[2]
- Plan may provide for participant loans.
- Nondiscrimination rules may apply if other employees are hired.[3]

Solo 401(k) Plan

- Employer contributions are not currently taxable to employee and earnings accumulate tax deferred.
- Most plans are self-directed (employee controls investments).
- Investment risk remains on employee.

Individual as Employee

- Elects to defer a portion of salary or bonus.
- Employee's elective contributions are limited to $15,500[4] per year (2008).
- Amounts deferred are subject to FICA and FUTA taxes but not current income tax.

Early Withdrawal

- A 10% penalty generally applies if withdrawals are made before age 59½.
- Some exceptions to the 10% penalty are available.
- Employee elective contributions can be withdrawn for financial hardship.[5]

Retirement

- Distributions must begin by specified date.[6]
- Funds may be distributed as a lump sum or as periodic payments.
- Earnings + deductible contributions are taxed as ordinary income in the year received.

Death

- Value of account is included in owner's gross estate.
- Proceeds can pass to surviving spouse with payments over the survivor's lifetime.
- Income and estate taxes can severely reduce funds left to nonspousal heirs.

---

[1] For 2008, the allocation total of employer contributions, forfeitures and employee deferrals to a participant's account may not exceed the lesser of 100% of compensation or $46,000.

[2] The total deduction is limited to 25% of covered payroll.

[3] Plans covering only the business owner (or the owner and spouse) effectively sidestep the nondiscrimination issue.

[4] In 2008, for those age 50 and older, additional "catch-up" contributions of $5,000 may be made.

[5] This assumes they are provided for by the plan. Under Treasury regulations, financial hardship is defined as "immediate and heavy financial need where funds are not reasonably available from other sources."

[6] For more than 5% owners, distributions must begin by April 1 of the year following the year in which the participant reaches age 70½.

403(b) Salary Deferral Plan
Tax-Sheltered Annuities

Eligibility

Employees of religious, charitable, educational, scientific and literary organizations described in IRC Sec. 501(c)(3) or public school systems are eligible.

Making Employer Contributions

While employer contributions are allowed, typically the employee agrees to have his or her salary reduced by the contribution amount. If the employer contributes its own funds, the arrangement is subject to many of the same rules that govern regular qualified plans.

Contribution Limits

The allocation total of employer contributions and employee deferrals to a participant's account may not exceed the lesser of 100% of compensation[1] (limited to a maximum of $230,000), or $46,000 per year. An employee's elective contributions to the plan are limited to $15,500[2] on a calendar-year basis. Total elective deferrals for employees of qualifying organizations with 15 years of service may be as high as $18,500.[2] For those age 50 or older, additional "catch-up" contributions of $5,000 may be made.

Federal law allows a 403(b) plan sponsor to modify plan provisions to allow participants the option to contribute to a Roth account. Contributions to a Roth 403(b) account are made with after-tax dollars and are subject to the same employee elective deferral limits as the 403(b) plan.

When to Setup a TSA

A TSA may be setup at any time during the year. However, salary-reduction agreements must be entered into before the reduced salary amounts are available to the employee. An employee can later modify the deferral amount, but only with respect to future income.

Investing Funds

There are three investments from which to choose.
1. Annuities (fixed or variable and individual or group)
2. Custodial accounts invested in mutual funds
3. Combination of whole life insurance[3] and annuities

---

[1] The term "compensation" includes deferrals to TSAs under IRC Sec. 403(b) as well as deferrals made to IRC Sec. 125 and IRC Sec. 457 plans.
[2] These are the maximum values for 2008. These values are subject to adjustment for inflation in future years.
[3] Under proposed regulations, life insurance is permitted only if the policy was issued before 02/14/05.

Continued

403(b) Salary Deferral Plan
Tax-Sheltered Annuities

Required Distributions

These funds are usually withdrawn at retirement. To avoid penalties, withdrawals must generally begin by April 1 following the calendar year in which the taxpayer became 70½ or, if later, by April 1 following the calendar year in which the employee actually retires.[1]

Borrowing TSA Funds

Participants can borrow funds from their TSA and later repay them without incurring a tax, if established conditions are met regarding maximum loan amount, amortization requirements, time period for repayments, etc.

Early Withdrawal Penalties

There is a 10% penalty for withdrawals prior to age 59½ and all withdrawals are taxed currently as ordinary income unless the distribution is rolled over; transferred to another TSA; or the annuitant is totally disabled, separates from service (after age 55) or dies.[2]

Financial Hardship

The salary-reduction amount (but not the earnings) is available for financial hardship; e.g., an immediate and heavy financial need which cannot be met with other assets.

The Death of a TSA Participant

When a participant dies, TSA proceeds become part of his or her taxable estate for federal estate tax purposes and they are generally considered as ordinary income to the beneficiary, except for any "pure" insurance proceeds provided by a 403(b) life insurance contract.

Changing from One TSA to Another

The transfer of funds from one 403(b) investment to another will not be considered a taxable distribution if the funds remain subject to the same distribution restrictions as on the prior investment. See Revenue Ruling 90-24. If proceeds from a TSA are rolled directly into an IRA, it will defer taxation. If a distribution is paid directly to the participant first, it will be subject to the mandatory 20% income tax withholding rule.

Federal Bankruptcy Impact

Federal bankruptcy law provides significant protection from creditors to participant accounts or accrued benefits in tax-exempt retirement plans.

---

[1] If the first distribution is delayed until April 1 of the following year, two distributions will be required in that year.
[2] Other 10% penalty exceptions may apply.

Continued...

403(b) Salary Deferral Plan
Tax-Sheltered Annuities

Counting Deferred Amounts as Current Compensation

Deferred amounts can be counted as current compensation in computing benefits under a separate qualified pension plan, if the qualified plan so provides.

End Result

- The employee avoids current income taxation on the deferred amount (except it is included in the Social Security base).

- The earnings on the accumulating funds are not taxed until they are distributed.

Comparison of Federal Income Tax Payable[1]

Without 403(b) Plan		With 403(b) Plan		Benefit
Taxable Income Before $5,000 Salary Reduction	Tax Due Without Annuity	Taxable Income After Reduction	Tax Due with Annuity	Current Income Tax Reduction
$25,000	$2,948	$20,000	$2,198	$750
35,000	4,448	30,000	3,698	750
45,000	5,948	40,000	5,198	750
55,000	7,448	50,000	6,698	750
85,000	13,938	80,000	12,688	1,250

Final 403(b) Regulations

On July 26, 2007, the IRS issued its long-awaited final 403(b) regulations. These are generally effective for plan years beginning after December 31, 2008, and require sponsoring non-profit employers or school districts to take on a greater role in the operation of their 403(b) plans. The following is a brief summary of some of the major points in these regulations:

1. The employer must have a written plan document. Among other requirements, the document will have to state plan eligibility requirements and coordinate operation of the plan among various 403(b) vendors. It will also have to state the type of funding vehicles offered. Previously, 403(b) arrangements that consisted of employee contributions only were not required to have a plan document.
2. The IRS will treat 403(b) custodial accounts as qualified retirement plans for purposes of governmental reporting requirements and limitations on death benefits offered in the plans.
3. Non discrimination rules apply to employer contributions, except for plans sponsored by state and local schools.

---

[1] Based on 2008 federal income tax rates and married filing jointly.

Continued..

403(b) Salary Deferral Plan
Tax-Sheltered Annuities

4. The right to make 403(b) contributions must be universally available to all employees of a sponsoring organization with few exceptions. Union employees are not excludable.
5. Two or more non-profit entities will be considered a single employer (a "controlled group"), if there is 80% or more overlap of directors or trustees.
6. 403(b) plans will have to follow rules applicable to other qualified retirement plans (such as 401(k) plans) relating to participant loans, dividing accounts due to divorce, hardship distributions, and age 70½ required minimum distributions.
7. The regulations clearly state that Roth-type contributions (contributed after-tax, distributable tax-free) and age 50-plus catch up contributions are available in 403(b) plans.
8. The definition of who may sponsor a 403(b) plan has been expanded to include health and welfare agencies such as adoption agencies and home health care service agencies.
9. Distributions are permitted upon stated events, such as attainment of a stated age, completion of a number of years of service, and termination of the 403(b) plan.

How a 403(b) Salary Deferral Plan Works

Employer[1]

- Contributions are tax deductible to the employer.
- May make discretionary contributions[1] from year to year so long as allocation is nondiscriminatory.

Sec. 403(b) Plan

- Employer contributions, if any, are not currently taxable to employee and earnings accumulate tax deferred.
- Plan is self-directed (employee controls investments).
- Investment risk remains on employee.

Employee

- Employee elects to defer a portion of salary.
- Amounts deferred subject to FICA and FUTA taxes but not current income tax.
- Employee's elective contributions limited to $15,500 per year (2008).[2]

Early Withdrawal

- A 10% penalty generally applies if withdrawals are made before age 59½.
- Some exceptions to 10% penalty are available.
- Employee elective contributions can be withdrawn for financial hardship.[3]

Retirement

- Distributions must begin by specified date.[4]
- Funds may be distributed as lump sum or periodic payments.
- Earnings + contributions taxed as ordinary income in year received.

Death

- Value of account is included in owner's gross estate.
- Proceeds can pass to surviving spouse, with payments over survivor's lifetime.
- Income and estate taxes can severely reduce funds left to nonspousal heirs.

---

[1] If there are employer contributions, the arrangement must generally satisfy the minimum participation requirements as well as the nondiscrimination rules applicable to employer-sponsored qualified plans.

[2] For those age 50 and older, additional "catch-up" contributions of $5,000 may be made.

[3] If provided for by the plan. Under Treasury regulations, financial hardship is defined as "immediate and heavy financial need where funds are not reasonably available from other sources."

[4] Withdrawals must begin in the later of the calendar year in which the taxpayer becomes age 70½, or, the calendar year in which the employee actually retires. The first distribution may be delayed until April 1 of the following year. If deferred, two distributions will be required in that year.

Stock Bonus Plan

The basics: Employer contributions to the plan are not dependent upon profits, and the plan may, but is not required to, invest primarily in employer stock.

How It Works

- Employer contributes to the plan.

- Employer contributions are tax deductible.

- Contributions are not taxed currently to the employee.

- Earnings accumulate income tax-deferred.

- Distributions are generally taxed as ordinary income. Distributions may be eligible for 10-year income averaging[1], or, at retirement from the current employer, rolled over to a Traditional or a Roth IRA[2] or to another employer plan if that plan will accept such a rollover.

Additional Considerations

- **Maximum annual deduction:** Up to 25% of covered payroll can be contributed and deducted by the corporation.

- **Individual limits:** The allocation of contributions to a participant's account may not exceed the lesser of 100% of includable compensation or $46,000 per year.

- **Employer contributions**
  - Most plans are discretionary as to the amount that the employer contributes.
  - If there are profits, the employer is expected to make "substantial and recurring"[3] contributions.

- **Excluding persons:** Certain persons can be eliminated on the basis of months of service, age, coverage in a union plan and salary base; for example, persons under age 21 can be excluded from the plan.

- **Investment of plan assets:** Investments must be diversified and prudent. Subject to plan provisions, plan assets can be invested in equity products like mutual funds or stocks; or debt instruments like T-Bills and CDs. Insurance products like life insurance and annuity policies may also be used. Stock bonus plans typically are heavily invested in employer stock. They are not, however, required to invest in employer stock as with an ESOP.

---

[1] Those born before 1936 may be able to elect 10-year averaging or capital gain treatment; these strategies are not available to those born after 1935.

[2] Beginning in 2008, distributions from qualified retirement plans, IRC Sec. 457 plans, and tax-sheltered annuities may be rolled directly into a Roth IRA. These rollover distributions are taxable events, subject to the same requirements as a Roth conversion.

[3] See IRS Reg. 1.401-1(b)(2).

Continued...

Stock Bonus Plan

- **Social Security integration:** Since the employer already contributes to the employee's Social Security retirement benefit, these contributions can be integrated into the contribution formula of the plan.

- **Parties which are favored:** Typically younger participants are favored because they have a longer time for their fund to grow.

- **Forfeitures:** As participants leave the company and separate from the plan, those less than 100% vested forfeit that part of the account in which they are not vested. The nonvested forfeitures may then be allocated to the remaining participants. Those participants who remain in the plan the longest will share in the most forfeitures, or forfeitures may reduce future employer contributions.

How Much Will There Be at Retirement?

This will depend upon three factors.
1. The frequency and amount of contributions,
2. The number of years until retirement, and
3. The investment return.

The risk of poor investment returns rests upon the employee. However, if the investment results are favorable, the participant will have a larger fund at retirement age.

An Example of What $10,000 Per Year Will Grow to Over Several Years at Various Rates of Growth Without Tax[1]				
Years	4.00%	6.00%	8.00%	10.00%
5	$54,163	$56,371	$58,666	$61,051
10	$120,061	$131,808	$144,866	$159,374
15	$200,236	$232,760	$271,521	$317,725
20	$297,781	$367,856	$457,620	$572,750
25	$416,459	$548,645	$731,059	$983,471
30	$560,849	$790,582	$1,132,832	$1,644,940
35	$736,522	$1,114,348	$1,723,168	$2,710,244

Top-Heavy Plans

If more than 60% of the plan assets are allocated to key employees[2], the employer must contribute at least as much for non-key participants as it does for key employees. This requirement applies only to a contribution of up to the first 3% of includible compensation (higher in some instances).

---

[1] The rates of return used in this illustration are not indicative of any actual investment and will fluctuate in value. An investment will not provide a consistent rate of return; years with lower (or negative) returns than the hypothetical returns shown may substantially affect the scenario presented.

[2] A "key" employee is someone who, at any time during the plan year was: (1) an officer of the employer whose compensation from the employer exceeded $150,000; or (2) a more than 5% owner; or (3) a 1% owner whose compensation from the employer exceeded $150,000.

Continued...

Stock Bonus Plan

Advantages to Employer

    A. Contributions are tax deductible.

    B. Contributions and costs are totally flexible.

    C. The plan is easy to understand by the employees.

    D. It can provide employees with permanent life insurance benefits that need not expire or require costly conversion at retirement age.

    E. Since all or substantially all of the assets are invested in employer's stock, this is a good method for raising additional capital without going to the marketplace.

    F. In effect, the corporation can raise capital with deductible contributions to its plan.

    G. If former participants do not provide the plan with distribution instructions, the plan may automatically distribute accounts less than $5,000. In the case of a plan that provides for such mandatory distributions, the plan must automatically roll an eligible distribution amount that exceeds $1,000 to a Rollover IRA in the former participant's name. A plan may allow direct rollovers of less than $1,000.

Advantages to Employees

    A. Annual employer contributions are not taxed to the participant.

    B. Earnings on the account are not currently taxed.

    C. Participants may also have a traditional, deductible IRA (subject to certain income limitations based on filing status), a traditional, nondeductible IRA, or a Roth IRA.

    D. There is the ability to purchase significant permanent life insurance, which is not contingent upon the company group insurance program. Purchase of life insurance will generate taxable income to the employee.

    E. Younger employees can accumulate a larger fund than with a Defined Benefit Plan.

    F. The forfeited, unvested portion of accounts of former participants may be allocated to the active participants' accounts. This can have a major impact on the future benefits.

    G. Participant may borrow from the plan within certain guidelines if provided for in the plan documents.

    H. Employee participates in employer's growth.

Continued...

Stock Bonus Plan

I. A potential market is created for stock of deceased shareholders.

J. At distribution, the gain on the stock is not taxed until it is sold.

K. Federal bankruptcy law provides significant protection from creditors to participant accounts or accrued benefits in tax-exempt retirement plans.

L. Upon distribution, for stock that is not readily tradable, the participant has the right to require the employer to repurchase the participant's stock.

Disadvantages to Employer

A. The stock bonus plan will generally not produce as large a contribution and deduction for older employees as will a defined benefit plan or other types of defined contribution plans.

B. Deductible contribution limits are set at 25% of covered payroll.

C. If a firm's stock is not publicly traded, the voting power of the stock must be passed through to the participants on matters requiring a majority vote of the shareholders.

D. The cost of re-valuing closely held stock each year may be expensive.

E. Future repurchases required by employee distributions may not come at a convenient time for company cash flow purposes.

Disadvantages to Employees

A. There is no guarantee as to future benefits.

B. Investment risks rest on the participant.

C. Older participants will not receive as large a benefit as with a defined benefit plan.

D. There is no assurance as to the frequency and amount of employer contributions.

E. The value of closely held stock may be difficult to determine at retirement age.

F. If the founder or other key people die, retire or terminate employment, the company stock may be worth very little.

G. The company may not be financially able to repurchase the stock, even though required to do so.

H. If the employer's stock is depressed in value at retirement time, there could be a significant loss in the retirement account.

Age-Weighted Profit Sharing Plan

The basics: Contributions are totally flexible and at the discretion of the employer, and need not be yearly, so long as they are "substantial and recurring."[1] Employer contributions are allocated to provide an equal assumed retirement benefit as a percentage of compensation at normal retirement age for all participants.

How It Works

- Employer contributions are tax deductible.

- Contributions not taxed currently to the employee.

- Earnings accumulate tax-deferred.

- Distributions are generally taxed as ordinary income. Distributions may be eligible for 10-year income averaging[2], or, at retirement from the current employer, rolled over to a Traditional or a Roth IRA[3], or to another employer plan if that plan will accept such a rollover.

Additional Considerations

- **Maximum annual deduction:** Up to 25% of covered payroll can be contributed and can be from current or past profits and deductible by the employer.

- **Individual limits:** The allocation of contributions to a participant's account may not exceed the lesser of 100% of includable compensation[4] or $46,000 per year.

- **Employer contributions**
  - Plans normally are discretionary as to the amount that the employer contributes.
  - If there are profits, the employer is expected to make "substantial and recurring" contributions.[1]

- **Excluding persons:** Certain persons can be eliminated on the basis of months of service, age or coverage in a union plan; for example, persons under age 21 can be excluded from the plan.

- **Investment of plan assets:** Plan assets can be invested in equity products like mutual funds, stocks and real estate; or in debt instruments like T-Bills and CDs; or in insurance products like life insurance and annuity products.

---

[1] See IRS Reg. 1.401-1(b)(2).
[2] Those born before 1936 may be able to elect 10-year averaging or capital gain treatment; these strategies are not available to those born after 1935.
[3] Beginning in 2008, distributions from qualified retirement plans, IRC Sec. 457 plans, and tax-sheltered annuities may be rolled directly into a Roth IRA. These rollover distributions are taxable events, subject to the same requirements as a Roth conversion.
[4] This rate applies to "net" self-employment income of the owner or partner, less the contribution and the deduction allowed for one-half of the self-employment tax.

Continued...

Age-Weighted Profit Sharing Plan

- **Social Security integration:** Since the employer already contributes to the employees' Social Security Retirement, the assumed retirement benefit can be integrated with Social Security, but seldom is.

- **Forfeitures:** As participants leave the company and separate from the plan, those less than 100% vested forfeit that part of the account in which they are not vested. The nonvested forfeitures may then be allocated to the remaining participants. Those participants who remain in the plan the longest will share in the most forfeitures, or forfeitures may be used to reduce future employer contributions.

- **Parties that are favored:** Older participants are favored from a contribution perspective because they are closer to retirement. However, all participants would receive the same projected retirement benefit as a percentage of compensation at age 65.

How Much Will There Be at Retirement?

This will depend upon three factors:

- The frequency and amount of contribution,
- The number of years until retirement, and
- The investment return.

The risk of poor investment return rests on the employee. However, if the investment results are favorable, the participant will have a larger fund at retirement age.

An Example of What $10,000 Per Year Will Grow to Over Several Years at Various Rates of Growth Without Tax[1]				
Years	4.00%	6.00%	8.00%	10.00%
5	$54,163	$56,371	$58,666	$61,051
10	$120,061	$131,808	$144,866	$159,374
15	$200,236	$232,760	$271,521	$317,725
20	$297,781	$367,856	$457,620	$572,750
25	$416,459	$548,645	$731,059	$983,471
30	$560,849	$790,582	$1,132,832	$1,644,940
35	$736,522	$1,114,348	$1,723,168	$2,710,244

Top-Heavy Plans

If more than 60% of the cumulative benefits are going to "key" employees[2], then the employer must contribute at least as much for "non-key" participants as for key employees. This requirement applies only to the first 3%[3] of compensation.

---

[1] The rates of return used in this illustration are not indicative of any actual investment and will fluctuate in value.

[2] A "key" employee is someone who, at any time during the plan year was: (1) an officer of the employer whose compensation from the employer exceeded $150,000; or (2) a more than 5% owner; or (3) a 1% owner whose compensation from the employer exceeded $150,000.

[3] The requirement will be greater than 3% in some instances.

Continue

Age-Weighted Profit Sharing Plan

Example – Allocation of Employer Contribution						
			Traditional			**Difference Between Age-Weighted and Nonintegrated**
Participant	**Age**	**Compensation**	**Non-integrated**	**Integrated at 5.7%**	**Age-Weighted**	
Owner A	55	$230,000	$32,282	$35,183	$46,000	$13,718
Owner B	50	150,000	21,053	20,923	19,951	-1,102
Employee 1	40	55,000	7,720	6,669	3,236	-4,484
Employee 2	35	30,000	4,211	3,637	1500[1]	-2,711
Employee 3	30	30,000	4,211	3,637	1500[1]	-2,711
Employee 4	25	30,000	4,211	3,637	1500[1]	-2,711
Totals		$525,000	$73,688	$73,686	$73,687	$0

The employer contributions are equal to 14.04% of $525,000 or $73,687. The age-weighted allocation, when accumulated to normal retirement age of 65, would purchase an equivalent retirement benefit as a percent of compensation. The projected retirement is important only to calculate the allocation of the employer contribution.

Advantages to Employer

A. Contributions are tax deductible.

B. Contributions and costs are totally flexible.

C. Forfeitures of terminating employees may reduce future costs or be reallocated among the accounts of those in the plan.

D. It can provide employees with permanent life insurance benefits that need not expire nor require costly conversion at retirement age.

E. The employer can direct investments.

F. If former participants do not provide the plan with distribution instructions, the plan may automatically distribute accounts less than $5,000. In the case of a plan that provides for such mandatory distributions, the plan must automatically roll an eligible distribution amount that exceeds $1,000 to a Rollover IRA in the former participant's name. A plan may allow direct rollovers of less than $1,000.

G. Plan can favor older employees.

Advantages to Employees

A. Annual employer contributions are not taxed to the participant.

---

[1] This is the "gateway" contribution at 5.0%.

Continued...

Age-Weighted Profit Sharing Plan

B. Earnings on the account are not currently taxed.

C. Federal bankruptcy law provides significant protection from creditors to participant accounts or accrued benefits in tax-exempt retirement plans.

D. Participants can have the right to direct investments.

E. Federal law allows a qualified plan to establish an "eligible investment advice arrangement" under which individually tailored investment advice is provided to plan participants. Any fees or commissions charged must not vary with the investment options chosen, or else a computer model meeting certain requirements must be used.

F. Participants may also have a traditional, deductible IRA (subject to certain income limitations based on filing status), a traditional, nondeductible IRA, or a Roth IRA.

G. There is the ability to purchase significant permanent life insurance, which is not contingent upon the company group insurance program. Purchase of life insurance will generate taxable income to the employee.

H. Older participants will receive a substantially greater allocation of the employer contribution than under traditional type of profit sharing plans.

I. The forfeited, unvested portion of accounts of former participants may be allocated to the active participants' accounts. This can have a major impact on future benefits.

J. If the plan so provides, vested balances may be withdrawn if the participant has a "financial hardship." Under Treasury regulations, this is defined as "immediate and heavy financial need where funds are not reasonably available from other sources." Safe harbor rules spell out the conditions and requirements for hardship distributions.

K. Participant may borrow from the plan within certain guidelines if provided for in the plan documents.

Disadvantages to Employer

A. The maximum deductible employer contribution is 25% of covered payroll.

B. If the key employees are younger than the other employees, they will not receive as large a proportion of the employer contribution.

C. It is more difficult to explain the plan to employees.

D. Administration costs will be higher.

Continue

Age-Weighted Profit Sharing Plan

Disadvantages to Employees

    A. There is no guarantee as to future benefits.

    B. Investment risks rest on the participant.

    C. There is no assurance as to the frequency and amount of employer contributions.

Fully-Insured Defined Benefit Plan
IRC Sec. 412(e)(3)[1]

Maximum Benefit

The maximum benefit under a defined benefit
plan is measured in two ways:

- **Percentage:** The retirement benefit cannot
  exceed 100% of the average of the highest
  three consecutive years of compensation.[2]
  This is reduced by 10% for each year of
  service less than 10.

- **Dollar amount:** The maximum dollar benefit is indexed at $185,000 per year (2008) for
  retirement at age 65, or at the Social Security normal retirement age, if later than 65.
  This amount is actuarially reduced for retirement more than three years prior to the
  normal Social Security retirement age. Retirement at age 55 would typically produce a
  maximum annual benefit of $100,000, depending on the assumptions used, cost of
  living adjustments, and number of years of participation. The dollar amount will also be
  increased for late retirement, subject to the percentage and dollar limitations. Lastly, if
  the individual has fewer than 10 years of participation at normal retirement age, the
  dollar amount is reduced proportionately.

First- and Subsequent-Year Contributions

The contribution will be the premium for the annuities or combination of annuities and life
insurance policies necessary to fund the benefit. This will almost always be higher than in
a traditional defined benefit plan when established and then may, or may not, decline as
real earnings exceed policy guarantees. The initial contribution for the benefit and future
benefit increases are based on the guaranteed rates in the policies. Future premiums will
reflect actual investment experience of the policies.

Methods of Defining the Benefit

- **Level percentage plan:** Example - The benefit is equal to 50% of compensation,[2]
  reduced by 1/25 for each year of participation less than 25 years.

- **Step rate service weighted for prior service:** Example - The benefit is equal to 8% of
  compensation for the first ten years of service plus 5.2% of compensation for all other
  years, but not to exceed a total of 33 years.[2]

- **Service plan:** Example - The benefit is 2.5% of compensation[2] for each year of service.
  Younger participants may also be favored if the benefit formula is service related.

- **Participation plan:** Example - The benefit is 5% of compensation[2] per year of
  participation with a maximum of 20 years.

---

[1] The Pension Protection Act of 2006 moved former IRC Section 412 (i) to a new code section, IRC Section 412(e)(3).
[2] For those self-employed, compensation is limited to net self-employment income, e.g., gross income less the
  contribution and the deduction allowed for one-half of the self-employment tax. In certain unusual circumstances, the
  required contribution may be more than the allowable deduction.

Continued

Fully-Insured Defined Benefit Plan
IRC Sec. 412(e)(3)

Top-Heavy Plans

If the present value of the accrued benefits of key employees[1] is 60% or more of the total value of all accrued benefits, the plan is top heavy. In that instance, the plan must provide for a minimum level of benefits for non-key participants.

Accrued Benefit

Each participant's accrued benefit is measured by the cash value of the policies purchased for each participant.

Special Requirements

For a plan to be considered as "fully insured" under IRC 412(e)(3), certain criteria must be met:

- The total benefits must be provided by one or more annuities or a combination of annuities and life insurance policies.

- The premium on the policies must be level from date of issue until scheduled retirement. Exception: "Dividends" or "excess earnings" may reduce such premium.

- Premiums must not be in default.

- There must be no outstanding policy loans.

Special Considerations

- If a plan qualifies, no actuarial certification is needed.

- If the plan is top-heavy, it may be necessary to fund top-heavy benefits with a separate "side fund." This would require an actuarial certification.

- To convert an existing plan to fully-insured status, several things must happen:
  - All existing assets must first be liquidated.
  - The net proceeds are then used to purchase single premium annuities for each participant based on their accrued benefits at time of conversion.
  - The difference between the projected retirement benefit and the benefit purchased by the single premium annuities is then funded.
  - It may prove difficult to convert from a fully-insured plan to a traditional defined benefit plan.

- In some cases, if care is not taken, the plan may become over funded.

- Because this is a specialized type of plan, someone with experience in this area is necessary to establish a fully-insured plan.

---

[1] A "key" employee is someone who, at any time during the plan year was: (1) an officer of the employer whose compensation from the employer exceeded $150,000; or (2) a more than 5% owner; or (3) a 1% owner whose compensation from the employer exceeded $150,000.

Continued...

Fully-Insured Defined Benefit Plan
IRC Sec. 412(e)(3)

- Converting to fully-insured status may help an "over-funded" defined benefit plan.

- The fully-insured plan is not a universal panacea but may be a useful tool in the right situation.

- In 2004, the IRS issued guidance designed to prohibit certain arrangements that it considers abusive. This guidance prohibits the plan from purchasing life insurance for a participant in excess of the death benefit provided by the plan, requires any policies distributed or purchased from the plan to be done so at full fair market value (not cash surrender value), and requires these plans to provide similar policies in a non-discriminatory manner to all plan participants.[1]

Advantages to Employer

A. Contributions are tax deductible.

B. It can reward long-term employees with a substantial retirement benefit even though they are close to retirement age.

C. Larger contributions for older employees may reduce corporate tax problem; e.g., excess accumulated earnings, high tax bracket current earnings, etc.

D. Forfeitures of terminating employees will reduce future costs.

E. It can provide employees with permanent life insurance benefits that need not expire or require costly conversion at retirement age.

F. A higher initial contribution will be produced than with a traditional DB plan.

G. If former participants do not provide the plan with distribution instructions, the plan may automatically distribute accounts less than $5,000. In the case of a plan that provides for such mandatory distributions, the plan must automatically roll an eligible distribution amount that exceeds $1,000 to a Rollover IRA in the former participant's name. A plan may allow direct rollovers of less than $1,000.

Advantages to Employees

A. Annual employer contributions are not taxed to the participant.

B. Earnings are not currently taxed.

C. Participants may also have a traditional, deductible IRA (subject to certain income limitations based on filing status), a traditional, nondeductible IRA, or a Roth IRA.

---

[1] See IRS press release IR-2004-21, February 13, 2004.

Continued.

Fully-Insured Defined Benefit Plan
IRC Sec. 412(e)(3)

D. Distributions may be eligible for 10-year income averaging[1], or, at retirement from the current employer, rolled over to a Traditional or a Roth IRA[2] or to another employer plan if that plan will accept such a rollover. Federal law allows retirement distributions to employees who are at least age 62 even if they have not separated from employment at the time distributions begin.

E. If the plan allows, there is the ability to purchase significant permanent life insurance under the plan. Purchase of life insurance will generate taxable income to the employee.

F. Employee is guaranteed a known retirement benefit.

G. Federal bankruptcy law provides significant protection from creditors to participant accounts or accrued benefits in tax-exempt retirement plans.

Disadvantages to Employer

A. In low profit or cash flow years, the employer is still obligated to make contributions, which may be substantial.

B. There is far less flexibility with the level of contribution even if profits are low, than with some other types of plans.

C. Even though an actuarial certification is not required, other administrative costs arise. The administrative costs will be similar to those in a traditional defined benefit plan.

D. Employer contributions may drop dramatically in future years.

E. The employer has no control over the investments.

F. Participants often do not understand the defined benefit plan as easily as they do other types of plans.

Disadvantages to Employees

A. Younger employees may not receive as great a benefit as they would under other plans.

B. The plan concept and details are more difficult to understand.

---

[1] Those born before 1936 may be able to elect 10-year averaging or capital gain treatment; these strategies are not available to those born after 1935.

[2] Beginning in 2008, distributions from qualified retirement plans, IRC Sec. 457 plans, and tax-sheltered annuities may be rolled directly into a Roth IRA. These rollover distributions are taxable events, subject to the same requirements as a Roth conversion.

Simplified Employee Pension (SEP)

The basics: A SEP provides an employer with a simplified way to make contributions to an employee's individual retirement account or individual retirement annuity.

- Employer contributions are made directly to SEP-IRAs set up for each employee with a bank, insurance company or other qualified financial institution.

- Employer contributions are tax deductible.

- Contributions are not taxed currently to the employee.

- Earnings accumulate income tax-deferred.

How Much Will There Be at Retirement?

This will depend upon three factors.
1. The frequency and amount of contributions,
2. The number of years until retirement, and
3. The investment return.

The risk of poor investment returns rests upon the employee. However, if the investment results are favorable, the participant will have a larger fund at retirement age. The following table illustrates the amount to which annual deposits of $10,000 will accumulate at various growth rates for various periods.

An Example of What $10,000 Per Year Will Grow to Over Several Years at Various Rates of Growth Without Tax[1]				
Years	4.00%	6.00%	8.00%	10.00%
5	$54,163	$56,371	$58,666	$61,051
10	$120,061	$131,808	$144,866	$159,374
15	$200,236	$232,760	$271,521	$317,725
20	$297,781	$367,856	$457,620	$572,750
25	$416,459	$548,645	$731,059	$983,471
30	$560,849	$790,582	$1,132,832	$1,644,940
35	$736,522	$1,114,348	$1,723,168	$2,710,244

Top-Heavy Plans

If more than 60% of the plan assets are allocated to key employees[2], then the employer must contribute at least as much for non-key participants as it does for key employees. This requirement applies only to a contribution of up to the first 3% of includable compensation (higher in some instances).

---

[1] The rates of return used in this illustration are not indicative of any actual investment and will fluctuate in value.
[2] A "key" employee is someone who, at any time during the plan year was: (1) an officer of the employer whose compensation from the employer exceeded $150,000; or (2) a more than 5% owner; or (3) a 1% owner whose compensation from the employer exceeded $150,000.

Continued

Simplified Employee Pension (SEP)

Additional Considerations

- **Annual contribution:** No annual contribution is required. If a contribution is made and IRS Form 5305-SEP is used as the plan document, the allocation must be the same percentage for each eligible employee. Allocation formulas that favor older employees may not be used. If integration with Social Security is desired, a custom plan or prototype document must be used.

- **Individual limits:** The allocation of excludable employer contributions to a participant's account may not exceed the lesser of 25% of compensation or $46,000. For the self-employed, these maximum values are effectively 20% and $46,000. For 2008, the maximum amount of compensation that may be considered in this calculation is $230,000.

- **Time of contribution:** Contributions can be made until the due date (plus extensions) of the employer's return.

- **Vesting:** Vesting must always be 100%.

- **Who may participate:** Any employee who is at least 21 years old and has performed service in at least three of the last five calendar years must be permitted to participate under the SEP unless his or her total compensation is less than $500[1] for the year for which the contribution will be made.

- **Investment of plan assets:** Plan assets can be invested in most equity products or debt instruments but may not be invested in life insurance, "hard" assets or collectibles. (Except for U.S. gold and silver coins.) Participants direct the funds contributed on their behalf.

- **Withdrawals:** Participants may withdraw or cash out at any time. However, withdrawals are included in taxable income in the year received. Withdrawals prior to age 59½ are subject to an additional 10% penalty tax. Exceptions to the 10% penalty apply if a distribution is made because of the participant's death or disability, or if a distribution is made as a series of substantially-equal periodic payments over the life expectancy of the SEP owner, or joint life expectancies of the owner and a designated beneficiary. Once the periodic payment format is chosen, it generally may not be modified without penalty before the later of five years, or the participant reaches age 59½. An additional exception to the 10% penalty applies for distributions made to pay medical expenses in excess of 7.5% of adjusted gross income. In certain cases, distributions to unemployed individuals for payment of health insurance premiums, or withdrawals made to pay certain first-time homebuyer or educational expenses, may also avoid the penalty.[2]

---

[1] This amount applies to 2008. This *de minimis* threshold is subject to change as indexed for inflation.
[2] See IRC Sec. 72(t).

Continued...

Simplified Employee Pension (SEP)

Advantages to Employer

A. Contributions are tax deductible.

B. Contributions and costs are very flexible.

C. Reporting is very minimal—no IRS or Dept. of Labor forms.

D. The plan is easy to understand by the employees.

E. The plan is easy to set up by merely completing IRS Model Form 5305-SEP[1], or the funding institution's plan.

F. There is little or no administrative expense.

G. There is no ongoing fiduciary liability to the employer for plan asset management.

Advantages to Employees

A. Annual contributions are not taxed currently to the participant.

B. Earnings on the account are not currently taxed.

C. Participants have the right to direct investments.

D. Federal law allows a qualified plan to establish an "eligible investment advice arrangement" under which individually tailored investment advice is provided to plan participants. Any fees or commissions charged must not vary with the investment options chosen, or else a computer model meeting certain requirements must be used.

E. Participants may also have a traditional, deductible IRA (subject to certain income limitations based on filing status), a traditional, nondeductible IRA, or a Roth IRA.

F. Funds can be withdrawn at any time; e.g., in the event of an emergency such as death or disability. Distributions are includable in taxable income in the year received. A 10% penalty tax may also apply if the participant is under age 59½ when a distribution is received.[2]

G. Federal bankruptcy law provides significant protection from creditors to participant accounts or accrued benefits in tax-exempt retirement plans. In traditional and Roth IRAs, generally, up to $1,000,000 is protected. However, funds in a SEP IRA are protected without any dollar limitation.

---

[1] This model form may not be used if employer has ever maintained a defined benefit plan or currently maintains any other qualified pension or profit sharing plan.

[2] See "Withdrawals" under "Additional Considerations," above.

Continued

Simplified Employee Pension (SEP)

Disadvantages to Employer

A. Contributions must be made for part-time and seasonal employees.

B. Employees can withdraw the funds as fast as they are put into the account.

C. Employees are always 100% vested—there are no forfeitures to reduce employer contributions.

D. Employees control investments.

E. Allocation methods that reduce employer costs may not be used; employee costs can be high compared to other types of plans. However, some plan documents used by investment vendors permit integration with social security, which will reduce employer contributions to some extent.

Disadvantages to Employees

A. There is no guarantee as to future benefits.

B. Investment risks rest on the participant.

C. There is no assurance as to the frequency and amount of employer contributions.

D. Special lump-sum tax treatment of distributions is not available.

E. There are no forfeitures to be reallocated.

F. Life insurance funding is not available.

Continued...

Simplified Employee Pension (SEP)

SEP vs. Profit Sharing Plan

Item	SEP	Profit Sharing
Maximum employer deduction for all plan participants	25% of covered compensation	25% of covered compensation
Maximum amount excludable from current taxation for employer	Lesser of 25% of compensation (limited to $230,000 in 2008) or $46,000	Lesser of 100% of compensation (limited to $230,000 in 2008) or $46,000
Included in employee gross income?	No	No
Eligibility	All categories of employees except union	Some flexibility
Waiting period	Age 21/any amount of service during 3 of last 5 calendar years	Age 21/1 year service (or 2 years if 100% vested)
Part-time employees	Must be included if they earn more than $500 in the year for which a contribution is made.	Excluded if less than 1,000 hours in plan year
Eligibility for contribution	If eligibility for plan is met, the employee is entitled to contribution whether or not employed on date of contribution	Determined by the plan document
Must annual contributions be made?	No – Discretionary	No – Discretionary
Deadline for making contributions	Tax filing date, including extensions	Tax filing date, including extensions
Reporting and disclosure (employer)	Minimal	Full ERISA requirements
Top-heavy regulations	Apply	Apply
Investments	Decided by employee; no hard assets or collectibles (except certain government coins)	Decided by trustee Plan may allow participants to direct investments
Allocation of contributions	Pro rata by compensation, but may be integrated with Social Security	Various Most favorable to highly paid and/or older participants
Protects from claims of bankruptcy creditors	Federal bankruptcy law provides significant protection from creditors.	Federal bankruptcy law provides significant protection from creditors.
Who controls withdrawals?	Employee	Terms of the plan trustee/administrator
Vesting requirements	Always 100% vested	May be graded up to six years

Continued

Simplified Employee Pension (SEP)

Item	SEP	Profit Sharing
Favorable taxation of lump-sum distribution	Not available	Maybe[1]
Employee withdrawals	Anytime, with penalty prior to age 59½	Generally, only on death, termination or retirement as provided by plan
Employee loans	No	Yes, provided legal guidelines are observed
Life insurance	Not permitted	Permitted within legal guidelines

---

[1] Those born before 1936 may be able to elect 10-year averaging or capital gain treatment; these strategies are not available to those born after 1935.

How a SEP-IRA Works

Employer

- Contributes for all qualified employees.[1]
- Contributions are tax deductible.
- Plan is flexible (contributions are not required each year).
- Generally little or no administrative expense.

SEP-IRA

- A separate IRA exists for each participant.
- Employer contributions are not currently taxable.
- Earnings accumulate tax-deferred.
- Plan is self-directed (employee controls investments).
- Investment risk remains on employee.

Employee

- Maximum 2008 allocation to a SEP for an employee is $46,000.[2] For a self-employed individual, the limit is also $46,000.[3]

Early Withdrawal

- A 10% penalty generally applies if withdrawals are made before age 59½.
- Some exceptions to 10% penalty are available.
- Earnings + deductible contributions taxed as ordinary income in year received.

Retirement

- Distributions must begin by April 1 of year following year owner reaches age 70½.
- Required minimum distribution rules apply.
- Earnings + deductible contributions taxed as ordinary income in year received.

Death

- Value of IRA is included in owner's gross estate.
- Proceeds can pass to surviving spouse with payments over survivor's lifetime.
- Income and estate taxes can severely reduce SEP-IRA funds left to nonspousal heirs.

---

[1] Any employee at least 21 years of age who has performed "service" in three of the last five years, and whose total compensation exceeds $500 for the year.
[2] For an employee, contributions may not exceed the lesser of 25% of compensation (maximum of $230,000) or $46,000.
[3] For a self-employed individual, contributions may not exceed the lesser of 20% of compensation (maximum of $230,000) or $46,000.

SIMPLE Retirement Plan

The Small Business Job Protection Act of 1996 created an entirely new type of retirement plan called "SIMPLE," an acronym that stands for Savings Incentive Match Plan for Employees. It is available for any business which:

- Has 100 or fewer employees (including employees of related entities);

- Does not maintain another tax-qualified retirement plan to which contributions are made; and

- Is either an incorporated or unincorporated firm.

How It Works

- Employee has the option of taking cash, or having it contributed to the trust for retirement. This is equivalent to the employee making a pre-tax contribution.

- Mandatory employer contributions are tax-deductible to the business.

- Employer contributions are not taxed currently to the participants.

- Earnings accumulate income tax deferred.

- The employer must deposit participant contributions within 30 days after the end of the month for which the contribution was made.[1]

- There are two different types of SIMPLE plans that, although similar, do have distinct differences. There is an IRA version and a 401(k) version.

Item	IRA Version	401(k) Version
Plan type	Individual IRA for each participant.	Cash or deferred profit sharing plan.
Participation	Any employee who received $5,000 or more of income during any 2 prior years and is expected to earn $5,000 during the current year must be eligible.	Regular qualified plan rules apply, such as: Minimum age of 21 1 year of service 1000 hours
Do cash or deferred nondiscrimination rules apply? [(401(k), 401(m)]	No	No, unless employer fails to contribute.
Top-heavy rules	They do not apply.	Do not apply unless employer fails to contribute.
ERISA reporting and disclosure rules	Simplified rules apply.	Regular rules apply.

---

[1] This provision of SIMPLE plans conflicts with current Department of Labor regulations, which prescribe a maximum 15-business-day time limit.

Continued...

SIMPLE Retirement Plan

Item	IRA Version	401(k) Version
Vesting	Always 100%	Always 100%
Employee contributions	Voluntary up to $10,500[1] (indexed for inflation) per year. May not exceed 100% of compensation. May stop at any time.	Voluntary up to $10,500[1] (indexed for inflation) per year. May not exceed 100% of compensation. May stop at any time.
Minimum participation requirements	There is no minimum number or percentage of eligible employees who must participate.	There is no minimum number or percentage of eligible employees who must participate.
Employer contributions	Employer must satisfy one of two alternatives. Election must be made at least 60 days before the start of the plan year.	Employer must satisfy one of two alternatives. Election must be made at least 60 days before the start of the plan year.
Alternative #1 -Matching contributions	Employer matches employee's elective deferral, dollar for dollar, up to 3.0% of compensation.	Employer matches employee's elective deferral, dollar for dollar, up to 3.0% of compensation.
	For any two years out of five, employer may have a lower match, but not less than 1.0%.	Not available.
	The $230,000 compensation limit does not apply.	The $230,000 compensation limit does apply.
	No conditions may be imposed on the right to the employer match such as minimum hours or end of year employment.	No conditions may be imposed on the right to the employer match such as minimum hours or end of year employment.
Alternative #2 - Nonelective contribution	Employer contribution is 2% of compensation to all eligible employees, whether they defer or not.	Employer contribution is 2% of compensation to all eligible employees, whether they defer or not.
	The $230,000 compensation limit does apply.	The $230,000 compensation limit does apply.
Employer contributions are due by:	Due date of employer's income tax return, plus filing extensions.	Due date of employer's income tax return, plus filing extensions.
Employee in-service withdrawals	These are allowed.	Rules are the same as for 401(k) plans. If plan provides for loans or hardship withdrawals, they are allowed.
Taxation of distributions	Generally, treated in the same fashion as withdrawals from a traditional IRA. Ordinary income. Penalty taxes may apply.	Same as 401(k) plans. Distribution is ordinary income. 10-Year averaging[2] may be available.
Additional employer contributions	Are not permitted.	Are not permitted.

---

[1] This is the 2008 limit. For those age 50 and older, additional "catch-up" contributions of $2,500 may be made.
[2] Those born before 1936 may be able to elect 10-year income averaging or capital gain treatment; these strategies are not available to those born after 1935.

Continue

SIMPLE Retirement Plan

Item	IRA Version	401(k) Version
May employer have another plan to which contributions are made or in which benefits accrue?	No	No
Rollovers	Allowed if to another SIMPLE IRA or, after 2 years of SIMPLE participation, to a traditional IRA.	These are allowed when made to a traditional IRA or qualified plan.
Taxation of premature (before age 59½) distributions within first two years of participation	Taxed as ordinary income, plus a 25% penalty, unless an exception applies.	Taxed as ordinary income, plus a 10% penalty, unless an exception applies.
Taxation of premature (before age 59½) distributions after first two years of participation	Taxed as ordinary income, plus a 10% penalty, unless an exception applies.	Taxed as ordinary income, plus a 10% penalty, unless an exception applies.
Reporting requirements	Plan trustee must provide employer with information on basic plan details.	Regular reporting and disclosure requirements apply. 5500 filing, Summary Plan Description and Summary Annual Report.
	Employer must notify employee of right to defer and provide above information.	
	By January 30, employer must give each participant a statement setting forth account balances as of December 31, and all activity during the calendar year.	401(k)-type of participant reports is required. Time limit is 9 months after the close of the plan year with Summary Annual Report.

Advantages to Employer

A. Unlike 401(k) plans, the employer knows in advance approximately what the financial commitment will be.

B. Employer contribution is tax deductible.

C. The plan is easily understood by employees.

D. The 401(k) version of the plan can provide employees with permanent life insurance benefits that need not expire nor require costly conversion at retirement age.

E. The employer can direct employer investments.

F. If former participants do not provide the plan with distribution instructions, the plan may automatically distribute accounts less than $5,000. In the case of a plan that provides for such mandatory distributions, the plan must automatically roll an eligible distribution amount that exceeds $1,000 to a Rollover IRA in the former participant's name. A plan may allow direct rollovers of less than $1,000.

Continued...

SIMPLE Retirement Plan

Advantages to Employees

A. Participant deferrals are made with pre-tax dollars.

B. Employer contributions are not currently taxable to participant.

C. In the 401(k) version, distributions may be eligible for 10-year income averaging[1] or, at retirement from the current employer, rolled over to a Traditional or a Roth IRA[2] or to another employer plan if that plan will accept such a rollover.

D. Distributions from the IRA version are taxed in the same manner as a traditional IRA, except for a 25% penalty for premature distributions in the first two years.

E. Participants have right to direct investment.

F. Federal law allows a qualified plan to establish an "eligible investment advice arrangement" under which individually tailored investment advice is provided to plan participants. Any fees or commissions charged must not vary with the investment options chosen, or else a computer model meeting certain requirements must be used.

G. Participants may also have a traditional, deductible IRA, or Roth IRA, subject to certain income limitations based on filing status.

H. In the 401(k) version there is the ability to purchase significant permanent life insurance which is not contingent upon the company group insurance program. Purchase of life insurance will generate taxable income to the employee.

I. Younger employees can accumulate a larger fund than with a defined benefit plan.

J. If the 401(k) plan permits, participants can borrow from the plan, within the requirements of the plan and the law.

K. In the 401(k) version, if the plan permits, participants can make hardship withdrawals within the requirements of the plan.

L. Federal bankruptcy law provides significant protection from creditors to participant accounts or accrued benefits in tax-exempt retirement plans. In traditional and Roth IRAs, generally, up to $1,000,000 is protected. However, funds in either a SIMPLE IRA or SIMPLE 401(k) are protected without any dollar limitation.

---

[1] Those born before 1936 may be able to elect 10-year averaging or capital gains treatment; these strategies are not available to those born after 1935.

[2] Beginning in 2008, distributions from qualified retirement plans, IRC Sec. 457 plans, and tax-sheltered annuities may be rolled directly into a Roth IRA. These rollover distributions are taxable events, subject to the same requirements as a Roth conversion.

Continued

SIMPLE Retirement Plan

Disadvantages to Employer

A. The employer is required to contribute.

B. The more highly paid participants may not be able to contribute sufficient funds to build an adequate retirement. This may bring pressure on the employer to provide additional retirement benefits.

C. While called a "SIMPLE" plan, in operation it is not nearly as simple as often thought.

Disadvantages to Employees

A. There is no guarantee as to future benefits.

B. Investment risk rests on the participant.

C. There are no forfeitures to reallocate as under other types of defined contribution plans.

D. For older employees, there may not be sufficient time to accumulate a decent retirement fund. Other types of defined contribution plans can provide a better retirement benefit for older workers.

How a SIMPLE IRA Works

Employer

- SIMPLE plans are only available to firms with 100 or fewer employees and which do not maintain another qualified retirement plan.
- Employer generally must match employee contributions dollar for dollar up to 3%.[2]
- Mandatory contributions are tax deductible to the business.

SIMPLE IRA

- A separate IRA exists for each participant.
- Employer contributions are not currently taxable to employee and earnings accumulate tax deferred.
- Most plans are self-directed (employee controls investments).
- Investment risk remains on employee.

Employee

- Employee may elect to defer a percentage of salary.
- Contributions are pre-tax, thus lowering total taxable income.
- For 2008, elective contributions cannot exceed $10,500 or 100% of compensation.[1]

Early Withdrawal

- A 25% penalty tax generally applies if withdrawals are made within two years and before age 59½.[3]
- Some exceptions to penalty tax are available.
- Earnings + deductible contributions are taxed as ordinary income in year received.

Retirement

- Distributions must begin by April 1 of year following year owner reaches age 70½.
- Required minimum distribution rules apply.
- Earnings + deductible contributions are taxed as ordinary income when received.

Death

- Value of IRA is included in owner's gross estate.
- Proceeds can pass to surviving spouse with payments over survivor's lifetime.
- Income and estate taxes can severely reduce IRA funds left to nonspousal beneficiaries.

---

[1] For those age 50 and older, additional "catch-up" contributions of $2,500 may be made.
[2] Alternately, employer may choose to contribute 2% of compensation to all eligible employees, whether they defer or not.
[3] Premature distributions (before age 59½) made after the first two years of participation are generally subject to a 10% penalty tax, unless an exception applies.

Qualified Plans Compared

Plan Type	Defined Benefit	Defined Contribution		
Benefit or Feature	Defined Benefit Plan	Nontraditional Defined Contribution Plan	401(k) Plan	SIMPLE IRA
Employer contributions deductible?	Yes	Yes	Yes	Yes
Employer contributions currently taxable to participant?	No	No	No	No
Earnings accumulate income tax deferred?	Yes	Yes	Yes	Yes
Distributions can be tax favored using 10-year income averaging?	Maybe[1]	Maybe[1]	Maybe[1]	No
Contribution benefit base is total compensation up to $230,000?	Yes	Yes	Yes	Effectively, $350,000[2]
Maximum employer annual contribution/deduction:	Determined by actuary	25% of covered payroll	25% of covered payroll excluding deferral, if plan specifies	Match up to 3% of covered payroll or 2% of covered payroll to all eligible employees
Employer contributions required?	Yes	Money purchase - yes Profit sharing - no	No	Yes at 2% of covered payroll to all eligible employees OR Dollar for dollar match up to 3% of compensation
Employer contributions discretionary?	No	Profit sharing - yes	Yes	No
Employer matching contributions allowed?	N/A	N/A	Yes	No. The employer contribution is mandatory.

---

[1] Those born before 1936 may be able to elect 10-year averaging or capital gain treatment; these strategies are not available to those born after 1935.
[2] The $350,000 amount is based on 3% of the 2008 contribution limit of $10,500 (or $10,500 divided by .03).

Continued...

Qualified Plans Compared

Plan Type	Defined Benefit	Defined Contribution		
Benefit or Feature	**Defined Benefit Plan**	**Nontraditional Defined Contribution Plan**	**401(k) Plan**	**SIMPLE IRA**
Employer contribution allocation	N/A	1. Age Weighted 2. Cross Tested 3. Super Integrated	1. Prorata by compensation; 2. Integrated with Soc. Sec.; 3. Age-weighted; or 4. Cross tested	Match up to 3% of compensation or 2% of compensation to all eligible employees
Employee contributions Required? Permitted?	No Rarely	No Rarely	No Yes	No Yes
Maximum participant benefits (defined benefit plans only)	Lesser of 100% of compensation or $185,000 annually	N/A	N/A	N/A
Maximum participant allocations (employer and employee) (defined contribution plans only)	N/A	Lesser of 100% of compensation or $46,000	Lesser of 100% of compensation or $46,000	Lesser of 100% of compensation or $21,000[1]
Catch-up provisions for those age 50 and older	N/A	No	Yes $5,000[2]	Yes $2,500[2]
Required discrimination tests Coverage? Benefits/Contributions? Deferral rates of highly compensated/nonhighly compensated?	Yes Yes N/A	Yes Yes N/A	Yes Yes Yes	No No N/A
Can exclude employees from plan participation on basis of age, length of service, part-time or union membership?	Yes	Yes	Yes	No ($5,000 income test applies)

[1] For 2008, includes a maximum employee contribution of $10,500, plus a dollar for dollar employer match.
[2] Applies to 2008.

Continued..

Qualified Plans Compared

Plan Type	Defined Benefit	Defined Contribution		
Benefit or Feature	**Defined Benefit Plan**	**Nontraditional Defined Contribution Plan**	**401(k) Plan**	**SIMPLE IRA**
Investments Self directed by participants or can be invested at participant discretion (most plans impose some practical considerations)	N/A	Yes	Yes	Yes
and/or Directed by the trustee, must be diversified and prudent	Yes	Yes	Yes	N/A
Self-dealing is prohibited between plan and a number of related persons?	Yes	Yes	Yes	Yes
Plan may recognize employer contributions or benefits of Social Security?	Yes	Yes	Yes	No
Participants who are favored	Older and closer to retirement	Highly compensated and older	Younger	Younger
How much will there be at retirement?				
Benefits specified in plan?	Yes	N/A	N/A	N/A
Investment return affects retirement benefits?	No	Yes	Yes	Yes
Benefits guaranteed at retirement?	Yes	No	No	No
Who bears investment risk?	Employer	Employee	Employee	Employee
Ease of understanding by participants	Difficult	Difficult to Easy	Easy	Easy

Continued...

Qualified Plans Compared

Plan Type / Benefit or Feature	Defined Benefit / Defined Benefit Plan	Defined Contribution		
		Nontraditional Defined Contribution Plan	401(k) Plan	SIMPLE IRA
Can life insurance be provided?	Yes	Yes	Yes	No
Can participants have a traditional, deductible IRA, or a Roth IRA, subject to income level limitations based on filing status?	Yes	Yes	Yes	Yes
Forfeitures are used to:	Reduce employer contribution	Reduce employer contribution or are reallocated among participants	Reduce employer contribution or are reallocated among participants	N/A
Can participants make loans subject to strict rules?	Yes	Yes	Yes	No
Are hardship withdrawals permitted under well-defined circumstances? (Participant cannot defer for 6 months thereafter.)	N/A	N/A	Yes	N/A
Top heavy requirements, if applicable[1]				
Defined benefit plans	Yes - 2% annual benefit for 10 years			
Defined contribution plans		Up to 3% of compensation[2]	Up to 3% of compensation[3]	No

---

[1] If more than 60% of the plan assets or accrued benefits are allocated to key employees, the plan is top heavy. A "Key" employee is someone who, at any time during the plan year was (1) an officer of the employer whose compensation from the employer exceeded $150,000; or (2) a more than 5% owner; or (3) a 1% owner whose compensation from the employer exceeded $150,000

[2] This amount may be greater in some circumstances.

[3] This amount depends on facts and circumstances.

Defined Contribution Plans Compared

Benefit or Feature	Plan Type			
	SEP	Traditional Defined Contribution Plan	401(k) Plan	SIMPLE IRA
Employer contributions deductible?	Yes	Yes	Yes	Yes
Employer contributions currently taxable to participant?	No	No	No	No
Earnings accumulate income tax deferred?	Yes	Yes	Yes	Yes
Distributions can be tax favored using 10-year income averaging?	No	Maybe[1]	Maybe[1]	No
Contribution benefit base is total compensation up to $230,000?	Yes	Yes	Yes	Effectively $350,000[2]
Maximum plan annual employer deduction	25%[3] of compensation of all covered participants	25% of compensation of all covered participants.	25% of compensation of all covered participants	Match deferral up to 3% of compensation or 2% of compensation to all eligible employees
Maximum participant allocation	Lesser of 25% of compensation or $46,000	Lesser of 100% of compensation or $46,000	Lesser of 100% of compensation or $46,000	Lesser of 100% of compensation or $21,000[4]
Catch-up provisions for those age 50 and older?	No	Yes $5,000	Yes $5,000	Yes $2,500
Employer contributions required?	No	Profit sharing No Money purchase Yes	No	Yes, at 2% of compensation to all eligible employees or dollar for dollar up to 3% of compensation

---

[1] Those born before 1936 may be able to elect 10-year averaging or capital gain treatment; these strategies are not available to those born after 1935.
[2] The $350,000 amount is based on 3% of the 2008 contribution limit of $10,500 (or $10,500 divided by .03).
[3] See the section in IRS Publication 590, Individual Retirement Arrangements (IRAs) on SEPs.
[4] For 2008, includes a maximum employee contribution of $10,500, plus a dollar for dollar employer match.

Continued...

Defined Contribution Plans Compared

Benefit or Feature	Plan Type			
	SEP	Traditional Defined Contribution Plan	401(k) Plan	SIMPLE IRA
Employer contributions discretionary?	Yes	Profit sharing = Yes Money purchase = No	Yes	No
Employer matching contributions allowed?	No	No	Yes	Yes[1]
How is employer non-matching contribution allocated?	Prorata by compensation	Prorata by compensation or integrated with Social Security	1. Prorata by compensation, or 2. Integrated with Social Security, or 3. Age-weighted, or 4. Cross tested	Prorata by compensation or up to 3% match on deferrals
Employee contributions				
Required?	No	No	No	No
Permitted?	No	Rarely	Yes	Yes
Employee vesting in employer contributions	Always 100%	May be graded over time	May be graded over time	Always 100%
Required discrimination test				
Coverage?	Yes	Yes	Yes	No
Contributions?	Yes	Yes	Yes	No
Deferral rates of highly compensated/nonhighly compensated?	N/A	N/A	Yes	N/A
Can exclude employees from plan participation on basis of age, length of service, part-time or union membership?	No.[2]	Yes	Yes	No[3]
Investments				
Self directed by participants (most plans impose some practical considerations)	Can only be directed by participants	Yes	Yes	Yes
and/or				
Directed by the trustee, must be diversified and prudent	N/A	Yes	Yes	N/A
Is self-dealing prohibited between the plan and a number of related persons?	Yes	Yes	Yes	Yes

---

[1] The employer is required to contribute, using one of these two methods: 1) at 2% of compensation to all eligible employees or 2) dollar-for-dollar up to 3% of compensation.
[2] Must participate if age 21, performed service in three of last five years and earned $500 in current year.
[3] $5,000 income test applies.

Continued

Defined Contribution Plans Compared

Benefit or Feature	Plan Type			
	SEP	Traditional Defined Contribution Plan	401(k) Plan	SIMPLE IRA
Plan may recognize employer contributions or benefits of Social Security?	Yes, but IRS form 5305 SEP may not be used	Yes	Yes	No
Participants who are favored	Younger	Younger	Younger	Younger
How much will there be at retirement?				
Investment return affects retirement benefits?	Yes	Yes	Yes	Yes
Benefits guaranteed at retirement?	No	No	No	No
Who bears investment risk?	Employee	Employee	Employee	Employee
Top heavy requirements, if applicable	Up to 3% of compensation	Up to 3% of compensation[1]	Up to 3% of compensation	No
Ease of understanding by participants	Easy	Easy	Easy	Easy
Can life insurance be provided?	No	Yes	Yes	No
Can participants have a traditional IRA or Roth IRA?[2]	Yes	Yes	Yes	Yes
Forfeitures are used for what purpose	N/A	Reduce employer contribution or are reallocated among participants	Reduce employer contribution or are reallocated among participants	N/A
Can participants make loans subject to strict rules?	No	Yes	Yes	No
Are hardship withdrawals permitted under well-defined circumstances? (Participant cannot defer for 6 months thereafter.)	No	Maybe[3]	Yes	No

---

[1] This amount may be greater in some circumstances.
[2] Subject to other requirements.
[3] Hardship withdrawals are permitted for profit sharing plans, but not for money purchase plans.

Combinations of Retirement Plans

Can an employer have more than one kind of tax-deductible retirement plan? Under current federal law the answer is yes. There are, however, certain limits imposed at both the individual plan level and at the combined plans level. In combining plans, an employer would not normally adopt more than one plan of the same type.

Individual Plan Limits

At the individual plan level, the maximum annual retirement benefit permitted under a defined benefit plan for a participant is the lesser of 100% of compensation or $185,000.[1] The maximum allocation to a participant under a defined contribution plan is the lesser of 100%[2] of compensation or $46,000.[2] If an employer adopts two plans of the same type, they would be aggregated for the purposes of these limits.

Combined Plan Deduction Limits

If an employer maintains both a defined contribution and a defined benefit plan at the same time, the individual plan limits discussed above apply separately to each type of plan. However, there is also an overall limitation to the deduction allowed to an employer for the combined plans. If any employee participates in both plans, the maximum employer deduction is limited to the greater of 25% of the total compensation of all employees participating in either plan or the normal cost of the defined benefit plan. This limit applies to employer-paid contributions, including pension, profit sharing, and matching contributions. 401(k) salary deferral contributions elected by employees are not subject to this 25% deduction limit.

Employer-paid contributions to a defined contribution plan that do not exceed 6% of total compensation of all employees participating in the defined contribution plan do not count toward this 25% deduction limit.

For example, assume an employer maintains both a defined benefit and a defined contribution plan, such as a profit sharing plan. Assume also that the total payroll of covered participants in either plan is $100,000 and that the required defined benefit contribution is $20,000. The most that could be contributed and deducted for the profit sharing plan is $11,000. (25% x $100,000 = $25,000; $25,000-$20,000 = $5,000; 6% x $100,000 = $6,000; $5,000 + $6,000 = $11,000). If the employer in this example were to contribute $13,500 to the profit sharing plan, $2,500 of the contribution would be nondeductible. There would also be a 10% excise tax on the non-deductible $2,500.

---

[1] These are 2008 limits. In some instances these limits may be reduced.
[2] These are 2008 limits.

Continued..

Combinations of Retirement Plans

If the required defined benefit plan contribution were $35,000, the employer could contribute and deduct the entire $35,000. However, the deductible contribution to the profit sharing plan would be limited to $6,000. If the defined contribution plan has a mandatory contribution (e.g., a target benefit or money purchase plan) a contribution is still required even though it may exceed the deductible limit and incur the 10% excise tax on the non-deductible portion.

Combined Plans with 401(k) Feature

Many different plan combinations are possible. One common arrangement is that of a defined benefit plan paired with a 401(k)/profit sharing plan. Consider what could be contributed and deducted in 2008 for an owner-only business, with the owner over age 50:

Individual	Compensation	Defined Benefit	Profit Sharing	401(k)	Total
Owner	$230,000	$200,000[1]	$13,800	$20,500	$234,300

If there are employees in addition to an owner-employee, the 401(k) might also provide for a safe harbor contribution and a tiered profit sharing contribution. With younger employees, and using a tiered 401(k) safe harbor plan with the defined benefit plan, the amount that could be contributed and deducted in 2008 would be:

Individual	Compensation	Defined Benefit	Safe Harbor & Profit Sharing	401(k)[2]	Total
Owner	$230,000	$120,000	$16,350	$20,500	$156,850
Employee 1	$50,000	$8,000	$1,500	-	$9,500
Employee 2	$35,000	$4,000	$1,050	-	$5,050
TOTAL	$315,000	$132,000[3]	$18,900	$20,500	$171,400

There is a special exception to the 25% deduction limit. If no single employee participates in both plans, the 25% deduction limit does not apply. If this occurs, however, other discrimination problems may arise unless the plans are properly designed to work together to satisfy IRS requirements.

Sequential Plans

Rather than adopting two different types of plans simultaneously, an employer may choose to use different types of plans, at different points in time. Prior to 2000, a complicated set of rules and limits effectively made it impossible for one employer to have different types of plans, even at different times. For plan years beginning January 1, 2000 and later, however, the former rules and limits no longer applied.

---

[1] Normal cost plus 50% funding cushion.
[2] The 401(k) deferrals shown are for the owner as part of the owner's contribution. No contribution is shown for the employees as they depend on individual employee elections and are not paid by the employer, but by the employee.
[3] Plus funding cushion of approximately 50% if desired.

Continued...

Combinations of Retirement Plans

In the mid-1980s, for example, many defined benefit plans were terminated because a change in the law made them fully funded. Under the new rules, an employer who terminated such a plan could now adopt a defined contribution plan, and contribute and deduct the maximum allowable for all eligible participants.

An employer may have chosen a defined contribution plan in the past because the key participants were younger. After many years these same key people could benefit more from a defined benefit plan. With the increased flexibility now available, the employer could switch to a defined benefit plan. Given the deduction limits applicable to combined plans, the employer could adopt a maximum defined benefit plan and either terminate the defined contribution plan or reduce its contribution to no more than 6% of compensation.

Allowable Combinations of Employer-Sponsored Plans

The table below lists the allowable combinations of employer-sponsored retirement plans:

Plan Type	Defined Benefit Plan	Defined Contribution Pension[1]	Defined Contribution Profit-Sharing[2]	Simple IRA	Simple 401(k)	SEP
Defined benefit plan	Yes	Yes	Yes	No	No	Maybe[3]
Defined contribution pension[1]	Yes	Yes	Yes	No	No	Yes
Defined contribution profit-sharing[2]	Yes	Yes	Yes	No	No	Yes
Simple IRA	No	No	No	No	No	No
Simple 401(k)	No	No	No	No	No	No
SEP	Maybe[3]	Yes	Yes	No	No	Yes

---

[1] Defined contribution money purchase or target benefit plans, including tiered or cross-tested varieties.
[2] Profit sharing plans such as 401(k), ESOPs and stock bonus plans, as well as tiered or cross-tested variations.
[3] Depends on whether this is allowed in the SEP plan documents.

Top-Heavy Plans

While large qualified retirement plans are rarely top heavy, most small plans are. In fact, the smaller the plan, the more likely it is to be top heavy.

When Is a Qualified Retirement Plan Top Heavy?[1]

- If the total present value of the accrued benefits for key participants in a defined benefit plan exceeds 60% of the present value of all benefits in the plan, the plan is top heavy.

- If the total account values for key employees in a defined contribution plan exceed 60% of the total value of all accounts, the plan is top heavy.

Key Participants

Key participants are any participants and participants' beneficiaries who, during the determination year.[2]

- are or were an officer of the sponsoring employer and earning more than $150,000[3];

- owned more than 5%[4] of the employer; or

- owned more than 1%[4] of the employer and received more than $150,000 of compensation from the employer.

Special Requirements for Top-Heavy Plans

- Vesting must either provide that a participant is fully vested after three years of service[5] or the vesting schedule must provide for graded vesting over six years of service[5] (0-20-40-60-80-100). More rapid vesting is permitted.

- For defined contribution plans, the employer must contribute and allocate to non-key participants the lesser of 3%[6] of compensation or the highest contribution percent of any key employee. Elective deferrals by a key employee under a 401(k) plan are considered to be an employer contribution.[7] The plan may require that a participant be employed at the end of the plan year; it may not require that the participant work a minimum number of hours.

---

[1] If there are multiple plans, they are generally aggregated together for determination purposes. Money rolled out or transferred is generally added back to the distributing plan as a key or non-key account for a period of five years (reduced to one year in 2002) and ignored by the receiving plan. In the case of mergers, the opposite is true.

[2] In-service distributions are subject to a five-year look-back period.

[3] This value applies to 2008.

[4] The family attribution rules of IRC Sec. 318 apply. Any participant is deemed to have the same ownership share as his or her spouse, children, parents and grandparents. In community property states spousal attribution may apply.

[5] In some instances, participation may be substituted for service.

[6] This may be higher in some circumstances.

[7] Beginning in 2002, matching contributions were credited to meeting the top-heavy minimum contribution requirement.

Continued...

Top-Heavy Plans

- For defined benefit plans, the employer must contribute and provide for a minimum benefit accrual of 2%[1] of average compensation for a maximum of ten years of participation. The plan may not require that a participant be employed at the end of the plan year; it may require that the participant perform 1,000 (or less) hours of service during the plan year.

- If the employer maintains multiple plans, top-heavy requirements do not have to be satisfied in all plans; special rules apply.

- If a plan is in the process of termination, top-heavy requirements continue to apply. Typically, this will apply only to defined benefit plans since the employer can take steps to cease contributions under a defined contribution plan.

- However, if a defined benefit plan is "frozen", the plan does not need to provide ongoing top-heavy benefit accruals.

- Depending on the plan document, the plan may or may not have to provide top-heavy contributions or benefits to key participants.

- Failure to provide the proper top-heavy benefit accruals or contributions will result in the plan being disqualified.

- If a plan has dual eligibility for different plan contributions, eligibility for any benefit makes a non-key employee eligible to receive a top-heavy benefit, if applicable. Example: A 401(k) plan has no service requirement for employee deferrals but requires one year of service for employer discretionary allocations. A 3% or more deferral by a key employee participant will trigger a 3% top-heavy contribution for all participants including those eligible for employee deferrals only.

---

[1] This percentage may be higher in some circumstances.

Fiduciary Standards and Responsibilities

One of the most important functions associated with all qualified retirement plans is the fiduciary role. The definition of fiduciary is a wide ranging one. Section 3 (21) (a) of ERISA[1] defines a fiduciary with respect to a plan to the extent he or she:

"exercises any discretionary authority or discretionary control respecting management of such plan or exercises any authority or control respecting management of its assets, renders investment advice for a fee or other compensation, direct or indirect, with respect to any moneys or other property of such plan or, has any discretionary authority or discretionary responsibility in the administration of such plan."

Department of Labor (DOL) Regulation 2510.3-21 exempts a securities broker or dealer if that person transacts the purchase or sale of securities on behalf of the plan, in the ordinary course of business as a broker or dealer, if the plan fiduciary is not the broker or dealer and the broker or dealer is operating under instructions from the plan. An insurance agent is similarly exempted if he or she provides the disclosure required in DOL Class Exemption 84-24.[2]

Duties of a Plan Fiduciary

- The fiduciary must follow the prudent man rule, but is held to a higher standard than the normal prudent man rule. ERISA[1] states that the fiduciary is required to discharge his duties "with the care, skill, prudence and diligence under circumstances then prevailing that a prudent man acting in a like capacity and familiar with such matters would use in the conduct of an enterprise of a like character and with like aims."[3]

- A fiduciary has the duty to diversify plan investments so as to minimize the risk of large losses, unless, under the circumstances, it is clearly not prudent to do so.[4] Investment of plan assets in a single bank or other pooled fund, mutual funds, annuity contracts, or life insurance contracts will satisfy the diversification rule if the fund itself is properly diversified.[5]

- The fiduciary is required to invest plan assets exclusively for the benefit of plan participants and beneficiaries.

- Fiduciaries must act in accordance with the plan documents unless that would violate the law.

- The fiduciary must arrange to purchase the bond required under ERISA.[1] The amount of the bond must be at least 10% of the value of the plan assets.

- Unless given a funding policy by the sponsoring employer or plan trustee, the fiduciary must develop a funding policy for the plan and measure results against such policy on an annual basis.

---

[1] ERISA refers to the Employee Retirement Income Security Act of 1974.
[2] See DOL Reg. 2510.3-21 and DOL Class Exemption 84-24 for more details.
[3] See ERISA Sec. 404(a)(1).
[4] See ERISA Sec. 404(a)(1)(C).
[5] See H Rep. No. 1280, 93rd Cong., 2nd Sess. 305 (1974).

Continued...

Fiduciary Standards and Responsibilities

- If there are multiple fiduciaries, each fiduciary is responsible for the acts of the other fiduciary(s) unless the fiduciary authority has been delegated in writing to another specific fiduciary(s).
- If assets do not have a readily determinable or ascertainable value, the fiduciary must annually have an independent appraisal to determine market value.
- A fiduciary may not engage (directly or indirectly) in the following activities between the fiduciary and the plan:
  - Sale, exchange or lease of property
  - Lending money or extending credit
  - Furnishing goods, services or facilities
  - The transfer of assets to or for the use of the fiduciary
  - Dealing with the plan assets for his or her own account
  - Receiving any payment from a party dealing with a transaction involving plan assets

CPA Audit Requirements

Plans with 100 or more participants at the beginning of the year must obtain an audit by a CPA for that plan year. There is one exception. If the plan in the prior year had less than 100 participants at the beginning of that year, and the current plan year has 120 or fewer participants at the beginning of the year, the CPA audit will not be required.

In addition, for plan years beginning on or after April 12, 2001, a CPA audit must be obtained regardless of the number of participants in the plan. If the plan meets either of the two following exceptions a CPA audit will not be required:

1. At least 95% of the plan assets as of the end of the prior plan year are "Qualifying Assets." Qualifying Assets are assets held by banks, insurance companies, broker dealers, mutual funds, or for an individually directed account plan, the participant may direct the investment of these assets and receive statements at least annually.

   In addition, the Summary Annual Report given to each must identify the financial institution holding those assets. If there is a bond for non-qualifying assets exceeding 5% of the plan assets, the surety company must be identified. Lastly, the participant must be notified that he or she may examine the bond or the financial reports issued by the qualifying institutions.

2. The plan may obtain a bond equal to 100% of the value of the non-qualifying assets as of the end of the prior plan year

It should be stressed that the plan must obtain both bonds if there are non-qualifying assets and the plan does not want to have a full CPA audit.

Failure to satisfy the CPA audit requirement or one of the exceptions for smaller plans means that the annual return is an incomplete filing resulting in penalties for non filing.

Prohibited Transactions Rules

Certain transactions between the plan and a disqualified person are prohibited.

Prohibited Transactions

- Sale, exchange or lease of property
- Lending money or extending credit
- Furnishing goods, services or facilities
- The transfer of assets to or for the use of

Additional Prohibitions

- A fiduciary is prohibited from dealing with plan assets for his or her own account.
- A fiduciary may not receive any payment from a party dealing with a transaction involving plan assets.

Penalties for Engaging in a Prohibited Transaction

There is a basic penalty leveled against the party engaging in the transaction equal to 15% of the value of the transaction. In the case of buying property, this would be the sale price. In the case of a loan, the value of the transaction is the interest charged for the first year.

Once made, the prohibited transaction is deemed to be a continuing one until corrected by undoing it; or a deficiency notice is delivered; or the penalty tax itself is levied. For example, if the prohibited transaction occurred in December of year one, in January of year two, it is deemed to occur again.

Not only is the 15% penalty levied again in year two but also there is a pyramiding that occurs when the prohibited transaction is not corrected. In year two, there is a 15% tax levied on the prohibited transaction that occurred in year one and that continued in year two. There is also a 15% penalty assessed for the same transaction in year two. Hence, the total penalty for the two years is 15% for the initial year plus another 30% for year two for a total of 45%.

If the prohibited transaction is not reversed by the time the IRS assesses this 15% excise tax, a tax of 100% of the amount involved in the prohibited transaction will be assessed.

Continued...

Prohibited Transactions Rules

Disqualified Persons

1. A plan fiduciary
2. Persons providing services to the plan
3. The employer of plan participants
4. Employee organizations with members in the plan
5. A 50% or more owner of the plan sponsor
6. A spouse, lineal descendant (or spouse) or ancestor of any person described above
7. A partnership, corporation, trust or estate of which 50% or more is owned, directly or indirectly, by a person described in items one through five
8. An officer, director, 10% or more shareholder, employee earning 10% or more of the yearly wages of the employer, or a person described in items three, four, five, and seven
9. A 10% or more partner or joint venturer of a person described in items three, four, five, and seven (IRC Section 4975(e)(2))

Exemptions

There are two types of exemptions.

- **Statutory:** IRC Section 4975(d), ERISA Secs. 407 and 408
- **Administrative:** This type is granted by the Department of Labor (DOL) either for individual transactions or on a class basis for repetitive or identical transactions. The DOL will not grant an exemption for an act that has already occurred. DOL exemptions are prospective only.

Qualified Plan Participant Loans

Most transactions between a qualified plan and its participants are prohibited transactions. One exception to the prohibited transaction rules concerns the granting of a loan to a plan participant.

Rules for Plan Loans

In order for the exception to apply, certain rules must be followed.

- The maximum loan must not exceed the lesser of 50% of the vested benefit of the participant or $50,000. The largest outstanding balance of any participant loan outstanding during the prior 12 months further reduces this amount.

- The loan must be fully amortized over a period not to exceed five years. In addition, the repayment must be on at least a quarterly basis. More commonly this will be done on a monthly or semi-monthly basis through payroll deduction.[1]

- The loan must bear a reasonable rate of interest. While the government does not give a specific guideline as to what is reasonable, a rule of thumb that has served through the years and has stood the test of time is that reasonable is prime plus 1% or 2%. The plan could also check with local banks for their rates on secured loans.

- If the participant borrowing from the plan is married, then that participant's spouse must also consent to the loan, if the plan or law so requires.

- If the loan is renegotiated during its term, it is considered a new loan. This will often cause additional problems with either the $50,000 maximum limit or the five year repayment period requirement.

- The plan must have a loan policy and qualification process for granting loans, including a reasonable effort to determine credit worthiness.

If these rules are not followed, then the participant loan falls outside of the exception and serious results can occur. The outstanding principal and any unpaid interest will be a deemed distribution[2] to the borrower and taxable as ordinary income to that participant in the year during which one or more of the rules are broken. It is entirely possible that the IRS could seek to disqualify the plan in an egregious situation. If this were to occur, the vested benefits of all participants could be immediately taxable to them.

---

[1] If the participant goes on active military duty, the loan repayments are suspended.
[2] While interest will continue to accrue on the defaulted loan, it will not create additional deemed income.

Unrelated Business Taxable Income
UBTI

Under the provisions of IRC Sec. 501(a), a qualified plan trust is treated as a tax-exempt organization. Income and gain from investments held in the trust are not currently taxed.

If, however, the trust operates a trade or business that is not substantially related to the trust's tax-exempt function (funding qualified plan benefits), any income or gain from this activity will be subject to current income taxation.[1] In other words, the trust may not operate an ongoing business, without the income received from the business being taxed to the trust each year.

However, the plan may deduct expenses against income in the year of occurrence. The plan is also entitled to a $1,000 exemption against income. If realized losses and expenses exceed income during the year, these may not be carried forward to future years.

IRC Sec. 514 provides that income earned through the use of debt financing by a tax-exempt organization is taxed currently as unrelated business taxable income (UBTI).

A common transaction that violates this rule is the purchase of securities on margin, using borrowed money. Borrowing the cash value from a life insurance policy to make an investment is another common violation. However, using the cash value to pay premiums on that policy is not a prohibited transaction.

Certain types of real estate transactions are exempt even though a property produces what would normally be considered unrelated business income. However, strict rules[2] must be followed to avoid having the income taxed as UBTI. These rules include:

- At the time of purchase, the sale price must be fixed.

- The timing of the repayment of the debt, or the amount of the debt itself, cannot be pegged to the income derived from the property or the profits arising from the property.

- The real estate cannot be purchased from a disqualified person[3] unless the seller is a fiduciary or provider of services. Furthermore, if such seller provides financing (owner financing), it must be on commercially-reasonable terms.

- Some sale/leaseback arrangements will trigger UBTI taxes. A sale/leaseback is permitted to an unrelated[4] party. If the seller is a related[4] party, then the amount of the leaseback may not exceed 25% of the rentable space in the building or complex. The lease must be on commercially reasonable terms.

---

[1] See IRC Secs. 511-513.
[2] See IRC Sec. 514(c)(9).
[3] See IRC Sec. 4975(e)(2).
[4] See IRC Sec. 267(b).

Continued.

Unrelated Business Taxable Income
UBTI

Calculating UBTI – An Example

After a $1,000 exemption, the income and gain are subject to income tax in the same ratio as the borrowing is to the total value of the asset.

Assume a qualified plan trust buys $100,000 of stock in High Flyer, Inc. To fund the purchase, half of the price, $50,000, is borrowed from the brokerage firm (on margin), with the remaining $50,000 coming from plan funds. The stock is held for two years, and is then sold for a total of $130,000.

The amount of UBTI is calculated as follows.

Value of stock when sold	$130,000
Purchase price	-$100,000
Gross profit	**$30,000**
Interest expense in year of sale	-$5,000
Net taxable income	**$25,000**
Percent of total value financed	50%
Amount subject to current tax	$12,500
Exemption	-$1,000
Net amount subject to income tax[1]	**$11,500**

---

[1] Capital gains are not relevant to the example.

Retirement Plan Distributions Before Age 59½

IRC Sec. 72(t)

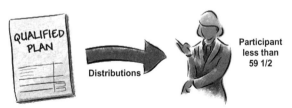

Distributions from qualified plans, 403(b) plans, SEPs, SIMPLE plans, and all IRAs may be subject to a 10% penalty tax if made before the participant reaches age 59½. The penalty tax is waived if the distribution is rolled over to an eligible recipient plan or if the participant is totally disabled or dies.[1] Since premature withdrawals are generally also subject to ordinary income tax, the extra 10% penalty could make the total tax very high.[2]

Possible Exceptions

There are several possible exceptions to this 10% penalty tax rule.

- For qualified employer plans, 403(b) plans, SIMPLE 401(k) plans, and distributions to participants who have separated from employment after age 55.

- When distributions are for deductible medical expenses, or pursuant to a qualified domestic relations order (QDROs), e.g., a divorce decree.[3]

- In certain situations, premature distributions from IRAs to pay health insurance premiums for unemployed individuals may also avoid the penalty tax.

- The Pension Protection Act of 2006 added two new exceptions to the 10% penalty tax:

  - Qualified reservists: Withdrawals from an IRA or qualified plan by military reservists called to active duty for more than 179 days, or indefinitely, between September 11, 2001 and December 31, 2007. Such withdrawals are subject to ordinary income tax and may be repaid within two years of the end of active duty.

  - Public safety officials: The 10% penalty does not apply to distributions from a qualified governmental defined benefit plan to a qualified public safety employee who separates from service (e.g. retires) after age 50.

- For IRAs there are two additional exceptions.

  - If the distribution is used to pay for qualified higher education expenses of the individual, spouse, child, or grandchild, then the 10% penalty tax is not assessed.

  - For a first-time homebuyer, there is a lifetime exemption of $10,000 from the 10% penalty tax. A first-time homebuyer is someone, or his or her spouse, who had no ownership in a principal residence in the two years prior to buying the new home.

---

[1] Distributions before age 59½ from SIMPLE IRA plans made within the first two years of participation are subject to a 25% penalty, rather than a 10% penalty, subject to the exceptions discussed above. If a premature distribution from a SIMPLE IRA is made after two years of participation, the 10% penalty applies, subject to the exceptions.

[2] The discussion here concerns federal income tax law. State or local income tax law may differ.

[3] The exception for QDROs does not apply to IRAs.

Continued

Retirement Plan Distributions Before Age 59½

IRC Sec. 72(t)

Health Savings Account (HSA) Funding Distributions From IRAs

The Tax Relief and Health Care Act of 2006 (TRHCA 2006) added a new provision to federal law allowing for tax-free transfers of certain amounts from traditional and Roth IRAs directly to HSAs. Because these distributions are excluded from income, by definition they avoid any 10% early withdrawal penalty that might otherwise apply under IRC Sec. 72(t).

Substantially-Equal Periodic Payments – IRC Sec. 72(t)(2)(A)(iv)

The substantially-equal periodic payments exception is available to any qualified plan, SEP, SIMPLE, 403(b) TSA plan, or IRA participant. This exception applies when the distribution is part of a scheduled series of substantially-equal periodic payments, made at least once a year, over the life (or life expectancy) of the participant, or the joint lives (or joint life expectancies) of the participant and a beneficiary. If the series of payments is subsequently modified (except because of death or disability) within a 5 year period, or, if later, age 59½, the 10% penalty tax will be re-applied and interest will be charged.

Calculating the Substantially-Equal Periodic Payment

In Notice 89-25, 11989-1, CB 662, Q&A-12 (March 20, 1989), the IRS listed three acceptable methods of calculating such a distribution.

- **Required minimum distribution:** The annual payment is determined using a method acceptable for calculating the required minimum distribution required under IRC Sec. 401(a)(9). In general, the account balance is divided by a life expectancy factor, resulting in a payment which fluctuates from year to year.

- **Fixed amortization method:** Payment under this method would be similar to the annual amount required to pay off a loan (equal to the amount in the plan at the start of distributions), at a reasonable interest rate, over the remainder of one's life. The dollar amount of the payment remains the same in each subsequent year.

- **Fixed annuitization:** An annuity factor is determined from a reasonable mortality table at an interest rate which is then reasonable for the age of the recipient of the distribution. The payment is determined for the first distribution and remains the same in each subsequent year.

Continued...

Retirement Plan Distributions Before Age 59½

IRC Sec. 72(t)

Revenue Ruling 2002-62

On October 3, 2002, the IRS released Revenue Ruling 2002-62, to address questions raised by taxpayers who had begun to receive distributions under IRC Sec. 72(t) and who had been adversely affected by the declining stock market. This ruling contained the following key points.

- It expanded the guidance given in Q&A 12 of IRS Notice 89-25 to, among other things, incorporate into the calculation process the new life expectancy tables issued in April, 2002, with regard to required minimum distributions from IRAs and qualified plans.

- Specified that if a participant who is using an acceptable method to calculate the required substantially-equal periodic payments exhausts the assets in an account prior to the required time period, the "cessation of payments will not be treated as a modification of the series of payments."

- Allows a participant who is using either of the fixed dollar amount methods (fixed amortization or fixed annuitization) to make a one-time change to the required minimum distribution method.

The guidance provided in Revenue Ruling 2002-62 replaces the guidance in Q&A 12 of IRS Notice 89-25 for any series of payments beginning on or after January 1, 2003, and may be used for distributions beginning in 2002. If distributions began before 2003 under any method that satisfied IRC Sec. 72(t)(2)(A)(iv), the participant may change to the required minimum distribution calculation method at any time.

Comparing the Three Methods[1]

Assumptions:
Plan or IRA account balance on 12/31 of the previous year: $400,000
Age of participant in distribution year: 50
Single life expectancy at age 50: 34.2[2]
Interest rate assumed: 4.5%
Distribution period: Single life only

- **Required minimum distribution method:** For the current year, the annual distribution amount is calculated by dividing account balance by the participant's life expectancy.

$$\$400,000 \, / \, 34.2 = \$11,695.51$$

- **Fixed amortization method:** Distribution amount is calculated by amortizing the account balance over the number of years of the participant's single life expectancy. The calculation is the same as in determining the payment required to pay off a loan.

$$\$400,000 \times (.045 \, / \, (1 - (1 + .045)^{\wedge -34.2})) = \$23,134.27$$

---

[1] The examples shown here were taken from the IRS web site, www.irs.gov, "FAQs regarding Revenue Ruling 2002-62," 12/27/02.
[2] Derived from the Single Life Table found in Q&A-1 of Reg. 1.401(a)(9)-9.

Continued

Retirement Plan Distributions Before Age 59½
IRC Sec. 72(t)

- **Fixed annuitization method:** The distribution amount is equal to the account balance divided by an annuity factor that for the present value of an annuity of one dollar per year paid over the life of a 50-year-old participant. Such annuity factors are typically calculated by an actuary. In this case, the age-50 annuity factor (17.462) is based on the mortality table in Appendix B of Rev. Rul. 2002-62 and an interest rate of 4.5%.

$400,000 / 17.462 = $22,906.88

Method	Annual Withdrawal
Required minimum distribution	$11,695.51
Fixed amortization	$23,134.27
Fixed annuitization	$22,906.88

Lump-Sum Distributions Before Age 59½

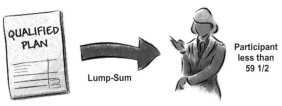

Qualified Plan Funds when Leaving an Employer

When terminating or changing employment prior to age 59½, a person often has several options as to what to do with the funds in his or her qualified retirement plan. He or she may choose from the following possible actions:

- **Leave funds in current plan:** If the current value exceeds $5,000, there may be some benefit to leaving the funds where they are. They will continue to grow tax-deferred and can be transferred at a later date to a rollover IRA or a new employer's eligible recipient plan.

- **Take cash in lump sum:** This option will require the entire amount (less participant after-tax contributions, if any) to be subject to income taxes in the participant's current tax bracket. There will be an additional 10% penalty tax for a participant under age 59½ unless he or she falls under certain exceptions.[1] The law requires that 20% of the taxable portion of the distribution be withheld for Federal Income Taxes.[2]

- **Rollover or transfer within 60 days:** Individuals who receive a cash, lump-sum distribution have a 60-day period during which funds may be transferred to either a rollover IRA or a new employer's qualified plan. Because this is a cash distribution, a 20% federal income tax withholding is required. Failure to transfer the funds within the 60-day period will result in the total amount (cash received plus the amount withheld) being added to taxable income for the year. Further, if an individual is under age 59½ at the time of distribution, the total amount will be subject to the 10% penalty tax on early distributions, unless an exception applies.[1]

- **Make a direct transfer:** The distribution can be transferred directly from the original, employer-sponsored qualified plan to another employer plan or to a rollover IRA. Since the participant does not actually receive the funds, there is no 20% withholding.

Potential Problem

However, if the plan withholds 20% for federal income taxes, which cannot be returned until after the tax returns for that year are filed, the participant may have to come up with additional funds to make a full rollover

---

[1] Distributions before age 59½ from SIMPLE IRA plans made within the first two years of participation are subject to a 25% penalty, rather than a 10% penalty subject to the usual exceptions. If a premature distribution from a SIMPLE IRA is made after two years of participation, the 10% penalty applies. See IRC Sec. 72(t)(6). SIMPLE IRAs are not subject to the 20% mandatory withholding requirement.

[2] State law may differ.

Continued..

Lump-Sum Distributions Before Age 59½

For example, assume a distribution of $100,000 made directly to a terminating employee. The employer would withhold 20%, or $20,000, for income tax purposes and the employee would receive only $80,000 in cash. If the employee decides within the 60-day period to roll the fund over into an IRA or a new employer's qualified plan, then he or she must come up with another $20,000 to make the full transfer.

If the funds are not found to make the full $100,000 transfer, then the $20,000 withheld becomes taxable to the employee as ordinary income. If the employee is under age 59½ when the distribution is made, a 10% penalty tax may also be due, unless certain exceptions apply.

Possible Solutions

To avoid this potential problem, the participant must make some decisions before the plan administrator prepares the check. If the transfer is made directly to a rollover IRA or a new qualified plan, the 20% is not withheld and the entire amount can be transferred.

An alternative might be for the participant to transfer the funds to a rollover IRA, and then elect to receive substantially-equal payments over his or her life expectancy and that of another person, if desired.

IRA Rollover of Qualified Plan Values
vs. Lump-Sum Tax Treatment

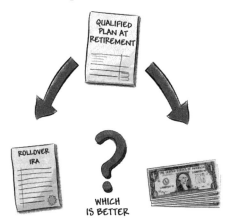

At the time of retirement, many persons are faced with the decision of whether to take a lump sum distribution from their qualified plan and pay the income tax or roll the funds into an IRA[1] and pay the tax only as funds are withdrawn.

Consideration	Rollover IRA	Lump-Sum Distribution from Qualified Plan[2]
Generally	Lump sum[3] distributions from qualified plans may be transferred to an individual retirement arrangement called a rollover IRA. To avoid the mandatory 20% federal income tax withholding rule, the payment must be made directly to the rollover IRA.	The taxpayer may choose to take all of a qualified retirement plan distribution outright and pay the tax.[4] IRC Sec. 402(d). There will be a mandatory 20% federal income tax withholding. Some states may also require income tax withholding.
Taxation at distribution	No tax is due at the time of the transfer to the IRA, but later distributions are taxed as ordinary income. The IRA must begin distribution by April 1 following the year in which the individual attains age 70½. Taxpayers over age 65 may also qualify for the credit for the elderly, as well as the higher standard deduction.	Taxpayers age 50 or more on 1/1/86 will have a choice at retirement age to: (1) Pay tax at capital gains rates (up to 20%) on pre-1974 portion and at ordinary income rates for the post-1973 portion, or (2) Elect 10-year averaging for the post-1973 portion or the entire amount (at 1986 rates).

---

[1] The comments in this report refer to a traditional IRA and not the Roth IRA. Beginning in 2008, distributions from qualified retirement plans, IRC Sec. 457 plans, and tax-sheltered annuities may be rolled directly into a Roth IRA. These rollover distributions will be taxable events, subject to the same requirements as a Roth conversion.

[2] Individuals must be at least age 59½ to avoid the 10% penalty for early withdrawals, subject to certain exceptions.

[3] There are special requirements for lump-sum distributions.

[4] If a lump-sum distribution from a qualified plan includes appreciated employer securities, the tax on the net unrealized appreciation may be deferred until the securities are disposed of in a taxable transaction. See IRC Sec. 402(e)(4)(B).

IRA Rollover as a Qualified Plan Conduit

When an employee leaves a job or a qualified plan is terminated, a special IRA – called a rollover or conduit - can be used to hold a qualified plan distribution until it is either transferred into a new qualified retirement plan or is later distributed to the employee.[1] Tax-sheltered annuity and IRC Sec. 457 plan distributions may also be transferred to an IRA rollover.

If the distribution is transferred to an IRA rollover[2] (or another qualified plan) in a direct rollover, no income tax is withheld and the employee avoids current income tax on the distribution.

If the distribution is first paid to the employee before being rolled over (it must be rolled over within 60 days) the plan administrator will withhold 20% of the distribution. In order to roll over the entire distribution and avoid current taxation (and a possible 10% penalty tax on the 20% of the distribution that was withheld), the employee will have to make up the 20% withholding from his or her separate funds.

Distributions from a traditional IRA, Roth IRA or SIMPLE IRA are not subject to the mandatory 20% tax withholding. However, if the distribution is not rolled to a plan of the same kind within 60 days, the entire distribution is generally taxable.[3]

Two Options

A qualified plan participant has two options when leaving a job.

- Participant may retain funds in an IRA[2] until age 70½ and then begin distributions.

- Participant may roll the funds over from the conduit IRA into another qualified plan (if permitted). This will requalify the funds for 10-year[4] averaging as long as no regular IRA contributions have been made to the conduit IRA.

Other Considerations

- Partial distributions can also qualify as eligible rollover distributions and can be tax deferred.

- Both deductible and nondeductible employee contributions may be rolled to the IRA.

---

[1] Based on federal law. State or local law may differ.
[2] The IRA referred to here is a traditional IRA, not a Roth IRA. Beginning in 2008, distributions from qualified retirement plans, IRC Sec. 457 plans, and tax-sheltered annuities may be rolled directly into a Roth IRA. These rollover distributions will be taxable events, subject to the same requirements as a Roth conversion.
[3] If a SIMPLE IRA is rolled to any other type of IRA within two years of the SIMPLE IRA being established, a 25% penalty tax is assessed.
[4] Those born before 1936 may be able to elect 10-year income averaging or capital gain treatment; these strategies are not available to those born after 1935.

Continued...

IRA Rollover as a Qualified Plan Conduit

- Noncash assets which are distributed can be sold and the cash proceeds transferred to the rollover IRA without realizing a current tax on any gain.

- Amounts received but not rolled over are generally included in taxable income in the year received and are subject to a 10% penalty tax if the employee is under age 59½. An exception to this 10% penalty applies if a distribution is made as substantially-equal periodic payments over the life or life expectancy of the IRA owner, or the joint lives or life expectancies of the IRA owner and a designated beneficiary.[1] The penalty tax is also not imposed in the event of death or disability. Amounts withheld and remitted as tax withholding are considered to be amounts received.

- The IRA conduit rollover should be distinguished from a direct transfer. In a direct transfer, the funds are transferred directly from one plan to another without going through a conduit rollover or being distributed to the participant.

- Federal bankruptcy law provides significant protection from creditors to participant accounts or accrued benefits in tax-exempt retirement plans. Generally, assets in IRA accounts are protected for amounts up to $1,000,000. In future years, this $1,000,000 limit will be indexed for inflation. However, funds rolled over from qualified plans are protected without limit.

---

[1] The 10% penalty is triggered retroactively if this periodic distribution schedule is modified within five years, or attainment of age 59½, if later.

IRA Rollover as a Qualified Plan Conduit

Funds can be transferred directly among all types of plans if the receiving plan permits such a transfer. If not, then a conduit IRA may be utilized.

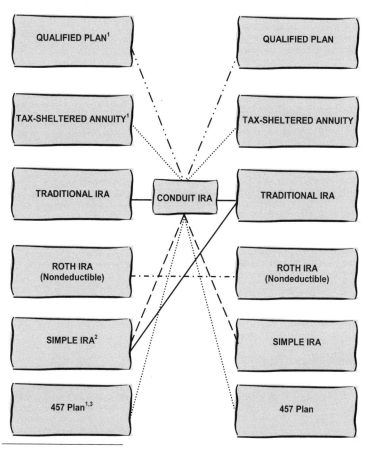

[1] In 2008, distributions from qualified retirement plans, IRC Sec. 457 plans, and tax-sheltered annuities may be rolled directly into a Roth IRA. These rollovers will be taxable events, with the same requirements as for a Roth conversion.

[2] If a SIMPLE IRA is rolled to any kind of IRA within two years of the SIMPLE IRA being established, there is a 25% penalty tax assessed on such a transfer. A direct transfer to another SIMPLE IRA during that period is not subject to the penalty.

[3] Rollovers to other plans are permitted from governmental 457(b) plans, but not from non-governmental 457(b) plans or from 457(f) plans. See IRC Sec. 457(e)(16).

Mandatory Withholding for Plan Distributions

Administrators of qualified plans making distributions which are eligible to be rolled over are required to give a written explanation to participants who are about to receive a plan distribution. This notice must be given at least 30 days (7 days for some plans) and not more than 180 days before the distribution.

This explanation[1] should cover the following.

- Special tax treatment for lump sum distributions, e.g., 10-year[2] averaging (not available for IRAs or TSAs).

- Potential tax penalties for distributions prior to age 59½.

- If the plan is a pension or profit sharing plan subject to the joint-and-survivor rules, an explanation of these rules must also be provided along with various waiver forms. This material allows a participant and spouse the option to elect out of the joint and survivor annuity requirement, if they so desire.

- Regular rollover rules: If the plan distribution is made directly to the participant, he or she has a 60-day period to roll the funds into an IRA[3] to defer the tax. However, the plan administrator is required to withhold 20% of the plan distribution made to individuals, even if the distribution is rolled into an IRA within the 60-day period. The amount withheld is sent to the IRS as an estimated income tax payment.

Potential Problem

Assume a hypothetical distribution of $100,000 from a qualified plan to the participant. The administrator is required to withhold 20% (or $20,000) of the distribution. If the participant takes the remaining $80,000 and rolls it into an IRA, he or she will be taxed on the $20,000 which was sent to the IRS because it is considered to be a taxable distribution. There may also be a penalty tax of 10% on the $20,000 if the recipient is less than age 59½, unless certain exceptions apply. To avoid this problem, the distributee could borrow $20,000 and thereby place the full $100,000 into the rollover IRA. The next year, the IRS would generally refund the $20,000 withheld and the loan could then be repaid.

Direct Rollover Option

To avoid the potential problem illustrated above, the administrator must notify plan distributees of the direct rollover option. The participant can elect to have the distribution made directly to the new IRA or a new qualified plan. This defers the tax and avoids the withholding rule.

---

[1] The IRS has issued sample text for this required explanation. See Notice 2002-3, IRB 2002-2, 289.
[2] Those born before 1936 may be able to elect either 10-year averaging or capital gain treatment.
[3] The comments in this report refer to a traditional IRA and not the Roth IRA. Beginning in 2008, distributions from qualified retirement plans, IRC Sec. 457 plans, and tax-sheltered annuities may be rolled directly into a Roth IRA. These rollover distributions will be taxable events, subject to the same requirements as a Roth conversion.

Net Unrealized Appreciation

Assets distributed from an employer's qualified retirement plan are often transferred directly to a rollover IRA to avoid being currently taxed. However, if the distribution includes employer securities, such as employer stock, automatically moving the employer securities into a rollover IRA is not always the wise thing to do.

If certain requirements are met, federal income tax law provides preferential treatment to such distributions of employer securities. In effect, this special tax treatment transforms ordinary income into long-term capital gain income. For the right person, this can result in significant income tax savings.[1] Because issues other than income taxes may also be important, a careful analysis is required before deciding to transfer employer securities to a rollover IRA, move them to a taxable securities account, or some mix of the two.

What Is Net Unrealized Appreciation (NUA)?

For income tax purposes, each share of employer stock you receive has two parts:

Part	Description
Appreciation	The value per share when distributed, minus the cost basis.
Cost Basis	How much was paid to purchase the share.

Until the shares are sold, the value represented by the appreciation is "unrealized."

How Is NUA Taxed Under Federal Income Tax Law?

Federal income tax treatment of employer securities, once distributed from the plan, depends on whether they are moved into a taxable securities account or a rollover IRA:

- **Taxable securities account:** The cost basis is taxable in the year of distribution as ordinary income, subject to marginal tax rates of up to 35.0%. Income tax on the appreciation is deferred until the securities are sold, when it is taxable as long-term capital gain. Currently, this type of long-term capital gain is subject to a maximum marginal tax rate of 15%. Any appreciation occurring after the securities are distributed is taxable as capital gain, either short-term or long-term, depending on how long they are held after being distributed.[2] If a distribution of employer securities is subject to the 10% penalty for early withdrawal, the 10% penalty applies only to the cost basis and not to the appreciation.

- **Rollover IRA:** Income tax on the cost basis, the appreciation, and any subsequent appreciation, is deferred until the securities are sold and the proceeds are distributed from the rollover IRA. Once distributed, all funds are taxable as ordinary income, at marginal tax rates of up to 35.0%.

---

[1] The discussion here concerns federal income tax law. State or local income tax law may vary widely.
[2] For federal income tax purposes, "long-term" is defined as holding an asset for more than 12 months. Short-term capital gain is taxed in the same manner as ordinary income.

Net Unrealized Appreciation

A Hypothetical Example

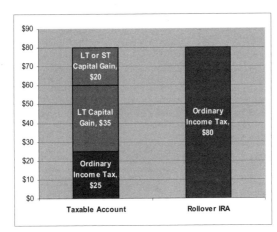

In this hypothetical example, stock was purchased at $25 a share inside the plan. At distribution, the stock had risen in value to $60 per share, giving rise to $35 of net unrealized appreciation. After distribution, the stock is held for a period of time before being sold. When finally sold, the share value had increased to $80 per share.

Lump-Sum Distribution Requirement

In order for NUA tax treatment to apply, a distribution from an employer's qualified plan must be a "lump-sum" distribution. A distribution is considered to be a lump-sum distribution if it is a distribution or payment within one taxable year of the recipient of the total balance to the credit of an employee and which becomes payable because of:

- The employee's death, or
- After the employee reaches age 59½, or
- Because the employee separates from service, or
- After the employee becomes disabled.

Without A Lump-Sum Distribution

If a distribution of employer securities is not part of a lump-sum distribution, NUA tax treatment applies only to appreciation attributable to <u>nondeductible employee contributions</u>, if any. If there are no nondeductible employee contributions, both the cost basis and the appreciation are taxable as ordinary income in the year of distribution.[1]

---

[1] Individuals who were born before January 1, 1936, may be eligible to use either 10-year forward averaging, at 1986 rates, or to pay the tax on any pre-1974 portion at capital gains rates of up to 20%.

Continued...

Net Unrealized Appreciation

Estate Planning and NUA

Some individuals may simply want to keep any employer securities and pass them on to their children or other heirs, rather than using them to generate retirement income. If the securities are distributed from the qualified plan into a taxable securities account, the income tax due on the cost basis is paid in the year the securities are distributed. Later, the heirs who ultimately receive the securities will be responsible for paying the income tax due on the NUA that occurred while the securities were inside the qualified plan.

However, any appreciation that occurs _after_ the securities are distributed from the employer plan will generally receive a stepped-up cost basis at death and will pass to the heirs free of federal income or capital gains taxes. Note that under current federal law, for one year, 2010, "carry-over" basis will generally replace "stepped-up" basis.

Issues To Consider

- **Income tax impact:** You, or your tax advisor, must "crunch the numbers" and calculate the potential income and/or estate tax impact of moving any qualified plan distribution into either a taxable account or a rollover IRA.
- **Future legislative changes:** Much of the benefit of the federal income tax treatment of NUA is due to the fact that the marginal tax rates currently levied on capital gains are lower than in the past. Under existing law, however, this relatively benign tax treatment is scheduled to end after 2010, when prior law will be reinstated. There are similar uncertainties with regard to the federal estate tax.
- **Need for portfolio diversification:** Is a large part of your retirement assets concentrated in employer stock? Perhaps a portion of the distribution should be transferred to a rollover IRA, with the remainder distributed to a taxable account. The employer securities inside the rollover IRA could then be sold, with no current tax impact, and the proceeds re-invested in a more diversified portfolio.
- **Time until needed:** Those individuals with a longer period of time before retirement begins will likely benefit more from the NUA approach as any employer securities will have a longer period of time for post-distribution gain.
- **Gifts to individuals:** An individual can gift up to $12,000[1] per year per person to any number of people, without incurring a gift tax. A gift of NUA securities within these limits has no immediate tax consequences to either the donor or the recipient. The gift transfers the donor's basis in the securities to the recipient and removes both the current value, and any future growth, from the donor's estate.
- **Charitable planning:** Highly appreciated employer stock may be a useful asset to contribute to a charitable trust.

Seek Professional Guidance

Because of the complexities involved, the advice and counsel of tax and financial professionals is highly recommended.

---

[1] The annual gift tax exclusion ($12,000 in 2008) is indexed for inflation in increments of $1,000.

Taxes on Qualified Plan Distributions at Death

Distributions from qualified plans at a participant's death are subject to federal estate taxation[1]. Also, the person receiving the distribution will incur additional income tax, subject to a deduction for the estate tax paid. The amount of the income tax will vary depending on whether the funds are taken in a lump sum or as an annuity.

Assume a Distribution of $100,000 at Time of Death[2]

Estate Size Including the Distribution	Federal Estate Tax after Applicable Credit	Portion of FET Attributed to Plan Distrib.	Distributed Amount Subject to Income Tax	Income Tax on the Balance		Lump-Sum Distribution with 10-year Averaging
				Paid as an Annuity at Beneficiary's Income Tax Bracket		
				25%	35%	
$2,000,000	$0	$0	$100,000	$25,000	$35,000	$14,470
3,000,000	450,000	45,000	55,000	13,750	19,250	7,220
4,000,000	900,000	45,000	55,000	13,750	19,250	7,220
5,000,000	1,350,000	45,000	55,000	13,750	19,250	7,220
6,000,000	1,800,000	45,000	55,000	13,750	19,250	7,220
7,000,000	2,250,000	45,000	55,000	13,750	19,250	7,220

Assume a Distribution of $500,000 at Time of Death[2]

Estate Size Including the Distribution	Federal Estate Tax after Applicable Credit	Portion of FET Attributed to Plan Distrib.	Distributed Amount Subject to Income Tax	Income Tax on the Balance		Lump-Sum Distribution with 10-year Averaging
				Paid as an Annuity at Beneficiary's Income Tax Bracket		
				25%	35%	
$2,000,000	$0	$0	$500,000	$125,000	$175,000	$143,680
3,000,000	450,000	225,000	275,000	68,750	96,250	58,270
4,000,000	900,000	225,000	275,000	68,750	96,250	58,270
5,000,000	1,350,000	225,000	275,000	68,750	96,250	58,270
6,000,000	1,800,000	225,000	275,000	68,750	96,250	58,270
7,000,000	2,250,000	225,000	275,000	68,750	96,250	58,270

Note: The 10-year averaging calculations must be based on 1986 single person rates and are available only to persons born before 1936. The 25% or 35% brackets used to illustrate the annuity method are presumed to remain the same throughout the period over which the annuity payments are received. State taxes are not considered here.

---

[1] Under the Tax Act of 2001, the federal estate tax is gradually phased out until its final repeal in the year 2010. If Congress does not act at that time to repeal it for the years following, it will automatically revert back to the rates in effect during the year 2001, with an exemption for the first $1,000,000 of assets.

[2] Assumes death occurs during 2008.

Taxes on Qualified Plan Distributions at Death

$100,000 Distribution from a $3,000,000 Estate[1]

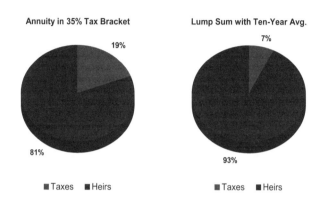

Annuity in 35% Tax Bracket

19%

81%

■ Taxes ■ Heirs

Lump Sum with Ten-Year Avg.

7%

93%

■ Taxes ■ Heirs

$500,000 Distribution from a $3,000,000 Estate[1]

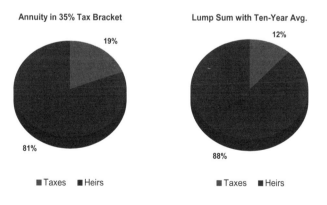

Annuity in 35% Tax Bracket

19%

81%

■ Taxes ■ Heirs

Lump Sum with Ten-Year Avg.

12%

88%

■ Taxes ■ Heirs

---

[1] Assumes death occurs in 2008.

541

Required Minimum Distributions
Lifetime Distributions from Traditional IRAs and Qualified Retirement Plans

Both traditional IRAs[1] and qualified retirement plans enjoy significant federal tax benefits.[2] Contributions are generally tax deductible and growth inside an account is tax-deferred. Federal law requires that certain amounts be paid out, generally beginning with the year an account owner turns age 70½. Funds become taxable when distributed.

- **Required minimum distributions:** These are the specified, minimum withdrawals that an account owner must make. The account owner is free to take larger amounts if desired.

- **Required beginning date:** This is the date by which an account owner must begin to make his or her required minimum distributions.

- **Penalty tax:** If an account owner does not make distributions that are large enough, or if distributions are not made at all, a penalty tax of 50% of the amount that should have been distributed is generally due.

Item	Traditional IRA[3]s	Qualified Plans
Required beginning date	By April 1 of the year following the year you attain age 70½.	By April 1 of the year following the later of (a) the year you reach age 70½, or (b) the year you retire. More than 5% owners must begin to receive distributions by April 1 of the year following the year they reach age 70½.
Initial distributions	If a required first withdrawal for 2008 is made by April 1, 2009, the required distribution for 2009 must be made by December 31, 2009. In effect there are two taxable distributions made in 2009. Each year thereafter, a distribution is required on or before December 31.	
More than one IRA or qualified retirement plan	If an individual has more than one IRA, the required minimum distribution must be determined for each IRA. However, the total required distribution may be made from any one or a combination of the IRAs. The IRAs may not be aggregated with employer-sponsored qualified retirement plans.	Generally, each plan must make its own separate required minimum distribution
Other	The minimum distribution rules do not apply to Roth IRAs during the owner's lifetime.	Qualified plans include TSA 403(b), Keogh, 401(k), SIMPLE 401(k), and pension and profit sharing plans.

---

[1] For required minimum distribution purposes "Traditional IRAs" include Simple IRAs and SEP IRAs
[2] This discussion concerns federal law only. State or local law may vary.
[3] The rules described here are for annual account withdrawals made from either an Individual Retirement Account or Individual Retirement Annuity. RMDs for *annuity* payments from Individual Retirement Annuities are subject to special rules. See Treasury Decision 9130, 6/15/04.

Continued

Required Minimum Distributions

Lifetime Distributions from Traditional IRAs and Qualified Retirement Plans

Calculating Required Minimum Distributions[1]

The actual amount that must be distributed each year is determined using:

- The balance in the account as of the previous December 31, and;

- The age of the account owner (and spouse, if married) at the end of the year.

The required minimum distribution is calculated by dividing the account balance by a theoretical life span taken from life expectancy tables provided by the Internal Revenue Service (IRS). The life expectancy table used will vary depending on the age of the account owner and, if married, his or her spouse. An individual's marital status is determined as of January 1 of the calendar year.

Single owner/spouse no more than 10 years younger: An IRA owner, age 75, has $100,000 in an IRA as of December 31of the prior year. The required minimum distribution for the current year would be $4,366.81, ($100,000 divided by 22.9). The divisor of 22.9 is taken from the *Uniform Lifetime Table for an individual age 75. The* calculation is the same for a single individual or a married individual with a spouse no more than 10 years younger than the IRA owner.

Spouse more than 10 Years Younger[2]: If the participant's spouse is more than 10 years younger than the participant, the minimum distribution factor used in calculating the required minimum distribution is found in the Joint and Last Survivor Table.

An IRA owner, age 75, has $100,000 in the IRA as of December 31of the prior year. His wife is age 63. The required minimum distribution would be $4,115.23, $100,000 divided by 24.3, the Joint and Last Survivor Table factor for an owner age 75 and a spouse age 63.

Seek Professional Advice

Given the complex and frequently changing nature of tax law, individuals faced with the need to make required distributions from IRAs or qualified retirement plans should seek the guidance of qualified professionals.

---

[1] The rules reviewed here are those contained in the final regulations issued by the Treasury Department on April 16, 2002, in Treasury Decision 8987.

[2] The spouse must be the sole beneficiary of the account.

The Basics of Required Minimum Distributions
Ensuring that Uncle Sam Gets His Due

The Benefits of Tax-Advantaged Savings

The benefits of retirement accounts such as a traditional IRA or a 401(k) are two-fold:

- Tax-deductible contributions allow individuals to reduce the size of their current tax burden while they are saving for retirement – which effectively lets them save more.

- Tax-deferred growth inside these accounts allows funds to accumulate without concern for an annual tax bill on that growth.

When It's Time to Pay Taxes

All good things must come to an end, however, and the IRS eventually must be paid. The tax benefits of these accounts are provided for one purpose: to help individuals save for retirement. Therefore, once an individual reaches retirement age, the same rules that provided the benefits now dictate that the funds must be used for retirement purposes and the taxes that have been avoided must be paid.

What does this mean? It means that the federal government has created a set of rules that require that a minimum amount of money must be withdrawn (distributed) from these accounts each year, starting at a specific age, known as the "required beginning date" (generally age 70½).

The amount to be distributed is determined by a special calculation that, in essence, takes the total amount in the account and divides it by the number of years the individual is expected to live. When the required minimum distribution amount is received, it is included as taxable income to the individual and Uncle Sam will, finally, get paid. But, one bit of good news is that the amount remaining in the account continues to grow tax deferred.

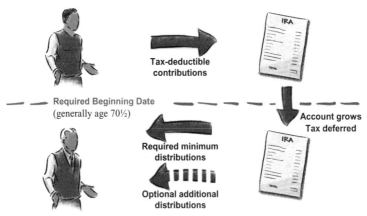

Required Minimum Distributions
Distributions from Traditional IRAs and Qualified Retirement Plans

Both traditional IRAs and qualified retirement plans enjoy significant federal tax benefits. Contributions to these retirement plans are generally tax-deductible and growth inside an account is tax-deferred. Federal law requires that certain amounts, calculated using IRS life expectancy tables, be paid out, with the first distribution generally being required for the year an account owner turns age 70½[1]. Funds become taxable when distributed.

Assumptions:

Calculation year:	2004
Account owner's age at end of calculation year:	54
Estimated rate of return:	6.00%

Life expectancy determined using the IRS Uniform Lifetime Table
Annual contribution: $3,000, increasing at 3.00%, ending at age 74

Account Owner's Age	Life Expectancy	Prior Year Account Balance	Required Minimum Distribution
75	22.9	$ 828,421	$36,176
76	22.0	$ 841,951	$38,270
77	21.2	$ 854,198	$40,292
78	20.3	$ 865,157	$42,619
79	19.5	$ 874,448	$44,843
80	18.7	$ 882,071	$47,170
81	17.9	$ 887,826	$49,599
82	17.1	$ 891,496	$52,134
83	16.3	$ 892,852	$54,776
84	15.5	$ 891,647	$57,526
85	14.8	$ 887,620	$59,974
86	14.1	$ 880,903	$62,475
87	13.4	$ 871,282	$65,021
88	12.7	$ 858,537	$67,601
89	12.0	$ 842,448	$70,204
90	11.4	$ 822,791	$72,175
91	10.8	$ 799,984	$74,073
92	10.2	$ 773,910	$75,874
93	9.6	$ 744,472	$77,549
94	9.1	$ 711,591	$78,197
95	8.6	$ 676,089	$78,615
96	8.1	$ 638,040	$78,770

---

[1] Except for 5% or more owners, participants in qualified plans such as 401(k)s or 403(b)s have the option of beginning required distributions at the later of age 70 ½ or the year they retire.

Required Minimum Distributions
Distributions from Traditional IRAs and Qualified Retirement Plans

Both traditional IRAs and qualified retirement plans enjoy significant federal tax benefits. Contributions to these retirement plans are generally tax-deductible and growth inside an account is tax-deferred. Federal law requires that certain amounts, calculated using IRS life expectancy tables, be paid out, with the first distribution generally being required for the year an account owner turns age 70½[1]. Funds become taxable when distributed.

Assumptions:

Calculation year:	2004
Account owner's age at end of calculation year:	54
Estimated rate of return:	6.00%

Life expectancy determined using the IRS Uniform Lifetime Table
Annual contribution: $3,000, increasing at 3.00%, ending at age 74

First Year's RMD Calculation

Item	Value
Age of Account Owner	75
Life Expectancy	22.9
Prior Year Account Balance	$ 828,421
RMD	$36,176

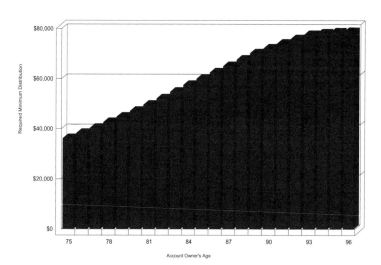

---

[1] Except for 5% or more owners, participants in qualified plans such as 401(k)s or 403(b)s have the option of beginning required distributions at the later of age 70 ½ or the year they retire.

Required Minimum Distributions After Death
Spousal Beneficiary

Funds in both traditional IRAs[1] and qualified retirement plans may not be kept inside these tax-deferred accounts indefinitely. Under federal law the money must eventually be distributed, and then taxed, through yearly "Required Minimum Distributions," or RMDs.[2]

The death of an account owner does not eliminate this requirement. However, the manner in which the assets must be distributed post-death will vary, depending primarily on:

- **Death before or after the required beginning date:** During life, an account owner must generally begin distributions no later than April 1 of the year following the year he or she reaches age 70½. This is known as the "Required Beginning Date," or RBD.[3]

- **Who inherits the assets:** The law mandates different distribution options depending on who inherits the assets in an account.

Surviving Spouse Options

If the surviving spouse is the sole designated beneficiary, or if there is no designated beneficiary, the funds must generally be distributed as shown in the tables below:

Owner Dies *Before* The Required Beginning Date

Situation	Distribution Requirement	Example
Rollover Account to Survivor's Name	The surviving spouse becomes the owner, with RMDs being taken under the normal "during lifetime" rules. No withdrawals are required until the surviving spouse reaches age 70½.	Assume that Kate's husband Jake dies in 2008 at age 67. Kate is age 65. Kate rolls the account over into her own name. Kate will not be required to take a distribution from the account until April 1 of the year after the year she reaches age 70½.
Leave Account in Deceased Spouse's Name – Surviving Spouse is Designated Beneficiary	RMDs for the beneficiary-spouse must begin by the later of: (a) 12/31 of the year the owner would have turned age 70½ had he or she lived, or (b) 12/31 of the year after the year of death. Distributions are made over the survivor's life expectancy.	Assume that Jake dies in 2008 at age 67. Kate is then age 65. Also assume that Jake would have reached age 70½ in 2011. Kate must take her first RMD by 12/31/11. This RMD is calculated by dividing the account balance on 12/31/10 by Kate's life expectancy (from the Single Life Table) for her age in 2011. If Kate turns 68 in 2011, this value is 18.6. For later years, her life expectancy is determined using her attained age in each year.
No Designated Beneficiary, the Owner's Estate, a Charity, or a Non-Qualifying Trust	The entire amount must be distributed by the end of the fifth year after the year the owner dies.	Jake dies on 01/01/08, at age 68, leaving his IRA to his estate. The entire IRA balance must be distributed by 12/31/13.

---

[1] For required minimum distribution purposes, the term "traditional IRA" also includes SIMPLE IRAs and SEP IRAs.
[2] This discussion concerns federal income tax law. State or local law may vary.
[3] The RBD for qualified plan participants is April 1 of the year following the later of (a) the year the participant reaches age 70½, or (b) the year he or she retires. More than 5% owners must begin to receive distributions by April 1 of the year following the year they reach age 70½.

Continued...

Required Minimum Distributions After Death
Spousal Beneficiary

Owner Dies *After* The Required Beginning Date

Situation	Distribution Requirement	Example
Rollover Account to Survivor's Name	A RMD must be made for the deceased owner for the year of death. The surviving spouse then becomes the owner, with RMDs being taken under the normal "during lifetime" rules. No withdrawals are required until the surviving spouse reaches age 70½.	Assume that Kate's husband Jake dies in 2008 at age 72. Kate is age 65. A distribution must be made for Jake for 2008. Since Kate is not more than 10 years younger than Jake, the life expectancy from the Uniform Lifetime Table is used.[1] The RMD is calculated by dividing the account balance on 12/31/07 by 25.6, the distribution period for a 72 year old account owner. After taking Jake's RMD for 2008, Kate can then roll the account into her own name and delay further distributions until April 1 of the year after the year she reaches 70½.
Leave Account in Deceased Spouse's Name – Surviving Spouse is Designated Beneficiary	A RMD must be made for the deceased owner for the year of death. RMDs for the beneficiary-spouse must begin by 12/31 of the year after the year of death, with distributions made over the survivor's life expectancy.	Assume Jake dies in 2008 at age 72. Kate is age 65. A distribution must be made for Jake for 2008, as discussed above. Distributions for Kate must begin by 12/31/09 based on her attained age in 2009. Assuming that Kate will turn 66 in 2009, the RMD for 2009 would be calculated by dividing the account balance on 12/31/08 by Kate's life expectancy (from the Single Life Table) of 20.2. For 2010, the RMD would be calculated by dividing the account balance as of 12/31/09 by Kate's 2010 life expectancy, at age 67, of 19.4.
No Designated Beneficiary, the Owner's Estate, a Charity, or a Non-Qualifying Trust	A RMD must be made for the deceased owner for the year of death. Thereafter, RMDs are based on the owner's theoretical life expectancy in the year of death.	Jake dies in 2008, at age 75, leaving his IRA entirely to charity. A RMD must be made for him for 2008, using his age 75 life expectancy (from the Uniform Lifetime Table) of 22.9. For later years, Jake's life expectancy in the year of his death (from the Single Life Table), reduced by one for each subsequent year, is used to calculate the RMD. For 2009, Jake's life expectancy would be 12.4, (his 2008 life expectancy at age 75 of 13.4-1). For 2010 the life expectancy used would be 11.4, (12.4-1).

---

[1] If Kate were more than 10 years younger than Jake, the factor shown on the Joint and Last Survivor Table would be used.

Continued

Required Minimum Distributions After Death
Spousal Beneficiary

Designated Beneficiary

IRAs and qualified plans allow an account owner to name a beneficiary or beneficiaries to receive the account proceeds should the owner die. From this pool of potential inheritors, IRS regulations require that the individual or group of individuals who will ultimately receive the funds, the "designated beneficiaries," be identified by September 30 of the year following the year of death. This time delay allows for a certain amount of post-death estate and income tax planning by "removing" a potential beneficiary through either a qualified disclaimer, a cash distribution, or by dividing the IRA or qualified plan into separate accounts.[1] The life expectancies of those beneficiaries who remain as of September 30 are then used to determine the RMDs for the years after death.

Entities without a measurable life span, such as the owner's estate, a charity, or a trust that does not meet certain IRS requirements, are not considered to be "designated beneficiaries" for RMD purposes. While such beneficiaries may inherit the funds in an account, distributions to these entities are generally made on less favorable terms.

Spousal Rollover

In order to roll the account into the name of the surviving spouse, the survivor must be the sole beneficiary and have an unlimited right to withdraw amounts from the account. If the spouse is not the sole beneficiary of an account, this requirement could be met by having other beneficiaries disclaim their interests on a timely basis. The surviving spouse could later name those individuals as beneficiaries of his or her own IRA.

The election to roll the account into the surviving spouse's name may be made at any time after the owner's death.

Trusts

In order for the beneficiaries of a trust to qualify as a "designated beneficiaries," the trust must meet certain requirements:

1. The trust must be valid under state law;
2. The trust must be irrevocable or will, under its terms, become irrevocable upon the death of the account owner;
3. The beneficiaries of the trust must be identifiable from the trust document; and
4. Certain documents must be provided to the plan administrator.[2]

If a trust does not meet these requirements, consideration should be given to reforming the trust, assigning or disclaiming an interest in the trust, cashing-out certain beneficiaries, or separating interests in the trust.

---

[1] Any separate accounts must generally be established by December 31 of the year following the year of the account owner's death.

[2] Generally, this must occur by October 31 of the year following the year of death.

Continued...

Required Minimum Distributions After Death
Spousal Beneficiary

Other Points

- **Marital status:** An account owner's marital status for the entire calendar year is determined as of January 1, even if the account owner and/or spouse die or divorce during the year.

- **Distributions from employer-sponsored qualified plans:** Post-death payments to beneficiaries of qualified plans are typically based on the individual provisions of a particular plan. A lump-sum distribution is perhaps the most frequently encountered option. A surviving spouse who takes a lump-sum distribution from a qualified plan has 60 days to move the funds tax-free into an IRA rollover.

- **Roth IRAs:** Roth IRAs do not have a lifetime distribution requirements. Because of this, a Roth IRA owner is always viewed as having died before the RBD. Post-death distributions from Roth IRAs are thus governed by the "death before RBD" rules.

Seek Professional Guidance

The body of law and regulation surrounding required minimum distributions is complex and often confusing. Further, the failure to correctly distribute the required amounts from an IRA or qualified plan can result in a federal excise tax of 50% of the amount that should have been distributed. Individual state or local law may also provide penalties.

The advice and guidance of qualified professionals is strongly recommended.

Required Minimum Distributions After Death
Non-Spouse Beneficiaries

Funds in both traditional IRAs[1] and qualified retirement plans may not be kept inside these tax-deferred accounts indefinitely. Under federal law the money must eventually be distributed, and then taxed, through yearly "Required Minimum Distributions," or RMDs.[2]

The death of an account owner does not eliminate this requirement. However, the manner in which the assets must be distributed post-death will vary, depending primarily on:

- **Death before or after required beginning date:** During life, an account owner must generally begin distributions no later than April 1 of the year following the year he or she reaches age 70½. This is known as the "required beginning date," or RBD.[3]

- **Who inherits the assets:** The law mandates different distribution options depending on who inherits the assets in an account.

Non-Spouse Beneficiary Options

If the designated beneficiary is not the account owner's spouse, or if there is no designated beneficiary, the funds must generally be distributed as shown in the following tables:

Owner Dies *Before* the Required Beginning Date

Situation	Distribution Requirement	Example
Individual Beneficiary	RMDs for the beneficiary must begin by 12/31 of the year after the year of death. Distributions are made over the beneficiary's life expectancy.	Paul dies in 2008 at age 67, leaving his IRA to his daughter Paulette, age 42. Paulette must begin to take RMDs by 12/31/09, using her age in 2009 of 43. The RMD for 2009 would be calculated by dividing the account balance on 12/31/08 by Paulette's age-43 life expectancy (from the Single Life Table) of 40.7.[4]
Multiple Beneficiaries[5]	RMDs for the beneficiaries must begin by 12/31 of the year after the year of death. Distributions are made over the oldest beneficiary's life expectancy.	Paul dies in 2008 at age 67, leaving his IRA to his brother Bob, age 76, and his daughter Paulette, age 42. RMDs to them must begin by 12/31/09 and must be made over Bob's life expectancy as of his birthday in the year after Paul's death. The RMD for 2009 would be calculated by dividing the account balance on 12/31/08 by Bob's 2009 (Single Life Table) life expectancy, for age 77, of 12.1.[4]
No Designated Beneficiary, the Estate, a Charity, or a Non-Qualifying Trust	The entire amount must be distributed by the end of the fifth year after the year the owner dies.	Paul dies on 01/01/08, at age 68, leaving his IRA to his estate. The entire IRA balance must be distributed by 12/31/13.

---

[1] For required minimum distribution purposes, the term "traditional IRA" also includes SIMPLE IRAs and SEP IRAs.
[2] This discussion concerns federal income tax law. State or local law may vary.
[3] The RBD for qualified plan participants is April 1 of the year following the later of (a) the year the participant reaches age 70½, or (b) the year he or she retires. More than 5% owners must begin to receive distributions by April 1 of the year following the year they reach age 70½.
[4] The life expectancy factor is reduced by one for each year after the year of the first required distribution.
[5] Assumes that the account is not divided into separate shares.

Continued...

Required Minimum Distributions After Death
Non-Spouse Beneficiaries

Owner Dies *After* the Required Beginning Date

Situation	Distribution Requirement	Example
Individual Beneficiary	A RMD must be made for the deceased owner for the year of death. RMDs for the beneficiary must begin by 12/31 of the year after the year of death. Distributions are made over the longer of the owner's theoretical life expectancy, or the beneficiary's life expectancy.	Paul dies in 2008 at age 72, leaving his IRA to his older brother Bob, age 76. Because Paul has already passed his RBD, a distribution must be made for him for 2008. The RMD for 2008 is determined by dividing the account balance as of 12/31/07 by 25.6, the life expectancy (from the Uniform Lifetime Table) for a 72-year-old account owner. For 2009 and later years, the RMDs are calculated using the longer of the Single Life Table life expectancy for Paul in the year of his death, reduced by one (age 72 =15.5-1=14.5) or Bob's life expectancy in the year after Paul's death (age 77=12.1). In this case, Paul's theoretical life expectancy is greater. The RMD for 2009 is calculated by dividing the account balance as of 12/31/08 by 14.5.[1]
Multiple Beneficiaries[2]	A RMD must be made for the deceased owner for the year of death. RMDs for the beneficiaries must begin by 12/31 of the year after the year of death, with distributions over the longer of the owner's theoretical life expectancy or the oldest beneficiary's life expectancy.	Paul dies in 2008 at age 72, leaving his IRA to his son Peter, age 46, and his daughter Paulette, age 42. Because Paul has already passed his RBD, a distribution for 2008 must be made for him. This distribution is calculated by dividing the account balance as of 12/31/07 by 25.6, the life expectancy (from the Uniform Lifetime Table) for a 72 year old. For 2009 and later years, the RMDs are calculated using the longer of the Single Life Table life expectancy for Paul in the year of his death, reduced by one (age 72=15.5-1=14.5) or Peter's life expectancy (he's older than Paulette) in the year after Paul's death (age 47=37.0). In this case, Peter's life expectancy is the greater. The RMD for 2009 is calculated by dividing the account balance as of 12/31/08 by 37.0.[1]
No Designated Beneficiary, the Estate, a Charity, or a Non-Qualifying Trust	A RMD must be made for the deceased owner for the year of death. Thereafter, RMDs are based on the owner's theoretical life expectancy in the year of death.	Paul dies in 2008, at age 75, leaving his IRA entirely to charity. A RMD must be made for him for 2008, calculated using his age 75 life expectancy (from the Uniform Lifetime Table) of 22.9. For 2009 and later years, Paul's life expectancy in the year of his death (from the Single Life Table), reduced by one for each subsequent year, is used to calculate the RMD. For 2009, Paul's life expectancy would be 12.4, (his 2008 life expectancy at age 75 of 13.4-1).[1]

---

[1] The life expectancy factor is reduced by one for each year after the year of the first required distribution.
[2] Assumes that the account is not divided into separate shares.

Continued

Required Minimum Distributions After Death
Non-Spouse Beneficiaries

Designated Beneficiary

IRAs and qualified plans allow an account owner to name a beneficiary or beneficiaries to receive the account proceeds should the owner die. From this pool of potential inheritors, IRS regulations require that the individual or group of individuals who will ultimately receive the funds, the "designated beneficiaries," be identified by September 30 of the year following the year of death. This time delay allows for a certain amount of post-death estate and income tax planning by "removing" a potential beneficiary through either a qualified disclaimer, a cash distribution, or by dividing the IRA or qualified plan into separate accounts.[1] The life expectancies of those beneficiaries who remain as of September 30 are then used to determine the RMDs for the years after death.

Entities without a measurable life span, such as the owner's estate, a charity, or a trust that does not meet certain IRS requirements, are not considered to be "designated beneficiaries" for RMD purposes. While such beneficiaries may inherit the funds in the account, distributions to these entities are generally made on less favorable terms.

Trusts

In order for the beneficiaries of a trust to qualify as a "designated beneficiaries," the trust must meet certain requirements:

1. The trust must be valid under state law;
2. The trust must be irrevocable or will, under its terms, become irrevocable upon the death of the account owner;
3. The beneficiaries of the trust must be identifiable from the trust document; and
4. Certain documents must be provided to the plan administrator.[2]

If a trust does not meet these requirements, consideration should be given to reforming the trust, assigning or disclaiming an interest in the trust, cashing-out certain beneficiaries, or separating interests in the trust.

---

[1] Any separate accounts must generally be established by December 31 of the year following the year of the account owner's death.

[2] Generally, this must occur by October 31 of the year following the year of death.

Continued...

Required Minimum Distributions After Death
Non-Spouse Beneficiaries

Other Points

- **Distributions from employer-sponsored qualified plans:** Post-death payments to beneficiaries of qualified plans are typically based on the individual provisions of a particular plan. A lump-sum distribution, with its heavy, immediate taxation, is perhaps the most frequently encountered option.

  The Pension Protection Act of 2006, effective for distributions after December 31, 2006, provides for a direct trustee-to-trustee transfer from a qualified plan to an IRA specifically designed to receive retirement assets inherited by a non-spouse beneficiary. The non-spouse beneficiary is not treated as the owner of the rolled-over assets and the assets may not be rolled-over to another account. Required minimum distributions are made from the "inherited IRA" in accordance with the normal rules applicable to non-spouse beneficiaries.

  Such an after-death transfer has the same result as if the decedent had moved the assets in his or her qualified plan into an IRA rollover prior to death.

- **Roth IRAs:** Roth IRAs do not have a lifetime distribution requirements. Because of this, a Roth IRA owner is always viewed as having died before the RBD. Post-death distributions from Roth IRAs are thus governed by the "death before RBD" rules.

Seek Professional Guidance

The body of law and regulation surrounding required minimum distributions is complex and often confusing. Further, the failure to correctly distribute the required amounts from an IRA or qualified plan can result in a federal excise tax of 50% of the amount that should have been distributed. Individual state or local law may also provide penalties.

The advice and guidance of qualified professionals is strongly recommended.

Stretch IRA

One major benefit of a traditional IRA[1] is that there is no federal[2] tax on growth in the account until the funds are distributed. This deferral of taxes generally allows for faster growth than would be possible if taxes had to be paid each year. Federal law does not allow this tax-deferral to continue forever; certain mandatory distributions (known as Required Minimum Distributions, or RMDs) must be made from these accounts once the owner reaches a specified age.

For traditional IRAs, distributions must begin no later than April 1 of the year following the year the owner reaches age 70½. Funds distributed from the account are generally taxable as ordinary income in the year received. Failure to make the minimum distributions when required can result in a significant income tax penalty.

The Stretch IRA - Extending the Period of Tax-Deferral

The term "stretch IRA" refers to a wealth transfer strategy that seeks to extend the period during which the assets in the IRA continue to grow tax-deferred. The stretch IRA concept is most often of interest to those who do not need extra income or those who wish to leave a legacy to their heirs in an income tax-efficient manner.

To begin, an IRA owner names a spouse or another (usually younger) person such as a child or grandchild, as the account beneficiary. Then, only the legally required, minimum distributions, (the RMDs), are taken from the account each year. Under IRS regulations, the methods used to calculate the RMDs can effectively extend the period over which the assets may be distributed.

The Pros and Cons of Stretch IRAs

Stretch IRAs have potential benefits as well as potential risks.

- **Benefits**
  - **Income for life:** A stretch IRA has the potential to provide lifetime income to a chosen beneficiary or beneficiaries.
  - **Minimize tax liability:** The income tax bite may be lessened by taking smaller distributions over a period of years, rather than as a single, large lump sum.
  - **Continue tax-deferred growth:** Extending the period over which distributions are made continues the benefits of tax-deferred growth, potentially increasing the wealth that can pass to the beneficiaries.

- **Risks**
  - **Beneficiary may die early:** A beneficiary may not live to normal life expectancy.
  - **Tax laws may change:** Tax laws or regulations may change, to the detriment of an IRA owner and/or beneficiaries.
  - **Poor investment returns:** Investment losses and inflation can both erode, or even eliminate, the value of future IRA distributions.

---

[1] The term "traditional IRA" includes SIMPLE IRAs and SEP IRAs.
[2] The discussion here concerns federal income tax law. State and/or local tax law may differ.

Continued...

Stretch IRA

The following hypothetical examples illustrate three ways that a stretch IRA might be arranged:

Spousal Beneficiary and a Single Inherited IRA

An IRA owner, age 68, makes his spouse, age 62, the sole beneficiary of his IRA. They have two adult children, ages 35 and 25.

When	What Happens
During the IRA owner's life	Beginning at age 70½, the IRA owner takes his required minimum distributions (RMDs).
IRA owner dies at age 75	The surviving spouse rolls the IRA over into her name. She names her two adult children as joint beneficiaries of her single rollover account.
Surviving spouse reaches age 70½	At age 70½, the surviving spouse begins taking her RMDs.
Surviving spouse dies at age 80	The children inherit the IRA assets. Each child receives RMDs based on the single life expectancy of the oldest child. They may not mix the funds with other IRA assets.

Spousal Beneficiary and Separate Inherited IRAs

An IRA owner, age 68, makes his spouse, age 62, the sole beneficiary of his IRA. They have two adult children, ages 35 and 25.

When	What Happens
During the owner's life	Beginning at age 70½, the IRA owner takes his required minimum distributions (RMDs).
IRA owner dies at age 75	The surviving spouse splits the IRA assets into two separate IRA rollover accounts. She names each of her two adult children as the sole beneficiary of one account.
Surviving spouse reaches age 70½	At age 70½, the surviving spouse begins taking her RMDs.
Surviving spouse dies at age 80	Each child inherits a separate IRA. Because there are two separate accounts, each child receives RMDs based on his or her individual life expectancy. They may not mix the funds with other IRA assets.

Continued...

Stretch IRA

Nonspousal Beneficiaries and Separate Inherited IRAs

An IRA owner, age 68, has two adult children, ages 35 and 25. He splits his IRA into two separate accounts and names each child as the sole beneficiary of one account.

When	What Happens
During the owner's life	Beginning at age 70½, the IRA owner takes his required minimum distributions (RMDs).
The owner dies at age 75	Each child inherits a separate IRA. Because there are two separate accounts, each child receives RMDs based on his or her individual life expectancy. They may not mix the funds with other IRA assets.

A married IRA owner may need to obtain his or her spouse's written consent before naming someone in place of (or in addition to) the spouse as the primary beneficiary of the IRA.

Post-Death Beneficiary Planning

The stretch IRA examples shown here illustrate situations in which the beneficiary planning takes place **prior** to the account owner's death. However, IRS regulations allow for a certain amount of **post-death** planning. From a pool of potential beneficiaries, those who will ultimately receive the assets must be identified by September 30 of the year following the owner's year of death. This time delay allows for the removal of a potential beneficiary either through a qualified disclaimer, a cash distribution, or by dividing the IRA into separate accounts. The life expectancies of those who remain as of September 30 are then used to determine the RMDs for the years after death.

Any separate accounts must generally be established by December 31 of the year following the year of the account owner's death.

Seek Professional Guidance

Setting up a stretch IRA requires careful consideration of a number of issues.

- Possible changes in tax law
- The impact of inflation
- The uncertainty of future investment results
- The need to integrate the stretch IRA into the overall estate plan
- The risks inherent in planning for an extended period into the future

The counsel and guidance of appropriate tax, legal, and investment advisors is highly recommended.

Stretch IRA
Spousal Beneficiary and a Single Inherited IRA

An IRA owner, age 68, makes his spouse, age 62, the sole beneficiary of his IRA. They have two adult children, ages 35 and 25.

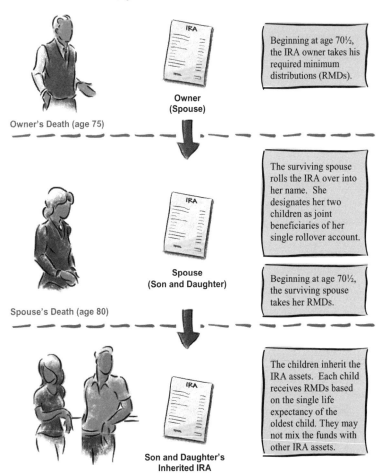

Owner (Spouse)

Beginning at age 70½, the IRA owner takes his required minimum distributions (RMDs).

Owner's Death (age 75)

Spouse (Son and Daughter)

The surviving spouse rolls the IRA over into her name. She designates her two children as joint beneficiaries of her single rollover account.

Beginning at age 70½, the surviving spouse takes her RMDs.

Spouse's Death (age 80)

Son and Daughter's Inherited IRA

The children inherit the IRA assets. Each child receives RMDs based on the single life expectancy of the oldest child. They may not mix the funds with other IRA assets.

Note: This is one example of how a stretch IRA might be structured. Professional guidance is strongly recommended.

Stretch IRA

Spousal Beneficiary and Separate Inherited IRAs

An IRA owner, age 68, makes his spouse, age 62, the sole beneficiary of his IRA. They have two adult children, ages 35 and 25.

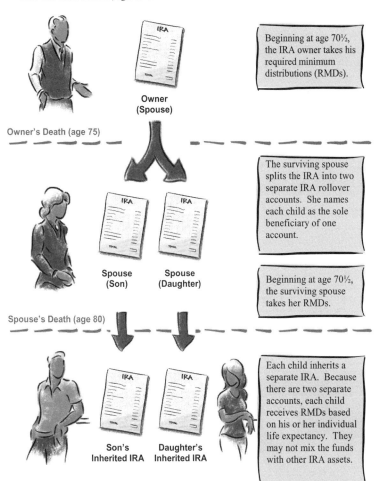

**Owner
(Spouse)**

Beginning at age 70½, the IRA owner takes his required minimum distributions (RMDs).

Owner's Death (age 75)

**Spouse
(Son)**   **Spouse
(Daughter)**

The surviving spouse splits the IRA into two separate IRA rollover accounts. She names each child as the sole beneficiary of one account.

Beginning at age 70½, the surviving spouse takes her RMDs.

Spouse's Death (age 80)

**Son's
Inherited IRA**   **Daughter's
Inherited IRA**

Each child inherits a separate IRA. Because there are two separate accounts, each child receives RMDs based on his or her individual life expectancy. They may not mix the funds with other IRA assets.

Note: This is one example of how a stretch IRA might be structured. Professional guidance is strongly recommended.

Stretch IRA

Non-Spouse Beneficiaries and Separate Inherited IRAs

Assume an IRA owner, age 68, has two adult children, ages 35 and 25.

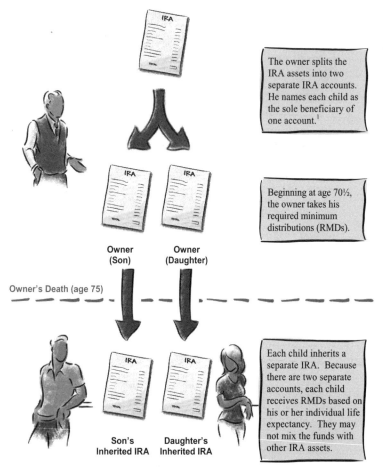

The owner splits the IRA assets into two separate IRA accounts. He names each child as the sole beneficiary of one account.[1]

Beginning at age 70½, the owner takes his required minimum distributions (RMDs).

Owner (Son)

Owner (Daughter)

Owner's Death (age 75)

Each child inherits a separate IRA. Because there are two separate accounts, each child receives RMDs based on his or her individual life expectancy. They may not mix the funds with other IRA assets.

Son's Inherited IRA

Daughter's Inherited IRA

Note: This is one example of how a stretch IRA might be structured. Professional guidance is strongly recommended.

---

[1] A married IRA owner may need to obtain his or her spouse's written consent before naming someone else in place of (or in addition to) the spouse as the beneficiary of the IRA.

Uniform Lifetime Table

IRS Reg. 1.401(a)(9)-9, Q+A-2

Age	Distribution Period
70	27.4
71	26.5
72	25.6
73	24.7
74	23.8
75	22.9
76	22.0
77	21.2
78	20.3
79	19.5
80	18.7
81	17.9
82	17.1
83	16.3
84	15.5
85	14.8
86	14.1
87	13.4
88	12.7
89	12.0
90	11.4
91	10.8
92	10.2
93	9.6
94	9.1
95	8.6
96	8.1
97	7.6
98	7.1
99	6.7
100	6.3
101	5.9
102	5.5
103	5.2
104	4.9
105	4.5
106	4.2
107	3.9
108	3.7
109	3.4
110	3.1
111	2.9
112	2.6
113	2.4
114	2.1
115 and over	1.9

Joint Life and Last Survivor Table

IRS Reg. 1.401(a)(9)-9, Q+A-3

Ages	20	21	22	23	24	25	26	27	28	29
20	70.1	69.6	69.1	68.7	68.3	67.9	67.5	67.2	66.9	66.6
21	69.6	69.1	68.6	68.2	67.7	67.3	66.9	66.6	66.2	65.9
22	69.1	68.6	68.1	67.6	67.2	66.7	66.3	65.9	65.6	65.2
23	68.7	68.2	67.6	67.1	66.6	66.2	65.7	65.3	64.9	64.6
24	68.3	67.7	67.2	66.6	66.1	65.6	65.2	64.7	64.3	63.9
25	67.9	67.3	66.7	66.2	65.6	65.1	64.6	64.2	63.7	63.3
26	67.5	66.9	66.3	65.7	65.2	64.6	64.1	63.6	63.2	62.8
27	67.2	66.6	65.9	65.3	64.7	64.2	63.6	63.1	62.7	62.2
28	66.9	66.2	65.6	64.9	64.3	63.7	63.2	62.7	62.1	61.7
29	66.6	65.9	65.2	64.6	63.9	63.3	62.8	62.2	61.7	61.2
30	66.3	65.6	64.9	64.2	63.6	62.9	62.3	61.8	61.2	60.7
31	66.1	65.3	64.6	63.9	63.2	62.6	62.0	61.4	60.8	60.2
32	65.8	65.1	64.3	63.6	62.9	62.2	61.6	61.0	60.4	59.8
33	65.6	64.8	64.1	63.3	62.6	61.9	61.3	60.6	60.0	59.4
34	65.4	64.6	63.8	63.1	62.3	61.6	60.9	60.3	59.6	59.0
35	65.2	64.4	63.6	62.8	62.1	61.4	60.6	59.9	59.3	58.6
36	65.0	64.2	63.4	62.6	61.9	61.1	60.4	59.6	59.0	58.3
37	64.9	64.0	63.2	62.4	61.6	60.9	60.1	59.4	58.7	58.0
38	64.7	63.9	63.0	62.2	61.4	60.6	59.9	59.1	58.4	57.7
39	64.6	63.7	62.9	62.1	61.2	60.4	59.6	58.9	58.1	57.4
40	64.4	63.6	62.7	61.9	61.1	60.2	59.4	58.7	57.9	57.1
41	64.3	63.5	62.6	61.7	60.9	60.1	59.3	58.5	57.7	56.9
42	64.2	63.3	62.5	61.6	60.8	59.9	59.1	58.3	57.5	56.7
43	64.1	63.2	62.4	61.5	60.6	59.8	58.9	58.1	57.3	56.5
44	64.0	63.1	62.2	61.4	60.5	59.6	58.8	57.9	57.1	56.3
45	64.0	63.0	62.2	61.3	60.4	59.5	58.6	57.8	56.9	56.1
46	63.9	63.0	62.1	61.2	60.3	59.4	58.5	57.7	56.8	56.0
47	63.8	62.9	62.0	61.1	60.2	59.3	58.4	57.5	56.7	55.8
48	63.7	62.8	61.9	61.0	60.1	59.2	58.3	57.4	56.5	55.7
49	63.7	62.8	61.8	60.9	60.0	59.1	58.2	57.3	56.4	55.6
50	63.6	62.7	61.8	60.8	59.9	59.0	58.1	57.2	56.3	55.4
51	63.6	62.6	61.7	60.8	59.9	58.9	58.0	57.1	56.2	55.3
52	63.5	62.6	61.7	60.7	59.8	58.9	58.0	57.1	56.1	55.2
53	63.5	62.5	61.6	60.7	59.7	58.8	57.9	57.0	56.1	55.2
54	63.5	62.5	61.6	60.6	59.7	58.8	57.8	56.9	56.0	55.1
55	63.4	62.5	61.5	60.6	59.6	58.7	57.8	56.8	55.9	55.0
56	63.4	62.4	61.5	60.5	59.6	58.7	57.7	56.8	55.9	54.9
57	63.4	62.4	61.5	60.5	59.6	58.6	57.7	56.7	55.8	54.9
58	63.3	62.4	61.4	60.5	59.5	58.6	57.6	56.7	55.8	54.8
59	63.3	62.3	61.4	60.4	59.5	58.5	57.6	56.7	55.7	54.8
60	63.3	62.3	61.4	60.4	59.5	58.5	57.6	56.6	55.7	54.7

Continued

Joint Life and Last Survivor Table

IRS Reg. 1.401(a)(9)-9, Q+A-3

Ages	20	21	22	23	24	25	26	27	28	29
61	63.3	62.3	61.3	60.4	59.4	58.5	57.5	56.6	55.6	54.7
62	63.2	62.3	61.3	60.4	59.4	58.4	57.5	56.5	55.6	54.7
63	63.2	62.3	61.3	60.3	59.4	58.4	57.5	56.5	55.6	54.6
64	63.2	62.2	61.3	60.3	59.4	58.4	57.4	56.5	55.5	54.6
65	63.2	62.2	61.3	60.3	59.3	58.4	57.4	56.5	55.5	54.6
66	63.2	62.2	61.2	60.3	59.3	58.4	57.4	56.4	55.5	54.5
67	63.2	62.2	61.2	60.3	59.3	58.3	57.4	56.4	55.5	54.5
68	63.1	62.2	61.2	60.2	59.3	58.3	57.4	56.4	55.4	54.5
69	63.1	62.2	61.2	60.2	59.3	58.3	57.3	56.4	55.4	54.5
70	63.1	62.2	61.2	60.2	59.3	58.3	57.3	56.4	55.4	54.4
71	63.1	62.1	61.2	60.2	59.2	58.3	57.3	56.4	55.4	54.4
72	63.1	62.1	61.2	60.2	59.2	58.3	57.3	56.3	55.4	54.4
73	63.1	62.1	61.2	60.2	59.2	58.3	57.3	56.3	55.4	54.4
74	63.1	62.1	61.2	60.2	59.2	58.2	57.3	56.3	55.4	54.4
75	63.1	62.1	61.1	60.2	59.2	58.2	57.3	56.3	55.3	54.4
76	63.1	62.1	61.1	60.2	59.2	58.2	57.3	56.3	55.3	54.4
77	63.1	62.1	61.1	60.2	59.2	58.2	57.3	56.3	55.3	54.4
78	63.1	62.1	61.1	60.2	59.2	58.2	57.3	56.3	55.3	54.4
79	63.1	62.1	61.1	60.2	59.2	58.2	57.2	56.3	55.3	54.3
80	63.1	62.1	61.1	60.1	59.2	58.2	57.2	56.3	55.3	54.3
81	63.1	62.1	61.1	60.1	59.2	58.2	57.2	56.3	55.3	54.3
82	63.1	62.1	61.1	60.1	59.2	58.2	57.2	56.3	55.3	54.3
83	63.1	62.1	61.1	60.1	59.2	58.2	57.2	56.3	55.3	54.3
84	63.0	62.1	61.1	60.1	59.2	58.2	57.2	56.3	55.3	54.3
85	63.0	62.1	61.1	60.1	59.2	58.2	57.2	56.3	55.3	54.3
86	63.0.0	62.1	61.1	60.1	59.2	58.2	57.2	56.2	55.3	54.3
87	63.0	62.1	61.1	60.1	59.2	58.2	57.2	56.2	55.3	54.3
88	63.0	62.1	61.1	60.1	59.2	58.2	57.2	56.2	55.3	54.3
89	63.0	62.1	61.1	60.1	59.1	58.2	57.2	56.2	55.3	54.3
90	63.0	62.1	61.1	60.1	59.1	58.2	57.2	56.2	55.3	54.3
91	63.0	62.1	61.1	60.1	59.1	58.2	57.2	56.2	55.3	54.3
92	63.0	62.1	61.1	60.1	59.1	58.2	57.2	56.2	55.3	54.3
93	63.0	62.1	61.1	60.1	59.1	58.2	57.2	56.2	55.3	54.3
94	63.0	62.1	61.1	60.1	59.1	58.2	57.2	56.2	55.3	54.3
95	63.0	62.1	61.1	60.1	59.1	58.2	57.2	56.2	55.3	54.3
96	63.0	62.1	61.1	60.1	59.1	58.2	57.2	56.2	55.3	54.3
97	63.0	62.1	61.1	60.1	59.1	58.2	57.2	56.2	55.3	54.3
98	63.0	62.1	61.1	60.1	59.1	58.2	57.2	56.2	55.3	54.3
99	63.0	62.1	61.1	60.1	59.1	58.2	57.2	56.2	55.3	54.3
100	63.0	62.1	61.1	60.1	59.1	58.2	57.2	56.2	55.3	54.3

Continued...

Joint Life and Last Survivor Table

IRS Reg. 1.401(a)(9)-9, Q+A-3

Ages	20	21	22	23	24	25	26	27	28	29
101	63.0	62.1	61.1	60.1	59.1	58.2	57.2	56.2	55.3	54.3
102	63.0	62.1	61.1	60.1	59.1	58.2	57.2	56.2	55.3	54.3
103	63.0	62.1	61.1	60.1	59.1	58.2	57.2	56.2	55.3	54.3
104	63.0	62.1	61.1	60.1	59.1	58.2	57.2	56.2	55.3	54.3
105	63.0	62.1	61.1	60.1	59.1	58.2	57.2	56.2	55.3	54.3
106	63.0	62.1	61.1	60.1	59.1	58.2	57.2	56.2	55.3	54.3
107	63.0	62.1	61.1	60.1	59.1	58.2	57.2	56.2	55.3	54.3
108	63.0	62.1	61.1	60.1	59.1	58.2	57.2	56.2	55.3	54.3
109	63.0	62.1	61.1	60.1	59.1	58.2	57.2	56.2	55.3	54.3
110	63.0	62.1	61.1	60.1	59.1	58.2	57.2	56.2	55.3	54.3
111	63.0	62.1	61.1	60.1	59.1	58.2	57.2	56.2	55.3	54.3
112	63.0	62.1	61.1	60.1	59.1	58.2	57.2	56.2	55.3	54.3
113	63.0	62.1	61.1	60.1	59.1	58.2	57.2	56.2	55.3	54.3
114	63.0	62.1	61.1	60.1	59.1	58.2	57.2	56.2	55.3	54.3
115+	63.0	62.1	61.1	60.1	59.1	58.2	57.2	56.2	55.3	54.3

Ages	30	31	32	33	34	35	36	37	38	39
30	60.2	59.7	59.2	58.8	58.4	58.0	57.6	57.3	57.0	56.7
31	59.7	59.2	58.7	58.2	57.8	57.4	57.0	56.6	56.3	56.0
32	59.2	58.7	58.2	57.7	57.2	56.8	56.4	56.0	55.6	55.3
33	58.8	58.2	57.7	57.2	56.7	56.2	55.8	55.4	55.0	54.7
34	58.4	57.8	57.2	56.7	56.2	55.7	55.3	54.8	54.4	54.0
35	58.0	57.4	56.8	56.2	55.7	55.2	54.7	54.3	53.8	53.4
36	57.6	57.0	56.4	55.8	55.3	54.7	54.2	53.7	53.3	52.8
37	57.3	56.6	56.0	55.4	54.8	54.3	53.7	53.2	52.7	52.3
38	57.0	56.3	55.6	55.0	54.4	53.8	53.3	52.7	52.2	51.7
39	56.7	56.0	55.3	54.7	54.0	53.4	52.8	52.3	51.7	51.2
40	56.4	55.7	55.0	54.3	53.7	53.0	52.4	51.8	51.3	50.8
41	56.1	55.4	54.7	54.0	53.3	52.7	52.0	51.4	50.9	50.3
42	55.9	55.2	54.4	53.7	53.0	52.3	51.7	51.1	50.4	49.9
43	55.7	54.9	54.2	53.4	52.7	52.0	51.3	50.7	50.1	49.5
44	55.5	54.7	53.9	53.2	52.4	51.7	51.0	50.4	49.7	49.1
45	55.3	54.5	53.7	52.9	52.2	51.5	50.7	50.0	49.4	48.7
46	55.1	54.3	53.5	52.7	52.0	51.2	50.5	49.8	49.1	48.4
47	55.0	54.1	53.3	52.5	51.7	51.0	50.2	49.5	48.8	48.1
48	54.8	54.0	53.2	52.3	51.5	50.8	50.0	49.2	48.5	47.8
49	54.7	53.8	53.0	52.2	51.4	50.6	49.8	49.0	48.2	47.5
50	54.6	53.7	52.9	52.0	51.2	50.4	49.6	48.8	48.0	47.3

Continued

Joint Life and Last Survivor Table

IRS Reg. 1.401(a)(9)-9, Q+A-3

Ages	30	31	32	33	34	35	36	37	38	39
51	54.5	53.6	52.7	51.9	51.0	50.2	49.4	48.6	47.8	47.0
52	54.4	53.5	52.6	51.7	50.9	50.0	49.2	48.4	47.6	46.8
53	54.3	53.4	52.5	51.6	50.8	49.9	49.1	48.2	47.4	46.6
54	54.2	53.3	52.4	51.5	50.6	49.8	48.9	48.1	47.2	46.4
55	54.1	53.2	52.3	51.4	50.5	49.7	48.8	47.9	47.1	46.3
56	54.0	53.1	52.2	51.3	50.4	49.5	48.7	47.8	47.0	46.1
57	54.0	53.0	52.1	51.2	50.3	49.4	48.6	47.7	46.8	46.0
58	53.9	53.0	52.1	51.2	50.3	49.4	48.5	47.6	46.7	45.8
59	53.8	52.9	52.0	51.1	50.2	49.3	48.4	47.5	46.6	45.7
60	53.8	52.9	51.9	51.0	50.1	49.2	48.3	47.4	46.5	45.6
61	53.8	52.8	51.9	51.0	50.0	49.1	48.2	47.3	46.4	45.5
62	53.7	52.8	51.8	50.9	50.0	49.1	48.1	47.2	46.3	45.4
63	53.7	52.7	51.8	50.9	49.9	49.0	48.1	47.2	46.3	45.3
64	53.6	52.7	51.8	50.8	49.9	48.9	48.0	47.1	46.2	45.3
65	53.6	52.7	51.7	50.8	49.8	48.9	48.0	47.0	46.1	45.2
66	53.6	52.6	51.7	50.7	49.8	48.9	47.9	47.0	46.1	45.1
67	53.6	52.6	51.7	50.7	49.8	48.8	47.9	46.9	46.0	45.1
68	53.5	52.6	51.6	50.7	49.7	48.8	47.8	46.9	46.0	45.0
69	53.5	52.6	51.6	50.6	49.7	48.7	47.8	46.9	45.9	45.0
70	53.5	52.5	51.6	50.6	49.7	48.7	47.8	46.8	45.9	44.9
71	53.5	52.5	51.6	50.6	49.6	48.7	47.7	46.8	45.9	44.9
72	53.5	52.5	51.5	50.6	49.6	48.7	47.7	46.8	45.8	44.9
73	53.4	52.5	51.5	50.6	49.6	48.6	47.7	46.7	45.8	44.8
74	53.4	52.5	51.5	50.5	49.6	48.6	47.7	46.7	45.8	44.8
75	53.4	52.5	51.5	50.5	49.6	48.6	47.7	46.7	45.7	44.8
76	53.4	52.4	51.5	50.5	49.6	48.6	47.6	46.7	45.7	44.8
77	53.4	52.4	51.5	50.5	49.5	48.6	47.6	46.7	45.7	44.8
78	53.4	52.4	51.5	50.5	49.5	48.6	47.6	46.6	45.7	44.7
79	53.4	52.4	51.5	50.5	49.5	48.6	47.6	46.6	45.7	44.7
80	53.4	52.4	51.4	50.5	49.5	48.5	47.6	46.6	45.7	44.7
81	53.4	52.4	51.4	50.5	49.5	48.5	47.6	46.6	45.7	44.7
82	53.4	52.4	51.4	50.5	49.5	48.5	47.6	46.6	45.6	44.7
83	53.4	52.4	51.4	50.5	49.5	48.5	47.6	46.6	45.6	44.7
84	53.4	52.4	51.4	50.5	49.5	48.5	47.6	46.6	45.6	44.7
85	53.3	52.4	51.4	50.4	49.5	48.5	47.5	46.6	45.6	44.7
86	53.3	52.4	51.4	50.4	49.5	48.5	47.5	46.6	45.6	44.6
87	53.3	52.4	51.4	50.4	49.5	48.5	47.5	46.6	45.6	44.6
88	53.3	52.4	51.4	50.4	49.5	48.5	47.5	46.6	45.6	44.6
89	53.3	52.4	51.4	50.4	49.5	48.5	47.5	46.6	45.6	44.6
90	53.3	52.4	51.4	50.4	49.5	48.5	47.5	46.6	45.6	44.6

Continued...

Joint Life and Last Survivor Table
IRS Reg. 1.401(a)(9)-9, Q+A-3

Ages	30	31	32	33	34	35	36	37	38	39
91	53.3	52.4	51.4	50.4	49.5	48.5	47.5	46.6	45.6	44.6
92	53.3	52.4	51.4	50.4	49.5	48.5	47.5	46.6	45.6	44.6
93	53.3	52.4	51.4	50.4	49.5	48.5	47.5	46.6	45.6	44.6
94	53.3	52.4	51.4	50.4	49.5	48.5	47.5	46.6	45.6	44.6
95	53.3	52.4	51.4	50.4	49.5	48.5	47.5	46.5	45.6	44.6
96	53.3	52.4	51.4	50.4	49.5	48.5	47.5	46.5	45.6	44.6
97	53.3	52.4	51.4	50.4	49.5	48.5	47.5	46.5	45.6	44.6
98	53.3	52.4	51.4	50.4	49.5	48.5	47.5	46.5	45.6	44.6
99	53.3	52.4	51.4	50.4	49.5	48.5	47.5	46.5	45.6	44.6
100	53.3	52.4	51.4	50.4	49.5	48.5	47.5	46.5	45.6	44.6
101	53.3	52.4	51.4	50.4	49.5	48.5	47.5	46.5	45.6	44.6
102	53.3	52.4	51.4	50.4	49.5	48.5	47.5	46.5	45.6	44.6
103	53.3	52.4	51.4	50.4	49.5	48.5	47.5	46.5	45.6	44.6
104	53.3	52.4	51.4	50.4	49.5	48.5	47.5	46.5	45.6	44.6
105	53.3	52.4	51.4	50.4	49.4	48.5	47.5	46.5	45.6	44.6
106	53.3	52.4	51.4	50.4	49.4	48.5	47.5	46.5	45.6	44.6
107	53.3	52.4	51.4	50.4	49.4	48.5	47.5	46.5	45.6	44.6
108	53.3	52.4	51.4	50.4	49.4	48.5	47.5	46.5	45.6	44.6
109	53.3	52.4	51.4	50.4	49.4	48.5	47.5	46.5	45.6	44.6
110	53.3	52.4	51.4	50.4	49.4	48.5	47.5	46.5	45.6	44.6
111	53.3	52.4	51.4	50.4	49.4	48.5	47.5	46.5	45.6	44.6
112	53.3	52.4	51.4	50.4	49.4	48.5	47.5	46.5	45.6	44.6
113	53.3	52.4	51.4	50.4	49.4	48.5	47.5	46.5	45.6	44.6
114	53.3	52.4	51.4	50.4	49.4	48.5	47.5	46.5	45.6	44.6
115+	53.3	52.4	51.4	50.4	49.4	48.5	47.5	46.5	45.6	44.6

Ages	40	41	42	43	44	45	46	47	48	49
40	50.2	49.8	49.3	48.9	48.5	48.1	47.7	47.4	47.1	46.8
41	49.8	49.3	48.8	48.3	47.9	47.5	47.1	46.7	46.4	46.1
42	49.3	48.8	48.3	47.8	47.3	46.9	46.5	46.1	45.8	45.4
43	48.9	48.3	47.8	47.3	46.8	46.3	45.9	45.5	45.1	44.8
44	48.5	47.9	47.3	46.8	46.3	45.8	45.4	44.9	44.5	44.2
45	48.1	47.5	46.9	46.3	45.8	45.3	44.8	44.4	44.0	43.6
46	47.7	47.1	46.5	45.9	45.4	44.8	44.3	43.9	43.4	43.0
47	47.4	46.7	46.1	45.5	44.9	44.4	43.9	43.4	42.9	42.4
48	47.1	46.4	45.8	45.1	44.5	44.0	43.4	42.9	42.4	41.9
49	46.8	46.1	45.4	44.8	44.2	43.6	43.0	42.4	41.9	41.4
50	46.5	45.8	45.1	44.4	43.8	43.2	42.6	42.0	41.5	40.9

Continued

Joint Life and Last Survivor Table

IRS Reg. 1.401(a)(9)-9, Q+A-3

Ages	40	41	42	43	44	45	46	47	48	49
51	46.3	45.5	44.8	44.1	43.5	42.8	42.2	41.6	41.0	40.5
52	46.0	45.3	44.6	43.8	43.2	42.5	41.8	41.2	40.6	40.1
53	45.8	45.1	44.3	43.6	42.9	42.2	41.5	40.9	40.3	39.7
54	45.6	44.8	44.1	43.3	42.6	41.9	41.2	40.5	39.9	39.3
55	45.5	44.7	43.9	43.1	42.4	41.6	40.9	40.2	39.6	38.9
56	45.3	44.5	43.7	42.9	42.1	41.4	40.7	40.0	39.3	38.6
57	45.1	44.3	43.5	42.7	41.9	41.2	40.4	39.7	39.0	38.3
58	45.0	44.2	43.3	42.5	41.7	40.9	40.2	39.4	38.7	38.0
59	44.9	44.0	43.2	42.4	41.5	40.7	40.0	39.2	38.5	37.8
60	44.7	43.9	43.0	42.2	41.4	40.6	39.8	39.0	38.2	37.5
61	44.6	43.8	42.9	42.1	41.2	40.4	39.6	38.8	38.0	37.3
62	44.5	43.7	42.8	41.9	41.1	40.3	39.4	38.6	37.8	37.1
63	44.5	43.6	42.7	41.8	41.0	40.1	39.3	38.5	37.7	36.9
64	44.4	43.5	42.6	41.7	40.8	40.0	39.2	38.3	37.5	36.7
65	44.3	43.4	42.5	41.6	40.7	39.9	39.0	38.2	37.4	36.6
66	44.2	43.3	42.4	41.5	40.6	39.8	38.9	38.1	37.2	36.4
67	44.2	43.3	42.3	41.4	40.6	39.7	38.8	38.0	37.1	36.3
68	44.1	43.2	42.3	41.4	40.5	39.6	38.7	37.9	37.0	36.2
69	44.1	43.1	42.2	41.3	40.4	39.5	38.6	37.8	36.9	36.0
70	44.0	43.1	42.2	41.3	40.3	39.4	38.6	37.7	36.8	35.9
71	44.0	43.0	42.1	41.2	40.3	39.4	38.5	37.6	36.7	35.9
72	43.9	43.0	42.1	41.1	40.2	39.3	38.4	37.5	36.6	35.8
73	43.9	43.0	42.0	41.1	40.2	39.3	38.4	37.5	36.6	35.7
74	43.9	42.9	42.0	41.1	40.1	39.2	38.3	37.4	36.5	35.6
75	43.8	42.9	42.0	41.0	40.1	39.2	38.3	37.4	36.5	35.6
76	43.8	42.9	41.9	41.0	40.1	39.1	38.2	37.3	36.4	35.5
77	43.8	42.9	41.9	41.0	40.0	39.1	38.2	37.3	36.4	35.5
78	43.8	42.8	41.9	40.9	40.0	39.1	38.2	37.2	36.3	35.4
79	43.8	42.8	41.9	40.9	40.0	39.1	38.1	37.2	36.3	35.4
80	43.7	42.8	41.8	40.9	40.0	39.0	38.1	37.2	36.3	35.4
81	43.7	42.8	41.8	40.9	39.9	39.0	38.1	37.2	36.2	35.3
82	43.7	42.8	41.8	40.9	39.9	39.0	38.1	37.1	36.2	35.3
83	43.7	42.8	41.8	40.9	39.9	39.0	38.0	37.1	36.2	35.3
84	43.7	42.7	41.8	40.8	39.9	39.0	38.0	37.1	36.2	35.3
85	43.7	42.7	41.8	40.8	39.9	38.9	38.0	37.1	36.2	35.2
86	43.7	42.7	41.8	40.8	39.9	38.9	38.0	37.1	36.1	35.2
87	43.7	42.7	41.8	40.8	39.9	38.9	38.0	37.0	36.1	35.2
88	43.7	42.7	41.8	40.8	39.9	38.9	38.0	37.0	36.1	35.2
89	43.7	42.7	41.7	40.8	39.8	38.9	38.0	37.0	36.1	35.2
90	43.7	42.7	41.7	40.8	39.8	38.9	38.0	37.0	36.1	35.2

Continued...

Joint Life and Last Survivor Table

IRS Reg. 1.401(a)(9)-9, Q+A-3

Ages	40	41	42	43	44	45	46	47	48	49
91	43.7	42.7	41.7	40.8	39.8	38.9	37.9	37.0	36.1	35.2
92	43.7	42.7	41.7	40.8	39.8	38.9	37.9	37.0	36.1	35.1
93	43.7	42.7	41.7	40.8	39.8	38.9	37.9	37.0	36.1	35.1
94	43.7	42.7	41.7	40.8	39.8	38.9	37.9	37.0	36.1	35.1
95	43.6	42.7	41.7	40.8	39.8	38.9	37.9	37.0	36.1	35.1
96	43.6	42.7	41.7	40.8	39.8	38.9	37.9	37.0	36.1	35.1
97	43.6	42.7	41.7	40.8	39.8	38.9	37.9	37.0	36.1	35.1
98	43.6	42.7	41.7	40.8	39.8	38.9	37.9	37.0	36.0	35.1
99	43.6	42.7	41.7	40.8	39.8	38.9	37.9	37.0	36.0	35.1
100	43.6	42.7	41.7	40.8	39.8	38.9	37.9	37.0	36.0	35.1
101	43.6	42.7	41.7	40.8	39.8	38.9	37.9	37.0	36.0	35.1
102	43.6	42.7	41.7	40.8	39.8	38.9	37.9	37.0	36.0	35.1
103	43.6	42.7	41.7	40.8	39.8	38.9	37.9	37.0	36.0	35.1
104	43.6	42.7	41.7	40.8	39.8	38.8	37.9	37.0	36.0	35.1
105	43.6	42.7	41.7	40.8	39.8	38.8	37.9	37.0	36.0	35.1
106	43.6	42.7	41.7	40.8	39.8	38.8	37.9	37.0	36.0	35.1
107	43.6	42.7	41.7	40.8	39.8	38.8	37.9	37.0	36.0	35.1
108	43.6	42.7	41.7	40.8	39.8	38.8	37.9	37.0	36.0	35.1
109	43.6	42.7	41.7	40.7	39.8	38.8	37.9	37.0	36.0	35.1
110	43.6	42.7	41.7	40.7	39.8	38.8	37.9	37.0	36.0	35.1
111	43.6	42.7	41.7	40.7	39.8	38.8	37.9	37.0	36.0	35.1
112	43.6	42.7	41.7	40.7	39.8	38.8	37.9	37.0	36.0	35.1
113	43.6	42.7	41.7	40.7	39.8	38.8	37.9	37.0	36.0	35.1
114	43.6	42.7	41.7	40.7	39.8	38.8	37.9	37.0	36.0	35.1
115+	43.6	42.7	41.7	40.7	39.8	38.8	37.9	37.0	36.0	35.1

Ages	50	51	52	53	54	55	56	57	58	59
50	40.4	40.0	39.5	39.1	38.7	38.3	38.0	37.6	37.3	37.1
51	40.0	39.5	39.0	38.5	38.1	37.7	37.4	37.0	36.7	36.4
52	39.5	39.0	38.5	38.0	37.6	37.2	36.8	36.4	36.0	35.7
53	39.1	38.5	38.0	37.5	37.1	36.6	36.2	35.8	35.4	35.1
54	38.7	38.1	37.6	37.1	36.6	36.1	35.7	35.2	34.8	34.5
55	38.3	37.7	37.2	36.6	36.1	35.6	35.1	34.7	34.3	33.9
56	38.0	37.4	36.8	36.2	35.7	35.1	34.7	34.2	33.7	33.3
57	37.6	37.0	36.4	35.8	35.2	34.7	34.2	33.7	33.2	32.8
58	37.3	36.7	36.0	35.4	34.8	34.3	33.7	33.2	32.8	32.3
59	37.1	36.4	35.7	35.1	34.5	33.9	33.3	32.8	32.3	31.8
60	36.8	36.1	35.4	34.8	34.1	33.5	32.9	32.4	31.9	31.3

Continued.

Joint Life and Last Survivor Table

IRS Reg. 1.401(a)(9)-9, Q+A-3

Ages	50	51	52	53	54	55	56	57	58	59
61	36.6	35.8	35.1	34.5	33.8	33.2	32.6	32.0	31.4	30.9
62	36.3	35.6	34.9	34.2	33.5	32.9	32.2	31.6	31.1	30.5
63	36.1	35.4	34.6	33.9	33.2	32.6	31.9	31.3	30.7	30.1
64	35.9	35.2	34.4	33.7	33.0	32.3	31.6	31.0	30.4	29.8
65	35.8	35.0	34.2	33.5	32.7	32.0	31.4	30.7	30.0	29.4
66	35.6	34.8	34.0	33.3	32.5	31.8	31.1	30.4	29.8	29.1
67	35.5	34.7	33.9	33.1	32.3	31.6	30.9	30.2	29.5	28.8
68	35.3	34.5	33.7	32.9	32.1	31.4	30.7	29.9	29.2	28.6
69	35.2	34.4	33.6	32.8	32.0	31.2	30.5	29.7	29.0	28.3
70	35.1	34.3	33.4	32.6	31.8	31.1	30.3	29.5	28.8	28.1
71	35.0	34.2	33.3	32.5	31.7	30.9	30.1	29.4	28.6	27.9
72	34.9	34.1	33.2	32.4	31.6	30.8	30.0	29.2	28.4	27.7
73	34.8	34.0	33.1	32.3	31.5	30.6	29.8	29.1	28.3	27.5
74	34.8	33.9	33.0	32.2	31.4	30.5	29.7	28.9	28.1	27.4
75	34.7	33.8	33.0	32.1	31.3	30.4	29.6	28.8	28.0	27.2
76	34.6	33.8	32.9	32.0	31.2	30.3	29.5	28.7	27.9	27.1
77	34.6	33.7	32.8	32.0	31.1	30.3	29.4	28.6	27.8	27.0
78	34.5	33.6	32.8	31.9	31.0	30.2	29.3	28.5	27.7	26.9
79	34.5	33.6	32.7	31.8	31.0	30.1	29.3	28.4	27.6	26.8
80	34.5	33.6	32.7	31.8	30.9	30.1	29.2	28.4	27.5	26.7
81	34.4	33.5	32.6	31.8	30.9	30.0	29.2	28.3	27.5	26.6
82	34.4	33.5	32.6	31.7	30.8	30.0	29.1	28.3	27.4	26.6
83	34.4	33.5	32.6	31.7	30.8	29.9	29.1	28.2	27.4	26.5
84	34.3	33.4	32.5	31.7	30.8	29.9	29.0	28.2	27.3	26.5
85	34.3	33.4	32.5	31.6	30.7	29.9	29.0	28.1	27.3	26.4
86	34.3	33.4	32.5	31.6	30.7	29.8	29.0	28.1	27.2	26.4
87	34.3	33.4	32.5	31.6	30.7	29.8	28.9	28.1	27.2	26.4
88	34.3	33.4	32.5	31.6	30.7	29.8	28.9	28.0	27.2	26.3
89	34.3	33.3	32.4	31.5	30.7	29.8	28.9	28.0	27.2	26.3
90	34.2	33.3	32.4	31.5	30.6	29.8	28.9	28.0	27.1	26.3
91	34.2	33.3	32.4	31.5	30.6	29.7	28.9	28.0	27.1	26.3
92	34.2	33.3	32.4	31.5	30.6	29.7	28.8	28.0	27.1	26.2
93	34.2	33.3	32.4	31.5	30.6	29.7	28.8	28.0	27.1	26.2
94	34.2	33.3	32.4	31.5	30.6	29.7	28.8	27.9	27.1	26.2
95	34.2	33.3	32.4	31.5	30.6	29.7	28.8	27.9	27.1	26.2
96	34.2	33.3	32.4	31.5	30.6	29.7	28.8	27.9	27.0	26.2
97	34.2	33.3	32.4	31.5	30.6	29.7	28.8	27.9	27.0	26.2
98	34.2	33.3	32.4	31.5	30.6	29.7	28.8	27.9	27.0	26.2
99	34.2	33.3	32.4	31.5	30.6	29.7	28.8	27.9	27.0	26.2
100	34.2	33.3	32.4	31.5	30.6	29.7	28.8	27.9	27.0	26.1

Continued...

Joint Life and Last Survivor Table

IRS Reg. 1.401(a)(9)-9, Q+A-3

Ages	50	51	52	53	54	55	56	57	58	59
101	34.2	33.3	32.4	31.5	30.6	29.7	28.8	27.9	27.0	26.1
102	34.2	33.3	32.4	31.4	30.5	29.7	28.8	27.9	27.0	26.1
103	34.2	33.3	32.4	31.4	30.5	29.7	28.8	27.9	27.0	26.1
104	34.2	33.3	32.4	31.4	30.5	29.6	28.8	27.9	27.0	26.1
105	34.2	33.3	32.3	31.4	30.5	29.6	28.8	27.9	27.0	26.1
106	34.2	33.3	32.3	31.4	30.5	29.6	28.8	27.9	27.0	26.1
107	34.2	33.3	32.3	31.4	30.5	29.6	28.8	27.9	27.0	26.1
108	34.2	33.3	32.3	31.4	30.5	29.6	28.8	27.9	27.0	26.1
109	34.2	33.3	32.3	31.4	30.5	29.6	28.7	27.9	27.0	26.1
110	34.2	33.3	32.3	31.4	30.5	29.6	28.7	27.9	27.0	26.1
111	34.2	33.3	32.3	31.4	30.5	29.6	28.7	27.9	27.0	26.1
112	34.2	33.3	32.3	31.4	30.5	29.6	28.7	27.9	27.0	26.1
113	34.2	33.3	32.3	31.4	30.5	29.6	28.7	27.9	27.0	26.1
114	34.2	33.3	32.3	31.4	30.5	29.6	28.7	27.9	27.0	26.1
115+	34.2	33.3	32.3	31.4	30.5	29.6	28.7	27.9	27.0	26.1

Ages	60	61	62	63	64	65	66	67	68	69
60	30.9	30.4	30.0	29.6	29.2	28.8	28.5	28.2	27.9	27.6
61	30.4	29.9	29.5	29.0	28.6	28.3	27.9	27.6	27.3	27.0
62	30.0	29.5	29.0	28.5	28.1	27.7	27.3	27.0	26.7	26.4
63	29.6	29.0	28.5	28.1	27.6	27.2	26.8	26.4	26.1	25.7
64	29.2	28.6	28.1	27.6	27.1	26.7	26.3	25.9	25.5	25.2
65	28.8	28.3	27.7	27.2	26.7	26.2	25.8	25.4	25.0	24.6
66	28.5	27.9	27.3	26.8	26.3	25.8	25.3	24.9	24.5	24.1
67	28.2	27.6	27.0	26.4	25.9	25.4	24.9	24.4	24.0	23.6
68	27.9	27.3	26.7	26.1	25.5	25.0	24.5	24.0	23.5	23.1
69	27.6	27.0	26.4	25.7	25.2	24.6	24.1	23.6	23.1	22.6
70	27.4	26.7	26.1	25.4	24.8	24.3	23.7	23.2	22.7	22.2
71	27.2	26.5	25.8	25.2	24.5	23.9	23.4	22.8	22.3	21.8
72	27.0	26.3	25.6	24.9	24.3	23.7	23.1	22.5	22.0	21.4
73	26.8	26.1	25.4	24.7	24.0	23.4	22.8	22.2	21.6	21.1
74	26.6	25.9	25.2	24.5	23.8	23.1	22.5	21.9	21.3	20.8
75	26.5	25.7	25.0	24.3	23.6	22.9	22.3	21.6	21.0	20.5
76	26.3	25.6	24.8	24.1	23.4	22.7	22	21.4	20.8	20.2
77	26.2	25.4	24.7	23.9	23.2	22.5	21.8	21.2	20.6	19.9
78	26.1	25.3	24.6	23.8	23.1	22.4	21.7	21.0	20.3	19.7
79	26.0	25.2	24.4	23.7	22.9	22.2	21.5	20.8	20.1	19.5
80	25.9	25.1	24.3	23.6	22.8	22.1	21.3	20.6	20	19.3

Continued..

Joint Life and Last Survivor Table
IRS Reg. 1.401(a)(9)-9, Q+A-3

Ages	60	61	62	63	64	65	66	67	68	69
81	25.8	25.0	24.2	23.4	22.7	21.9	21.2	20.5	19.8	19.1
82	25.8	24.9	24.1	23.4	22.6	21.8	21.1	20.4	19.7	19.0
83	25.7	24.9	24.1	23.3	22.5	21.7	21.0	20.2	19.5	18.8
84	25.6	24.8	24.0	23.2	22.4	21.6	20.9	20.1	19.4	18.7
85	25.6	24.8	23.9	23.1	22.3	21.6	20.8	20.1	19.3	18.6
86	25.5	24.7	23.9	23.1	22.3	21.5	20.7	20.0	19.2	18.5
87	25.5	24.7	23.8	23.0	22.2	21.4	20.7	19.9	19.2	18.4
88	25.5	24.6	23.8	23.0	22.2	21.4	20.6	19.8	19.1	18.3
89	25.4	24.6	23.8	22.9	22.1	21.3	20.5	19.8	19.0	18.3
90	25.4	24.6	23.7	22.9	22.1	21.3	20.5	19.7	19.0	18.2
91	25.4	24.5	23.7	22.9	22.1	21.3	20.5	19.7	18.9	18.2
92	25.4	24.5	23.7	22.9	22.0	21.2	20.4	19.6	18.9	18.1
93	25.4	24.5	23.7	22.8	22.0	21.2	20.4	19.6	18.8	18.1
94	25.3	24.5	23.6	22.8	22.0	21.2	20.4	19.6	18.8	18.0
95	25.3	24.5	23.6	22.8	22.0	21.1	20.3	19.6	18.8	18.0
96	25.3	24.5	23.6	22.8	21.9	21.1	20.3	19.5	18.8	18.0
97	25.3	24.5	23.6	22.8	21.9	21.1	20.3	19.5	18.7	18.0
98	25.3	24.4	23.6	22.8	21.9	21.1	20.3	19.5	18.7	17.9
99	25.3	24.4	23.6	22.7	21.9	21.1	20.3	19.5	18.7	17.9
100	25.3	24.4	23.6	22.7	21.9	21.1	20.3	19.5	18.7	17.9
101	25.3	24.4	23.6	22.7	21.9	21.1	20.2	19.4	18.7	17.9
102	25.3	24.4	23.6	22.7	21.9	21.1	20.2	19.4	18.6	17.9
103	25.3	24.4	23.6	22.7	21.9	21.0	20.2	19.4	18.6	17.9
104	25.3	24.4	23.5	22.7	21.9	21.0	20.2	19.4	18.6	17.8
105	25.3	24.4	23.5	22.7	21.9	21.0	20.2	19.4	18.6	17.8
106	25.3	24.4	23.5	22.7	21.9	21.0	20.2	19.4	18.6	17.8
107	25.2	24.4	23.5	22.7	21.8	21.0	20.2	19.4	18.6	17.8
108	25.2	24.4	23.5	22.7	21.8	21.0	20.2	19.4	18.6	17.8
109	25.2	24.4	23.5	22.7	21.8	21.0	20.2	19.4	18.6	17.8
110	25.2	24.4	23.5	22.7	21.8	21.0	20.2	19.4	18.6	17.8
111	25.2	24.4	23.5	22.7	21.8	21.0	20.2	19.4	18.6	17.8
112	25.2	24.4	23.5	22.7	21.8	21.0	20.2	19.4	18.6	17.8
113	25.2	24.4	23.5	22.7	21.8	21.0	20.2	19.4	18.6	17.8
114	25.2	24.4	23.5	22.7	21.8	21.0	20.2	19.4	18.6	17.8
115+	25.2	24.4	23.5	22.7	21.8	21.0	20.2	19.4	18.6	17.8

Continued...

Joint Life and Last Survivor Table

IRS Reg. 1.401(a)(9)-9, Q+A-3

Ages	70	71	72	73	74	75	76	77	78	79
70	21.8	21.3	20.9	20.6	20.2	19.9	19.6	19.4	19.1	18.9
71	21.3	20.9	20.5	20.1	19.7	19.4	19.1	18.8	18.5	18.3
72	20.9	20.5	20.0	19.6	19.3	18.9	18.6	18.3	18.0	17.7
73	20.6	20.1	19.6	19.2	18.8	18.4	18.1	17.8	17.5	17.2
74	20.2	19.7	19.3	18.8	18.4	18.0	17.6	17.3	17.0	16.7
75	19.9	19.4	18.9	18.4	18.0	17.6	17.2	16.8	16.5	16.2
76	19.6	19.1	18.6	18.1	17.6	17.2	16.8	16.4	16.0	15.7
77	19.4	18.8	18.3	17.8	17.3	16.8	16.4	16.0	15.6	15.3
78	19.1	18.5	18.0	17.5	17.0	16.5	16.0	15.6	15.2	14.9
79	18.9	18.3	17.7	17.2	16.7	16.2	15.7	15.3	14.9	14.5
80	18.7	18.1	17.5	16.9	16.4	15.9	15.4	15.0	14.5	14.1
81	18.5	17.9	17.3	16.7	16.2	15.6	15.1	14.7	14.2	13.8
82	18.3	17.7	17.1	16.5	15.9	15.4	14.9	14.4	13.9	13.5
83	18.2	17.5	16.9	16.3	15.7	15.2	14.7	14.2	13.7	13.2
84	18.0	17.4	16.7	16.1	15.5	15.0	14.4	13.9	13.4	13.0
85	17.9	17.3	16.6	16.0	15.4	14.8	14.3	13.7	13.2	12.8
86	17.8	17.1	16.5	15.8	15.2	14.6	14.1	13.5	13.0	12.5
87	17.7	17.0	16.4	15.7	15.1	14.5	13.9	13.4	12.9	12.4
88	17.6	16.9	16.3	15.6	15.0	14.4	13.8	13.2	12.7	12.2
89	17.6	16.9	16.2	15.5	14.9	14.3	13.7	13.1	12.6	12.0
90	17.5	16.8	16.1	15.4	14.8	14.2	13.6	13.0	12.4	11.9
91	17.4	16.7	16.0	15.4	14.7	14.1	13.5	12.9	12.3	11.8
92	17.4	16.7	16.0	15.3	14.6	14.0	13.4	12.8	12.2	11.7
93	17.3	16.6	15.9	15.2	14.6	13.9	13.3	12.7	12.1	11.6
94	17.3	16.6	15.9	15.2	14.5	13.9	13.2	12.6	12.0	11.5
95	17.3	16.5	15.8	15.1	14.5	13.8	13.2	12.6	12.0	11.4
96	17.2	16.5	15.8	15.1	14.4	13.8	13.1	12.5	11.9	11.3
97	17.2	16.5	15.8	15.1	14.4	13.7	13.1	12.5	11.9	11.3
98	17.2	16.4	15.7	15.0	14.3	13.7	13.0	12.4	11.8	11.2
99	17.2	16.4	15.7	15.0	14.3	13.6	13.0	12.4	11.8	11.2
100	17.1	16.4	15.7	15.0	14.3	13.6	12.9	12.3	11.7	11.1
101	17.1	16.4	15.6	14.9	14.2	13.6	12.9	12.3	11.7	11.1
102	17.1	16.4	15.6	14.9	14.2	13.5	12.9	12.2	11.6	11.0
103	17.1	16.3	15.6	14.9	14.2	13.5	12.9	12.2	11.6	11.0
104	17.1	16.3	15.6	14.9	14.2	13.5	12.8	12.2	11.6	11.0
105	17.1	16.3	15.6	14.9	14.2	13.5	12.8	12.2	11.5	10.9
106	17.1	16.3	15.6	14.8	14.1	13.5	12.8	12.2	11.5	10.9
107	17.0	16.3	15.6	14.8	14.1	13.4	12.8	12.1	11.5	10.9
109	17.0	16.3	15.5	14.8	14.1	13.4	12.8	12.1	11.5	10.9
110	17.0	16.3	15.5	14.8	14.1	13.4	12.7	12.1	11.5	10.9

Continued...

Joint Life and Last Survivor Table

IRS Reg. 1.401(a)(9)-9, Q+A-3

Ages	70	71	72	73	74	75	76	77	78	79
111	17.0	16.3	15.5	14.8	14.1	13.4	12.7	12.1	11.5	10.8
112	17.0	16.3	15.5	14.8	14.1	13.4	12.7	12.1	11.5	10.8
113	17.0	16.3	15.5	14.8	14.1	13.4	12.7	12.1	11.4	10.8
114	17.0	16.3	15.5	14.8	14.1	13.4	12.7	12.1	11.4	10.8
115+	17.0	16.3	15.5	14.8	14.1	13.4	12.7	12.1	11.4	10.8

Ages	80	81	82	83	84	85	86	87	88	89
80	13.8	13.4	13.1	12.8	12.6	12.3	12.1	11.9	11.7	11.5
81	13.4	13.1	12.7	12.4	12.2	11.9	11.7	11.4	11.3	11.1
82	13.1	12.7	12.4	12.1	11.8	11.5	11.3	11.0	10.8	10.6
83	12.8	12.4	12.1	11.7	11.4	11.1	10.9	10.6	10.4	10.2
84	12.6	12.2	11.8	11.4	11.1	10.8	10.5	10.3	10.1	9.9
85	12.3	11.9	11.5	11.1	10.8	10.5	10.2	9.9	9.7	9.5
86	12.1	11.7	11.3	10.9	10.5	10.2	9.9	9.6	9.4	9.2
87	11.9	11.4	11.0	10.6	10.3	9.9	9.6	9.4	9.1	8.9
88	11.7	11.3	10.8	10.4	10.1	9.7	9.4	9.1	8.8	8.6
89	11.5	11.1	10.6	10.2	9.9	9.5	9.2	8.9	8.6	8.3
90	11.4	10.9	10.5	10.1	9.7	9.3	9.0	8.6	8.3	8.1
91	11.3	10.8	10.3	9.9	9.5	9.1	8.8	8.4	8.1	7.9
92	11.2	10.7	10.2	9.8	9.3	9.0	8.6	8.3	8.0	7.7
93	11.1	10.6	10.1	9.6	9.2	8.8	8.5	8.1	7.8	7.5
94	11.0	10.5	10.0	9.5	9.1	8.7	8.3	8.0	7.6	7.3
95	10.9	10.4	9.9	9.4	9.0	8.6	8.2	7.8	7.5	7.2
96	10.8	10.3	9.8	9.3	8.9	8.5	8.1	7.7	7.4	7.1
97	10.7	10.2	9.7	9.2	8.8	8.4	8.0	7.6	7.3	6.9
98	10.7	10.1	9.6	9.2	8.7	8.3	7.9	7.5	7.1	6.8
99	10.6	10.1	9.6	9.1	8.6	8.2	7.8	7.4	7.0	6.7
100	10.6	10.0	9.5	9.0	8.5	8.1	7.7	7.3	6.9	6.6
101	10.5	10.0	9.4	9.0	8.5	8.0	7.6	7.2	6.9	6.5
102	10.5	9.9	9.4	8.9	8.4	8.0	7.5	7.1	6.8	6.4
103	10.4	9.9	9.4	8.8	8.4	7.9	7.5	7.1	6.7	6.3
104	10.4	9.8	9.3	8.8	8.3	7.9	7.4	7.0	6.6	6.3
105	10.4	9.8	9.3	8.8	8.3	7.8	7.4	7.0	6.6	6.2
106	10.3	9.8	9.2	8.7	8.2	7.8	7.3	6.9	6.5	6.2
107	10.3	9.8	9.2	8.7	8.2	7.7	7.3	6.9	6.5	6.1
108	10.3	9.7	9.2	8.7	8.2	7.7	7.3	6.8	6.4	6.1
109	10.3	9.7	9.2	8.7	8.2	7.7	7.2	6.8	6.4	6.0
110	10.3	9.7	9.2	8.6	8.1	7.7	7.2	6.8	6.4	6.0

Continued...

Joint Life and Last Survivor Table
IRS Reg. 1.401(a)(9)-9, Q+A-3

Ages	80	81	82	83	84	85	86	87	88	89
111	10.3	9.7	9.1	8.6	8.1	7.6	7.2	6.8	6.3	6.0
112	10.2	9.7	9.1	8.6	8.1	7.6	7.2	6.7	6.3	5.9
113	10.2	9.7	9.1	8.6	8.1	7.6	7.2	6.7	6.3	5.9
114	10.2	9.7	9.1	8.6	8.1	7.6	7.1	6.7	6.3	5.9
115+	10.2	9.7	9.1	8.6	8.1	7.6	7.1	6.7	6.3	5.9

Ages	90	91	92	93	94	95	96	97	98	99
90	7.8	7.6	7.4	7.2	7.1	6.9	6.8	6.6	6.5	6.4
91	7.6	7.4	7.2	7.0	6.8	6.7	6.5	6.4	6.3	6.1
92	7.4	7.2	7.0	6.8	6.6	6.4	6.3	6.1	6.0	5.9
93	7.2	7.0	6.8	6.6	6.4	6.2	6.1	5.9	5.8	5.6
94	7.1	6.8	6.6	6.4	6.2	6.0	5.9	5.7	5.6	5.4
95	6.9	6.7	6.4	6.2	6.0	5.8	5.7	5.5	5.4	5.2
96	6.8	6.5	6.3	6.1	5.9	5.7	5.5	5.3	5.2	5.0
97	6.6	6.4	6.1	5.9	5.7	5.5	5.3	5.2	5.0	4.9
98	6.5	6.3	6.0	5.8	5.6	5.4	5.2	5.0	4.8	4.7
99	6.4	6.1	5.9	5.6	5.4	5.2	5.0	4.9	4.7	4.5
100	6.3	6.0	5.8	5.5	5.3	5.1	4.9	4.7	4.5	4.4
101	6.2	5.9	5.6	5.4	5.2	5.0	4.8	4.6	4.4	4.2
102	6.1	5.8	5.5	5.3	5.1	4.8	4.6	4.4	4.3	4.1
103	6.0	5.7	5.4	5.2	5.0	4.7	4.5	4.3	4.1	4.0
104	5.9	5.6	5.4	5.1	4.9	4.6	4.4	4.2	4.0	3.8
105	5.9	5.6	5.3	5.0	4.8	4.5	4.3	4.1	3.9	3.7
106	5.8	5.5	5.2	4.9	4.7	4.5	4.2	4.0	3.8	3.6
107	5.8	5.4	5.1	4.9	4.6	4.4	4.2	3.9	3.7	3.5
108	5.7	5.4	5.1	4.8	4.6	4.3	4.1	3.9	3.7	3.5
109	5.7	5.3	5.0	4.8	4.5	4.3	4.0	3.8	3.6	3.4
110	5.6	5.3	5.0	4.7	4.5	4.2	4.0	3.8	3.5	3.3
111	5.6	5.3	5.0	4.7	4.4	4.2	3.9	3.7	3.5	3.3
112	5.6	5.3	4.9	4.7	4.4	4.1	3.9	3.7	3.5	3.2
113	5.6	5.2	4.9	4.6	4.4	4.1	3.9	3.6	3.4	3.2
114	5.6	5.2	4.9	4.6	4.3	4.1	3.9	3.6	3.4	3.2
115+	5.5	5.2	4.9	4.6	4.3	4.1	3.8	3.6	3.4	3.1

Continued

Joint Life and Last Survivor Table
IRS Reg. 1.401(a)(9)-9, Q+A-3

Ages	100	101	102	103	104	105	106	107	108	109
100	4.2	4.1	3.9	3.8	3.7	3.5	3.4	3.3	3.3	3.2
101	4.1	3.9	3.7	3.6	3.5	3.4	3.2	3.1	3.1	3.0
102	3.9	3.7	3.6	3.4	3.3	3.2	3.1	3.0	2.9	2.8
103	3.8	3.6	3.4	3.3	3.2	3.0	2.9	2.8	2.7	2.6
104	3.7	3.5	3.3	3.2	3.0	2.9	2.7	2.6	2.5	2.4
105	3.5	3.4	3.2	3.0	2.9	2.7	2.6	2.5	2.4	2.3
106	3.4	3.2	3.1	2.9	2.7	2.6	2.4	2.3	2.2	2.1
107	3.3	3.1	3.0	2.8	2.6	2.5	2.3	2.2	2.1	2
108	3.3	3.1	2.9	2.7	2.5	2.4	2.2	2.1	1.9	1.8
109	3.2	3.0	2.8	2.6	2.4	2.3	2.1	2.0	1.8	1.7
110	3.1	2.9	2.7	2.5	2.3	2.2	2.0	1.9	1.7	1.6
111	3.1	2.9	2.7	2.5	2.3	2.1	1.9	1.8	1.6	1.5
112	3.0	2.8	2.6	2.4	2.2	2.0	1.9	1.7	1.5	1.4
113	3.0	2.8	2.6	2.4	2.2	2.0	1.8	1.6	1.5	1.3
114	3.0	2.7	2.5	2.3	2.1	1.9	1.8	1.6	1.4	1.3
115+	2.9	2.7	2.5	2.3	2.1	1.9	1.7	1.5	1.4	1.2

Ages	110	111	112	113	114	115
110	1.5	1.4	1.3	1.2	1.1	1.1
111	1.4	1.2	1.1	1.1	1.0	1.0
112	1.3	1.1	1.0	1.0	1.0	1.0
113	1.2	1.1	1.0	1.0	1.0	1.0
114	1.1	1.0	1.0	1.0	1.0	1.0
115+	1.1	1.0	1.0	1.0	1.0	1.0

Single Life Table

IRS Reg. 1.401(a)(9)-9, Q+A-1

Age	Life Expectancy	Age	Life Expectancy	Age	Life Expectancy
0	82.4	38	45.6	76	12.7
1	81.6	39	44.6	77	12.1
2	80.6	40	43.6	78	11.4
3	79.7	41	42.7	79	10.8
4	78.7	42	41.7	80	10.2
5	77.7	43	40.7	81	9.7
6	76.7	44	39.8	82	9.1
7	75.8	45	38.8	83	8.6
8	74.8	46	37.9	84	8.1
9	73.8	47	37.0	85	7.6
10	72.8	48	36.0	86	7.1
11	71.8	49	35.1	87	6.7
12	70.8	50	34.2	88	6.3
13	69.9	51	33.3	89	5.9
14	68.9	52	32.3	90	5.5
15	67.9	53	31.4	91	5.2
16	66.9	54	30.5	92	4.9
17	66.0	55	29.6	93	4.6
18	65.0	56	28.7	94	4.3
19	64.0	57	27.9	95	4.1
20	63.0	58	27.0	96	3.8
21	62.1	59	26.1	97	3.6
22	61.1	60	25.2	98	3.4
23	60.1	61	24.4	99	3.1
24	59.1	62	23.5	100	2.9
25	58.2	63	22.7	101	2.7
26	57.2	64	21.8	102	2.5
27	56.2	65	21.0	103	2.3
28	55.3	66	20.2	104	2.1
29	54.3	67	19.4	105	1.9
30	53.3	68	18.6	106	1.7
31	52.4	69	17.8	107	1.5
32	51.4	70	17.0	108	1.4
33	50.4	71	16.3	109	1.2
34	49.4	72	15.5	110	1.1
35	48.5	73	14.8	111+	1.0
36	47.5	74	14.1		
37	46.5	75	13.4		

RMD Amounts – A Moving Target
Traditional IRAs and Qualified Retirement Plans

RMD Amount – A Moving Target

Over the past few years the Internal Revenue Service (IRS) has issued three sets of rules concerning the required minimum distributions (RMDs) from Traditional IRAs and qualified retirement plans:

- **1987 Proposed Regulations:** In 1987, the IRS issued proposed regulations which were never made final. These 1987 proposed regulations generally calculate the RMD amounts using the life expectancies found in Reg.1.72-9, Table V (one life) or Table VI (joint and survivor)[1].

- **2001 Proposed Regulations:** In January 2001, the IRS issued new proposed RMD regulations in Reg-130477-00 and Reg-130481-00. Under these proposed regulations, the RMD is generally calculated using the participant's attained age and a minimum distribution factor. This factor is based on the joint life expectancy of the participant and a theoretical beneficiary (whether there is one or not) who is assumed to be exactly 10 years younger than the participant.

- **2002 Final Regulations:** Final regulations regarding RMDs were issued by the Treasury Department on April 16, 2002, in Treasury Decision 8987. These final regulations generally retained the rules outlined in the 2001 proposed regulations, but provided updated life expectancy tables. The new regulations were effective for distributions made in calendar years beginning on or after January 1, 2003. For required distributions during calendar 2002, a taxpayer could calculate the RMD amount using the 1987 proposed regulations, the 2001 proposed regulations, or the 2002 final regulations.

RMD Under 1987 Proposed Regulations

Single Individual: A participant age 75 has $100,000 remaining (as of December 31 of the prior year) in his IRA. From Table V, the expected return multiple for an individual age 75 is 12.5. The amount that must be withdrawn is $8,000, ($100,000 ÷ 12.5).

Joint and Survivor: An IRA participant, age 75, has $100,000 in the IRA as of December 31 of the prior year. His wife is age 63. From Table VI, the expected return multiple for an individual age 75 and a beneficiary age 63 is 23.1. The amount that must be withdrawn is $4,329.00 ($100,000 ÷ 23.1).

---

[1] Both Table V and Table VI are too large to be reproduced here.

Continued...

RMD Amounts – A Moving Target
Traditional IRAs and Qualified Retirement Plans

RMD Under 2001 Proposed Regulations

Example Using the 2001 Proposed Regulations: An IRA participant, age 75, has $100,000 in the IRA as of December 31 of the prior year. The minimum distribution factor for an individual age 75 is 21.8. The required minimum distribution for the current year would thus be $4,587.16 ($100,000 divided by 21.8).

If the participant's spouse is more than 10 years younger than the participant, and the spouse is the sole beneficiary of the account for the entire calendar year, the minimum distribution factor used in calculating the required minimum distribution is determined in accordance with Reg.1.72-9, using the values shown in Annuity Table VI.[1]

Spouse more than 10 Years Younger: An IRA participant, age 75, has $100,000 in the IRA as of December 31 of the prior year. His wife is age 63. The required minimum distribution for the current year would be $4,329.00 ($100,000 divided by 23.1, the Table VI factor for a participant age 75 and a spouse age 63).

2001 Proposed Regulations – Minimum Distribution Factors

Age	Divisor	Age	Divisor	Age	Divisor
70	26.2	86	13.1	102	5.0
71	25.3	87	12.4	103	4.7
72	24.4	88	11.8	104	4.4
73	23.5	89	11.1	105	4.1
74	22.7	90	10.5	106	3.8
75	21.8	91	9.9	107	3.6
76	20.9	92	9.4	108	3.3
77	20.1	93	8.8	109	3.1
78	19.2	94	8.3	110	2.8
79	18.4	95	7.8	111	2.6
80	17.6	96	7.3	112	2.4
81	16.8	97	6.9	113	2.2
82	16.0	98	6.5	114	2.0
83	15.3	99	6.1	115 and older	1.8
84	14.5	100	5.7		
85	13.8	101	5.3		

---

[1] See Prop. Treas. Reg. Sec. 1.401(a)(9)-5, Q&A4(b).

Continue

RMD Amounts – A Moving Target
Traditional IRAs and Qualified Retirement Plans

RMD Under 2002 Final Regulations

Example Using the 2002 Final Regulations: An IRA participant, age 75, has $100,000 in the IRA as of December 31 of the prior year. The required minimum distribution for the current year would be $4,366.81 ($100,000 divided by 22.9).

If the participant's spouse is more than 10 years younger than the participant, the minimum distribution factor used in calculating the required minimum distribution is determined in accordance with the Joint and Last Survivor Table specified in Reg. 1.401(a)(9)-9, Q&A3[1]. The participant's marital status is determined on January 1 of the calendar year.

Spouse more than 10 Years Younger: An IRA participant, age 75, has $100,000 in the IRA as of December 31 of the prior year. His wife is age 63. The required minimum distribution for the current year would be $4,115.23 ($100,000 divided by 24.3, the Joint and Last Survivor Table factor for a participant age 75 and a spouse age 63).

2002 Final Regulations - Uniform Lifetime Table

Age	Divisor	Age	Divisor	Age	Divisor
70	27.4	86	14.1	102	5.5
71	26.5	87	13.4	103	5.2
72	25.6	88	12.7	104	4.9
73	24.7	89	12.0	105	4.5
74	23.8	90	11.4	106	4.2
75	22.9	91	10.8	107	3.9
76	22.0	92	10.2	108	3.7
77	21.2	93	9.6	109	3.4
78	20.3	94	9.1	110	3.1
79	19.5	95	8.6	111	2.9
80	18.7	96	8.1	112	2.6
81	17.9	97	7.6	113	2.4
82	17.1	98	7.1	114	2.1
83	16.3	99	6.7	115 and older	1.9
84	15.5	100	6.3		
85	14.8	101	5.9		

---

[1] The Joint and Last Survivor Table covers ages 0 to 115 and is too large to be reproduced here. The table can be found in Appendix C of IRS Publication 590, Individual Retirement Arrangements (IRAs).

Continued...

RMD Amounts – A Moving Target

Traditional IRAs and Qualified Retirement Plans

Summary

The table below summarizes the RMD amounts that would be required for the examples discussed earlier, under the various sets of regulations.

Situation	1987 Proposed Regs.	2001 Proposed Regs.	2002 Final Regs.
Individual age 75, $100,000 balance in the IRA as of December 31 of the previous year	$8,000.00	$4,587.16	$4,366.81
Individual age 75, spouse age 63, $100,000 balance in the IRA as of December 31 of the previous year	$4,329.00	$4,329.00	$4,115.23

Seek Professional Advice

Given the complex and frequently changing nature of tax law, individuals faced with the need to make required distributions from IRAs or qualified retirement plans should seek the professional guidance of competent tax or accounting advisors.

Annuity Table V

Ordinary Life Annuities - One Life - Expected Return Multiples
IRS Reg. 1.72-9

Age	Multiple	Age	Multiple	Age	Multiple
5	76.6	42	40.6	79	10.0
6	75.6	43	39.6	80	9.5
7	74.7	44	38.7	81	8.9
8	73.7	45	37.7	82	8.4
9	72.7	46	36.8	83	7.9
10	71.7	47	35.9	84	7.4
11	70.7	48	34.9	85	6.9
12	69.7	49	34.0	86	6.5
13	68.8	50	33.1	87	6.1
14	67.8	51	32.2	88	5.7
15	66.8	52	31.3	89	5.3
16	65.8	53	30.4	90	5.0
17	64.8	54	29.5	91	4.7
18	63.9	55	28.6	92	4.4
19	62.9	56	27.7	93	4.1
20	61.9	57	26.8	94	3.9
21	60.9	58	25.9	95	3.7
22	59.9	59	25.0	96	3.4
23	59.0	60	24.2	97	3.2
24	58.0	61	23.3	98	3.0
25	57.0	62	22.5	99	2.8
26	56.0	63	21.6	100	2.7
27	55.1	64	20.8	101	2.5
28	54.1	65	20.0	102	2.3
29	53.1	66	19.2	103	2.1
30	52.2	67	18.4	104	1.9
31	51.2	68	17.6	105	1.8
32	50.2	69	16.8	106	1.6
33	49.3	70	16.0	107	1.4
34	48.3	71	15.3	108	1.3
35	47.3	72	14.6	109	1.1
36	46.4	73	13.9	110	1.0
37	45.4	74	13.2	111	.9
38	44.4	75	12.5	112	.8
39	43.5	76	11.9	113	.7
40	42.5	77	11.2	114	.6
41	41.5	78	10.6	115	.5

Annuity Table VI

Ordinary Joint Life and Last Survivor Annuities - Two Lives -
Expected Return Multiples - IRS Reg. 1.72-9

Age 55 - 64

Ages	55	56	57	58	59	60	61	62	63	64
55	34.4	33.9	33.5	33.1	32.7	32.3	32.0	31.7	31.4	31.1
56	33.9	33.4	33.0	32.5	32.1	31.7	31.4	31.0	30.7	30.4
57	33.5	33.0	32.5	32.0	31.6	31.2	30.8	30.4	30.1	29.8
58	33.1	32.5	32.0	31.5	31.1	30.6	30.2	29.9	29.5	29.2
59	32.7	32.1	31.6	31.1	30.6	30.1	29.7	29.3	28.9	28.6
60	32.3	31.7	31.2	30.6	30.1	29.7	29.2	28.8	28.4	28.0
61	32.0	31.4	30.8	30.2	29.7	29.2	28.7	28.3	27.8	27.4
62	31.7	31.0	30.4	29.9	29.3	28.8	28.3	27.6	27.3	26.9
63	31.4	30.7	30.1	29.5	28.9	28.4	27.6	27.3	26.9	26.4
64	31.1	30.4	29.8	29.2	28.6	28.0	27.4	26.9	26.4	25.9
65	30.9	30.2	29.5	28.9	28.2	27.6	27.1	26.5	26.0	25.5
66	30.6	29.9	29.2	28.6	27.9	27.3	26.7	26.1	25.6	25.1
67	30.4	29.7	29.0	28.3	27.6	27.0	26.4	25.8	25.2	24.7
68	30.2	29.5	28.8	28.1	27.4	26.7	26.1	25.5	24.9	24.3
69	30.1	29.3	28.6	27.8	27.1	26.5	25.8	25.2	24.6	24.0
70	29.9	29.1	28.4	27.6	26.9	26.2	25.6	24.9	24.3	23.7
71	29.7	29.0	28.2	27.5	26.7	26.0	25.3	24.7	24.0	23.4
72	29.6	28.8	28.1	27.3	26.5	25.8	25.1	24.4	23.8	23.1
73	29.5	28.7	27.9	27.1	26.4	25.6	24.9	24.2	23.5	22.9
74	29.4	28.6	27.8	27.0	26.2	25.5	24.7	24.0	23.3	22.7
75	29.3	28.5	27.7	26.9	26.1	25.3	24.6	23.8	23.1	22.4
76	29.2	28.4	27.6	26.8	26.0	25.2	24.4	23.7	23.0	22.3
77	29.1	28.3	27.5	26.7	25.9	25.1	24.3	23.6	22.8	22.1
78	29.1	28.2	27.4	26.6	25.8	25.0	24.2	23.4	22.7	21.9
79	29.0	28.2	27.3	26.5	25.7	24.9	24.1	23.3	22.6	21.8
80	29.0	28.1	27.3	26.4	25.6	24.8	24.0	23.2	22.4	21.7
81	28.9	28.1	27.2	26.4	25.5	24.7	23.9	23.1	22.3	21.6
82	28.9	28.0	27.2	26.3	25.5	24.6	23.8	23.0	22.3	21.5
83	28.8	28.0	27.1	26.3	25.4	24.6	23.8	23.0	22.2	21.4
84	28.8	27.9	27.1	26.2	25.4	24.5	23.7	22.9	22.1	21.3
85	28.8	27.9	27.0	26.2	25.3	24.5	23.7	22.8	22.0	21.3
86	28.7	27.9	27.0	26.1	25.3	24.5	23.6	22.8	22.0	21.2
87	28.7	27.8	27.0	26.1	25.3	24.4	23.6	22.8	21.9	21.1
88	28.7	27.8	27.0	26.1	25.2	24.4	23.5	22.7	21.9	21.1
89	28.7	27.8	26.9	26.1	25.2	24.4	23.5	22.7	21.9	21.1
90	28.7	27.8	26.9	26.1	25.2	24.3	23.5	22.7	21.8	21.0

Note: The tables shown here are a partial extract from Annuity Table VI. The full table covers ages 5 - 115.

Continue

Annuity Table VI

Ordinary Joint Life and Last Survivor Annuities - Two Lives -
Expected Return Multiples - IRS Reg. 1.72-9

Ages	55	56	57	58	59	60	61	62	63	64
91	28.7	27.8	26.9	26.0	25.2	24.3	23.5	22.6	21.8	21.0
92	28.6	27.8	26.9	26.0	25.2	24.3	23.5	22.6	21.8	21.0
93	28.6	27.8	26.9	26.0	25.1	24.3	23.4	22.6	21.8	20.9
94	28.6	27.7	26.9	26.0	25.1	24.3	23.4	22.6	21.7	20.9
95	28.6	27.7	26.9	26.0	25.1	24.3	23.4	22.6	21.7	20.9
96	28.6	27.7	26.9	26.0	25.1	24.2	23.4	22.6	21.7	20.9
97	28.6	27.7	26.8	26.0	25.1	24.2	23.4	22.5	21.7	20.9
98	28.6	27.7	26.8	26.0	25.1	24.2	23.4	22.5	21.7	20.9
99	28.6	27.7	26.8	26.0	25.1	24.2	23.4	22.5	21.7	20.9
100	28.6	27.7	26.8	26.0	25.1	24.2	23.4	22.5	21.7	20.8
101	28.6	27.7	26.8	25.9	25.1	24.2	23.4	22.5	21.7	20.8
102	28.6	27.7	26.8	25.9	25.1	24.2	23.3	22.5	21.7	20.8
103	28.6	27.7	26.8	25.9	25.1	24.2	23.3	22.5	21.7	20.8
104	28.6	27.7	26.8	25.9	25.1	24.2	23.3	22.5	21.6	20.8
105	28.6	27.7	26.8	25.9	25.1	24.2	23.3	22.5	21.6	20.8
106	28.6	27.7	26.8	25.9	25.1	24.2	23.3	22.5	21.6	20.8
107	28.6	27.7	26.8	25.9	25.1	24.2	23.3	22.5	21.6	20.8
108	28.6	27.7	26.8	25.9	25.1	24.2	23.3	22.5	21.6	20.8
109	28.6	27.7	26.8	25.9	25.1	24.2	23.3	22.5	21.6	20.8
110	28.6	27.7	26.8	25.9	25.1	24.2	23.3	22.5	21.6	20.8
111	28.6	27.7	26.8	25.9	25.0	24.2	23.3	22.5	21.6	20.8
112	28.6	27.7	26.8	25.9	25.0	24.2	23.3	22.5	21.6	20.8
113	28.6	27.7	26.8	25.9	25.0	24.2	23.3	22.5	21.6	20.8
114	28.6	27.7	26.8	25.9	25.0	24.2	23.3	22.5	21.6	20.8
115	28.6	27.7	26.8	25.9	25.0	24.2	23.3	22.5	21.6	20.8

Note: The tables shown here are a partial extract from Annuity Table VI. The full table covers ages 5 - 115.

Continued...

Annuity Table VI

Ordinary Joint Life and Last Survivor Annuities - Two Lives -
Expected Return Multiples - IRS Reg. 1.72-9

Age 65 - 74

Ages	65	66	67	68	69	70	71	72	73	74
65	25.0	24.6	24.2	23.8	23.4	23.1	22.8	22.5	22.2	22.0
66	24.6	24.1	23.7	23.3	22.9	22.5	22.2	21.9	21.6	21.4
67	24.2	23.7	23.2	22.8	22.4	22.0	21.7	21.3	21.0	20.8
68	23.8	23.3	22.8	22.3	21.9	21.5	21.2	20.8	20.5	20.2
69	23.4	22.9	22.4	21.9	21.5	21.1	20.7	20.3	20.0	19.6
70	23.1	22.5	22.0	21.5	21.1	20.6	20.2	19.8	19.4	19.1
71	22.8	22.2	21.7	21.2	20.7	20.2	19.8	19.4	19.0	18.6
72	22.5	21.9	21.3	20.8	20.3	19.8	19.4	18.9	18.5	18.2
73	22.2	21.6	21.0	20.5	20.0	19.4	19.0	18.5	18.1	17.7
74	22.0	21.4	20.8	20.2	19.6	19.1	18.6	18.2	17.7	17.3
75	21.8	21.1	20.5	19.9	19.3	18.8	18.3	17.8	17.3	16.9
76	21.6	20.9	20.3	19.7	19.1	18.5	18.0	17.5	17.0	16.5
77	21.4	20.7	20.1	19.4	18.8	18.3	17.7	17.2	16.7	16.2
78	21.2	20.5	19.9	19.2	18.6	18.0	17.5	16.9	16.4	15.9
79	21.1	20.4	19.7	19.0	18.4	17.8	17.2	16.7	16.1	15.6
80	21.0	20.2	19.5	18.9	18.2	17.6	17.0	16.4	15.9	15.4
81	20.8	20.1	19.4	18.7	18.1	17.4	16.8	16.2	15.7	15.1
82	20.7	20.0	19.3	18.6	17.9	17.3	16.6	16.0	15.5	14.9
83	20.6	19.9	19.2	18.5	17.8	17.1	16.5	15.9	15.3	14.7
84	20.5	19.8	19.1	18.4	17.7	17.0	16.3	15.7	15.1	14.5
85	20.5	19.7	19.0	18.3	17.6	16.9	16.2	15.6	15.0	14.4
86	20.4	19.6	18.9	18.2	17.5	16.8	16.1	15.5	14.8	14.2
87	20.4	19.6	18.8	18.1	17.4	16.7	16.0	15.4	14.7	14.1
88	20.3	19.5	18.8	18.0	17.3	16.6	15.9	15.3	14.6	14.0
89	20.3	19.5	18.7	18.0	17.2	16.5	15.8	15.2	14.5	13.9
90	20.2	19.4	18.7	17.9	17.2	16.5	15.8	15.1	14.5	13.8
91	20.2	19.4	18.6	17.9	17.1	16.4	15.7	15.0	14.4	13.7
92	20.2	19.4	18.6	17.8	17.1	16.4	15.7	15.0	14.3	13.7
93	20.1	19.3	18.6	17.8	17.1	16.3	15.6	14.9	14.3	13.6
94	20.1	19.3	18.5	17.8	17.0	16.3	15.6	14.9	14.2	13.6
95	20.1	19.3	18.5	17.8	17.0	16.3	15.6	14.9	14.2	13.5
96	20.1	19.3	18.5	17.7	17.0	16.2	15.5	14.8	14.2	13.5
97	20.1	19.3	18.5	17.7	17.0	16.2	15.5	14.8	14.1	13.5
98	20.1	19.3	18.5	17.7	16.9	16.2	15.5	14.8	14.1	13.4
99	20.0	19.2	18.5	17.7	16.9	16.2	15.5	14.7	14.1	13.4
100	20.0	19.2	18.4	17.7	16.9	16.2	15.4	14.7	14.0	13.4

Note: The tables shown here are a partial extract from Annuity Table VI. The full table covers ages 5 - 115.

Continue

Annuity Table VI

Ordinary Joint Life and Last Survivor Annuities - Two Lives -
Expected Return Multiples - IRS Reg. 1.72-9

Ages	65	66	67	68	69	70	71	72	73	74
101	20.0	19.2	18.4	17.7	16.9	16.1	15.4	14.7	14.0	13.3
102	20.0	19.2	18.4	17.6	16.9	16.1	15.4	14.7	14.0	13.3
103	20.0	19.2	18.4	17.6	16.9	16.1	15.4	14.7	14.0	13.3
104	20.0	19.2	18.4	17.6	16.9	16.1	15.4	14.7	14.0	13.3
105	20.0	19.2	18.4	17.6	16.8	16.1	15.4	14.6	13.9	13.3
106	20.0	19.2	18.4	17.6	16.8	16.1	15.3	14.6	13.9	13.3
107	20.0	19.2	18.4	17.6	16.8	16.1	15.3	14.6	13.9	13.2
108	20.0	19.2	18.4	17.6	16.8	16.1	15.3	14.6	13.9	13.2
109	20.0	19.2	18.4	17.6	16.8	16.1	15.3	14.6	13.9	13.2
110	20.0	19.2	18.4	17.6	16.8	16.1	15.3	14.6	13.9	13.2
111	20.0	19.2	18.4	17.6	16.8	16.0	15.3	14.6	13.9	13.2
112	20.0	19.2	18.4	17.6	16.8	16.0	15.3	14.6	13.9	13.2
113	20.0	19.2	18.4	17.6	16.8	16.0	15.3	14.6	13.9	13.2
114	20.0	19.2	18.4	17.6	16.8	16.0	15.3	14.6	13.9	13.2
115	20.0	19.2	18.4	17.6	16.8	16.0	15.3	14.6	13.9	13.2

Note: The tables shown here are a partial extract from Annuity Table VI. The full table covers ages 5 - 115.

Continued...

Annuity Table VI

Ordinary Joint Life and Last Survivor Annuities - Two Lives -
Expected Return Multiples - IRS Reg. 1.72-9

Age 75 - 84

Ages	75	76	77	78	79	80	81	82	83	84
75	16.5	16.1	15.8	15.4	15.1	14.9	14.6	14.4	14.2	14.0
76	16.1	15.7	15.4	15.0	14.7	14.4	14.1	13.9	13.7	13.5
77	15.8	15.4	15.0	14.6	14.3	14.0	13.7	13.4	13.2	13.0
78	15.4	15.0	14.6	14.2	13.9	13.5	13.2	13.0	12.7	12.5
79	15.1	14.7	14.3	13.9	13.5	13.2	12.8	12.5	12.3	12.0
80	14.9	14.4	14.0	13.5	13.2	12.8	12.5	12.2	11.9	11.6
81	14.6	14.1	13.7	13.2	12.8	12.5	12.1	11.8	11.5	11.2
82	14.4	13.9	13.4	13.0	12.5	12.2	11.8	11.5	11.1	10.9
83	14.2	13.7	13.2	12.7	12.3	11.9	11.5	11.1	10.8	10.5
84	14.0	13.5	13.0	12.5	12.0	11.6	11.2	10.9	10.5	10.2
85	13.8	13.3	12.8	12.3	11.8	11.4	11.0	10.6	10.2	9.9
86	13.7	13.1	12.6	12.1	11.6	11.2	10.8	10.4	10.0	9.7
87	13.5	13.0	12.4	11.9	11.4	11.0	10.6	10.1	9.8	9.4
88	13.4	12.8	12.3	11.8	11.3	10.8	10.4	10.0	9.6	9.2
89	13.3	12.7	12.2	11.6	11.1	10.7	10.2	9.8	9.4	9.0
90	13.2	12.6	12.1	11.5	11.0	10.5	10.1	9.6	9.2	8.8
91	13.1	12.5	12.0	11.4	10.9	10.4	9.9	9.5	9.1	8.7
92	13.1	12.5	11.9	11.3	10.8	10.3	9.8	9.4	8.9	8.5
93	13.0	12.4	11.8	11.3	10.7	10.2	9.7	9.3	8.8	8.4
94	12.9	12.3	11.7	11.2	10.6	10.1	9.6	9.2	8.7	8.3
95	12.9	12.3	11.7	11.1	10.6	10.1	9.6	9.1	8.6	8.2
96	12.9	12.2	11.6	11.1	10.5	10.0	9.5	9.0	8.5	8.1
97	12.8	12.2	11.6	11.0	10.5	9.9	9.4	8.9	8.5	8.0
98	12.8	12.2	11.5	11.0	10.4	9.9	9.4	8.9	8.4	8.0
99	12.7	12.1	11.5	10.9	10.4	9.8	9.3	8.8	8.3	7.9
100	12.7	12.1	11.5	10.9	10.3	9.8	9.2	8.7	8.3	7.8
101	12.7	12.1	11.4	10.8	10.3	9.7	9.2	8.7	8.2	7.8
102	12.7	12.0	11.4	10.8	10.2	9.7	9.2	8.7	8.2	7.7
103	12.6	12.0	11.4	10.8	10.2	9.7	9.1	8.6	8.1	7.7
104	12.6	12.0	11.4	10.8	10.2	9.6	9.1	8.6	8.1	7.6
105	12.6	12.0	11.3	10.7	10.2	9.6	9.1	8.5	8.0	7.6
106	12.6	11.9	11.3	10.7	10.1	9.6	9.0	8.5	8.0	7.5
107	12.6	11.9	11.3	10.7	10.1	9.6	9.0	8.5	8.0	7.5
108	12.6	11.9	11.3	10.7	10.1	9.5	9.0	8.5	8.0	7.5
109	12.6	11.9	11.3	10.7	10.1	9.5	9.0	8.4	7.9	7.5
110	12.6	11.9	11.3	10.7	10.1	9.5	9.0	8.4	7.9	7.4
111	12.5	11.9	11.3	10.7	10.1	9.5	8.9	8.4	7.9	7.4
112	12.5	11.9	11.3	10.6	10.1	9.5	8.9	8.4	7.9	7.4
113	12.5	11.9	11.2	10.6	10.0	9.5	8.9	8.4	7.9	7.4
114	12.5	11.9	11.2	10.6	10.0	9.5	8.9	8.4	7.9	7.4
115	12.5	11.9	11.2	10.6	10.0	9.5	8.9	8.4	7.9	7.4

Note: The tables shown here are a partial extract from Annuity Table VI. The full table covers ages 5 - 115.

Annuity Table VI

Ordinary Joint Life and Last Survivor Annuities - Two Lives -
Expected Return Multiples - IRS Reg. 1.72-9

Age 85 - 94

Ages	85	86	87	88	89	90	91	92	93	94
85	9.6	9.3	9.1	8.9	8.7	8.5	8.3	8.2	8.0	7.9
86	9.3	9.1	8.8	8.6	8.3	8.2	8.0	7.8	7.7	7.6
87	9.1	8.8	8.5	8.3	8.1	7.9	7.7	7.5	7.4	7.2
88	8.9	8.6	8.3	8.0	7.8	7.6	7.4	7.2	7.1	6.9
89	8.7	8.3	8.1	7.8	7.5	7.3	7.1	6.9	6.8	6.6
90	8.5	8.2	7.9	7.6	7.3	7.1	6.9	6.7	6.5	6.4
91	8.3	8.0	7.7	7.4	7.1	6.9	6.7	6.5	6.3	6.2
92	8.2	7.8	7.5	7.2	6.9	6.7	6.5	6.3	6.1	5.9
93	8.0	7.7	7.4	7.1	6.8	6.5	6.3	6.1	5.9	5.8
94	7.9	7.6	7.2	6.9	6.6	6.4	6.2	5.9	5.8	5.6
95	7.8	7.5	7.1	6.8	6.5	6.3	6.0	5.8	5.6	5.4
96	7.7	7.3	7.0	6.7	6.4	6.1	5.9	5.7	5.5	5.3
97	7.6	7.3	6.9	6.6	6.3	6.0	5.8	5.5	5.3	5.1
98	7.6	7.2	6.8	6.5	6.2	5.9	5.6	5.4	5.2	5.0
99	7.5	7.1	6.7	6.4	6.1	5.8	5.5	5.3	5.1	4.9
100	7.4	7.0	6.6	6.3	6.0	5.7	5.4	5.2	5.0	4.8
101	7.3	6.9	6.6	6.2	5.9	5.6	5.3	5.1	4.9	4.7
102	7.3	6.9	6.5	6.2	5.8	5.5	5.3	5.0	4.8	4.6
103	7.2	6.8	6.4	6.1	5.8	5.5	5.2	4.9	4.7	4.5
104	7.2	6.8	6.4	6.0	5.7	5.4	5.1	4.8	4.6	4.4
105	7.1	6.7	6.3	6.0	5.6	5.3	5.0	4.8	4.5	4.3
106	7.1	6.7	6.3	5.9	5.6	5.3	5.0	4.7	4.5	4.2
107	7.1	6.6	6.2	5.9	5.5	5.2	4.9	4.6	4.4	4.2
108	7.0	6.6	6.2	5.8	5.5	5.2	4.9	4.6	4.3	4.1
109	7.0	6.6	6.2	5.8	5.5	5.1	4.8	4.5	4.3	4.1
110	7.0	6.6	6.2	5.8	5.4	5.1	4.8	4.5	4.3	4.0
111	7.0	6.5	6.1	5.7	5.4	5.1	4.8	4.5	4.2	4.0
112	7.0	6.5	6.1	5.7	5.4	5.0	4.7	4.4	4.2	3.9
113	6.9	6.5	6.1	5.7	5.4	5.0	4.7	4.4	4.2	3.9
114	6.9	6.5	6.1	5.7	5.3	5.0	4.7	4.4	4.1	3.9
115	6.9	6.5	6.1	5.7	5.3	5.0	4.7	4.4	4.1	3.9

Note: The tables shown here are a partial extract from Annuity Table VI. The full table covers ages 5 - 115.

587

Business Owner Planning Needs

Below is a list of concerns that may be of particular interest to you, the business owner. Indicate the level of importance of each item with a check mark.

	Level of Importance		
	High	**Medium**	**Low**
Business Concerns			
Business Succession Planning			
Key Employee Planning			
Executive Benefit Planning			
Estate Concerns			
Planning Estate Distributions			
Estate Tax Planning			
Charitable Planning			
Survivorship Needs Planning			
Retirement Concerns			
Planning for Your Retirement			
Qualified Retirement Plans			
Traditional IRA/Roth IRA			
Investment Risk Analysis			
Other			
Long-term Care Planning			
Education Planning			
Disability Income Planning			
Life Insurance Planning			

Retirement and the Business Professional
Don't Put All Your Eggs in One Basket

Many entrepreneurs who start or purchase a business do so for a number of reasons, both emotional and financial. Social status, the freedom to be your own boss and the potential for a high income are a few of the reasons commonly cited.

For some, business ownership is also seen as a primary way to pay for retirement. If everything goes as planned, the business owner works hard and, over time, the business grows and becomes more valuable. When the owner reaches a certain age the business is sold, with the proceeds from the sale funding the retirement years.

The Realities of Business Ownership

Using the business as the sole means of achieving financial independence amounts to placing a bet that the owner will be able to sell at the right time, the right price and under the right terms. There are several reasons why this may not happen:

- **Business failure:** Despite good intentions and hard work, businesses do fail. In 2003, for example, there were 612,296 new, small (less than 500 employees) businesses started in the United States; in the same year, 540,658 small businesses closed their doors, and 35,037 filed for bankruptcy.[1]

- **Timing of the sale:** Selling a business is a complex, often time-consuming procedure. The actual process of finding a buyer, negotiating the deal, arranging financing and finally closing the sale may extend over months or even years.

- **Proceeds:** Depending on market conditions, the amount realized may not be enough to pay for retirement. Income taxes will inevitably consume some of the proceeds. The owner may have to accept installment payments, rather than a lump sum.

- **"I am the business":** The value of a business may depend largely on the skills and/or customer relationships of a particular owner.

Diversification to Reduce Risk

A business owner who seeks to reduce risk will view his or her business as one asset among many. In addition to the business, a diversified portfolio could include the following.

- **Qualified retirement plans:** Business income is used to fund employer-sponsored qualified plans with a current deduction for contributions and tax-deferred growth.

- **Nonqualified plans:** Nonqualified deferred compensation plans are often used to reward selected employees and serve to supplement qualified retirement plans.

- **General investment portfolio:** A business owner can develop a general investment portfolio, outside of the framework of the business.

---

[1] Source: U.S. Small Business Administration, Office of Advocacy: "Frequently Asked Questions." See http://www.sba.gov/advo/frequentlyaskedquestions, accessed 3/02/07.

Basic Types of Business Organizations

	Sole Proprietor	Partnership	C Corporation	S Corporation	Limited Liability Company
Creation	No written document is necessary.	Created by oral or written agreement.	Articles of incorporation filed with state.	Articles of incorporation filed with state.	Operating agreement/articles of organization filed with state.
Life span	Expires when owner dies.	Agreement can set time. Otherwise, dissolved at death of any partner.	Continues on after shareholder's death.	Continues on after shareholder's death.	May dissolve on a member's death, retirement, bankruptcy, resignation or expulsion.
Management responsibility	Rests with sole proprietor.	Rests with Partners.	Rests with board of directors who are elected by shareholders.	Rests with board of directors who are elected by shareholders..	Rests with managers.
Liability	Sole proprietor is personally liable for all debts.	Each partner is personally liable for all business debts or liabilities.	Liability is limited to the assets of the corporation, not shareholder's assets.	Liability is limited to the assets of the corporation, not shareholder's assets.	Liability is limited to the assets of the company, not member's assets.
Income taxes	All income and expenses are reported on tax return of sole proprietor.	Partnership prepares information return, but income is taxable to partners.[1]	Corporation pays tax on net income. Reasonable salaries are deductible to corporation and taxable to employees.	Corporation files information return, but income is taxed to shareholders.[1]	Company files information return, but income is taxed to the owners (members).[1]
Sale or transfer during lifetime	Sole proprietor may sell or give away any asset.	A transfer will dissolve the partnership, unless remaining partner(s) agree(s) to new partner.	Stock is transferrable. Remaining shareholders may have a first right of refusal prior to a sale to an outsider.	Restricted to 100 shareholders who are resident U.S. citizens, estates and certain types of trusts.	Members owning substantially all of the company may transfer interests without consent.
Sale or transfer at death	Is usually dissolved. Estate may sell or operate it.	Automatically dissolved, unless agreement to the contrary.	Stock can be transferred to heirs. Stock can also be sold or retained, unless a buy-sell agreement exists.	Estate is eligible shareholder only during estate administration. Otherwise, same as above.	Deceased's estate is an eligible shareholder. Otherwise, same as above.

[1] State law will vary: some states tax partnership, S corporations and LLC income.

Advantages and Disadvantages of Corporations

A corporation is an artificial person created through state charter. As a legal person, the corporation can enter contracts, own property, and hire employees. A corporation is a separate taxpayer from its owners, the shareholders.

Advantages of Incorporation

- **Limited liability:** The shareholders are not generally liable for the debts and liabilities of the corporation beyond their contributions to capital. However, lenders will usually require personal guarantees by the shareholders on loans to the corporation.

- **Continuity:** The corporation continues in existence, even if its shareholders die.

- **Ease of transfer:** Shares of stock can be transferred to children or other buyers to raise capital or for estate distribution purposes.

- **Centralized management:** The shareholders elect the Board of Directors, who manages the affairs of the corporation, including appointment of officers.

- **Tax and fringe benefits**
  - Tax-qualified retirement plans
  - Medical and disability plans
  - Group life insurance
  - Split-dollar insurance plans
  - Salary continuation plans

Disadvantages of Incorporation

- Cost to establish a corporation

- Need to observe corporate formalities

- Double taxation of income if dividends are paid. Possible tax on excess corporate accumulated earnings.

S Corporations

Corporations that elect to be taxed as small business corporations under IRC Sec. 1362 are taxed similarly to a partnership. The corporation (as long as it qualifies for S corporation status) generally pays no tax.[1] All profits and losses flow through the corporation to the shareholders and they are taxed on the profits whether or not they are taken out of the corporation.

The S corporation is often used to spread corporate income among family members who own the company stock (after employees receive adequate salaries).

Business losses, often incurred in the early years of a business, can be passed through to the shareholders and can be used to offset other ordinary income. Deductible losses are limited to shareholder's basis in stock including loans to the corporation.

Requirements to Elect S Corporation Treatment

- Election must be made on or before the 15th day of the 3rd month of a corporation's tax year to be effective for that year.

- The number of shareholders cannot exceed 100, with all members of a family (and their estates) automatically being treated as one shareholder. The members of a family include a common ancestor, lineal descendent of the common ancestor, and the spouses, or former spouses, of such lineal descendents or common ancestor, spanning no more than six generations. See IRC Sec. 1361(c)(1).

- Each shareholder must be an individual, a decedent's estate, a bankrupt's estate or certain trusts specified in IRC Sec. 1361(c)(2), including a qualified subchapter S trust provided for by IRC Sec. 1361(d)(1).[2] Eligible shareholders also include an electing small business trust,[3] charities, and qualified pension, profit sharing and stock bonus plans,[4] and certain IRAs holding bank corporation stock.[5]

- There must not be more than one class of stock, although there can be voting and nonvoting shares.

- All stockholders must consent to the election.

---

[1] Some states impose a tax on income.
[2] A shareholder's agreement can be used to prevent stockholders from transferring S corporation stock to a nonqualifying trust.
[3] Each beneficiary of the trust is counted in determining whether the shareholder limit has been exceeded. An interest in these trusts must be acquired by gift or bequest (not purchased).
[4] See IRC Secs. 1361(b)(1)(B) and 1361(c)(6).
[5] IRC Sec. 1361(c)(2)(A)(vi).

Continued.

S Corporations

Termination of the S Election[1]

- S corporation status is automatically terminated if any event occurs that would prohibit the corporation from making the election in the first place. The election terminates as of the date of the disqualifying event.

- The S election can be revoked with the consent of more than 50% of the outstanding stock held by shareholders.

- If a corporation, for three consecutive years, has both accumulated earnings and profits, as well as passive investment income exceeding 25% of its gross receipts, its election will be revoked beginning with the following tax year.

---

[1] If the election is terminated or revoked, the corporation cannot re-elect S status without IRS consent until the 5th year after the year the termination or revocation is effective.

Limited Liability Companies

The limited liability company (LLC) is, for federal income tax purposes, a pass-through entity like a partnership or S corporation, but it includes the limited liability of a corporation.

| | Partnership | | Corporation | | |
	General	Limited	C Type	S Type	LLC
Personal liability for business	Yes fully liable	Only limited	Only limited	Only limited	Only limited
Participate in management	Yes	No[1]	Yes	Yes	Yes
Any type or number of shareholders	Yes	Yes	Yes	No[2]	Yes
Avoids double taxation	Yes	Yes	No[3]	Yes	Yes

LLCs are created by statute and vary from state to state. The operating agreement sets forth the relationship of its members (owners) and governs how the LLC will be operated, allocation of earnings, capital contributions and distributions. The formalities found in the corporate business organization, like directors meetings, written minutes, etc., may not be required.

Federal Income Taxation of LLCs

Federal income tax law[4] provides some flexibility as to how an LLC and its members are taxed:

- **Single member LLC:** An LLC with a single member by default is "Disregarded as an entity separate from its owner..". For LLCs with a single <u>individual</u> member, this means that income and expenses are generally reported on the individual's personal return on Schedule C, E, or F. An LLC with a single individual member may elect to report income and expenses as a corporation. For LLCs with a single <u>corporate</u> member, income and expenses are typically reported on the corporation's return.

- **Multiple member LLC:** An LLC with two or more members (individual or corporate) by default reports income and expenses as a partnership. Such an LLC may elect to report income and expenses as a corporation.

State income tax law can vary and does not necessarily follow federal law.

---

[1] Limited partners cannot participate in management.
[2] The S corporation is currently limited to 100 shareholders and there can be only one class of stock.
[3] C corporation's net income is subject to the corporate federal income tax up to 35%.
[4] See IRC Reg. 301.7701-3.

Qualified Deferred Compensation Plan
IRC Sec. 457

Employees (or independent contractors) of
state and local governments and tax-exempt
employers can elect to defer future income
(and taxation) under an eligible deferred
compensation plan described in IRC Sec.
457.

Eligible Deferred Compensation Plan

- The plan must be established and maintained by an eligible employer, which includes
  states, political subdivisions of states, agencies of state and local governments, as well
  as any other organization exempt from income tax under IRC Sec. 501(c); e.g.,
  charitable organizations, trade associations, farmers cooperatives, etc.

- The Small Business Job Protection Act of 1996 requires the assets of state and local
  government plans to be held in a trust or custodial account.

- In general, the plan cannot provide for distribution of amounts payable prior to the
  participant's separation from service or attainment of age 70½, unless the participant is
  faced with an unforeseeable emergency. However, the plan may adopt provisions
  permitting in-service distribution of benefits if the total benefit is less than a specified
  amount, currently $5,000. Such in-service distributions may be either voluntary or
  involuntary and are subject to strict conditions.

- The plan must provide that the amounts of income deferred, plus assets purchased with
  those funds, plus the income earned on those assets remain the property of the
  employer. However, the IRS has permitted the use of a rabbi trust to prevent the
  employer from using the funds for other purposes. See Ltr. Rul. 9205002.

- There must be a limit of $15,500[1] of income that can be deferred in one year. For
  individuals who are participants in state or local government plans, and who are at least
  age 50, catch-up contributions of $5,000 may also be made.[1] The age 50 and over
  catch-up contributions are not available to participants in plans sponsored by tax-
  exempt organizations.

- During the three years prior to normal retirement age, other catch-up limits apply.[2]

- Plan loans can be made under the same rules that apply to qualified plans.

Excise and Penalty Taxes

The 10% penalty tax on early distributions from qualified plans and 403(b) plans does not
apply to IRC Sec. 457 plans. However, the minimum distribution rules effective at age
70½ or later retirement do apply.

---

[1] 2008 value.
[2] These other limits are two times the normal contribution limits.

Continued...

Qualified Deferred Compensation Plan
IRC Sec. 457

Life Insurance

The premium paid for life insurance in an IRC Sec. 457 plan will not be taxable to the insured if:

- The employer retains all incidents of ownership in the policy,
- The employer is the beneficiary, and
- There is no requirement to transfer the policy or its proceeds.

The death benefits paid from an IRC Sec. 457 plan to an employee's heirs are included as taxable income to those heirs under deferred compensation rules. See Treasury Reg. 1.457-10(d).

Nonqualified Deferred Compensation Plan

	Corporation	Key Employee
Agreement	Agrees to pay compensation for a set period after a stated date or death.	Agrees to continue service until specified date (e.g., normal retirement age). Optional: After separation, agrees not to compete and/or to provide consultation services.
Advantages	Corporation retains key employee.	Employee (or heirs) receives extra retirement benefit when tax bracket may be lower.
Taxation	Benefits paid to employee (or heirs) are deductible to corporation when paid or constructively received.	Benefits are taxed when payments are made or constructively received.

How It Works

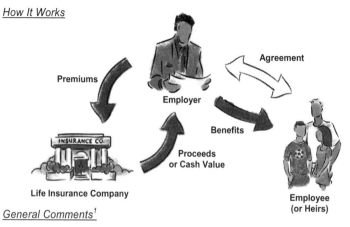

Premiums

Agreement

Employer

Benefits

Proceeds or Cash Value

Life Insurance Company

Employee (or Heirs)

General Comments[1]

- Deferral must generally be agreed upon before the compensation is earned.

- If the plan is unfunded, the compensation is not taxable until received.

- If the plan is funded, the employee's rights must be subject to substantial risk of forfeiture and they must be nontransferable. If they are not subject to such risk or are transferable, the payments become currently taxable.

- Employer can pick and choose which employees to benefit. However, if they are not highly compensated, the plan may be subject to ERISA requirements.

- A cash value life insurance contract can be used to informally fund an agreement. It can provide the necessary funds at either death or distribution.[2]

- Nonqualified plans are not subject to the pre-age 59½ distribution penalties or the age-based mandatory distribution rules imposed on qualified plans, IRAs, etc.

---

[1] The AJCA of 2004 significantly changed nonqualified deferred compensation plan rules. If a plan fails to meet the new requirements, compensation deferred under the plan becomes currently taxable and penalties and interest apply.
[2] Under the provisions of IRC Sec. 101(j), added by the Pension Protection Act of 2006, death proceeds from a life insurance policy owned by an employer on the life of an employee are generally includable in income unless certain requirements are met. Until the full scope of this new law is clarified, caution is advised. State or local law may vary.

Rabbi Trust
Protecting Deferred Compensation

Money which is set aside by an employer to fund future deferred compensation arrangements with employees must be subject to the claims of company creditors to avoid current taxation to the employee. However, employees often feel more threatened by potential changes in company management and the subsequent use of these funds for business objectives of the new officers.

One way to reduce these fears is for the employer to establish a rabbi trust (so called because the first IRS ruling involved a rabbi). Assets transferred to the rabbi trust are still available to the general creditors of the employer in the event of insolvency, but not for other company uses.

Some employers may not wish to make contributions to the trust each year, preferring to pay non-qualified deferred compensation benefits from cash flow as they come due. To ease employee concerns over the effect of any change in company control on these unfunded benefits, the agreement could provide for an initial funding of the trust with a nominal dollar amount. If a potential change of control occurs, the company is then obligated to contribute to the trust the present value of the future benefits. If the change of control does not take place within a certain period, e.g., one year, the funds could then be returned to the employer. See IRS Letter Ruling 8907034.[1]

The employer receives a deduction only upon distribution to the employee, who at that time is also subject to income taxation on the payment.

The IRS has issued a model rabbi trust for those who desire a safe harbor when establishing a non-qualified deferred compensation plan. (See Rev. Proc. 92-64.)

The model rabbi trust form can be used by the employer with the assurance that the contributions to the trust will not be taxable to the executive. Generally, the IRS will no longer issue advance rulings as to the tax treatment of non-qualified deferred compensation plans informally funded through a trust unless the employer uses the model rabbi trust or there is a rare and unusual circumstance.

IRC Sec. 409A

The American Jobs Creation Act of 2004 included new IRC Sec. 409A, which added to federal income tax law numerous requirements that a nonqualified deferred compensation plan must meet to avoid having deferred amounts treated as being constructively received in the current year. If these requirements are not met, all current and past-deferred compensation, plus any earnings, are included in the employee's gross income for the current tax year. Further, an additional 20% tax is levied, plus an underpayment interest penalty. State or local law may differ.

---

[1] An IRS Private Letter Ruling is applicable only to the taxpayer who requested it and may not be cited as precedent.

Secular Trust
Protecting Deferred Compensation

Nonqualified deferred compensation plans are often used as a fringe benefit to recruit and retain key executives.

Even if funds are set aside by the employer to meet its future obligation, the company's creditors may reach the funds if there is financial difficulty.

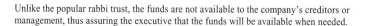

In order to protect these funds, an irrevocable arrangement commonly known as a secular trust can be established. The employer pays the agreed upon contributions to the trust, which invests the funds until the executive's retirement, disability or death.

Unlike the popular rabbi trust, the funds are not available to the company's creditors or management, thus assuring the executive that the funds will be available when needed.

Tax Consequences

- Funds are taxable to the employee during the year they are contributed to the plan, if vested. See IRC Secs. 83 and 402(b).

- The contributions are deductible to the corporation in the same year. See IRC Sec. 404(a)(5).

Many advisors feel that future tax rates will increase and that payment of the lower tax now will result in a larger fund at the executive's retirement. One disadvantage, however, is that the executive's taxes will increase, but his or her current available income does not. The employer may wish to provide an additional cash bonus to pay the extra taxes.

The possible tax advantage, combined with the separation of the fund from potential corporate creditors, makes the secular trust attractive to many executives.

Private Letter Rulings from the IRS have raised doubts regarding secular trusts and should be considered before drafting the trust. See PLR 9206009 and 9207010.[1]

IRC Sec. 409A

The American Jobs Creation Act of 2004 included new IRC Sec. 409A, which added to federal income tax law numerous requirements that a nonqualified deferred compensation plan must meet to avoid having deferred amounts treated as being constructively received in the current year. If these requirements are not met, all current and past-deferred compensation, plus any earnings, are included in the employee's gross income for the current tax year. Further, an additional 20% tax is levied, plus an underpayment interest penalty. State or local law may differ.

---

[1] An IRS Private Letter Ruling is applicable only to the taxpayer who requested it and may not be cited as precedent.

Nonqualified Deferred Compensation

Avoiding Constructive Receipt

Nonqualified deferred compensation (NQDC) plans are commonly used to provide additional benefits to selected key employees or executives. In a typical plan, an employee enters into an agreement with the employer to defer a portion of his or her compensation until a future date or event. Such plans are "nonqualified" because they do not meet the requirements of "qualified" plans under the Internal Revenue Code (IRC).[1] There are two broad categories of NQDC plans:

- **Funded:** The employer sets funds aside, beyond the reach of its general creditors, to guarantee payment of the amounts deferred. The money is deductible to the employer, and is included in the employee's gross income, in the year set aside.

- **Unfunded:** The deferred compensation is generally secured only by the employer's promise to pay. It is deductible to the employer, and is included in the employee's gross income, in the year that the funds are either actually or "constructively" received by the employee. Constructive receipt typically occurs when the employee has an unlimited right to the funds (received or not), with no "substantial risk of forfeiture."

Avoiding current taxation on deferred amounts is highly desirable as it generally results in a larger benefit when the funds are received by the employee in the future.

Avoiding Constructive Receipt – IRC Sec. 409A

The American Jobs Creation Act of 2004 (AJCA) included new IRC Sec. 409A, which added to federal income tax law a number of requirements that a NQDC plan must meet to avoid having deferred amounts treated as being constructively received in the current year. If these requirements are not met, all current and past-deferred compensation, plus any earnings, are included in the employee's gross income for the current tax year. An additional 20% tax is levied, plus an underpayment interest penalty.

IRC Sec. 409A was effective January 1, 2005 and generally applied to amounts deferred after December 31, 2004. Certain amounts deferred before January 1, 2005 are considered "grandfathered" under the prior rules and are exempt from IRC Sec. 409A. If the plan under which these grandfathered amounts were deferred is "materially modified" on or after October 3, 2004, IRC Sec. 409A then applies to the grandfathered amounts.

In the years following passage of the AJCA, the Internal Revenue Service (IRS) issued a series of announcements on how the new law would be applied. Taxpayers were expected to comply "in good faith" with this transitional guidance. On April 10, 2007, the IRS released TD 9321, containing most of the final IRC Sec. 409A regulations.[2] These regulations, which generally apply to tax years beginning on or after January 1, 2008, required plan sponsors to conform with the final regulations no later than December 31, 2007. Notice 2007-86, issued by the IRS on October 22, 2007, generally allowed employers until December 31, 2008, to bring their plans into compliance with the statute.

---

[1] The discussion here concerns federal income tax law. State or local income tax law may differ.
[2] At the same time, the government also released IRS Notice 2007-34, providing general guidance on the applicability of IRC Sec. 409A to split-dollar arrangements.

Continued

Nonqualified Deferred Compensation
Avoiding Constructive Receipt

Key Concepts

There are a number of key concepts involved in understanding NQDC plans:

- **Deferral of compensation:** Under the final regulations a very broad definition of "deferral of compensation" is used, ".......if, under the terms of the plan and the relevant facts and circumstances, the service provider has a legally binding right during a taxable year to compensation that, pursuant to the terms of the plan, is or may be payable to (or on behalf of) the service provider in a later year."[1]

IRC Sec. 409A May Apply To:
Agreements covering a change in control
Certain incentive or bonus plans
Employment and separation agreements
Phantom or restricted stock plans
Split-dollar arrangements
Stock options/rights granted at less than FMV
Supplemental Executive Retirement Plans (SERPS)

- **Service provider:** The person or entity who provides services. Generally, any cash-basis taxpayer including: (1) an individual; (2) a corporation;[2] or (3) a partnership.[3]

- **Service recipient:** Any person, organization, or entity to whom services are provided.[3]

- **Substantial risk of forfeiture:** Generally, a substantial risk of forfeiture exists when receipt of the deferred compensation depends on the employee performing "substantial future services", or the "occurrence of a condition related to the compensation, and the risk of forfeiture is substantial."[4]

Exceptions and Special Situations

The final regulations exempt a number of types of compensation from IRC Sec. 409A:

- **Short-term deferrals:** Certain deferrals paid no later than 2-1/2 months after the first tax year the amounts are no longer subject to a substantial risk of forfeiture.

- **Separation pay plans:** Applicable to limited amounts of compensation, paid within a specified time period, and payable only as a result of separation from service. The final regulations carefully define the situations to which this exception applies.

- **Qualified and welfare benefit plans:** Excepted from Section 409A are many qualified pension, profit sharing, and stock bonus plans. Bona fide plans providing welfare benefits such as medical, sick leave, vacation, or disability are also excluded.

---

[1] Reg. Sec. 1.409A-1(b)(1)
[2] Including a C corporation, an S corporation, or a personal service corporation.
[3] For the sake of simplicity, this report uses the term "employee" for "service provider" and "employer" for "service recipient." The terms used in the final regulations are broad and intended to cover a wide range of relationships.
[4] Reg. Sec. 1.409A-1(d).

Continued...

Nonqualified Deferred Compensation
Avoiding Constructive Receipt

- **Stock options and stock appreciation rights:** The exercise price of the option or stock right can never be less than the FMV of the stock on the day the option or right is granted. A stock option or stock right plan may not include any deferral feature. Incentive stock options and options granted under employee stock purchase plans (statutory stock rights) are excluded from Section 409A.

- **Independent contractor:** Except for corporate directors and those providing management services, independent contractors are generally exempt from Section 409A.

- **Educational benefits:** Covering expenses such as tuition and books paid for education for the service provider (not for family members).

- **Foreign plans:** Applicable to nonresident aliens or U.S. citizens working abroad.

Election to Defer Compensation

- **Generally:** The election must be made no later than the end of the previous tax year.

- **First year of eligibility:** The deferral election must be made within 30 days of an employee's first becoming eligible to participate in the plan.

- **Performance-based compensation:** If an employee's compensation is performance based, over a period of at least 12 months, the election to defer compensation must be made no later than six months before the end of the 12 month period.

Distributions

The timing and manner in which the deferred compensation will be paid out must be decided at the time the initial deferral election is made. Generally, distributions may be made only when one of the following events occurs:

- The employee separates from service.[1]

- Upon the employee's death or disability.

- At a specific time, or according to a fixed schedule.

- Because of a change in ownership or effective control of the employing corporation.

- Because of an unforeseeable emergency.

If a plan allows an employee to later choose to delay or change the form of payment, the new election may not be effective until 12 months after it is made. If the change relates to (1) separation from service; or (2) according to a fixed schedule or at a fixed point in time; or (3) because of a change in the service recipient's ownership, any payment made under the new election must be delayed at least <u>five years</u> beyond when it would have otherwise

---

[1] Distributions to a "specified" employee may not be made until six months after the employee separates from service (or, if earlier, the date of the employee's death). A specified employee is a "key" employee, as that term is defined in IRC Sec. 416(i), of a corporation whose stock is publicly traded.

Continued...

been made. Distributions made because of death, disability, or unforeseen emergency may be delayed for periods less than five years.

Acceleration of Benefits

Under the final regulations, benefit payments may be accelerated only in certain, narrow situations, and only when done either automatically (under the terms of the plan) or upon a decision by the service recipient:

1. **De minims distributions:** Amounts which do not exceed specified limits.
2. **Certain legal requirements:** Such as paying required income or employment taxes, complying with a divorce decree or domestic relations order, or meeting conflict of interest or ethics standards.
3. **At plan termination:** Specific requirements must be met.

Other Tax Issues

The Pension Protection Act of 2006 (PPA 2006) added two provisions to the federal income tax code which have a potentially heavy impact on NQDC plans:

- **Employer-owned life insurance contracts:** NQDC plans are sometimes funded with life insurance. Generally, amounts received under a life insurance contract paid by reason of the death of the insured are excluded from income. Under the provisions of PPA 2006, however, death proceeds from a life insurance policy owned by an employer on the life of an employee are generally includable in income, unless certain requirements are met. This law was effective for contracts issued after August 17, 2006, except for policies acquired in an IRC Sec. 1035 exchange. Until the full scope of this new legislation is clarified by the IRS, caution is advised. See IRC Sec. 101(j).

- **"At-risk" qualified plans:** Effective for funds transferred or set aside after August 17, 2006, PPA 2006 added restrictions on executive nonqualified deferred compensation at firms with under-funded qualified retirement plans. This law generally provides that during any period in which a qualified retirement plan is "at-risk", any funds set aside in a NQDC plan for high-level executives will become taxable in the year of transfer. An underpayment interest penalty and a 20% penalty tax also apply. Further, the employer is denied a deduction for such transfers. See IRC Sec. 409A(b)(3).

Seek Professional Guidance

Given the complexities involved, and because the tax and other penalties for not meeting the requirements of the Internal Revenue Code are significant, professional guidance is strongly recommended.

Split-Dollar Arrangement

The term "split-dollar arrangement" refers to a method of paying for life insurance. In a typical contract, an employer and employee agree to split the cost (premiums) and benefits (cash-value and death benefits) of a permanent life insurance policy.

The agreement between the employee and employer can take many forms. The elements commonly found in split-dollar agreements are outlined below.

Policy Ownership

There are two basic forms of policy ownership[1] for split-dollar plans.

- **Endorsement method:** The employer owns the policy but a written endorsement is added to the policy which splits the benefits between the employer and the employee.

- **Collateral assignment:** The employee owns the policy and assigns certain interests in the policy to the employer as collateral for payments made by the employer.

Splitting the Cost (premiums)

Dividing the cost of a policy can be done in any manner desired. Listed below are several typical payment arrangements:

- **Classic method**
  - Employer pays an amount equal to the annual cash-value buildup.
  - Employee pays the balance.
- **Employer-pay-all method**
  - Employer pays the entire premium.
  - Employee is taxed on the value of the economic benefit received.

Making the Payment

- **Employer pay all:** The employer pays the entire premium; the employee pays tax on the value of the economic benefits received.

- **Executive bonus plan:** The employer pays a bonus to the employee. From the bonus, the employee pays the economic benefit portion of the premium. The bonus payment is a deductible expense to the employer and taxable income to the employee. Some agreements provide an extra bonus amount to cover the additional tax due.

---

[1] This report highlights split-dollar arrangements in the employer and employee context. Split-dollar arrangements are also possible between other parties, for example between a corporation and a shareholder, an employer and an independent contractor, a partnership and a partner, or a private individual and a trust.

Continued...

Split-Dollar Arrangement

Splitting the Benefits

The employer and employee can decide to split the policy benefits in any way they wish.

- **Classic method**
  - **Employer's share:** At death, the employer receives the greater of the cash value or the total premiums paid.
  - **Employee's share:** The employee's beneficiary receives the balance of the proceeds, e.g., the face amount less the amount repaid to the employer.

- **Employer-pay-all method**
  - **Employer's share:** At death, the employer recovers the agreed-upon amount.
  - **Employee's share:** The employee's beneficiary receives the balance of the proceeds, e.g., the face amount less the sum paid to the employer.

A Few Uses of Split-Dollar

- **Fringe benefit:** Since the employer can pick and choose those employees who will benefit, split-dollar can be used to attract and retain key executives.

- **Estate planning:** When the estate is large enough to incur a federal estate tax (a taxable estate in excess of $2,000,000[1]), an estate owner may consider removing life insurance from the estate. One way of reducing death taxes is the irrevocable life insurance trust.

- **Business continuation:** In a family-owned business there is a risk of adverse tax treatment when the corporation redeems the deceased owner's stock. See IRC Secs. 302 and 318. The proceeds of corporate owned life insurance might also create a corporate AMT problem. Under a corporate stock redemption the surviving stockholders would own stock worth more, but with an unchanged cost basis. Using a cross-purchase buy-sell agreement funded with life insurance can eliminate these problems. Differences between the owners in age and/or percentage of ownership may cause the life insurance premiums to be expensive for some stockholders. A split-dollar arrangement may assist each stockholder in purchasing enough insurance on the other stockholder(s).

- **Group term replacement:** Nondiscrimination rules can limit the amount of group term insurance available to key executives. With a split-dollar plan, executives can have increased protection now and substantial benefits at retirement.

---

[1] The applicable exclusion amount is the dollar value of assets protected from federal estate tax by an individual's applicable credit amount. It is scheduled to change as follows: $2,000,000 for 2007-2008; $3,500,000 for 2009, zero federal estate tax for the year 2010; and $1,000,000 for 2011 and thereafter (unless permanently repealed or otherwise modified).

Continued...

Split-Dollar Arrangement

Federal Taxation of Split-Dollar Arrangements

Split-dollar arrangements are subject to a complex web of federal income tax law[1] and regulation, including:

- **Treasury Decision 9092:** Under the final federal regulations contained in Treasury Decision 9092, issued on September 11, 2003, many of the economic benefits of a split-dollar arrangement will be treated as currently taxable. Such taxable benefits may include: (1) the value of current life insurance protection; (2) accrued cash value; (3) imputed loan interest; or (4) premium contributions from the non-owner of the policy. Depending on the relationship between the parties to a split-dollar arrangement, the economic benefits may be treated for tax purposes as compensation, dividends, a capital contribution, a gift, or "a transfer having a different tax character." Under certain circumstances, death benefits paid to a beneficiary (other than a policy owner) will be taxable income.

- **IRC Sec. 409A – nonqualified deferred compensation:** IRC Sec. 409A concerns the federal income tax treatment of nonqualified deferred compensation agreements. Income deferred under an arrangement which does not meet the requirements of IRC Sec. 409A is generally subject to income taxation in the current year, including substantial penalties and interest. In some instances, a split-dollar arrangement may be deemed to come under the provisions of IRC Sec. 409A. See Treasury Decision 9321 and Notice 2007-34 for further details.

- **Employer-owned life insurance contracts:** Under federal law, amounts received under a life insurance contract paid by reason of the death of the insured are generally excluded from income. Under the provisions of the Pension Protection Act of 2006, however, death proceeds from a life policy owned by an employer on the life of an employee are generally includable in income, unless certain requirements are met. This law was effective for contracts issued after August 17, 2006, except for policies acquired in an IRC Sec. 1035 exchange. Until the full scope of this new legislation is clarified by the IRS, caution is advised. See IRC Sec. 101(j).

Seek Professional Guidance

Split-dollar arrangements involve complex legal, tax and insurance questions. The guidance of appropriate advisors is strongly recommended.

---

[1] The discussion here concerns federal income tax law; state or local law may vary.

Federal Taxation of Split-Dollar Arrangements

On September 11, 2003, the Treasury Department and the Internal Revenue Service (IRS) released Treasury Decision 9092, containing final regulations on the taxation of split-dollar arrangements for the purpose of federal income, employment, self-employment and gift taxes.[1] The issuance of these final regulations came after several years of regulatory review and largely follow proposed regulations issued in 2002 and 2003.

The final regulations were effective for split-dollar arrangements entered into after September 17, 2003, and to arrangements entered into before September 18, 2003, but later materially modified. Certain "grandfathering" and "safe harbor" provisions apply to arrangements entered into before September 17, 2003.

What Is a Split-Dollar Arrangement?

In general terms, a split-dollar arrangement is an agreement between two or more parties to share the benefits and/or costs of a permanent life insurance policy. Under the final regulations, it is generally any arrangement with the following elements:

- **Parties:** Includes the owner of the life insurance contract and a non-owner.

- **Premium payer:** Either party pays all or part of the premiums.

- **Premium recovery:** One of the parties paying the premiums is entitled to recover (conditionally or otherwise) all or any portion of those premiums.

- **Premium security:** Recovery of premiums paid is made from, or secured by, the proceeds of the life insurance policy.

This definition covers a wide range of relationships, including those between employer and employee, service recipient and service provider, corporation and shareholder, or donor and donee.

Who Owns the Policy?

The benefits of split-dollar arrangements will be taxed under one of two mutually-exclusive "regimes", depending on who owns the life insurance policy. Generally, if the employer, service recipient, corporation, or donor is the owner, the "economic benefit" regime applies. If the employee, service provider, shareholder, or donee is the owner, the "loan" regime applies.

The "owner" is generally the person or entity named in the life insurance contract as the owner. Under a major exception to this rule, an employer, service recipient, or donor will be treated as the owner (regardless of who actually owns the contract) if, at all times, the only benefit available to an employee, service provider, or donee is the value of current life insurance protection. The final regulations include ownership attribution rules for certain compensatory split-dollar arrangements. A "non-owner" is generally any person or entity other than the contract owner who has an interest in the policy.

---

[1] The rules discussed here concern federal law; state and local law may differ.

Continued...

Federal Taxation of Split-Dollar Arrangements

Economic Benefit Regime

Under the economic benefit regime, the owner of the policy is considered to be providing economic benefits to the non-owner. This regime generally applies to split-dollar agreements traditionally described as "endorsement" arrangements.

Depending on the relationship between the owner and non-owner, these economic benefits could be treated for tax purposes as compensation, dividends, a capital contribution, a gift, or "a transfer having a different tax character." The value of these benefits, reduced by any consideration paid by the non-owner to the owner, is generally measured on the last day of the non-owner's taxable year[1] and may include the following:

- **Current life insurance protection:** The value of current life insurance protection is generally calculated using an IRS-provided premium factor, published in the Internal Revenue Bulletin. Currently, this is Table 2001. If certain requirements are met, the insurer's one-year term rates may be used.

- **Cash values available to the non-owner:** Defined as cash values to which the non-owner has current[2] access, to the extent not taken into account in a prior taxable year.

- **Other:** These include the value of any other economic benefits provided to the non-owner, to the extent not taken into account in a prior taxable year.

There are a number of other tax consequences to keep in mind:

- **Non-owner payments are income to the owner:** Any amount paid by the non-owner to the owner for any economic benefit is included in the owner's gross income.

- **Investment in the contract:** In a split-dollar arrangement, only the owner of a life insurance policy may have a basis in the contract. Therefore, a non-owner has no basis in the policy until the policy (or an undivided interest) is transferred to the non-owner.

- **Amounts received under the life insurance contract:** The final regulations provide that any amount received under the life contract (other than an amount received by reason of death) and provided to the non-owner is treated as though paid by the insurance company to the owner and then by the owner to the non-owner. Death benefits paid to a beneficiary (other than the owner of the policy) are excluded from income under IRC Sec. 101(a) only to the extent such amounts are due to current life insurance protection provided to the non-owner under the agreement, the cost of which was paid by the non-owner, or which the non-owner has taken into account as an economic benefit.

---

[1] As an alternative, the parties could agree to use the policy anniversary date.
[2] In general, these are cash values to which the non-owner has a current or future right, which are directly or indirectly accessible by the non-owner, and which are inaccessible to the owner or the owner's general creditors.

Continued

Federal Taxation of Split-Dollar Arrangements

Loan Regime

Under this regime, the non-owner is viewed as making an interest-bearing loan to the owner. The loan regime generally applies to "collateral assignment" arrangements. A payment made pursuant to a split-dollar life insurance arrangement is a split-dollar loan, and the owner and non-owner are treated, respectively, as borrower and lender, if:

- **Payments:** A payment is made (directly or otherwise) from the non-owner to the owner;

- **Payment is a loan:** The payment is a loan under general federal tax principles, or a reasonable person would expect the payment to be repaid in full; and

- **Payment source:** The repayment is to be made from (or is secured by) the policy's death benefit, cash surrender value, or both.

Each premium payment under a split-dollar arrangement is a separate loan for federal tax purposes. If a split-dollar loan does not provide for an adequate rate of interest, it is considered a "below-market" loan and is recharacterized as a loan with interest at the applicable federal rate (AFR). The regulations presume a transfer by the lender to the borrower of the interest shortfall, and further presume this amount to be repaid to the lender as interest due. Other regulations with regard to forgiven interest apply.

Gift-Tax Treatment of Private Split-Dollar Arrangements

The final regulations make clear that the same general principles apply to private split-dollar arrangements. Premium payments in private split-dollar arrangement may be considered gifts or loans, with consequent federal tax results.

Sarbanes-Oxley Act of 2002

One section of the Sarbanes-Oxley Act of 2002 prohibits publicly traded companies from making certain loans to directors and executives. The final IRS split-dollar regulations leave the interpretation and administration of Sarbanes-Oxley to the Securities and Exchange Commission (SEC). In the absence of any guidance from the SEC, it remains unclear as to whether or not Sarbanes-Oxley applies to split-dollar arrangements.

IRC Sec. 409A – Nonqualified Deferred Compensation

IRC Sec. 409A concerns the federal income tax treatment of nonqualified deferred compensation arrangements. Income deferred under an arrangement which does not meet the requirements of IRC Sec. 409A is generally subject to taxation in the current year, including substantial penalties and interest. Most of the final regulations concerning IRC Sec. 409A were released in TD 9321, on April 10, 2007.

Continued...

Federal Taxation of Split-Dollar Arrangements

Notice 2007-34, released at the same time as the final 409A regulations, provides general guidance regarding on how IRC Sec. 409A applies to split-dollar arrangements. As explained in the notice, split-dollar arrangements which provide only death benefits are generally exempt from IRC Sec. 409A. Arrangements which provide for certain short-term (2-1/2 months) deferrals of compensation are also generally exempt.

Notice 2007-34 also listed examples of split-dollar arrangements to which IRC Sec. 409A would apply. For example, an endorsement split-dollar arrangement, taxed under the economic benefit regime, would come under IRC Sec. 409A if it includes a promise by the employer to transfer a policy's cash value to the employee at retirement. A split-dollar arrangement taxed under the loan regime would come under IRC. Sec. 409A if it provides that loan amounts can be waived, cancelled, or forgiven in the future.

Because both the federal law and regulation are complex, caution is advised to ensure that a split-dollar arrangement does not come within the scope of IRC Sec. 409A.

Employer-Owned Life Insurance Contracts

Under federal law, amounts received under a life insurance contract paid by reason of the death of the insured are generally excluded from income. Under the provisions of the Pension Protection Act of 2006, however, death proceeds from a life policy owned by an employer on the life of an employee are generally includable in income, unless certain requirements are met. This law was effective for contracts issued after August 17, 2006, except for policies acquired in an IRC Sec. 1035 exchange. Until the full scope of this new legislation is clarified by the IRS, caution is advised. See IRC Sec. 101(j).

Seek Professional Guidance

Given the complexities involved, those considering or involved in a split-dollar arrangement are advised to seek the help of appropriate professional counselors.

Split-Dollar Arrangement
Collateral Assignment Method

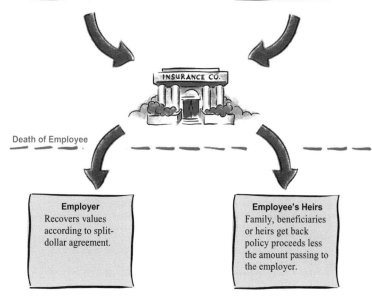

Employer
Pays the portion of the premium in excess of what the employee pays.

Employee assigns right to collect amounts paid after his or her death.

Employee
Pays the portion of the premium equal to the economic benefit[1] he or she receives.

INSURANCE CO.

Death of Employee

Employer
Recovers values according to split-dollar agreement.

Employee's Heirs
Family, beneficiaries or heirs get back policy proceeds less the amount passing to the employer.

Notes: This diagram illustrates a very basic variety of split-dollar arrangement which can be modified to meet the needs of both employer and employee.

---

[1] Under Treasury Decision 9092, (September 11, 2003) many economic benefits of a split-dollar arrangement are currently taxable; death benefits paid to a beneficiary other than the policy owner may also be taxable. Under Treasury Decision 9321 and IRS Notice 2007-34, (April 10, 2007), some split-dollar arrangements may come under the requirements of IRC Sec. 409A concerning nonqualified deferred compensation. Those considering a split-dollar arrangement should first consult with their legal and/or tax advisors. State or local law may vary.

Split-Dollar Arrangement
Endorsement Method

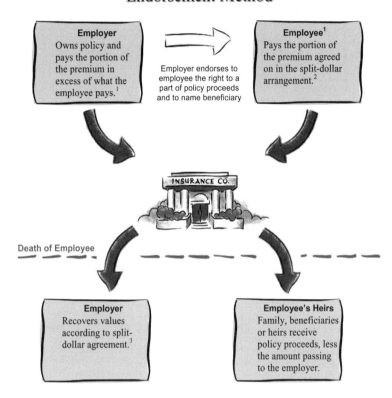

Employer
Owns policy and pays the portion of the premium in excess of what the employee pays. [1]

Employer endorses to employee the right to a part of policy proceeds and to name beneficiary

Employee[1]
Pays the portion of the premium agreed on in the split-dollar arrangement. [2]

INSURANCE CO.

Death of Employee

Employer
Recovers values according to split-dollar agreement. [3]

Employee's Heirs
Family, beneficiaries or heirs receive policy proceeds, less the amount passing to the employer.

Note: This diagram illustrates a very basic variety of split-dollar arrangement, in the employer and employee context. Split-dollar arrangements are also possible between other parties, for example, between a corporation and a shareholder, an employer and an independent contractor, a partnership and a partner, or a private individual and a trust. Split-dollar arrangements can be modified to meet the specific needs of the parties involved.

---

[1] Under Treasury Decision 9092, (September 11, 2003) many economic benefits of a split-dollar arrangement are currently taxable; death benefits paid to a beneficiary other than the policy owner may also be taxable. Under Treasury Decision 9321 and IRS Notice 2007-34, (April 10, 2007), some split-dollar arrangements may come under the requirements of IRC Sec. 409A concerning nonqualified deferred compensation. Those considering a split-dollar arrangement should first consult with their legal and/or tax advisors. State or local law may vary.
[2] In an employer-pay-all agreement, the employee pays nothing.
[3] Under federal law, amounts received under a life insurance contract paid by reason of the death of the insured are generally excluded from income Under the provisions of the Pension Protection Act of 2006, death proceeds from a life insurance policy owned by an employer on the life of an employee are generally includable in income, unless certain requirements are met. The law was effective for contracts issued after August 17, 2006, except for contracts acquired in an IRC Sec. 1035 exchange. Until the full scope of this new law is clarified by the IRS, caution is advised.

Split-Dollar Arrangement
Funding an Irrevocable Life Insurance Trust

Since the federal estate tax is imposed on all the assets inside an estate, many people prefer to reduce this tax by arranging to have some of their assets outside of their estate. One method of achieving this is the irrevocable life insurance trust (ILIT), a type of trust designed primarily to own life insurance policies. At death, the policy proceeds are used to provide additional dollars for estate liquidity needs. Such a trust takes maximum advantage of the gift tax laws and at the same time ensures that the proceeds of any policies inside the trust are received free of federal income and estate taxes.[1]

A split-dollar life insurance arrangement can help a key employee achieve this important estate-planning goal.

During Life

In general, the following steps would be taken.

- The employee establishes an irrevocable life insurance trust.

- The trustee of the trust obtains life insurance on the life of the employee, naming the trust as beneficiary of the policy.

- The employer and the trust enter into a split-dollar agreement, providing for a sharing of the premiums and death benefits of the policy owned by the trust. Typically the trust will pay that portion of the premium equal to the economic benefit[2] received. The employer pays the remaining balance. As a part of the agreement, the trust assigns the policy to the employer as security for the repayment of premiums advanced.

- The employee gifts funds to the trust, to allow the trust to pay its portion of the premium. The employer may, if desired, bonus sufficient funds to the employee to cover these gifts.

At Death

- The insurance company typically returns to the employer the amounts specified in the split-dollar agreement.

- The balance of the policy proceeds is paid directly to the trustee of the irrevocable life insurance trust. The trust (if trust provisions so provide) may then lend the funds to the employee's estate, or may use them to purchase assets from the estate. The executor would then have the cash necessary to pay the estate settlement costs without increasing the taxable estate.

- Ultimately, assets in the trust are distributed to the employee's beneficiaries.

---

[1] State or local law may vary.

[2] Under Treasury Decision 9092, (September 11, 2003) many economic benefits of a split-dollar arrangement are currently taxable; death benefits paid to a beneficiary other than the policy owner may also be taxable. Under Treasury Decision 9321 and IRS Notice 2007-34, (April 10, 2007), some split-dollar arrangements may come under the requirements of IRC Sec. 409A concerning nonqualified deferred compensation. Those considering a split-dollar arrangement should first consult with their legal and/or tax advisors. State or local law may vary.

Split-Dollar Arrangement
Funding an Irrevocable Life Insurance Trust

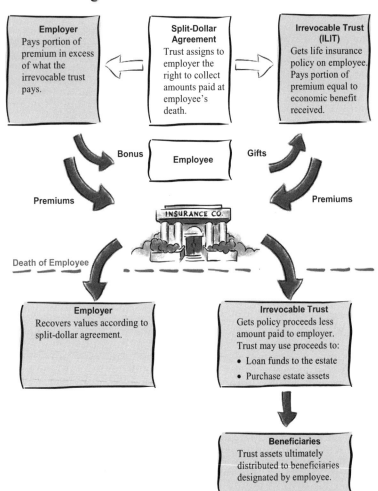

Employer
Pays portion of premium in excess of what the irrevocable trust pays.

Split-Dollar Agreement
Trust assigns to employer the right to collect amounts paid at employee's death.

Irrevocable Trust (ILIT)
Gets life insurance policy on employee. Pays portion of premium equal to economic benefit received.

Bonus

Employee

Gifts

Premiums

Premiums

INSURANCE CO.

Death of Employee

Employer
Recovers values according to split-dollar agreement.

Irrevocable Trust
Gets policy proceeds less amount paid to employer. Trust may use proceeds to:
- Loan funds to the estate
- Purchase estate assets

Beneficiaries
Trust assets ultimately distributed to beneficiaries designated by employee.

Note: Under Treasury Decision 9092, (September 11, 2003) many economic benefits of a split-dollar arrangement are currently taxable; death benefits paid to a beneficiary other than the policy owner may also be taxable. Under Treasury Decision 9321 and IRS Notice 2007-34, (April 10, 2007), some split-dollar arrangements may come under the requirements of IRC Sec. 409A concerning nonqualified deferred compensation. Those considering a split-dollar arrangement should first consult with their legal and/or tax advisors. State or local law may vary.

Split-Dollar Arrangement
Funding a Cross-Purchase Agreement

In order to ensure the orderly continuation of a business, co-shareholders will frequently enter into a cross-purchase agreement, in which each agrees to purchase the ownership interest of the other in case of death. A split-dollar life insurance arrangement can be used to fund such a need.

During Life

In general, the following steps would be taken.

- The shareholders of a corporation, acting as individuals, enter into a cross-purchase agreement with each other, agreeing to purchase the ownership interest of a shareholder who dies.

- Each shareholder, acting as an individual, purchases a life insurance policy on the life of the other shareholder.

- Each shareholder, as an employee of the corporation, enters into a separate split-dollar agreement with the company, providing for a sharing of premiums and death benefits on the policy. Each shareholder pays that portion of the premium equal to the economic benefit[1] received. The corporation pays the remaining balance. As a part of the agreement, each shareholder assigns the policy to the corporation as security for the repayment of premiums advanced.

At Death

- The insurance company typically pays to the corporation the amounts specified in the split-dollar agreement.

- The balance of the policy proceeds is paid to the surviving shareholder. These funds are used to purchase the deceased shareholder's stock from his or her estate.

---

[1] Under Treasury Decision 9092, (September 11, 2003) many economic benefits of a split-dollar arrangement are currently taxable; death benefits paid to a beneficiary other than the policy owner may also be taxable. Under Treasury Decision 9321 and IRS Notice 2007-34, (April 10, 2007), some split-dollar arrangements may come under the requirements of IRC Sec. 409A concerning nonqualified deferred compensation. Those considering a split-dollar arrangement should first consult with their legal and/or tax advisors. State or local law may vary.

Split-Dollar Arrangement
Funding a Cross-Purchase Agreement

During Life

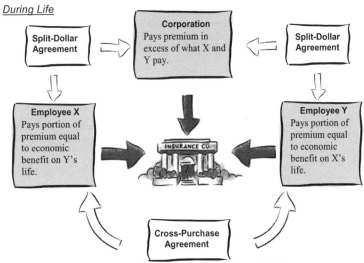

Employees X and Y each buy life insurance policies on the other's life.

— — — At The Death of Employee X — — — — — — — —

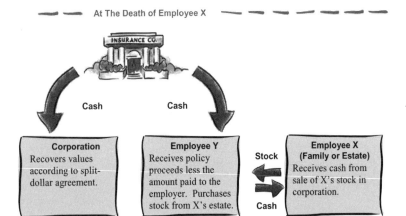

Note: Under Treasury Decision 9092, (September 11, 2003) many economic benefits of a split-dollar arrangement are currently taxable; death benefits paid to a beneficiary other than the policy owner may also be taxable. Under Treasury Decision 9321 and IRS Notice 2007-34, (April 10, 2007), some split-dollar arrangements may come under the requirements of IRC Sec. 409A concerning nonqualified deferred compensation. Those considering a split-dollar arrangement should first consult with their legal and/or tax advisors. State or local law may vary.

Reverse Split-Dollar Arrangement
A Key Person/Retirement Benefit Combination

The purpose of this technique is to protect the corporation in the event of the loss of a key employee while binding the employee to the corporation until retirement by providing a substantial tax favored build-up of cash value available at that time.[1]

How It Works

- **Prior to retirement**
  - **Owner:** Employee owns policy from the beginning.
  - **Beneficiary:** Corporation is named beneficiary of its agreed-upon interests in the cash values and death benefit.
  - **Premium payer:** Corporation is receiving the economic benefit and is responsible for paying the death benefit costs. Employee pays any balance.
  - **Reverse split-dollar agreement:** Limits rights to internal values (i.e., right to borrow, assign, withdraw, etc.) until termination of plan.

- **At retirement:** The employee/owner simply changes the beneficiary. The agreement expires, eliminating restrictions on the values. There is no further economic benefit to the corporation. Nothing is owed to the corporation.

- **At death:** The death benefit is received by beneficiaries free of income taxation, but is a part of the employee's estate (less the portion paid to the employer).

Besides protection from the loss of a key person, other corporate uses include:

- Sec. 303 or stock redemption funding,

- Salary continuation or death benefit only funding, and

- Corporate loan protection.

Note: The Internal Revenue Service, in IRS Notice 2002-59, August 16, 2002, effectively eliminated the legal authority for reverse split-dollar arrangements.

---

[1] Under Treasury Decision 9092 (September 11, 2003), many economic benefits of a split-dollar arrangement are currently taxable. These benefits may include: (1) value of current life insurance protection; (2) accrued cash value; (3) imputed loan interest, or (4) premium contributions from a non-policy owner. Death benefits paid to a beneficiary (other than policy owner) may be taxable. 9092 contained other split-dollar rules not addressed here and those considering split-dollar arrangements should consult legal/tax advisors. State or local law may vary.

Split-Dollar Arrangement
Deferred Compensation - Collateral Assignment Method

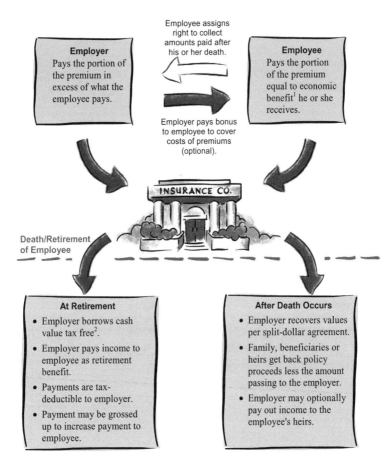

Employee assigns right to collect amounts paid after his or her death.

Employer pays bonus to employee to cover costs of premiums (optional).

Employer
Pays the portion of the premium in excess of what the employee pays.

Employee
Pays the portion of the premium equal to economic benefit[1] he or she receives.

INSURANCE CO.

Death/Retirement of Employee

At Retirement
- Employer borrows cash value tax free[2].
- Employer pays income to employee as retirement benefit.
- Payments are tax-deductible to employer.
- Payment may be grossed up to increase payment to employee.

After Death Occurs
- Employer recovers values per split-dollar agreement.
- Family, beneficiaries or heirs get back policy proceeds less the amount passing to the employer.
- Employer may optionally pay out income to the employee's heirs.

Note: This diagram illustrates a very basic variety of split-dollar plan which can be modified to meet the needs of both employer and employee. A separate agreement is required to address the deferred compensation aspect of this arrangement.

---

[1] Under Treasury Decision 9092, (September 11, 2003) many economic benefits of a split-dollar arrangement are currently taxable; death benefits paid to a beneficiary other than the policy owner may also be taxable. Under Treasury Decision 9321 and IRS Notice 2007-34, (April 10, 2007), some split-dollar arrangements may come under the requirements of IRC Sec. 409A concerning nonqualified deferred compensation. Those considering a split-dollar arrangement should first consult with their legal and/or tax advisors. State or local law may vary.

[2] Interest charges may apply. Loans reduce death benefits. Borrowed amounts may be taxable and subject to a 10% penalty if the policy is a MEC. For details see policy information and insurance ledger.

Private Split-Dollar Arrangement

A private split-dollar arrangement is a way for individuals and trusts to split the ownership, premium payments and benefits of a cash value life insurance policy. Such arrangements use the same underlying concept found in employer-employee split-dollar transactions and apply it to family or private relationships.

One Example of a Private Split-Dollar Arrangement

A private split-dollar arrangement can take many forms. One private split-dollar arrangement, reviewed by the Internal Revenue Service (IRS) in Private Letter Ruling (PLR) 9636033,[1] was set up with the following general structure.

- **Insured spouse:** One spouse was chosen as the insured. The insured spouse created an irrevocable life insurance trust (ILIT) and made a cash gift (subject to gift tax) to the trust. Because the couple resided in a community property state, and to avoid any question of the policy proceeds being included in the estate of the non-insured spouse, the cash gift to the ILIT was made from the insured's separate funds.

- **Irrevocable life insurance trust (ILIT):** The ILIT purchased a life insurance policy on the life of the insured spouse. The trust, as the policy owner, entered into an agreement with the non-insured spouse to split the premium payments. The sharing agreement specified that the trust would pay annual premiums equal to the economic benefit received.

- **Non-insured spouse:** The non-insured spouse agreed to pay the balance of the premiums, also from separate funds. In return for these payments, the non-insured spouse received certain rights from the trust, including the right to borrow from the policy, receive the cash surrender value (less outstanding loans, if any) if the policy is surrendered before death and recover premiums paid at the death of the insured. The IRS concluded that the premium payments by the non-insured spouse were not gifts to the trust, because of the right to be reimbursed for the payments.

Before the Insured's Death

Under the agreement reviewed by the IRS, if additional funds are needed,[2] the non-insured spouse has the right to borrow the accumulated cash values from the policy. If the non-insured spouse dies before the insured spouse, the gross estate of the non-insured spouse will include the value of premiums paid (or the value of the right to recover them). The non-insured spouse could leave these rights to the ILIT or to other heirs.

If these rights were left to the insured spouse, the insured spouse would have an incident of ownership in the policy, which could subject the death benefit to potential federal estate tax[3].

---

[1] Private Letter Rulings are not legal precedents and are only applicable to the taxpayer who requested the ruling.
[2] For example, additional funds might be needed because of an emergency or to meet daily living expenses.
[3] Under the Tax Act of 2001, the federal estate tax is gradually phased out until its final repeal in the year 2010. If Congress does not act at that time to repeal it for the years following, it will automatically revert back to the rates in effect during the year 2001, with an exemption for the first $1,000,000 of assets.

Continued...

Private Split-Dollar Arrangement

At the Death of the Insured

The PLR also covered the tax results at the death of the insured.

- **Estate of insured:** The insured spouse will not have any incidents of ownership in the life insurance policy. Thus, the policy death benefits will not be includable in the insured's gross estate.

- **Non-insured spouse:** The surviving, non-insured spouse will receive, free of income and estate taxes, a portion of the death benefit. Under the premium splitting agreement, the non-insured spouse is entitled to the greater of the net cash value or total premiums paid.

- **Irrevocable life insurance trust (ILIT):** The ILIT will receive the balance of the death proceeds, also income and estate tax free. The trustee of the ILIT could be given authority to distribute trust principal and/or interest to the non-insured spouse or other heirs.

Second-to-Die Policies

Private Letter Ruling 9636033, discussed above, involved the use of a private split-dollar arrangement where only one spouse was the insured. In PLR 9745019[1], the IRS reviewed a private split-dollar arrangement involving a second-to-die policy covering the lives of a husband and wife. This separate ruling involved a collateral assignment split-dollar agreement between a married couple and the trustee of an irrevocable life insurance trust, as the owner and beneficiary of a second-to-die policy.

Other Uses for Private Split-Dollar

Other uses of a private split-dollar arrangement might include the following.

- **Generation skipping transfers:** Such as might occur when a grandparent wants to transfer assets to a grandchild. The grandparent would be the insured and the premium (and beneficiary) split could be between the grandparent and grandchild.

- **Help a child obtain insurance:** A parent may want to use private split-dollar to help a child obtain permanent life insurance. The parent and child agree to split the premium. The parent retains control of the policy cash value and endorses to the child the right to name the beneficiary of a portion of the death benefit.

---

[1] Private Letter Rulings are not legal precedents and are only applicable to the taxpayer who requested the ruling.

Continued...

Private Split-Dollar Arrangement

Treasury Decision 9092

On September 11, 2003, the Treasury Department and the Internal Revenue Service (IRS) issued Treasury Decision 9092, effective September 17, 2003, containing final federal[1] regulations on the taxation of split-dollar arrangements. Although primarily intended to address split-dollar arrangements in other contexts, TD 9092 makes it very clear that the regulations apply equally to private split-dollar arrangements.

Under these regulations, many of the economic benefits of a split-dollar arrangement will be treated as currently taxable. Such taxable benefits may include: (1) the value of current life insurance protection; (2) accrued cash value; (3) imputed loan interest; or (4) premium contributions from the non-owner of the policy. Under certain circumstances, death benefits paid to a beneficiary (other than a policy owner) will be taxable income.

Seek Professional Guidance

Given the complexities involved, individuals considering a private-split dollar arrangement, as well as those involved in existing arrangements, are strongly advised to seek the guidance of appropriate legal, tax and insurance advisors.

---

[1] The discussion here concerns federal tax law. State and local law may vary.

Executive Carve-Out Plan
An Alternative to Group Term

Executive Carve Out Defined

An executive carve-out plan is a plan which provides life insurance coverage on selected employees, by carving out all or a portion of their coverage under an employer-sponsored group term plan, and also provides them with individual policies.

Primary Objectives

- Provide additional benefits to the employee in the form of accumulated cash values and post retirement coverage.

- Reduce the employer's cost of providing the benefit with level premium and/or split-dollar cost recovery.

- Reduce the employee's taxable benefit.

Plan Design

The plan may be designed either as:

- A bonus plan [IRC Sec. 162(a)], or

- A split-dollar arrangement.

Advantages	IRC Sec. 162 Bonus Plans	Split-Dollar Arrangements
Employer cost tax deductible	Yes	No
Employer cost recoverable	No	Yes
Reduce employee's reportable income	See Footnote[1]	Maybe[2]
Cash value available to employee	Yes	Maybe[3]
Post retirement benefits	Yes	Yes
Employer discretion for coverage	Yes	Yes

---

[1] The employer may decide to reduce or increase the employee's reportable income compared to group term plan.

[2] Under Treasury Decision 9092, (September 11, 2003) many economic benefits of a split-dollar arrangement are currently taxable; death benefits paid to a beneficiary other than the policy owner may also be taxable. Under Treasury Decision 9321 and IRS Notice 2007-34, (April 10, 2007), some split-dollar arrangements may come under the requirements of IRC Sec. 409A concerning nonqualified deferred compensation. Those considering a split-dollar arrangement should first consult with their legal and/or tax advisors. State or local law may vary.

[3] Depends upon how the split-dollar arrangement is structured.

Executive Bonus Plan
IRC Sec. 162

An executive bonus plan is a method of
compensating selected key employees by paying
the premiums of a life insurance policy on the
employee's life.

Some Requirements to Make the Plan Work

- Employer cannot be the beneficiary, either
  directly or indirectly, of the insurance. See
  IRC Sec. 264(a)(1).

- The amount of the premium is additional
  compensation to the executive. (Subject to unreasonable compensation rules.)

- There should be a written agreement between employer and employee.

- Executive must pay current income tax on the amount of the net premium paid by the
  employer. (Employer can bonus the extra money needed to pay the tax or it can be paid
  by policy loans or withdrawals.)

Benefits to Employer

- Can reward key executives.

- Selective participation is allowed (no discrimination rules).

- Premium costs are tax-deductible.

- Creation of plan is simple.

- No administration.

- Amounts of coverage on various employees can differ.

- Plan can be terminated without IRS approval or restrictions.

Benefits to Executive

- Executive owns the policy[1] and cash values. If he or she changes employers, the policy
  is not lost.

- Accumulating cash values will help in emergencies, at retirement or for personal
  investments.

- The death benefit may be income tax free. See IRC Sec. 101(a).

- Proceeds may be used for estate settlement costs.

---

[1] Some tax practitioners feel that an executive could agree (through a policy endorsement) not to change ownership or
borrow against the policy without the employer's consent.

How an Executive Bonus Plan Works
IRC Sec. 162

Employer
- Pays premium.
- Includes the premium in the employee's taxable income.[1]
- Deducts the premium as a business expense.[2]

Employee
- Purchases and owns the policy.
- Pays the tax on the premium.
- Names beneficiaries.
- Can borrow against cash values.[3]

After Death Occurs

Employee's Heirs
Family or other named beneficiaries receive the policy proceeds at the death of the executive.[4]

---

[1] Employer may also choose to bonus the tax amounts to the employee, creating a net-no-cost scenario for the employee.
[2] See Reg. 1.162-9, Bonuses to Employees.
[3] Some tax practitioners feel than an executive could agree (through a policy endorsement) not to change ownership or borrow against the policy without the employer's consent.
[4] Death benefit is generally received free of income tax. See IRC Sec. 101(a).

Table 2001

Valuing Life Insurance Protection – Single Life

Table 2001 is an IRS-provided table[1] of one-year term premiums used to calculate the value of current life insurance protection in split-dollar arrangements.

Table 2001 One-year Term Premiums for $1,000 of Life Insurance Protection

Age	Premium	Age	Premium	Age	Premium	Age	Premium
0	$0.70	25	$0.71	50	$2.30	75	$33.05
1	$0.41	26	$0.73	51	$2.52	76	$36.33
2	$0.27	27	$0.76	52	$2.81	77	$40.17
3	$0.19	28	$0.80	53	$3.20	78	$44.33
4	$0.13	29	$0.83	54	$3.65	79	$49.23
5	$0.13	30	$0.87	55	$4.15	80	$54.56
6	$0.14	31	$0.90	56	$4.68	81	$60.51
7	$0.15	32	$0.93	57	$5.20	82	$66.74
8	$0.16	33	$0.96	58	$5.66	83	$73.07
9	$0.16	34	$0.98	59	$6.06	84	$80.35
10	$0.16	35	$0.99	60	$6.51	85	$88.76
11	$0.19	36	$1.01	61	$7.11	86	$99.16
12	$0.24	37	$1.04	62	$7.96	87	$110.40
13	$0.28	38	$1.06	63	$9.08	88	$121.85
14	$0.33	39	$1.07	64	$10.41	89	$133.40
15	$0.38	40	$1.10	65	$11.90	90	$144.30
16	$0.52	41	$1.13	66	$13.51	91	$155.80
17	$0.57	42	$1.20	67	$15.20	92	$168.75
18	$0.59	43	$1.29	68	$16.92	93	$186.44
19	$0.61	44	$1.40	69	$18.70	94	$206.70
20	$0.62	45	$1.53	70	$20.62	95	$228.35
21	$0.62	46	$1.67	71	$22.72	96	$250.01
22	$0.64	47	$1.83	72	$25.07	97	$265.09
23	$0.66	48	$1.98	73	$27.57	98	$270.11
24	$0.68	49	$2.13	74	$30.18	99	$281.05

---

[1] See Treasury Decision 9092, September 11, 2003, IRS Notice 2002-8, IRB 2002-4, 398, and IRS Notice 2001-10, IRB 2001-5, 459 for the regulatory history of this table.

P.S. 58 Table - Economic Benefit to Employee

Item Description	Value
Age of employee	45
Death benefit of policy	$ 250,000
Cash value portion	$50,000
Insurance protection to employee	$ 200,000
P.S. 58 rate per $1,000 of insurance	6.30
Term rate of recommended insurer, if lower	44.00
Benefit to employee	$1,260
Contribution by employee	$ 200
Amount reportable as income by employee	**$1,060**

P.S. 58 rates are a federal-government-provided table of uniform, one-year term insurance premiums used to measure the cost of pure life insurance protection. In the past, the P.S. 58 rates were one standard used to measure the economic benefit of life insurance protection acquired in conjunction with split-dollar arrangements or inside of qualified retirement plans.

On September 11, 2003, the Treasury Department and the Internal Revenue Service (IRS) issued Treasury Decision 9092 containing final regulations on the federal taxation of split-dollar arrangements, including the standards to be used in measuring the value of current life insurance protection. With the exception of certain arrangements in existence prior to its effective date of September 17, 2003,[1] TD 9092 effectively eliminated P.S. 58 as a standard by which to calculate the value of current life insurance protection.

---

[1] Certain grandfathering and safe-harbor rules apply to agreements in existence prior to September 17, 2003. See IRS Notice 2002-8, IRB 2002-1 CB, January 3, 2002.

P.S. 58 Rates
Valuing Life Insurance Protection – Single Life

P.S. 58 rates are a federal government provided table of uniform, one-year term insurance premiums, used to measure the cost of pure life insurance protection. In the past, P.S. 58 rates were one standard employed to measure the economic benefit of life insurance protection acquired in conjunction with split-dollar arrangements or inside of qualified retirement plans.

On September 11, 2003, the Treasury Department and the Internal Revenue Service (IRS) issued Treasury Decision 9092, containing final regulations on the federal taxation of split-dollar arrangements, including the standards to be used in measuring the value of life insurance protection. With the exception of certain arrangements in existence prior to its effective date of September 17, 2003,[1] TD 9092 effectively eliminated P.S. 58 as a standard by which to determine the value of current life insurance protection.

One-year Term Premiums for $1,000 of Life Insurance Protection

Age	Premium	Age	Premium	Age	Premium
15	$1.27	38	$3.87	61	$22.53
16	$1.38	39	$4.14	62	$24.50
17	$1.48	40	$4.42	63	$26.63
18	$1.52	41	$4.73	64	$28.98
19	$1.56	42	$5.07	65	$31.51
20	$1.61	43	$5.44	66	$34.28
21	$1.67	44	$5.85	67	$37.31
22	$1.73	45	$6.30	68	$40.59
23	$1.79	46	$6.78	69	$44.17
24	$1.86	47	$7.32	70	$48.06
25	$1.93	48	$7.89	71	$52.29
26	$2.02	49	$8.53	72	$56.89
27	$2.11	50	$9.22	73	$61.89
28	$2.20	51	$9.97	74	$67.33
29	$2.31	52	$10.79	75	$73.23
30	$2.43	53	$11.69	76	$79.63
31	$2.57	54	$12.67	77	$86.57
32	$2.70	55	$13.74	78	$94.09
33	$2.86	56	$14.91	79	$102.23
34	$3.02	57	$16.18	80	$111.04
35	$3.21	58	$17.56	81	$120.57
36	$3.41	59	$19.08		
37	$3.63	60	$20.73		

Note: The rate is applied to the death benefit less the cash value of the policy at the end of the year.

---

[1] Certain grandfathering and safe-harbor rules apply to agreements in existence prior to September 17, 2003. See also IRS Notice 2002-8, IRB 2002-4, 398.

U.S. 38 Rates

Reportable Economic Benefit For Split-Dollar
Survivorship Life Arrangements

The factors below are based on average ages of the couple insured under a survivor life (second-to-die) insurance policy.

Average Age of Couple	Income Reportable Per $1,000 at Risk	Average Age of Couple	Income Reportable Per $1,000 at Risk
40	0.02	62	0.62
41	0.02	63	0.73
42	0.03	64	0.86
43	0.03	65	1.02
44	0.04	66	1.20
45	0.04	67	1.43
46	0.05	68	1.69
47	0.05	69	2.00
48	0.06	70	2.37
49	0.07	71	2.80
50	0.09	72	3.32
51	0.10	73	3.93
52	0.12	74	4.65
53	0.14	75	5.50
54	0.16	76	6.50
55	0.19	77	7.68
56	0.23	78	9.07
57	0.27	79	10.71
58	0.32	80	12.64
59	0.37	81	14.90
60	0.44	82	17.55
61	0.52	83	20.65

Income Tax Impact

Age 70	
Regular P.S. 58 Costs Single Life Split-Dollar	Survivorship[1] Split-Dollar
$48.06	$2.37

In the past, U.S. 38 rates were used to measure the reportable economic benefit in split-dollar arrangements covering more than one life. Following Treasure Decision 9092 (September 11, 2003) and IRS Notice 2002-8 (January 1, 2002), the U. S. 38 rates may no longer be used.[2] Rather, the single life rates shown in Table 2001 are to be used, with "appropriate adjustments" for multiple life situations.

---

[1] Based on U.S. Life Table 38 and IRS accepted formula.
[2] Certain grandfathering and safe-harbor rules apply to split-dollar agreements in existence prior to September 17, 2003.

Meet the Business Planning Team

Business planning, especially for the succession of the business, is a very complex discipline and will generally require the efforts of more than one professional.

A business planning team might consist of two or more of the following persons:

The CEO of the Team

You are the Chief Executive Officer of this team. You will make all of the final decisions after carefully reviewing the recommendations of the various members of your team.

Estate and Business Planning Attorney

Most attorneys can draft a will or establish a small corporation. However, it may be wise to choose one who specializes in estate planning and business continuation. Your choice could mean the difference between successfully achieving your goals and failure of the business plan.

Life Underwriter

Life insurance is very often a key element in the smooth transfer of a business to either heirs or surviving business associates. An insurance professional will be able to assist you in determining the best type of policy and the amount required to meet your goals.

Certified Public Accountant (CPA)

Almost all successful businesses require the services of a qualified accountant. The CPA designation is an indication that a person has passed rigorous examinations and has been in practice for a number of years. Some CPAs have pursued additional studies in the complex areas of business valuation methods.

Business Appraisal Expert

In the event of a disagreement with the IRS as to the value of the business interest, it would be prudent to possess a detailed appraisal by a trained and qualified expert. There are experts who specialize exclusively in this field.

Financial Advisor

Sometimes the life agent, accountant or other member of the businesss planning team may have special training in financial planning. Other times a person who specializes in financial planning may be a part of your team. This broader knowledge may help to coordinate the efforts of the team.

Importance of a Business Continuation Plan

Competing Interests of Heirs and Surviving Owners

These interests are many and may include the following.

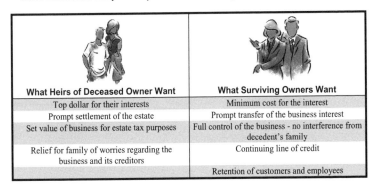

What Heirs of Deceased Owner Want	What Surviving Owners Want
Top dollar for their interests	Minimum cost for the interest
Prompt settlement of the estate	Prompt transfer of the business interest
Set value of business for estate tax purposes	Full control of the business - no interference from decedent's family
Relief for family of worries regarding the business and its creditors	Continuing line of credit
	Retention of customers and employees

Potential Problems Without a Written Agreement

Frequent results include:

- Heated conflicts among the remaining owners and the decedent's family;
- Unhappiness on all sides, and sometimes litigation;
- Delays in settling the estate and continuing business growth;
- Loss of customers; and
- Possible liquidation of the business which may bring less than full value.

The Solution: A Written Agreement (and cash)

Taking the time now to see that the business will pass in an orderly manner at time of death will benefit all parties and their heirs. A written agreement can provide:

- An orderly transfer of the business;
- A mutually agreeable sales price;
- Mutually agreeable terms of sale;
- A value that is binding on the IRS for federal estate tax purposes[1]; and
- Stability for customers, staff, creditors and investors.

An agreement which is favorable to all parties can be more easily drafted prior to a crisis.

---

[1] Under the Tax Act of 2001, the federal estate tax is gradually phased out until its final repeal in the year 2010. If Congress does not act at that time to repeal it for the years following, it will automatically revert back to the rates in effect during the year 2001, with an exemption for the first $1,000,000 of assets.

Commonly Asked
Business Continuation Questions

The following are commonly asked business continuation
questions. Each question is followed by an answer that
highlights the issues involved and the importance of taking
action.

Question: What's the problem?

Answer: Think about the essence of a closely held business.
If it's like most firms, it has these characteristics.

- The majority stockholders operate the business.

- The majority stockholders receive most of their income from salary or bonuses.

- Stockholders have limited creditor liabilities.

- If a stockholder were to die or become permanently disabled, the legal structure of the business would survive.

- If a stockholder were to die or become permanently disabled, the personnel structure would be significantly changed.

The problem is, when a business owner dies, the business often dies too: not because
anything wrong has been done but because nothing has been done, and that's wrong!

At death (or disability), no asset tends to deteriorate as quickly or as totally as a business.
Often, the precipitous drop in value is staggering!

Think about it. If a friend owned a car or a home or almost any other tangible asset, one
month after that friend died, the value of that car or home would be relatively the same.
But if the friend owned a restaurant that didn't reopen for a month or was a doctor whose
practice was closed for a month or owned a manufacturing plant which produced no goods
for a month, what would the business be worth at the end of that month?

Question: Why can't leaving the business to the proper parties in a will solve the problem?

Answer: Leaving the business to successors at death through will provisions does not
answer the key problems. A disgruntled heir or a dissatisfied spouse may attack a will.
Often, part of the business ends up in the hands of inactive heirs who can add little to the
business but who want income equal to working stockholders. The result is an increased
probability of business failure and inevitable family discord. Most importantly, a will
cannot address the central problems created when a business owner dies or becomes
permanently disabled.

Continued...

Commonly Asked
Business Continuation Questions

Look at these four points, seen from the perspective of a surviving stockholder and the decedent's survivors.

Surviving Stockholder	Decedent's Survivors
Continue reasonable salaries	Pay dividends and hire family
Build and expand the business	Pay dividends and hire family
Maintain a long-term outlook	Pay dividends and hire family
Build a strong cash reserve	Pay dividends and hire family

A surviving stockholder doing his or her own job, and probably that of the deceased co-stockholder as well, would want at least the same salary as before, if not a greater salary, in recognition of the increased responsibilities. And the surviving stockholder may want profits plowed back into the business rather than being paid out as dividends.

On the other hand, the heirs of a deceased stockholder would want the corporation to pay dividends and/or hire one or more family members at the highest possible salary. Typically, lots of income will be needed to maintain the current living standard and to pay the unexpectedly high debts, taxes, and expenses that accompany death.

This is why the death or long-term disability of a stockholder almost always creates conflicting interests and dissension.

Question: What happens after a stockholder's death or disability?

Answer: When a working stockholder dies or becomes permanently disabled, there is inevitably a reorganization of the business.

The remaining stockholders generally must:

- Buy out the heirs;

- Sell out to the heirs;

- Accept the purchasers of their stock as business associates; or

- Take the heirs into the business and share profits and decisions.

Is it possible to take one of these courses of action now? Given a choice, which course of action is realistically the most appealing?

Continued

Commonly Asked
Business Continuation Questions

Question: Can one be more specific about the problems and objectives of the heirs?

Answer: This can be answered by thinking about the following questions.

- If the heirs are invited to take an active part in the operation and management of the business, will they have the training, experience, and willingness to carry their load and earn their salaries?

- Will all the surviving stockholders be comfortable with the new arrangement?

- If the heirs decide to trust the surviving stockholder to run the business and take care of them and remain inactive, will the dividends the firm pays be sufficient for their needs and meet their expectations?

- Will the heirs panic if business income must be re-invested back in the business rather than paid out as dividends?

- How will the heirs react if the surviving stockholder decides to sell stock to an outside party? Where will that leave them?

- If the heirs decide to sell their stock to an outside party, will they obtain a price they feel is fair and adequate, or will the price they need for the stock be more than a knowledgeable buyer is willing to pay?

- Do the heirs know the true value of the stock?

- Can the heirs find a buyer at a reasonable price, or at any price, if they hold only a minority interest?

- Will the surviving stockholder lose his or her job if the heirs own, and then sell, their majority interest?

Question: What are the objectives of the surviving stockholder when another stockholder dies or becomes permanently disabled?

Answer: Typically, a surviving stockholder will want to retain control. Retaining control and preventing outsiders from interfering in the management of the business and its affairs will be crucial objectives. If the business has elected S Corporation treatment (pass through of taxation), the surviving stockholder will want to be sure that election is not lost (which could easily happen if the stock falls into the wrong hands). Further, it will also be desirable to have the cash to guarantee a fair payment to buy out the deceased co-stockholder's heirs.

Continued...

Commonly Asked
Business Continuation Questions

Question: What are the odds that death or disability could actually occur between two co-stockholders?

Answer: If either event does occur, the probability against it happening doesn't really matter, does it? But it is helpful to at least know what the actuaries know.

Probability of Death Prior to Age 65[1]

Probability of Death Prior to Age 65	Ages of Business Owners
48.5%	30/30
47.4%	35/35
44.8%	40/40
43.5%	45/45
39.8%	50/50
38.0%	30/35
46.6%	40/45
44.7%	40/45
41.7%	45/50

Note: Statistics courtesy of NumberCruncher Software (610.527.5216).

Question: What's the solution to all of these problems?

Answer: A legal agreement called a buy-sell is often the best solution. The document, prepared by an attorney, is a legal instrument which requires the corporation (in the case of a stock redemption agreement) or the remaining stockholders (in the case of a cross-purchase agreement) to buy the stock of a deceased, retiring, or permanently disabled stockholder. It would require the estate of the stockholder to sell under a formula devised while both parties are alive and well.

There is even a type of buy-sell that combines the flexibility of both the stock redemption and the cross purchase. This is called the wait-and-see buy-sell. With it one can wait and see the best course of action, tax-wise, and then take it, even many years after the agreement is drafted.

---

[1] The probablity that one of two business owners in average physical condition will die prior to age 65 is illustrated.

Continued...

Commonly Asked
Business Continuation Questions

Question: How is this agreement funded? Is there a perfect buy-sell funding mechanism?

Answer: There's no free lunch or perfect buy-sell funding vehicle. The ideal is a method that will facilitate a trouble-free transfer of the business interest and provide funds for that purchase in a manner that:

- Is relatively inexpensive;
- Is easy to administer; and
- Will not adversely affect the business or the surviving stockholder's working capital or credit position.

Since two of the most common causes of ownership termination are death and long-term disability, the financial mechanism chosen must provide ample amounts of cash, at the time needed most, whenever that occurs!

Question: What are the various funding alternatives?

Answer: There are four ways to fund a buy-sell. They are using cash on hand, borrowing, making installment payments, and through life and/or disability insurance.

Here are some thoughts and questions that should be discussed with the business planning team.

- **Cash**
  - How much cash will be required and will it be available when needed?
  - When will that cash be needed?
  - Will after-tax dollars need to be kept on hand to finance the purchase?
  - Will a higher alternative rate of return have to be sacrificed in order to keep adequate cash on hand?

- **Borrowing**
  - Will the firm or the surviving stockholders be able to borrow money after the death or long-term disability of a stockholder/employee?
  - What rate of interest will be required and would it be deductible?
  - How serious will the cash drain impact be on corporate or personal reserves?

Continued...

Commonly Asked
Business Continuation Questions

- **Installment payments**
    - Can the decedent's family afford to leave substantial sums of money at the risk of the business?
    - Where will the deceased stockholder's family obtain cash to pay taxes, debts, and other immediate estate settlement costs?
    - What rate of interest will the decedent's family want to charge on the unpaid balance? Will that interest be deductible?
    - What will the total cost be?
    - Can the business carry the extra debt and still find future growth?

- **Insurance**
    - Will the buyers be guaranteed that the event which creates the need, death or disability, will create sufficient cash to satisfy that need?
    - Will this method reduce or eliminate the strain on future working capital in return for relatively small, predictable annual transfer of cash to cash values?
    - Can policy cash values be used, before an insured's death, for a corporate emergency or opportunity?

A question commonly arises at this point, "Where does the IRS come in?"

The answer is that the IRS (and the state inheritance tax people) typically value a business as a going concern. They take the highest sustainable value and add that to the value of all other assets. The total may be subject to federal estate tax[1] rates as high as 45%[2]. Without the cash to pay the tax on the estate, the tax may absorb most of the estate, including the business.

The son of a business owner was recently quoted as saying:

"You can't inherit a family business anymore. If it's got any value at all, you've got to sell it just to pay inheritance taxes."

It should be obvious that setting up a buy-sell agreement can be crucial to the survival of a business, as well as essential to guarantee the economic security that the business represents to family and loved ones. Such an undertaking involves a considerable amount of time, thought, and background experience in many areas, as well as teamwork and cooperation among all the members of your advisory team.

---

[1] Under the Tax Act of 2001, the federal estate tax is gradually phased out until its final repeal in the year 2010. If Congress does not act at that time to repeal it for the years following, it will automatically revert back to the rates in effect during the year 2001, with an exemption for the first $1,000,000 of assets.
[2] The top bracket will be 45% in 2007 through 2009 with zero taxes in 2010. If Congress does not act at that time to repeal the federal estate tax for the years following, in the year 2011 the top bracket of 55% will automatically return.

Buy-Sell Agreement

In order to guarantee a buyer for the interest in a business (particularly a minority interest which may be of very little value to one's heirs), consideration should be given to a lifetime agreement among the business owners as to how to dispose of the business.

Entity Plan

Under an entity plan the corporation (or partnership) buys the interest of the deceased business owner. This type of arrangement is often used when there are several owners.

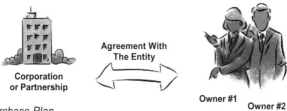

Corporation or Partnership

Agreement With The Entity

Owner #1   Owner #2

Cross-Purchase Plan

Under this plan each surviving owner agrees to buy the interest of any deceased owner.

Agreement Between Owners

Owner #1   **Owner #2**

An attorney should be consulted in deciding which plan is better.

Advantages of Buy-Sell Agreements

- Guarantees a buyer for an asset that probably will not pay dividends to one's heirs.

- Can establish a value for federal estate tax purposes that is binding on the IRS. See IRC Sec. 2703.

- Spells out the terms of payment and is easily funded with life insurance and disability insurance, if desirable.[1]

- Provides a smooth transition of complete control and ownership to those who are going to keep the business going.

---

[1] Buy-sell agreements are frequently funded with life insurance. Under the provisions of IRC Sec. 101(j), added by the Pension Protection Act of 2006, death proceeds from a life insurance policy owned by an employer on the life of an employee are generally includable in income, unless certain requirements are met. Until the full scope of this new law is clarified by the IRS, caution is advised. State or local law may vary.

Buy-Sell Agreement - Partnership

At death, the disposition of a partner's interest depends upon several key factors.

- Does the partner want his/her interest sold or retained by the heirs?
- Will death costs force the sale of the business?
- Can the remaining partners afford to buy the deceased partner's interest?
- Can the partners operate without each other?

In the absence of a continuation agreement, a partnership is dissolved at the death of a partner. The surviving partner(s) becomes the liquidation trustee, who is responsible by law for dissolving and terminating the business.

Common Problems During Dissolution

During the dissolution process, the liquidating trustee partner can expect problems.

- Creditors may become worried and may want to be paid immediately.
- Operating the business may be difficult without the deceased partner's skills.
- Debtors may not pay.
- The remaining partner may be forced to sell assets.
- Good will may be lost.
- Deceased partner's family may not understand why the income has stopped.

A Better Solution Is a Binding Buy-Sell Agreement

- **Entity plan:** Under this arrangement, the partnership purchases the deceased or withdrawing partner's interest.

Partnership

Agreement with
the Partnership

Partner #1

Partner #2

- **Cross-purchase plan:** Under this arrangement, the surviving partners purchase the deceased or withdrawing partner's interest.

Partner #1

Agreement
Between Owners

Partner #2

Note: An attorney should be consulted in deciding which plan is better and in preparing the agreement.

Continued

Buy-Sell Agreement - Partnership

A Buy-Sell Agreement Benefits All Parties[1]

Benefits to Deceased's Family	Benefits to Buyer of Business	Additional Lifetime Benefits
• Freed of business worries. • Not forced to sell assets. • Family gets a fair price for business interest. • Probate estate is settled more quickly.	• The owner has full control of the business and its future earning potential. • May alleviate concerns of creditors or suppliers.	• The agreement can cover a buy out at retirement, disability or disagreement. • It produces a sense of security that heirs are protected and that the business will continue.

---

[1] Buy-sell agreements are frequently funded with life insurance. Under the provisions of IRC Sec. 101(j), added by the Pension Protection Act of 2006, death proceeds from a life insurance policy owned by an employer on the life of an employee are generally includable in income, unless certain requirements are met. Until the full scope of this new law is clarified by the IRS, caution is advised. State or local law may vary.

Buy-Sell Agreement - Sole Ownership

The Death of a Sole Owner

When the sole owner of a business dies, his or her executor has several choices, some of which have potential problems.

- **The executor can continue the business.**
  - The executor may be unfamiliar with the business.
  - There can be some loss in good will.
  - The executor may be liable for any business losses.
  - Creditors will typically want to be paid immediately.
  - Subsequent sale may bring less than the value determined for federal estate tax[1] purposes.

- **The executor can close down the business.**
  - Loyal employees are out of work.
  - Family income ceases.
  - Accounts receivable may be very difficult to collect.

- **The business can be transferred by will to the heirs.**
  - Heirs may not have the desire or ability to run business.
  - There can be some loss of good will.
  - The business may have to be sold to pay the taxes and expenses.
  - Creditors will typically want to be paid immediately.
  - Accounts receivable may be very difficult to collect.

- **The executor can liquidate the business.**
  - Buyers may pay only a fraction of the going-concern value.
  - Good will is totally lost.
  - Creditors will want to be paid immediately.
  - Accounts receivable may be very difficult to collect.
  - Family income is eliminated.

---

[1] Under the Tax Act of 2001, the federal estate tax is gradually phased out until its final repeal in the year 2010. If Congress does not act at that time to repeal it for the years following, it will automatically revert back to the rates in effect during the year 2001, with an exemption for the first $1,000,000 of assets.

Continue

Buy-Sell Agreement - Sole Ownership

A Better Solution

There is a better solution - a binding buy-sell agreement which benefits all parties.

- **Benefits to the deceased's family.**
  - Freed from business worries.
  - Not forced to sell assets.
  - Family gets a fair price.
  - Probate estate is more quickly settled.
- **Benefits to the buyer of business** (usually a key employee).
  - He or she still has a job and his or her income continues.
  - He or she owns the business and controls its future success.

Lifetime Benefits

In addition to the benefits explained above, there are also various benefits which occur during the lifetime of the owner.

- Knowing the business will continue gives employees a more stable feeling.
- Knowing that he or she may some day own the business, the prospective buyer works harder.
- Key employee can be put in charge when owner retires.

Buy-Sell Agreement - Corporation

When a stockholder dies, the disposition of his stock depends upon several key factors.

- Is the decedent a majority or minority stockholder?
- Is retention or sale of stock desired?
- Will death costs force the sale?
- Is there a market for the stock?

Ownership Situation	Additional Considerations
Decedent was minority owner	A minority interest in a corporation has little value to an owner who is not an employee. Close corporations rarely pay dividends. Without an agreement the estate is in a poor bargaining position. Minority stockholders can cause problems.
Decedent was equal owner	Decedent's spouse or children may have a vote equal to the shareholder who is running the business.
Decedent was majority owner	Can a minority stockholder afford the buyout? Are the payments tied to the success of the business? Can a minority stockholder keep the business successful?
Decedent was sole owner	Who will buy the stock? Child? Key employee? Competitor? How will he or she pay for it if the business fails?

A Buy-Sell Agreement Brings Certainty[1]

The best way to bring certainty to these unanswered questions is a binding buy-sell agreement which benefits all parties.

- **Benefits to the deceased's family**
  - They receive a fair price for the stock.
  - They are free from business worries.

- **Benefits to the buyer of business**
  - He or she has control of business and its future earning potential.

- **Price and terms**
  - These are established prior to the crisis.

- **Additional lifetime benefits**
  - Prospective owners work harder if the business may someday be theirs.
  - The agreement can cover a buyout at retirement, disability or disagreement.

---

[1] Buy-sell agreements are frequently funded with life insurance. Under the provisions of IRC Sec. 101(j), added by the Pension Protection Act of 2006, death proceeds from a life insurance policy owned by an employer on the life of an employee are generally includable in income, unless certain requirements are met. Until the full scope of this new law is clarified by the IRS, caution is advised. State or local law may vary.

Types of Corporate Continuation Plans

If the owners want to keep the business in the family, but money is needed to pay estate taxes or other estate settlement costs, a partial stock redemption under IRC Sec. 303 should be considered. If the business interest is to be passed to others, several choices are available.[1]

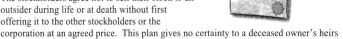

Continuation Plans in Brief

- **First offer of stock to existing stockholder(s):** The stockholders agree not to sell their stock to an outsider during life or at death without first offering it to the other stockholders or the corporation at an agreed price. This plan gives no certainty to a deceased owner's heirs and will not peg the value for federal estate tax purposes.

- **Option to buy:** An agreement giving the corporation (and/or surviving stockholders) an option to purchase a deceased stockholder's shares. Since the estate is required to sell if the option is exercised, the value for federal estate tax purposes may be pegged. The heirs have no certainty since the corporation is not required to purchase the stock.

- **Cross-purchase buy-sell agreement:** A written agreement among the stockholders to purchase each other's shares at the death of an owner. The price is either stated in the agreement, set by a formula, or provides for the use of independent appraisers

- **Stock redemption plan:** Stockholders enter into an agreement with the corporation to have their estates sell their shares back to the corporation at death. The company usually carries key employee insurance policies to finance the payments for the stock.

- **Wait-and-see plan:** A written agreement among the stockholders and the corporation, generally giving the corporation an option to buy the stock. If it elects not to purchase, the surviving stockholders may buy it and, if they don't, the corporation may be required to buy the shares.

Considerations in Choosing a Plan

- What is the value of the corporation and who can afford to buy it?

- How many owners are there and how old are they? What percentage of ownership does each person have?

- What is the net worth of each owner? Are the owners related?

- Are they all insurable?

- What are the individual tax brackets and the corporate tax bracket?

- Does the non-active spouse have any rights, e.g., community property interest?

---

[1] Many types of corporate continuation plans are funded with life insurance. Under the provisions of IRC Sec. 101(j), added by the Pension Protection Act of 2006, death proceeds from a life insurance policy owned by an employer on the life of an employee are generally includable in income, unless certain requirements are met. Until the full scope of this new law is clarified by the IRS, caution is advised. State or local law may vary.

Buy-Sell Agreement - Cross-Purchase vs. Corporate Stock Redemption

	Cross-Purchase Buy-Sell	Corporate Stock Redemption
Parties to the plan	A cross-purchase plan is between the shareholders themselves.	A stock redemption plan is between the corporation and the stockholders.
Income tax treatment at a later sale of stock by the surviving shareholders	Purchasing stockholders get a new basis in acquired stock, which is used to measure taxable gain at a later sale of the stock.	The surviving stockholders own a larger percentage of the outstanding shares, but their basis in the stock does not change, causing a higher capital gain at a later sale of the stock.
State laws restricting stock redemptions	Only applies to redemptions by the corporation.	State laws may require that redemptions of stock can be made only from surplus.
Family attribution rules IRC Sec. 318	Only applies to redemptions by the corporation.	These rules may cause what appears to be a total redemption of a decedent's stock, to be treated as a taxable dividend.
Are life insurance policies available to corporate creditors?	Not usually. It is possible if the creditor is, for some reason, able to pierce the corporate veil.	The cash values and the proceeds would generally be available to the creditors of the corporation.
Who pays the premiums on insured plans?	The shareholders. If corporation pays, it must be treated as additional compensation.[1]	Corporation is the policy owner, beneficiary, and the premium payer.[1]
Are there problems when transferring the policies which the decedent owned on other shareholders?	A purchase of these policies by a surviving shareholder will create a transfer for value which may cause the proceeds to be partially subject to income taxation.	Policies are owned by the corporation. No need to make a transfer when one shareholder dies.
What if the corporation needs the proceeds?	Available only if the surviving shareholders are willing to lend the proceeds to the corporation.	Corporation has the right to collect the proceeds at date of death.
Which is easier to understand?	At death, there may be multiple buyers of the decedent's shares. In an insured plan this also means multiple policies on each shareholder.	Generally thought to be easier to understand. At time of death, only one buyer (the corporation) and one seller (the deceased shareholder's estate).
What's wrong with multiple insurance policies?	The plan may require many policies. The formula is: (number of shareholders) times (number of shareholders - 1). For example, if there were 5 shareholders, you would need 20 life insurance policies, i.e., 5 X (5-1)	Need only one policy for each shareholder.

---

[1] Both cross-purchase and stock-redemption agreements are frequently funded with life insurance. Under the provisions of IRC Sec. 101(j), added by the Pension Protection Act of 2006, death proceeds from a life insurance policy owned by an employer on the life of an employee are generally includable in income, unless certain requirements are met. Until the full scope of this new law is clarified by the IRS, caution is advised. State or local law may vary.

Continued.

Buy-Sell Agreement - Cross-Purchase vs. Corporate Stock Redemption

	Cross-Purchase Buy-Sell	Corporate Stock Redemption
Other considerations	• If a Stockholder is having trouble paying the premium, he or she may allow the policy to lapse. • Insurance may cost more if the corporation is in a lower tax bracket than the individuals.	• It permits the pooling of premium obligations.[1] • No question arises as to unreasonable compensation. This often occurs when salaries are increased to pay the premiums for life insurance used to fund a cross-purchase agreement. • Life insurance proceeds are included in adjusted current earnings for purposes of the alternative minimum tax. • The voting power could be altered in an undesirable way.[2]

Wait-and-See Buy-Sell Agreement

If it seems difficult to make the decision as to which plan to use, one may consider what is called a wait-and-see buy-sell agreement.

A. Stockholders and corporation agree to the following.

- The surviving shareholders have the option[3] to purchase the shares of the deceased shareholder, and

- The corporation has the obligation to redeem the shares to the extent they are not purchased by the shareholders.

B. Funding should be as in a cross-purchase plan.

C. When a shareholder dies, the survivors elect one of two options.

- Option one
  - Collect insurance proceeds.
  - Buy the shares individually.

---

[1] When one stockholder is older and/or the majority owner and the other is younger and/or a minority owner, the insurance premiums may be vastly different.
[2] Example: Father owns 30%, son owns 30% and unrelated key man owns 40%. A combined vote of father and son controls the business. If father's stock is redeemed at his death, the unrelated key man would own a majority of the outstanding stock and control the business.
[3] The wait-and-see plan is generally most desirable, however, if a shareholder is obligated to purchase stock and doesn't, a later purchase by the corporation would likely be a dividend.

Continued...

Buy-Sell Agreement - Cross-Purchase vs. Corporate Stock Redemption

- Option two
  - Collect insurance proceeds.
  - Lend proceeds to the corporation.
  - Cause the corporation to redeem the shares.
  - Corporation issues interest-bearing notes to repay loans.

D. An alternative arrangement

- The corporation has the first option to purchase the stock at the price or formula set in the agreement.
- If the corporation fails to exercise its option, the surviving shareholders have a second option to purchase the stock.
- If the survivors fail to purchase the stock, or only purchase a portion of it, then the corporation is required to purchase the remainder.

Buy-Sell Agreement - S Corporation

Cross-Purchase

A cross-purchase buy-sell agreement would be
basically the same in an S corporation as with a
regular C corporation.

Stock Redemption

Because of the tax treatment of the S corporation,
the stock redemption plan has a few different
considerations:

- Since most income passes through to the shareholders, there is little opportunity to manipulate the corporate and individual tax brackets.

- Accumulation of funds by the S corporation would be taxed at the shareholders' top marginal tax brackets. Life insurance would lessen this problem because the premiums are so much less than the amount needed for the buyout. Applicable state insurance laws must be reviewed to make sure shareholders have an "insurable interest" in the other shareholders.

- If stock passes to too many persons in addition to the existing shareholders, currently limited to 100 persons, the S corporation election may be lost.

- A beneficiary who inherits S corporation stock (so that he or she then owns more than 50% of the shares) could possibly revoke the election, contrary to the wishes of the other shareholders.

- Life insurance proceeds may be income tax exempt to both the S corporation and individual shareholders[1]; the basis of stock held by each shareholder is increased by his or her share of the proceeds. See IRC Secs. 1366(a)(1)(A) and 1367(a)(1)(A). Income from a stock redemption may be treated as a mix of taxable dividend and capital gain, or it may be treated solely as a capital gain transaction. See IRC Sec. 1368.

---

[1] Buy-sell agreements are frequently funded with life insurance. Under the provisions of IRC Sec. 101(j), added by the Pension Protection Act of 2006, death proceeds from a life insurance policy owned by an employer on the life of an employee are generally includable in income, unless certain requirements are met. Until the full scope of this new law is clarified by the IRS, caution is advised. State or local law may vary.

Cross-Purchase Buy-Sell Agreement

A cross-purchase buy-sell agreement involves shareholders entering into an agreement with each other, rather than with the corporation, to insure an orderly disposition of their stock in the event of an untimely death or disability.

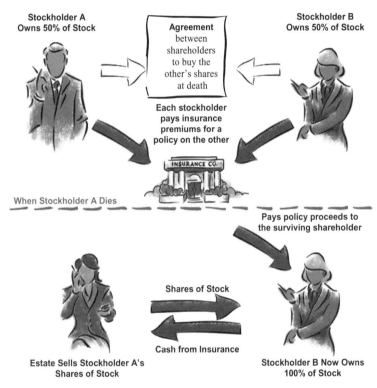

Advantages	Disadvantages
The transferred shares receive a new income tax basis equal to the price paid. This will mean a tax savings, if the stock is later sold at a higher price.	Plan is more difficult to administer if more than two or three shareholders.
No problem with state laws restricting redemptions.	Requires more policies, e.g., 12 policies for 4 shareholders, 20 policies for 5 shareholders, etc.
No problem with IRC Sec. 318 attribution rules.	Some policies may lapse if owner doesn't make the payments.
Life policies may be insulated from the corporation's creditors.	Life insurance proceeds may be taxable if the provisions of IRC Sec. 101(j) apply.

Cross-Purchase Buy-Sell Agreement
with Three or More Owners

A cross-purchase buy-sell agreement involves stockholders entering into an agreement
with each other, rather than with the corporation, to insure an orderly disposition of their
stock in the event of an untimely death or disability. Unless certain requirements are met,
life insurance proceeds may be includable in income. See IRC Sec. 101(j).

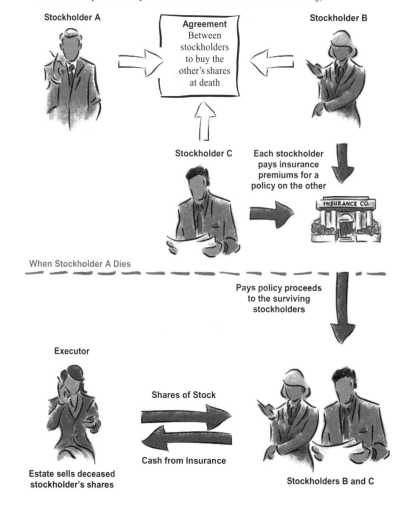

Stockholder A

Agreement
Between
stockholders
to buy the
other's shares
at death

Stockholder B

Stockholder C

Each stockholder
pays insurance
premiums for a
policy on the other

INSURANCE CO.

When Stockholder A Dies

Pays policy proceeds
to the surviving
stockholders

Executor

Shares of Stock

Cash from Insurance

Estate sells deceased
stockholder's shares

Stockholders B and C

Stock Redemption Plan

A stock redemption plan involves shareholders entering into an agreement with the corporation to ensure an orderly disposition of their stock in the event of an untimely death or disability.

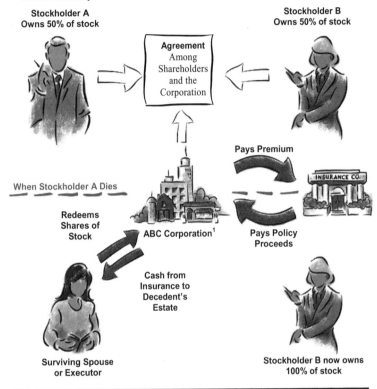

Advantages	Disadvantages
Usually easier to understand than the cross purchase plan.	Possible accumulated earnings tax on earnings retained to fund the buyout.
Fewer policies in insured plans.	Possibility that family attribution rules will make the buyout a dividend.
No questions as to unreasonable compensation.	Voting power may be altered unfavorably.
	Strict state redemption laws must be followed.
	Value of survivor's shares increase, but not basis.
	Possible increase in corporate AMT

---

[1] Unless certain requirements are met, life insurance proceeds may be includable in income. See IRC Sec. 101(j).

Wait-And-See Buy-Sell Agreement

The decision as to whether a cross purchase buy-sell agreement or a stock redemption plan is better may be difficult at the time it is drafted. Many business owners use the wait-and-see approach to defer this choice until after a death occurs.

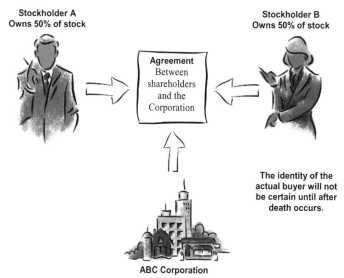

Stockholder A
Owns 50% of stock

Stockholder B
Owns 50% of stock

Agreement
Between
shareholders
and the
Corporation

The identity of the
actual buyer will not
be certain until after
death occurs.

ABC Corporation

Typical Plan

- The corporation has the first option to purchase the stock at the price or formula set in the agreement.

- If the corporation fails to exercise its option, the surviving shareholders have a second option to purchase the stock.

- If they fail to purchase the stock, or only purchase a portion of it, then the corporation is required to purchase the remainder.

- If the insurance policies[1] are owned by and payable to the shareholders, the surviving shareholders may decide to lend the proceeds to the corporation after a death occurs, if they determine that a stock redemption would be most advantageous.

- When the corporation pays back the loan, it will not be considered income to the shareholder, except for interest which is paid on the loan.

- On the other hand, if a cross purchase plan is more advantageous the corporation will not exercise its first option to buy the stock.

---

[1] Unless certain requirements are met, life insurance proceeds may be includable in income. See IRC Sec. 101(j).

Trusteed Corporate Buy-Sell Agreement

One of the advantages of a cross-purchase buy-sell agreement is that each surviving stockholder gets a new income tax basis on the stock which he or she purchases from the deceased (or departing) shareholder. The new basis would be equal to the amount paid for the stock. This will reduce income taxes if the business is later sold for a higher amount.

One disadvantage to insurance-funded cross-purchase buy-sell plans becomes apparent when there are several owners. For example, if there were five owners, each of them would have to own a policy on each of the other four owners. This would mean that a total of 20 different policies would be required. To get the benefits of the increased tax basis and a fewer number of polices, one should consider a trusteed buy-sell agreement.

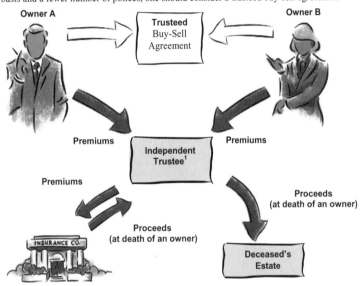

During Life	At Death
Each owner signs an agreement with an independent trustee to do the following: • Endorse their stock certificates in blank and deliver them to the trustee. • Agree to allow the trustee to take out an insurance contract on his or her life. • Contribute funds to pay the premiums on the policies on the lives of the other owners.	• The trustee collects the insurance proceeds on the decedent's life and delivers them to his or her estate. • The trustee, under the terms of the agreement, sees that the corporation issues new shares to each of the surviving owners in exchange for the shares which belonged to the deceased owner.

Note: In situations involving three or more co-stockholders, the death of the first stockholder to die can create a "transfer for value" problem for the surviving stockholders under IRC Sec. 101(a)(2)(B).

---

[1] Unless certain requirements are met, life insurance proceeds may be includable in income. See IRC Sec. 101(j).

Making Buy-Sell Agreements
Acceptable to the IRS
IRC Sec. 2703

When a business owner dies, there is a risk that the
IRS will include his or her business interest in the
gross estate at a value that exceeds the price at which
it is actually sold to a new buyer. To reduce the
possibility of such a hardship, many business owners
enter into a buy-sell agreement, while they are still
living.

If the new buyer happens to be the business owner's son or daughter, it is easy to imagine
the parent directing his executor to sell the business to that child at a value which is far
below fair market value. This would cause the estate to have a lower value and thus the
government would collect a smaller federal estate tax. Therefore, buy-sell agreements
between family members are generally subject to very close scrutiny by the IRS.

The government recognizes the use of buy-sell agreements to peg the value of a business
for estate tax purposes, so long as there is no abuse in the area of valuing the business.

Rules for Business Valuation

The Internal Revenue Code provides the following rules for business valuation in IRC
Sec. 2703.

- The agreement must be a bona fide business arrangement.

- It must not be merely a device to transfer the business interest to family members[1] for
  less than full and adequate consideration.

- The terms of the agreement must be comparable to those found in similar arrangements
  entered into by persons in an arm's length transaction.

If the parties to the agreement are not related to one another and are not the natural objects
of each other's bounty, they can set the value of their stock for federal estate tax purposes,
with a buy-sell agreement which contains a formula, a fixed price or provides for
independent appraisals.

If the parties to the agreement are related,[1] they must use a reasonable formula in the
agreement or agree to the use of independent appraisals after death occurs in order to
establish a binding value. An experienced professional business appraiser who is familiar
with the industry should choose the formula.

Note: Under the Tax Act of 2001, the federal estate tax is gradually phased out until its final repeal in the year
2010. If Congress does not act at that time to repeal it for the years following, it will automatically revert back
to the rates in effect during the year 2001, with an exemption for the first $1,000,000 of assets.

---

[1] Family members are defined in the regulations to include one's spouse, parents of either spouse and their lineal
descendants (and their spouses), and other individuals who would be the natural objects of the transferor's bounty.
See Reg. Sec. 25.2701-1, 25.2701-2.

Corporate Distributions to Redeem Stock

General rule: The purchase by a corporation of its own stock is treated as a dividend taxable as ordinary income to the selling stockholder and not deductible by the corporation.

IRC Sec. 302 provides three exceptions to this rule. Redemptions which qualify are treated as a sale or exchange of stock subject to capital gain treatment.

Since the stock in the decedent's estate gets a new basis at the decedent's death (IRC Sec. 1014), a subsequent sale at that price would result in no tax.[1]

Purchase Price

When a Redemption Will Be Treated as a Sale

- **Is not essentially equivalent to a dividend** (IRC Sec. 302(b)(1)): This first exception to the dividend treatment of stock redemptions is perhaps the most difficult for which to qualify. The IRS must be convinced on the basis of facts and circumstances. This section should be relied upon only if the others are not available. A private ruling should be sought from the IRS.

- **Is a complete redemption of all the stockholder's interest in the corporation** (IRC Sec. 302(b)(3)): If all of stockholder's shares (voting, nonvoting, preferred and common) are redeemed, the redemption will qualify for capital gain treatment. In determining how many shares the stockholder owns, add to the shares actually owned those "constructively owned" under the IRC Sec. 318 Attribution Rules.

- **Is substantially disproportionate** (IRC Sec. 302(b)(2)): A redemption will receive capital gain treatment if immediately after the redemption the following three mathematical tests are met:

  - The stockholder owns less than 50% of the total combined voting power of all classes of stock entitled to vote.

  - The stockholder's percentage of voting stock must be less than 80% of his percentage of voting stock prior to the redemption.

  - The stockholder's percentage of common stock (voting and nonvoting) must be less than 80% of his percentage of voting stock prior to the redemption.

---

[1] Under the Tax Act of 2001, the federal estate tax is gradually phased out until its final repeal in the year 2010. If Congress does not act at that time to repeal it for the years following, it will automatically revert back to the rates in effect during the year 2001, with an exemption for the first $1,000,000 of assets. In place of the federal estate tax, the Tax Act of 2001 provides for a capital gain tax on the appreciation portion of assets owned by the decedent. There are certain adjustments to increase the basis so that estates smaller than $1,300,000 will not be affected by the tax. There are additional basis increases for assets passing to one's spouse, as well as for the decedent's capital losses, net operating losses, etc.

Continued.

Corporate Distributions to Redeem Stock

Formula to Determine Number of Shares to Be Redeemed

$$\frac{\text{(number of shares owned}^1 \quad \text{x} \quad \text{total shares outstanding)}}{\text{(5 x total shares)} \quad - \quad \text{(4 x shares owned)}} = \underline{\hspace{3cm}}$$

Number of shares
which must be
redeemed to qualify

For example: 1,000 shares outstanding and B owns 600 shares

$$\frac{600 \quad \text{x} \quad 1,000}{(5 \times 1,000) \quad - \quad (4 \times 600)} = \frac{600,000}{2,600} = 230.76 \text{ shares}$$

Therefore, at least 231 shares should be redeemed to be "substantially disproportionate."

IRC Sec. 318 Attribution Rules

The attribution rules of IRC Secs. 302(c) and 318 apply to both of the following.

- Complete redemptions
- Substantially disproportionate redemptions

These provisions are meant to give capital gain treatment only when there is a substantial change in the ownership of the corporation. Some redemptions do not, in reality, change the control or ownership and are, therefore, treated as dividends.

The attribution rules can be divided into two groups.

- Family
- Other entities (e.g., partnerships, estates, trusts, corporations, etc.)

---

[1] Refers to shares actually and constructively owned under IRC Sec. 318.

Corporate Stock Redemption
IRC Sec. 303

IRC Sec. 303 permits a corporation to redeem a portion of a decedent's stock without it being considered a dividend and thus use corporate surplus to meet the deceased shareholder's estate settlement costs.

Purchase Price

- The amount of stock which can be redeemed cannot exceed in value the total of federal and state death taxes (plus interest) and funeral and administration expenses of the deceased.

- The redemption must generally occur within three years and 90 days after filing the federal estate tax return. See IRC Sec. 303(b)(1).

- In order for the stock to qualify for favorable tax treatment, the value of the stock must exceed 35% of the adjusted gross estate[1] (gross estate less the sum of debts, losses, funeral and administration expenses). If the decedent owns 20% or more of the value of each of two or more corporations, they can be combined to meet the 35% requirement.

- The Internal Revenue Code also requires that the person whose shares are redeemed must bear the burden of the federal estate taxes, the state death taxes, and administration expenses in an amount at least equal to the amount of the stock redemption. In an AB type credit shelter trust, the marital or survivor's trust does not bear these expenses. Therefore, if the stock were redeemed from the marital trust, it would not qualify under Sec. 303 capital gains treatment. Likewise, if stock passes by joint tenancy to the surviving spouse and the will directs the executor to pay all death taxes and expenses of administration from the residue of the probate estate, the redemption will not qualify under Sec. 303.

- Even if the corporation has no liquid assets, the surviving spouse or adult child may lend the money to the corporation to fund a redemption. Then future corporate earnings can be paid out to the surviving spouse or child as payment of a corporate debt. The lender may receive these monies through life insurance on the life of the deceased owner.

- Care must be exercised in accumulating cash in the corporation for such a redemption. The IRS may determine it to be an unreasonable accumulation and subject to a penalty tax. A life insurance policy is an excellent method to fund the plan without accumulating large sums of cash.

Note: Under the Tax Act of 2001, the federal estate tax is gradually phased out until its final repeal in the year 2010. If Congress does not act at that time to repeal it for the years following, it will automatically revert back to the rates in effect during the year 2001, with an exemption for the first $1,000,000 of assets.

---

[1] Gifts made within three years of death (in excess of the annual gift tax exclusion) are brought back into the gross estate for purposes of qualifying under Sec. 303. This is to prevent the making of deathbed gifts in order to qualify the remaining estate for Sec. 303.

Family Attribution

Under IRC Sec. 318(a)(1) a redeeming stockholder "constructively" owns stock directly owned by or for his spouse, children, grandchildren or parents.

Note: A stockholder is not deemed to own stock of his brothers, sisters or grandparents.

The family attribution rules can be waived if after a complete redemption the following conditions are satisfied.

- Immediately after the redemption, the redeeming stockholder can have no interest in the corporation as an officer, director or employee (creditor is all right).[1]

- The stockholder must not acquire an interest in the corporation within 10 years after the redemption except by inheritance.

- An agreement must be filed by the redeeming stockholder or his executor agreeing to notify the IRS of any stock acquisition which would violate the above rule and agreeing to maintain necessary records.

- The redeeming stockholder did not acquire the redeemed stock within 10 years before the redemption from a family member whose stock ownership would be attributed to him under the attribution rules.

- At the time of the redemption there is not a stockholder related under the attribution rules who has acquired stock from the redeeming stockholder in the prior 10 years.

Note: The last two conditions above may not apply if the IRS can be convinced tax avoidance was not a principal purpose of the transaction or that the redeeming stockholder inherited the shares.

Prohibited Interests

- Serving as custodian of stock held in an account under the Uniform Gifts to Minors Act. See Rev. Rul. 81-233, 1981-2 CB 83. However, the spouse of redeemed stockholder may act as custodian. See LR 7931043.

- Acting as officer, director or employee. See IRC Sec. 302(c)(2).

- Having an interest in a trust that owns stock of the redeeming corporation. See IRC Sec. 318(a).

- Acting as an independent contractor for corporation. See Lynch, CA-9, 86-2 USTC Paragraph 9731 (1986).

---

[1] A few interests which the redeeming stockholder can have and still not cause a loss of the waiver of family attribution rules include:
   a. Lease property from the corporation. See PLR 8328088, 4/14/83; PLR 8301035, 9/30/82; and Rev. Rul. 77-467, 1977-2 CB 92. An IRS Private Letter Ruling (PLR) is applicable only to the taxpayer who requested it and may not be cited as precedent.
   b. Purchase insurance under company's health plan. See LR 8236037, 6/8/82.
   c. Continue life insurance under company group term life plan. See LR 8314018, 12/23/82.

Continued...

Family Attribution

Entity Attribution

In addition to the family attribution rules, the redeeming stockholder is also treated as owning a proportionate part of the stock that is actually owned by the following entities.

- A partnership in which he or she is a partner
- An estate of which he or she is a beneficiary
- A trust of which he or she is a beneficiary
- A corporation in which he or she owns 50% or more of the outstanding stock

The attribution rules are highly complex and should be dealt with only with the assistance of appropriate tax and legal advisors.

Methods of Funding a Buy-Sell Agreement

In the event of a business owner's death, there are several options to consider for funding a Buy-Sell agreement.

- **Personal funds of buyers:** Most successful business people do not keep large sums of liquid assets on hand. They have their money working in their businesses.

- **Sinking fund in the business:** Such a fund will be inadequate if death is premature and the time of need is uncertain. A corporation may develop an accumulated earnings tax problem.

- **Borrowed funds:** Loss of key person (an owner) may impair the credit worthiness of the business and other partners or shareholders. Interest costs may be excessive, and interest expense of shareholders or partners may not be deductible.

- **Installment payments to heirs by buyer:** The business may fail and the payments stop. The principal and interest payments may be too burdensome.

- **Life insurance owned by the buyer:**
  - Complete financing guaranteed from the beginning.
  - Proceeds may be free from income tax; see IRC Sec. 101(j).
  - Cash values can be used for a buyout due to retirement or disability.
  - It is generally the most economical method.
  - Credit position is strengthened.

Who Should Own the Policy?

Improper ownership of insurance policies that are used to fund buy-sell agreements can cause serious problems for the survivors.

The following hypothetical situation illustrates the proper ownership of policies:

Assumptions:
Owners: A, B and C
Ownership: 60%, 30%, 10%
Business value: $2,000,000
Funding vehicle: Life insurance

Cross-Purchase Plan				Entity Plan		
Insured	Owner, Beneficiary and Premium Payer	Amount and Number of Policies		Insured	Owner, Beneficiary and Premium Payer	Amount and Number of Policies
A (60%)	B C	$600,000 $600,000		**A** (60%)	The Business	$1,200,000
B (30%)	A C	$300,000 $300,000		**B** (30%)	The Business	$600,000
C (10%)	A B	$100,000 $100,000		**C** (10%)	The Business	$200,000

Note: Premiums for life insurance (or disability insurance to fund a buyout) are not deductible to the individuals or to the business entity. However, the policy proceeds are generally received income-tax-free by the beneficiary.[1]

---

[1] If the corporation pays the premiums on policies used by the stockholders to fund a cross-purchase plan, there will likely be constructive dividend problems. For a C corporation, policy values payable to the corporation may be subject to the corporate alternative minimum tax.

Taxes on Premiums Paid by a Corporation

Situation	Tax Treatment of Premiums	Legal Reference
Cross-purchase buy-sell Corporation pays the premiums directly on behalf of stockholder or policyholder.	If payment is intended to be additional compensation (corporate minutes should reflect this) the corporation can deduct it and the policy owner would report additional income.	IRC Sec. 162(a)
	If payment were considered as unreasonable compensation, it would be treated as a dividend and not deducted by the corporation.	*Atlas Heating & Ventilating Co. vs. Comm.,* 18 BTA 389
	If it were clear that the policies are to fund a cross-purchase buy-sell agreement, the premiums paid by the corporation would be treated as dividends.	Rev. Rul. 59-184, 1959-1 CB 65; *Thomas F. Doran vs. Comm.,* 246 F2d 934 (9th Cir. 1957)
Cross-purchase buy-sell Corporation pays the premiums under a classic split-dollar agreement.	Premium payments by the corporation are generally treated as interest-bearing loans to the shareholder.[1]	Treasury Decision 9092
Stock redemption buy-sell by corporation Corporation pays the premiums directly for policies on the lives of the stockholders.	Premiums are not deductible by the corporation and not a dividend to the stockholder or policyholder.	Rev. Rul. 59-184 1959-1 CB 65; *Sanders vs. Fox,* 253 F2d 855 (10th Cir. 1958); and *Prunier vs. Comm.,* 248 F2d 818 (1st Cir. 1957)

When an individual or corporation collects the proceeds of a policy by reason of the death of the insured, they are generally not subject to income taxation. See IRC Sec. 101(a).[2] For a C corporation, increases in policy values on policies owned by the corporation and death benefits payable to the corporation may be subject to the corporate alternative minimum tax.

---

[1] Under Treasury Decision 9092 (September 11, 2003), many economic benefits of a split-dollar arrangement are currently taxable. These benefits may include: (1) value of current life insurance protection; (2) accrued cash value; (3) imputed loan interest, or (4) premium contributions from a non-policy owner. Death benefits paid to a beneficiary (other than policy owner) may be taxable. 9092 contained other split-dollar rules not addressed here and those considering split-dollar arrangements should consult legal/tax advisors. State or local law may vary.

[2] An exception would be a lifetime transfer of an insurance policy which violates the transfer-for-value rules of IRC Sec. 101(a)(2).

Transfers for Value

Life insurance death proceeds are typically exempt from income taxation under IRC sec. 101(a)(1). The gift of a policy during the insured's lifetime does not affect this exemption; however, the sale of a policy may subject part of the proceeds to income taxation when the insured dies. If a policy is transferred for value to a non-exempt transferee, the portion included as taxable income will be the face amount less any consideration (purchase price and subsequent premiums) paid by the transferee.

Exempt Transferees

Parties who can purchase a policy from another and are exempt transferees include the following (no exceptions).

- The insured

- A partner of the insured

- A partnership of which the insured is a partner

- Corporation of which insured is a shareholder/officer

- Any person where the basis is determined by reference to the transferor's basis; e.g., a gift

Typical Violations of this Rule

- A policy owner agrees to name another person as a beneficiary in exchange for valuable consideration. See Reg. Sec. 1.101-1(b)(1).

- When two persons assign policies on their own lives to each other at about the same time, the question of a transfer for valuable consideration is raised.

- A corporation changes its buy-sell agreement from a stock redemption plan to a cross purchase plan and transfers key person insurance policies to stockholders other than the insured.

- For estate planning reasons, a corporate key man life insurance policy is transferred to the insured's adult child or an irrevocable trust to keep the proceeds out of the estate.[1] Since she or he is not an employee, the policy is usually purchased for its current cash value.

---

[1] Under the Tax Act of 2001, the federal estate tax is gradually phased out until its final repeal in the year 2010. If Congress does not act at that time to repeal it for the years following, it will automatically revert back to the rates in effect during the year 2001, with an exemption for the first $1,000,000 of assets.

Continued

Transfers for Value

Problem: The child or trustee is not an exempt party. Under the transfer-for-value rule the proceeds may be out of the estate, but are partially includable as ordinary income in the year received by the beneficiary.

A better way: Have the insured purchase the policy from the corporation (the insured is an exempt party). He is now free to make a gift of the policy to the child or trust; however, the donor/insured must survive the 3-year contemplation of death period. See IRC Sec. 2035.

Where there is a non-exempt party owning a purchased policy, it may be wise to have the insured purchase it back for its cash value and then, by a later gift, transfer it back to the non-exempt party. This will remove the taint. See Reg. Sec. 1.101-1(b)(2).

When changing from a corporate stock redemption plan to a cross purchase buy-sell arrangement, consider a separate partnership. See Letter Rulings 9328010, 9328012, 9328017, 9328019 and 9328020.

The Cost of Borrowing
When Interest is Deductible

The table of borrowing costs below assumes a $100,000 loan at various interest rates, years for repayment and borrower tax brackets.

Loan Duration	Interest Rate	Annual Payment	Total Payments	Interest Portion	Annual Pretax Earnings Required[1] in a Marginal Tax Bracket of		
					15.00%	28.00%	33.00%
5 years	3.00%	$21,835	$109,177	$9,177	$25,365	$29,613	$31,686
	5.00%	$23,097	$115,487	$15,487	$26,627	$30,875	$32,948
	7.00%	$24,389	$121,945	$21,945	$27,918	$32,167	$34,240
	9.00%	$25,709	$128,546	$28,546	$29,239	$33,487	$35,560
	12.00%	$27,741	$138,705	$38,705	$31,270	$35,519	$37,592
10 years	3.00%	$11,723	$117,231	$17,231	$13,488	$15,612	$16,648
	5.00%	$12,950	$129,505	$29,505	$14,715	$16,839	$17,876
	7.00%	$14,238	$142,378	$42,378	$16,002	$18,127	$19,163
	9.00%	$15,582	$155,820	$55,820	$17,347	$19,471	$20,507
	12.00%	$17,698	$176,984	$76,984	$19,463	$21,587	$22,624
15 years	3.00%	$8,377	$125,650	$25,650	$9,553	$10,969	$11,660
	5.00%	$9,634	$144,513	$44,513	$10,811	$12,227	$12,918
	7.00%	$10,979	$164,692	$64,692	$12,156	$13,572	$14,263
	9.00%	$12,406	$186,088	$86,088	$13,582	$14,998	$15,689
	12.00%	$14,682	$220,236	$120,236	$15,859	$17,275	$17,966
20 years	3.00%	$6,722	$134,431	$34,431	$7,604	$8,666	$9,184
	5.00%	$8,024	$160,485	$60,485	$8,907	$9,969	$10,487
	7.00%	$9,439	$188,786	$88,786	$10,322	$11,384	$11,902
	9.00%	$10,955	$219,093	$119,093	$11,837	$12,899	$13,417
	12.00%	$13,388	$267,758	$167,758	$14,270	$15,332	$15,851
25 years	3.00%	$5,743	$143,570	$43,570	$6,449	$7,298	$7,713
	5.00%	$7,095	$177,381	$77,381	$7,801	$8,651	$9,065
	7.00%	$8,581	$214,526	$114,526	$9,287	$10,137	$10,551
	9.00%	$10,181	$254,516	$154,516	$10,887	$11,736	$12,151
	12.00%	$12,750	$318,750	$218,750	$13,456	$14,306	$14,720

Example: Assume you borrow $100,000 for five years at a 7.00% rate of interest. Your annual payment would be $24,389 for five years or a total of $121,945. If you were in a marginal tax bracket of 28.00%, you would have to earn an extra $32,167 annually to pay off the loan.

Interest incurred or paid in a trade or business is generally deductible, as is qualified residence interest. This illustration assumes that the interest on the loan is fully deductible.

---

[1] Required earnings are only estimates, since the interest deduction will vary from year to year as the amount of the loan decreases.

The Cost of Borrowing
When Interest is Deductible

Although borrowing is often necessary and desirable, one should be aware of the effects of interest payments.

Assume a $100,000 loan at various interest rates to be paid back in 15 years and a marginal income tax bracket of 28.00%.

The Impact of a Higher Interest Rate

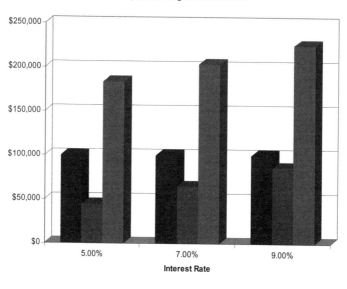

■ Amount Borrowed   ■ Total Interest   ■ Total Earnings Req'd to Pay

The Cost of Borrowing
When Interest is Not Deductible

The table of borrowing costs below assumes a $100,000 loan at various interest rates, years for repayment and borrower tax brackets.

Loan Duration	Interest Rate	Annual Payment	Total Payments	Interest Portion	Annual Pretax Earnings Required in a Marginal Tax Bracket of		
					15.00%	28.00%	33.00%
5 years	3.00%	$21,835	$109,177	$9,177	$25,689	$30,327	$32,590
	5.00%	$23,097	$115,487	$15,487	$27,174	$32,080	$34,474
	7.00%	$24,389	$121,945	$21,945	$28,693	$33,874	$36,402
	9.00%	$25,709	$128,546	$28,546	$30,246	$35,707	$38,372
	12.00%	$27,741	$138,705	$38,705	$32,636	$38,529	$41,404
10 years	3.00%	$11,723	$117,231	$17,231	$13,792	$16,282	$17,497
	5.00%	$12,950	$129,505	$29,505	$15,236	$17,987	$19,329
	7.00%	$14,238	$142,378	$42,378	$16,750	$19,775	$21,250
	9.00%	$15,582	$155,820	$55,820	$18,332	$21,642	$23,257
	12.00%	$17,698	$176,984	$76,984	$20,822	$24,581	$26,416
15 years	3.00%	$8,377	$125,650	$25,650	$9,855	$11,634	$12,502
	5.00%	$9,634	$144,513	$44,513	$11,334	$13,381	$14,379
	7.00%	$10,979	$164,692	$64,692	$12,917	$15,249	$16,387
	9.00%	$12,406	$186,088	$86,088	$14,595	$17,230	$18,516
	12.00%	$14,682	$220,236	$120,236	$17,273	$20,392	$21,914
20 years	3.00%	$6,722	$134,431	$34,431	$7,908	$9,336	$10,032
	5.00%	$8,024	$160,485	$60,485	$9,440	$11,145	$11,977
	7.00%	$9,439	$188,786	$88,786	$11,105	$13,110	$14,088
	9.00%	$10,955	$219,093	$119,093	$12,888	$15,215	$16,350
	12.00%	$13,388	$267,758	$167,758	$15,750	$18,594	$19,982
25 years	3.00%	$5,743	$143,570	$43,570	$6,756	$7,976	$8,571
	5.00%	$7,095	$177,381	$77,381	$8,347	$9,855	$10,590
	7.00%	$8,581	$214,526	$114,526	$10,095	$11,918	$12,808
	9.00%	$10,181	$254,516	$154,516	$11,977	$14,140	$15,195
	12.00%	$12,750	$318,750	$218,750	$15,000	$17,708	$19,030

Example: Assume you borrow $100,000 for five years at 7.00% rate of interest. Your annual payment would be $24,389 for five years or a total of $121,945. If you were in a marginal tax bracket of 28.00%, you would have to earn an extra $33,874 annually to pay off the loan.

This illustration assumes that the loan is a personal loan and the interest is not deductible on your income tax return.

The Cost of Borrowing
When Interest is Not Deductible

Although borrowing is often necessary and desirable, one should be aware of the effects of interest payments.

Assume a $100,000 loan at various interest rates to be paid back in 15 years and a marginal income tax bracket of 28.00%.

The Impact of a Higher Interest Rate

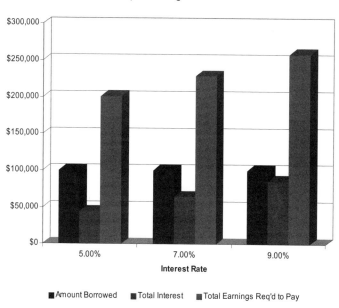

■Amount Borrowed   ■Total Interest   ■Total Earnings Req'd to Pay

Reasons to Value a Business

The following are a few of the most common reasons to value a business.

- Establish a purchase price in a buy-sell agreement.
- Determine the size of the gross estate for death tax purposes.[1]
- Determine if the estate qualifies for tax relief provisions.
  - IRC Sec. 303 stock redemption
  - Installment payments of death taxes (IRC Sec. 6166)
  - IRC Sec. 2032A current use valuation of business owned real estate
  - IRC Sec. 2057 qualified family-owned business interest (QFOBI) deduction[2]
- Plan for an equitable disposition of the estate among children where some are active in the business and some are not.
- Determine the value of lifetime gifts of the business.

Other reasons include private annuities, installment sales, recapitalizations, mergers, divorce settlements, charitable contributions, etc.

Fair Market Value

Treasury regulations set forth the following definition for fair market value.

"...the net amount which a willing purchaser... would pay for the interest to a willing seller, neither being under any compulsion to buy or to sell and both having reasonable knowledge of relevant facts." See Reg. Sec. 20.2031-3.

---

[1] Under the Tax Act of 2001, the federal estate tax is gradually phased out until its final repeal in the year 2010. If Congress does not act at that time to repeal it for the years following, it will automatically revert back to the rates in effect during the year 2001, with an exemption for the first $1,000,000 of assets.

[2] Under the provisions of The Economic Growth and Tax Relief Reconciliation Act of 2001, The QFOBI deduction will not be available to the estates of decedents dying in 2004-2010.

Business Valuation Factors

The value of a business interest is generally based on two things:

1. What the company owns, which is reflected on the balance sheet, and
2. What the company earns, which is reflected in the income statement.

The IRS is guided by the factors set forth in Revenue Ruling 59-60[1] in valuing a business for tax purposes.

The Nature and History of the Business

Consideration is given to the following.

- Size and consistency of the growth rate
- Stability of the business or lack thereof
- Products, services and company assets
- Record of sales
- Management - especially recent changes
- Diversity of operations

Economic Outlook

The general economic outlook and condition of the particular industry in which the business operates will affect how a business is valued. Common questions to be considered include the following.

- Is it a growth industry?
- How competitive is this company in the industry?
- What would be the economic effect of the loss of a key employee?

The Book Value of the Stock

- Based on assets minus liabilities - to show liquidity position.
- Believed to be unreliable in valuing most businesses.

---

[1] See Revenue Ruling 59-60, 1959-1 CB 237. Also see Rev. Rules. 65-192, 1965-2 CB 259; 65-193, 1965-2 C. B. 370 and 77-287, 1977-2 CB 319

Continued...

Business Valuation Factors

The Earning Capacity of the Company

This is perhaps the most significant factor.

- Earning capacity is average earnings over a five-year period multiplied by a capitalization rate.

- There is no standard table of capitalization rates.

- Capitalization rates are usually based on price-earnings ratios of similar, publicly traded companies.

The Dividend Paying Capacity

This is considered to be a primary factor.

- This does not mean dividends actually paid, but the capacity to pay.

- The IRS recognizes the need to retain a reasonable portion of the profits for expansion needs.

Goodwill and Other Intangible Values

- Goodwill is based on earning capacity.

- It represents an excess of net earnings over and above a fair return on the net tangible assets of the business.

- Other intangibles include the following.
  - Ownership of a trade or brand name
  - Prestige and renown of the business
  - Prolonged successful operation in a particular locality

Prior Sales and Size of Block

- Prior sales may be meaningful if they were arms-length transactions.

- Small isolated sales or distress sales are not significant.

- Valuation of a controlling interest may carry a premium value.

- Valuation of a minority interest should include a discount.

Continued

Business Valuation Factors

Similar Companies

How the business performs in comparison to its competitors is another consideration in valuing the business. For example, the valuation may consider the market price of stocks in similar, publicly traded corporations as a way of assessing performance.

- Companies must be sufficiently comparable.

- The comparative appraisal method examines price-earnings, price-book value and price-dividend ratios of each corporation.

Weight to Be Given to Each Factor

Some factors will carry more weight in the valuation than others. There is no exact mathematical formula that can be applied.

A study by Standard Research Consultants[1] showed that in 74 tax cases the most frequently used factors were:

- Sale price in 33 cases;

- Book value in 24 cases; and

- Earning power in 17 cases.

Earnings will typically have more importance in companies selling products and services, whereas net worth will be more important in real estate holding companies.

---

[1] Study by Standard Research Consultants, as quoted in the CLU Journal, Vol. 34, No. 2, April 1980, pp. 61-70.

Valuation Methods Explained

Since no single method can be applied in determining the value of every business, a number of approaches have developed over the years. The American Society of Appraisers has grouped these approaches into three classifications.

1. Income based
2. Market based
3. Asset based

Valuation Techniques

- **Income approach:** This approach attempts to measure the stream of benefits coming into the business. The two most commonly used methods are capitalized returns and discounted future returns.

  - **Capitalized returns method:** This method examines the company's history of earnings or cash flow (either gross or net), generally over the previous five or more years. The average annual return is determined and then divided by a capitalization rate selected for the particular kind of business being valued.

  - **Discounted future returns method:** This method looks at projected future earnings of the company and then applies a discount to them to determine the current or present value of the projected income stream.

- **Market approach:** This approach is similar to that used in valuing residential real estate, wherein a house is compared to similar houses which have recently sold (after adjustments for any differences). With the market approach, a search is made for similar companies with publicly traded stock and then the selling price of its shares is adjusted to account for any differences between the two companies. Comparisons will commonly look at one or more of the following factors.

  - Price/earnings ratio
  - Ratio of price to dividends
  - Gross cash flow
  - Book value
  - Revenues
  - Net asset value

A major problem with these methods is that it is often difficult to find similar publicly traded companies. Another problem is that comparing a closely held or privately held company with that of a publicly traded firm where the above information is readily available is often a case of comparing apples with oranges. Publicly held firms are accountable to their stockholders, where closely held or privately held firms are accountable to their owners and, as a result, are often managed entirely differently.

Continued

Valuation Methods Explained

- **Asset based approach:** This approach is more concerned with the underlying net value of the company's tangible assets. If the business is to be continued after the owner's death, the fair market value of the assets is commonly used. If, however, the business were to be liquidated, a lower value would be used to compensate for the loss which generally occurs with the forced sale of assets.
  - **Book value:** Book value is company assets minus liabilities as shown on the balance sheet.
  - **Book value or adjusted book value:** These methods are most frequently used with companies which own many tangible assets, like a real estate holding company or with a company that has very low or negative earnings.
  - **Excess earnings method:** This method is also called Treasury method because it was developed by the Treasury Department in the 1930's. It is based on Rev. Rul. 68-609, 1968-2 CB 327 and considers both the adjusted book value and a capitalization of earnings in excess of a fair return on the company's assets.

Weighting the Methods

When several valuation methods are used, some are generally more accurate in determining the true value of the business. For example, in high asset/low income companies, more weight would probably be given to the adjusted book value than to the capitalization of earnings. Because of the influence that weighting methods have in the outcome of the business valuation, a CPA, attorney, valuation specialist or other business advisor should be consulted to arrive at the appropriate weightings.

Ownership Premium or Discount

Adjustments to the estimated value of the business are made to reflect unique circumstances which may affect its marketability. These may include location, degree of specialty required to run the business, presumed availability of buyers and other factors which could affect the sale price if offered on the open market. For example, a closely held business is often discounted in value to reflect the control that other owners may exercise over a single owner's ability to sell his or her interest.

There are no specific rules or guidelines associated with these adjustments. Frequently they serve as a reality check to help influence the outcome of the valuations or better approximate the expectations of the valuation specialist, CPA, attorney, owners or other business advisors. As a result, the discount or premium applied to the business will usually be arrived at as a consensus of opinion among the business advisors. Particular care should be applied in selecting a rate of adjustment and, whenever possible, the rate should be provided by a valuation specialist experienced in the specific market for which the business is being valued.

Advantages and Disadvantages
of Valuation Methods

There are many different methods for valuing a
business, with some better suited to a specific
type of business than others. A key task of the
valuation specialist is to select the most
appropriate method for valuing a particular
business. The method chosen should provide a
reasonable estimate of value, be suitable for the
intended purpose and be able to face legal
challenges by the IRS or other opposing parties.

As a part of the process, a valuation specialist will
often employ several different methods and average the results to arrive at a "ballpark"
estimate. Because each method has strengths and weaknesses, business owners and their
advisors should be familiar with the most commonly used valuation techniques.

Net Asset Value

The value is based on a sale at fair market value (FMV) of the firm's assets on a going-
concern basis.

- **Strengths**
  - Data required to perform the valuation are usually easily available.
  - Allows for adjustments (up and down) in estimating FMV.
  - Suitable for firms with heavy tangible investments (e.g. equipment, land).
  - Helpful when the firm's future is in question or where the firm has a brief or volatile
    earnings record.

- **Weaknesses**
  - Can understate the value of intangible assets such as copyrights or goodwill.
  - Does not take into account future changes (up or down) in sales or income.
  - Balance sheet may not accurately reflect all assets.

Discounted Future Earnings

The value of the firm is equivalent to the capital required to produce income equal to a
projected future income stream from continuing operations of the firm. The rate of return
used is adjusted to take into account the level of risk assumed by a buyer in purchasing the
business as a going concern.

- **Strengths**
  - The value of the firm is based on projected future results, rather than assets.
  - Can be used with either net earnings or net cash flow.
  - Useful when future results are expected to be different (up or down) from recent
    history.

Continued

Advantages and Disadvantages
of Valuation Methods

- **Weaknesses**
  - May understate the value of balance sheet assets.
  - Discounts the valuation based on the level of risk. A business perceived as riskier typically receives a lower valuation than a more stable business.
  - Projections are not guarantees; unforeseen future events can cause income or earnings projections to be completely invalid.

Excess Earnings (Treasury Method)

The value of the firm is determined by adding the estimated market value of its tangible assets to the capitalized value of projected income resulting from goodwill.

- **Strengths**
  - Takes into account both tangible and intangible assets.
  - Includes projected future values of income resulting from goodwill.
  - Is based on IRS Rev. Rul. 68-609, 1968 CB 327.

- **Weaknesses**
  - Relies on estimate of period for which goodwill is expected to last, which is often difficult to assess. Projections based on this value can be unreliable.
  - May understate future revenues or value of intangible assets.
  - Though based on IRS rulings, the IRS cautions that the method can be relied on "only if there is no better basis therefore available."

Capitalization of Earnings

Value is equivalent to the capital (invested at a reasonable rate of return) required to generate an income equal to an average of the firm's recent, historical results.

- **Strengths**
  - A simplified approach that arrives at an easily determined value.
  - Does not rely on projections, but on an average of results from the recent past.
  - Most useful for businesses with stable, predictable cash flows and earnings.

- **Weaknesses**
  - May understate value for firms using aggressive strategies to reduce taxable income.
  - May overlook value of tangible or intangible assets.
  - Reliance on past earnings may ignore potential future growth.

Business Valuation

Revenue Ruling 59-60, 1959-1 CB 237 sets forth the factors to be considered in valuing a closely held business for death tax purposes. They are as follows:

- The history and nature of the business; i.e., the risk and the stability of the business
- The economic outlook in general, as well as for this industry
- The book value of the company
- The company's earning capacity
- The capacity to pay dividends (not its dividend paying history)
- The goodwill of the company
- Any recent sales of company stock
- The value of similar businesses which are publicly traded

A Formula for Valuing Goodwill

1.	Value of tangible assets	$ _____
2.	Liabilities	(_____)
3.	**= Net value of tangible assets**	_____
4.	x Industry percentage return [1]	x _____ %[1]
5.	**= Annual earnings attributable to assets** (line 3 x line 4)	_____
6.	Average annual earnings of company[2]	_____ [2]
7.	**Earnings from goodwill** (line 6 minus 5)	_____
8.	÷ Capitalization rate[3]	_____ %[3]
9.	**= Goodwill** (line 7 ÷ line 8)	_____
10.	**Goodwill plus net value of assets** (line 9 + line 3)	$ _____

Projected Future Growth

___Years	_____% Growth	$ _____	x _____	= _____
		Current Business Value	Compound Interest Factor	Projected Business Value

Note: This is not intended to replace a qualified appraisal.

---

[1] Industry percentage return: 8% should be used with stable, low-risk businesses and 10% with more hazardous, high-risk businesses.

[2] The average annual net earnings amount is computed on all the years of operation up to five. This should be before taxes and personal compensation to the owners.

[3] Revenue Ruling 68-609 recommends a capitalization rate of 15% for low-risk, stable businesses and 20% for hazardous, high-risk businesses.

Discount and Capitalization Rates
A Brief Explanation

Some business valuation methods attempt to compute the present value of a company based on either projected or historic earnings. These valuation methods include the discounted future earnings method, excess earnings method and capitalization of earnings method. These valuation methods rely on computed discount rates or capitalization rates to find a company's value.

While the uses of discount rates and capitalization rates in these valuation methods seem similar, there are significant differences. It is important to understand the differences and how to apply them.

What Is a Discount Rate?

There are times when a company's current or historic earnings do not fairly represent its future earnings. In these cases it may be more reasonable to rely on the company's projected earnings to compute its present value. A valuation method using a discount rate approach may be appropriate in these cases.

A discount rate is the rate of return a buyer would expect from owning a business, given an expected level of risk of ownership. The higher the risk, the higher the discount rate goes. The lower the risk and the more certain the return, the lower the discount rate.

In applying a discount rate, the higher the discount rate, the lower will be the computed value of a company. On the other hand, the lower the discount rate, the higher will be the computed value of a company.

Determining a Discount Rate

One way to determine a discount rate is to build it from available risk factors. The first factor is the risk-free rate. The 20-year Treasury bond rate as of the valuation date is generally accepted as a basic risk-free rate. This rate is readily available and is routinely published in the newspaper.

Added to the risk-free rate is an appropriate risk factor or, in some cases, multiple risk factors. Some guidance to understanding these risk factors can be learned from referring to the Schilt's Risk Premium Table.[1]

More likely than not, a specific valuation situation will differ from the general descriptions provided in Schilt's table. For this reason, the business owner should seek the assistance of a trained valuation expert to compute an appropriate discount rate.

---

[1] James H. Schilt, "A Rational Approach to Capitalization Rates for Discounting the Future Income Stream of a Closely Held Company." *The Financial Planner*, January 1982. Reprinted with permission of James H. Schilt, ASA. (415) 986-1057.

Continued...

Discount and Capitalization Rates
A Brief Explanation

Schilt's Risk Premium for Discounting Projected Income Streams[1]

Category	Description	Risk Premium
1.	Includes established businesses with a strong trade position, are well financed, have depth in management, whose past earnings have been stable and whose future is highly predictable.	6 - 10%
2.	Includes established businesses in a more competitive industry that are well financed, have depth in management, have stable past earnings and whose future is fairly predictable.	11 - 15%
3.	Includes businesses in a highly-competitive industry requiring little capital to enter, no management depth and element of risk is high although past record may be good.	16 - 20%
4.	Includes small businesses that depend on the special skill(s) of one or two people and larger, established businesses that are highly cyclical. In both cases, future earnings may be expected to deviate widely from projections.	21 - 25%
5.	Includes small, one-person businesses of a personal service nature where the transferability of the income stream is in question.	26 - 30%

What Is a Capitalization Rate?

Sometimes a company's historic earnings are reasonably believed to represent the company's future earnings. This can be true of long-established businesses as well as businesses in mature industries. In these cases, a valuation method using a capitalization rate approach may be appropriate. One method for computing a capitalization rate is based on the company's discount rate. Using this method, you subtract the company's growth rate from the discount rate. The following table helps to illustrate the relationship between the growth rate and capitalization rate:

Note: Assume a Discount Rate of 22%

If the company's growth rate is...	Then the company's capitalization rate will be	Growth Rate	Capitalization Rate
Less than zero	Greater than the discount rate	-2%	24%
Zero	equal to the discount rate	0%	22%
Greater than zero	less than the discount rate	+2%	20%

For example, if a company's discount rate is 22% and its growth rate is +2%, the capitalization rate is 20% (22%-2%=20%) using this method. If the average earnings are $50,000, the company's computed value (using the straight capitalization of earnings method) would be $250,000 ($50,000 divided by 20% equals $250,000).

The use of discount rates and capitalization rates to compute the value of a business can be very difficult and misleading. Often, important adjustments must be made to these rates to reflect unique or unusual circumstances. Business owners should rely on qualified business valuation specialists in using these rates.

---

[1] Table is intended for use with pre-tax earnings.

Business Valuation Per Share
Using The Courtroom Method
The Most Expensive Method

Title of Case	Taxpayer (Estate)	IRS	Court	% Above Estate	
				IRS	Court
Bader v. U.S.	$ 521.83	$ 1,250.00	$ 643.00	240%	123%
Baltimore National Bank v. U.S.	1,509.64	2,500.00	2,300.00	166%	152%
Braverman. Est. of Morris v. Comm.	2,058.25	4,000.00	2,724.92	194%	132%
Brush. Est. of Marjorie Gilbert v. Comm.	3.00	7.38	5.50	246%	183%
Burda. Est. of L.J.	3.00	20.00	5.00	667%	167%
Damon, Est. of Robert Hosken v. Comm.	3.00	6.00	3.75	200%	125%
Ewing. Est. of Anna C. v. Comm.	2,400.00	6,530.00	4,750.00	272%	198%
Fitts, Est. of Cora Russell v. Comm.	150.00	600.00	375.00	400%	250%
Garrett, Est. of Jessie Ring v. Comm.	50.39	285.65	285.65	567%	567%
Gessell v. Comm.	310.00	475.00	475.00	153%	153%
Hanscom, Meiville	50.00	100.00	100.00	200%	200%
Heinhold, Est. of Matthew	3.17	10.00	8.00	315%	252%
Huntington, Est. of Henry E.	10,638.35	16,559.67	16,100.99	156%	151%
Kuhn, Est. of Harold L. v. U.S.	1,290.43	1,700.00	1,355.00	132%	105%
Levenson, Est. of David J. v. Comm.	252.85	1,033.00	900.00	409%	356%
Leyman, Est. of Harry Stole v. Comm.	536.00	700.00	630.00	131%	118%
Louis, John J. Jr. Exr. v. U.S.	3.25	20.00	5.34	615%	164%
Luckenbach, Est. of Edgar F. v. Comm.	114.75	229.52	175.00	200%	153%
Maxcy, Est. of Hugh G. v. Comm.	7,018.68	9,358.24	7,018.68	133%	100%
Miller, Est. of Mary K. v. Comm.	500.00	1,150.00	860.00	230%	172%
Mitchell, Est. of Julian v. Comm.	700.00	980.00	800.00	140%	114%
Obermer. Nesta v. U.S.	3,350.00	5,921.67	3,947.78	177%	118%
Reynolds. Est. of Pearl Gibbons v. Comm.	316.67	2,637.50	1,600.00	833%	505%
Ridgely. Est. of Mabel Lloyd v. U.S.	106.00	115.00	115.00	108%	108%
Righter. Est. of Jessie H. v. U.S.	424.00	1,000.00	700.00	236%	165%
Rothgery. Est. of Bernard Anthony v. U.S.	60.72	582.00	582.00	958%	958%
Russell. William E. Exr. v. U.S.	1,360.00	2,100.00	2,100.00	154%	154%
Schneider-Paas. Est. of A. Johannes v. Comm.	4,761.90	38,500.00	23,809.00	809%	500%
Snodgross. Est. of John Milton v. U.S.	53.00	65.00	53.00	123%	100%
Thompson. Est. of Barbara F. v. Comm.	225.00	535.00	283.50	238%	126%
Tompkins. Est. of Lida R. v. Comm.	834.00	12,725.85	5,500.00	1,526%	659%
Wallace. Est. of Marvin R. v. U.S.	64.23	147.00	91.50	229%	142%
Worthen. Exr. (Stone) v. U.S.	100.00	175.00	104.00	175%	104%
Yeazel. Gilbert A. Exr. V. Coyle	304.11	450.00	400.00	148%	132%

When the IRS challenges a business valuation and the estate defends itself in court, the result can be a higher valuation and higher estate taxes. In the cases above, court valuations averaged 227% higher than the estate's. Had the estate not gone to court, IRS valuations averaged 338% higher, but court costs for attorneys, accountants, appraisers, etc., made the total costs of the court valuation and IRS valuation similar.

Time Delay in Closing Contested Estates

When the value of a business interest in an estate is challenged by the IRS, the loss to the heirs may be substantial. Part of that loss is due to the delay in getting distribution of the assets from the estate. The delay may also have a harmful effect on the morale of employees, vendors and customers.

Title of Case	Years	Months	Days
Atkins, Estate of Charles H.M. v. Comm.	3	6	4
Bader v. U.S.	7	9	24
Bendet, Estate of Louis	4	1	23
Bank of Calif. v. Comm.	6	9	15
Brush, Estate of Marjorie Gilbert v. Comm.	5	3	2
Damon, Estate of Robert Hosken v. Comm.	7	10	11
Ewing, Estate of Anna C. v. Comm.	7	6	24
Fitts, Estate of Cora Russell v. Comm.	6	7	20
Garrett, Estate of Jessie Ring v. Comm.	6	6	16
Goodall, Estate of Robert A. v. Comm.	11	7	13
Gold v. Grongquist	2	10	28
Harrison, Florence M. et al., v. Comm.	5	7	3
Heinold, Estate of Matthew I. v. Comm.	6	4	2
Houghton, Albert B. v. U.S.	8	11	25
Laird, Mary Du Pont	10	10	29
Louis, John J. Jr. Exr. v. U.S.	7	8	26
Luckenbach, Est. of Edgar F. v. Comm.	14	10	11
Maxcy, Est. of Gregg v. Comm.	8	11	21
Maxcy, Est. of Hugh G. v. Comm.	6	2	7
Miller, Est. of Mary K. v. Comm.	7	0	29
Moore, Anna H.	6	10	22
Nathan's Estate, In re	7	4	11
Patton, Estate of Walter L.	7	3	16
Perlick, Est. of Hilbert R. v. U.S.	6	11	9
Reynolds, Est. of Pearl Gibbons v. Comm.	7	10	22
Ridgely, Est. of Mabel Lloyd v. U.S.	4	8	9
Righter, Est. of Jessie H. v. U.S.	9	10	25
Rothgery, Est. of Bernard Anthony v. U.S.	10	10	0
Russell, William 11E. Exr. v. U.S.	6	6	5
Schneider-Pass, Est. of Alfred Johannes v. Comm.	11	1	19
Snodgross, Est. of John Milton v. U.S.	5	5	6
Tomkins, Estate of	8	10	24
Wilber National Bank	7	2	15

Average time delay in above cases was 7½ years. A buy-sell agreement could have avoided this problem.

Odds of Disability

Insurance claims studies indicate that the odds of becoming disabled for 90 days or longer are much greater than dying during one's working years. Studies also suggest that, as the number of business owners or key employees increases, so do the odds that one of them will suffer a long-term disability.

Probability of at Least One Long-Term Disability Prior to Age 65

Age	Number of People in the Age Group					
	1	2	3	4	5	6
25	58%	82%	92%	97%	99%	99%
30	54%	79%	90%	96%	98%	99%
35	50%	75%	88%	94%	97%	98%
40	45%	70%	84%	91%	95%	97%
45	40%	64%	78%	87%	92%	95%
50	33%	55%	70%	80%	86%	91%
55	25%	43%	57%	68%	76%	82%

Note: Based on the 1985 Commissioners Individual Disability Table.

Determining Odds of Disability Among People of Different Ages

Use the following table and worksheet to determine the risk of a long-term disability among your business owners or key employees.

	Age						
	25	30	35	40	45	50	55
Value	.42	.46	.50	.55	.60	.67	.75

Step 1: For each owner or key employee you wish to include in your analysis, choose the value from the table above that corresponds to the age closest to the actual age of the owner or key employee, and include the value in the space below.

Step 2: Multiply all of the values by each other to arrive at a single value.

_____ x _____ x _____ x _____ x _____ = _____

Step 3: Multiply the single value by 100 to convert it to a percent.

100 x _____ = _____%

Step 4: Subtract the single value from 100% to determine the odds of long-term disability for any one of the groups of owners or key employees in your company.

100% - _____ = _____ %

Note: You can perform this analysis for any number of owners or key employees, not just the five shown in this worksheet.

Disability of a Business Owner

Many business owners have created buy-sell
agreements to protect themselves and their
businesses in case of an untimely death. These
agreements are often funded with life insurance to
ensure that the cash to purchase the business is
available when needed.

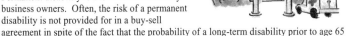

Permanent disability is another threat faced by
business owners. Often, the risk of a permanent
disability is not provided for in a buy-sell
agreement in spite of the fact that the probability of a long-term disability prior to age 65
is greater than the probability of death.

To provide for this risk, business owners can amend existing buy-sell agreements or create
separate agreements. Special disability insurance policies can be used to fund a disability
buy-sell agreement. These policies can be set up to pay a lump sum, a series of payments,
or a combination of the two.

Key Elements to Consider

- **Definition of disability:** How disability is defined in the agreement is very important
  and should probably be tied to the definition in the disability insurance policy.

- **Elimination period:** The period of time between the first day of the disability and the
  trigger date; e.g., 12 months to 24 months are frequent options.

- **Trigger date:** This is the date at the end of the elimination period when the buyout
  begins and the insurance company begins paying on the policy.

- **Successive disability:** A disabled person may temporarily return to work but thereafter
  have a recurrence of the disability. In many plans, successive disability periods can be
  tied together to meet the elimination period.

- **Funding period:** The period over which the buyout payments are made. It can be an
  immediate lump sum or spread out over a period of months, or a combination of both.
  The funding period set in the policy should match the terms of the buy-sell agreement.

- **Recover from disability:** The recovery of a disabled person after the buyout has begun
  can raise several questions, among them: Does the funding stop? Can the person return
  to work with the same company? Lump sum settlement plans, in some cases, can
  remove some of the uncertainty.

- **Buy-sell agreement:** The buy-sell agreement must be in force at the time of disability
  in order for payments to be made from the policy.

- **Converting to individual coverage:** Sometimes the disability plan will be convertible
  to individual coverage if the business has no further need for the coverage, the owner
  needs additional individual coverage, and he or she meets certain requirements.

- **Involvement in the business:** Many insurers require that the business owner be actively
  involved in the business.

Continued

Disability of a Business Owner

Tax Basics for Disability Buyouts

	Corporation		Partnership	
	Stock Redemption by the Corporation	**Cross Purchase by the Stockholders**	**Entity Buy-Sell by the Partnership**	**Cross Purchase by the Partners**
Are premiums for a disability policy to fund a buyout deductible?	No IRC Sec. 265(a)(1)	No IRC Sec. 265(a)(1)	No IRC Sec. 265(a)(1)	No IRC Sec. 265(a)(1)
Are the proceeds from a disability policy taxable income?	No IRC Sec. 104(a)(3)	No IRC Sec. 104(a)(3)	No IRC Sec. 104(a)(3)	No IRC Sec. 104(a)(3)
Are payments from the corporation or partnership to individual owner deductible to the entity?	No	N/A	No	N/A
How are benefits taxed to the individual receiving them?	If a complete redemption, it is treated as a sale or exchange. IRC Sec. 302(b)(3)	Capital gain on excess of purchase price over his or her basis in the stock. IRC Secs. 1001; 1221; 1222	Return of basis is nontaxable. Excess is generally taxed as ordinary income. IRC Sec. 736(b)	Capital gain on excess of purchase price over his or her basis in the partnership.
Can the sale qualify as an installment sale to prorate the gains over the years in which payments are received?	Yes IRC Sec. 453	Yes IRC Sec. 453	Yes IRC Sec. 453	Yes IRC Sec. 453

Continued...

Disability of a Business Owner

Business Overhead Expense

Another form of disability insurance specially suited to the business owner is Business Overhead Expense (BOE). BOE policies are designed to reimburse certain business expenses of the owner while he or she is totally or partially disabled. The funds provided by the BOE policy help the business survive during the time of the owner's disability. Often, the BOE policy is the reason the owner has a business to return to after the disability. Should the disability appear permanent, the owner usually has additional time to make decisions regarding the future of the business.

Generally speaking, there are only certain types of business owners who qualify for BOE coverage. These include owners of closely held businesses, owners of small businesses and professionals with their own practices.

Some of the expenses typically covered by a BOE policy include the following.

- Legal and accounting fees
- Utilities
- Principal payments on debt
- Leased equipment
- Business insurance premiums
- Office supplies
- Salaries of non-owner, non-family employees
- Professional dues
- Business taxes
- Rent
- Workers compensation

In no instance is there any payment from a BOE policy to the business owner. Instead, these funds must come from his or her own disability plan.

Tax Basics for Disability Buyouts

	Corporation		Partnership	
	Stock Redemption by the Corporation	**Cross Purchase by the Stockholders**	**Entity Buy-Sell by the Partnership**	**Cross Purchase by the Partners**
Are premiums for a disability policy to fund a buyout deductible?	No IRC Sec. 265(a)(1)	No IRC Sec. 265(a)(1)	No IRC Sec. 265(a)(1)	No IRC Sec. 265(a)(1)
Are the proceeds from a disability policy taxable income?	No IRC Sec. 104(a)(3)	No IRC Sec. 104(a)(3)	No IRC Sec. 104(a)(3)	No IRC Sec. 104(a)(3)
Are payments from the corporation or partnership to individual owner deductible to the entity?	No	N/A	No	N/A
How are benefits taxed to the individual receiving them?	If a complete redemption, it is treated as a sale or exchange. IRC Sec. 302(b)(3)	Capital gain on excess of purchase price over his or her basis in the stock. IRC Secs. 1001; 1221; 1222	Return of basis is nontaxable. Excess is generally taxed as ordinary income. IRC Sec. 736(b)	Capital gain on excess of purchase price over his or her basis in the partnership.
Can the sale qualify as an installment sale to prorate the gains over the years in which payments are received?	Yes IRC Sec. 453	Yes IRC Sec. 453	Yes IRC Sec. 453	Yes IRC Sec. 453

Business Overhead Expense

Business overhead expense (BOE) is a form of disability insurance specially suited to the business owner. BOE policies are designed to reimburse certain business expenses of the owner while he or she is totally or partially disabled. The funds provided by the BOE policy help the business survive during the period of the owner's disability. Often, the BOE policy is the reason the owner has a business to return to after the disability. Should the disability appear permanent, the owner usually has additional time to make decisions regarding the future of the business.

Generally speaking, there are only certain types of business owners who qualify for BOE coverage. These include owners of closely held businesses, owners of small businesses and professionals with their own practices.

Some of the expenses typically covered by a BOE policy include the following.

- Legal and accounting fees
- Utilities
- Principal payments on debt
- Leased equipment
- Business insurance premiums
- Office supplies
- Salaries of non-owner, non-family employees
- Professional dues
- Business taxes
- Rent
- Workers compensation

In no instance is there any payment from a BOE policy to the business owner. Instead, these funds must come from his or her own disability plan.

Disability Buy-Out Cross-Purchase Agreement

A cross-purchase buy-sell agreement involves business owners entering into an agreement with each other to assure an orderly disposition of their business interest in the event of disability.

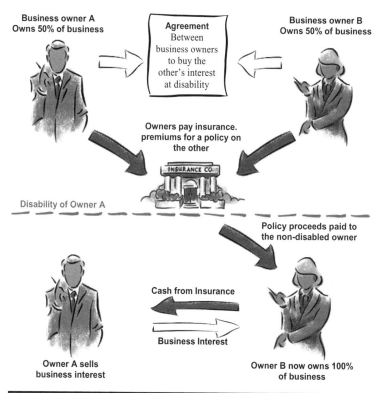

Advantages	Disadvantages
The transferred interests receive a new income tax basis equal to the price paid. This will mean a tax savings, if the interest is later sold at a higher price.	Plan is more difficult to administer if more than two or three business owners.
No problem with state laws restricting redemptions.	Requires more policies, e.g., 12 policies for 4 owners, 20 policies for 5 owners, etc.
Disability policies may be insulated from the company's creditors.	Policies may lapse if owner doesn't make the payments.

Disability Buy-Out Stock Redemption Plan

A stock redemption plan involves stockholders entering into an agreement with the corporation to insure an orderly disposition of their stock in the event of disability.

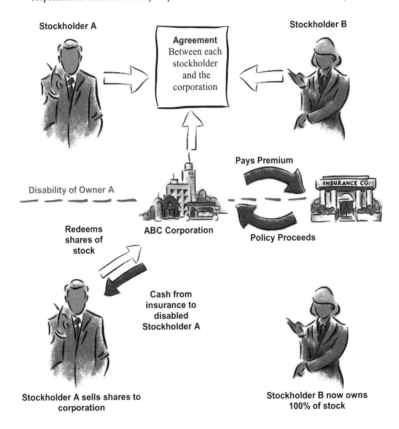

Advantages	Disadvantages
Usually easier to understand than the cross-purchase plan.	Voting power may be altered unfavorably.
Fewer policies in insured plans.	Strict state redemption laws must be followed.
No questions as to unreasonable compensation issues when agreement is properly written.	Value of non-disabled owner's shares increase but not basis.

Key Employee Insurance

The untimely death of a key employee or a business owner who is also a key employee can have a disastrous effect on a business. Some of the "costs" of such an event might include the following.

- A weakening of the company's credit rating

- The financial cost (in time and dollars) to find, hire, and train a replacement

- The distraction of other employees, resulting in deadlines not met, deteriorating morale, or a higher level of personality conflicts

- A need for cash to fulfill promises made to the deceased employee's spouse or family, such as salary continuation or deferred compensation

- The inability to seize a business opportunity, because cash reserves are being used to recruit and train a new employee

- A loss of confidence among both suppliers and customers

Additional problems may exist if key employee is an owner.

- Disagreements between the heirs and the surviving business owners or key employees

- Lack of cash to buy the interest of a deceased owner, requiring a sale of the business to an unknown, outside third party

- Surviving owners may be forced to work with someone who is either not competent or not motivated enough to make the business thrive.

- The business may have to be sold to pay estate taxes[1].

---

[1] Under the Tax Act of 2001, the federal estate tax is gradually phased out until its final repeal in the year 2010. If Congress does not act at that time to repeal it for the years following, it will automatically revert back to the rates in effect during the year 2001, with an exemption for the first $1,000,000 of assets.

Methods of Valuing a Key Employee

There is no easy mathematical formula to determine the value of a key employee. However, over the years business owners have frequently used three different methods to estimate the worth of an employee to their company.

- **The cost of replacement method:** Totals the direct, out-of-pocket costs involved in finding, hiring and training a replacement, as well as the estimated loss-of-opportunity costs.

- **The contribution to profits method:** Estimates the impact a key employee has on the company's net profit. The firm first calculates the expected profit from a normal return on capital, e.g., the net book value of assets. Profit in excess of this normal return is assumed to result from the efforts of the key employees. An estimate is made of the percentage of profit attributable to each key employee. This percentage is then multiplied by total excess profit, to determine the dollar amount of excess profit from each key employee. This sum is then multiplied times the number of years needed to find and train a competent replacement.

- **The multiple of compensation method:** Assumes that an employee's value is accurately reflected in his or her total compensation package. The multiple that is used (for example: 2 x annual compensation), will depend on the type of business and the estimated difficulty in finding a qualified replacement. This method is perhaps the easiest way to estimate the potential loss to the firm.

Financing the Replacement of a Key Employee

Replacing an employee – particularly a key employee – can be expensive. It is better to prepare ahead of time for this potential cost.

There are a number of methods commonly used to finance the hiring and training of a new key employee.

1. **Pay in cash:** However, most businesses do not keep large amounts of cash sitting idle; the money is typically working in the business. The need to raise cash quickly may result in "distress sales" of valuable assets, at a price below normal market value.

2. **Establish a sinking fund:** However, dollars kept in a savings account represent lost business opportunities. For example, if each $1.00 put into a marketing campaign returns $10.00 in sales and the company has a 15% profit margin, the return on each $1.00 invested in marketing is $1.50. On an annual basis, this would be a 50% return. If the same dollar (along with the profits) were reinvested two or three times a year, with a similar increase, the ultimate return would be many times that earned in a bank account.

   Therefore, a sinking fund may be very costly when one considers the loss of business opportunities.

3. **Borrow the funds:** This option assumes that the loss of a key employee does not seriously damage the firm's credit worthiness. Each dollar borrowed must be repaid, with interest. If the loan were amortized over a 10-year period, at 12% interest, for each $1,000 borrowed the company would repay a total of $1,770.

   Here, too, the business owner must take into account the "opportunity cost" of missed growth and profits, had the money used to repay the loan been reinvested in the company instead.

4. **Life insurance policies:** Many business owners choose life insurance to protect against the loss of a key employee. The premiums are small compared to the lump sum which would have to be quickly raised, either out of earnings or by borrowing, when a death does occur.[1]

If permanent type policies are used there will also be a cash value build up, which can be available for the business in time of need, regardless of the firm's credit worthiness.

---

[1] Under the provisions of IRC Sec. 101(j), added by the Pension Protection Act of 2006, death proceeds from a life insurance policy owned by an employer on the life of an employee are generally includable in income, unless certain requirements are met. The law was effective for contracts issued after August 17, 2006, except for contracts acquired under an IRC Sec. 1035 Exchange. Until the full scope of this new law is clarified by the IRS, caution is advised. State or local law may vary.

Key Employee Coverage Issues

Both the IRS and the courts have long recognized that the loss of a manager, scientist, salesperson or other key individual will almost always have a serious effect on the earning power and sometimes on the very stability of a business. Although the principle applies in publicly held businesses, it is particularly true in a closely held corporation where profits are dependent on the ability, initiative, judgment or business connections of a single person or small group of owner/employees. The death or disability of a key person at the wrong time can have a dramatic impact in a smaller business.

There is no universally recognized and accepted formula for computing the economic effect of the loss of a key person. One method used in several court cases utilizes a discount approach in which a percentage discount is taken from the going concern value of the business.

Some authorities feel that if the business will survive the death of the key employee and, in time, a competent successor can be found, a discount factor of from fifteen to twenty percent should be used. Where the business is likely to fail or be placed in serious jeopardy upon the death (or disability) of the key employee, a discount of from twenty to forty five percent is more appropriate. The exact discount factor should be arrived at through consultation with the officers of the company and the firm's accounting and legal advisers.

Some questions to ask in determining the factor (or range of factors) to be used include the following.

- How long will it take for a new person to reach the efficiency of the key individual?

- How much will it cost to locate and situate a replacement?

- Will the new employee demand more salary?

- How much will it cost to train the new person?

- What mistakes is a replacement likely to make during the break-in period and how much are those mistakes likely to cost the company?

- What proportion of the firm's current net profit is attributable to the key employee?

- Is the employee engaged in any projects that, if left unfinished at death or disability, would prove costly to the business? If so, how costly?

- Would a potentially profitable project have to be abandoned or would a productive department have to be closed?

- Would the employee's death result in the loss of clientele or personnel attracted to the business because of his or her personality, social contacts, unique skills, talents or managerial ability?

- What effect would the key employee's death have on the firm's credit standing?

- What proportion of the firm's actual loss is it willing to self-insure, if any?

Protecting Against the Loss of a Key Employee

Business owners frequently use life insurance to protect their company from many of the potential problems which may otherwise damage or destroy what has taken years to build.

Life insurance is unique in that it will generally pay the pre-determined amount no matter when the death occurs.

The premiums are usually small compared to the potential death benefit. Also, if policies are used which develop cash values, they can be shown as business assets on the balance sheet, contributing to the value of the business and potentially to its borrowing power.

Borrowing against cash values may also be a lifesaving source in times of financial crisis.[2]

How Key Employee Insurance Works

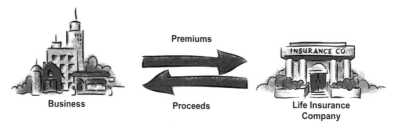

Business **Premiums** → ← **Proceeds** **Life Insurance Company**

- Company owns the policy
- Company pays the premiums
- After death, the company collects the policy proceeds[1]

Potential Uses for Proceeds

- Purchasing stock from the decedent's estate

- Honoring salary continuation arrangements to surviving spouse

- Finding, recruiting, and training a new employee

- Paying any necessary bills and strengthening the credit position

- Funding expansion of the business

- Adding income-tax free corporate surplus

---

[1] Under the provisions of IRC Sec. 101(j), added by the Pension Protection Act of 2006, death proceeds from a life insurance policy owned by an employer on the life of an employee are generally includable in income, unless certain requirements are met. The law was effective for contracts issued after August 17, 2006, except for contracts acquired under an IRC Sec. 1035 Exchange. Until the full scope of this new law is clarified by the IRS, caution is advised. State or local law may vary.

[2] Policy loans and interest will reduce the payable death benefit of a policy. If a policy lapses or is surrendered with a loan outstanding, the loan will be treated as taxable income in the current year, to the extent of gain in the policy.

Key Employee Disability Plans

Frequently a business will retain key employee
life insurance coverage. In doing so, the owners
express their understanding that a business may
suffer financially if a key person dies.

Often overlooked in their decision, however, is
what will happen to the business if a key person
is disabled. In this instance, the business may
confront the same financial issues it would face if
the key employee were to die. Some of these issues include the following.

- The costs to recruit a replacement

- The costs to train a replacement

- The opportunity costs of lost business from the disability of the key employee

The key person disability plan will protect the business by providing funds to help cover
the potential lost profits and the costs of finding and training a replacement.

Some of these plans offer a replacement benefit which will reimburse the company for
some percentage of the replacement costs, up to certain limits, for the first 12 to 24
months after the key person's disability occurs.

Sometimes the key person disability plan will be convertible to individual coverage if the
business has no further need for the coverage, the insured needs additional individual
coverage and the insured meets certain income and, possibly, physical requirements.

Note: Key employee disability insurance has become a specialty product and providers of this important coverage
are becoming more difficult to find.

The Need for Estate Planning

At a person's demise there are certain
typical problems which, if not planned for,
create a burden on those who are left behind.

Proper estate planning can eliminate or
reduce these problems.

Financial Burdens

- **Estate settlement costs are too high:**
  These costs consist primarily of probate
  fees and death taxes.

  - **Probate fees:** These are generally paid to the executor of the estate and the attorney
    who assists with the probate.

  - **Death taxes:** Estates that exceed certain amounts may be subject to both state and
    federal death taxes.

- **Estate assets are improperly arranged:**

  - **Liquidity:** There are not enough liquid
    (cash type) assets to pay estate settlement
    costs.

  - **Cash flow:** There is not enough income to
    care for loved ones left behind; e.g., spouse
    and minor children.

Transfer of Assets

- Estate assets may be subject to probate delays and expense.

- Assets transferred to minors may be in cumbersome guardianship accounts until they
  attain age 18 (or 21 in some states) and are then distributed outright to the children.

- Additional death taxes may be paid because there was no pre-
  death planning.

Care of Minors

- **Guardians:** Parents can nominate a guardian for their minor
  children in a will.

- **Asset management:** If the wrong persons are chosen to
  manage the assets left for the minors, the assets may be lost or
  unnecessarily reduced.

Key Estate Planning Considerations

Planning your estate requires thoughtful consideration of a number of key issues.

Transfer of Assets

A primary objective is to insure that your assets go to those you want to receive them. Your attorney can advise you as to the best way to distribute your assets.

Method	Description
Will	A legal document, prepared under state law, that names those who should receive your property. After death a "probate" will be required, a process in which the property listed in the will is distributed under court supervision. An "executor" is generally named in the will to carry out the decedent's wishes. If you die without a will (termed "intestate"), your property will be distributed according to state law, which may not be what you want.
Trust	In simple terms, a "trust" is a relationship in which the owner of an asset transfers legal title of the asset to someone else, called the "trustee", to manage for the benefit of the owner or a third party, such as your children. In estate planning, trusts come in many forms and have many uses, including probate avoidance, estate tax reduction, and asset management.
Joint Ownership	Assets held in joint tenancy pass at the time of death to the joint owner, if living, otherwise they must be probated.
Beneficiary Designations	Some assets, such as life insurance policies and qualified retirement plans, allow the owner to name a "beneficiary" to receive the asset. When the owner dies, title to the asset immediately passes to the named individual or organization under automatic operation of law.

Minimizing Transfer Costs

If proper planning is not done, legal costs, probate expenses, and federal and/or state estate or inheritance taxes can consume a large portion of your assets.

- **Probate:** The use of trusts, as well as making appropriate use of situations where assets can pass directly to joint tenants or named beneficiaries, can help reduce probate and legal expenses.

- **Estate taxes:** A number of strategies can be used to reduce the impact of estate taxes:

  - Lifetime gifts – each individual has an annual gift tax exclusion, currently $12,000 per person per year,[1] generally allowing for tax-free transfers to others.[2]
  - Marital deduction – under federal law, spouses who are both U.S. citizens can gift any amount to each other, generally with no estate or gift tax consequences.
  - Charitable giving – gifts to charities, during life or at death, are an effective way to reduce the size of a estate.

---

[1] Applicable to 2008. This value is subject to adjustment for inflation each year.
[2] The discussion here refers to federal income and estate tax law; state or local law may differ.

Continued

Key Estate Planning Considerations

- Credit shelter trust – also known as a "bypass trust", a credit shelter trust makes sure the applicable credit amount of the first to die in a married couple, currently $780,800,[1] is not wasted. This is equivalent to the first $2,000,000[1] of his or her assets. This amount can provide income and other benefits to the surviving spouse without being included in the survivor's estate.
- Irrevocable life insurance trusts – trusts which are designed to provide liquidity while keeping the proceeds of life insurance policies outside of the taxable estate.

Caring for Survivors

Your survivors – a spouse, minor children, or a disabled child of any age – must also be considered in the estate plan.

- **Life Insurance:** Life insurance may be needed to create an estate and provide the liquid assets needed to keep the family financially intact.

- **A guardian for dependents:** In case both parents are deceased, a guardian (and one or more alternates) should be named to care for minor children or other dependents.

- **Asset management:** Professional asset management may be necessary to insure that financial resources are not squandered. Working with your investment advisor, you may need to rearrange some of your assets to provide increased liquidity to your estate.

Who Makes Medical Decisions When I Cannot?

Modern medicine can now keep someone "alive" in situations that formerly would have resulted in death. Those who do not wish to have their lives artificially prolonged by such techniques must plan ahead and put their wishes in writing.

- **"Living Will":** Also known as a "Directive to Physicians", this document provides guidance as to the type of medical treatment to be provided or withheld and the general circumstances under which the directive applies.

- **Durable power of attorney for health care:** Many states have laws allowing a person to appoint someone to make health care decisions for them if they become unable to do so for themselves.

Outside the Legal Framework

Many of the documents involved in an estate plan are legal in nature, typically prepared by an attorney. However, not all documents involved in an estate plan are legal ones.

- **Letter of Instructions:** A "Letter of Instructions" is an informal document that can include information such as your wishes regarding disposition of your remains, contact information for key advisors and family members, the location of important documents, the description and location of assets, or notes on family history. It is used to provide, in a private manner, direction and guidance to your family or executor in the settling and administration of your estate.

---

[1] Applicable to 2008. These values are subject to change each year.

Continued...

Key Estate Planning Considerations

- **Ethical Will:** While a legal will or a trust are used to distribute assets, an "Ethical Will" serves to transfer values and beliefs. It is a very personal expression of the writer's life and values as well as the people, events, and experiences that influenced that life. In a very real sense, an ethical will is a spiritual legacy to future generations

Seek Professional Guidance

Although an estate plan can be as simple as a set of hand-written instructions, there are a number of situations where legal guidance is considered vital:

- **To create a will or trust:** An experienced attorney, familiar with local law, can prepare the legal documents needed to meet the needs of your individual situation.

- **Estate taxes:** If your estate is large enough to be subject to estate tax, your attorney can suggest ways to lighten the tax burden.

- **Squabbling heirs:** Planning may be needed to minimize potential conflicts between your heirs or beneficiaries. Such disputes can occur when siblings don't get along or there are children from more than one marriage.

- **Property elsewhere:** If you own property in more than one state or country, there may be a need for an ancillary probate. Living trusts are often used to transfer these assets and avoid the additional probate.

In addition to your attorney, your estate planning "team" will likely include experts from other disciplines such as income tax, life insurance, trust administration, charitable giving, and investment management. The professional guidance provided by such advisors is a key part of creating and implementing a successful estate plan.

Periodic Review

Because tax law and personal lives are never static, don't just put your estate plan in a drawer and forget about it. Many financial professionals recommend a periodic estate plan review.

Estate Settlement Costs Funnel

What Happens to Your Estate at Death?

At a person's demise, his or her assets are subject to a number of expenses that can significantly reduce the size of the estate left for the heirs. Proper estate planning can minimize these expenses and determine in advance how the costs that remain will be paid.

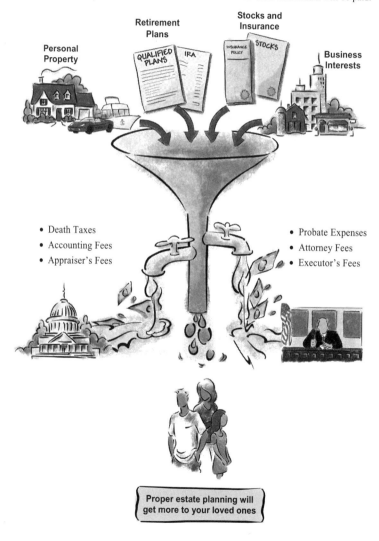

Retirement Plans

Stocks and Insurance

Personal Property

Business Interests

- Death Taxes
- Accounting Fees
- Appraiser's Fees

- Probate Expenses
- Attorney Fees
- Executor's Fees

Proper estate planning will get more to your loved ones

Estate Settlement Costs

Shortly after the death of an individual, certain costs of settling the estate must be paid in cash. Two primary goals of estate planning are to minimize these costs and decide in advance how the costs that remain will be paid.

Estate Settlement Costs

- **Decedent's last illness, funeral and burial expenses and debts**

- **Probate administration expenses** (see below): Expenses include attorney's fees, executor's commissions, appraiser's fees, court costs, tax return preparation, etc. Some states determine the fees based on the value of the assets passing through probate. Assets that typically do not pass through probate would include: joint tenancy, life insurance, assets in living trusts, etc.

- **Death taxes:** A federal estate tax is imposed on estates exceeding the applicable exclusion amount of $2,000,000.[1] Individual states may also impose an inheritance or estate tax.

Probate Administration Fees[2]

Probate Assets	Fee to Each	Probate Assets	Fee to Each
$10,000	$400	$700,000	$17,000
40,000	1,600	750,000	18,000
80,000	3,200	800,000	19,000
100,000	4,000	900,000	21,000
120,000	4,600	1,000,000	23,000
160,000	5,800	1,250,000	25,500
200,000	7,000	1,500,000	28,000
250,000	8,000	1,750,000	30,500
300,000	9,000	2,000,000	33,000
350,000	10,000	2,500,000	38,000
400,000	11,000	2,750,000	40,500
450,000	12,000	3,000,000	43,000
500,000	13,000	3,500,000	48,000
550,000	14,000	4,000,000	53,000
575,000	14,500	4,500,000	58,000
600,000	15,000	5,000,000	63,000
625,000	15,500	10,000,000	113,000
650,000	16,000	15,000,000	163,000
675,000	16,500	25,000,000	TBD[3]

Typical Statutory Formula

4% on the 1st $15,000

3% on the next $85,000

2% on the next $900,000

1% on amount over $1,000,000

---

[1] The applicable exclusion amount is the dollar value of assets protected from federal estate tax by an individual's applicable credit amount. It is scheduled to change as follows: $2,000,000 for 2007-2008; $3,500,000 for 2009, zero federal estate tax for the year 2010; and $1,000,000 for 2011 and thereafter (unless permanently repealed or otherwise modified).

[2] This table illustrates typical statutory attorney's fees and executor's commissions for probating an estate.

[3] A reasonable amount to be determined by the court.

The High Cost of Dying When Estate is Probated
Assumes Death Occurs During 2008

Probate is a legal process in which the terms of a decedent's will are carried out under court supervision. The probate process is a matter of public record and can be expensive both in terms of time (six months is typically the minimum needed) and money. Probate expenses may include fees paid to both the executor and attorney (in some states these fees are set by law, based on the value of the probated assets), appraisers fees, court costs, and tax preparation

fees. The federal estate tax is a tax on a person's right to transfer property to others at death. It is generally imposed on estates larger than $2,000,000[1].

(A) Estate Size	(B) Administration Expense[2]	(C) Taxable Estate (A – B)	(D) Federal Estate Taxes	(E) Total Costs (B + D)
$1,000,000	$60,000	$940,000	$0	$60,000
$1,500,000	$85,000	$1,415,000	$0	$85,000
$2,000,000	$110,000	$1,890,000	$0	$110,000
$2,500,000	$135,000	$2,365,000	$164,250	$299,250
$3,000,000	$160,000	$2,840,000	$378,000	$538,000
$3,500,000	$185,000	$3,315,000	$591,750	$776,750
$4,000,000	$210,000	$3,790,000	$805,500	$1,015,500
$5,000,000	$260,000	$4,740,000	$1,233,000	$1,493,000
$6,000,000	$310,000	$5,690,000	$1,660,500	$1,970,500
$8,000,000	$410,000	$7,590,000	$2,515,500	$2,925,500
$10,000,000	$510,000	$9,490,000	$3,370,500	$3,880,500
$15,000,000	$760,000	$14,240,000	$5,508,000	$6,268,000
$20,000,000	$1,010,000	$18,990,000	$7,645,500	$8,655,500
$30,000,000	$1,510,000	$28,490,000	$11,920,500	$13,430,500
$40,000,000	$2,010,000	$37,990,000	$16,195,500	$18,205,500
$50,000,000	$2,510,000	$47,490,000	$20,470,500	$22,980,500
$100,000,000	$5,010,000	$94,990,000	$41,845,500	$46,855,500

Note: Under the Tax Act of 2001, the federal estate tax is gradually phased out until its final repeal in the year 2010. If Congress does not act at that time to repeal it for the years following, it will automatically revert back to the rates in effect during the year 2001, with an exemption for the first $1,000,000 of assets.

The top bracket will be 45% in 2007 through 2009 with zero taxes in 2010. If Congress does not act at that time to repeal the federal estate tax for the years following, in the year 2011 the top bracket of 55% will automatically return.

---

[1] The applicable exclusion amount is the dollar value of assets protected from federal estate tax by an individual's applicable credit amount. It is scheduled to change as follows: $2,000,000 for 2007-2008; $3,500,000 for 2009, zero federal estate tax for the year 2010; and $1,000,000 for 2011 and thereafter (unless permanently repealed or otherwise modified).

[2] Administration expense is assumed to be 5.0% of Estate Size, plus $10,000 for last illness and burial costs. Administration fees (such as executor's commissions and attorney's fees) and last illness and burial expenses are deductible in determining the federal estate tax. The actual total cost could be more or less than the amount shown.

The High Cost of Dying When Estate is Not Probated
Assumes Death Occurs During 2008

Successfully avoiding probate can result in a larger inheritance for beneficiaries and heirs. Holding title to property in forms such as Joint Tenancy, Community Property with Right of Survivorship, and Transfer on Death is one way to achieve this. Naming a beneficiary for assets such as life insurance or retirement plan accounts, where the property is transferred automatically by contract, is another. A third way to effectively avoid probate is by setting up a revocable living trust (also called an inter-vivos trust).

(A) Estate Size	(B) Administration Expense[1]	(C) Taxable Estate (A − B)	(D) Federal Estate Taxes	(E) Total Costs (B + D)
$1,000,000	$10,000	$990,000	$0	$10,000
$1,500,000	$10,000	$1,490,000	$0	$10,000
$2,000,000	$10,000	$1,990,000	$0	$10,000
$2,500,000	$10,000	$2,490,000	$220,500	$230,500
$3,000,000	$10,000	$2,990,000	$445,500	$455,500
$3,500,000	$10,000	$3,490,000	$670,500	$680,500
$4,000,000	$10,000	$3,990,000	$895,500	$905,500
$5,000,000	$10,000	$4,990,000	$1,345,500	$1,355,500
$6,000,000	$10,000	$5,990,000	$1,795,500	$1,805,500
$8,000,000	$10,000	$7,990,000	$2,695,500	$2,705,500
$10,000,000	$10,000	$9,990,000	$3,595,500	$3,605,500
$15,000,000	$10,000	$14,990,000	$5,845,500	$5,855,500
$20,000,000	$10,000	$19,990,000	$8,095,500	$8,105,500
$30,000,000	$10,000	$29,990,000	$12,595,500	$12,605,500
$40,000,000	$10,000	$39,990,000	$17,095,500	$17,105,500
$50,000,000	$10,000	$49,990,000	$21,595,500	$21,605,500
$100,000,000	$10,000	$99,990,000	$44,095,500	$44,105,500

Note: Under the Tax Act of 2001, the federal estate tax is gradually phased out until its final repeal in the year 2010. If Congress does not act at that time to repeal it for the years following, it will automatically revert back to the rates in effect during the year 2001, with an exemption for the first $1,000,000 of assets.

The top bracket will be 45% in 2007 through 2009 with zero taxes in 2010. If Congress does not act at that time to repeal the federal estate tax for the years following, in the year 2011 the top bracket of 55% will automatically return.

---

[1] Administration expense is assumed to be 5.0% of Estate Size, plus $10,000 for last illness and burial costs. Administration fees (such as executor's commissions and attorney's fees) and last illness and burial expenses are deductible in determining the federal estate tax. The actual total cost could be more or less than the amount shown.

Potential Savings by Avoiding Probate
Assumes Death Occurs During 2008

The table below illustrates the potential savings realized by not having to pay the expenses typically associated with passing an estate through the probate process. Changing title to assets so that property transfers automatically at death, naming beneficiaries for assets such as life insurance or retirement plans, or using a revocable living trust are effective ways of achieving these potential savings.

| (A) Estate Size | Total Estate Settlement Costs | | (D) Potential Savings (B - C) |
	(B) With Probate[1]	(C) W/O Probate[2]	
$1,000,000	$60,000	$10,000	$50,000
$1,500,000	$85,000	$10,000	$75,000
$2,000,000	$110,000	$10,000	$100,000
$2,500,000	$299,250	$230,500	$68,750
$3,000,000	$538,000	$455,500	$82,500
$3,500,000	$776,750	$680,500	$96,250
$4,000,000	$1,015,500	$905,500	$110,000
$5,000,000	$1,493,000	$1,355,500	$137,500
$6,000,000	$1,970,500	$1,805,500	$165,000
$8,000,000	$2,925,500	$2,705,500	$220,000
$10,000,000	$3,880,500	$3,605,500	$275,000
$15,000,000	$6,268,000	$5,855,500	$412,500
$20,000,000	$8,655,500	$8,105,500	$550,000
$30,000,000	$13,430,500	$12,605,500	$825,000
$40,000,000	$18,205,500	$17,105,500	$1,100,000
$50,000,000	$22,980,500	$21,605,500	$1,375,000
$100,000,000	$46,855,500	$44,105,500	$2,750,000

Note: Under the Tax Act of 2001, the federal estate tax is gradually phased out until its final repeal in the year 2010. If Congress does not act at that time to repeal it for the years following, it will automatically revert back to the rates in effect during the year 2001, with an exemption for the first $1,000,000 of assets.

The top bracket will be 45% in 2007 through 2009 with zero taxes in 2010. If Congress does not act at that time to repeal the federal estate tax for the years following, in the year 2011 the top bracket of 55% will automatically return.

---

[1] Federal estate tax, plus administration expenses assumed to be $10,000 for last illness and burial costs, plus probate equal to 5% of the estate. The actual total cost could be more or less than the amount shown.
[2] Federal estate tax, plus administration expenses assumed to be $10,000 for last illness and burial costs. There would likely be some charges for appraisal fees, tax return preparation and other miscellaneous expenses. The actual total cost could be more or less than the amount shown.

The High Cost of Dying
with a $5,000,000 Gross Estate

Administration and Probate Costs[1]

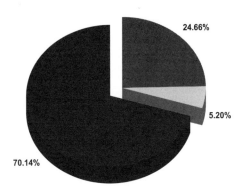

24.66%

5.20%

70.14%

■ Federal Estate Tax ▦ Admin. Costs ■ Amount to Heirs

Administration Costs Only - No Probate[1]

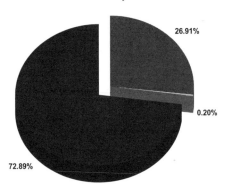

26.91%

0.20%

72.89%

■ Federal Estate Tax ▦ Admin. Costs ■ Amount to Heirs

---

[1] Assumes death occurs in 2008, with no marital deduction. Administration costs assume $10,000 for last illness and burial. Probate costs assume 5% of gross estate. Percentages may not equal 100% due to rounding. Under the Tax Act of 2001, the federal estate tax is gradually phased out until its final repeal in the year 2010. If Congress does not act at that time to repeal it for the years following, it will automatically revert back to the rates in effect during the year 2001, with an exemption for the first $1,000,000 of assets.

The Federal Estate Tax

An Overview for 2008

The federal estate tax is an excise tax on the right to transfer property at date of death. The gross estate includes the fair market value of all assets owned by the decedent as of the date of death, including life insurance policies. The top estate tax bracket is 45%[1] on taxable estates over $2,000,000.

The tax applies only to taxable estates that exceed the applicable exclusion amount ($2,000,000[2] for 2008).

Transfers between spouses generally qualify for the unlimited marital deduction and are free of current tax. See IRC Sec. 2056.

The estate tax return (Form 706) and any taxes due are generally payable nine months after date of death. In some situations, a portion of the taxes may be paid to the IRS in installments. See IRC Secs. 6161 and 6166.

If the value of the estate assets declines during the first six months after death (which often happens if the decedent owned a business), the value (for all assets) as of six months after death may be used on the tax return.

Lifetime gifts that exceed the annual gift tax exclusion ($12,000 per donee per year)[3] will also reduce the estate owner's applicable credit amount.

Some transfers made during one's lifetime may be brought back into the decedent's estate. A few examples are listed below.

- Gifts of life insurance policies within three years prior to death. See IRC Sec. 2035.

- Transfer of an asset from which the donor retains an income for his or her life. See IRC Sec. 2036.

- Transfer of an asset where donor retains the right to alter or terminate the transfer. See IRC Sec. 2038.

- Assets placed in joint tenancy with another are included in the gross estate.

Note: Under the Tax Act of 2001, the federal estate tax is gradually phased out until its final repeal in the year 2010. If Congress does not act at that time to repeal it for the years following, it will automatically revert back to the rates in effect during the year 2001, with an exemption for the first $1,000,000 of assets.

---

[1] The top bracket will be 45% in 2007 through 2009 with zero taxes in 2010. If Congress does not act at that time to repeal the federal estate tax for the years following, in the year 2011 the top bracket of 55% will automatically return.

[2] The applicable exclusion amount is the dollar value of assets protected from federal estate tax by an individual's applicable credit amount. It is scheduled to change as follows: $2,000,000 for 2007-2008; $3,500,000 for 2009, zero federal estate tax for the year 2010; and $1,000,000 for 2011 and thereafter (unless permanently repealed or otherwise modified).

[3] The annual gift tax exclusion ($12,000 in 2008) is indexed for inflation in increments of $1,000.

How the Federal Estate Tax Works

A Simplified Illustration

1. Determine the gross estate.

Total the fair market value of all assets the decedent owned.
- Residence, real estate
- Business interests, stocks, bonds
- Life insurance, personal property, etc.

2. Subtract the deductions.

Certain items may be deducted to determine the taxable estate amount.
- Assets passing to surviving spouse
- Debts of the decedent
- Probate and burial expenses
- Bequests to charities, etc.

3. Calculate the tax.

Using the taxable estate amount, calculate the federal estate tax.

Graduated tax rates are used, with the highest marginal rate in 2008 being 45%.

4. Take applicable credits.

For assets passing to someone other than a spouse, reduce the tax by the applicable credit amount.

Also, a state death tax credit and other credits may apply.

5. Pay the tax.

After subtracting the credits, any remaining tax is due nine months after death – in cash.

Due in Cash

Federal Estate Tax Worksheet

Assumes Death Occurs During 2008

A. Fair market value of real estate and business property $_____

B. Fair market value of investments, stocks, bonds, funds, etc.   _____

C. Fair market value of personal and other property   _____

     D. **Gross estate** (sum of items A, B and C)   _____

E. Administration expenses (funeral expenses, etc.)   _____

F. Debts of decedent   _____

G. Marital deduction (assets to spouse)   _____

H. Charitable deduction (bequests to charity)   _____

I. State death taxes[1]   _____

     J. **Total deductions** (sum of items E through I)   (_____)

     K. **Taxable estate** (item D minus item J)   _____

L. Adjusted taxable gifts (gifts made during life)   _____

M. Estate tax base amount (sum of items K and L)   _____

     N. **Gross estate tax** (on item M from table below)   _____

O. Unified credit (maximum of $780,800)   _____

P. Gift taxes paid on lifetime gifts   _____

     Q. **Total credits** (sum of items O and P)   (_____)

     R. **Net federal estate tax** (item N minus item Q)   _____

Estate Tax Table

If Estate Tax Base Amount...		Tentative Tax Is...		
Over...	But Not Over...	Tax	Plus %	Of Excess Over...
$0	$10,000	$0	18.00%	$0
10,000	20,000	1,800	20.00%	10,000
20,000	40,000	3,800	22.00%	20,000
40,000	60,000	8,200	24.00%	40,000
60,000	80,000	13,000	26.00%	60,000
80,000	100,000	18,200	28.00%	80,000
100,000	150,000	23,800	30.00%	100,000
150,000	250,000	38,800	32.00%	150,000
250,000	500,000	70,800	34.00%	250,000
500,000	750,000	155,800	37.00%	500,000
750,000	1,000,000	248,300	39.00%	750,000
1,000,000	1,250,000	345,800	41.00%	1,000,000
1,250,000	1,500,000	448,300	43.00%	1,250,000
1,500,000	2,000,000	555,800	45.00%	1,500,000
2,000,000	2,500,000	780,800	45.00%	2,000,000
2,500,000	and up	1,005,800	45.00%	2,500,000

[1] For years 2005-2010, death taxes paid to a state will be allowed as a deduction from the gross estate, rather than a credit against the federal estate tax.

Federal Estate Tax Tables

For Individuals Dying in 2008

Under the provisions of the Economic Growth and Tax Relief Reconciliation Act of 2001 (EGTRRA), the top federal estate tax rate will change for each year between 2002-2010. The first table below shows the federal estate tax rates for 2008. EGTRRA also provided for a changing applicable credit amount, as shown in the second table. If Congress does not act to change current law, in 2011, a top marginal rate of 55% will apply, with an applicable credit amount of $345,800.

Federal Estate Tax Table: 2008

If Taxable Estate...		Tentative Tax Is...		
Is Over...	But Not Over...	Tax	Plus %	Of Excess Over...
$ 0	$ 10,000	$ 0	18%	$ 0
10,000	20,000	1,800	20%	10,000
20,000	40,000	3,800	22%	20,000
40,000	60,000	8,200	24%	40,000
60,000	80,000	13,000	26%	60,000
80,000	100,000	18,200	28%	80,000
100,000	150,000	23,800	30%	100,000
150,000	250,000	38,800	32%	150,000
250,000	500,000	70,800	34%	250,000
500,000	750,000	155,800	37%	500,000
750,000	1,000,000	248,300	39%	750,000
1,000,000	1,250,000	345,800	41%	1,000,000
1,250,000	1,500,000	448,300	43%	1,250,000
1,500,000	2,000,000	555,800	45%	1,500,000
2,000,000	and higher	780,800	45%	2,000,000

Applicable Credit Amount: 2001 - 2011

Year	Applicable Credit Amount	Applicable Exclusion Amount	Top Federal Estate Tax Rate
2001	$ 220,550	$ 675,000	55%
2002	345,800	1,000,000	50%
2003	345,800	1,000,000	49%
2004	555,800	1,500,000	48%
2005	555,800	1,500,000	47%
2006	780,800	2,000,000	46%
2007	780,800	2,000,000	45%
2008	780,800	2,000,000	45%
2009	1,455,800	3,500,000	45%
2010	No FET	No FET	0%
2011	345,800	1,000,000	55%

Federal Estate Tax Approximator

Assumes Death Occurs in 2008

Item Description	Value
Estimated gross estate at death	$10,000,000
Debts, probate, mortgages, etc.	- $2,500,000
Net estate at death	**$7,500,000**
Assets passing to spouse	- $5,000,000
Assets passing to charities	- $1,000,000
Taxable estate	**$1,500,000**
Adjusted taxable gifts made after 1976	$ 100,000
Adjusted taxable estate	**$1,600,000**
Tentative federal estate tax	$ 600,800
Gift taxes paid after 1976	-$10,000
Applicable (unified) credit amount	- $ 600,800
Federal estate tax due	**-$10,000**

Note: Under the Tax Act of 2001, the federal estate tax is gradually phased out until its final repeal in the year 2010. If Congress does not act at that time to repeal it for the years following, it will automatically revert back to the rates in effect during the year 2001, with an exemption for the first $1,000,000 of assets.

Valuation of Estate Assets

Assets belonging to the deceased estate owner are included in his or her estate at their fair market value on the date of death or if the executor elects, their value six months after date of death.[1]

A Few Selected Assets

Type of Assets	How Asset Is Valued	Reference
Listed stocks and bonds (including over the counter)	The mean between highest and lowest quoted selling prices on the valuation date.	Reg. Sec. 20.2031-2(b)(1)
Mutual funds	Valued at their bid price or redemption value (i.e., the amount the fund would pay the shareholder if it redeemed the shares on the valuation date).	Regs. Secs. 20.2031-8 (b) and 25. 2512-6(b); *U.S. vs. Cartwright,* 411 U.S. 546 (1973)
Survivor's annuity (under a joint and survivor annuity contract)	The amount that the same insurance company would require for a single life annuity on the survivor, as of the applicable valuation date.	Reg. Sec. 20.2031-8
Close corporation stock	Fair market value is based on history and nature of business, economic outlook, book value, earning capacity, dividend paying capacity, goodwill, recent sales of stock and similar publicly traded company stock.	Rev. Rul. 59-60, 1959-1 CB 237
Real estate	Fair market value of real estate in the United States or in a foreign country.	IRC Secs. 2031, 2032A, 2033
Real estate (farm or corporate owned)	Value may be determined by actual use rather than on its highest and best use if certain conditions are met.	IRC Sec. 2032A
Mortgages and notes	The amount of the unpaid principal plus accrued interest, unless a lower value can be proven (i.e., an insolvent debtor).	Reg. Sec. 20.2031-4
Life insurance on the decedent's life	Amount receivable by the estate or by a named beneficiary, if the deceased insured had incidents of ownership in the policy.	Reg. Sec. 20.2042-1

---

[1] The "six months after date of death" is referred to as the alternate valuation date. (IRC Sec. 2032) If elected, assets sold or distributed during this six-month period are valued at the date of the sale or distribution. All other assets must be valued at the six-month date except assets that diminish in value due to the mere lapse of time (e.g., an annuity). If elected, it must reduce both the value of the decedent's gross estate and the federal estate tax liability. See IRC Sec. 2032(c).

Continued

Valuation of Estate Assets

Type of Assets	How Asset Is Valued	Reference
Life insurance policy owned by decedent on the life of another person	The cost of buying another policy of the same value and same type on the same insured.	Reg. Sec. 20.2031-8
Joint tenancy with a spouse	One-half of the value of property owned jointly by spouses is included in the estate of the first spouse to die.	IRC Sec. 2040(b)
Joint tenancy with other than spouse (general rule)	Entire value of property less the original contribution of the survivor is included in the estate of the first joint tenant to die.	IRC Sec. 2040(a)

Note: Under the Tax Act of 2001, the federal estate tax is gradually phased out until its final repeal in the year 2010. If Congress does not act at that time to repeal it for the years following, it will automatically revert back to the rates in effect during the year 2001, with an exemption for the first $1,000,000 of assets.

Federal Credit for State Death Tax Paid

Prior to 2002, a decedent who lived in a state that imposed a state death tax was allowed a credit against his or her federal estate tax liability for some or all of this state tax. Many states "piggy-backed" on the federal estate tax and collected as a death tax the amount of the maximum federal credit allowed. The amount of the federal credit was calculated using the table shown below.

State Death Tax Credit for Federal Estate Tax

Adjusted Taxable Estate[1]		Credit on Column 1	Plus %	Of Excess Over...
At Least...	But Less Than...			
$0	$40,000	$0	0.0%	$0
$40,000	$90,000	$0	0.8%	$40,000
$90,000	$140,000	$400	1.6%	$90,000
$140,000	$240,000	$1,200	2.4%	$140,000
$240,000	$440,000	$3,600	3.2%	$240,000
$440,000	$640,000	$10,000	4.0%	$440,000
$640,000	$840,000	$18,000	4.8%	$640,000
$840,000	$1,040,000	$27,600	5.6%	$840,000
$1,040,000	$1,540,000	$38,800	6.4%	$1,040,000
$1,540,000	$2,040,000	$70,800	7.2%	$1,540,000
$2,040,000	$2,540,000	$106,800	8.0%	$2,040,000
$2,540,000	$3,040,000	$146,800	8.8%	$2,540,000
$3,040,000	$3,540,000	$190,800	9.6%	$3,040,000
$3,540,000	$4,040,000	$238,800	10.4%	$3,540,000
$4,040,000	$5,040,000	$290,800	11.2%	$4,040,000
$5,040,000	$6,040,000	$402,800	12.0%	$5,040,000
$6,040,000	$7,040,000	$522,800	12.8%	$6,040,000
$7,040,000	$8,040,000	$650,800	13.6%	$7,040,000
$8,040,000	$9,040,000	$786,800	14.4%	$8,040,000
$9,040,000	$10,040,000	$930,800	15.2%	$9,040,000
$10,040,000		$1,082,800	16.0%	$10,040,000

EGTRRA – State Death Tax Credit Phase Out 2002-2004

Under the Economic Growth and Tax Relief Reconciliation act of 2001 (EGTRRA), the federal credit for state death taxes was gradually phased out (see table below) until 2005, when it was eliminated.

Year	Credit from Table	Adjustment Factor	Adjusted Credit
2002	$ _____	x .75	$ _____
2003	$ _____	x .50	$ _____
2004	$ _____	x .25	$ _____

---

[1] The adjusted taxable estate is the taxable estate reduced by $60,000.

Continued.

Federal Credit for State Death Tax Paid

How Will the States Be Affected?

Many of the states do not have a separate inheritance or estate tax. In the past they were able to rely on what was termed the "pick-up" or "sponge" tax, i.e., the amount of the state death tax credit allowed by federal law. Because this federal credit does not exist during 2005-2010, the revenue it brought to the states disappears during those years.

The chart below illustrates how a theoretical $10,000,000 estate would be taxed during the period 2001 thru 2011 and where the tax revenues would go.

Year of Death	Total Estate Tax	Amount to State	Amount to Federal Gov't
2001	$4,920,250	$1,067,600	$3,852,650
2002	$4,430,000	$800,700	$3,629,300
2003	$4,355,000	$533,800	$3,821,200
2004	$4,065,000	$266,900	$3,798,100
2005	$3,985,000	$0	$3,985,000
2006	$3,680,000	$0	$3,680,000
2007	$3,600,000	$0	$3,600,000
2008	$3,600,000	$0	$3,600,000
2009	$2,925,000	$0	$2,925,000
2010	$0	$0	$0
2011	$4,795,000	$1,067,600	$3,727,400

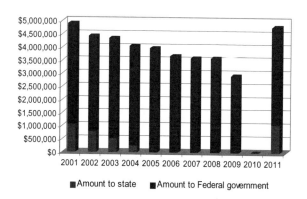

Amount to state　　■Amount to Federal government

So even though the federal estate tax will decrease over this period, the total amount the federal government actually receives will go up. It is the states that will take the loss.

Many state legislatures will likely consider reinstating prior inheritance and state estate tax laws that were repealed in exchange for the "pick-up" tax.

Planning Your Estate with Uncertain Tax Laws
Crystal Ball Estate Planning

The enactment of the Tax Act of 2001 introduced a considerable amount of uncertainty into the estate planning process. Under this law, the federal estate tax (FET) is only repealed for the year 2010, unless the Congress in session at that time takes the initiative to finalize the repeal. Predicting who will be in control of Congress, as well as what the monetary requirements of the government programs and the actual budget surplus/deficit will be at that time, is, of course, impossible.

The year following 2010 (the one year that the FET is actually repealed) is the year that the first baby boomers reach age 65 and become entitled to Social Security and Medicare. The demands on the Treasury in the years that follow will be substantial. A look at recent history tells us that Congress changes the tax law almost every year. If the demands for government services rise, increased taxes are almost certain.

Estate Settlement Costs

If we are dealing with the question of liquidity for estate tax purposes, most of the reductions to the FET do not come until the year before the repeal (2009) when the applicable exclusion amount reaches $3.5 million. The table below illustrates the taxation of a hypothetical estate.

Assumptions:
Current estate size: $10,000,000
Annual growth rate: 7.0%
Repeal of FET is not extended past 2010

Year	Estate Size	Applicable Exemption Amt	Federal Estate Tax Due
2001	$10,000,000	$675,000	$4,920,250
2002	$10,700,000	$1,000,000	$4,780,000
2003	$11,449,000	$1,000,000	$5,065,010
2004	$12,250,430	$1,500,000	$5,145,206
2005	$13,107,960	$1,500,000	$5,445,741
2006	$14,025,517	$2,000,000	$5,531,778
2007	$15,007,304	$2,000,000	$5,853,287
2008	$16,057,815	$2,000,000	$6,326,017
2009	$17,181,862	$3,500,000	$6,156,838
2010	$18,384,592	$0	$0
2011	$19,671,514	$1,000,000	$10,473,533

Continued

Planning Your Estate with Uncertain Tax Laws
Crystal Ball Estate Planning

Planning for the Future

Regarding liquidity to pay potential estate settlement costs, some have said you can make a "little mistake" or you can make a "big mistake," and only you can choose which.

If you adhere to the argument that the estate tax will probably be reinstated (it affects a very small percentage of the voting public), you will likely create (or retain) an estate plan that provides for sufficient liquidity for your estate to pay the anticipated federal estate tax.

Alternatively, if you take a more optimistic approach and feel that finally Congress has given us a good law and whoever controls the legislature in 2010 will likely vote to finalize the repeal and you feel you are likely to live another 10 years, liquidity to pay a federal estate tax would not factor into your estate plan.

The second approach certainly will appeal to some, but for those who have spent a lifetime building an estate, which they would like to pass to their heirs, will find it fraught with uncertainty.

The "little mistake" would be to plan that the 2010 Congress will not repeal the federal estate tax. If it is repealed, you will have extra liquidity to benefit heirs and/or your favorite charity, or use for your own retirement.

The "big mistake" would be to plan that the federal estate tax will still be repealed in 2011 (it currently only dies for the year 2010) and not provide for sufficient estate liquidity. Since many people use life insurance to provide liquidity for estate taxes, they must consider whether or not they will be in poor health in 2011 and thus precluded from using this liquidity tool. Even if they are in good health, the annual premiums will likely be much higher than they are today.

Will the Federal Estate Tax Repeal Last?

Prior to June 2001, only two percent of persons dying were subject to any federal estate taxes. During 1997, about one-half of all death taxes imposed were on the wealthiest one person of every 1,000 who died. This 1/10th of 1% of the population will, of course, benefit the most from the repeal of the federal estate tax.

Estate tax laws were enacted in 1797 (Federal Stamps for Wills and Estates), 1862 (during the Civil War), and 1898 (to pay for the Spanish-American War). These were all repealed a few years later. Our current law was enacted in 1916 and has been frequently modified over the years. Will it change again even before the repeal scheduled for the year 2010? If not, will the Congress then in session have the votes required to finalize the repeal? And if they do, will the President veto their bill, as President Clinton did in 2000?

Death Taxes under the Tax Act of 2001 for a $5,000,000 Estate

Under the Tax Act of 2001, there is a federal estate tax (FET) on estates exceeding a $2,000,000 applicable exclusion amount. This $2,000,000 figure will increase periodically until 2010. In 2010 the FET will be repealed and the current, full step-up in basis of a decedent's assets will be replaced with a limited[1] step-up in basis. In 2011 the FET returns, with the same rates as were in effect during 2001 and a $1,000,000 applicable exclusion amount. If, however, the government acts to permanently repeal the estate tax after 2010, it would likely be replaced with a capital gains tax on the amount in excess of the basis carried over when an asset is sold.

The example below clearly illustrates that the tax burden on inherited assets would not be completely eliminated with any permanent repeal of the federal estate tax.

Assumptions:
    Current estate size: $5,000,000
    Annual growth rate: 7%
    Capital gains rate: 20%
    Cost basis of estate assets: $1,000,000

Year of Death	Net Taxable Estate[2]	Federal Estate Taxes Due Until 2010 under Tax Act	
2001	$5,000,000	$2,170,250	
2002	5,350,000	2,105,000	
2003	5,724,500	2,260,005	
2004	6,125,215	2,205,103	
2005	6,553,980	2,365,371	
2006	7,012,759	2,305,869	
2007	7,503,652	2,476,643	
2008	8,028,907	2,713,008	
2009	8,590,931	2,290,919	
2010	$9,192,296	$1,378,459 Cap. Gains Tax[2]	
		FET Repealed Cap. Gains Tax[3]	**FET Remains** Current Law
2011	$9,835,757	$1,507,151	$4,704,666
2012	10,524,260	1,644,852	5,109,556
2013	11,260,958	1,792,192	5,551,575
2014	12,049,225	1,949,845	6,024,535
2015	12,892,671	2,118,534	6,530,603

[1] Step-up in basis is limited to $1,300,000, plus $3,000,000 for surviving spouses.
[2] Net taxable estate is the total estate passing to a non-spouse heir, less debts and bequests.
[3] The capital gains tax is incurred for inherited, appreciated assets. The tax is not due until the assets are sold.

Death Taxes under the Tax Act of 2001
for a $10,000,000 Estate

Under the Tax Act of 2001, there is a federal estate tax (FET) on taxable estates exceeding a $2,000,000 applicable exclusion amount. This $2,000,000 figure will increase periodically until 2010. In 2010 the FET will be repealed and the current, current full step-up in basis of a decedent's assets will be replaced with a limited[1] step-up in basis. In 2011 the FET returns, with the same rates as were in effect during 2001 and a $1,000,000 applicable exclusion amount. If, however, the government acts to permanently repeal the estate tax after 2010, it would likely be replaced with a capital gains tax on the amount in excess of the basis carried over when an asset is sold.

The example below clearly illustrates that the tax burden on inherited assets would not be completely eliminated with any permanent repeal of the federal estate tax.

Assumptions:
Current estate size: $10,000,000
Annual growth rate: 7%
Capital gains rate: 20%
Cost basis of estate assets: $2,000,000

Year of Death	Net Taxable Estate[2]	Federal Estate Taxes Due Until 2010 under Tax Act	
2001	$10,000,000	$4,920,250	
2002	10,700,000	4,780,000	
2003	11,449,000	5,065,010	
2004	12,250,430	5,145,206	
2005	13,107,960	5,445,741	
2006	14,025,517	5,531,738	
2007	15,007,304	5,853,287	
2008	16,057,815	6,326,017	
2009	17,181,862	6,156,838	
2010	$18,384,592	$3,016,918 Cap. Gains Tax[2]	
		FET Repealed Cap. Gains Tax[3]	**FET Remains** Current Law
2011	$19,671,514	$3,274,303	$10,473,533
2012	21,048,520	3,549,704	11,230,886
2013	22,521,916	3,844,383	12,041,254
2014	24,098,450	4,159,690	12,908,348
2015	25,785,342	4,497,068	13,836,138

---

[1] Step-up in basis limited to $1,300,000, plus $3,000,000 for surviving spouses.
[2] Net taxable estate is the total estate passing to a non-spouse heir, less debts and bequests.
[3] The capital gains tax is incurred for inherited, appreciated assets. The tax is not due until the assets are sold.

Federal Estate Taxes under the Tax Act of 2001

Under the Tax Act of 2001, the federal estate tax is repealed for the year 2010 and then reverts back to the rates in effect during 2001 (with an applicable exclusion amount of $1,000,000). The graph below illustrates the federal estate tax due on three different estate sizes with the year of death ranging from 2001 through 2015. Note that in year 2010, while there is no FET due, substantial capital gains tax may be due and payable by the heir(s), if inherited assets are sold.

Assumptions:
Current estate size: $5,000,000, $10,000,000 and $15,000,000
Annual estate growth rate: 7%

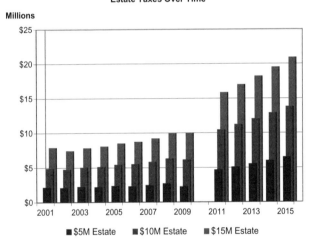

Estate Taxes Over Time

Carry-Over Income Tax Basis After 2010

The Dilemma

If Congress finalizes the repeal of the federal
estate tax before the end of 2010, it will be
replaced with what is called "carry-over
basis." If the federal estate tax is not repealed
for those years following 2010, then the Tax
Act of 2001 includes a "sunset" provision that
will cause the taxation methods and rates to
revert to those in effect during 2001.

Current Law

Under current law, most appreciated assets belonging to a decedent receive a new,
stepped-up income tax basis at death. This means that the beneficiary can sell the asset for
its value at the date of death and not pay any capital gain tax. This remains the law until
2010, at which time it will be replaced by a modified carry-over basis.

Law After Repeal of Estate Tax

Assuming that the federal estate tax is finally repealed for years following 2010,
appreciated assets passing to one's spouse or other heirs will carry with them the same
income tax basis that the decedent had. Basis usually begins with the purchase price of
the asset and then may be decreased for depreciation taken and increased for expenditures
to improve the asset (like an addition to an office building).

When the heir later sells the asset, he or she must determine the gain based on the
decedent's adjusted income tax basis. (See below for an example of adjusted income tax
basis.)

Adjustments to Basis

The heirs are entitled to further increase the basis of the inherited assets by up to
$1,300,000 (as allocated by the executor). There is an additional basis increase of
$3,000,000 for assets passing to the surviving spouse. Unused capital losses and net
operating losses may also increase the basis of the asset.

Need to Keep Records

It will become more important than ever to keep records regarding assets, since the burden
of establishing the income tax basis will rest with the heirs. The executor will be subject
to penalties for failure to file timely returns on estates transferring property with a
cumulative value of more than $1,300,000. In addition, if the decedent received
appreciated property within three years of death, it must also be reported to the IRS and
these assets will not be eligible for the increase in basis.

Continued...

Carry-Over Income Tax Basis After 2010

An Example of the Income Tax Carry-Over Basis

The following example will help explain the effect of the carry-over income tax basis, should it become the law in 2010. For this example, we will assume the following facts.

John purchased an office building many years ago for $1,500,000. Over the years, he has depreciated it for income tax purposes so that the adjusted cost basis at the time of his demise in 2011 is only $1,000,000. The fair market value (FMV) is $10,000,000 and there is a willing buyer waiting to purchase it from the heirs.

	If Assets Pass to Spouse		If Assets Pass to Other Heir	
	FET Not Repealed	FET Repealed	FET Not Repealed	FET Repealed
Current fair market value	$10,000,000	$10,000,000	$10,000,000	$10,000,000
Basis to heir	$10,000,000	$1,000,000	$10,000,000	$1,000,000
Increase to basis	Full step up	$1,300,000	Full step up	$1,300,000
Spousal basis increase	Full step up	$3,000,000	Full step up	For spouse only
Adjusted basis to heir	$10,000,000	$5,300,000	$10,000,000	$2,300,000
Capital gain if sold at FMV	$0	$4,700,000	$0	$7,700,000
Capital gain tax at 20%	$0	$940,000	$0	$1,540,000
Federal estate tax	$0	$0	$4,795,000	$0
Estimated liability	**$0**	**$940,000**	**$4,795,000**	**$1,540,000**

The Tax Act of 2001 has made it somewhat difficult to plan for the future. Will John's heir(s) owe $0, $940,000, $1,540,000 or $4,795,000? In larger estates there could be substantial capital gains taxes even on transfers to one's spouse.

If Congress fails to repeal the federal estate tax beyond 2010, it may it be too late to provide the proper liquidity needed to pay the federal estate tax due.

Estates of Famous People

Estate settlement costs can be very costly and are paid even by the rich and famous. The following examples are from public probate records of individuals who have died.

The following estates made use of the marital deduction:[1]

Name	Gross Estate	Settlement Costs	Net Estate	Percent Shrinkage
Stan Laurel	$91,562	$8,381	$83,181	9%
Goodwin Knight	$102,049	$21,585	$80,464	21%
W.C. Fields	$884,680	$329,793	$554,887	37%
Nelson Eddy	$472,715	$109,990	$362,725	23%
Dixie Crosby	$1,332,571	$781,953	$550,618	59%
Franklin D. Roosevelt	$1,940,999	$574,867	$1,366,132	30%
Humphrey Bogart	$910,146	$274,234	$635,912	30%
Clark Gable	$2,806,526	$1,101,038	$1,705,488	30%
Dean Witter	$7,451,055	$1,830,717	$5,620,338	25%
Henry J. Kaiser, Sr.	$5,597,772	$2,488,364	$3,109,408	44%
Henry J. Kaiser, Jr.	$55,910,373	$1,030,415	$54,879,958[2]	2%
Al Jolson	$4,385,143	$1,349,066	$3,036,077	31%
Gary Cooper	$4,984,985	$1,530,454	$3,454,531	31%
Myford Irvine	$13,445,552	$6,012,685	$7,432,867	45%
Walt Disney	$23,004,851	$6,811,943	$16,192,908	30%
Harry M. Warner	$8,946,618	$2,308,444	$6,638,174	26%
William E. Boeing	$22,386,158	$10,589,748	$11,796,410	47%

Estates where the marital deduction was not used or not available:

Name	Gross Estate	Settlement Costs	Net Estate	Percent Shrinkage
William Frawley	$92,446	$45,814	$46,632	49%
"Gabby" Hayes	$111,327	$21,963	$89,364	20%
Hedda Hopper	$472,661	$165,982	$306,679	35%
Marilyn Monroe	$819,176	$448,750	$370,426	55%
Erle Stanley Gardner	$1,795,092	$636,705	$1,158,387	35%
Cecil B. DeMille	$4,043,607	$1,396,064	$2,647,543	35%
Elvis Presley	$10,165,434	$7,374,635	$2,790,799	73%
J.P. Morgan	$17,121,482	$11,893,691	$5,227,791	69%
John D. Rockefeller, Sr.	$26,905,182	$17,124,988	$9,780,194	64%
John D. Rockefeller, Jr.	$160,598,584	$24,965,954	$135,632,630[2]	16%
Alwin C. Ernst, CPA	$12,642,431	$7,124,112	$5,518,319	56%
Frederick Vanderbilt	$76,838,530	$42,846,112	$33,992,418	56%

---

[1] Under current laws, the costs would be different. Under the Tax Act of 2001, the federal estate tax is gradually phased out until its final repeal in the year 2010. If Congress does not act at that time to repeal it for the years following, it will automatically revert back to the rates in effect during the year 2001, with an exemption for the first $1,000,000 of assets.

[2] Over $50,000,000 of Henry J. Kaiser's estate went to the Kaiser Family Foundation. Most of the estate of John D. Rockefeller, Jr. went to the Rockefeller Brothers Fund, Inc.

Estates of Four Famous People

Marital Deduction Was Used

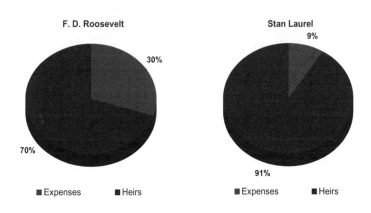

F. D. Roosevelt

30%

70%

■ Expenses   ■ Heirs

Stan Laurel

9%

91%

■ Expenses   ■ Heirs

Marital Deduction Was Not Available or Not Used

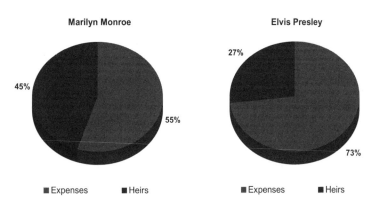

Marilyn Monroe

45%

55%

■ Expenses   ■ Heirs

Elvis Presley

27%

73%

■ Expenses   ■ Heirs

Basic Steps in the Estate Planning Process

There are several basic steps to take in planning your estate. A typical program would be as follows.

The Basic Steps

1. **Choose your team:** Choose, as needed, your attorney, tax professional, insurance professional, trust officer, planned-giving specialist or financial advisor.
2. **Gather information:** A completed fact finder serves to list your goals and objectives, shows names, ages, assets and liabilities, desired heirs; goals and objectives.
3. **Analyze data:** Pretend death occurred yesterday. What happens to your estate, your business, and your family? What if you die 10 years from now? Your team analyzes the data to provide you with the results.
4. **Team makes recommendations:** Review the suggestions made by your team to overcome current plan shortcomings.
5. **Decide and implement:** Select the plan that best fits your needs and goals. Sign essential documents (e.g. wills and trusts), purchase needed insurance, and change investments as necessary.
6. **Periodic review:** Starting the cycle over. Because the world (and your estate) is constantly changing, many advisors recommend an annual planning review.

Meet the Estate Planning Team

Estate planning is a complex field that covers many areas including wills, trusts, insurance, accounting, business continuation, and estate, gift and income taxes. It would be difficult to find one person who is a trained and licensed expert in all of these areas. Most often, the needed skills and knowledge are available only by bringing together an Estate Planning Team. The various members of the team can then work closely to preserve the estate and pass it on to the heirs with the least amount of expense and aggravation.

You Are the Captain of Your Team

Possible Team members may include the following:

- Attorney
- Tax Professional
- Insurance Professional
- Trust Administrator
- Charitable Advisor
- Financial Advisor

Choose the Estate Planning Team

Estate planning is a complex field that covers many areas including wills, trusts, insurance, accounting, business continuation, and estate, gift and income taxes. It would be difficult to find one person who is a trained and licensed expert in all of these areas. Most often, the needed skills and knowledge are available only by bringing together an Estate Planning Team. The various members of the team can then work closely to preserve the estate and pass it on to the heirs with the least  amount of expense and aggravation. Potential members of the team may include the following.

Estate Planning Attorney

Most attorneys can draft a basic will. However, one who specializes in estate planning law will be more familiar with the various tools and techniques available to save you and your heirs thousands of dollars in taxes, probate and administration expenses.

Tax Professional

Federal and state laws require that a number of income and estate tax returns be filed shortly after your demise. Even in the simplest of situations, properly completing these tax returns can be a complex and confusing process. These returns will be even more involved if you own a business or rental real estate.

Insurance Professional

Life insurance is often utilized in estate planning solutions. Contracts differ greatly and are issued by companies with varying degrees of financial strength.

A professional life insurance agent will help you choose a financially strong company, the correct type of policy for your situation and the correct amount of insurance. Determining who will be the owner of a life insurance policy is a key question. The answer can add or avoid hundreds of thousands of dollars in estate taxes.

Trust Administrator

If you select a corporate fiduciary (a bank or trust company) as executor of your will or trustee of your trust, you should consider involving them in the development of your estate plan.

Sometimes they have important provisions which should be added to the will or trust document to help them administer the estate.

Continued...

Choose the Estate Planning Team

Planned-Giving Specialist

Charitable organizations often have planned-giving specialists who are well versed in methods of making lifetime gifts or bequests at the time of death, which can benefit you and your heirs.

Financial Advisor

Sometimes the life agent, accountant or other member of the estate planning team may have special training in financial planning. Other times, a person who specializes in financial planning may be part of your team. If so, he or she will often take a very active part in directing the formation of the overall estate plan.

The Captain of the Team

You are the captain of the team. The final decisions must be made by you after carefully reviewing the recommendations of the other members of your estate planning team.

How Often Should Legal Documents Be Reviewed?

Once a legal document is completed and signed, it is often carefully laid to rest in a safe deposit box or file drawer and comes out again only when a party dies or a conflict arises.

Prudent persons periodically review and update their legal documents. Just how often depends, of course, on the document and which circumstances have changed. The following list sets forth some events that may require the updating of a legal document.

Life Events

- Marriage
- Dissolution of a marriage (divorce)
- Death of a spouse
- A substantial change in estate size
- A move to another state
- Death of executor, trustee or guardian
- Birth or adoption
- Serious illness of family member
- Change in business interest
- Retirement
- Change in health
- Change in insurability for life insurance
- Acquisition of property in another state
- Changes in tax, property or probate and trust law
- A change in beneficiary attitudes
- Financial responsibility of a child

If there is any question as to the effect of a change in circumstances on your will, trust, buy-sell agreement, asset titles and beneficiary designations, etc., contact the appropriate member of your team and have it reviewed before a crisis arises.

Choosing an Attorney

Choosing an attorney is a key part of your personal financial life. Unfortunately, the process of finding the right individual can be confusing and frustrating. First of all, you need to be able to find someone who is qualified in the area of the law with which you need help. Secondly, you should be comfortable working with that person.

Always remember that your attorney works for you. Your attorney has a professional and ethical duty to put your interests first. The attorney's primary role is to provide advice and guidance; the final decision as to what action should be taken is yours.

How to Find an Attorney

Talk to people you know and ask about their experience. Another good idea is to check with the local bar association because they often have a referral program.

What Criteria Should Be Used?

In simple terms, the goal is to find the best qualified person you can afford.

On your part, you need to know exactly what it is you wish to accomplish. Do you want to set up a trust? Do you need help in settling an estate? Do you have a dispute with the IRS? Are you filing for divorce? Were you injured in an accident? Have you been charged with a crime? Do you need to draft documents and contracts for your business?

No one individual can be proficient in all areas of the law. That's why most attorneys tend to concentrate their efforts in a specific area of expertise, which can facilitate your search.

What Does Being Licensed Mean?

An individual must pass the state bar exam to practice law in a particular state. Each state is different and has its own examination. Therefore, being licensed in one state does not allow an attorney to practice law in another state. Passing a state's bar means that the individual has demonstrated that he or she possesses a minimum level of legal knowledge and is therefore authorized to represent clients before the courts of that state.

An attorney should be willing to furnish you with his or her state bar number. You can then check with the state bar to verify that the attorney is licensed. In some states, you can find out if he or she has been disciplined for past misconduct. Of course, merely being licensed is no assurance that a particular attorney is the best person to handle your case.

Interview the Attorney

Interview your attorney as you would anyone you were considering hiring for a job. Your attorney should be someone you are comfortable with and with whom you can communicate freely. Even more important, your attorney must be someone you can trust.

Continue

Choosing an Attorney

Experience

Ask the attorney about his or her legal background and experience. Although many state bar associations do not require an attorney to be experienced or qualified in a specific area of law to practice in that area, some states do recognize highly specialized areas of legal expertise. At a minimum, you should know if your attorney has ever handled the type of matter you need help with.

Next, you should ask about your attorney's non-law background and experience. Most attorneys have had a life outside of law school. The most important experience relating to your matter may not be law or even law related.

Large Firm vs. Individual Practitioner

Since most attorneys tend to specialize in their practice of law, they often find that they can not provide all the services a client may require. Therefore, an attorney generally has two choices: work with a large firm and refer the client to specialists within the firm; or develop a list of outside attorneys to refer clients to for matters they choose not to handle. From the client's point of view, this decision is a matter of personal choice.

- **Large firms**: Advantages: One-stop shopping, generally good in-house expertise and can usually handle a variety of concerns. Disadvantages: May lack understanding of you and your business; sometimes more expensive.

- **Individual Practitioner**: Advantages: More likely to take the time to fully understand you and your needs; generally lower hourly rates. Disadvantages: Limited expertise, may hit time constraints when doing trials. In addition, you may need to work with more than one office to handle all matters.

Items to Discuss Before Meeting with an Attorney

There are several topics that persons should consider prior to meeting with the attorney who will draft a will or a trust.

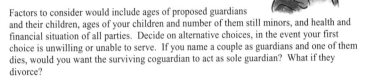

Guardians for Minor Children

Who is best able to cope with the raising of your minor children? A brother, sister or a close friend may be a better choice than a grandparent.

Factors to consider would include ages of proposed guardians and their children, ages of your children and number of them still minors, and health and financial situation of all parties. Decide on alternative choices, in the event your first choice is unwilling or unable to serve. If you name a couple as guardians and one of them dies, would you want the surviving coguardian to act as sole guardian? What if they divorce?

Executor of the Estate

If all or part of your estate passes through probate, whom do you want to handle the details of paying your debts and death taxes and distributing the remaining assets to the beneficiaries named in your will?

Living Trust

Is it important to you to avoid probate? Make a list of your assets and approximate values, along with a list of mortgages on any property. Your attorney can give you an estimate of what it will cost your heirs to pass your estate through probate.

The living trust is frequently used to avoid or reduce probate expenses. Ask your attorney to explain the advantages and disadvantages of this type of trust.

Trustee

If you have a trust, either in your will or a separate living trust, you will need to name a trustee to manage investments, pay taxes, make distributions, etc. In the event he or she dies, you will want to provide for one or more successor trustees.

Continued

Items to Discuss Before Meeting with an Attorney

A Corporate or Individual Fiduciary

Executors and trustees are referred to as
fiduciaries because of the higher standard of
care which is required of them in managing
the assets of another person. Discuss the
facts of your own estate relative to the list of
advantages shown below.

- **Advantages of a corporate fiduciary**
  - They don't die or become disabled – permanence.
  - They are financially accountable for their mistakes.
  - They are impartial as to the children. This may prevent the children from becoming bitter towards an individual trustee who happens to be a friend or relative and who doesn't make distributions every time the children ask for something.
  - They have investment expertise, tax and accounting abilities, and computer capabilities. Studies show that they save many dollars in the average estate.
  - They refuse loans to hard-up friends of the trustee.
  - They keep current with the constant changes in the law.

- **Advantages of an individual fiduciary**
  - A relative or friend may not charge a fee.
  - A relative or friend may have a more personal interest.
  - An individual may have special expertise (i.e., running the family business).

Suggestion: Some people prefer the use of an individual and a corporate trustee, as co-trustees, to obtain the advantages of each.

Distributions to Children

If you do not want your assets distributed outright to your
children in the event of your demise, they should probably be
held in a trust. The trustee will take care of their needs as
instructed in the trust. However, at some future time you will
probably want to distribute the assets to them.

Many people like to distribute a portion of the estate at several
different times; e.g., 1/3 at age 21, 1/3 at age 25 and 1/3 at age
30; or 1/2 at age 30 and 1/2 at age 35, etc. Your preference:
___ at age ___; ___ at age ___; ___ at age ___.

Continued...

Items to Discuss Before Meeting with an Attorney

Final Heirs

In the event your children pass away prior to inheriting your estate, to whom would you want your estate to pass? For example, one could pass ½ to the husband's side of the family (e.g., parents, brothers, sisters, etc.) and ½ to the wife's side.

Charitable Bequests

Would you be interested in making any charitable bequests, especially if it reduced your income and death taxes?[1]

Other Questions

Would you want your children to remain in the present house?

Is it important to reduce your death tax obligation?

---

[1] Under the Tax Act of 2001, the federal estate tax is gradually phased out until its final repeal in the year 2010. If Congress does not act at that time to repeal it for the years following, it will automatically revert back to the rates in effect during the year 2001, with an exemption for the first $1,000,000 of assets.

Advantages of a Will

Avoids Distribution Under the Law of Intestacy

The state intestacy law will pass property to certain relatives of
the decedent. These laws have been drafted to be fair in the
average situation, but most persons would like to choose who
will receive their estate when they die.

Permits the Nomination of a Guardian for Minor Children

Without a nomination in a will, the court will appoint a guardian of the person for minor
children. Relatives are not always the best choice for a guardian and consideration must
be given to the financial situation of the potential guardian, as well as his or her health,
age, willingness and ability to care for your children.

Waiver of the Probate Bond

In the absence of a will, the court will require a fiduciary bond to be posted by the
administrator (executor) of the estate to guarantee the replacement of any funds embezzled
or diverted by him. Since this additional cost must be borne by the estate, the estate owner
may want to waive the bond requirement in the will. Great care should be used in
selecting an executor.

Choosing the Executor

The duties of the executor of an estate can be very time consuming and frustrating,
especially to a spouse who has just lost his or her mate. In the will, a qualified individual
and/or a corporate trust company can be chosen to handle these responsibilities.

Making Specific Bequests to Individuals

An individual may bequeath specific items of jewelry, heirlooms and furniture, or make
cash bequests, and be certain that they will pass to the proper persons. Without a will,
written or oral instructions may not be followed.

Sale of Assets During the Administration of Probate

Additional expense to the estate can generally be avoided by permitting the sale of assets
without the executor having to publish a notice of sale in the newspaper. A sale of assets
may be necessary in order to pay death taxes and expenses of probate.

Continued...

Advantages of a Will

Authorizing the Continuation of a Business

Unless the will authorizes the continuation of a business, the executor must operate it at his or her own risk. Many executors may elect not to administer the estate unless this risk is borne by the estate.

Deferring Distributions to Minors

When parents die leaving minor children, each child's share of the estate must be held in a guardianship account until he or she attains the age of 18 (or 21), at which time the entire remaining share is distributed outright. Trust provisions can be placed in the will to defer these distributions until a more mature age.

Tax Savings

Certain, substantial tax savings are possible through the use of trusts. The will can be used to create trusts after death. Such trusts are known as testamentary credit shelter trusts. Similar tax savings, as well as probate savings, can be achieved through the use of trusts established during life, known as living credit shelter trusts.[1]

Peace of Mind

Although this advantage cannot be measured in dollars and cents, when the estate is in order an emotional load is lifted from the person who is concerned for his or her family's well being.

---

[1] Under the Tax Act of 2001, the federal estate tax is gradually phased out until its final repeal in the year 2010. If Congress does not act at that time to repeal it for the years following, it will automatically revert back to the rates in effect during the year 2001, with an exemption for the first $1,000,000 of assets.

Types of Wills and Trusts

There are many varieties of wills and trusts to fit the needs of each individual. Only a qualified attorney should draft these documents.

A few of the more common documents are listed below.

- **Basic will:** A basic or simple will generally gives everything outright to a surviving spouse, children or other heirs. Sometimes called an "I Love You" will.

- **Will with contingent trust:** Frequently, married couples with minor children will pass everything to their spouse, if living, and if not, to a trust for their minor children until they become more mature.

- **Pour-over will:** The so-called pour-over will is generally used in conjunction with a living trust. It picks up any assets that were not transferred to the trust during the person's lifetime and pours them into the trust upon death. The assets will generally be subject to probate administration, however.

- **Tax-saving will:** A will may be used to create a testamentary credit shelter trust. This trust provides lifetime benefits to the surviving spouse, without having those trust assets included in the survivor's estate at his or her subsequent death.

- **Living trust without tax planning:** Generally, the surviving spouse has full control of the principal and income of this type of trust. Its main purpose is to avoid probate. If required, the trust can also be used to manage the assets for beneficiaries who are not yet ready to inherit the assets outright, because they lack experience in financial and investment matters.

- **Living credit shelter trust:** This type of trust avoids probate and also makes certain that both spouses use their applicable credit amount. Estates of up to $4,000,000[1] can be passed to children or other heirs, without probate expense or death tax, by a married couple using this type of trust.

---

[1] This value is two times the current applicable exclusion amount. The applicable exclusion amount is the dollar value of assets protected from federal estate tax by an individual's applicable credit amount. It is scheduled to change as follows: $2,000,000 for 2007-2008; $3,500,000 for 2009, zero federal estate tax for the year 2010; and $1,000,000 for 2011 and thereafter (unless permanently repealed or otherwise modified).

Continued...

Types of Wills and Trusts

- **QTIP trust:** A type of trust known as a QTIP trust allows the first spouse to die to specify who will receive his or her assets after the surviving spouse dies. Use of a QTIP also permits the deferral of death taxes on the assets until the death of the surviving spouse.

QTIP means qualified terminable interest property. The income earned on assets in a QTIP trust must be given to the surviving spouse for his or her lifetime. After the death of the surviving spouse, however, the assets then pass to beneficiaries chosen by the first spouse to die, frequently children of a prior marriage.

Even if there are no children of a prior marriage, some estate owners use this type of trust to prevent a subsequent spouse of the survivor from diverting or wasting estate assets. A QTIP trust can only hold certain qualifying property. For this reason, it is often used in tandem with a credit shelter trust.

- **Qualified domestic trust:** Transfers at death to a noncitizen spouse will not qualify for the marital deduction unless the assets pass to a qualified domestic trust (QDOT). The QDOT rules require a U.S. Trustee (unless waived by the IRS) and other measures that help ensure collection of a death tax at the surviving noncitizen spouse's later demise.

Note: Additional trusts may be used for current income tax savings or to remove life insurance from the taxable estate, but the above-described documents are generally at the center of a person's estate plan.

Various Estate Planning Arrangements
A Summary of Benefits

Benefits	No Will	Basic Will	Trust Will	Basic Living Trust	CST[1] with Living Trust	CST and QTIP with Living Trust
1. Allows you to select:						
a. Beneficiaries of estate,	No	Yes	Yes	Yes	Yes	Yes
b. Executor of will,	No	Yes	Yes	Yes[2]	Yes[2]	Yes[2]
c. Guardians for children, and	No	Yes	Yes	Yes[2]	Yes[2]	Yes[2]
d. Trustees of trust.	No	No	Yes	Yes	Yes	Yes
2. Avoids probate costs.[3]	No	No	No	Yes	Yes	Yes
3. Provides asset management for children over age 18.	No	No	Yes	Yes	Yes	Yes
4. Protects estate owner from a conservatorship.	No	No	No	Yes	Yes	Yes
5. Designed to save death taxes for couples.	No	No	Maybe[4]	No	Yes	Yes
6. Allows the first spouse to die to determine the ultimate beneficiaries of the estate in excess of $2,000,000[5], while still deferring the death taxes.	No	No	Yes	No	No	Yes

Brief Description of Arrangement

- **No will:** Your estate passes to heirs picked by the legislature.

- **Basic will:** Generally passes everything to your spouse, if living, otherwise to your children when they reach age 18.

- **Trust will:** May contain credit shelter and QTIP trusts or may pass everything to your spouse, if living, otherwise for children.

- **Basic living trust:** Designed to avoid probate and provide asset management. Used for smaller estates and single persons.

- **CST with living trust:** Designed to use the applicable credit amounts of both spouses. Can often save a significant amount of money in death taxes and probate fees.

- **CST and QTIP with living trust:** Same as the CST with living trust, plus it gives the first spouse to die more control over who will eventually receive his or her assets after the surviving spouse dies. Also called a QTIP trust.

---

[1] CST stands for credit shelter trust. QTIP stands for qualified terminable interest property trust.

[2] Each living trust is generally accompanied by a "pour over" type of will which picks up assets not put into the trust during lifetime and transfers them after death. Executors/guardians are named in a will.

[3] If all of the assets are in the living trust, probate is not necessary. However, there will usually be some expense for legal advice or the transfer of assets not in the trust. Without a trust, probate costs may exceed 5% of the total estate.

[4] Some trust wills contain credit shelter trusts designed to save death taxes, while others merely manage assets.

[5] The applicable exclusion amount is the dollar value of assets protected from federal estate tax by an individual's applicable credit amount. It is scheduled to change as follows: $2,000,000 for 2007-2008; $3,500,000 for 2009, zero federal estate tax for the year 2010; and $1,000,000 for 2011 and thereafter (unless permanently repealed or otherwise modified).

No Will? No Problem!

State Drawn Will in Common Law States

LAST WILL OF PAUL PROCRASTINATOR

First: I direct the Probate Judge to appoint anyone of his choosing to administer all property in my name and distribute it under the terms of this will.

Second: I direct that all of my assets be converted to cash, all of my debts paid, including taxes, probate fees, administrative fees, and attorney's fee.

Third: I direct that one-half (if I am survived by one child) or one-third (if I am survived by two or more children) of my separate property, be paid to my spouse.

Fourth: I direct that the balance of my estate be distributed outright, and in cash, in equal shares to my children. If any child be a minor, I direct that his share be held by a guardian for his benefit. The guardian may be anyone of the Probate Judge's choosing.

Fifth: When each of my minor children attains age 18, I direct that his share be then paid to him outright, regardless of his financial or emotional maturity.

Sixth: In the event that my spouse does not survive me, I direct that his/her share be added to the children's shares created under Articles Fourth and Fifth.

Seventh: If none of my children survive me but my spouse does, I direct that the remainder under Article Third be distributed outright in the following manner:

    a. One-half of my separate property to my spouse.

    b. The balance to my parents, if living, otherwise to my brothers and sisters or their heirs.

Eighth: If I am not survived by my spouse, children or parents, I direct the Probate Court to seek out my closest blood relatives and divide my estate among them in a way which gives an equal share to my closest relatives or their descendants

Ninth: If no relatives are located, I direct that all of my property go to the State.

(No Witnesses are Necessary) No Signature Necessary to
Put This Document In Force

_____   _____

Note: This is not a legal document, but rather a summary of a typical state law.

No Will? No Problem!
State Drawn Will in Community Property States

LAST WILL OF PAUL PROCRASTINATOR

First: I direct the Probate Judge to appoint anyone of his choosing to administer all property in my name and distribute it under the terms of this will.

Second: I direct that all of my assets be converted to cash, all of my debts paid, including taxes, probate fees, administrative fees, and attorney's fee.

Third: I direct that all our community property and one-half (if I am survived by one child) or one-third (if I am survived by two or more children) of my separate property, be paid to my spouse.

Fourth: I direct that the balance of my estate be distributed outright, and in cash, in equal shares to my children. If any child be a minor, I direct that his share be held by a guardian for his benefit. The guardian may be anyone of the Probate Judge's choosing.

Fifth: When each of my minor children attains age 18, I direct that his share be then paid to him outright, regardless of his financial or emotional maturity.

Sixth: In the event that my spouse does not survive me, I direct that his/her share be added to the children's shares created under Articles Fourth and Fifth.

Seventh: If none of my children survive me but my spouse does, I direct that the remainder under Article Third be distributed outright in the following manner:

    a. One-half of my separate property and all of our community property to my spouse.

    b. The balance to my parents, if living, otherwise to my brothers and sisters or their heirs.

Eighth: If I am not survived by my spouse, children or parents, I direct the Probate Court to seek out my closest blood relatives and divide my estate among them in a way which gives an equal share to my closest relatives or their descendants.

Ninth: If no relatives are located, I direct that all of my property go to the State.

(No Witnesses are Necessary)   No Signature Necessary to
                                            Put This Document In Force

_____   _____

Note: This is not a legal document, but rather a summary of a typical state law.

Duties of an Executor

The executor of an estate is named in one's will and has
many duties and responsibilities. Some of the more
important tasks include:

- Find the latest will and read it.

- File a petition with the court to probate the will.

- Assemble all of the decedent's assets.
  - Take possession of safe deposit box contents.
  - Consult with banks and savings and loans in the area to find all accounts of the
    deceased. Also check for cash and other valuables hidden around the home.
  - Transfer all securities to his or her name (as executor) and continue to collect
    dividends and interest on behalf of the heirs of the deceased.
  - Find, inventory and protect household and personal effects and other personal
    property.
  - Collect all life insurance proceeds payable to the estate.
  - Find and inventory all real estate deeds, mortgages, leases and tax information.
    Provide immediate management for rental properties.
  - Arrange ancillary administration for out-of-state property.
  - Collect monies owed the deceased and check interests in estates of other deceased
    persons.

- Find and safeguard business interests, valuables, personal property, important papers,
  the residence, etc.

- Inventory all assets and arrange for appraisal of those for which it is appropriate.

- Determine liquidity needs. Assemble bookkeeping records. Review investment
  portfolio. Sell appropriate assets.

- Pay valid claims against the estate. Reject improper claims and defend the estate, if
  necessary.

- Pay state and federal taxes due.
  - File income tax returns for the decedent and the estate.
  - Determine whether the estate qualifies for special use valuation under IRC Sec.
    2032A, the qualified family-owned business interest deduction under IRC Sec. 2057
    or deferral of estate taxes under IRC Secs. 6161 or 6166.
  - If the surviving spouse is not a U.S. citizen, consider a qualified domestic trust to
    defer the payment of federal estate taxes.
  - File federal estate tax return[1] and state death and/or inheritance tax return.

---

[1] Under the Tax Act of 2001, the federal estate tax is gradually phased out until its final repeal in the year 2010. If
Congress does not act at that time to repeal it for the years following, it will automatically revert back to the rates in
effect during the year 2001, with an exemption for the first $1,000,000 of assets.

Continued...

Duties of an Executor

- Prepare statement of all receipts and disbursements. Pay attorney's fees and executor's commissions. Assist the attorney in defending the estate, if necessary.

- Distribute specific bequests and the residue; obtain tax releases and receipts as directed by the court. Establish a testamentary trust (or pour over into a living trust), where appropriate.

Steps in a Probate
An Overview

Executor/Administrator

Submits Will for Probate

Probate Court

---

1. Takes control of estate assets.

- Makes an inventory.
- Has assets appraised.
- Maintains insurance on assets.

2. Notifies creditors of probate.

- Sells assets, if necessary.
- Pays valid creditor's claims.
- Defends against frivolous claims.

3. Prepares tax returns.

- Prepares final income tax return.
- Prepares federal estate tax return (if estate exceeds $2,000,000 in 2008).

4. Petitions court to:

- Pay attorney and executor fees, and
- Distribute remaining assets to beneficiaries (or their trusts).

Note: Steps will vary with each state in which assets are owned.

Avoiding Probate

The probating of a will permits a court of law to supervise the transfer of assets from the decedent to his heirs. A typical probate lasts about one year, with six months generally being a minimum time if everything proceeds according to schedule.

Because of high attorney's fees, executor's commissions and court costs, and the often-unwanted publicity and the time delay involved in probating an estate, many people attempt to avoid probate administration. Some of the methods of avoidance are listed below.

Joint Tenancy

Joint tenancy is a form of title arrangement, usually between spouses. Title passes automatically to the surviving joint tenant. There may be income tax disadvantages to this arrangement and the joint tenancy is dissolved after one tenant dies. Creditors of either joint tenant can attach the asset. It may also frustrate estate tax savings which are anticipated from carefully drafted wills and trusts.

Community Property with Rights of Survivorship

Title passes automatically to the surviving spouse with no income tax disadvantages as with joint tenancy.

Totten Trust

A Totten trust is a vehicle for passing savings accounts to heirs. Passbook accounts are held in trust for another. Typical wording would be: "John Doe, in trust for Johnny Doe."

Life Insurance

The proceeds of life insurance are rarely subject to probate administration, unless the insured's estate is the beneficiary or all of the named beneficiaries pre-decease the insured.

Lifetime Gifts

Even gifts made shortly prior to death will avoid probate. However, they may be brought back into the estate for death tax purposes. Also, gifts carry the donor's basis to the donee, whereas appreciated assets in the decedent's estate will generally get a new or stepped-up basis.[1]

---

[1] Under the Tax Act of 2001, the rules regarding basis of inherited property will change for individuals dying in 2010. If Congress does not act at that time to repeal these rules for the years following, they will automatically revert back to the rules in effect during the year 2001.

Continued...

Avoiding Probate

Revocable Living Trust

The revocable living trust is an effective method of avoiding probate. It has the additional advantage of providing management of the funds for the heirs for some time after the decedent's demise. Also, in the event the person setting up the living trust (also called an inter-vivos trust) becomes mentally incompetent or otherwise incapacitated, a successor trustee can take over management of the estate. Generally, this type of trust will not produce any estate tax savings.

Transfer on Death (TOD)

Many states have adopted the provisions of the Uniform TOD Security Registration Act, which permits securities and securities accounts to be registered so that ownership automatically passes to named beneficiaries at the death of the owner(s).

Transfer on Death

Many states have adopted a version of the Uniform TOD Security Registration Act. TOD is an acronym that stands for "transfer on death". The provisions of the Act permit securities and securities accounts to be registered so that ownership automatically passes to named beneficiaries upon the death of the owner or the last-to-die of multiple owners. In general, the result is a simplified, nonprobate transfer similar to pay-on-death (POD) transfers of bank accounts or Totten trusts. Assets transferred via TOD registration generally receive a full step-up in cost basis.

In the case of multiple owners, the property must be titled so that ownership will vest in the survivor of them before the asset passes to the named beneficiary. Thus, the owners may hold the property as joint tenants, as tenants by the entireties, or as "owners of community property held in survivorship form." A disadvantage of multiple ownership is that all parties must sign for any future account changes.

Beneficiary Designations

Beneficiary designations determine who receives the assets at death. The Act allows naming a contingent beneficiary to receive the assets if the beneficiary fails to survive. It also provides that "lineal descendants per stirpes[1]" may be substitute beneficiaries.

Acronyms Approved in Statute	Example of Use
TOD = transfer on death	John S. Doe TOD John S. Doe, Jr.
POD = pay on death	John S. Doe POD John S. Doe, Jr.
JT TEN = joint tenants	John S. Doe Mary B. Doe JT TEN TOD John S. Doe, Jr.
SUB BENE = substitute beneficiary	John S. Doe TOD John S. Doe, Jr. SUB BENE Peter Doe
LDPS = lineal descendants per stirpes	John S. Doe Mary B. Doe TOD John S. Doe, Jr. LDPS

Creditor and Third-Party Claims

Generally, the Act does not provide any protection against the claims of third parties such as creditors, or individuals with other interests, such as a spouse's community property interest. A creditor or other party asserting a conflicting interest can do so simply by giving notice to the registering entity (the broker-dealer). As a practical matter, this will usually block transfer of the asset until the conflict is resolved.

Seek Professional Guidance

As a general rule, TOD registration as an estate planning tool is most useful in smaller estates, those without estate tax problems, or in situations involving a single estate owner with a single beneficiary. Estate owners are advised to seek the advice and counsel of a competent estate planning attorney in their state of residence before making any decisions regarding the use of TOD registration.

---

[1] "Per stirpes" is a Latin term meaning "in the stirrups of." In estate planning it refers to a common method of dividing an estate among the heirs of an estate owner.

Holding Title

Separate Property

Property owned by either a husband or wife that is not owned by the other is called separate property. This generally includes property acquired by either spouse prior to marriage, by gift, will or inheritance, or as money damages for personal injury, and all of the rents, issues and profits thereof.

Community Property

Both real and personal property earned or accumulated during marriage through the efforts of either husband or wife living together in a community property state. Deceased spouse's will has control over one-half of the community property.

Community Property With Right of Survivorship

Both real and personal property earned or accumulated during marriage through the efforts of either husband or wife living together in a community property state. At the first death, title automatically passes to the surviving spouse by operation of law.

Joint Tenancy

Joint ownership of equal shares by two or more persons with right of survivorship. A person's last will has no effect upon such joint tenancy assets.

Tenancy by the Entirety

Joint ownership of an asset between a husband and wife (with right of survivorship) that generally cannot be terminated without the consent of both parties.

Tenancy in Common

Ownership by two or more persons who hold undivided interests without right of survivorship. Interests need not be equal and will pass under the terms of the owner's will.

Severalty

Ownership held by one person only. This can be a natural person or a legal person, such as a corporation.

Continued

Holding Title

Tenancy-in-Partnership

Method by which property is owned by a partnership. Specific interest in the property cannot be conveyed by one partner alone.

Custodian for a Minor

Under the Uniform Gifts to Minors Act or Uniform Transfers to Minors Act, an adult person can hold title to property for the benefit of a minor.

Trustee

The trustee of a living or testamentary trust holds legal title to property for beneficiaries, who have equitable title.

Life Estate

A use of ownership in real property that terminates upon the death of the life tenant.

Note: Advice as to how to hold title to specific assets is the practice of law. These laws vary from state to state.

Joint Tenancy

Could joint tenancy, one of the most common forms of holding title to assets, lead to an estate planning disaster for your heirs? Joint tenancy is a form of holding equal interests in an asset by two or more persons. If one joint tenant dies, his or her share generally passes automatically to the other joint tenant by right of survivorship.

Advantages of Joint Tenancy

- **Probate avoidance:** Title to assets held in joint tenancy passes automatically at the death of one joint tenant to the others. There is no need for a formal probate (unless all the joint tenants die).

- **Convenience:** Bank accounts held in joint tenancy can be withdrawn by any joint tenant. This may be an advantage if one party becomes incompetent due to an accident, a stroke, advanced age, etc.

Potential Disadvantages of Joint Tenancy

- **Loss of control:** Your will (or trust) will have no effect on joint tenancy assets, even if you change your mind as to the persons you would like to receive your share when you die. Also, the entire asset may be available to the creditors of either joint tenant.

- **Assets may not reach your children:** Quite often assets passing to a surviving joint tenant spouse end up in joint tenancy with a new spouse. The new spouse may ultimately receive all of the assets rather than your children.

  Also, if the first joint tenant to die had children of a prior marriage they can be easily cut out of any inheritance by the surviving joint tenant.

- **Potential tax problems**
  - **Gift tax:** The creation of a joint tenancy in some assets may be subject to gift taxation if the value exceeds the $12,000 annual gift tax exclusion.[1] Gifts to one's spouse are generally not taxable.
  - **Estate tax:** A credit shelter trust is often used to reduce estate taxes when a married couple dies. Holding assets in joint tenancy can completely upset this type of estate tax planning, by passing assets outside the trust.
  - **Income tax:** When appreciated assets are sold, a "capital gains" tax is generally paid on the difference between the cost basis and the appreciated sales price. Assets included in one's estate receive a new, stepped-up cost basis at the time of death, namely the value at which the assets are included in the decedent's estate.[2] If these assets are then sold at this higher value, there is no gain, and thus no capital gains tax is due. However, assets held in joint tenancy title receive only a partial step-up in basis, on the decedent's share. IRC Sec. 1014(b)(9). If the decedent owns the asset alone or as community property, the basis of the entire asset will be stepped-up. See IRC Secs. 1014(a) and 1014(b)(6).

Note: State income tax laws should also be examined before changing the form of ownership.

---

[1] The annual gift tax exclusion ($12,000 in 2008) is indexed for inflation in increments of $1,000.
[2] This applies to persons dying in years other than 2010. For deaths during 2010, there will be a limit on the step up in basis.

Continued.

Joint Tenancy

Dissolving an Unwanted Joint Tenancy

After careful examination, if it is decided to dissolve a joint tenancy in real property, it is generally done by creating a new deed by which the joint tenants transfer their interests to themselves as tenants in common or community property.

It may also be possible to change title by a separate written agreement between the parties. Since the transfer of real estate is governed by the law of the state in which it is situated, local legal counsel should be sought prior to any change of title.

Note: The changing of title to assets can have very serious tax consequences and should be undertaken only after competent professional advice.

Should One Hold Appreciated Assets in Community Property or Joint Tenancy?

For Persons Owning Real Property or Appreciated Personal Property in Community Property States

(AK, AZ, CA, ID, LA, NM, NV, TX, WA, WI)

Assumptions:
You bought land as an investment in 1975 for $40,000 (your basis). Today, it is worth $220,000.

Capital Gains

If you were to sell the land today for $220,000, you would incur a taxable gain on $180,000, the difference between your basis ($40,000) and your sale price ($220,000). Such profits are subject to income tax at capital gains rates.

Stepped-Up Basis

If, instead, you died and your surviving spouse then sold the land, the tax picture would be different. At the date of death, IRC Sec. 1014(b) permits the basis of a decedent's property to be stepped-up to its value as of date of death.[1]

The Surviving Spouse's Half of the Investment

If the title is in joint tenancy, the survivor's share will retain its original cost basis. In our example this would be $20,000. (See IRC Sec. 1014(b)(9).) If the title is in community property, the survivor's share will get a stepped-up basis. In our example this would be $110,000. See IRC Sec. 1014(b)(6).

	If Joint Tenancy		If Community Property	
	Decedent	**Survivor**	**Decedent**	**Survivor**
Original Cost Basis	$20,000	$20,000	$20,000	$20,000
Today's Value	$110,000	$110,000	$110,000	$110,000
- Death Occurs -	-	-	-	-
Basis of Decedent's Half	$110,000	-	$110,000	-
Basis of Survivor's Half	-	$20,000	-	$110,000
Taxable Amount (capital gain if sold by survivor for $220,000)	$0	$90,000	$0	$0
Total Taxable Amount	$90,000		$0	

The result: If the land were sold shortly after death, holding title in joint tenancy could subject $90,000 to income tax, as shown above.

---

[1] For persons dying in the year 2010, there will be a limit on the step up in basis, under current law.

750

Revocable Living Trust
(Inter-vivos Trusts)

A trust is created when one person (the trustor or grantor) transfers to another person or a corporation (the trustee) a property interest to be held for the benefit of himself or others (the beneficiaries).

If the trust is created during the trustor's lifetime, rather than in his will, it is an inter-vivos or living trust. When the trustor retains the right to dissolve the trust arrangement, it is a revocable living trust.

What Are Some of the Advantages?

- Assets in the trust are not subject to probate administration. This usually saves executor's and attorney's fees. It also grants more privacy as to who gets the trust assets, when they receive them and how much they get.

- Professional management is available if the trustor becomes incompetent, disabled or wants to be free of the worries of management.

- Should the trustor (also usually the original trustee) die, or be unable to serve, a successor trustee can step in and manage the trust assets without delay or red tape.

- Annual court accountings, with accompanying legal fees, are not required, although some states do not require annual accountings for testamentary trusts (will trusts), either.

- The trustee can collect life insurance proceeds immediately after the trustor dies and can (if permitted under the trust document) use the proceeds to care for family members without any need for court approval.

What Are Some of the Disadvantages?

- Creditors may not be cut off as quickly as they are in probated estates; e.g., four months in some states.

- A little more effort is required to transfer assets into the trust and records should be kept of transactions by the trustee.

- The attorney usually charges a higher fee to establish a living trust, as opposed to a will with a testamentary trust. There may also be ongoing administrative charges.

Note: Assets in a revocable living trust are included in one's gross estate for federal estate tax purposes.

Funding Your Revocable Living Trust

Many people have established living trusts in an effort to avoid probate administration, reduce death taxes, or provide management of assets for minor children.

A great number of these trusts are completely unfunded. In other words, title to the person's assets has never been transferred into the name of the trust. In order to avoid probate, the assets must be in the trust (the trust must be the legal owner of the assets) at the time the estate owner dies. Individuals who have established living trusts should periodically check the title of their assets to verify that they are held in the trust name.

- Savings and loan and bank accounts can be easily changed into the trust name by the institution.

- Real estate is generally transferred into the trust name by having an attorney prepare a new deed.

- Promissory notes and deeds of trust can be assigned to the trust.

- Personal effects, furniture, furnishings, clothing, jewelry and items that have no certificate of ownership can be transferred with a deed of gift or assignment of personal property.

- A stockbroker can assist you in transferring your securities.

- Certificates of limited partnership should be examined for instructions and requirements for making the transfer.

- Closely held corporation stock must be changed into the trustee's name. If there is a buy-sell agreement, it must be reviewed for any prohibition against this type of transfer. Also, if the corporation is either an S corporation or a professional corporation, special rules must be followed.

- General partnership interests can be put into the trust if the partnership agreement permits such transfers.

- Sole proprietorships require a bill of sale or an assignment of interest, which includes the goodwill of the business.

- Life insurance proceeds made payable to the living trust will be managed for the benefit of your heirs along with the other assets in the trust until such time as they are to be distributed.

- Qualified plan benefits and IRAs should be paid to the surviving spouse, if living; otherwise they may be paid to the living trust. Retirement benefits paid to a living trust will be subject to faster payout requirements unless the trust is also qualified as a designated beneficiary trust.

Note: Check with an attorney concerning all transfers to your trust. The transfer of various assets after death with an affidavit may be permitted.

Durable Power of Attorney

A power of attorney is a written document which one person (the principal) uses to empower another person (the agent or attorney-in-fact) to act on his or her behalf.

**Principal
(competent adult)**

**Agent
(attorney-in-fact)**

Powers Which May Be Included

Non-Tax Powers	Tax-Related Powers
• To buy, sell or lease assets • To sue on the principal's behalf • To collect from creditors • To change provisions in a living trust • To operate the principal's business	• The power to make gifts to the spouse (to equalize the estates) and to children, grandchildren, etc. (to utilize the annual gift tax exclusions) • The power to make disclaimers • The power to create living trusts to benefit the principal, spouse and heirs • The power to complete transfers to a living trust if the principal becomes incompetent • The power to join the competent spouse in signing income and gift tax returns • The power to exercise special powers of appointment

Additional Considerations

Some powers, such as the power to execute and revoke a will, can not be given to another individual. In addition, powers of attorney are usually notarized and those affecting real property may need to be recorded.

A power can be a "general" power, giving the agent all powers held by the principal; a "limited" power restricts the agent to performing only those actions specifically listed.

The document can be written to empower the agent now, or to become effective only upon the occurrence of a specific event, such as the principal's incapacity (sometimes referred to as a "springing" power). A durable power of attorney may save the often-considerable costs of a conservatorship. A conservatorship, however, has the benefit of court supervision.

Note: Significant powers may be granted under a power of attorney. Before using a preprinted form, legal advice should be obtained.

Who Makes Medical Decisions When I Cannot?

Today's advanced medical technology allows physicians to keep a person "alive" in situations that formerly would have resulted in death. Individuals who do not wish their lives to be prolonged by such artificial techniques must plan ahead and put their desires in writing.

In the now famous case of <u>Cruzan v. Dir. Mo. Dept. of Health</u>, 110 S. Ct. 2841 1990, the U.S. Supreme Court held that a state may demand clear and convincing proof of a person's wish to refuse or withdraw medical support. Ms. Cruzan was an accident victim who had not made clear her desire to have medical support withdrawn. Because of this failure, she could have been kept alive, in a vegetative state, for years, at an estimated cost of $200,000 per year.

When Should Medical Treatment Be Withheld?

As the following examples are read, one might ask, "Would I want medical support withdrawn in this situation?"

- In a coma with no hope of recovery

- In a coma with a small likelihood of recovery with permanent brain damage

- Afflicted with brain damage or disease, severe in nature, and a terminal illness

- Afflicted with brain damage or disease, severe in nature, but without terminal illness

In these situations, and others, difficult decisions must be made as to the treatment to be provided or withheld (for example, artificial respiration, medicine, food, water, etc.).

When a patient is incapable of expressing his or her wishes, some other way must be found to guide the decision making process. The "living will" and "durable power of attorney for health care" (advance health care directives) are useful in this regard.

Living Will

Most states recognize some form of what has been called a "living will", or "directive to physicians." Such a document sets down in writing a person's wishes as to the type of medical treatment to be provided, or withheld, and the general circumstances under which the directive applies.

Durable Power of Attorney for Health Care

Many states also have provision for a durable power of attorney for health care, which allows an individual to appoint another person to make health care decisions for them if they became unable to do so. The agent is generally empowered to make decisions beyond end-of-life issues, such as admission to a nursing home, consent for surgical operations, and care in the event of senility or other disability.

Advance Health Care Directives
End-of-Life Decision Making

Modern medicine can now keep a person alive in situations that, in years past, would have resulted in the individual's death. Frequently, a patient in such a condition is unable to communicate his or her wishes with regard to the type of medical care to be provided. In the absence of any other guidance, the attending physician will typically use all available means to keep the individual alive, even when death is certain, with no hope of recovery.

However, many individuals feel that once death is inevitable, life should not be artificially prolonged through the use of such technology. The decision to start or withdraw such life-sustaining support, although always difficult, can be made easier with advance planning.

The term "advance health care directives" is commonly used to describe two key documents (sometimes combined into one) designed to address these end-of-life decisions:

- **Living Will**

- **Durable Power of Attorney for Health Care**

Individual state law governs the use of these documents, and such legislation can vary widely. Individuals who live in more than one state may need to execute a living will and a durable power of attorney for health care for each state.

Living Will

A living will, also known as a "directive to physicians," is a written statement of the individual's health care wishes should he or she become seriously ill and unable to communicate. The document is designed to provide guidance to someone else appointed to make health care decisions for the individual, or to the attending physician if there is no health care agent. A living will might include:

- Directions as to pain medication.

- Directions as to when to provide, withhold, or withdraw artificial nutrition and hydration, and all other forms of health care, including cardiopulmonary resuscitation.

- A discussion of any religious beliefs that might impact medical treatment.

- Instructions for funeral and burial services.

Because it is impossible to foresee the future, the living will should be written in the broadest possible manner, to cover a wide range of situations.

Continued...

Advance Health Care Directives
End-of-Life Decision Making

Durable Power of Attorney for Health Care

In a durable power of attorney for health care, sometimes known as a "health care proxy," an individual (the principal) appoints another person (the agent) to make health care decisions if the principal is incapable of doing so.[1] A durable power of attorney may employ a "springing" power, which means that the power "springs" into life when the principal becomes incapacitated.[2] Additional powers granted to the agent could include:

- Access to medical records.
- Authority to transfer the principal to another facility or to another state.
- Ability to authorize a "Do Not Resuscitate" (DNR) order.
- Postmortem powers to dispose of the remains, to authorize an autopsy, or to donate all or part of the principal's body for transplant, education, or research purposes.

Other Points

- **Talk about the issues** - the individual should spend time talking with family, friends, clergy, and physician about his or her wishes in end-of-life decisions.
- **Make the documents available** – if a living will and/or a durable power of attorney exist, be sure that those involved know where to locate the documents.
- **Revocation** – an individual can generally revoke a living will or durable power of attorney at any time.

Additional Resources

Non-profit organizations such as the following provide support and education on end-of-life issues:

- **National Hospice and Palliative Care Organization** – (800) 658-8898, on the internet at: www.nhpco.org

Seek Professional Guidance

The counsel and guidance of legal, religious, and medical professionals is essential to the successful preparation of advance health care directives.

---

[1] Many states have provision in their laws for the appointment of a surrogate such as a spouse, domestic partner, or other close family member to make health care decisions for the principal, in situations where no durable power of attorney for health care exists.

[2] Under the Health Insurance Portability and Accountability Act (HIPAA), a physician is prohibited from discussing a patient's medical condition without the patient's consent. Thus, if an individual becomes incapacitated, the person named as agent under a durable power of attorney for health care may not have access to the principal's health-care information. Without this information, the agent would be unable to legally establish that the principal had become incapacitated, and would not be able to trigger any "springing" power. A HIPPA authorization can be used to give the agent access to the principal's health-care information.

Lifetime Gifts

Lifetime gifts and transfers at death are taxed using a tax schedule that has cumulatively progressive rates. Each taxable transfer, including the final transfer at death, begins in the tax bracket attained by the prior gift.

Prior to EGTRRA 2001, both lifetime gifts and transfers at death were taxed under a unified estate and gift tax system. Against this tax each taxpayer had a "unified credit" which could be used fully or in part during lifetime, with any remaining portion available at death. For 2001, for example, the unified credit was $220,550, equivalent to $675,000 of assets. EGTRRA 2001 however, introduced a "split" in the amount of assets exempt from tax, beginning in 2004. The table below shows how the exemption amount (the applicable exclusion amount) will change.

Calendar Year	At-death Exemption	Gift Tax Exemption
2002	$1,000,000	$1,000,000
2003	1,000,000	1,000,000
2004	1,500,000	1,000,000
2005	1,500,000	1,000,000
2006	2,000,000	1,000,000
2007	2,000,000	1,000,000
2008	2,000,000	1,000,000
2009	3,500,000	1,000,000
2010	Tax Repealed	1,000,000
2011	1,000,000	1,000,000

Because of a "sunset" provision in EGTRRA 2001, if Congress does not act to repeal the federal estate tax for years following 2010, the law will automatically revert back to its state in 2001 with an exemption for the first $1,000,000 of assets.

Annual Gift Tax Exclusion

Each taxpayer is allowed to transfer/gift a certain amount of assets each year, without concern for gift taxes. This "annual exclusion amount" is currently $12,000[1] per donor and a gift of this amount can be given to each of any number of donees. If husband and wife agree, they can "split" gifts and give twice this amount to each of any number of children, grandchildren, etc.

Marital Deduction

There is an unlimited marital deduction for gifts of separate or community property passing from one spouse to another. Transfers to spouses who are not U.S. citizens are not protected by the gift tax marital deduction, but a non-citizen spouse is entitled to a $128,000 (in 2008) per year special annual gift tax exclusion if such a gift would qualify for the marital deduction if the spouse were a U.S. citizen.

---

[1] The annual gift tax exclusion ($12,000 in 2008) is indexed for inflation in increments of $1,000.

Continued...

Lifetime Gifts

Educational or Medical Expenses

A donor may give, free of gift tax consequences, unlimited amounts for a donee's school tuition (not books, supplies, or other expenses) or qualified medical expenses. Such gifts must be made directly to the school or health care provider, and not to the donee.

Deductibility for Income Tax Purposes

Gifts or gift taxes are not deductible for income tax purposes, unless contributed to a qualified charity.

Gift Tax Returns

These returns are filed annually, generally by April 15 of the year following the gift for amounts in excess of the annual gift tax exclusion.

Includability of Gifts in the Estate

Gifts made within three years of death are not considered in the computation of the taxable estate. However, if they exceed the annual gift tax exclusion, they may be added to the taxable estate as adjusted taxable gifts. This, in effect, pushes the assets remaining in the taxable estate into the higher tax brackets; however, the appreciation on the assets from date of gift until date of death is not brought into the computation.

Gifts of life insurance policies, however, are still included if made within three years of death. Certain incomplete transfers (e.g., retained life estates, revocable transfers, etc.) will also be included in the gross estate without regard to when they were made.

All taxable transfers made within three years (except gifts that qualify for the annual gift tax exclusion) will be included for determining whether an estate qualifies for an IRC Sec. 303 stock redemption, the IRC Sec. 2032A special use valuation or the IRC Sec. 6166 deferral of estate tax payment. Restrictions on gifts also apply to the IRC Sec. 2057 qualified family-owned business interest deduction.

Advantages of Making Gifts

- Gifts put future appreciation of assets out of the estate.
- The gift tax paid reduces the taxable estate.[1]
- Making gifts of income-producing assets may reduce current income taxes.
- Probate administration is not necessary for gifted assets.
- The donor can see the beneficiaries enjoy the assets while he or she is still living.

---

[1] Under the Tax Act of 2001, the federal estate tax is gradually phased out until its final repeal in the year 2010. If Congress does not act at that time to repeal it for the years following, it will automatically revert back to the rates in effect during the year 2001, with an exemption for the first $1,000,000 of assets. If there is a possibility that the federal estate tax will be permanently repealed in 2011, it may not be prudent to make lifetime gifts that incur a gift tax, unless they fall within the applicable exclusion amount for gifts ($1,000,000 in 2002 and thereafter).

The Federal Gift Tax

Assumptions:
Year intended gift is made: 2008
Value of intended gift (in excess of the annual gift tax exclusion amount)[1]: $1,000,000
Value of taxable gifts made in prior years: $ 100,000
Applicable (unified) credit used in prior years: $10,000

Item Description	Value
Total current and prior taxable gifts	$1,100,000
Total gift tax computed on current and prior taxable gifts	$ 386,800
Total gift tax computed on prior taxable gifts only	23,800
Tentative tax due on this gift (difference)	$ 363,000
Applicable (unified) credit available for this gift	$ 345,800
Applicable (unified) credit used in prior years	10,000
Remaining credit applied to this gift (no greater than tax due)	$ 335,800
Net gift tax due	**$27,200**

---

[1] Does not include gifts to spouse or charity, or gifts of less than the annual exclusion amount to any number of persons. The annual gift tax exclusion ($12,000 in 2008) is indexed for inflation in increments of $1,000.

Annual Exclusion Gifts
Reducing the Federal Estate Tax

By following a consistent program of annual lifetime gifts to children, grandchildren, etc., an estate owner can dramatically reduce his or her taxable estate. The following chart illustrates the results of such a gifting program. It assumes that the gifts are made at the beginning of each year and will grow at 6% annually outside the parent's estate. A person can give up to $12,000[1] per year to any number of people without incurring a gift tax.

Annual Gift	Number of Years Over Which Gifts Are Made				
	5 Years	10 Years	15 Years	20 Years	25 Years
$12,000	$71,704	$167,660	$296,070	$467,913	$697,877
24,000	143,408	335,319	592,141	935,825	1,395,753
36,000	215,111	502,979	888,211	1,403,738	2,093,630
48,000	286,815	670,639	1,184,281	1,871,651	2,791,506
60,000	358,519	838,299	1,480,352	2,339,564	3,489,383
72,000	430,223	1,005,958	1,776,422	2,807,476	4,187,260
84,000	501,927	1,173,618	2,072,492	3,275,389	4,885,136
96,000	573,631	1,341,278	2,368,563	3,743,302	5,583,013
108,000	645,334	1,508,937	2,664,633	4,211,214	6,280,889
120,000	717,038	1,676,597	2,960,703	4,679,127	6,978,766

_____	x	_____%	= _____
Potential amount removed from your estate (See chart above.)		Estimated top estate tax bracket (See below.)	Approximate savings which could pass to your heirs

Top Federal Estate Tax Brackets

Years	Top Bracket	Applied to Amounts Over...
2001	55%	$3,000,000
2002	50%	2,500,000
2003	49%	2,000,000
2004	48%	2,000,000
2005	47%	2,000,000
2006	46%	2,000,000
2007-2009	45%	1,500,000
2010	0%	0
2011	55%	3,000,000

Note: If some of the annual gift amounts are used to purchase life insurance outside of the estate, the potential wealth-building effect becomes very dramatic.

Beginning in 2002, the applicable exclusion amount for gifts is $1,000,000 even if the federal estate tax is repealed in 2010.

---

[1] The annual gift tax exclusion ($12,000 in 2008) is indexed for inflation in increments of $1,000.

Effect of Annual Exclusion Gifting Program

This calculation assumes that the sunset provision of the Economic Growth and Tax Relief Reconciliation Act of 2001 will take effect.

Assumptions:
Current net estate size: $1,000,000
Estimated estate growth rate: 4.50%
Estimated year of (second) death: 10
Number of donors: 1
Number of persons to receive gifts: 2
Level annual amount per donor to each beneficiary: $ 555

Item Description	Value
Total gifts first year	$1,110
Number of years gifts will continue	5
Total gifts	**$5,550**
Growth during the gifting period	**$ 796**
Growth after the gifting period	**$1,562**
Total amount removed from the estate	**$7,908**

	Without Gifts	With Gifts
Potential estate size at death	$1,552,969	$1,545,061
Federal estate tax on estate	$ 233,836	$ 230,278
Potential savings from gift program		**$3,559**

Federal Gift Taxes After 2009

Assuming Congress Fails to Repeal FET

For taxpayers dying after 2009, there will continue to be a federal gift tax on total gifts in excess of the annual gift tax exclusion of $12,000 (per donor, per donee, per year).[1] The lifetime exemption amount is $1,000,000, which can be used to offset gifts that exceed the annual exclusion limits.

The table below is applied to this total amount of current and prior gifts to determine whether a gift tax is due. The applicable exclusion amount ($330,800) and any prior gift taxes paid will be applied to determine the amount of gift tax due, if any.

If Taxable Gift...		Tentative Tax Is...		
Is Over...	But Not Over...	Tax	Plus %	Of Excess Over...
$0	$10,000	$0	18%	$0
10,000	20,000	1,800	20%	10,000
20,000	40,000	3,800	22%	20,000
40,000	60,000	8,200	24%	40,000
60,000	80,000	13,000	26%	60,000
80,000	100,000	18,200	28%	80,000
100,000	150,000	23,800	30%	100,000
150,000	250,000	38,800	32%	150,000
250,000	500,000	70,800	34%	250,000
500,000		155,800	35%	500,000

Worksheet for Gifts Made After 2009

1. Current taxable gifts[2] $ _____
2. Prior taxable gifts $ _____
3. **Total taxable gifts**
   (item 1 plus item 2) $ _____
4. Gift tax
   (See table above.) $ _____
5. Applicable exclusion amount ($330,800)
6. **Remaining tax**
   (item 4 less item 5) $ _____
7. Gift tax paid in prior years $ _____
8. **Net gift tax due**
   (item 6 less item 7) $ _____

---

[1] The annual gift tax exclusion ($12,000 in 2008) is indexed for inflation in increments of $1,000.
[2] Current taxable gifts would be those in excess of the annual exclusion, those to charity and those to one's spouse.

Tax-Free Gifts and Bequests
If Congress Fails to Repeal FET after 2010[1]

Gifts made during lifetime or bequests at time of death may be subject to federal gift or estate taxes if they exceed certain exempt amounts.

Under the Tax Law of 2001, these exempt amounts are subject to the following phase-in schedule:

Millions

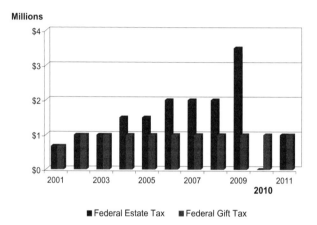

■ Federal Estate Tax   ■ Federal Gift Tax

Amounts subject to federal gift taxes during lifetime are those that exceed the annual gift tax exclusion amount of $12,000[2] (per donor, per donee, per year). Taxable lifetime gifts from prior years must be added to current gifts to determine when the exemption amount has been exceeded.

In calculating the federal estate tax, any taxable lifetime gifts are added back into the estate prior to determining the tax due. A credit is allowed for any gift tax actually paid during lifetime.

---

[1] During the year 2010, there is no federal estate tax. Lifetime gifts, however, continue to be subject to the $1,000,000 exemption amount.
[2] The annual gift tax exclusion ($12,000 in 2008) is indexed for inflation in increments of $1,000.

IRC Sec. 2503(c) Trust for Minors

Estate owners often seek to reduce the size of their estates by making gifts to their minor children or grandchildren. Because most minors cannot manage such gifts, there is a need to provide supervision for gifted assets until the donees reach adulthood.

One possible solution is to set up a trust, with minor children or grandchildren as trust beneficiaries. Because assets in a trust are typically not distributed to the beneficiaries until a future date, such gifts are usually considered to be gifts of a "future" interest.

The Gift Tax Problem

Gifts in excess of $12,000 per donor[1] to any donee are subject to a gift tax. Gifts under $12,000 may be subject to gift taxes if they are considered to be a future interest instead of a present interest[2] to the beneficiary.

IRC Sec. 2503(c) provides an exception to the general rule that gifts made in trust are gifts of a future interest. Gifts meeting the requirements of this code section qualify as gifts of a present interest, and thus qualify for the annual gift tax exclusion of $12,000.

The Requirements of IRC Sec. 2503(c)

- Principal and income may be expended for the minor by the trustee[3] before the minor reaches age 21[4].

- Any principal and income not expended will pass to the minor at age 21.

- Should the minor die prior to age 21, the trust principal and any accumulated income will be paid to the minor's estate or to whomever he or she appoints.

Income Tax Issues

Trust income is taxable to the trust or, if distributed, to the minor. However, for certain children, unearned income in excess of $1,800 per year is subject to taxation at the parents' top marginal income tax bracket.[5]

Seek Professional Guidance

When considering gifts to minors, the advice and counsel of professional estate and income tax specialists is strongly recommended.

---

[1] Gifts meeting the requirements of IRC Sec. 2503(b) qualify for an annual gift tax exclusion of $12,000 per donee (2008). Client and spouse can combine gifts for a total of $24,000.

[2] A gift generally qualifies as a "present interest" if the recipient has an unrestricted right to use, enjoy, or possess the gift.

[3] The trustee's ability to distribute funds for the benefit of the minor(s) should not be restricted.

[4] Local state law may provide that an individual reaches his or her majority at an age younger than 21. The gift tax exclusion of IRC Sec. 2503(c), however, is based on an individual reaching age 21.

[5] The Small Business and Work Opportunity Tax Act of 2007 expanded the "kiddie tax" to include a child up to age 18, or a child who is a full-time student age 19 to 23. Children who are age 18 or who are full-time students age 19-23, and whose earned income exceeds one-half of the amount of their support, are exempt from the tax. This legislation is effective for tax years beginning after May 25, 2007. State or local law may vary.

How an IRC Sec. 2503(c) Trust Works

A donor may seek to reduce the size of his or her estate by gifting assets to minor children or grandchildren. If the gifts are made through a trust, a trustee can manage the assets until the children reach adulthood. If the trust meets the requirements of IRC Sec. 2503(c), gifts to the trust qualify for the annual gift tax exclusion of $12,000 per year.

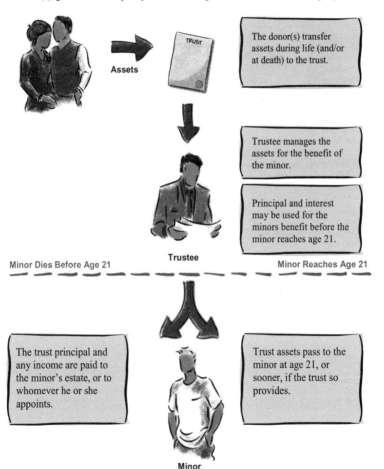

Assets

The donor(s) transfer assets during life (and/or at death) to the trust.

Trustee manages the assets for the benefit of the minor.

Principal and interest may be used for the minors benefit before the minor reaches age 21.

Minor Dies Before Age 21   **Trustee**   **Minor Reaches Age 21**

The trust principal and any income are paid to the minor's estate, or to whomever he or she appoints.

Trust assets pass to the minor at age 21, or sooner, if the trust so provides.

Minor

Note: The annual gift tax exclusion ($12,000 in 2008) is indexed for inflation in increments of $1,000.

Uniform Gifts to Minors Act

The Uniform Gifts to Minors Act (UGMA) provides a simple and inexpensive method of making gifts to minors, which will qualify as a present interest for the annual gift tax exclusion of $12,000 per year for each minor.[1]

Transfer assets during lifetime or at death to a custodian	For the benefit of a Minor	
Donor	**Custodian**	**Minor**

The asset is placed in the name of an adult as custodian under the UGMA. Legal title, however, vests in the minor.

The custodian is to use the assets during the child's minority for support, education and maintenance of the minor.

The custodianship terminates when the child reaches his majority, which is 18 in most states.

Assets that can be conveyed under UGMA are generally limited to money, securities, life insurance and annuity contracts.

Income on the assets is taxable to the minor, whether distributed or accumulated. For certain children, unearned income in excess of $1,800 is subject to taxation at the parents' top marginal income tax bracket.[2]

If the donor appoints himself custodian, the assets will be part of his estate should he die before distribution to the minor. To remove the asset from the gross taxable estate, a third party should be named as custodian. See Rev. Rul. 57-366, 1957-2 CB 618; Rev. Rul. 59-357, 1959-2 CB 212.[3]

Note: Almost all states have changed to UTMA, which is more flexible as to distribution ages and assets which can be held in custodial name.

---

[1] The annual gift tax exclusion ($12,000 in 2008) is indexed for inflation in increments of $1,000.

[2] The Small Business and Work Opportunity Tax Act of 2007 expanded the "kiddie tax" to include a child up to age 18, or a child who is a full-time student age 19 to 23. Children who are age 18 or who are full-time students age 19-23, and whose earned income exceeds one-half of the amount of their support, are exempt from the tax. This legislation is effective for tax years beginning after May 25, 2007. State or local law may vary.

[3] Under the Tax Act of 2001, the federal estate tax is gradually phased out until its final repeal in the year 2010. If Congress does not act at that time to repeal it for the years following, it will automatically revert back to the rates in effect during the year 2001, with an exemption for the first $1,000,000 of assets.

Uniform Transfers to Minors Act

The Uniform Transfers to Minor's Act (UTMA) provides a simple and inexpensive method of making a gift or bequest to a minor without the expense of a trust.

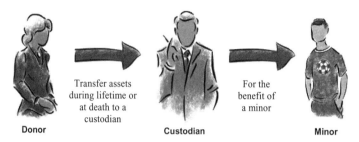

Donor

Transfer assets
during lifetime or
at death to a
custodian

Custodian

For the
benefit of
a minor

Minor

Duties of the Custodian

- Collect, hold, manage, invest and reinvest the assets.
- Deal with assets as a prudent person would.

Payments by Custodian

- Make payments to the minor (or for his or her benefit) in whatever amounts the custodian considers advisable.
- Consideration need not be made as to:
  - Another's duty or ability to support the minor, or
  - Any other income available to the minor.

Life Insurance Rules for Policies Held in Custodianship

- Life or endowment policies on the minor's life must name his or her estate as the sole beneficiary.
- The minor, his or her estate, or the custodian (as custodian for the minor) must be the irrevocable beneficiary of policies on the life of someone other than the minor.

Termination of a Custodianship

The custodianship is generally ended when the minor becomes of age (18 or 21). A few states have provisions allowing the custodianship to be extended to age 25.[1] Some states permit the donor to select any age between 18 and 21 to distribute the assets.

---

[1] If the donor specifies that the custodianship will extend past the child's reaching age 21, the transfer will not qualify as a gift of a present interest.

Continued...

Uniform Transfers to Minors Act

Further Considerations

- Both real and personal property can be transferred.

- The donor may be the custodian. Sometimes a transfer of possession and control to a third party is necessary to establish one's intent to complete the transfer. If notice is given to the appropriate third person (e.g., bank, insurance company, etc.) or is made a public record, as with the recording of a deed, the donor can be the custodian. However, if the donor dies prior to distributing the assets to the minor, the value of the assets will be included in his or her gross estate.

- A transfer may be for only one minor and only one person may act as custodian at a time. Successor custodians may be appointed. Title to the property vests in the minor and he or she is subject to income tax on the earnings or gain. For certain children, unearned income in excess of $1,800 is subject to taxation at the parents' top marginal income tax bracket.[1]

- These rules may vary slightly from state to state.

---

[1] The Small Business and Work Opportunity Tax Act of 2007 expanded the "kiddie tax" to include a child up to age 18, or a child who is a full-time student age 19 to 23. Children who are age 18 or who are full-time students age 19-23, and whose earned income exceeds one-half of the amount of their support, are exempt from the tax. This legislation is effective for tax years beginning after May 25, 2007. State or local law may vary.

How a Custodial Account Works
Gifts under the UGMA or UTMA

A custodial account provides a simple and inexpensive method of making gifts to minors.

Donor   **Donor's Assets**

The doner transfers the assets during his or her lifetime (or at death) to the custodian.

Custodian

The custodian manages the assets for the benefit of the minor child.

Adulthood

Title generally passes to the minor, when he or she reaches adulthood (under state law).

Adult Child

Special Needs Trust

In order to preserve the public assistance benefits of a person with a disability, such as a child with a developmental disability, etc., many people use a special needs trust.

Medicaid, which pays medical expenses for the poor, has limits on the amount of assets that a recipient can own or can earn during each year that welfare benefits are paid.

In order to qualify for the program prior to spending down one's estate, some individuals attempt to give their assets to relatives or invest them into an exempt form, such as a personal residence in which the spouse resides. Single persons sometimes transfer their residence to their children and retain the right to live in the house for the remainder of their lifetime.

The law denies persons eligibility for Medicaid benefits if assets were transferred less than 60 months[1] before applying for benefits. This is a complicated, changing area of the law.

Trusts for Children with Disabilities

A parent of a child with a disability should review each asset to see whether or not it will pass to that child at time of the parent's death. For example, life insurance, annuities, IRAs, pension benefits, joint bank accounts, etc., often pass to persons other than those named in one's will or trust. If such assets pass to a disabled child, however, he or she may lose current government benefits.

One must also decide whether or not to disinherit a child with a disability or use a special-needs type of trust.

Special needs trusts are generally established by the parents or other relatives of the disabled child. The trustee should have absolute discretion over how to expend the trust funds for the benefit of the disabled child.

- **Government benefits** - Government benefits should be used to meet basic needs such as food, clothing, and shelter.

- **Special needs trust** - The funds from the trust should be used for supplementary needs such as utilities, medical care, special equipment, education, job training or entertainment.

Seek Professional Guidance

Since the laws in this area are very complex and vary from state to state, experienced, knowledgeable legal counsel should be retained to draft the appropriate documents.

---

[1] Effective February 8, 2006, the Deficit Reduction Act of 2005 significantly tightened the requirements to qualify for Medicaid.

How a Special Needs Trust Works

Special needs trusts allow family members to provide some benefits to a disabled child without causing him or her to lose government benefits.

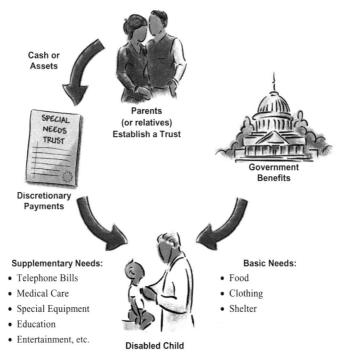

Cash or Assets

SPECIAL NEEDS TRUST

Parents (or relatives) Establish a Trust

Government Benefits

Discretionary Payments

Supplementary Needs:
- Telephone Bills
- Medical Care
- Special Equipment
- Education
- Entertainment, etc.

Disabled Child

Basic Needs:
- Food
- Clothing
- Shelter

Items to Consider

- Parents can act as the trustees
- Trust should be separate from the family trust
- The trust may be revocable or irrevocable
- Final beneficiaries should be named to receive the trust assets after the disabled child dies
- Family members should discuss the future management of the trust and how it will be funded

This is a highly specialized document and should be drafted by an attorney who is experienced in the areas of disability, government benefits, and estate planning.

Estate Summary
Simple Will

In the absence of a simple will, state law will pass property to certain relatives of a deceased party. The state will also appoint a guardian for minor children. The court may also require a fiduciary bond to be posted by the administrator of the estate, at a cost to the estate.

A simple will allows a person to select the executor of an estate, bequeath specific items or a specific amount to individuals or organizations, and to select the guardian for minor children.

The following illustrates the estate tax consequences with only a simple will in place.

At Elle 's death in 2012		At Luke's death in 2017	
Gross estate	$ 164,967	Gross estate	$ 660,026
Debt	- 11,110	Debt	0
Taxes[1] and fees	- 28,407	Taxes and fees	-382,967
		ILIT	0
Assets to partner	116,296		
Amount to Others	**$9,154**	**Total to Heirs**	**$ 277,059**

At Luke's death in 2017

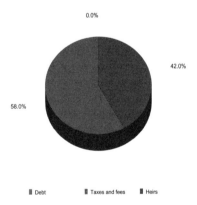

0.0%

42.0%

58.0%

▌ Debt   ▌ Taxes and fees   ▌ Heirs

---

[1] The federal estate tax estimates shown are based on estate and gift tax provisions contained in the Economic Growth and Tax Relief Reconciliation Act of 2001 (EGTRRA). Unless Congress changes the law, these provisions will be in effect only through 12/31/2010, after which prior law will be reinstated.

Estate Summary
Simple Will

In the absence of a simple will, state law will pass property to certain relatives of a deceased party. The state will also appoint a guardian for minor children. The court may also require a fiduciary bond to be posted by the administrator of the estate, at a cost to the estate.

A simple will allows a person to select the executor of an estate, bequeath specific items or a specific amount to individuals or organizations, and to select the guardian for minor children.

The following illustrates the estate tax consequences with only a simple will in place.

At Elle 's death in 2012

Gross estate	$ 164,967
Debt	- 11,110
Taxes[1] and fees	- 28,407
ILIT	0
Total to Heirs	**$ 125,450**

At Elle 's death in 2012

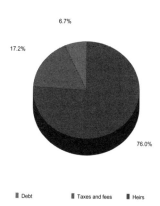

6.7%

17.2%

76.0%

▌ Debt   ▌ Taxes and fees   ▌ Heirs

---

[1] The federal estate tax estimates shown are based on estate and gift tax provisions contained in the Economic Growth and Tax Relief Reconciliation Act of 2001 (EGTRRA). Unless Congress changes the law, these provisions will be in effect only through 12/31/2010, after which prior law will be reinstated.

Estate Analysis
Simple Will

Elle 's Estate

	Value today	Assumed annual growth rate	Value in 5 years
Assets			
Joint Ownership			
Cash	$22	5.00%	$28
Other assets	22	5.00%	28
Residence	0	5.00%	0
Non - Joint Ownership			
Retirement plans	5,555	6.00%	7,434
Cash	55,511	5.00%	70,848
Other assets	55,511	5.00%	70,848
Residence	4,444	5.00%	5,672
Total Assets			154,857
Life insurance owned by Elle			10,110
Gross Estate			164,967
Less			
Debt			11,110
Final expenses			5,000
Administration fees			5,928
Probate fees			5,898
State estate tax deduction			0
Taxable Estate			137,032
Federal estate tax[1]			0
State tax			11,581
Estate after Taxes			**$ 125,450**

---

[1] The federal estate tax estimates shown are based on estate and gift tax provisions contained in the Economic Growth and Tax Relief Reconciliation Act of 2001 (EGTRRA). Unless Congress changes the law, these provisions will be in effect only through 12/31/2010, after which prior law will be reinstated.

Continued

Estate Analysis
Simple Will

Estate Taxes at Second Death

Luke's Estate

	Value today	Assumed annual growth rate	Value in 5 years
Assets			
Joint Ownership			
Cash	$22	5.00%	$28
Other assets	22	5.00%	28
Residence	0	5.00%	0
Non - Joint Ownership			
Retirement plans	55,555	6.00%	74,345
Cash	0	5.00%	0
Other assets	0	5.00%	0
Residence	0	5.00%	0
Total Assets Inside Estate			**74,401**

Life insurance proceeds payable to Luke	5,555
Assets from Elle 's estate	116,296
Total Assets	**196,253**
Asset growth rate assumed after first death	25.00%
Asset value at second death	598,916
Insurance owned by Luke	61,110
Gross Estate	**660,026**

Less	
Debt	0
Final expenses	5,000
Administration fees	23,990
Probate fees	23,960
State estate tax deduction	0
Taxable Estate	**607,077**

Federal estate tax[1]	0
State tax	330,018
Irrevocable life insurance trust	0
Total to Heirs	**$ 277,059**

---

[1] The federal estate tax estimates shown are based on estate and gift tax provisions contained in the Economic Growth and Tax Relief Reconciliation Act of 2001 (EGTRRA). Unless Congress changes the law, these provisions will be in effect only through 12/31/2010, after which prior law will be reinstated.

Estate Analysis
Simple Will

Elle 's Estate

	Value today	Assumed annual growth rate	Value in 5 years
Assets			
Retirement plans	$5,555	6.00%	$7,434
Cash	55,511	5.00%	70,848
Other assets	55,511	5.00%	70,848
Residence	4,444	5.00%	5,672
Total Assets			154,857
Life insurance owned by Elle			10,110
Gross Estate			164,967
Less			
Debt			11,110
Final expenses			5,000
Administration fees			5,928
Probate fees			5,898
State estate tax deduction			0
Taxable Estate			137,032
Federal estate tax[1]			0
State tax			11,581
Irrevocable life insurance trust			0
Total to Heirs			**$ 125,450**

---

[1] The federal estate tax estimates shown are based on estate and gift tax provisions contained in the Economic Growth and Tax Relief Reconciliation Act of 2001 (EGTRRA). Unless Congress changes the law, these provisions will be in effect only through 12/31/2010, after which prior law will be reinstated.

Estate Summary
Irrevocable Life Insurance Trust

All assets in an estate are subject to taxation. One way to have assets pass to heirs is to change ownership so that the assets are passed to the intended beneficiaries outside of the estate. Life insurance trusts are a way to increase the amount of your estate that passes to your heirs. The trust is irrevocable and serves as both the owner and beneficiary of the life insurance policy. Generally the grantor makes annual gifts to the trust and the trustee pays the premiums.

The following illustrates the use of an irrevocable life insurance trust.

At Elle 's death in 2012		**At Luke's death in 2017**	
Gross estate	$ 164,967	Gross estate	$ 660,026
Debt	- 11,110	Debt	0
Taxes[1] and fees	- 28,407	Taxes and fees	-382,967
		ILIT[2]	330,018
Assets to partner	116,296		
Amount to Others	**$9,154**	**Total to Heirs**	**$ 607,077**

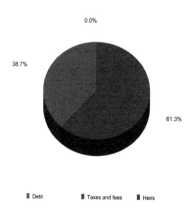

At Luke's death in 2017

0.0%

38.7%

61.3%

■ Debt   ■ Taxes and fees   ■ Heirs

---

[1] The federal estate tax estimates shown are based on estate and gift tax provisions contained in the Economic Growth and Tax Relief Reconciliation Act of 2001 (EGTRRA). Unless Congress changes the law, these provisions will be in effect only through 12/31/2010, after which prior law will be reinstated.

[2] The Life Insurance illustrated above assumes an annual premium of $18,151 that is payable for 3 years.

Estate Analysis
Irrevocable Life Insurance Trust

Elle 's Estate

	Value today	Assumed annual growth rate	Value in 5 years
Assets			
Joint Ownership			
Cash	$22	5.00%	$28
Other assets	22	5.00%	28
Residence	0	5.00%	0
Non - Joint Ownership			
Retirement plans	5,555	6.00%	7,434
Cash	55,511	5.00%	70,848
Other assets	55,511	5.00%	70,848
Residence	4,444	5.00%	5,672
Total Assets			**154,857**
Life insurance owned by Elle			10,110
Gross Estate			**164,967**
Less			
Debt			11,110
Final expenses			5,000
Administration fees			5,928
Probate fees			5,898
State estate tax deduction			0
Taxable Estate			**137,032**
Federal estate tax[1]			0
State tax			11,581
Estate after Taxes			**$ 125,450**

---

[1] The federal estate tax estimates shown are based on estate and gift tax provisions contained in the Economic Growth and Tax Relief Reconciliation Act of 2001 (EGTRRA). Unless Congress changes the law, these provisions will be in effect only through 12/31/2010, after which prior law will be reinstated.

Continued

Estate Analysis
Irrevocable Life Insurance Trust

Luke's Estate

	Value today	Assumed annual growth rate	Value in 5 years
Assets			
Joint Ownership			
Cash	$22	5.00%	$28
Other assets	22	5.00%	28
Residence	0	5.00%	0
Non - Joint Ownership			
Retirement plans	55,555	6.00%	74,345
Cash	0	5.00%	0
Other assets	0	5.00%	0
Residence	0	5.00%	0
Total Assets Inside Estate			**74,401**
Life insurance proceeds payable to Luke			5,555
Assets from Elle 's estate			116,296
Total Assets			**196,253**
Asset growth rate assumed after first death			25.00%
Asset value at second death			598,916
Insurance owned by Luke			61,110
Gross Estate			**660,026**
Less			
Debt			0
Final expenses			5,000
Administration fees			23,990
Probate fees			23,960
State estate tax deduction			0
Taxable Estate			**607,077**
Federal estate tax[1]			0
State tax			330,018
Irrevocable life insurance trust[2]			330,018
Total to Heirs			**$ 277,059**

---

[1] The federal estate tax estimates shown are based on estate and gift tax provisions contained in the Economic Growth and Tax Relief Reconciliation Act of 2001 (EGTRRA). Unless Congress changes the law, these provisions will be in effect only through 12/31/2010, after which prior law will be reinstated.

[2] The Life Insurance illustrated above assumes an annual premium of $18,151 that is payable for 3 years.

Estate Summary
Irrevocable Life Insurance Trust

All assets in an estate are subject to taxation. One way to have assets pass to heirs is to change ownership so that the assets are passed to the intended beneficiaries outside of the estate. Life insurance trusts are a way to increase the amount of your estate that passes to your heirs. The trust is irrevocable and serves as both the owner and beneficiary of the life insurance policy. Generally the grantor makes annual gifts to the trust and the trustee pays the premiums.

The following illustrates the use of an irrevocable life insurance trust.

At Elle 's death in 2012

Gross estate	$ 164,967
Debt	- 11,110
Taxes[1] and fees	- 28,407
ILIT[2]	11,581
Total to Heirs	**$ 137,032**

At Elle 's death in 2012

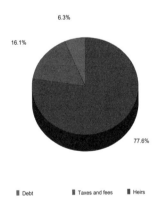

6.3%

16.1%

77.6%

▮ Debt   ▮ Taxes and fees   ▮ Heirs

---

[1] The federal estate tax estimates shown are based on estate and gift tax provisions contained in the Economic Growth and Tax Relief Reconciliation Act of 2001 (EGTRRA). Unless Congress changes the law, these provisions will be in effect only through 12/31/2010, after which prior law will be reinstated.

[2] The Life Insurance illustrated above assumes an annual premium of $637 that is payable for 3 years.

Estate Analysis
Irrevocable Life Insurance Trust

Elle 's Estate

	Value today	Assumed annual growth rate	Value in 5 years
Assets			
Retirement plans	$5,555	6.00%	$7,434
Cash	55,511	5.00%	70,848
Other assets	55,511	5.00%	70,848
Residence	4,444	5.00%	5,672
Total Assets			**154,857**
Life insurance owned by Elle			10,110
Gross Estate			**164,967**
Less			
Debt			11,110
Final expenses			5,000
Administration fees			5,928
Probate fees			5,898
State estate tax deduction			0
Taxable Estate			**137,032**
Federal estate tax[1]			0
State tax			11,581
Irrevocable life insurance trust[2]			11,581
Total to Heirs			**$ 137,032**

---

[1] The federal estate tax estimates shown are based on estate and gift tax provisions contained in the Economic Growth and Tax Relief Reconciliation Act of 2001 (EGTRRA). Unless Congress changes the law, these provisions will be in effect only through 12/31/2010, after which prior law will be reinstated.
[2] The Life Insurance illustrated above assumes an annual premium of $637 that is payable for 3 years.

Estate Options

There are many options available that allow you to pass the maximum amount of assets to your heirs, while minimizing the amount of estate taxes that must be paid. Choosing which options are best depends upon your personal situation. Most of these options are complicated and must be established carefully.

The following illustrates the amounts that will pass to heirs using a simple will and then adding an irrevocable life insurance trust.

Amount to Heirs

	Simple Will	ILIT[1]
At Elle 's death in 2012	$9,154	$9,154
At Luke's death in 2017	$ 277,059	$ 607,077
Total	**$ 286,213**	**$ 616,231**

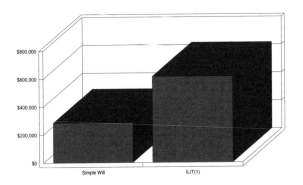

---

[1] The Life Insurance illustrated above assumes an annual premium of $18,151 that is payable for 3 years.

Estate Options

There are many options available that allow you to pass the maximum amount of assets to your heirs, while minimizing the amount of estate taxes that must be paid. Choosing which options are best depends upon your personal situation. Most of these options are complicated and must be established carefully.

The following illustrates the amounts that will pass to heirs using a simple will and then adding an irrevocable life insurance trust.

Amount to Heirs

	Simple Will	ILIT[1]
At Elle 's death in 2012	$ 125,450	$ 137,032

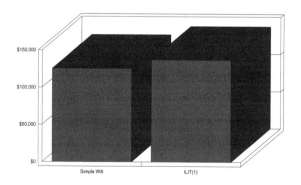

---

[1] The Life Insurance illustrated above assumes an annual premium of $637 that is payable for 3 years.

How Are Death Taxes Paid?

Death taxes are due and payable in cash within nine months after the taxpayer's death.

Five Ways to Provide Money for Death Taxes

- **The executor may borrow the cash:** This only defers the problem, since the money will have to be repaid with interest. This includes installment payments to the government.

- **The taxpayer may pay in cash:** Rarely does a person accumulate large sums of cash. If he or she does, he or she probably will forego many profitable investment opportunities in order to keep the estate in a liquid position.

- **The taxpayer may sell stock market investments:** This may be a wise choice if the market is "up" when the stocks or bonds need to be converted to cash and the taxpayer has been investing long enough to accumulate the necessary amount.

- **The executor may liquidate other assets:** If there is not a ready market, however, the assets may be sold at a great loss.

- **The taxpayer can pay his or her estate settlement costs with life insurance.**

Advantages of Life Insurance

- The insured's heirs almost always get back more than he or she paid in.

- Payment of benefit is prompt.

- There is generally no income tax on the proceeds.

- Proceeds may be free of estate tax.

- Payments can be spread out rather than paid all at once.

- It avoids many of the problems of the other four methods set forth above.

- The proceeds are generally not subject to probate.

- Life insurance provides cash for a predictable and certain need which will arise at some unpredictable moment.

Note: Under the Tax Act of 2001, the federal estate tax is gradually phased out until its final repeal in the year 2010. If Congress does not act at that time to repeal it for the years following, it will automatically revert back to the rates in effect during the year 2001, with an exemption for the first $1,000,000 of assets.

Taxation of Life Insurance Proceeds

Income Taxation

Death proceeds of a life insurance policy are almost always income tax free. See IRC Sec. 101.

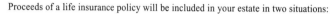

Federal Estate Taxation[1]

Proceeds of a life insurance policy will be included in your estate in two situations:

- If your estate is named as the beneficiary, or

- If you have incidents of ownership in the policy (for example, if you have the power to change beneficiaries, borrow against the cash values, surrender the policy, etc.). See IRC Sec. 2042.

Transfers Within Three Years Prior to Death

If you make a gift of a life insurance policy and then die within three years, the full face amount of the policy will be included in your gross estate for estate tax purposes. See IRC Sec. 2035.

Should You Cross-Own Policies?

Prior to 1982, married couples would frequently own the life insurance policies on each other's life. This technique often kept the insurance from being taxed when the first spouse died.

Since January 1, 1982, however, federal law has provided for an unlimited marital deduction. This means that any amount of assets transferred to one's spouse are not subject to estate or gift taxation. Therefore, any life insurance policies payable to the surviving spouse (no matter which spouse owns them) will not be taxed because of the unlimited marital deduction.

The Problem

When the surviving spouse later dies, his or her estate will have been enlarged by the insurance proceeds collected at the death of the first spouse. Now there may be a substantial tax problem.

An irrevocable life insurance trust or ownership of the policies by children or grandchildren can remove the proceeds from the insured's estate, as well as the estate of the surviving spouse.

---

[1] Under the Tax Act of 2001, the federal estate tax is gradually phased out until its final repeal in the year 2010. If Congress does not act at that time to repeal it for the years following, it will automatically revert back to the rates in effect during the year 2001, with an exemption for the first $1,000,000 of assets.

Irrevocable Life Insurance Trust for a Single Person

Since estate taxes[1] are imposed upon all the assets in the estate, many people prefer to pay the taxes by rearranging some of these assets instead of relying on their current income.

One method of achieving this goal is the irrevocable life insurance trust (ILIT). To prevent inclusion in the estate, an irrevocable trust cannot be revoked or amended by the grantor.

- **Funded irrevocable insurance trusts:** This trust has income-producing assets transferred into it, which will pay the premiums on the insurance policy from the income earned. Irrevocable life insurance trusts are typically not funded with a single, lump-sum payment because the gift taxes on the assets transferred are the same as the federal estate taxes on assets remaining in the estate. Also, if the trust is a "grantor trust" for income tax purposes, the income earned on the assets would still be included on the income tax return of the insured grantor. See IRC Sec. 677(a)(3).

- **Unfunded irrevocable insurance trusts:** Although this trust is not totally unfunded, it usually just owns an insurance policy and the grantor makes annual gifts to the trust with which the trustee can pay the premiums.

Some Areas of Concern

- **Trust is irrevocable:** This means that the grantor cannot get anything out once it is put into the trust. Some suggest that a special power of appointment in the hands of the insured's child would permit that child to appoint the trust assets back out to the insured or others. If the federal estate tax is repealed after 2010, this flexibility may be very desirable. The trustee would need to be authorized to reappoint trust assets without liability to the trust beneficiaries.

- **Annual gift tax exclusion may be lost:** Contributions to the trust are future interests instead of present interests. Future interests typically do not qualify for the $12,000 (in 2008) annual gift tax exclusion. This concern can be overcome by granting to the beneficiaries a limited power to withdraw certain sums from the trust for a short time after the grantor makes the contribution. This is sometimes referred to as a Crummey provision after the case which decided the validity of this technique [*Crummey vs. U.S.*, 397 F.2d 82 (CA-9, 1968)]. The rules set forth in this case and subsequent rulings must be carefully followed. Crummey power holders should be actual trust beneficiaries; however, the tax court allowed contingent beneficiaries (e.g., children, grandchildren, etc.) to qualify in Est. of Maria Cristofani vs. Comm., 97 T.C. 74 (1991).[2]

---

[1] Under the Tax Act of 2001, the federal estate tax is gradually phased out until its final repeal in the year 2010. If Congress does not act at that time to repeal it for the years following, it will automatically revert back to the rates in effect during the year 2001, with an exemption for the first $1,000,000 of assets.

[2] The IRS has continued to attack the conclusion reached in the *Cristofani* case, using a substance-over-form argument. Individuals planning an irrevocable trust similar to that involved in *Cristofani* are advised to consult an attorney on the steps needed to avoid having the IRS conclude that gifts to an irrevocable trust are not gifts of a present interest.

Continued

Irrevocable Life Insurance Trust
for a Single Person

- **Non-exercise of withdrawal powers:** The failure of a beneficiary to withdraw the amounts permitted under the Crummey provision will cause a lapse of that power. Lapsed amounts in excess of the specified limit[1] are generally considered to be taxable gifts from the beneficiary. However, if the beneficiary is given a limited power to appoint the amount in excess of these limits (in his or her will), the power is deemed not to lapse and therefore no gift tax is due.

  Another strategy to deal with this problem is referred to as a "hanging" power. It limits the amount which lapses each year to the larger of $5,000 or 5% of the trust assets. Any amount in excess of this limit "hangs" or carries over to later years. The IRS has, in one situation, stated its opposition to this method. See TAM 8901004.

- **Three-year rule:** If an existing life policy is gifted by the insured to an irrevocable life insurance trust and the insured dies within three years of the transfer, the policy proceeds will be included in the insured's estate. IRC Sec. 2035. On the other hand, if the trustee uses cash in the trust to purchase a new policy on the insured's life and the insured dies within the three-year period, the proceeds will generally be excluded from his or her estate. Care should be taken to make certain that the insured has no incidents of ownership in the policy or control over the trustee.

---

[1] The limit is the greater of $5,000 or 5% of the value of the assets subject to the power.

Irrevocable Life Insurance Trust
for a Single Person

Any increase in the taxable estate due to additional life insurance proceeds will be taxed at one's marginal estate tax bracket, unless the policies are owned outside the estate. Brackets range from 18% to 45% on taxable estates in excess of the applicable exclusion amount of $2,000,000.[3]

Example

Assumptions:
Your estate at date of death: $3,000,000
Recommended new insurance amounts: $1,000,000
Potential estate with new insurance: $4,000,000

If New Insurance Is Included in One's Estate	Projected Marginal Tax Bracket 45%[1]	If New Insurance Is Outside One's Estate[2]
Portion of increased estate to the IRS **$450,000** Portion to heirs **$550,000**		All of new life insurance goes to one's beneficiaries **$1,000,000**

Federal estate tax on	$4,000,000	=	$900,000
Federal estate tax on	$3,000,000	=	450,000
Difference		=	$450,000
Additional amount to heirs		=	**$450,000**

Note: Taxes indicated above assume full applicable credit amount is available.

Under the Tax Act of 2001, the federal estate tax is gradually phased out until its final repeal in the year 2010. If Congress does not act at that time to repeal it for the years following, it will automatically revert back to the rates in effect during the year 2001, with an exemption for the first $1,000,000 of assets.

---

[1] This is the current marginal tax bracket on a $2,000,000 taxable estate (assuming death in 2008). The top bracket will be 45% in 2007 through 2009 with zero taxes in 2010. If Congress does not act at that time to repeal the federal estate tax for the years following, in the year 2011 the top bracket of 55% will automatically return.

[2] Typically, to keep insurance proceeds out of the estate, either adult beneficiaries or an irrevocable life insurance trust (ILIT) should own the policy.

[3] The applicable exclusion amount is the dollar value of assets protected from federal estate tax by an individual's applicable credit amount. It is scheduled to change as follows: $2,000,000 for 2007-2008; $3,500,000 for 2009, zero federal estate tax for the year 2010; and $1,000,000 for 2011 and thereafter (unless permanently repealed or otherwise modified).

Irrevocable Life Insurance Trust
for a Married Couple

Since estate taxes[1] are imposed upon all of the assets in the estate, many people prefer to pay the taxes by rearranging some of these assets instead of relying on their current income.

One method of achieving this goal is the irrevocable life insurance trust (ILIT). To prevent inclusion in the estate, an irrevocable trust cannot be revoked or amended by the grantor.

- **Funded irrevocable insurance trusts:** This trust has income-producing assets transferred into it which will pay the premiums on the insurance policy from the income earned. Irrevocable life insurance trusts are typically not funded with a single, lump-sum payment because the gift taxes on the assets transferred are the same as the federal estate taxes on assets remaining in the estate. Also, if the trust is a "grantor trust" for income tax purposes, the income earned on the assets would still be included on the income tax return of the insured grantor. See IRC Sec. 677(a)(3).

- **Unfunded irrevocable insurance trusts:** Although this trust is not totally unfunded, it usually just owns an insurance policy and the grantor makes annual gifts to the trust with which the trustee can pay the premiums.

Additional Considerations

- **Trust is irrevocable:** This means that the grantor cannot get anything out once it is put into the trust. Some suggest that a special power of appointment in the hands of the insured's child would permit that child to appoint the trust assets back out to the insured or others. If the federal estate tax is repealed after 2010, this flexibility may be very desirable. The trustee would need to be authorized to reappoint trust assets without liability to the trust beneficiaries.

- **Annual gift tax exclusion may be lost:** Contributions to the trust are future interests instead of present interests. Future interests typically do not qualify for the $12,000 (in 2008) annual gift tax exclusion. This concern can be overcome by granting to the beneficiaries a limited power to withdraw certain sums from the trust for a short time after the grantor makes the contribution. This is sometimes referred to as a Crummey provision after the case which decided the validity of this technique (Crummey vs. U.S., 397 F.2d 82 (CA-9, 1968)). The rules set forth in this case and subsequent rulings must be carefully followed. Crummey power holders should be actual trust beneficiaries; however, the tax court allowed annual gift tax exclusions for contingent beneficiaries (e.g., children, grandchildren, etc.) who were given withdrawal rights (Est. of Maria Cristofani vs. Comm., 97 T.C. 74 (1991)).[2]

---

[1] Under the Tax Act of 2001, the federal estate tax is gradually phased out until its final repeal in the year 2010. If Congress does not act at that time to repeal it for the years following, it will automatically revert back to the rates in effect during the year 2001, with an exemption for the first $1,000,000 of assets.

[2] The IRS has continued to attack the conclusion reached in the *Cristofani* case, using a substance-over-form argument. Individuals planning an irrevocable trust similar to that involved in *Cristofani* are advised to consult an attorney on the steps needed to avoid having the IRS conclude that gifts to an irrevocable trust are not gifts of a present interest.

Continued...

Irrevocable Life Insurance Trust
for a Married Couple

- **Non-exercise of withdrawal powers:** The failure of a beneficiary to withdraw the amounts permitted under the Crummey provision will cause a lapse of that power. Lapsed amounts in excess of the specified limit[1] are generally considered to be taxable gifts from the beneficiary. However, if the beneficiary is given a limited power to appoint the amount in excess of these limits (e.g., in his or her will), the power is deemed not to lapse and therefore no gift tax is due.

  Another strategy used to deal with this problem is referred to as a "hanging" power. It limits the amount which lapses each year to the larger of $5,000 or 5% of trust assets. Any amount in excess of this limit "hangs" or carries over to later years. The IRS has, in one situation stated its opposition to this method. See TAM 8901004.

- **Three-year rule:** If an existing life policy is gifted by the insured to an irrevocable life insurance trust and the insured dies within three years of the transfer, the policy proceeds will be included in the insured's estate. IRC Sec. 2035. On the other hand, if the trustee uses cash in the trust to purchase a new policy on the insured's life and the insured dies within the three-year period, the proceeds will generally be excluded from his or her estate. Care should be taken to make certain that the insured has no incidents of ownership in the policy or control over the trustee.

- **Second-to-die policies:** Second-to-die or survivor life policies do not pay the proceeds until both spouses are deceased, which is when the death taxes generally become due. Premiums on a single second-to-die policy are generally lower than the combined premiums on two individual policies, allowing a couple to obtain a larger face amount of insurance. If the surviving spouse will need policy proceeds to live on, however, this type of policy should generally not be used.

---

[1] The limit is the greater of $5,000 or 5% of the value of the assets subject to the power.

Credit Shelter and Irrevocable Insurance Trusts

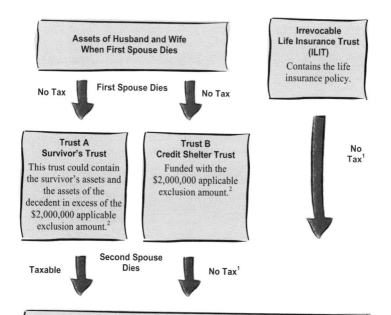

Assets of Husband and Wife When First Spouse Dies

Irrevocable Life Insurance Trust (ILIT)
Contains the life insurance policy.

No Tax | First Spouse Dies | No Tax

Trust A Survivor's Trust
This trust could contain the survivor's assets and the assets of the decedent in excess of the $2,000,000 applicable exclusion amount.[2]

Trust B Credit Shelter Trust
Funded with the $2,000,000 applicable exclusion amount.[2]

No Tax[1]

Taxable | Second Spouse Dies | No Tax[1]

Assets Pass to Children or Other Heirs
- Assets from the survivor's trust are taxable if they exceed $2,000,000 or the applicable exclusion amount at that time.[2]
- Assets from the credit shelter trust should not be taxable.
- Life insurance in the irrevocable life insurance trust is outside of the taxable estate.

Note: Under the Tax Act of 2001, the federal estate tax is gradually phased out until its final repeal in the year 2010. If Congress does not act at that time to repeal it for the years following, it will automatically revert back to the rates in effect during the year 2001, with an exemption for the first $1,000,000 of assets.

---

[1] The tax savings from either the credit shelter trust or the irrevocable life insurance trust can be very substantial.
[2] The applicable exclusion amount is the dollar value of assets protected from federal estate tax by an individual's applicable credit amount. It is scheduled to change as follows: $2,000,000 for 2007-2008; $3,500,000 for 2009, zero federal estate tax for the year 2010; and $1,000,000 for 2011 and thereafter (unless permanently repealed or otherwise modified).

Paying Estate Costs with Estate-Tax-Free Dollars

Since estate taxes are imposed upon the value of the assets in one's estate, many people prefer to pay for these taxes by repositioning these assets, rather than trying to solve the problem entirely from their current earnings.

The following method of systematically transferring small amounts of capital from the estate appeals to many estate owners.

Assume an estate of $3,500,000, with death occurring in 2008.

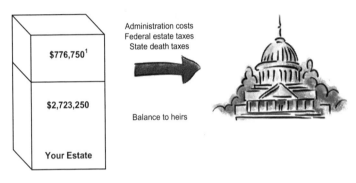

$776,750[1]

$2,723,250

Your Estate

Administration costs
Federal estate taxes
State death taxes

Balance to heirs

With a little planning,
the entire estate may be kept intact.

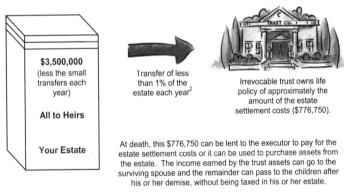

$3,500,000
(less the small transfers each year)

All to Heirs

Your Estate

Transfer of less than 1% of the estate each year[2]

Irrevocable trust owns life policy of approximately the amount of the estate settlement costs ($776,750).

At death, this $776,750 can be lent to the executor to pay for the estate settlement costs or it can be used to purchase assets from the estate. The income earned by the trust assets can go to the surviving spouse and the remainder can pass to the children after his or her demise, without being taxed in his or her estate.

---

[1] Under the Tax Act of 2001, the federal estate tax is gradually phased out until its final repeal in the year 2010. If Congress does not act at that time to repeal it for the years following, it will automatically revert back to the rates in effect during the year 2001, with an exemption for the first $1,000,000 of assets.
[2] Assumes approximate cost of a permanent type life insurance policy on a 50-year-old male. Actual amount will vary.

Using Life Insurance to Pay Estate Costs

Shortly after a death occurs the executor of the estate is responsible for paying the costs of settling the deceased's estate. These costs include probate administration fees, state inheritance or estate taxes, attorney's fees, federal estate taxes, executor's commissions, and appraisal fees.

Many people use life insurance proceeds to pay these expenses. If life insurance is purchased outside one's estate (for example, by adult children or an irrevocable life insurance trust), it need not be subject to either income or estate taxation. Transfer of the premiums from the estate will further reduce the taxable estate.

A Hypothetical Comparison

Assumptions:

Single person (or 2nd spouse to die)
Current estate size: $3,000,000
Estate growth rate: 7.2%
Estimated years until death: 10

Face amount of insurance: $800,000[1]
Annual insurance premium: $25,000
Number of years until paid up: 8

Plan A - Without Life Insurance		
Yr.	Taxable Estate Plus Growth	Federal Estate Tax[2]
2008	$3,216,000	$547,200
2009	3,447,552	0
2010	3,695,776	0
2011	3,961,872	1,474,030
2012	4,247,126	1,630,919
2013	4,552,919	1,799,105
2014	4,880,730	1,979,402
2015	5,232,142	2,172,678
2016	5,608,856	2,379,871
2017	6,012,694	2,601,982

Assets after estate taxes: $3,410,712
Plus life insurance: $0
Total to heirs: $3,410,712

Plan B - With Life Insurance				
Yr.	Taxable Estate Plus Growth	Less Insurance Premium	Net Taxable Estate	Federal Estate Tax[2]
2008	$3,216,000	$25,000	$3,191,000	$535,950
2009	3,420,752	25,000	3,395,752	0
2010	3,640,246	25,000	3,615,246	0
2011	3,875,544	25,000	3,850,544	1,412,799
2012	4,127,783	25,000	4,102,783	1,551,531
2013	4,398,183	25,000	4,373,183	1,700,251
2014	4,688,053	25,000	4,663,053	1,859,679
2015	4,998,792	25,000	4,973,792	2,030,586
2016	5,331,905	0	5,331,905	2,227,548
2017	5,715,803	0	5,715,803	2,438,692

Assets after estate taxes: $3,277,111
Plus life insurance: $800,000[3]
Total to heirs: $4,077,111

Arrangements	Assets at Death	Federal Estate Tax	Amount to Heirs	Additional Assets to Heirs
1. No Insurance	$6,012,694	$2,601,982	$3,410,712	$0
2. Insurance in the Estate	6,515,803	2,878,296	3,637,507	226,795
3. Insurance outside the Estate	6,515,803	2,438,692	4,077,111	666,399

---

[1] Life insurance amount and premiums will vary with insurance company, type of policy, and age and health of insured.
[2] Under the Tax Act of 2001, the federal estate tax is gradually phased out until its final repeal in the year 2010. If Congress does not act at that time to repeal it for the years following, it will automatically revert back to the rates in effect during the year 2001, with an exemption for the first $1,000,000 of assets.
[3] Assumes life insurance is excluded from the estate.

Effect of Life Insurance Transfers
on Federal Estate Taxes

This calculation assumes that the sunset provision of the Economic Growth and Tax Relief
Reconciliation Act of 2001 will take effect.

Assumptions:
Current net estate (less life insurance): $1,000,000
Estimated estate growth rate: 4.50%
Estimated year of death: 10
Current life insurance inside the estate: $ 200,000
Amount of current life insurance available to transfer outside the estate: $ 200,000
Proposed new life insurance: $ 500,000

	With Life Insurance Inside Estate	With Life Insurance Outside Estate
Potential estate size at death	$2,252,969	$1,552,969
Federal estate taxes	$ 558,955	$ 233,836
Savings with life insurance outside of estate		**$ 325,119**

Payment of premiums on policies outside the estate will further reduce the estate size.

Gifts of Life Insurance Policies

Valuation (market value) of Policies

Type of Policy	Value for Gift Tax Purposes
Whole life	The interpolated terminal reserve plus unearned premium
Whole life (paid up)	Present cost of comparable policy at present age
New policy	The gross premium just paid
Term policy	The unearned premium

Federal Tax Status of Gifted Policies – Three Situations

Assumes husband (insured) is now deceased.

Owner/Applicant (Original Owner)	Person Assigned to	Person Who Paid Premiums	Federal Gift/Estate Tax Status	Cases or Rulings
Husband	Anyone within three years prior to death	Husband or employer-paid premiums	Full face amount includable in gross estate	IRC Sec. 2035(d)
Husband	Anyone more than three years prior to death	Husband or employer paid premiums	Premiums paid in excess of $12,000 are taxable gifts[1]	IRC Sec. 2035(d)
Wife, children or irrevocable trust	No transfer of policy in this situation	Husband, wife, child or irrevocable trust	Proceeds not includable in estate	*Estate of Joseph Leder, 90-1 USTC Para. 60,001 (10th Cir. 1989); Estate of Eddie L. Headrick vs. Comm., 90-2 USTC Para. 60,049 (6th Cir. 1990); Estate of Frank M. Perry, Sr. vs. Comm., 91-1 USTC Para. 60,064 (5th Cir. 1991).*

Every precaution should be taken in establishing and funding irrevocable insurance trusts if the desired tax benefits are to be realized. If there is any connection between the insured and the insurance policy, the IRS may try to establish that the trustee is merely an agent of the insured.

Note: Under the Tax Act of 2001, the federal estate tax is gradually phased out until its final repeal in the year 2010. If Congress does not act at that time to repeal it for the years following, it will automatically revert back to the rates in effect during the year 2001, with an exemption for the first $1,000,000 of assets.

---

[1] The annual gift tax exclusion ($12,000 in 2008) is indexed for inflation in increments of $1,000. If the policy is assigned to the wife, the unlimited marital deduction will probably defer any gift tax. See IRC Sec. 2523(a). If a policy has more than one owner, premiums paid or deemed paid by another person are gifts of a future interest and are not eligible for the annual gift tax exclusion.

Adult Children's Insurance Trust

When life insurance is owned by the insured, it is generally included in his or her gross estate (or the estate of his or her spouse).[1]

In order to avoid the loss of up to 45%[2] of the insurance proceeds for additional estate taxes, many people take steps to have these proceeds excluded from their taxable estates.

Most Common Methods

The most common methods used to exclude life insurance from one's taxable estate are:

- An irrevocable life insurance trust, and
- Ownership of the policies by adult children.

Potential Problems

The irrevocable life insurance trust requires special care to make certain that the money contributed for the payment of the premiums qualifies for the annual gift tax exclusion.

In order to qualify for the annual gift tax exclusion, the gift must be a present interest. This is generally difficult to accomplish in an irrevocable trust unless the beneficiaries are given the right to withdraw the funds each time the grantor contributes to the trust. This right is sometimes called a Crummey provision. The trustee must notify the beneficiaries each time they have such a right to withdraw funds.

Also, if the contributions exceed a certain limit[3] per year per beneficiary and the beneficiary fails to withdraw the funds, the tax code states that a lapse has occurred and may subject the beneficiaries to a gift tax problem. Careful drafting of the trust can generally avoid this problem.[4]

Even with these inconveniences, the irrevocable life insurance trust is a very valuable estate planning tool, especially when there is a desire to provide income for a surviving spouse or the insured's children are still minors.

---

[1] If the surviving spouse is the beneficiary, there may not be an estate tax due at the first death because of the unlimited marital deduction. However, the policy proceeds would then be part of the surviving spouse's estate to the extent they were not consumed prior to his or her demise.

[2] This is the current marginal tax bracket on a $2,000,000 taxable estate (assuming death in 2008). The top bracket will be 45% in 2007 through 2009 with zero taxes in 2010. If Congress does not act at that time to repeal the federal estate tax for the years following, in the year 2011 the top bracket of 55% will automatically return.

[3] The limit is the greater of $5,000 or 5% of the value of the assets subject to the power.

[4] In certain situations, the tax status of gifts to an irrevocable life insurance trust is unclear. Individuals planning an irrevocable trust are advised to consult an attorney on the steps needed to avoid having the IRS conclude that gifts to the trust are not gifts of a present interest and thus be ineligible for the annual gift tax exclusion.

Continued...

Adult Children's Insurance Trust

When children are adults, the same tax result can often be reached without the need for a trust document.

- Existing life insurance policies can be transferred to an adult child named as the owner and beneficiary. If, however, there is more than one child, there may be problems of multiple owners on the policy:
  - A gift of an existing life insurance policy to more than one owner will always be a gift of a future interest, as no single owner can exercise any right or access any policy values without the consent of all co-owners.
  - With multiple owners, the annual gift tax exclusion will not apply to the transfer of ownership nor to any premiums subsequently paid by the transferor.
- If only one child is named as owner, and two or more children are named as beneficiaries, there will be a gift tax on the portions passing to the non-owner beneficiaries at the insured's demise. As a further complication, the child named as owner could change beneficiaries at any time.

As an alternative, cash can be given to the children to purchase a new life insurance policy.

One potential problem is that some of the children may elect not to use the funds to solve estate liquidity problems by withholding the insurance proceeds from the executor.

A Possible Solution

The estate owner can encourage his or her children to set up a revocable living insurance trust with the children acting as grantors. The trustees could then apply for insurance on the estate owner's life.

After the insured's demise, the trust could be permitted to lend money to the executor of the estate or purchase assets from the estate. This procedure provides cash proceeds where they are needed most without increasing the size of the taxable estate.

The children generally follow the desires of the estate owner when they know that this trust is only part of the inheritance which they could receive.

Death Tax Reduction

The federal estate tax, which is imposed on taxable estates exceeding $2,000,000[1], can be reduced through various techniques.

- **Lifetime gifts:** Each person can make annual gifts of $12,000[2] ($24,000 per couple, if married) to any number of donees; e.g., children or grandchildren, without incurring a gift tax.

- **Charitable transfers:** Bequests at death or lifetime charitable gifts can reduce the estate size and thus reduce the death tax. Charitable gifts made during life provide the added benefit of an income tax deduction. Gifts can be of a partial interest; for example, one can retain the right to income for life.

- **Marital transfers:** Generally, neither lifetime gifts nor bequests at death to one's spouse are subject to death taxes. This in effect defers the tax until the surviving spouse dies. Special rules apply to noncitizen spouses.

- **Credit shelter trusts:** The credit shelter trust makes certain that the applicable credit amounts of both spouses are used. This can bring significant savings to many estates.

- **Estate value freezing techniques:** Corporate recapitalizations, personal holding companies and multi-tier family partnerships which previously transferred future growth of a business to a younger generation while still retaining power to control the business, have been almost eliminated.

- **Private annuity:** Generally, a private annuity is the sale of an asset to a younger generation in exchange for an unsecured promise to pay annual amounts for the seller's lifetime. This removes the assets from the estate; however, the payments, if accumulated, could build up over the seller's life expectancy to the size of the asset which was transferred.[3]

- **Life insurance trusts:** By transferring small amounts of the estate (equal to the insurance premium) to an irrevocable life insurance trust, an estate owner can reduce his or her current estate while creating a much larger asset outside the estate. The proceeds of the policy will not be subject to income taxes or federal estate taxes at the estate owner's demise. See IRC Sec. 101(a).

---

[1] The applicable exclusion amount is the dollar value of assets protected from federal estate tax by an individual's applicable credit amount. It is scheduled to change as follows: $2,000,000 for 2007-2008; $3,500,000 for 2009, zero federal estate tax for the year 2010; and $1,000,000 for 2011 and thereafter (unless permanently repealed or otherwise modified).

[2] The annual gift tax exclusion ($12,000 in 2008) is indexed for inflation in increments of $1,000.

[3] On October 17, 2006, the IRS issued proposed regulations (NPRM REG-141901-5) on the exchange of appreciated property for an annuity contract. These proposed regulations treat the transaction as if the transferor had sold the property for cash and then used the proceeds to purchase an annuity contract. The proposed regulations are generally effective for transactions occurring after October 18, 2006.

The Marital Deduction

For both gift tax (IRC Sec. 2523) and estate tax (IRC Sec. 2056) purposes, a deduction is allowed for the value of gifts between spouses.[1]

The deduction is unlimited; i.e., 100% of qualified transfers such as the following.

A. Outright gifts or bequests

B. Gifts or bequests in trust

- **General power of appointment trust:** The spouse has the right to all income plus the right to determine during life and/or at death who receives the remaining principal.

- **Revocable trust:**[2] Spouse has right to all income and to revoke or amend the trust at any time in his or her favor.

- **Estate trust:** Income accumulates during surviving spouse's lifetime. The spouse has the right (through the use of a will) to determine at death who gets the accumulated income and principal.

- **Qualified terminable interest property (QTIP) trust:** Spouse has the right to all income during life. No one else can benefit from the principal, but the donor (or decedent) can direct who will get the principal at the surviving spouse's later demise.

- **Qualified domestic trust:** If the surviving spouse is not a U.S. citizen, the marital deduction will not be allowed unless the assets pass to a qualified domestic trust which meets four conditions:

  - The trust requires at least one U.S. trustee (unless waived by the IRS) who approves all distributions.
  - Spouse must have an interest which would otherwise qualify for the marital deduction if he or she were a citizen.
  - Must meet Treasury requirements designed to ensure collection of tax at surviving spouse's demise.
  - Executor makes irrevocable election on federal estate tax return to defer the tax.

A noncitizen spouse who becomes a U.S. citizen before the estate tax return is filed and was a resident from the decedent's death through the filing of the return is eligible for the marital deduction.

Any distributions of principal will be taxed at the same rate as if they were included in the decedent's estate.

---

[1] Under the Tax Act of 2001, the federal estate tax is gradually phased out until its final repeal in the year 2010. If Congress does not act at that time to repeal it for the years following, it will automatically revert back to the rates in effect during the year 2001, with an exemption for the first $1,000,000 of assets.

[2] At death, the trust becomes irrevocable. The surviving spouse has as much (or as little) flexibility as provided for by the grantor.

Credit Shelter Trust

The Problem

Under current law, a person can pass any size estate to his or her U.S. citizen spouse without concern for a federal estate tax because of the unlimited marital deduction. See IRC Sec. 2056.

However, when the surviving spouse later dies and passes the combined estate to his or her heirs, there is only that spouse's applicable credit amount to reduce the death tax. Therefore, the applicable credit amount of the first spouse to die was wasted.

The Solution

To preserve the applicable credit amount of the first spouse to die, many couples use a credit shelter trust (also called an exemption or by-pass trust). When the first spouse dies, up to $2,000,000[1] is placed into the credit shelter trust. This trust is neither taxed at that time nor at the later death of the surviving spouse, even though it may appreciate greatly in value.

The surviving spouse, however, can have access to the income from the trust for life and can use the principal if necessary for his or her health, education, support and maintenance.

Estates of married couples (including life insurance) which are smaller than the applicable exclusion amount now and are not likely to exceed these amounts in the future, will generally not benefit tax-wise from this type of trust.

---

[1] The applicable exclusion amount is the dollar value of assets protected from federal estate tax by an individual's applicable credit amount. It is scheduled to change as follows: $2,000,000 for 2007-2008; $3,500,000 for 2009, zero federal estate tax for the year 2010; and $1,000,000 for 2011 and thereafter (unless permanently repealed or otherwise modified).

Credit Shelter Trust

The credit shelter trust is designed to make use of the applicable credit amount of each spouse, while allowing the surviving spouse to have use of the assets of the deceased spouse. The credit shelter trust is generally not taxed at either death. The survivor's trust is generally taxed when the surviving spouse later dies.

Current Estate

First Spouse Dies

Trust A Survivor's Trust		Trust B Credit Shelter Trust
(all assets not in credit shelter trust)		(up to $2,000,000[2])
- Remains Revocable[1] - **Survivor Gets**	**No Tax**	**- Becomes Irrevocable -** **Survivor Can Have**
• All income • All principal • Right to amend • Unlimited power to appoint principal to anyone		• All income • Principal for health, support and maintenance • Limited power to appoint principal among heirs

Tax on Assets Over $2,000,000[2]

Surviving Spouse Dies

No Tax

Children's Trust

• Assets can be held in this trust while the children are growing in maturity.

• The trustee manages estate and distributes it to children at specified ages.

---

[1] Trust may be irrevocable if it is a general power of appointment trust or an estate trust.
[2] The applicable exclusion amount is the dollar value of assets protected from federal estate tax by an individual's applicable credit amount. It is scheduled to change as follows: $2,000,000 for 2007-2008; $3,500,000 for 2009, zero federal estate tax for the year 2010; and $1,000,000 for 2011 and thereafter (unless permanently repealed or otherwise modified).

Credit Shelter and QTIP Trusts

The Problem

Under current law, a person can pass any size estate to his or her U.S. citizen spouse without concern for a federal estate tax because of the unlimited marital deduction. See IRC Sec. 2056.

However, when the surviving spouse later dies and passes the combined estate to his or her heirs, there is only that spouse's applicable credit amount to reduce the death tax. Therefore, the applicable credit amount of the first spouse to die was wasted.

The Solution

To preserve the applicable credit amount of the first spouse to die, many couples use a credit shelter trust (also called an exemption or by-pass trust). When the first spouse dies, up to $2,000,000[1] is placed into the credit shelter trust. It is not subject to estate tax at that time nor at the later death of the surviving spouse, even though it may appreciate greatly in value.

The surviving spouse, however, can have access to the income from the trust for life and can use the principal if necessary for his or her health, education, support and maintenance.

Additional Planning

Sometimes a third trust, called a QTIP trust, is added to the credit shelter trust. QTIP stands for qualified terminable interest property trust. The QTIP allows the first spouse to die to give lifetime benefits (like income earned on the trust assets) to his or her spouse while still retaining the right to name the persons who will ultimately receive the trust assets.

This trust is particularly useful in protecting children of a prior marriage from being cut off by the surviving stepparent spouse.

It also reduces the possibility of the estate passing to a subsequent marriage partner or close friend of the surviving spouse.

Careful drafting is required to make certain the QTIP trust qualifies for the marital deduction. Special language may be required if the QTIP trust is the beneficiary of an IRA. See Rev. Rul. 89-89, 1989-2 CB 231.

Estates of married couples which are less than the applicable exclusion amounts now (including life insurance) and are not likely to exceed these amounts in the future will generally not benefit tax wise from this type of trust.

---

[1] The applicable exclusion amount is the dollar value of assets protected from federal estate tax by an individual's applicable credit amount. It is scheduled to change as follows: $2,000,000 for 2007-2008; $3,500,000 for 2009, zero federal estate tax for the year 2010; and $1,000,000 for 2011 and thereafter (unless permanently repealed or otherwise modified).

Credit Shelter and QTIP Trusts

The combination of credit shelter and QTIP trusts is designed to make use of the applicable credit amount of each spouse, while giving the first to die the power to choose who receives his or her estate. The credit shelter trust is generally not taxed at either death. The survivor's and QTIP trusts are generally taxed when the surviving spouse dies.

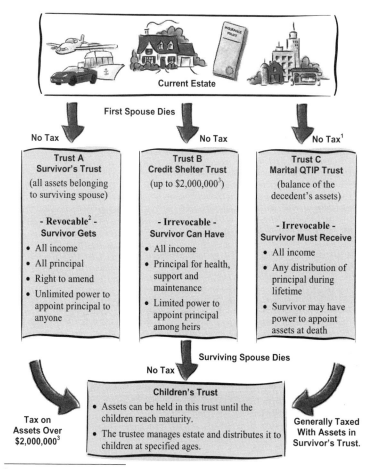

Current Estate

First Spouse Dies

No Tax   No Tax   No Tax[1]

Trust A **Survivor's Trust** (all assets belonging to surviving spouse)	**Trust B** **Credit Shelter Trust** (up to $2,000,000[3])	**Trust C** **Marital QTIP Trust** (balance of the decedent's assets)
- Revocable[2] - **Survivor Gets** • All income • All principal • Right to amend • Unlimited power to appoint principal to anyone	**- Irrevocable -** **Survivor Can Have** • All income • Principal for health, support and maintenance • Limited power to appoint principal among heirs	**- Irrevocable -** **Survivor Must Receive** • All income • Any distribution of principal during lifetime • Survivor may have power to appoint assets at death

Surviving Spouse Dies

No Tax

Tax on Assets Over $2,000,000[3]

Children's Trust
• Assets can be held in this trust until the children reach maturity.
• The trustee manages estate and distributes it to children at specified ages.

Generally Taxed With Assets in Survivor's Trust.

---

[1] The executor may choose to have the QTIP trust taxed at the death of the first spouse, or after surviving spouse dies.
[2] Trust may be irrevocable if it is a general power of appointment trust or an estate trust.
[3] The applicable exclusion amount is the dollar value of assets protected from federal estate tax by an individual's applicable credit amount. It is scheduled to change as follows: $2,000,000 for 2007-2008; $3,500,000 for 2009, zero federal estate tax for the year 2010; and $1,000,000 for 2011 and thereafter (unless permanently repealed or otherwise modified).

Lifetime QTIP Trust
For Couples with Unequal Estates

If a married couple has unequal estates, there may be a larger death tax if the less-wealthy spouse dies first. For example, assume that a husband has a net worth of $4,000,000 and his wife has assets with only very nominal value. Further assume that the husband's will or living trust provides for a QTIP/credit shelter trust at his demise. The following table illustrates the problem if his wife dies first.

Order of Death	Amount Which Would Go to the Survivor's or QTIP Trust	Amount Which Would Go to the Credit Shelter Trust	Federal Estate Tax at the Death of the Surviving Spouse[1]
If husband dies first	$2,000,000	$2,000,000	$0
If wife dies first	4,000,000	0	900,000

This result is caused by not fully using the wife's applicable credit amount — $900,000 will pass to the government for taxes rather than to the children or other beneficiaries. The husband could solve this tax problem by transferring $2,000,000 of assets to his wife while they are both still living. However, once she has the assets, he loses control over who the ultimate beneficiaries will be; e.g., their children, his children of a prior marriage, her children, a favorite charity, etc.

A possible solution that gives the tax benefit without the loss of control over the ultimate beneficiary is a lifetime QTIP trust.

How It Works

- The husband has a net worth of $4,000,000. He gifts $2,000,000 to a lifetime QTIP trust (no gift tax because of the unlimited marital deduction). To qualify for no-tax treatment, a QTIP election must be made by the donor. See IRC Sec. 2523(f).

- The trustee pays the income to the wife for her lifetime and then to the beneficiaries previously selected by the husband at her later demise.

At the wife's death the trust principal will be included in her estate (IRC Sec. 2044), but her applicable credit amount will offset the tax (assuming her estate has not grown above the applicable exclusion amount of $2,000,000[2]).

---

[1] These values assume death occurs in 2008.
[2] The applicable exclusion amount is the dollar value of assets protected from federal estate tax by an individual's applicable credit amount. It is scheduled to change as follows: $2,000,000 for 2007-2008; $3,500,000 for 2009, zero federal estate tax for the year 2010; and $1,000,000 for 2011 and thereafter (unless permanently repealed or otherwise modified).

Continued

Lifetime QTIP Trust
For Couples with Unequal Estates

Lifetime QTIP Trust Diagram

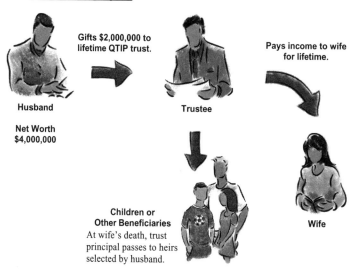

Gifts $2,000,000 to lifetime QTIP trust.

Husband

Net Worth $4,000,000

Trustee

Pays income to wife for lifetime.

Wife

Children or Other Beneficiaries
At wife's death, trust principal passes to heirs selected by husband.

Potential Tax Savings

The amount of potential tax savings will depend upon the marginal federal estate tax bracket of the wealthy spouse and the amount of assets owned by the less wealthy spouse.

Estate of Wealthy Spouse		Federal Estate Tax Savings[1]
Before the Transfer	After the Transfer	
$4,000,000	$2,000,000	$900,000
4,250,000	2,250,000	900,000
4,500,000	2,500,000	900,000
4,750,000	2,750,000	900,000
5,000,000	3,000,000	900,000
5,250,000	3,250,000	900,000
5,500,000	3,500,000	900,000

Note: Under the Tax Act of 2001, the federal estate tax is gradually phased out until its final repeal in the year 2010. If Congress does not act at that time to repeal it for the years following, it will automatically revert back to the rates in effect during the year 2001, with an exemption for the first $1,000,000 of assets.

---

[1] This assumes death occurs in 2008 and that the less wealthy spouse had only nominal assets and that there was no tax incurred at his or her demise. These savings will vary as the applicable exclusion amount is periodically increased.

Credit Shelter Trust vs. Simple Will
A Tax Comparison

The credit shelter trust utilizes the applicable credit amounts of both spouses. The tax savings will vary depending on the year of death, the size of the estate, the rate of growth for estate assets between the deaths of the two spouses and the applicable exclusion amount[1] in effect at date of death.

The chart below illustrates the approximate savings in a variety of estates. (Assumes no growth of assets between deaths.)

Federal Estate Taxes after Both Spouses Die

Estate Size	Tax with All-to-Spouse Arrangement[3]	Tax with Credit Shelter Trust[3]	Credit Shelter Trust with 50/50 Division[2]		
			Demise of First Spouse to Die	Demise of Second Spouse to Die	Combined Deaths
$1,000,000	$0	$0	$0	$0	$0
1,500,000	0	0	0	0	0
2,000,000	0	0	0	0	0
2,500,000	225,000	0	0	0	0
3,000,000	450,000	0	0	0	0
3,500,000	900,000	0	0	0	0
4,000,000	1,125,000	0	0	0	0
5,000,000	1,350,000	450,000	225,000	225,000	450,000
6,000,000	1,800,000	900,000	450,000	450,000	900,000
7,000,000	2,250,000	1,350,000	675,000	675,000	1,350,000
8,000,000	2,700,000	1,800,000	900,000	900,000	1,800,000
9,000,000	3,150,000	2,250,000	1,125,000	1,125,000	2,250,000
10,000,000	3,600,000	2,700,000	1,350,000	1,350,000	2,700,000

Note: Under the Tax Act of 2001, the federal estate tax is gradually phased out until its final repeal in the year 2010. If Congress does not act at that time to repeal it for the years following, it will automatically revert back to the rates in effect during the year 2001, with an exemption for the first $1,000,000 of assets.

---

[1] The applicable exclusion amount is the dollar value of assets protected from federal estate tax by an individual's applicable credit amount. It is scheduled to change as follows: $2,000,000 for 2007-2008; $3,500,000 for 2009, zero federal estate tax for the year 2010; and $1,000,000 for 2011 and thereafter (unless permanently repealed or otherwise modified).

[2] With a trust that splits the estate in half when the first spouse dies (typical of credit shelter trusts created prior to 1982), a portion of the tax must be paid when the first spouse dies. Even though the overall combined death tax may be less, most estate owners prefer to defer taxation until the death of the second spouse, especially since the federal estate tax may be permanently repealed in 2011.

[3] Tax is paid after the death of the second spouse to die.

Life Insurance and the Applicable Credit Amount
Which Spouse Should Be Insured?

Married couples with estates of unequal size should examine the question of which spouse to insure from a tax standpoint.

For example, assume the following.

- Husband has assets of $2,000,000 (no insurance).

- Wife has assets of $200,000 (no insurance).

- The agreed upon life insurance need is $500,000.

Important question: Which spouse should be insured?

- **If husband dies first:** Assuming the use of an AB type credit shelter trust and using the marital deduction and applicable credit amount of each spouse, the result should be a zero death tax.[1]

- **If wife dies first:** Assuming the use of an AB type credit shelter trust, the matter of which spouse was insured will determine the tax consequence.

The table below illustrates what would result in these two instances.

	$500,000 Policy on Husband's Life (wealthier spouse)	$500,000 Policy on Wife's Life (less wealthy spouse)
Wife's demise		
Estate size	$200,000	$700,000
Death tax	0	0
Husband's later demise		
Estate size	$2,500,000[2]	$2,000,000
Death tax	225,000	0
Combined death taxes	$225,000	$0

Note: If neither spouse's estate exceeds the applicable exclusion amount, consider life insurance on each spouse to pass the maximum amount to heirs with no death tax. Also, consider an irrevocable life insurance trust to avoid death taxes if the taxable estate exceeds $4,000,000 ($2,000,000 x 2).

---

[1] This assumes the combined estates do not exceed $4,000,000. The applicable exclusion amount is the dollar value of assets protected from federal estate tax by an individual's applicable credit amount. It is scheduled to change as follows: $2,000,000 for 2007-2008; $3,500,000 for 2009, zero federal estate tax for the year 2010; and $1,000,000 for 2011 and thereafter (unless permanently repealed or otherwise modified).

[2] Assumes death occurs in 2008. Includes the husband's $2,000,000 applicable exclusion amount plus $500,000 of life insurance on husband's life.

Exhausting the Applicable Credit Amount Today

Assets growing at about 5% per year will double in value in about 15 years. As the size of one's estate grows, so does the amount of estate tax which will one day come due.

Under federal law, only taxable estates larger than the applicable exclusion amount[1] are subject to the federal estate tax.

Rather than wait until death to make a gift, some taxpayers choose to make large, taxable lifetime gifts. The major benefit of this approach is that it can remove any future appreciation in the gifted assets from the donor's estate.

Consider the following example.

Assumptions:
    Estate size: $5,000,000
    Years until death: 10
    Growth rate: 6%
    Current gift amount: $2,000,000

	Assumes No Current Use of the Applicable Credit Amount	Assume a Current Gift of $2,000,000
Current estate size	$5,000,000	$5,000,000
Current gift	-0	-2,000,000
Balance in estate	$5,000,000	$3,000,000
Estate in 10 years at 6%	8,954,238	5,372,543
Add back gift at death	0	2,000,000
Taxable estate	$8,954,238	$7,372,543
Federal estate tax[2]	$3,129,407	$2,417,644
Potential tax savings	**$711,763**	

---

[1] The applicable exclusion amount is the dollar value of assets protected from federal estate tax by an individual's applicable credit amount. It is scheduled to change as follows: $2,000,000 for 2007-2008; $3,500,000 for 2009, zero federal estate tax for the year 2010; and $1,000,000 for 2011 and thereafter (unless permanently repealed or otherwise modified).

[2] Calculated as through death occurs in 2008.

Qualified Family-Owned Business Interest

IRC Sec. 2057 provides for a deduction from the gross estate of qualified family-owned business interest property (QFOBI). Under this provision, if more than 50% of an estate's assets are qualified family-owned business interests and certain other requirements are met, up to $675,000 of such property may be deducted from the gross estate.[1] Act Section 512(d) of the Tax Act of 2001 repeals the QFOBI deduction, effective for decedents dying after 12/31/2003. Under the sunset provisions of the act, the QFOBI provisions will be reinstated for decedents dying after 12/31/2010.

The estate tax savings provided by this Code section can be lost if certain requirements are not met during the 10-year period following the decedent's death.

Qualified Family-Owned Business Interest

Business interests include sole proprietorships as well as other entities such as corporations, LLCs and partnerships. In general, the following are required to qualify for the deduction.

- **Ownership and material participation:** The decedent or family members[2] must have owned and materially participated in the business for at least five of the eight years prior to death.

- **Location of business:** The principal place of business must be located in the United States.

- **Percentage of estate assets:** The qualified family-owned business interest must make up more than 50% of the decedent's adjusted gross estate.

- **Decedent, executor and heirs:** At the time of death, the decedent must have been either a U.S. citizen or resident. The executor must choose to have the deduction apply to the estate and each qualified heir[3] with an interest in the business must sign a recapture agreement.

---

[1] This was effective for estates of decedents dying after 12/31/97. The IRS Restructuring and Reform Act of 1998 amended the original QFOBI law and redesignated IRC Sec. 2033A as IRC Sec. 2057.

[2] Family members include the decedent's spouse, ancestors, lineal descendants and parents' lineal descendants, or spouses of any of these.

[3] Qualified heirs include actual family members, as well as any person who has been actively employed by the business for at least 10 years prior to the date of the decedent's death. The IRS Restructuring and Reform Act of 1998 clarified that a trust may be treated as a qualified heir if all trust beneficiaries are qualified heirs.

Continued...

Qualified Family-Owned Business Interest

- **Ownership percentage:**[1] At the time of death, the decedent must have had an interest at least equal to one of the following.

One Family	Two Families	Three Families
50% owned by the Decedent (and family)	**70%** owned by the Decedent (and family) **AND** one other family, with the Decedent (and family) owning at least **30%**	**90%** owned by the Decedent (and family) **AND** two other families, with the Decedent (and family) owning at least **30%**

Deduction Amount

If all requirements are met, the executor may elect to deduct the lesser of the value of the QFOBI property or $675,000.

Interaction with Applicable Credit Amount

Under the provisions of IRC Sec. 2057(a), the amount of the QFOBI deduction is coordinated with the applicable credit amount. The applicable credit amount protects a specified amount of property, known as the applicable exclusion amount, from estate taxes. This amount of protected property is scheduled to increase over time.

Year	Maximum Applicable Exclusion Amount	Maximum Deduction for QFOBI
2000 – 2001	$675,000	$675,000
2002 – 2003	$1,000,000	$675,000
2004 – 2005	$1,500,000	QFOBI repealed
2006 – 2008	$2,000,000	QFOBI repealed
2009	$3,500,000	QFOBI repealed
2010	Federal estate tax repealed	
2011	$1,000,000	$675,000

The law limits the maximum amount that may be protected from estate tax by the combination of the QFOBI deduction and the applicable exclusion amount to $1,300,000. If the maximum QFOBI deduction is taken, the applicable exclusion amount is limited to $625,000 ($1,300,000 - $675,000 = $625,000).

---

[1] Corporate stockholders need the appropriate percentage of both share ownership and voting power. Partners need the required percentage of both the capital interest and the profits interest. Special look-through rules apply to businesses which own other business interests.

Continue

Qualified Family-Owned Business Interest

If QFOBI assets are less than $675,000, the applicable exclusion amount is increased by the difference between the QFOBI assets and $675,000, but not beyond what it would have been (under the scheduled increases) without the QFOBI deduction.

The following hypothetical examples illustrate this interaction.

A Year of Death	B QFOBI Value in Estate	C QFOBI Deduction Taken	D Applicable Exclusion Amount Maximum	E Applicable Exclusion Amount Allowed	F Total Sheltered (C + E)
2001	$475,000	$475,000	$675,000	$675,000	$1,150,000
2003	$450,000	$450,000	$1,000,000	$850,000	$1,300,000

Recapture of Benefits

The new law recaptures the federal estate tax savings if any of the following events occur during the 10-year period after the decedent's death.

- The material-participation requirements of IRC Sec. 2032A(c)(6)(B) are not met. In general, this Code section requires a qualified heir or family member to materially participate in the trade or business for at least five years of any eight-year period.

- A qualified heir disposes of any portion of the inherited business interest, except through a disposition to a member of the qualified heir's family or qualified conservation contribution.

- The qualified heir loses U.S. citizenship.

- The principal place of business ceases to be the United States.

If the event causing the recapture occurs between six and 10 years after death, only a partial recapture will be required.

Other Requirements to Qualify for the Deduction

- If the business is a corporation, its stock must not have been publicly traded within the three years before death. Personal holding company interests do not qualify for the deduction.

- If the business holds passive assets, such as publicly traded stock or cash in excess of reasonable day-to-day working capital needs, the value of such assets must be reduced for QFOBI purposes.

- The business must meet a liquidity test which looks at the business interests passing to qualified heirs at the time of death and certain lifetime gifts.

Continued...

Qualified Family-Owned Business Interest

Planning for the QFOBI Deduction

In order to meet the percentage requirements to qualify for the QFOBI deduction, an estate owner may wish to consider reducing nonbusiness assets in the gross estate. However, transfers of assets to a spouse are not effective unless completed more than 10 years prior to death. Transfers to others, except for nontaxable transfers to other family members, must be completed more than three years prior to death.

The requirements to qualify for the QFOBI deduction are complex. An estate owner should seek competent legal and tax guidance to make certain that all requirements are complied with.

Qualifying for the QFOBI Deduction
A Check List of Requirements

In the right situation, the qualified family-owned business interest (QFOBI) deduction can be a useful estate planning and business continuation tool. The requirements to qualify, however, are complex. This checklist of major requirements can help you decide if further investigation into this estate cost reduction strategy would be useful.

Requirements to Qualify for the Deduction

In order for the estate to qualify for the deduction, you must first be able to answer yes to each of the following requirements.

- **Ownership and material participation:** The decedent or family members must have owned and materially participated in the business for at least five of the eight years before death. **Yes / No**

- **Business location:** The principal place of business must be in the U.S. **Yes / No**

- **Percentage of estate assets:** The QFOBI asset must be more than 50% of the decedent's adjusted gross estate at the time of death. **Yes / No**

- **Citizenship/residency:** At the time of death, the decedent must be a citizen or resident of the United States. **Yes / No**

- **The QFOBI deduction option is not automatic:** The executor must elect to have the exclusion apply to the estate. **Yes / No**

- **Recapture agreement:** Each qualified heir must agree in writing to repay the benefits received through the QFOBI deduction, if certain after-death requirements are not met. **Yes / No**

- **Ownership percentage:** At the time of death, the decedent must have held an interest equal to at least one of the following:
  - 50% owned by the decedent and family; or **Yes / No**
  - 70% owned by the decedent and family and one other family (decedent and family owning at least 30%); or **Yes / No**
  - 90% owned by decedent and family and two other families (decedent and family owning at least 30%). **Yes / No**

After Making the Election

There are severe consequences, including repayment of the avoided federal estate taxes (with penalties and interest), if the heirs do not meet certain requirements during the 10-year period following the decedent's death.

- **Material participation:** At least one qualified heir or family member must materially participate in the trade or business for at least five years of any eight-year period. **Yes / No**

- **Other recapture events:** A qualified heir disposes of the business interest; a qualified heir loses U.S. citizenship; the principal place of business ceases to be the United States. **Yes / No**

Special Use Valuation
IRC Sec. 2032A

Valuation of Farm and Business Real Estate

For federal estate tax purposes, real estate is normally valued at its highest and best use. This can produce unfair results when valuing certain real property, such as farmland which is adjacent to highly developed and very valuable land. For this reason, Congress enacted IRC Sec. 2032A to allow certain real estate to be valued at its actual use rather than its best possible use. This special use valuation can reduce the gross estate up to $960,000.[1]

Requirements to Qualify for IRC Sec. 2032A

- The real property must be in the United States and must be in use for trade or business or as a farm for farming purposes on the date of the decedent's demise.

- The adjusted value[2] of the real and personal property used in the business or farming operation must be at least 50% of the adjusted value of the gross estate.

- At least 25% of the decedent's adjusted gross estate must consist of qualified real property.

- The decedent or a member of his or her family must have been a material participant in the operation of the farm or other business for at least five of the eight years preceding his or her death, disability or retirement (with Social Security benefits).

- The property must pass to a qualified heir (i.e., spouse, parents, lineal descendants or aunts and uncles and their descendants).

Valuation

If the requirements are met to qualify under IRC Sec. 2032A, the law provides two specific techniques for valuation. One is based on a special formula [IRC Sec. 2032A(e)(7)] and the other is based on a number of specified factors [Sec. 2032A(e)(8)].

---

[1] This is the value for the year 2008. This limit is subject to adjustment for inflation in future years.
[2] Adjusted value means the market value of the property less unpaid mortgages or other indebtedness against the property.

Continued..

Special Use Valuation
IRC Sec. 2032A

Possible Recapture

If the qualified heir disposes of the property within 10 years of the decedent's death, the law imposes an additional tax, unless the property is transferred to another qualified heir who is also a member of the decedent's family. Also, if the qualified heir does not actively manage the operation of the farm or business for more than three of any eight consecutive years, the qualified status will cease. There is a two-year grace period, immediately following the decedent's death during which the qualified heir does not need to commence use of the property.

A like-kind exchange of qualified real property for other qualified real property to be used for the same qualified use will not incur an additional estate tax.

A possible disadvantage of using the special use valuation is that the heirs receive a lower basis in property for capital gains purposes.

If a technical defect is made in filing for the election (e.g., failure to include certain required information), the executor of the decedent's estate can have a reasonable time (not exceeding 90 days) to correct the flaw. See IRC Sec. 2032A(d)(3).

The Taxpayer Relief Act of 1997 amended IRC Sec. 2032A to allow both surviving spouses and lineal descendents of the deceased to lease specially valued property on a net cash basis to certain family members. New IRC Sec. 2032A(c)(7)(E), effective for leases entered into after 12/31/76.

Note: Under the Tax Act of 2001, the federal estate tax is gradually phased out until its final repeal in the year 2010. If Congress does not act at that time to repeal it for the years following, it will automatically revert back to the rates in effect during the year 2001, with an exemption for the first $1,000,000 of assets.

Deferring Payment of Federal Estate Taxes
IRC Sec. 6161 and IRC Sec. 6166

Federal estate taxes are due nine months after a person dies. Because of the hardships, which this sometimes causes in estates containing nonliquid assets, Congress provided two code sections to permit deferred installment payments when certain requirements and conditions are met.

Qualification under IRC Sec. 6161 is at the discretion of the IRS for hardship situations. An estate can generally qualify under IRC Sec. 6166 if it meets all of the requirements.

	IRC Sec. 6161	IRC Sec. 6166
Maximum period of tax spread out	10 years	14 years (Interest only on tax for the first four years).[1] Installment payments over a five-year period apply to certain holding company, and lending and finance business interests.
Portion of tax affected	Total federal estate tax	Only tax attributable to qualifying business,[2] less the applicable credit amount
Interest rate	Same as for deficiencies. Changes periodically.	2% on the portion of tax attributable to first $1,280,000[3] of the taxable value of the business. Interest on any remainder is at 45% of the rate for deficiencies.
Requirements to qualify under each code section	Demonstrate reasonable cause as to why tax cannot be paid when due.	• Business value is greater than 35% of the adjusted gross estate.[4] • Businesses can be combined if decedent owned 20% or more of each. • Business must be closely held: 45[4] or fewer shareholders/partners, or 20% or more voting ownership.

Possible Pitfalls Using Secs. 6161 or 6166

- The deferred payment alternative is not available under IRC Sec. 6166 for federal estate taxes attributable to nonbusiness interests. A business owner's estate which currently qualifies for the IRC Sec. 6166 election may cease to qualify before his or her death because the nonbusiness assets appreciate faster than the business or the business may decline in value.

- The executor can be released of further liability on the unpaid tax if a bond is posted or if parties with an interest in the estate sign a special lien and agreement. However, it appears that parties with an interest would include children and grandchildren named as remaindermen in an AB type credit shelter trust.

---

[1] A principal payment is due in the fifth year.
[2] In one situation, the IRS has determined that the term business does not include active management of one's own real estate portfolio. (See IRS Letter Ruling 9621007, 2/13/96.) The Tax Act of 2001 included certain stock in qualifying lending and finance businesses as qualifying business interests.
[3] This is the value for the year 2008. This amount will be indexed for inflation in future years.
[4] Gifts made within three years of death (in excess of the annual gift tax exclusion) are brought back into the gross estate for purposes of qualifying under IRC Sec. 6166. This prevents deathbed gifts designed to make the estate qualify for the benefits of IRC Sec. 6166.

Continued.

Deferring Payment of Federal Estate Taxes
IRC Sec. 6161 and IRC Sec. 6166

- In certain situations, the IRS may require either the posting of a surety bond or the granting by the executor of a special extended estate tax lien, before agreeing to installment payments under IRC Sec. 6166. See IRS Notice 2007-90, 11/13/07.

- An Internal Revenue Service lien on a business might impair the business in the raising of additional funds for expansion or in periods of financial stress.

- The benefit of the 2% rate is not available to certain holding company stock and non-readily tradable business interests. The interest rate for installment payments of estate tax attributable to such property is 45% of the rate for underpayment of tax. See IRC Secs. 6166(b)(7)(A)(iii) and 6166 (b)(8)(A)(iii)[1].

- The tax due will be accelerated if one-half or more of an interest in the business is sold, exchanged, distributed or withdrawn. This does not apply to transfers by will or transfers involved in an IRC Sec. 303 stock redemption if the redemption proceeds are used to pay the estate tax.

- The remaining tax due will be accelerated if an installment payment of tax or interest is missed. If delinquent payments are paid within six months, the tax will not be accelerated, but the favorable interest rate will be lost for the payment and a 5% per month penalty will be imposed. See IRC Sec. 6166(g)(3)(B).

- Neither of these sections is available for the payment of state inheritance taxes or administration expenses, unless provided by specific state laws.

Life insurance proceeds are often the least expensive method of paying the estate settlement costs. Life insurance removes the risk and uncertainty that the estate may not qualify under the deferral elections or that the cash flow might not be sufficient to meet the annual obligation. Also, the proceeds are generally income tax free and can be arranged to be free of estate taxes too.

---

[1] Includes amendments made by the IRS Restructuring and Reform Act of 1998.

Deferring Payment of Federal Estate Taxes
IRC Sec. 6161 and IRC Sec. 6166

Item Description	Value
Value of gross estate	$10,000,000
Debts, last illness, burial and probate costs	$2,500,000
Adjusted gross estate	$7,500,000
35% of Adjusted Gross Estate	$2,625,000
Value of Business Interest in the Estate	$5,000,000
Is Business a Corporation?	Yes
Estate QUALIFIES for a Section 303 Redemption.	

Estate QUALIFIES for 6166 deferral treatment.

Powers of Appointment

A power of appointment may allow an estate owner to transfer to another person; e.g., spouse, child, etc., the power to decide at some future time the ultimate beneficiary of his or her estate.

This may be important when the beneficiaries are minors and the donor is not certain as to their spending habits, wealth from other sources, future needs, undesirable personal habits, etc.

The creation and exercise or non-exercise of these powers may incur certain tax liabilities and must, therefore, be carefully planned and drafted.

General Powers of Appointment

A general power of appointment is a power that permits the holder to appoint the assets to himself or herself, his or her creditors, his or her estate, or the creditors of his or her estate. Assets subject to a general power of appointment are included in the estate of the person who possesses it. If the power is released during lifetime, it may subject the assets to gift taxation. General powers of appointment created after October 21, 1942 are included in the gross estate whether exercised or permitted to lapse. See IRC Sec. 2041(a)(2). The value of the property which can be appointed is includable in the gross estate of the holder of the power.

Exception to the Rule Regarding General Powers

A person can die owning a power of appointment and not have it included in his or her estate if its use is limited by an ascertainable standard relating to the person's health, education, support or maintenance. In drafting an ascertainable standard provision, the cautious estate planner will follow the provisions set forth in the IRC Sec. 2041(b)(1)(A). Do not use words like comfort, welfare or happiness. See Treas. Reg. Sec. 20.2041-1(c)(2).

These limited powers are sometimes called special powers of appointment and, since they are generally not subject to estate or gift taxation, can be very flexible estate planning tools.

This type of power is often used with the AB type credit shelter trust (also called an exemption or by-pass trust). A special power of appointment is any power to appoint to persons other than the donee of the power or his or her creditors, or the donee's estate or its creditors.

Continued...

Powers of Appointment

Lapse of a General Power and the 5-and-5 Rule

Usually the non-exercise (or lapse) of a general power of appointment is considered to be a release of the power and hence a taxable gift. However, to the extent that the property which could have been appointed does not exceed the greater of $5,000 or 5% of the total value of the assets subject to the power, the lapse will not be a taxable transfer. See IRC Secs. 2041(b)(2) and 2514(e).

Disclaimer of a General Power of Appointment

A person who properly disclaims a power of appointment will not have the power included in his or her gross estate.

Caveat: This is a complex area of the law. The estate planner and owner must be careful to avoid unintentionally creating or exercising general powers of appointment. Also, state law should be examined for additional tax consequences.

Note: Under the Tax Act of 2001, the federal estate tax is gradually phased out until its final repeal in the year 2010. If Congress does not act at that time to repeal it for the years following, it will automatically revert back to the rates in effect during the year 2001, with an exemption for the first $1,000,000 of assets.

Disclaimers

Disclaimers are a means of renouncing a gift or inheritance so that it passes to a third party without being taxed to the intended beneficiary.

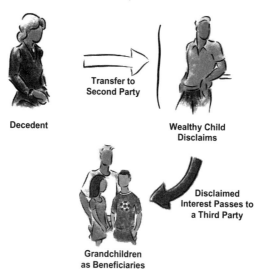

Decedent

Transfer to Second Party

Wealthy Child Disclaims

Disclaimed Interest Passes to a Third Party

Grandchildren as Beneficiaries

Requirements for a Successful Disclaimer

IRC Sec. 2518 sets forth the tests that must be met for a successful disclaimer.

- The refusal to accept the interest must be irrevocable and unqualified.

- It must generally[1] be made within nine months after the transfer creating the interest (i.e., death) or nine months after disclaimant's 21st birthday, if that is later.

- It must be in writing.

- The disclaimant may not have accepted any benefits from the disclaimed interest.

- Without any direction on the part of the disclaimant, the interest must pass to another person or entity (i.e., spouse, children, charity, etc.). A written transfer of an entire interest in property to the person(s) who would have received the same had it been disclaimed will be treated as an effective disclaimer provided the other listed requirements are met.

---

[1] See Reg. 25.2518-2(c)(4), as amended by TD8744 (12/31/97), for an exception to the nine-month rule for certain jointly owned property.

Continued...

Disclaimers

Situations Which May Be Improved with a Disclaimer

- A wealthy child inherits from his parents and by disclaiming the interest it will pass to his children, thus by-passing his generation for estate tax purposes (subject to potential generation-skipping transfer tax).

- A surviving spouse is given the entire estate under the unlimited marital deduction; and by disclaiming a portion of the interest equal to the applicable credit amount of the deceased spouse, he or she can avoid having that portion taxed in his or her estate when he or she later dies.

- A surviving spouse or child is given a general power of appointment over an interest, which will make it includable in his or her estate. This power can be disclaimed to avoid the additional tax.

Note: Under the Tax Act of 2001, the federal estate tax is gradually phased out until its final repeal in the year 2010. If Congress does not act at that time to repeal it for the years following, it will automatically revert back to the rates in effect during the year 2001, with an exemption for the first $1,000,000 of assets.

Generation-Skipping Transfer Tax

Estate owners can often reduce death taxes
by skipping a generation of heirs; e.g.,
bypass their children or give the children
only a right to income for their lifetime
with the remainder passing to their
grandchildren.

Under prior law, when a child died under
such an arrangement, the assets were not
subject to federal estate tax and therefore a
generation of death taxes was skipped.

In order to reduce the loss of this tax in larger estates, Congress enacted the generation-skipping transfer tax in 1976. This very complex law was repealed in 1986 but was replaced with a similar law set forth in IRC Secs. 2601-2663.

Two Common Types of Transfers

- **Generation-sharing transfers:** The transferor (e.g., grandparent) typically places assets in a trust which pays income to his or her child for life and then the remainder passes to grandchildren after the child is deceased.

- **Direct generation skip:** The transferor bypasses his or her children and gives the asset either directly to the grandchildren or a trust for their benefit.

Exempt Transfer

Each transferor has a $2,000,000[1] exemption which can be allocated between gifts made during his or her lifetime and transfers made at time of death.

Rate of Tax

Generation-skipping transfers which exceed the exemptions shown above will be subject to the maximum estate tax rate of 45%.[2] This tax is in addition to the federal estate and gift tax, and is reported on IRS Forms 706GS(D), 706GS(T) or 709. See Treas. Reg. 26.2662-1.

Note: Under the Tax Act of 2001, the federal estate tax is gradually phased out until its final repeal in the year 2010. If Congress does not act at that time to repeal it for the years following, it will automatically revert back to the rates in effect during the year 2001, with an exemption for the first $1,000,000 of assets.

---

[1] The exemption is $2,000,000 for 2007-2008. It changes to $3,500,000 in 2009; to zero in 2010; and back to $1,000,000 (with an adjustment for inflation) in 2011.

[2] This is the current marginal tax bracket on a $2,000,000 taxable estate (assuming death in 2008). The top bracket will be 45% in 2007 through 2009 with zero taxes in 2010. If Congress does not act at that time to repeal the federal estate tax for the years following, in the year 2011 the top bracket of 55% will automatically return.

Continued...

Generation-Skipping Transfer Tax

Reducing the Impact of the Generation-Skipping Transfer Tax

- Married couples should consider a three-trust plan. The first spouse to die could divide his or her $2,000,000 GST exemption between a credit shelter trust (usually equivalent to the applicable exclusion amount) and a QTIP GST-exempt trust. The remaining assets could pass to a QTIP GST-nonexempt trust.

- Consider making full use of the annual gift tax exclusion of $12,000[1] to any number of donees; e.g., children, grandchildren, in-laws, etc.

- Encourage children or grandchildren (or trusts for their benefit) to purchase and own large life insurance policies on the parent or grandparent. At death, the insurance proceeds would not generally be subject to federal estate tax or the generation-skipping transfer tax.

Note: In order to keep the assets of an irrevocable life insurance trust from being subject to the generation-skipping transfer tax, care must be taken to see that transfers (after 3/31/88) to the trust by the insured qualify for the annual gift tax exclusion and that the insured correctly allocates part of his or her $2,000,000 exemption to each transfer.

The generation-skipping transfer tax is a very complex area of the law. Documents must be carefully drafted to avoid this tax in larger estates. For more information, examine IRS Forms 706 GS(D), (D-1) and (T) and their instructions.

---

[1] The annual gift tax exclusion ($12,000 in 2008) is indexed for inflation in increments of $1,000.

Income in Respect of a Decedent
Federal[1] Income and Estate[2] Taxes

For estate tax purposes, a cash basis taxpayer who dies after becoming entitled to income, but who had not actually received it before death, is generally required to include this income in his or her taxable estate. Such income is termed income in respect of a decedent, or IRD. Common sources of IRD include earned-but-unpaid wages, untaxed interest on U. S. savings bonds and untaxed distributions from qualified plans and IRAs.

For income tax purposes, however, the decedent is not allowed to include the IRD on his or her final income tax return. Rather, it is the ultimate recipients of IRD (the heirs) who generally must include it as taxable income, in the year received. A recipient of IRD is allowed a deduction for the amount of estate tax attributable to the IRD included in the decedent's estate.

Assumptions:
   Total taxable estate: $5,000,000
   IRD assets included in taxable estate: $2,000,000
   Year of death: 2004
   Assumed marginal federal income tax rate: 39.60%

Item	With IRD Assets	Without IRD Assets
Taxable estate	$5,000,000	$3,000,000
Federal estate tax before credits[2]	$2,220,800	$1,260,800
Applicable (unified) credit amount	- $ 555,800	- $ 555,800
State death tax credit	-$97,900	-$45,500
Net federal estate tax	**$1,567,100**	**$ 659,500**
Federal estate tax with IRD assets	$1,567,100	
Federal estate tax without IRD assets	- $ 659,500	
Estate tax due to IRD assets	**$ 907,600**	
Total IRD assets	$2,000,000	
Federal estate tax on IRD assets	- $ 907,600	
IRD subject to federal income tax	**$1,092,400**	
Assumed marginal federal income tax rate	39.60%	
Federal income tax on IRD	**$ 432,590**	

---

[1] The discussion here concerns federal law. State or local tax treatment of IRD may differ.
[2] Under the Tax Act of 2001, the federal estate tax is gradually phased out until its final repeal in the year 2010. If Congress does not act at that time to repeal it for the years following, it will automatically revert back to the rates in effect during the year 2001, with an exemption for the first $1,000,000 of assets.

Income in Respect of a Decedent

Under the Internal Revenue Code (IRC), a cash basis taxpayer is generally required to recognize income for federal income tax purposes when the income is actually received. If, however, a cash basis taxpayer dies after becoming entitled to an item of income, but before actually receiving it, the income may not be included on his or her final income tax return because it has not been received.

Such income is termed income in respect of a decedent (IRD).[1] In general, the ultimate recipient of the IRD (e.g., the decedent's estate or heirs) must include the IRD as taxable income for income tax purposes when received. Also, the decedent's estate must include the value of the IRD, for estate tax purposes, as property in which the decedent had an interest.[2]

The Nature of IRD

Although not defined in the IRC,[3] the regulations (Reg. 1.691(a)-1(b)) describe IRD as "those amounts to which a decedent was entitled as gross income, but which were not properly includible in computing his taxable income for the taxable year ending with the date of his death or for a previous taxable year under the method of accounting employed by the decedent." IRD also includes the following:

- All accrued income of a cash basis decedent

- Income accrued solely by reason of the decedent's death, if the decedent reported under the accrual method

- Income to which the decedent had a contingent claim at the time of death[4]

The regulations also specify that IRD includes income in respect of a prior decedent. If the present decedent received the right to income from a prior decedent and the amount was not properly includible in computing the present decedent's taxable income for the year ending on the date of his or her death, the amount is income in respect of the present decedent when it is paid.

Common Sources of IRD

Income in respect of a decedent can arise from a number of common situations. A few frequently encountered sources of IRD are listed below.

- **Wages or other employee compensation:** Such as renewal commissions or deferred compensation, earned by a cash basis decedent, but unpaid at the time of death.

- **Interest on U.S. savings bonds:** Under certain circumstances, untaxed interest on U.S. savings bonds is IRD.

---

[1] Only in very limited situations will the activities of accrual basis taxpayers generate IRD.
[2] See IRC Secs. 691(a) and 2033, respectively.
[3] State or local tax treatment of IRD may differ from federal law.
[4] The regulations do not explain the meaning of the term contingent claim. Instead, the courts must be relied upon to interpret this term.

Continued.

Income in Respect of a Decedent

- **Dividend income:** This income is created if the decedent dies between the date of record and the date of payment.

- **Rental income:** If paid after death and attributable to the period before death, rental income is IRD.

- **Distributions from qualified plans and IRAs:** These are usually considered IRD. Spousal beneficiaries of distributions from IRAs may elect to treat a decedent's IRA as his or her own and avoid having the distribution classified as IRD.

- **Partnership interests:** A decedent's share of partnership income prior to death is considered IRD.

- **S corporations:** For the estates of decedents dying after August 20, 1996, IRD can result from inheriting S corporation stock.

Deductions in Respect of a Decedent

The law allows the recipient of IRD to deduct certain expenses incurred by the decedent but not yet paid at the time of death. Such expenses are termed deductions in respect of a decedent (DRD) and are allowable as deductions for both estate and income tax purposes.[1] IRC Sec. 691(b) identifies five types of expenses and one type of credit, which qualify as DRD.

- The deduction for ordinary and necessary business expenses under IRC Sec. 162

- The interest deduction allowed under IRC Sec. 163

- Deductible taxes under IRC Sec. 164

- Expenses incurred for the production of income under IRC Sec. 212

- The deduction for depletion under IRC Sec. 611

- Foreign tax credits under IRC Sec. 27

Income Tax Deduction for Estate Tax Paid

IRC Sec. 691(c) allows, for income tax purposes, the recipient of IRD a deduction for the federal estate tax attributable to the amount of IRD included in the decedent's estate. The amount of estate tax attributable to the IRD is determined by first calculating the estate tax due on the gross estate, which includes the IRD, and then calculating the estate tax due on the gross estate excluding the IRD.

The deduction for estate tax paid is allowed to the recipient in the year in which the IRD is actually received. For individual taxpayers, the deduction is taken as a miscellaneous itemized deduction (not subject to the 2% of AGI limitation) on Schedule A.

Note: Under the Tax Act of 2001, the federal estate tax is gradually phased out until its final repeal in the year 2010. If Congress does not act at that time to repeal it for the years following, it will automatically revert back to the rates in effect during the year 2001, with an exemption for the first $1,000,000 of assets.

---

[1] See IRC Sec. 642(g).

Potential Combined Tax Disaster
with a Child as the Beneficiary
For Qualified Plan Distributions to a Child During 2008

Through a combination of the federal estate tax and regular income tax paid by the beneficiary, the government may tax a hard-earned qualified plan fund very heavily.

Assumptions:
Qualified plan balance: $2,000,000
Beneficiary: Child
Federal estate tax[1] bracket: 45%
Child's marginal income tax bracket: 35.0%

Beginning balance in qualified plan	$2,000,000
Federal estate tax @ 45%	-900,000
Amount left after federal estate tax	$1,100,000
Income tax payable by the beneficiary on $1,100,000 at 35.0%	**-385,000**
Amount to Child[2]	**$715,000**

Note: This is a hypothetical example to illustrate the potential cumulative impact of these two taxes.

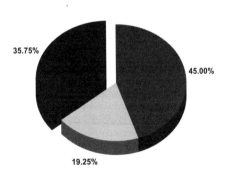

35.75%

45.00%

19.25%

■ Federal Estate Tax ▨ Income Tax ■ Child

---

[1] Under the Tax Act of 2001, the federal estate tax is gradually phased out until its final repeal in the year 2010. If Congress does not act at that time to repeal it for the years following, it will automatically revert back to the rates in effect during the year 2001, with an exemption for the first $1,000,000 of assets.
[2] This calculation does not consider any state income tax.

Potential Combined Tax Disaster
with a Grandchild as the Beneficiary
For Qualified Plan Distributions to a Grandchild During 2008

Through a combination of the federal estate tax, the generation-skipping transfer (GST) tax and regular income tax paid by the beneficiary, the government may tax a hard-earned qualified plan fund very heavily.

Assumptions:
  Qualified plan balance: $2,000,000
  Beneficiary: Grandchild
  Federal estate tax[1] bracket: 45%
  Grandchild's marginal income tax bracket: 35.0%
  GST tax rate: 45%

Beginning balance in qualified plan	$2,000,000
Federal estate tax (FET) @ 45%	-900,000
Generation-skipping transfer tax @ 45%[2]	-495,000
Amount left after FET and GSTT	$605,000
Income tax payable by the beneficiary on $605,000 at 35.0%	-211,750
Amount to Grandchild[3]	**$393,250**

Note: This is a hypothetical example to illustrate the potential cumulative impact of these three taxes.

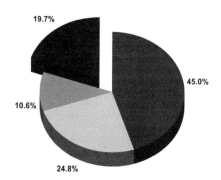

19.7%

45.0%

10.6%

24.8%

■ Federal Estate Tax　▨ GSTT　▨ Income tax　■ Grandchild

---

[1] Under the Tax Act of 2001, the federal estate tax is gradually phased out until its final repeal in the year 2010. If Congress does not act at that time to repeal it for the years following, it will automatically revert back to the rates in effect during the year 2001, with an exemption for the first $1,000,000 of assets.
[2] Assumes $2,000,000 exemptions have been used.
[3] This calculation does not consider any state income tax.

Effects of Skipping a Generation

The long-term effect of skipping a generation of estate taxes can be very substantial. Each estate owner has a $2,000,000[1] exemption from the generation-skipping transfer tax (GSTT). The chart below compares three possible plans for removing $2,000,000 from your estate.

Plan A: A gift of $2,000,000 to your child.

Plan B: A gift of $2,000,000 to your grandchild.

Plan C: A Gift of $2,000,000 to your grandchild who pays $50,000 per year for 10 years (a total of $500,000) for an insurance policy on your life in the amount of $2,000,000.[2] The remaining $1,500,000 the grandchild (or a trust) retains and invests.

Comparison of Three Plans

	Plan A	Plan B	Plan C
Current gift to child[3]	$2,000,000	$0	$0
Current gift to grandchild[3]	0	2,000,000	2,000,000
Additional amount in child's estate	2,000,000	0	0
Growth for 20 years at 5%	5,306,595	0	0
Additional estate tax at child's death	2,918,627	0	0
(assumes 55% tax bracket)			
Amount passing to grandchild	2,387,968	0	0
Additional amount in grandchild's estate			
• Transferred at child's death	2,387,968		
Invested at 5% for 20 years	6,335,990		
• Gift to grandchild now			
Non-insurance portion	0	2,000,000	1,500,000
Growth at 5% for 40 years	0	14,079,977	10,559,983
Portion used to purchase life insurance	0	0	500,000
Insurance face amount	0	0	2,000,000
Growth at 5% for 30 years[4]	0	0	8,643,885
Total amount at grandchild's death	6,335,990	14,079,977	19,203,868
Federal estate tax (at 55%)	3,484,794	7,743,988	10,562,127
Net to great grandchildren	$2,851,195	$6,335,990	$8,641,741

Note: Assumes child or grandchild is in 55% bracket before gifts. Under current law, the 55% bracket returns in 2011.

---

[1] This value applies to 2008.

[2] The insurance that can be purchased will vary greatly depending on age, health, etc. (Assumes 60-year old male.)

[3] A federal gift tax will be due at the time of the gift on any amount in excess of the applicable exclusion amount. The applicable exclusion amount is the dollar value of assets protected from federal estate tax by an individual's applicable credit amount. It is scheduled to change as follows: $2,000,000 for 2007-2008; $3,500,000 for 2009, zero federal estate tax for the year 2010; and $1,000,000 for 2011 and thereafter (unless permanently repealed or otherwise modified).

[4] Assumes the insured dies 10 years after the gift.

Generation-Skipping Transfers and the QTIP Trust

The QTIP trust is a useful technique for a married couple to defer the payment of death taxes until the surviving spouse dies, without regard to the size of the first spouse's estate.

A QTIP, or "C" trust, is typically used in combination with two other trusts: an "A" trust, generally containing any assets belonging to the surviving spouse; and the "B", or credit shelter trust (CST). The CST generally contains enough assets to take advantage of the first spouse's applicable credit amount (in 2007, $2,000,000[1] worth of assets). Assets in this trust are usually not taxed at the death of either spouse.

The QTIP trust holds the balance of the first spouse's assets. If the estate's executor so elects, the federal estate tax on these assets can be deferred until the survivor later dies.

Before 2004 - Potential Generation-Skipping Transfer Tax Problem

Each person who transfers assets during life or at death has an exemption from the generation-skipping transfer tax (GSTT). In 2007, for example, a person can transfer $2,000,000[2] to his or her grandchild and not pay the GSTT on it even though a generation that might pay an estate tax on the assets (the transferor's child) has been skipped.

Assets in a credit shelter trust usually qualify for the first spouse's GSTT exemption. Generally, however, only an amount of assets equivalent to the applicable credit amount in effect in the year of death is transferred to this trust.

In years before 2004 a potential problem was created because there was a difference between the applicable credit amount and the GSTT exemption amount. For 2003, for example, the applicable credit amount was $1,000,000. The GSTT exemption amount was $1,120,000. Since the assets in the QTIP trust are normally considered to be transferred by the surviving spouse, and without proper planning, the remaining portion of the first spouse's $1,120,000 GSTT exemption ($120,000) could have been lost.

The Internal Revenue Code allows the executor of the estate to make what is sometimes called a "reverse" QTIP election as it pertains to the GSTT exemption. See IRC Sec. 2652(a)(3). This means that all of the assets in the QTIP trust would be treated as if the first spouse were the transferor and thus qualify for his or her GSTT exemption. However, if the total amount of assets in both the credit shelter trust and the QTIP trust exceeded (in 2003) $1,120,000, the excess above $1,120,000 would be subject to the GSTT.

---

[1] The applicable exclusion amount is the dollar value of assets protected from federal estate tax by an individual's applicable credit amount. It is scheduled to change as follows: $2,000,000 for 2006-2008; $3,500,000 for 2009, zero federal estate tax for the year 2010; and $1,000,000 for 2011 and thereafter (unless permanently repealed or otherwise modified).

[2] The exemption is $2,000,000 for 2006-2008. It changes to $3,500,000 in 2009; to zero in 2010; and back to $1,000,000 (with an adjustment for inflation) in 2011.

Continued...

Generation-Skipping Transfers and the QTIP Trust

Before 2004 – A Potential Solution

One solution to this potential problem was to create two QTIP trusts. One trust (the "exempt" QTIP) would contain an amount which, when combined with the assets in the credit shelter trust, would equal the GSTT exemption. The other trust (the "nonexempt" QTIP) would contain the first spouse's remaining assets. When the surviving spouse later died, his or her GSTT exemption could be applied to the non-exempt QTIP and/or any other separate assets.

As an example, assume the husband has an estate of $2,240,000 and the wife has only nominal assets. The chart below illustrates the potential estate and GSTT liability when the husband dies first. The example assumes death in 2003.

| Type of Trust | Amount to the Credit Shelter Trust | QTIP Trusts | | Amount Subject to Generation-Skipping Transfer Tax when Surviving Spouse Dies |
		Amount to Exempt QTIP	Amount to Nonexempt QTIP	
One QTIP trust and one credit shelter trust	$1,000,000	$0	$1,240,000	$1,240,000 of which $120,000 would be subject to the GSTT of 49%.[1]
Two QTIP trusts and one credit shelter trust	1,000,000	120,000	1,120,000	$1,120,000, all of which should be protected by the survivor's GSTT exemption.
Federal estate tax treatment	No estate tax at the death of either spouse	The QTIP is generally taxed at the death of the surviving spouse.		

2004-2010

Under the Economic Growth and Tax Relief Reconciliation Act of 2001(EGTRRA), between 2004 – 2009, the applicable exclusion amount for federal estate taxes (FET) and the GSTT exemption amount will be the same in each year:

Year	FET Exemption	GST Exemption
2004	$1,500,000	$1,500,000
2005	1,500,000	1,500,000
2006	2,000,000	2,000,000
2007	2,000,000	2,000,000
2008	2,000,000	2,000,000
2009	3,500,000	3,500,000

The fact that these two amount are the same means that, for 2004 – 2009, there should be no loss of any part of the GSTT exemption of the first spouse to die.

---

[1] This is the amount in excess of the surviving spouse's $1,120,000 generation-skipping transfer tax exemption.

Continued

Generation-Skipping Transfers and the QTIP Trust

2011 and Later – The Problem Returns

EGTRRA of 2001 also provides that both the federal estate tax and the GSTT are repealed for 2010, to be replaced with a capital gains tax. Unless Congress makes the current law permanent, however, both of these taxes return in 2011, with the same applicable exclusion amount and GSTT exemption amount as existed in 2003, adjusted for inflation.

In this situation, it is likely that the GSTT exemption amount will exceed the applicable exclusion amount. This difference could once again present estate owners with the possibility of losing part of the GSTT exemption, unless proper estate planning is done.

Seek Professional Guidance

Given the changing nature of federal estate tax law, estate owners are advised to regularly review their estate plans with an experienced estate planning attorney.

Transfers to Noncitizen Spouses

When a U.S. citizen dies, his or her assets are subject to federal estate taxes if they exceed the applicable exclusion amount. The applicable exclusion amount for 2008 is $2,000,000.[1]

Assets passing to a U.S. citizen spouse can generally qualify for an unlimited marital deduction that will defer any estate tax until he or she later dies. However, if the surviving spouse is not a U.S. citizen, the transfer will not qualify for the unlimited marital deduction, unless passed to a Qualified Domestic Trust (QDOT).

Transfers During Life

U.S. citizens can transfer assets of unlimited value to their citizen spouse during lifetime. If, however, the spouse is a noncitizen, any gifts in excess of $128,000 per year will be subject to federal gift tax.

Transfers at Time of Death

As noted above, transfers at the death of a U.S. citizen to a noncitizen spouse will be subject to federal estate taxes, unless the assets pass to a QDOT. The requirements for a QDOT are set forth in IRC Sec. 2056A(a) and related Treasury Regulations. The essential elements are:

- The QDOT must have at least one trustee who is an individual U.S. citizen or a domestic corporation.

- The U.S. trustee must be able to withhold taxes due on any distributions of the trust principal.

- The trust must meet the requirements set forth by the U.S. Treasury to ensure the collection of the federal estate tax.[2]

- The QDOT must also satisfy the rules which qualify interspousal transfers for the marital deduction for citizen spouses, i.e., a QTIP Trust, a general power of appointment trust or an estate trust. See IRS Letter Ruling 9021037.

- The executor of the estate must make both the QTIP trust election (if applicable) and QDOT election to qualify for the marital deduction. See IRC Sec. 2056A(b)(14) and IRS Letter Ruling 9032014.

Note: Under the Tax Act of 2001, transfers at death to noncitizens who are nonresidents will be treated as a sale or exchange after 2009.

---

[1] The applicable exclusion amount is the dollar value of assets protected from federal estate tax by an individual's applicable credit amount. It is scheduled to change as follows: $2,000,000 for 2007-2008; $3,500,000 for 2009, zero federal estate tax for the year 2010; and $1,000,000 for 2011 and thereafter (unless permanently repealed or otherwise modified).

[2] If the QDOT has assets exceeding $2,000,000, the U.S. trustee must be a bank, or the individual U.S. trustee must furnish a bond for 65% of the value of the QDOT assets at the transferor's demise or must furnish an irrevocable letter of credit to the U.S. government for 65% of the value. Up to $600,000 of the value of the personal residence (in the QDOT) may be excluded in determining whether the $2,000,000 threshold has been reached. See Reg. Sec. 20.2056A-2(d).

Continued...

Transfers to Noncitizen Spouses

What if Death Occurs Without a QDOT?

If the death of a U.S. citizen results in a direct transfer of assets to a noncitizen spouse, the surviving noncitizen spouse may voluntarily establish a QDOT and transfer the assets to the trust before the date on which the tax return is due; i.e., nine months after date of death. See IRC Sec. 2056(d)(2)(B) and Reg. Sec. 20.2056A-2(b)(2).

If the surviving spouse becomes a U.S. citizen before the estate tax return is due, the requirement for a QDOT disappears. Also, if citizenship is obtained after the filing of the tax return and no taxable distributions were made from the QDOT, the surviving spouse may provide the trustee with evidence of citizenship and thereby relax the requirements for a U.S. trustee, etc. See Reg. 20.2056A-10(a).

Trusts that qualify for the marital deduction, but not for the QDOT, may be reformed in court to make them meet the requirements of the Code. See IRC Sec. 2056(d)(5) and Reg. Sec. 20.2056A-4(a)(2).

Distributions from a QDOT

Distributions to a surviving noncitizen spouse of trust income (or distributions of principal on account of hardship) are not subject to the QDOT tax. However, other distributions of trust principal will be subject to federal estate taxes calculated at the marginal estate tax rate of the deceased citizen spouse.

When a U.S. resident noncitizen spouse dies, he or she is entitled to the same applicable credit amount available to U.S. citizens. In 2008, the applicable credit amount is $780,800, equivalent to $2,000,000 of assets. See IRC Sec. 2010. If the noncitizen spouse is a nonresident alien, at death he or she is generally entitled to an applicable exclusion amount of only $13,000, equivalent to $60,000 of assets. See IRC Sec. 2102.[1]

Special Rules for Canadian Spouses

The U.S. imposes an estate tax on the worldwide assets of its residents and citizens. Canada, however, does not impose an estate tax. Instead, capital property of a Canadian resident decedent is deemed to have been disposed of immediately before death for its full fair market value and 50% of any appreciation is subject to Canadian income tax.

The U.S. system is an estate tax system; the Canadian system is an income tax system. Because of the inconsistency of the two tax systems and the possibility of a double tax being imposed on a single asset, the U.S. and Canada have entered into a tax treaty which specifies a series of credits available to residents of one country for taxes paid to the other country.

---

[1] See Estate of Barkat A. Khan v. Commissioner, TC Memo 1998-22.

Continued...

Transfers to Noncitizen Spouses

A modification (Protocol) to the U.S. - Canada tax treaty provides for reciprocal tax credits, significantly reducing the double taxation arising from the imposition of both the U.S. federal estate tax and the Canadian income tax, upon the death of an individual.

Some highlights of this protocol include the following.

- The Protocol became effective on November 9, 1995 and was retroactively effective for deaths occurring after November 10, 1988.

- Canadian citizens and residents are allowed a larger applicable credit amount than is generally available to nonresident, alien decedents.

- Instead of a marital deduction, a credit is allowed against U.S. estate tax for property passing to a Canadian spouse.

- A credit is allowed against U.S. estate tax for income tax paid to Canada as a result of the decedent's death.

- U.S. estate tax will not be imposed on most Canadian resident decedents whose estates are worth $1,200,000 (U.S. dollars) or less, unless those estates include real property or business interests located in the U.S.

- A Canadian spousal rollover is available to U.S resident decedents.

- A credit is provided against Canadian income tax for U.S. estate tax paid on property located in the U.S. or generating income from the U.S.

- Because it applied retroactively, the Protocol allowed estates in both the U.S. and Canada to file refund claims within one year of its effective date or within the ordinary statute of limitations.

Seek Professional Guidance

The United States has entered into a number of tax treaties with foreign countries. Individuals with a non-U.S. citizen spouse or individuals with property in foreign countries are advised to seek professional guidance and counsel when planning their estates.

Estate Freezing Generally

When an estate reaches $2,000,000, it enters the top estate tax bracket.

When 45% of each additional dollar of estate growth is earmarked for estate taxes, many estate owners look for methods of freezing the growth of their present estate.

Techniques developed over the years can be classified in three categories.

- **Gifts of assets**
  - Lifetime gifts to children of $12,000[1] or less per year are generally free of gift taxes.
  - Gifts to an irrevocable life insurance trust can create very large amounts of capital which are not subject to estate or income tax.
  - Gifts to charities can produce both income and estate tax savings.

- **Intrafamily sales of assets**
  - An installment sale of an asset to a child in exchange for secured promissory notes will put future growth of the asset in the child's estate.
  - A private annuity is the sale of an asset for an unsecured promise to pay annual amounts for the seller's lifetime.

- **Changes in business organizations**
  - Corporate recapitalizations
  - Personal holding company
  - Multi-tier family partnerships

The Revenue Reconciliation Act of 1990 repealed the so-called antifreeze provision of the IRC Sec. 2036(c) and replaced it with a new Chapter 14 entitled "Special Valuation Rules." See IRC Secs. 2701 – 2704.

The purpose of this new chapter is to impose a gift tax at the time an estate-freezing transaction occurs rather than waiting until the taxpayer dies.

IRC Sec. 2701 establishes a valuation rule for estate-freezing techniques involving interests in corporations and partnerships; e.g., recapitalizations.

Note: Under the Tax Act of 2001, the federal estate tax is gradually phased out until its final repeal in the year 2010. If Congress does not act at that time to repeal it for the years following, it will automatically revert back to the rates in effect during the year 2001, with an exemption for the first $1,000,000 of assets.

---

[1] The annual gift tax exclusion ($12,000 in 2008) is indexed for inflation in increments of $1,000.

Family General Partnership

Family partnerships are often used as a method of dividing business income with children in lower tax brackets and shifting future appreciation out of one's estate.

The rules set forth in IRC Sec. 704(e) deal with partnerships where capital is a material income-producing factor, as opposed to businesses which earn income by providing services.

Family members can either purchase an interest in the business or receive it by gift. If the value exceeds the annual gift tax exclusion amount, currently $12,000,[1] there may be gift taxes due. The donor parent may use his or her applicable credit amount to eliminate or reduce gift taxes on amounts exceeding the annual gift tax exclusion.

A trust for minors can be a partner if the trust is administered solely for the beneficiaries' best interests. See Treas. Reg. Sec. 1.704-1(e)(2)(vii).

Why Consider a Family Partnership?

What is the effect of shifting estate growth to a younger generation? Assume a sole proprietorship currently valued at $200,000 which has a growth potential of 10%.

	Retain as Sole Proprietorship	Set Up a Family Partnership
1. Current value of business	$200,000	$200,000
2. Amount transferred to children	0	100,000
3. Amount remaining in the estate	200,000	100,000
4. Growth of business (10 years at 10%)	518,748	259,374
5. Federal estate tax at 45%	233,436	116,718
Potential estate tax savings		**$116,718**
6. Growth of business (20 years at 10%)	$1,345,500	$672,750
7. Federal estate tax at 45%	605,475	302,737
Potential estate tax savings		**$302,737**

Family Partnerships Are Not for Everyone

Before proceeding with a family partnership arrangement, business owners must ask if they really want to have a child involved in their business. What effect will the reduced income have on their lifestyle? Will there be a gift tax due and payable when the transfer is made? Will the tax savings compensate for the increased complexity?

---

[1] The annual gift tax exclusion ($12,000 in 2008) is indexed for inflation in increments of $1,000.

Family Limited Partnership

Family limited partnerships (FLP) can be used
with business, personal or investment assets.
Their traditional purpose has been to divide
investment income with children in lower income
tax brackets and increase the family's net
spendable income.

They have also been used for long-range estate
planning. Closely held businesses, along with
other assets, are subject to Federal estate and generation skipping transfer taxes. These taxes
can effectively prevent the transfer of a family business from one generation to the next.
The FLP provides a valuable estate planning tool to lessen these tax burdens.[1]

In recent years, such partnerships have also been employed as a method of protecting
family assets from creditors.

IRC Sec. 704(e) effectively limits FLPs to business/investment activities where capital is a
material income-producing factor, as contrasted with activities which earn income by
providing services.

How It Works

The parents set up a FLP and transfer capital assets into the partnership. Within the
partnership structure, the parents act as the general partners; the children (or
grandchildren) are the limited partners.

In a limited partnership, the general partners often own only a small proportion of the
partnership (for example 5%), while the limited partners own the majority interest. The
general partners have complete responsibility and control of partnership activities, as well
as the liability for partnership debts and losses.

The limited partners have no control or management rights. Their liability is limited to the
amount of their contribution to the partnership.

One of the most attractive features of the FLP is its flexibility. Some estate planning
strategies must be irrevocable in order to be effective. Once set up, these irrevocable tools
cannot be changed or undone. By contrast, the FLP document can be modified to respond
to changes in the family or business structure.

---

[1] Under the Tax Act of 2001, the federal estate tax is gradually phased out until its final repeal in the year 2010. If Congress
does not act at that time to repeal it for the years following, it will automatically revert back to the rates in effect during the
year 2001, with an exemption for the first $1,000,000 of assets.

Continued...

Family Limited Partnership

Reasons to Consider a Family Limited Partnership

There are three primary reasons for creating an FLP.

- **Income tax benefits:** Income generated by a limited partnership is often allocated according to ownership. With the limited partners (the children or grandchildren) owning the majority interest, most of the income generated could flow through to them and be taxed at their lower marginal tax rate.

- **Estate planning benefits:** When the parents contribute assets to the partnership, they are transferring asset value and shifting asset growth from themselves to a younger generation.

Consider the following hypothetical example in which an asset has a current value of $200,000 and is expected to grow by 10% per year. Over time, the parents transfer 90% of the business to the children.

	Retain for Parents	Contribute to FLP
Current value	$200,000	$200,000
Amount transferred to children	$0	$180,000
Amount remaining in estate	$200,000	$20,000
Asset value in 20 years	$1,345,500	$134,550
Federal estate tax assumed at 45%	$605,475	$60,548
Potential estate tax savings	**$544,928**	

Often a gifted ownership interest can receive a discounted value because the interest is either a minority interest or lacks marketability. This minority interest issue should be carefully reviewed with your legal advisor.

- **Protecting assets from lawsuits:** Most state limited partnership statutes prevent the creditors of a limited partner from attaching partnership assets. While the creditors may get a charging order against the debtor's partnership interest, as a practical matter it is very difficult to collect the debt. The FLP may provide one of the most effective asset protection structures available today.

Family Limited Partnerships Are Not for Everyone

Before considering a FLP, there are a number of questions that the parent or parents must answer. Do they really want to have a child involved in their business? Will the income shared with the child affect the parents' lifestyle? Will a gift tax be due and payable when the transfer is made to the child? Will the income tax savings compensate for the increased complexity?

Additionally, legal counsel must be obtained. Because of the complexity involved, FLPs are not appropriate for every situation. The documentation for such a partnership must be carefully designed to avoid problems with both federal law and the law of the state under which the limited partnership is being created.

Family Limited Partnership

Family limited partnerships (FLP) can be used
with business, personal or investment assets.
Their traditional purpose has been to divide
investment income with children in lower income
tax brackets and increase the family's net
spendable income.

They have also been used for long range estate
planning. Closely held businesses, along with
other assets, are subject to federal estate and generation skipping transfer taxes. These taxes
can effectively prevent the transfer of a family business from one generation to the next.
The FLP provides a valuable estate planning tool to lessen these tax burdens.[1]

In recent years, such partnerships have also been employed as a method of protecting
family assets from creditors.

IRC Sec. 704(e) effectively limits FLPs to business/investment activities where capital is a
material, income-producing factor, as contrasted with activities which earn income by
providing services.

How It Works

The parents set up a FLP and transfer capital assets into the partnership. Within the
partnership structure, the parents act as the general partners; the children (or
grandchildren) are the limited partners.

In a limited partnership, the general partners often own only a small proportion of the
partnership (for example 5%), while the limited partners own the majority interest. The
general partners have complete responsibility and control of partnership activities, as well
as the liability for partnership debts and losses.

The limited partners have no control or management rights. Their liability is limited to the
amount of their contribution to the partnership.

One of the most attractive features of the FLP is its flexibility. Some estate planning
strategies must be irrevocable in order to be effective. Once set up, these irrevocable tools
cannot be changed or undone. By contrast, the FLP document can be modified to respond
to changes in the family or business structure.

---

[1] Under the Tax Act of 2001, the federal estate tax is gradually phased out until its final repeal in the year 2010. If Congress
does not act at that time to repeal it for the years following, it will automatically revert back to the rates in effect during the
year 2001, with an exemption for the first $1,000,000 of assets.

Continued...

Family Limited Partnership

Why Consider a Family Limited Partnership?

There are three primary reasons for creating an FLP.

- **Income tax benefits:** Income generated by a limited partnership is often allocated according to ownership. With the limited partners (the children or grandchildren) owning the majority interest, most of the income generated could flow through to them and be taxed at their lower marginal tax rate.

- **Estate planning benefits:** When the parents contribute assets to the partnership, they are transferring asset value and shifting asset growth from themselves to a younger generation.

  Consider the following hypothetical example in which an asset has a current value of $1,000,000 and is expected to grow by 2.00% per year. Over time, the parents transfer 50% of the business to the children.

	Retain for Parents	Contribute to FLP
Current value	$1,000,000	$1,000,000
Amount transferred to children	$0	$ 500,000
Amount remaining in estate	$1,000,000	$ 500,000
Asset value in 10 years	$1,218,994	$ 609,497
Federal estate tax assumed at 40.00%	$ 487,598	$ 243,799
Potential estate tax savings	**$ 243,799**	

  Often a gifted ownership interest can receive a discounted value because the interest is either a minority interest or lacks marketability. This minority interest issue should be carefully reviewed with your legal advisor.

- **Protecting assets from lawsuits:** Most state limited partnership statutes prevent the creditors of a limited partner from attaching partnership assets. While the creditors may get a charging order against the debtor's partnership interest, as a practical matter it is very difficult to collect the debt. The FLP may provide one of the most effective asset protection structures available today.

Family Limited Partnerships Are Not for Everyone

Before considering a FLP, there are a number of questions that the parent or parents must answer. Do they really want to have a child involved in their business? Will the income shared with the child affect the parents' lifestyle? Will a gift tax be due and payable when the transfer is made to the child? Will the income tax savings compensate for the increased complexity?

Additionally, legal counsel must be obtained. Because of the complexity involved, FLPs are not appropriate for every situation. The documentation for such a partnership must be carefully designed to avoid problems with both federal law and the law of the state under which the limited partnership is being created.

Family Limited Partnership

Consider the following hypothetical example in which an asset has a current value of $1,000,000 and is expected to grow by 2.00% per year. Over time, the parents transfer 50% of the business to the children.

	Retain for Parents	Contribute to FLP
Current value	$1,000,000	$1,000,000
Amount transferred to children	$0	$ 500,000
Amount remaining in estate	$1,000,000	$ 500,000
Asset value in 10 years	$1,218,994	$ 609,497
Federal estate tax assumed at 40.00%	$ 487,598	$ 243,799
Potential estate tax savings	**$ 243,799**	

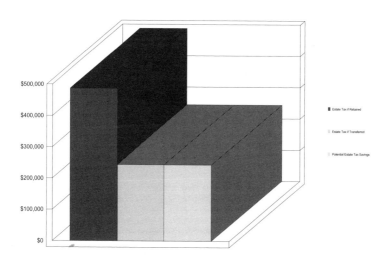

Installment Sale

The installment sale method allows a taxpayer to spread the profit on a sale over the entire period during which the payments are received. Each payment received is treated as part return of investment and part profit and interest. This relieves the seller of paying tax on income not yet received.

The seller must either use the installment method or elect not to use it and include all of the gain in the current year.

Imputed Interest

If no interest is charged under the terms of the agreement, the IRS imputes interest to the transaction. This means that even if the seller does not collect any interest on the transaction, the IRS will pretend that he or she does and require him or her to include the imputed interest in his or her annual income.

Depreciable Property

If the property sold has been subject to excess depreciation (i.e., greater than straight-line depreciation), any recapture of the excess depreciation must be reported in the year of the sale. Any gain in excess of the recaptured amount may be eligible for installment treatment. When the parties are related, installment sale treatment is only available for sales of depreciated property if it can be demonstrated that tax avoidance was not a principal purpose for the installment sale.

Sales to Related Parties

Any installment sale to a related party[1] who then sells (or otherwise disposes of) the property may cancel the installment reporting of the first sale unless at least two years have passed since the first sale and the property is not marketable securities. See IRC Sec. 453(e).

---

[1] Related parties generally include one's spouse, ancestors, descendants, brothers, sisters and business entities or trusts controlled by any of them. See IRC Sec. 453(f)(1).

Continued...

Installment Sale

Sales by Dealers

Sales of real or personal property by a dealer or anyone who regularly sells property on the installment plan cannot be reported on the installment method. Neither can sales of personal property that would have to be included in business inventory if it were on hand at the end of the tax year.

Advantages of Installment Sales

If installment-sale reporting is available, it has several important advantages.

- By spreading income over two or more tax years, it may allow the gain to be taxed in lower tax brackets.

- Even if no taxes are saved, if the payment can be postponed for one or more years, the deferred tax dollars can earn income until they become due.

- Potential future appreciation of the asset may be removed from the seller's estate.

- One may be able to shift high-income-producing assets to a family member in a lower tax bracket.

Notes: An installment sale of an interest in a corporation or partnership should not be regulated by the special valuation rules of IRC Sec. 2701.

In some situations there may be interest due on deferred tax liabilities. See IRC Sec. 453A.

Private Annuity

A private annuity is a contract between two individuals to exchange a valuable asset for a lifetime income.

A Typical Example

Parent
(annuitant)

Transfers valuable assets
(usually highly appreciated)

An unsecured promise to pay an
annual sum for lifetime of annuitant

Child
(payor)

Formula

| Fair Market Value of Asset | ÷ | Annuity Factor for Age and Sex of Annuitant (See IRC Sec. 7520.) | = | Annual Payment Necessary to Avoid Gift Tax |

- If the annuity payment is large enough, there will be no gift tax.
- The annuity factor is dependent upon the parent's age.
- Parent can make annual gifts to child to assist in meeting the annual payments.
- Payments to annuitant are partially income tax-free with the remainder taxed as ordinary income, but they are not deductible to the payer.[1]

Estate Planning Considerations

Advantages	Disadvantages
• The asset and future appreciation may be removed from the annuitant's estate without gift tax or estate tax liability. • The annuitant gets a lifetime income. • Some of the payments will be considered a return of capital and not taxable.	• Annuitant may live too long with the payer paying too much for the asset, thus increasing the size of annuitant's estate. • Payments are not tax deductible. • If payer dies, it may be difficult to collect the payments. A life policy could guarantee funds.

---

[1] On 10/17/06, the IRS issued proposed regulations (NPRM REG-141901-5) on the exchange of appreciated property for an annuity contract. These proposed regulations treat the transaction as if the transferor had sold the property for cash and then used the proceeds to purchase an annuity contract. The proposed regulations are generally effective for transactions occurring after 10/18/06, with a six-month delay until 04/18/07 for certain types of transactions.

Corporate Recapitalization

Recapitalization is a reorganization of the corporation's capital structure by readjusting the amount and type of stock outstanding. Typically, the corporation issues both voting preferred stock and common stock in exchange for the owner's currently held common stock.

Prior to 1987, most of the value of the company at the time of the recapitalization was assigned to the preferred stock. The common stock, therefore, had very little value and could be gifted to or sold to the children with very little, if any, gift tax consequence. Since the future appreciation of the business would be reflected in the common stock, the parents could transfer all of the future appreciation while still effectively retaining control of the business until their deaths.

In 1987, Congress effectively eliminated recapitalizations as an estate freezing device by enacting IRC Sec. 2036(c).

Rules Under IRC Sec. 2701

The Revenue Reconciliation Act of 1990 repealed IRC Sec. 2036(c) and enacted IRC Sec. 2701, which specifically deals with valuation in the transfer of business interests. Recapitalization freezes may be beneficial under this law if all the rules are carefully followed.

First, the business must be valued using appraisal standards acceptable to the IRS.

Second, the preferred stock, which the owner will retain, must be valued.

- Some privileges are assigned a zero value; e.g., voting rights, conversion rights, etc.

- At least 10% of the business value must be allocated to the common stock (if the family owns 50% or more of the business).

- The value is based on the dividends which must be paid to the preferred stockholders. Higher dividends will increase the value of the preferred stock, but they also drain the working capital of the business.

Finally, the value of the preferred stock is subtracted from the appraised value of the entire business, and the difference will be the value of the common stock.

If dividends are missed, they will be added back into the value of the preferred stock when the owner dies. If dividends are not paid for four consecutive years, interest will accrue and will also be added onto the value of the preferred stock.

Note: Under the Tax Act of 2001, the federal estate tax is gradually phased out until its final repeal in the year 2010. If Congress does not act at that time to repeal it for the years following, it will automatically revert back to the rates in effect during the year 2001, with an exemption for the first $1,000,000 of assets.

Joint Purchase of Assets

The technique of a joint purchase of certain assets by a parent and child brought some very attractive tax results; however, in most cases it has been eliminated as a family wealth-transfer technique. Here's how it might still work.

- A parent and child find a qualified property. Joint purchases by family members must be limited to a personal residence or tangible property, such as artwork.[1]

- The parent purchases the life income interest and the child purchases the remainder interest. The IRS Table S gives the following percentages at an 8% rate. This rate varies from month to month as provided under IRC Sec. 7520.

Values	Age of Parents					
	50	55	60	65	70	75
Value of Remainder	18%	23%	28%	35%	42%	50%
Value of Life Income	82%	77%	72%	65%	58%	50%

Note: Numbers have been rounded to the nearest percent. See Reg. Sec. 25.2512-5.

Assume a father aged 55 wants to purchase a personal residence with his son under this type of arrangement. The father must invest 77% and the son only 23%. At the father's demise, his life income expires and the asset is not included in his estate—the entire 77% that he paid into the property, plus any appreciation, would be excluded.

Potential Problems

- The return on the child's investment may not be very high if the parent lives beyond life expectancy.

- If the parent gives the money to the child to make the initial purchase, there will be estate and gift tax problems. The IRS will likely treat the transaction as a purchase by the father with a gift of a future interest (the remainder) to the child. Future interests do not qualify for the annual gift tax exclusion. Furthermore, since the father retained a life income, the IRS may attempt to include the asset in his estate.

Note: Under the Tax Act of 2001, the federal estate tax is gradually phased out until its final repeal in the year 2010. If Congress does not act at that time to repeal it for the years following, it will automatically revert back to the rates in effect during the year 2001, with an exemption for the first $1,000,000 of assets.

---

[1] Some analysts feel the IRS will include the asset in the parent's estate under IRC Sec. 2702.

Grantor-Retained Interest Trust
(GRIT)

Grantor makes irrevocable gift

Grantor receives a fixed payment

Grantor (parent)

(irrevocable trust)

At the end of the designated time period, the remainder passes to the grantor's children.

Children

The use of the grantor-retained interest trust (GRIT) under the Revenue Reconciliation Act of 1990 is limited to those trusts which either pay the grantor a fixed payment at least annually (an annuity) or pay a fixed percentage of the trust assets as computed annually (a unitrust).

The intrafamily GRIT allowed under the prior law currently has only a limited usefulness in the areas of tangible property (e.g., art work) and personal residences which are exempt from the special valuation rules. Such a GRIT is still usable in situations involving unrelated individuals, as well as those including non-lineal descendants such as nieces, nephews and cousins.

To avoid confusion between the GRIT prior to the change in law and the type of trusts which are now permitted, we have two new forms of GRITs called GRATs and GRUTs.

The GRAT is a grantor-retained annuity trust and the GRUT is a grantor-retained unitrust.

By following the new rules, senior family members may transfer assets with growth potential to junior family members with minimal payment of gift taxes.

In localities where real estate values are depressed, a personal residence GRIT may be very useful in transferring future appreciation potential to one's children.

Note: Under the Tax Act of 2001, the federal estate tax is gradually phased out until its final repeal in the year 2010. If Congress does not act at that time to repeal it for the years following, it will automatically revert back to the rates in effect during the year 2001, with an exemption for the first $1,000,000 of assets.

Grantor-Retained Interest Trust
(GRIT)

Grantor makes irrevocable gift

Grantor receives a fixed payment

Grantor (parent)

(irrevocable trust)

At the end of the designated time period, the remainder passes to the grantor's children.

Children

The value of the transferred asset minus the value of the retained income interest will equal the value of the remainder interest which is subject to gift taxation.

The example below illustrates the potential tax benefits of a term trust for 10 years.

Assumptions:
Value of asset: $1,000,000
Age of grantor at beginning of trust: 55
Term of the trust:[1] 10 years
Federal discount rate:[2] 7.00%

Value of remainder interest	$ 508,349
Probability of living 10 years	88.69%
Amount of taxable gift: $ 450,862	

Assuming the grantor lives beyond the 10 -year period, he or she will have removed a $1,000,000 asset (plus its growth potential during the 10 years) from the taxable estate.

The cost of the transfer would be the gift tax on the value of the taxable gift. The gift is of a future interest and does not qualify for the annual gift tax exclusion. The gift tax on assets up to $1,000,000 is first offset by an individual's applicable credit amount. The tax on gifts which exceed the $1,000,000 must be paid in cash in the year the gift is made.

---

[1] If death occurs before 10 years, the value of the trust assets is includable in the grantor's gross taxable estate.
[2] This rate generally changes monthly.

Grantor-Retained Interest Trust
(GRIT)

The following example illustrates the potential tax benefits of a term trust for 10 years.

Assumptions:
Value of asset: $1,000,000
Age of grantor at beginning of trust: 55
Term of the trust:[1] 10 years
Federal discount rate:[2] 7.00%

Value of remainder interest	$ 508,349
Probability of living 10 years	88.69%
Amount of taxable gift: $ 450,862	

Assuming the grantor lives beyond the 10 -year period, he or she will have removed a $1,000,000 asset (plus its growth potential during the 10 years) from the taxable estate.

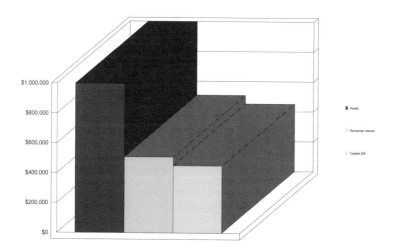

---

[1] If death occurs before 10 years, the value of the trust assets is includable in the grantor's gross taxable estate.
[2] This rate generally changes monthly.

Grantor-Retained Annuity Trust
GRAT

An estate owner may use the GRAT to transfer assets and future appreciation to his or her children.

Grantor
(parent)

Parent transfers remainder interest in an asset to trust.

(irrevocable trust)

Parent retains right to receive a fixed payment (at least annually) for 10 years.[1]

At the end of the designated time period, the remainder passes to the grantor's children.

Children

The value of the transferred asset minus the value of the retained annuity interest will equal the value of the remainder interest that is subject to gift taxation.

Assumptions:
Value of asset placed in GRAT: $500,000
Age of grantor: 65
Type of payment: End of year
Term of payment: 10 years
Federal discount rate (changes monthly): 4.0%

Annual Payment to the Grantor	First-Year Payment as a Percentage of the Asset[2]	Value of the Retained Interest	Gift Tax Value of the Remainder Interest
$30,000	6%	$243,327	$256,673
$40,000	8%	$324,436	$175,564
$50,000	10%	$405,545	$94,455
$60,000	12%	$486,654	$13,346

The cost of the transfer would be the gift tax on the value of the remainder interest. The gift is of a future interest and does not qualify for the annual gift tax exclusion. The gift tax on assets up to $1,000,000 is first offset by an individual's applicable credit amount. The tax on gifts that exceed $1,000,000 must be paid in cash in the year the gift is made.

---

[1] The payment period can be for the life of the grantor, for two or more joint lives or for a set number of years.
[2] In subsequent years the dollar amount of annual payment would remain the same but the percentage of trust assets distributed would vary.

Grantor-Retained Annuity Trust
GRAT

An estate owner may use the GRAT to transfer assets and future appreciation to his or her children.

**Grantor
(parent)**

**Parent transfers
remainder interest in an
asset to trust.**

**Parent retains right to
receive a fixed payment (at
least annually) for 10 years.** [1]

GRAT

(irrevocable trust)

**At the end of the designated
time period, the remainder
passes to the grantor's children.**

Children

The value of the transferred asset minus the value of the retained annuity interest will equal the value of the remainder interest which is subject to gift taxation.

Assumptions:
Value of asset placed in GRAT: $1,000,000
Type of payment: End of year
Term of payment: 10 years
Federal discount rate (changes monthly): 7.00%

Annual Payment to the Grantor	First-Year Payment as a Percentage of the Asset[2]	Value of the Retained Annuity Interest	Gift Tax Value of the Remainder Interest
$60,000	6.00%	$ 421,415	$ 578,585
$80,000	8.00%	$ 561,887	$ 438,113
$ 100,000	10.00%	$ 702,358	$ 297,642
$ 120,000	12.00%	$ 842,830	$ 157,170

The cost of the transfer would be the gift tax on the value of the remainder interest. The gift is of a future interest and does not qualify for the annual gift tax exclusion. The gift tax on assets up to $1,000,000 is first offset by the applicable credit amount. The tax on gifts which exceed $1,000,000 must be paid in cash in the year the gift is made.

---

[1] The payment period can be for the life of the grantor, for two or more joint lives or for a set number of years.
[2] In subsequent years the dollar amount of annual payment would remain the same but the percentage of trust assets distributed would vary.

Grantor-Retained Annuity Trust
GRAT

The GRAT may be used by an estate owner to transfer assets and future appreciation to his or her children.

Assumptions:
Value of asset placed in GRAT: $1,000,000
Type of payment: End of year
Term of payment: 10 years
Federal discount rate (changes monthly): 7.00%

Annual Payment to the Grantor	First-Year Payment as a Percentage of the Asset[1]	Value of the Retained Annuity Interest	Gift Tax Value of the Remainder Interest
$60,000	6.00%	$ 421,415	$ 578,585
$80,000	8.00%	$ 561,887	$ 438,113
$ 100,000	10.00%	$ 702,358	$ 297,642
$ 120,000	12.00%	$ 842,830	$ 157,170

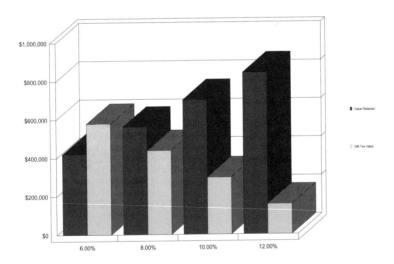

[1] In subsequent years the dollar amount of annual payment would remain the same but the percentage of trust assets distributed would vary.

Grantor-Retained Unitrust
GRUT

An estate owner may use the GRUT to transfer assets to his or her children.

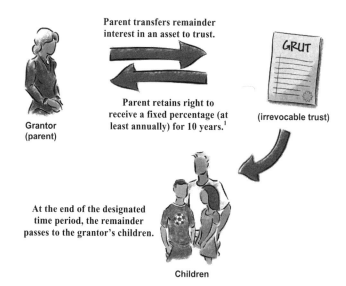

Parent transfers remainder interest in an asset to trust.

GRUT

Parent retains right to receive a fixed percentage (at least annually) for 10 years.[1]

(irrevocable trust)

Grantor (parent)

At the end of the designated time period, the remainder passes to the grantor's children.

Children

The value of the transferred asset minus the value of the retained unitrust interest will equal the value of the remainder interest that is subject to gift taxation.

For example, if the payout rate is 6%, the trustee will pay the grantor 6% of the value of the trust assets each year. If the trust assets earn more than the 6% payout, there will be a higher payment the following year.

For this reason, the GRUT is not as effective as the grantor-retained annuity trust (GRAT) in shifting asset appreciation to younger generations.

However, for persons desiring to transfer assets to children while retaining an increasing annual return of income, the GRUT should be considered.

The cost of the transfer would be the gift tax on the value of the remainder interest. The gift is of a future interest and does not qualify for the annual gift tax exclusion. The gift tax on assets up to $1,000,000 is first offset by the applicable credit amount. The tax on gifts which exceed $1,000,000 must be paid in cash in the year the gift is made.

---

[1] The payment period can be for the life of the grantor or a set number of years.

Grantor-Retained Unitrust
GRUT

An estate owner may use the GRUT to transfer assets to his or her children.

**Grantor
(parent)**

**Parent transfers remainder
interest in an asset to trust.**

**Parent retains right to
receive a fixed percentage (at
least annually) for 10 years.**

(irrevocable trust)

**At the end of the designated
time period, the remainder
passes to the grantor's children.**

Children

The value of the transferred asset minus the value of the retained unitrust interest will equal the value of the remainder interest that is subject to gift taxation.

Assumptions:
Value of asset placed in grantor-retained unitrust: $1,000,000
Type of payment: End of year
Term of payment:[1] 10 years
Federal discount rate (changes monthly): 7.00%

First-Year Payment to the Grantor	First-Year Payment as a Percentage of the Asset[2]	Value of the Retained Interest	Gift Tax Value of the Remainder Interest
$60,000	6.00%	$ 461,385	$ 538,615
$80,000	8.00%	$ 565,612	$ 434,388
$ 100,000	10.00%	$ 651,322	$ 348,678
$ 120,000	12.00%	$ 721,499	$ 278,501

The cost of the transfer would be the gift tax on the value of the remainder interest. The gift is of a future interest and does not qualify for the annual gift tax exclusion. The gift tax on assets up to $1,000,000 is first offset by the applicable credit amount. The tax on gifts that exceed $1,000,000 must be paid in cash in the year the gift is made.

---

[1] Although the payment period for a GRUT can be for the life of the grantor, or a set number of years, this example assumes a set number of years.

[2] In subsequent years the dollar amount of annual payment would vary but the percentage of trust assets distributed would remain the same.

Grantor-Retained Unitrust
GRUT

The GRUT may be used by an estate owner to transfer assets to his or her children.

Assumptions:
Value of asset placed in grantor-retained unitrust: $1,000,000
Type of payment: End of year
Term of payment: 10 years
Federal discount rate (changes monthly): 7.00%

First-Year Payment to the Grantor	First-Year Payment as a Percentage of the Asset[1]	Value of the Retained Interest	Gift Tax Value of the Remainder Interest
$60,000	6.00%	$ 461,385	$ 538,615
$80,000	8.00%	$ 565,612	$ 434,388
$ 100,000	10.00%	$ 651,322	$ 348,678
$ 120,000	12.00%	$ 721,499	$ 278,501

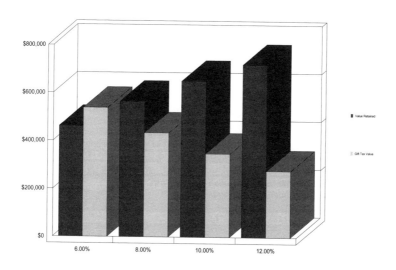

[1] In subsequent years the dollar amount of annual payment would remain the same but the percentage of trust assets distributed would vary.

Personal Residence GRIT

The GRIT is a grantor-retained income trust. This planning technique allows a person (the grantor) to transfer assets to a trust and retain the income for a number of years, after which the remaining trust assets pass to others; e.g., children, grandchildren, etc.

By retaining the rights to the income, the value of the remaining interest is reduced, along with the potential gift tax. If the grantor lives beyond the term of years selected to receive the income, the asset will be totally removed from his or her taxable estate.

Although the use of this device was limited by the Tax Act of 1990, it is still useful when used with a personal residence of the grantor.

Qualified Personal Residence Trust

The following example illustrates the potential tax benefits of this type of trust, with a term of 10 years or the death of the grantor, should it occur earlier:

Assumptions:
Value of residence: $500,000
Age of grantor at beginning of trust: 65
Term of the trust: 10 years
Gov't. rate for valuing remainder interest: 7.4%[1]

Value of remainder interest	$244,865
Probability of living 10 years	76.02%
Amount of taxable gift = $186,142	

Assuming the grantor lives beyond the 10-year period, he or she will have removed a $500,000 asset (plus its growth potential during the 10 years) from the taxable estate.[2]

The trust instrument should be drafted so that it is a grantor trust. This makes the trust income taxable to the grantor but also allows him or her to deduct mortgage interest and property tax payments made by the trustee.

Note: The grantor's applicable credit amount may be used to avoid paying a gift tax on the taxable portion.

---

[1] This rate generally changes monthly.
[2] If death occurs before 10 years, the value of the trust assets is includable in the grantor's gross taxable estate.

Personal Residence GRIT

The GRIT is a grantor-retained income trust. This planning technique allows a person (the grantor) to transfer assets to a trust and retain the income for a number of years, after which the remaining trust assets pass to others; e.g., children, grandchildren, etc.

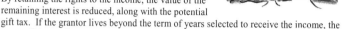

By retaining the rights to the income, the value of the remaining interest is reduced, along with the potential gift tax. If the grantor lives beyond the term of years selected to receive the income, the asset will be totally removed from his or her taxable estate.

Although the use of this device was limited by the Tax Act of 1990, it is still useful when used with a personal residence of the grantor.

Qualified Personal Residence Trust

The following example illustrates the potential tax benefits of this type of trust, with a term of 10 years or the death of the grantor, should it occur earlier.

Assumptions:
Value of residence: $1,000,000
Age of grantor at beginning of trust: 55
Term of the trust:[1] 10 years
Federal discount rate:[2] 7.00%

Value of remainder interest	$ 508,349
Probability of living 10 years	88.69%
Amount of taxable gift: $ 450,862	

Assuming the grantor lives beyond the 10 -year period, he or she will have removed a $1,000,000 asset (plus its growth potential during the 10 years) from the taxable estate.

The trust instrument should be drafted so that it is a grantor trust. This makes the trust income taxable to the grantor but also allows him or her to deduct mortgage interest and property tax payments made by the trustee.

Note: The grantor's applicable credit amount may be used to avoid paying a gift tax on the taxable portion.

---

[1] If death occurs before 10 years, the value of the trust assets is includable in the grantor's gross taxable estate. Under the Tax Act of 2001, the federal estate tax is gradually phased out until its final repeal in the year 2010. If Congress does not act at that time to repeal it for the years following, it will automatically revert back to the rates in effect during the year 2001, with an exemption for the first $1,000,000 of assets.
[2] This rate generally changes monthly.

Personal Residence GRIT

The following example illustrates the potential tax benefits of this type of trust, with a term of 10 years or the death of the grantor, should it occur earlier.

Assumptions:
Value of residence: $1,000,000
Age of grantor at beginning of trust: 55
Term of the trust:[1] 10 years
Federal discount rate:[2] 7.00%

Value of remainder interest	$ 508,349
Probability of living 10 years	88.69%
Amount of taxable gift: $ 450,862	

Assuming the grantor lives beyond the 10 -year period, he or she will have removed a $1,000,000 asset (plus its growth potential during the 10 years) from the taxable estate.

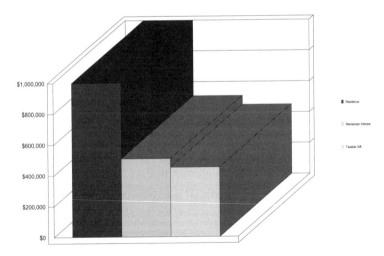

[1] If death occurs before 10 years, the value of the trust assets is includable in the gross taxable estate of the grantor. Under the Tax Act of 2001, the federal estate tax is gradually phased out until its final repeal in the year 2010. If Congress does not act at that time to repeal it for the years following, it will automatically revert back to the rates in effect during the year 2001, with an exemption for the first $1,000,000 of assets.
[2] This rate generally changes monthly.

Considering a Charitable Gift

Areas of need in society, such as health, education, general welfare, etc., which are not addressed by private enterprise or charitable organizations, may eventually become a government responsibility.

Many people are concerned with the growth of government and its increasing involvement in their lives. Assisting the charities of one's choice can decrease the need for government involvement in these areas of society.

Reasons for Making a Charitable Gift

Many persons make gifts or bequests to charitable organizations for a number of reasons. Some of the more common motivations would include the following.

- Compassion for those in need
- Religious and spiritual commitment
- Perpetuation of one's beliefs, values and ideals
- Support for the arts, sciences and education
- A desire to share one's good fortune with others

Whatever the reasons, U.S. tax law is designed to encourage these gifts.

Different Types of Charitable Gifts

Some donors prefer to make outright gifts of cash or other valuable assets to their favorite charities.

Other individuals, although they would like to make an outright gift, depend on the income from their assets for their daily needs. Often, such donors decide to wait until they die to transfer assets to a charity, through a will or trust.

However, there are methods which allow a donor to make a gift now, while still retaining an income for life. The most popular of these methods are listed below.

- Charitable remainder annuity trust
- Charitable remainder unitrust
- Pooled income fund
- Charitable gift annuity

Another gifting technique assigns an income interest to the charity for a period of years (or the lifetime of a person), after which the remainder passes to the donor's heirs. Gifts made in this manner involve what are known as charitable lead trusts.

Continued...

Considering a Charitable Gift

Potential Financial Benefits of Charitable Gifts

- Can provide an income tax deduction
- In many cases can avoid or delay payment of capital gains tax
- May increase personal after-tax cash flow
- May increase the amount passing to one's heirs[1]

---

[1] Under the Tax Act of 2001, the federal estate tax is gradually phased out until its final repeal in the year 2010. If Congress does not act at that time to repeal it for the years following, it will automatically revert back to the rates in effect during the year 2001, with an exemption for the first $1,000,000 of assets.

Charitable Giving Techniques

Gifts to charity during lifetime or at death will reduce the size of the gross taxable estate. An additional benefit of lifetime gifts is that an income tax deduction is available within certain percentage limitations.

Split-Interest Gifts

If the estate owner is not willing or able to contribute the entire asset during lifetime, he or she may consider a split-interest, deferred gift.

The ownership interests in an asset can be split or divided into two parts, a stream of income payable for one or more lifetimes or a term of years (the income interest) and the principal remaining after the income term (the remainder interest).[1] In a split-interest gift, one portion is given in trust for the charity and the other portion is retained.

Charitable Remainder Plans

When the estate owner retains the right to the income but transfers his or her rights in the remainder to a trust, it is called a charitable remainder trust.

To qualify for an income tax deduction the trust must be a unitrust, an annuity trust, a pooled income fund or a charitable gift annuity.

- **Charitable remainder unitrust:** In this type of trust the donor usually retains a right to a fixed percentage of the fair market value of the trust assets, re-valued annually. If the value of the assets increases, so does the annual payout and vice versa. See IRC Sec. 664(d)(2).

- **Charitable remainder annuity trust:** This trust is similar to the unitrust but instead pays a fixed dollar amount year after year. The increases or decreases in the value of the trust do not affect the payments. See IRC Sec. 664(d)(1).

- **Pooled income fund:** Assets are transferred to a common investment fund maintained by the charity. Each donor receives annually a share of the income from the fund, in proportion to the contribution made. These annual payments continue for the lifetimes of the donor and spouse. At death, the corpus of the donor's gift, together with any capital gains, passes to the charity. Payments will increase or decrease with the investment performance of the fund. See IRC Sec. 642(c)(5).

- **Charitable gift annuity:** The donor transfers the asset directly to the charity in exchange for the charity's agreement to pay a fixed lifetime annuity.

The amount of the income tax deduction is dependent upon the percentage of the income interest and the period over which it will be paid (usually the life of the donor and his or her spouse). This is determined from the mortality tables published by the government.

---

[1] Technically, the present value of the income share and the present value of the remainder interest.

Continued...

Charitable Giving Techniques

Charitable Income Trusts

The charitable income or lead trust is the reverse of the charitable remainder trust.

The income interest is assigned to the charity, usually for a period of years, and then the remainder generally passes to the donor's heirs. The amount of the estate tax deduction and the amount left for the heirs will depend upon the number of years and percentage of the annual payments and the investment results of the trustee.

Asset Replacement Trust

The combination of a charitable remainder trust (CRT) and an asset replacement insurance trust can greatly benefit you, your heirs and your favorite charity.

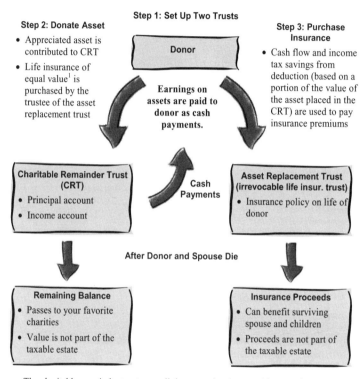

Step 1: Set Up Two Trusts

Step 2: Donate Asset
- Appreciated asset is contributed to CRT
- Life insurance of equal value[1] is purchased by the trustee of the asset replacement trust

Donor

Earnings on assets are paid to donor as cash payments.

Step 3: Purchase Insurance
- Cash flow and income tax savings from deduction (based on a portion of the value of the asset placed in the CRT) are used to pay insurance premiums

Charitable Remainder Trust (CRT)
- Principal account
- Income account

Cash Payments

Asset Replacement Trust (irrevocable life insur. trust)
- Insurance policy on life of donor

After Donor and Spouse Die

Remaining Balance
- Passes to your favorite charities
- Value is not part of the taxable estate

Insurance Proceeds
- Can benefit surviving spouse and children
- Proceeds are not part of the taxable estate

- The charitable remainder trust can sell the appreciated asset without paying any income tax on the capital gain. By reinvesting this larger amount, the trust can pay to the donor (and spouse, if desired) a fixed percentage of the trust assets, e.g., 5%, 6%, 8%, etc., for the remainder of their lives.

- The charitable deduction is based on the ages of the donor and spouse at the time of transfer, current interest rates and the percentage cash return received each year.

The result: An appreciated asset has been given away which will eventually benefit a charity. Additionally, cash flow has increased for life. The value of the asset has been replaced with life insurance payable to the heirs. This combination is a true win-win-win situation.

---

[1] Where the donated asset faces a significant potential estate tax, some practitioners recommend insurance equal to the after-tax (after paying the estate tax) value of the asset rather than 100%.

865

Charitable Income Tax Deduction

Federal income tax law allows a deduction for gifts to qualified charitable organizations, such as churches, colleges, hospitals, charitable foundations, etc. The actual amount of the deduction is dependent upon several factors.

- **Type of charity:** Does the organization benefit the general public or does it have a more limited or private purpose?

- **Type of asset:** Is the donated item cash, a capital asset with untaxed appreciation, tangible personal property, etc.?

- **Portion of asset given:** Is it a gift of the entire asset or only an interest in the asset, like a remainder interest, which will pass to the charity at some time in the future?

- **When gift is given:** Is the gift being made now or will it occur at some future date, as under the terms of a will or trust?

Income Tax Savings

The gift of an asset to a charity generally results in a federal income tax deduction,[1] which should decrease the tax due and increase the amount of net after-tax income for the year. However, charitable contributions are not always 100% deductible against an individual's federal income tax liability.

Limits on Annual Charitable Deduction

Federal law limits the amount that is deductible for the year in which the gift is made, based upon one's adjusted gross income (AGI). If the limit is exceeded for the year, any excess deduction can generally be carried forward for up to five years.

If combined charitable contributions for the year do not exceed 20% of AGI, they may all be deducted. If, however, contributions exceed 20% of AGI, the deduction may be limited to 50%, 30% or 20% of AGI, depending upon the type of property given and the type of charitable organization receiving the gift. In no event can the deduction exceed 50% of the donor's adjusted gross income for the year.

- **50% limit:** This limit applies to contributions to public charities, (i.e. most churches, hospitals, colleges, etc.), unless the gift is of capital gain[2] property and the deduction is taken for the fair market value, in which case a 30% limit will apply. The 50% limit is available for gifts of capital gain property if the deduction is limited to the cost basis of the asset.

---

[1] The discussion here concerns federal tax law. State or local income tax law can vary.
[2] Capital gain property as used here applies to capital assets held long-term (at least 12 months and one day).

Continue

Charitable Income Tax Deduction

- **30% limit:** This limit applies to gifts for the use of any charitable organization and gifts (other than capital gain property) to non-50% type charities.

- **20% limit:** This limit applies to gifts of capital gain property to non-50% type charities.

- **Patents and Intellectual Property:** The American Jobs Creation Act of 2004 established special rules for charitable donations of patents and other intellectual property. Effective for gifts made after June 3, 2004, a donor's deduction for gifts of patents and other intellectual property is limited to the lesser of the taxpayer's basis or the fair market value of the property. An additional deduction may be available for a limited number of future years if the donee organization realizes income from the gifted property, and certain requirements are met. See IRC Sec. 170.

Limits on Itemized Deductions

As AGI increases, federal law also acts to reduce certain itemized deductions, including charitable contributions.

Under EGTRRA of 2001, however, this reduction in deductibility is gradually phased-out, by one-third in 2006-2007, and by two-thirds in 2008-2009. In 2010 there is no reduction to any itemized deduction, regardless of the level of income. However, unless the law is changed, the prior rules will again apply in 2011.

Income Tax Deduction for Split-Interest Gifts

Determining the federal income tax deduction for a "split-interest" gift, (i.e. a charitable remainder or charitable lead trust), can be complicated. The key factors involved are:

- How long the charity must wait before it benefits; and

- How much income is paid to the beneficiaries each year; and

- The prevailing interest rates at the time of the gift (as indicated by the applicable federal rate).

Seek Professional Guidance

The counsel and guidance of a CPA, IRS Enrolled Agent, or other qualified tax professional is strongly recommended.

Charitable Gifts and Estate Taxation

Gifts to a charity or to a charitable remainder trust can reduce one's taxable estate by not only the value of the gift but also its potential appreciation.

If the donor retains the right to the income, as in a charitable remainder trust, the estate tax savings will not be as large. However, the donor (or donors) may choose to make gifts of the income each year to children, grandchildren or to a trust on their behalf.

If certain requirements are met, these gifts will qualify for the annual gift tax exclusion of $12,000[1] from each donor to as many qualified beneficiaries as there are under the terms of the trust.

The chart below illustrates the potential savings, based on a hypothetical situation.

Assumptions:
Current estate size: $2,500,000
Estate growth rate: 6.00%
Value of charitable gift: $250,000
Year of death: 2008
Applicable credit: $780,800
Congress will not permanently repeal the FET

Years From Now	Taxable Estate		Federal Estate Tax		Savings in Federal Estate Taxes With Gift
	Without the Gift	With the Gift	Without the Gift	With the Gift	
Now	$2,500,000	$2,250,000	$225,000	$112,500	$112,500
5	3,345,564	3,011,008	605,504	454,953	150,550
10	4,477,119	4,029,407	1,114,704	913,233	201,470
15	5,991,395	5,392,256	1,796,128	1,526,515	269,613
20	8,017,839	7,216,055	2,708,027	2,347,225	360,803
25	10,729,677	9,656,709	3,928,355	3,445,519	482,835
30	14,358,728	12,922,855	5,561,428	4,915,285	646,143
35	19,215,217	17,293,695	7,746,848	6,882,163	864,685

Note: If both the income from the trust and the income tax savings from the charitable deduction are given to an irrevocable trust (or to adult children) to purchase life insurance on the life of the donor, one is able to transfer a substantial amount of money to one's heirs which is not subject to either income tax or estate tax.

---

[1] The annual gift tax exclusion ($12,000 in 2008) is indexed for inflation in increments of $1,000.

Qualified Conservation Easement

Protecting undeveloped land for the preservation of wildlife or the public enjoyment of nature can be one of the most meaningful legacies an individual can make. Few people, however, want to make an outright gift of their ranch or farm property for such purposes.

One possible solution to this dilemma involves creating a qualified conservation easement, and then donating the easement to a charitable conservation organization or government agency. The easement effectively restricts future development and use of the land, while allowing a donor to retain ownership and possession. If the easement meets certain requirements, the donor can be eligible for both income and estate tax benefits.

Federal Income and Estate Tax Benefits

The tax[1] benefits of a qualified conservation easement can be substantial:

- **Income tax benefits:** If a qualified easement is donated during life, the property owner is eligible for an income tax deduction equal to the value of the easement. In 2006 and 2007,[2] for individuals, the deduction is limited to 50% of the donor's adjusted gross income (AGI) in the year the donation is made; any excess may be carried forward and deducted for up to 15 years. For "qualified farmers or ranchers," the allowable deduction is generally 100% of AGI, with a 15 year carry-forward of any unused deductions.[3] In 2008, for all taxpayers, the deduction will be limited to 30% of the donor's AGI, with a five-year carry-forward of any unused deductions.

No income tax deduction is allowed if an easement is donated upon the owner's death.

- **Estate tax benefits:** There are two: (1) the property value for estate tax purposes will be lower; and (2) under IRC Sec. 2031(c), an exclusion from the taxable estate is allowed for up to 40% of the remaining property value (maximum of $500,000) in the estate. Both are available regardless of when the easement is donated, during life or at death.

Terms and Requirements

The terms of a conservation easement are typically determined by the property owner and the organization that is to receive the easement. There are several requirements that must be met in order for the easement to be considered a "qualified" conservation easement, as shown in the table on the following page:

---

[1] The discussion here concerns federal law; state and local law may differ.
[2] The Pension Protection Act of 2006 provided for a "temporary" increase in the general deduction allowed for the donation of a conservation easement.
[3] Special requirements may apply to individual and corporate "farmers and ranchers."

Continued...

Qualified Conservation Easement

Issues	Requirements
Location & Purpose	• Property must be located in the United States. • Easement must be permanent and established for at least one of the following: (1) outdoor recreation or education of the general public; (2) protection of a natural ecosystem; (3) preservation of open space for scenic enjoyment or pursuant to a governmental conservation policy that will yield a significant public benefit; or (4) preservation of a historically important land area or certified historic structure[1].
Charitable Organization	• Donation must be to a qualified charitable or governmental organization with a commitment to protect the easement's purpose. • Easement must contain legally enforceable restrictions that the charitable organization can (and has the resources to) enforce.

Donor's Retained Usage

The donor can retain the right to occupy and use the property, to conduct farm operations, to construct residences and related buildings, or farm buildings, all without losing tax benefits. However, the tax benefits may be reduced or lost if the donor retains the right to subdivide or develop the property, to use it for commercial purposes other than farming, or to use the land in a way that threatens the conservation purposes of the easement.

Valuation of a Conservation Easement

A conservation easement is generally valued by appraising the property before and after the donation of the easement. The difference between the two appraisals is the value of the easement. A proportional amount of the donor's income tax basis will be allocated to the easement.

Impact on a Donor's Estate

The donation of a conservation easement can impact a donor's estate in several ways:

- **Reduction in estate size:** The reduction in the value of land means that the size of a donor's estate will be reduced, potentially resulting in a lower estate tax bill.

- **Estate exclusion:** IRC Sec. 2031(c) provides that up to 40% of the post-easement value of the property, up to a maximum of $500,000, may be excluded from the taxable estate. If the easement is worth at least 30% of the original, pre-easement value of the property, the full 40% exclusion is available. If the easement is worth less than 30%, the exclusion will be reduced according to a statutory schedule.

---

[1] A historically-important land area or certified historic structure is not a qualified conservation purpose for the estate exclusion under IRC Sec. 2031(c).

Continue

Qualified Conservation Easement

- **No step-up in basis:** Under current law, property received by inheritance generally receives a full step-up in basis to its fair market value on the decedent's date of death. However, property excluded from the estate under IRC Sec. 2031(c) does not receive a step-up in basis. Depending on the situation, there may be circumstances where it would not make sense to use the IRC Sec. 2031(c) exclusion.

Wealth Replacement Trust

Some of the income tax savings from a conservation easement created and donated during life can be used to fund a wealth replacement trust to benefit the donor's family. A wealth replacement trust is an irrevocable life insurance trust which owns either a life insurance policy on the life of the donor or a survivorship policy on the donor and his or her spouse. If the trust is properly structured, the life insurance proceeds can be fully excluded from federal estate taxes.

Seek Professional Guidance

Estate planning for certain land owners (farmers, ranchers, and rural business owners) presents unique estate planning challenges and opportunities. The counsel and guidance of appropriate legal, tax, and financial professionals is strongly recommended.

Unrelated Business Taxable Income

Unrelated business taxable income (UBTI) can cause serious income tax problems in a charitable remainder trust (CRT).[1]

Through the end of 2006, a CRT that had any UBTI for the year lost its tax exemption for that year and, instead, was taxed as a regular complex trust.

Beginning in 2007, however, a new set of rules applied. Under the provisions of the Tax Relief and Health Care Act of 2006, a charitable remainder trust which has unrelated business taxable income is subject to a 100% excise tax on such income. For example, if a CRT had $50 of UBTI, the tax would be equal to $50. This new tax treatment replaces the former loss of tax exemption for the year.

What Is Unrelated Business Taxable Income?

UBTI is defined in IRC Sec. 512. Generally, it is income derived by a charity from any unrelated trade or business carried on by it and not specifically excluded by statute.

Typically, investment income or capital gains are not UBTI (unless the asset is debt financed). Revenue from an active trade or business, however, is generally considered to be UBTI.

Many limited partnerships generate UBTI and should be avoided in CRT funding and investment. There is danger when a highly appreciated asset is sold in a CRT and, in the same tax year, the trustee invests in or accepts from the donor a limited partnership interest which just happens to produce a little UBTI. Even one dollar of UBTI in a year can trigger income tax problems. Besides limited partnerships, donors should avoid unincorporated business transfers, participating leases on rental properties, etc.

Debt-Financed Property

Indebtedness on property can be a problem when creating a CRT. In all debt-encumbered property transfers, the donor is considered to have received proceeds from a sale in the amount of the indebtedness. The IRS rationale is that relief from debt is the same as receiving income, and is a taxable event. At best, one has taxable income (in the amount of the debt relief) with a partial, offsetting charitable deduction for the equity in the property.

However, for some time now the IRS has indicated that the UBTI problems discussed above would apply to indebted property transfers to a CRT unless the debt was "old and cold." An exception was allowed when the debt had been placed on the property, and the donor had held the property, more than five years before transfer.

---

[1] The discussion here concerns federal income tax law; state or local law may differ.

Continued

Unrelated Business Taxable Income

However, even this limited exception has been overruled. The IRS, in a private letter ruling,[1] completely disqualified a CRT funded with "old and cold" indebted property. The service contended that the grantor trust rules applied; i.e., the grantor is treated as the owner of the trust if income from the trust is used to discharge a legal obligation of the grantor.

To be safe, the donor should payoff the debt or move it to other property prior to the transfer to a charitable trust. If the debt is too substantial for this, the donor may have to use a different charitable income instrument, such as a charitable gift annuity, rather than a charitable remainder trust.

Seek Professional Guidance

Given the complexities involved, the advice and guidance of competent tax and financial advisors is strongly recommended.

---

[1] See PLR 9015049 dated 1/16/90. A IRS Private Letter Ruling is applicable only to the taxpayer who requested it and may not be cited as precedent.

Charitable Remainder Annuity Trust
CRAT

A charitable remainder annuity trust (CRAT) is an irrevocable trust which pays a fixed dollar amount each year to a beneficiary, such as the donor of the trust assets, his or her spouse, child, etc. This fixed dollar amount is determined by applying the trust's stated percentage payout, e.g., 5%, 6%, etc., to the value[1] of the assets initially transferred by the donor.

After the death of the income beneficiaries or at the end of a set number of years,[2] whatever assets remain in the trust are distributed to the charities named in the trust. If additional contributions are desired in later years, new trusts must be established.

Income Tax Considerations

The charitable income tax deduction is based on the current value of the charity's right to receive the trust assets at some time in the future (a remainder interest). There are several factors in determining this value.

- The first factor is the estimated length of time which the charity must wait; for example, a term of years (like 10, 15, 20, etc.) or for the donor's or other person's lifetime.

- Another factor is the percentage rate payable to the income beneficiaries each year and how frequently it is paid; e.g., annually, monthly, etc. Obviously, the higher the rate of payout, the less there will be for the charity; and, therefore, the smaller the charitable deduction will be.

- The current rate of return on investments as determined by the applicable federal (midterm) rates (AFR) is also an important factor.[3]

All of these factors are applied to government tables to determine the current value of the charitable deduction. If the charitable deduction exceeds a certain percentage of the donor's adjusted gross income for the year of the gift, that portion must be carried over into future years.

Gift Tax Considerations

If the income from the CRAT is payable to someone other than the donor, it may be subject to federal gift taxation. If certain requirements are met, the income gift can be made to qualify for the annual gift tax exclusion of $12,000[4] per beneficiary. Also, the marital deduction will usually eliminate any gift tax on payments to the donor's spouse.

---

[1] In cases of hard to value assets like real estate, a qualified appraisal is required to support the values.
[2] If a set number of years is chosen to determine the term of the trust (instead of the lifetime(s) of one or two beneficiaries), the maximum term is 20 years.
[3] This rate changes monthly.
[4] The annual gift tax exclusion ($12,000 in 2008) is indexed for inflation in increments of $1,000.

Continue

Charitable Remainder Annuity Trust
CRAT

Estate Tax Considerations

The value of the interest passing to the charity is deductible from the gross estate. If there are income beneficiaries other than the donor and his or her spouse, there may be an estate tax on the value of this income interest.[1]

Some states allow a surviving spouse to "elect" to receive a portion of the deceased spouse's estate. Such laws are designed to prevent the surviving spouse from being completely disinherited. If state law allows assets in a CRAT to be used to satisfy the surviving spouse's election, the CRAT could cease to qualify as a charitable trust under federal law. As a result, previous income tax deductions can be lost and the assets in the trust could be added back to the deceased spouse's estate. The IRS originally provided a "safe harbor" for this situation in Revenue Procedure 2005-24, with a grandfather date of June 28, 2005. In Notice 2006-15, however, the federal government extended the June 28, 2005 date until "further guidance is issued by the Internal Revenue Service."

Almost Everyone Benefits

A taxpayer can contribute an asset (usually highly appreciated and low income producing) to a CRAT and receive a current income tax deduction.

The CRAT can sell the appreciated asset without paying any capital gain tax and can then reinvest the entire proceeds at a higher rate of return.

The trust will often pay out a higher return than the donor previously received. This, coupled with the income tax deduction, can create a substantial increase in cash flow.

Thus far, the only ones to lose are the donor's heirs. To solve this problem, many taxpayers use a portion of the increased cash flow to purchase a life insurance policy (outside of the estate) to replace all or part of the value of the asset placed in the trust. This arrangement lets almost everyone benefit.

Party	Benefit
Donor (and spouse)	Increased cash flow during retirement years
Children/heirs	Same size or larger inheritance (with insurance)
Favorite charity	Receives remaining assets after donor's death
Internal Revenue Service	Receives less income and estate tax

---

[1] Under the Tax Act of 2001, the federal estate tax is gradually phased out until its final repeal in the year 2010. If Congress does not act at that time to repeal it for the years following, it will automatically revert back to the rates in effect during the year 2001, with an exemption for the first $1,000,000 of assets.

Charitable Remainder Annuity Trust
CRAT

The donor transfers an asset to the trustee of the charitable remainder annuity trust (CRAT) and receives a fixed dollar amount for each year thereafter. A current income tax deduction is also available.

When the donor or other named beneficiary dies, the remaining trust assets pass to the designated charity.

Donor		CRAT
• Transfers asset to CRAT. • Receives fixed dollar amount each year.[1] • Receives income tax deduction.[2]	**Asset** **Annual Annuity Payout** **Income Tax Deduction**	• Trustee sells asset and reinvests for greater return. • Pays no capital gain tax on the appreciation at the time of sale. • Trustee pays fixed dollar amount yearly.

After the beneficiary is deceased, remaining trust assets pass to the charity.[3]

Charitable Organization

• Receives any assets remaining in the trust when the beneficiary is deceased.

---

[1] The annual annuity payout is taxed under a four-tier system, as specified in IRC Sec. 664(b). Generally speaking, ordinary income is paid first, followed by capital-gain, other income, and trust principal.

[2] The income tax deduction is based on a government determined applicable federal rate and may have to be spread over more than one year, if it exceeds certain percentage of income limitations.

[3] If a surviving spouse "elects" to claim a part of a deceased spouse's estate, the income and estate tax benefits of a CRAT will likely be lost. See the "safe harbor" provisions of Revenue Procedure 2005-24 and Notice 2006-15.

Charitable Remainder Unitrust
CRUT

A charitable remainder unitrust (CRUT) is an irrevocable trust which pays a fixed percentage of the value of its holdings each year to a beneficiary such as the donor of the trust assets, his or her spouse, child, etc. Unlike the fixed dollar payment of a charitable remainder annuity trust, the unitrust payments will fluctuate with the changing asset balance in the trust, reflecting year-to-year investment performance[1].

After the death of the income beneficiaries or at the end of a set number of years (no more than 20), whatever assets remain in the trust are distributed to the charities named in the trust. Additional contributions can be made to the trust in later years if desired.

CRUT Variations

The standard form of CRUT requires payment of the full stated percentage throughout the life of the trust, even if assets must be liquidated. Other CRUT variations include:

- **Net-Income CRUT:** A CRUT may be drafted to pay out less than the established percentage if the trust income during the year is less than the required payout percentage. This shortage can be made up in later years when the trust earns more than the required payout percentage.

- **Flip CRUT:** Under IRS regulations, a CRUT may begin life as a net-income trust, and, at some pre-determined future date or triggering event, permanently convert ("flip") to a standard unitrust. A "flip" CRUT is an option for an individual seeking a current income tax deduction, tax-deferred buildup and increased income at a later date.

Income Tax Considerations

The charitable income tax deduction is based on the current value of the charity's right to receive the trust assets at some time in the future. Three factors are involved:

- The estimated length of time, which the charity must wait; for example, a term of years (like 10, 15, 20, etc.) or for the donor's or other person's lifetime.

- The percentage rate payable to the income beneficiaries each year and how frequently it is paid; e.g., annually, monthly, etc. The higher the rate of payout, the less there will be for the charity; and, therefore, the smaller the charitable deduction.

- The current investment return, as determined by the IRS. These are called the IRC 7520 mid-term rates.[2]

These factors are applied to government tables to determine the current value of the charitable deduction. If the charitable deduction exceeds a certain percentage of the donor's adjusted gross income in the year of the gift, the excess must be carried over to future years.

---

[1] Assets must be revalued each year to determine the payout amount.
[2] This rate changes monthly.

Continued...

Charitable Remainder Unitrust
CRUT

Gift Tax Considerations

If the income from the CRUT is payable to someone other than the donor, it may be subject to federal gift taxation. If certain requirements are met, the income gift can be made to qualify for the annual gift tax exclusion of $12,000[1] per beneficiary. Also, the marital deduction will usually eliminate any tax on payments to the donor's spouse.

Estate Tax Considerations

The value of the interest passing to the charity is deductible from the gross estate. If there are income beneficiaries other than the donor and his or her spouse, there may be an estate tax on the value of this income interest.[2]

Some states allow a surviving spouse to "elect" to receive a portion of the deceased spouse's estate. Such laws are designed to prevent the surviving spouse from being completely disinherited. If state law allows assets in a CRUT to be used to satisfy the surviving spouse's election, the CRUT could cease to qualify as a charitable trust under federal law. As a result, previous income tax deductions can be lost and the assets in the trust could be added back to the deceased spouse's estate.[3]

Almost Everyone Benefits

A taxpayer can contribute an asset (usually highly appreciated and low income producing) to a CRUT and receive a current income tax deduction. The CRUT can sell the appreciated asset without paying any capital gain tax and can then reinvest the entire proceeds at a higher rate of return. The trust will often pay out a higher return than the donor previously received. This, coupled with the federal income tax deduction, can create a substantial increase in cash flow.

Thus far, the only ones to lose are the donor's heirs. To solve this problem, many taxpayers use a portion of the increased cash flow to purchase a life insurance policy (outside of the estate) to replace the value of the asset placed in the trust. This arrangement lets almost everyone benefit.

Party	Benefit
Donor (and spouse)	Increased cash flow during retirement years
Children/heirs	Same size or larger inheritance (with insurance)
Favorite charity	Receives remaining assets after donor's death
Internal Revenue Service	Receives less income and estate tax

---

[1] The annual gift tax exclusion ($12,000 in 2008) is indexed for inflation in increments of $1,000.

[2] Under the Tax Act of 2001, the federal estate tax is gradually phased out until its final repeal in the year 2010. If Congress does not act at that time to repeal it for the years following, it will automatically revert back to the rates in effect during the year 2001, with an exemption for the first $1,000,000 of assets.

[3] The IRS originally provided a "safe harbor" for this situation in Revenue Procedure 2005-24, with a grandfather date of June 28, 2005. In Notice 2006-15, however, the federal government extended the June 28, 2005 date until "further guidance is issued by the Internal Revenue Service."

Charitable Remainder Unitrust
CRUT

The donor transfers an asset to the trustee of the charitable remainder unitrust (CRUT) and receives a set percentage of the trust value for each year thereafter. A current income tax deduction is also available.

When the donor or other named beneficiary dies, the remaining trust assets pass to the designated charity.

Donor		**CRUT**
• Transfers asset to CRUT. • Receives annual payout.[1] • Receives income tax deduction.[2]	**Asset** **% of Trust Annually** **Income Tax Deduction**	• Trustee sells asset and reinvests for greater return. • Pays no capital gain tax due on the appreciation at the time of sale. • Trustee pays a percentage of trust assets as valued each year.

After the beneficiary is deceased, remaining trust assets pass to the charity.[3]

Charitable Organization
• Receives any assets remaining in the trust when the beneficiary is deceased.

---

[1] The annual annuity payout is taxed under a four-tier system, as specified in IRC Sec. 664(b). Generally speaking, ordinary income is paid first, followed by capital-gain, other income, and trust principal.

[2] This deduction may have to be spread over more than one year, if it exceeds certain percentage of income limitations.

[3] If a surviving spouse "elects" to claim a part of a deceased spouse's estate, the income and estate tax benefits of a CRUT will likely be lost. See the "safe harbor" provisions of Revenue Procedure 2005-24 and Notice 2006-15.

Charitable Remainder Trust Numerical Tests

Charitable remainder trusts (CRTs), which include both
charitable remainder annuity trusts and charitable remainder
unitrusts, are subject to a maze of law and regulation. The
failure of a CRT to meet all requirements can result in a trust
being disqualified as a charitable remainder trust, with negative
income, gift and federal estate tax consequences. The loss of
charitable status would also defeat a donor's charitable intent.

Some of these requirements involve numerical tests, several of
which have long been a part of the qualifying conditions for
CRTs. The Taxpayer Relief Act of 1997 (TRA '97), which became law on August 5,
1997, introduced two additional numerical tests.

Pre-TRA '97 Numerical Tests

Prior to TRA '97, there were two key numerical tests for CRTs: the 5% probability test
and the 5% minimum payment test.

- **5% probability test:** This test, which applies only to charitable remainder annuity
  trusts (CRATs), measures the theoretically possibility that a noncharitable beneficiary
  will live long enough to exhaust the assets in the trust, leaving nothing for charity.[1]
  Using a complicated mathematical formula and government interest and longevity
  tables, a probability of exhausting the trust assets is calculated at the time property is
  transferred to the trust. If the probability of exhaustion is higher than 5%, no income or
  estate tax deduction is allowed.[2]

- **5% minimum payment test:** This test concerns the minimum annual payment which
  must be made from a CRT. IRC Sec. 664(d)(1)(A), relating to CRATs, requires the
  payment to be not less than five percent of the initial net fair market value of all
  property placed in trust. IRC Sec. 664(d)(2)(A), concerning charitable remainder
  unitrusts (CRUTs), specifies the minimum payment to be a fixed percentage (which is
  not less than five percent) of the net fair market value of its assets, valued annually.

Taxpayer Relief Act of 1997

TRA '97 added two new required numerical tests: the 50% payout limitation test and the
10% minimum charitable benefit test.

- **50% payout limitation test:** TRA '97 amended IRC Sec. 664 to limit the annual
  payment that can be made from a CRT. For CRATs, the new legislation limits annual
  payments to no more than 50% of the initial net fair market value of property in the
  trust. For CRUTs, the new law establishes a similar cap, limiting annual payments to no
  more than 50% of the net fair market value of the trust's assets, valued annually. A
  CRT which fails this test will be treated as a complex trust, with all income taxed to
  either the trust or its beneficiaries. This new test applies to transfers in trust after June
  18, 1997.

---

[1] With a charitable remainder unitrust, exhaustion of trust assets is considered impossible as payments from the trust are
based on a percentage of trust assets.
[2] See Rev. Rul. 77-374, 1977-2, CB 329; Rev. Rul. 70-452, 1970-2 CB 199; and Reg. Para 20.2055-2(b)(1).

Continued.

Charitable Remainder Trust Numerical Tests

- **10% minimum charitable benefit:** TRA '97 also set, for the first time, a minimum charitable benefit that must ultimately pass to the charity. For CRATs, this minimum is 10% of the initial net fair market value of all property placed in the trust. For CRUTs, the remainder interest passing to the charity must be at least 10% of the net fair market value of such property as of the date such property is contributed to the trust.[1] The 10% minimum charitable benefit requirement generally applies to transfers in trust after July 28, 1997.

Relief Provisions

TRA '97 provided several relief provisions for trusts which would meet all CRT requirements, except the 10% minimum charitable benefit requirement.[2] The law provides that a trust may be declared void ab initio (from the beginning). Under this option, no charitable tax deduction is permitted to the donor for the transfer and any income or capital gains created by property transferred to the CRT become income and capital gain of the donor.

The new law also allows a donor to reform a trust, by modifying either the annual payout or the term of a CRT (or both), to allow the trust to meet the 10% minimum charitable benefit. Strict time limits have been imposed for this reformation.[3]

Seek Professional Guidance

The laws and regulations surrounding charitable remainder trusts can be complex and confusing. Individuals facing decisions concerning the tax and estate planning implications of a CRT are strongly advised to consult with an attorney, CPA, IRS enrolled agent or other competent professional.

---

[1] For both CRATs and CRUTs, the 10% remainder interest valuation is determined in accordance with the provisions of IRC Sec. 7520.
[2] See new IRC Sec. 2055(e)(3)(J).
[3] See IRC Sec. 2055(e)(3)(C)(iii).

Charitable Gift Annuity
CGA

When a donor transfers an asset to a charity[1] in exchange for an income for one or two lives, it is called a charitable gift annuity.

The income tax deduction from this arrangement will vary depending on the age of the donor, the payout rate and the applicable (mid-term) federal rate (AFR) (which is determined monthly).

The following charts illustrate the income tax deduction at various ages and AFRs. Each example assumes a cash gift of $100,000. The payouts vary with the age of the donor.[2]

AFR Table Rate	Age 55 / 5.5% / $5,500 ← Recommended Payout → 5.7% / $5,700 / Age 60			
	Total Charitable Deduction	Income Excluded from Taxation[3]	Total Charitable Deduction	Income Excluded from Taxation[3]
4%	$18,309	$2,866	$24,197	$3,145
5%	26,512	2,578	31,052	2,861
6%	33,401	2,337	36,911	2,617

AFR Table Rate	Age 65 / 6.0% / $6,000 ← Recommended Payout → 6.5% / $6,500 / Age 70			
	Total Charitable Deduction	Income Excluded from Taxation[3]	Total Charitable Deduction	Income Excluded from Taxation[3]
4%	$29,908	$3,522	$34,981	$4,089
5%	35,528	3,240	39,518	3,804
6%	40,415	2,994	43,531	3,551

AFR Table Rate	Age 75 / 7.1% / $7,100 ← Recommended Payout → 8.0% / $8,000 / Age 80			
	Total Charitable Deduction	Income Excluded from Taxation[3]	Total Charitable Deduction	Income Excluded from Taxation[3]
4%	$40,809	$4,773	$46,406	$5,701
5%	44,327	4,490	49,053	5,420
6%	47,492	4,234	51,474	5,162

Note: Table calculated using ACGA "recommended" Single Life Gift Annuity rates effective 07/01/04.

---

[1] In most states, a charity must be licensed to grant a gift annuity.
[2] Many charities follow the suggested payout rates developed by the American Council on Gift Annuities, 233 McCrea, Suite #400, Indianapolis, IN 46225-1030; Tel: (317) 269-6271.
[3] The amount shown represents that portion of the annual payment due to recovery of the donor's basis in the annuity. Once the basis has been completely recovered, all additional payments are fully taxable.

Charitable Gift Annuity
CGA

The donor transfers an asset to a charity and receives a fixed dollar amount, set at the time the gift is made, each year thereafter. A current income tax deduction is also available.

When the donor or other named beneficiary dies, the charity has no further financial obligations to pay.

Donor		CGA
• Transfers asset to charity	**Asset**	• Charity sells asset and reinvests for greater return
• Receives annual payout[1]		• Charity pays no capital gain tax on the appreciation at the time of sale[3]
• Receives income tax deduction[2]	**Annual Annuity** 	
	Income Tax Deduction	• Charity pays a fixed dollar amount, established at time of gift each year for lifetime of beneficiary

After the beneficiary is deceased the charity has no further obligations to pay.

---

[1] Annuity payments are part return of principal (nontaxable), part ordinary income and (if any) part capital gain. Once a donor has recovered his or her basis, the annuity payments are fully taxable.

[2] This deduction may have to be spread over more than one year if it exceeds certain percentage of income limitations.

[3] If certain requirements are met, the donor may recognize any capital gain ratably over the time period the annuity is expected to be received. Otherwise, the donor must recognize all capital gain in the year the annuity transaction is entered into.

Taxation of a Charitable Gift Annuity

Payments received from charitable gift annuities are taxed in the same manner as commercial annuities; i.e., using the annuity exclusion ratio. This often gives them an advantage over payments from pooled income funds or charitable remainder trusts, from which the income may be fully taxable.

A portion of each payment from an annuity is considered to be a return of principal and is, therefore, exempt from income tax. Also, a portion of the payment may be taxed at capital gains rates.

Payment Allocation

The chart below illustrates the allocation of payments from a charitable gift annuity as various types of income. The examples are based on the following set of assumptions.

Assumptions:
- Amount contributed: $100,000
- Age of beneficiary: 75
- Payout rate: 7.1%[1]
- Applicable federal rate (AFR): 3.0%

Assuming a Cash Contribution with Basis of $100,000

Years	Annual Income	Ordinary Income	Exempt Income	Long-Term Capital Gain
1-12.5	$7,100	$2,010	$5,090	$0
Thereafter	$7,100	$7,100	$0	$0

Assuming a Stock Contribution with Basis of $50,000

Years	Annual Income	Ordinary Income	Exempt Income	Long-Term Capital Gain
1-12.5	$7,100	$2,010	$2,545	$2,545
Thereafter	$7,100	$7,100	$0	$0

Note: The donor will also receive a current income tax deduction of nearly $37,000.

Appreciated Capital Assets

Appreciated capital assets held long-term may be exchanged for a charitable gift annuity without taxation of the unrealized capital gain at time of transfer (much like a charitable remainder trust) unless an income beneficiary other than the donor and his or her spouse is named. In such cases, the full, unrealized gain is taxable to the donor/grantor.

---

[1] This would be $7,100 per year, paid quarterly.

Pooled Income Fund
PIF

A pooled income fund (PIF) is similar to a charitable remainder trust to which more than one donor is able to make contributions.

A public charity must establish and maintain a common investment fund into which donors transfer assets while retaining a share of the annual income in proportion to his or her contribution.

The federal income tax deduction is based on the ages of the beneficiaries and the highest rate of return paid by the fund over the last three years.[1]

The frequency of payments, e.g., monthly, quarterly, etc., does not affect the tax deduction.

Pooled income funds may not invest in tax-exempt securities nor accept them as contributions. Also, neither donor nor beneficiary may serve as trustee.

Estate and Gift Taxation

If the donor causes the income to be paid to another person (like a child or a parent) there would be a taxable gift. If certain requirements are met, the income gift can be made to qualify for the annual gift tax exclusion of $12,000[2] per beneficiary.

The value of the asset passing to the PIF is removed from the donor's gross estate.[3] Periodic payments, if received by the donor, will, however, tend to increase the estate size unless they are otherwise consumed.

After the life income beneficiaries die, the remaining assets pass to the charity.

---

[1] If the fund has been in existence for less than three years, the rate used is based on interest rates provided by the federal government. See Rev. Rul. 94-41, IRB 1994-26,5.

[2] The annual gift tax exclusion ($12,000 in 2008) is indexed for inflation in increments of $1,000.

[3] Under the Tax Act of 2001, the federal estate tax is gradually phased out until its final repeal in the year 2010. If Congress does not act at that time to repeal it for the years following, it will automatically revert back to the rates in effect during the year 2001, with an exemption for the first $1,000,000 of assets.

Pooled Income Fund
PIF

The donor transfers an asset to the trustee of the pooled income fund (PIF) and receives a proportionate share of the trust's income for each year thereafter. A current income tax deduction is also available.

When the donor or other named beneficiary dies, the remaining trust assets pass to the designated charity.

Donor		PIF
• Transfers asset to PIF. • Receives annual payout. • Receives income tax deduction.[1]	Asset Annual Payment Income Tax Deduction	• Trustee sells asset and reinvests for greater return. • Pays no capital gain tax due on the appreciation. • Trustee pays a proportionate share of the fund's income each year for lifetime of beneficiary.

After the beneficiary is deceased remaining trust assets pass to the charity.

Charitable Organization

• Receives any assets remaining in the trust when the beneficiary is deceased.

---

[1] This deduction is based on life expectancy and the highest rate paid by the fund over the last three years. The deduction may have to be spread over more than one year, if it exceeds certain percentage of income limitations.

Charitable Lead Annuity Trust
CLAT

In General

A donor may transfer assets to an irrevocable charitable lead annuity trust (CLAT). The trust then pays a fixed dollar amount to a qualified charity for either a set number of years or the lifetimes of individuals. When the trust term has ended, the remaining assets are distributed to the donor, his or her spouse, heirs or others.

The trust must pay out the same dollar amount each year, without regard to its earnings. If the trust earns more than it pays out to the charitable beneficiary, those extra earnings (or asset appreciation) will pass to the non-charitable beneficiaries (children, grandchildren, others) without additional estate or gift taxes.

Valuation of assets is required only at the time the assets are transferred to the CLAT. A new trust will be required if additional contributions are made in later years. Ideally, assets in the CLAT should have both income potential (to make the required payments to the charitable beneficiary) and growth potential (to pass long-term appreciation to the ultimate beneficiaries with a minimum of estate or gift taxes).

After the lead (or income) period has expired, if the beneficiary of the trust is other than the donor or his or her spouse, there may be a taxable gift. The gift tax would be based on the present value of the beneficiaries' right to receive the trust remainder at some future time. This calculation is dependent upon the term of the trust, the amount payable each year to the charity and the AFR (applicable federal rate) at the time of the transfer.

Planning Considerations

A donor establishing a CLAT needs to consider several key questions.

- **Income tax deduction:** If certain requirements are met, an income tax deduction is allowed for the value of the income passing to charity.[1] With a grantor trust the donor is considered the owner of the trust (taxable on the income under the grantor trust rules of IRC Secs. 671-677) and is allowed the tax deduction, subject to certain percentage of AGI limitations. If the trust is a non-grantor trust, the trust itself is permitted an unlimited tax deduction for distributions to qualified charities. If these requirements are not met, no charitable income tax deduction is allowed to either the donor or the trust.

- **Remainder interest:** At the end of the trust term, should the assets remaining in the trust revert to the donor or pass to other individuals such as the donor's heirs?

- **Generation-Skipping Transfer Tax (GSTT):** A taxable event for GSTT purposes will occur if the individuals who ultimately receive the assets when the trust terminates are the donor's grandchildren or a later generation.

---

[1] See IRS Reg. 1.170A-6.

Continued...

Charitable Lead Annuity Trust
CLAT

Estate Tax Reduction

Frequently, CLATs are set up as non-grantor trusts, with the ultimate beneficiary of the trust assets being someone other than the donor or his or her spouse. Such CLATs typically provide no income deduction to the donor, but do provide a means of transferring assets to children or grandchildren, with substantial valuation discounts. For example, at a 4.2% AFR, a 10-year CLAT, paying 5% annually[1] to a charity, offers a 40.7% discount from market value. The same trust, over a 15-year term, offers a 55.7% discount from market value; over 20 years a 67.8% discount from market value is achieved.

The CLAT is an excellent way for affluent individuals to meet charitable obligations, as well as make discounted, deferred transfers to heirs.[2]

---

[1] 5% of the value of the assets, as measured at the time of the transfer into the CLAT. For example, given assets worth $1,000,000 at the time of transfer, a 5% payment would yield a fixed payment to charity of $50,000 per year, for the term of the trust.

[2] Under the Tax Act of 2001, the federal estate tax is gradually phased out until its final repeal in the year 2010. If Congress does not act at that time to repeal it for the years following, it will automatically revert back to the rates in effect during the year 2001, with an exemption for the first $1,000,000 of assets.

Charitable Lead Annuity Trust
CLAT

The donor transfers an asset to the trustee of the charitable lead annuity trust (CLAT), which pays the same fixed dollar amount for each year thereafter to a selected charity. A current income tax deduction is generally allowed for the present value of the income interest paid to the charity.

At the end of the term of the trust, the remaining assets pass to the donor's heirs, spouse, or sometimes back to the donor, if living.

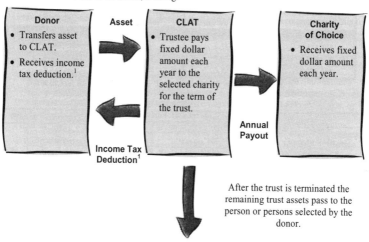

Donor
- Transfers asset to CLAT.
- Receives income tax deduction.[1]

Asset

CLAT
- Trustee pays fixed dollar amount each year to the selected charity for the term of the trust.

Charity of Choice
- Receives fixed dollar amount each year.

Annual Payout

Income Tax Deduction[1]

After the trust is terminated the remaining trust assets pass to the person or persons selected by the donor.

Final Beneficiaries

These beneficiaries could be the donor, if the trust was set to last only a term of years, or it could be the donor's spouse, children, grandchildren[2], etc., which may also produce an estate tax reduction.[3]

---

[1] The income tax deduction, allowable only to grantor trusts, is based on a government determined applicable federal rate and may have to be spread over more than one year, if it exceeds certain percentage of income limitations.

[2] Choosing grandchildren (or later descendants) to receive the assets when the trust terminates may trigger the Generation-Skipping Transfer Tax (GSTT).

[3] Under the Tax Act of 2001, the federal estate tax is gradually phased out until its final repeal in the year 2010. If Congress does not act at that time to repeal it for the years following, it will automatically revert back to the rates in effect during the year 2001, with an exemption for the first $1,000,000 of assets.

Charitable Lead Unitrust
CLUT

In General

A donor may transfer assets to an irrevocable charitable lead unitrust (CLUT) – sometimes referred to as a charitable income unitrust. The trust then pays a fixed percentage of its assets to a qualified charity for either a set number of years or the lifetimes of individuals. When the term of the trust has ended, the remaining assets are distributed to the donor, his or her spouse, heirs or other individuals.

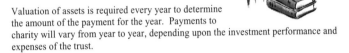

Valuation of assets is required every year to determine the amount of the payment for the year. Payments to charity will vary from year to year, depending upon the investment performance and expenses of the trust.

After the lead (or income) period has expired, if the beneficiary of the trust is other than the donor or his or her spouse, there may be a taxable gift. The gift tax would be based on the present value of the beneficiaries' right to receive the trust remainder at some future time. This calculation is dependent upon the term of the trust, the amount payable each year to the charity and the AFR (applicable federal rate) at the time of the transfer.

Planning Considerations

A donor establishing a CLUT needs to consider several key questions:

- **Income tax deduction:** If certain requirements are met, an income tax deduction is allowed for the value of the income passing to charity.[1] With a grantor trust the donor is considered the owner of the trust (taxable on the income under the grantor trust rules of IRC Secs. 671-677) and is allowed the tax deduction, subject to certain percentage of AGI limitations. If the trust is a non-grantor trust, the trust itself is permitted an unlimited tax deduction for distributions to qualified charities. If these requirements are not met, no charitable income tax deduction is allowed to either the donor or the trust.

- **Remainder interest:** At the end of the trust term, should the assets remaining in the trust revert to the donor or pass to other individuals such as the donor's heirs?

- **Generation-Skipping Transfer Tax (GSTT):** A taxable event for GSTT purposes will occur if the individuals who ultimately receive the assets when the trust terminates are the donor's grandchildren or a later generation.

---

[1] See IRS Reg. 1.170A-6.

Continued

Charitable Lead Unitrust
CLUT

Estate Tax Reduction

Frequently, CLUTs are set up as non-grantor trusts, with the ultimate beneficiary of the trust assets being someone other than the donor or his or her spouse. Such CLUTs typically provide no income deduction to the donor, but do provide a means of transferring assets to children or grandchildren, with substantial valuation discounts. For example, at a 4.2% AFR, a 10-year CLUT, paying 5% annually[1] to a charity, offers a 39.3% discount from market value. The same trust, over a 15-year term, offers a 52.7% discount from market value; over 20 years a 63.2% discount from market value is achieved.

The CLUT is an excellent way for affluent individuals to meet charitable obligations, as well as make discounted, deferred transfers to heirs.[2]

---

[1] This amount is 5% of the value of the assets, as revalued each year.
[2] Under the Tax Act of 2001, the federal estate tax is gradually phased out until its final repeal in the year 2010. If Congress does not act at that time to repeal it for the years following, it will automatically revert back to the rates in effect during the year 2001, with an exemption for the first $1,000,000 of assets.

Charitable Lead Unitrust
CLUT

The donor transfers an asset to the trustee of the charitable lead unitrust (CLUT), which pays a fixed percentage of the trust assets as valued each year thereafter to a selected charity. A current income tax deduction is generally allowed for the present value of the income interest paid to the charity.

At the end of the term of the trust, the remaining assets pass to the donor's heirs, spouse or sometimes back to the donor, if living.

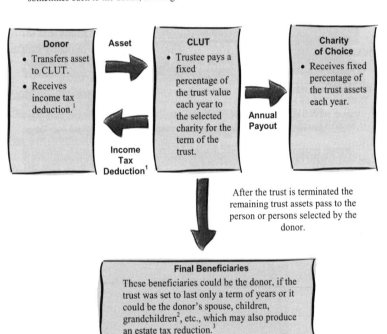

Donor	Asset	CLUT		Charity of Choice
• Transfers asset to CLUT. • Receives income tax deduction.[1]		• Trustee pays a fixed percentage of the trust value each year to the selected charity for the term of the trust.	Annual Payout	• Receives fixed percentage of the trust assets each year.

Income Tax Deduction[1]

After the trust is terminated the remaining trust assets pass to the person or persons selected by the donor.

Final Beneficiaries

These beneficiaries could be the donor, if the trust was set to last only a term of years or it could be the donor's spouse, children, grandchildren[2], etc., which may also produce an estate tax reduction.[3]

---

[1] The income tax deduction, allowable only to grantor trusts, may have to be spread over more than one year if it exceeds certain percentage of income limitations.

[2] Choosing grandchildren (or later descendants) to receive the assets when the trust terminates may trigger the Generation-Skipping Transfer Tax (GSTT).

[3] Under the Tax Act of 2001, the federal estate tax is gradually phased out until its final repeal in the year 2010. If Congress does not act at that time to repeal it for the years following, it will automatically revert back to the rates in effect during the year 2001, with an exemption for the first $1,000,000 of assets.

Supplementing Retirement Income
With a Charitable Remainder Unitrust

Another Way to Fund Retirement

In many instances, a charitable remainder trust is set up just before retirement, with the donor making a single, large gift to the trust. Such a trust allows an individual who is on the verge of retirement to combine charitable goals with retirement income planning.

A charitable remainder unitrust (CRUT) can be established some years before retirement. The CRUT allows additional annual gifts to the trust. For a person who is a number of years away from retirement, this type of trust can combine charitable objectives with retirement asset accumulation goals.

Who Should Consider a CRUT to Accumulate Retirement Assets?

A person who:

- Has a high level of current income;

- Has at least five to ten years before retirement and desires to put away more for the golden years;

- Has reached the maximum level of contributions to his or her qualified retirement plan, and/or

- Needs to shelter retirement funds from current income taxation.

The "Flip" CRUT – A Typical Example

- The donor establishes a charitable remainder unitrust with income for life or for the lives of the donor and/or spouse. Payouts are set at the annual minimum 5.0% of the net fair market value of assets or the income generated by the trust, whichever is less. The trust document specifies that the trust will convert ("flip") from its net income format to a standard form of unitrust at some pre-determined date or other triggering event. At that point, the trustee will distribute a full 5% of the trust's then value using both income and corpus if required.

- The donor makes annual gifts to the trust.

- In the early years, the trustee invests the annual gifts in capital gain assets which generate little or no current income.

- At the death of the last income beneficiary, the trust assets pass directly to the charity.

The result: Due to very small (perhaps zero) payouts in the pre-retirement years, the assets in the trust can grow much larger. When the 5.0% payments begin, the annual income can be substantially higher.

Continued...

Supplementing Retirement Income
With a Charitable Remainder Unitrust

How It Works – A Hypothetical Example

Assumptions:
Married couple aged 45 and 42. First spouse dies at age 77, second spouse at age 81
Gifts of $25,000 per year are made each year for 20 years.
Net income CRUT for 20 years paying out less than 5% of the trust value, flipping to a standard 5%
payout thereafter. 7.0% total return each year.
Years 1 through 20 assume 1% paid as income, with 6.0% as growth
Years 21 through 40 assume 5.0% paid as income, with 2.0% as growth.

Pre-Retirement Period – Maximize Capital Accumulation, Minimized Income and Taxes

Year	Total Contributions to CRUT at $25,000/Year	Cumulative Deduction Allowed	Cumulative Pre-Retirement Income	CRUT Year-End Value
1	$25,000	$3,447	$250	$26,500
5	$125,000	$18,952	$4,064	$149,383
10	$250,000	$42,772	$16,548	$349,291
15	$375,000	$72,460	$40,302	$616,813
20	$500,000	$109,057	$79,135	$974,818

Post-Retirement ("flip") Period – Maximize Income, Charitable Legacy

Year	Total Contributions to CRUT	Current-Year Income	Cumulative Post-Retirement Income	CRUT Year-End Value
22	$500,000	$49,716	$98,457	$1,014,201
24	$500,000	$51,724	$200,891	$1,055,175
26	$500,000	$53,814	$307,464	$1,097,804
28	$500,000	$55,988	$418,312	$1,142,155
30	$500,000	$58,250	$533,700	$1,188,298
32	$500,000	$60,603	$653,718	$1,236,305
34	$500,000	$63,052	$778,585	$1,286,252
36	$500,000	$65,599	$908,497	$1,338,216
38	$500,000	$68,249	$1,043,657	$1,392,280
40	$500,000	$71,006	$1,184,277	$1,488,529

Total post-retirement income...$1,184,277
Charitable legacy (remainder)......................................$1,488,529

Life Insurance Charitable Plan

For the individual who would like to make a substantial bequest to his or her favorite charity, but does not have sufficient assets to fulfill this desire, a charitable plan consisting of a life policy should be considered.

The policy owner (typically, the insured) can transfer an existing life insurance policy to the charity or contribute the funds necessary to purchase a new policy. Additional tax-deductible contributions can be made to help the charity pay the annual premium. This not only spreads out the amount to be given, but allows one to experience the feeling that comes from sharing with others on a more frequent basis.

You Receive	Gift of Policy[1]	Charity Receives
• An income tax deduction, and • A feeling of satisfaction.	⟹	• A large sum in the future.

If circumstances change, the insured can discontinue making the gifts and the charity will either continue the payments or surrender the policy for the cash values.

Note: Merely naming a charity as a beneficiary of a policy will not produce an income tax deduction, since the owner (insured) still has the power to surrender the policy. IRC Sec. 170(f)(3)

The income tax deduction is limited to the lesser of:

- Donor's cost basis (premiums paid less dividends received in cash and policy loans outstanding); or

- The policy's value, which varies with type of policy.
  - **Ordinary life:** The interpolated terminal reserve (roughly cash value) plus any pre-paid premium.
  - **Paid-up policy:** Present cost of a comparable policy at the donor's current age.
  - **New policy:** The gross premium just paid.
  - **Term insurance:** The portion of premium that is still unearned by the insurer.

Note: Revenue Ruling 59-195 approves the use of the applicable regulations for estate (Reg. Sec. 20.2031-8) and gift tax (Reg. Sec. 25.2512-6) to be used for determining the income tax deduction.

---

[1] This is generally funds to purchase a new policy and a small annual contribution to pay premiums.

Private Foundations

People give money and property to charity for a
number of reasons. Among the most common are the
following.

- The desire to help society by funding a worthy
  cause

- To enjoy the income and estate tax benefits derived
  from charitable giving[1]

Despite these benefits, one concern a donor may have
is the loss of control over money and property gifted
to a charity. To meet this concern, a donor can create
a private foundation that will distribute its donations and income to charitable causes
favored by the donor.

What Is a Private Foundation?

A private foundation is a charitable organization created and funded by a donor (during
life or at death) which is designed to achieve one or more specific charitable purposes.
Overall management of the foundation is provided by a board of directors or trustees often
selected by the donor. The directors or trustees can be paid reasonable compensation for
their services.

Technically, tax law describes a private foundation as a charitable organization exempt
from income tax under IRC Sec. 501(c)(3) other than the following.

- Organizations that generally receive a substantial part of their support from the general
  public or from the government

- Religious organizations

- Educational institutions with regular learning facilities, a student body and a specific
  curriculum

- Organizations devoted to promoting public safety

In addition, a private foundation does not include any charitable organization which[2]:

- Receives more than one-third of its support from the sum total of gifts, grants,
  contributions, membership fees and receipts from a permissible business or activity;
  and/or

- Receives one-third or less of its support each year from the sum of gross investment
  income and excess unrelated business income.

---

[1] Under the Tax Act of 2001, the federal estate tax is gradually phased out until its final repeal in the year 2010. If
Congress does not act at that time to repeal it for the years following, it will automatically revert back to the rates in
effect during the year 2001, with an exemption for the first $1,000,000 of assets.
[2] See IRC Sec. 509(a).

Continued.

Private Foundations

Choice of Entity

A private foundation can be structured as either a corporation or a trust. There are advantages to each type of arrangement.

- A corporation may be more flexible than a trust, to meet changing circumstances. Corporations operate through a board of directors and officers, who can be easily hired or replaced.

- Trustees may be held to a higher degree of responsibility than corporate officers, with respect to liability.

- It may be easier to establish a trust; an important point if a donor wants to realize a tax deduction before a tax year closes.

- The filing requirements for a trust may be simpler than for a corporation, which could reduce administrative costs.

Tax Deduction for Contributions to a Private Foundation

Contributions to a private foundation are generally deductible as follows.

- Cash contributions are generally deductible up to 30% of a donor's adjusted gross income (AGI). See IRC Sec. 170(b)(1)(B).

- Gifts of appreciated property are generally deductible up to 20% of a donor's AGI. See IRC Sec. 170(b)(1)(D).

- Gifts of qualified appreciated stock are fully deductible up to fair market value. IRC Sec. 170(e)(5), as amended by the Tax and Trade Relief Extension Act of 1998.[1] The deduction for full market value of qualified appreciated stock by one donor is limited to 10% of the stock of a corporation. See IRC Sec. 170(e)(5)(C).

- All appreciated property (other than qualified stock) contributed by a donor is deductible only up to cost basis.

- Testamentary (at death) bequests are fully deductible from the decedent's AGI.

- Lifetime gifts of cash or appreciated property, which exceed the applicable 20% or 30% of AGI limitation, can be carried forward for up to five years. See IRC Sec. 170(b)(1)(D)(ii).

Note: The contribution and deduction limitations described above are unique to private foundations. Gifts to public charities are treated differently under federal tax law.

---

[1] Effective July 1, 1998.

Continued...

Private Foundations

Special Rules for Private Foundations

Private foundations are subject to a variety of complex tax rules that must be carefully followed to avoid additional income taxes and/or penalties. Some of the most important rules include:

- **Failure to distribute income:** If a private foundation fails to distribute its annual income by the end of the subsequent year, it is subject to a tax of 15%. See IRC Sec. 4942(a). The tax can increase to 100% if the income is not distributed by the date the tax is assessed or by the date the IRS issues a warning (90-day letter). See IRC Sec. 4942(b).

- **Self dealing:** An excise tax is triggered when a disqualified person[1] engages in any of the following activities[2].
  - Selling, exchanging or leasing property
  - Lending money or providing credit
  - Furnishing goods or services
  - Paying compensation or reimbursing expenses
  - Transferring foundation income or assets to or for the use of a disqualified person
  - Furnishing foundation money or property to a government official.
    A disqualified person who conducts an act of self-dealing is subject to an initial penalty tax of 5% of the amount involved and a 200% additional tax if the self-dealing isn't corrected in a timely manner. Foundation managers who knowingly participate in acts of self-dealing are subject to a tax of 2½%. If he, she or they fail to correct an act, an additional penalty of 50% may be imposed.

- **Excess business holdings:** A private foundation that possesses any excess business holdings is subject to a tax of 5%. See IRC Sec. 4943(a).

- **Net investment income:** A private foundation is liable for an excise tax of 2% on its net investment income. See IRC Sec. 4940(a).

- **Investment jeopardizes charitable purpose:** An excise tax of 5% is imposed if the foundation invests its income and funds in such a way that its charitable purpose is jeopardized. See IRC Sec. 4944(a).

- **Legislative activities:** An excise tax of 10% is imposed if funds are used for legislative activities or for engaging in propaganda. In addition, foundation managers who authorize such expenditures can be liable for an additional 2½% tax. See IRC Sec. 4945(a).

---

[1] Under current law, a disqualified person is an individual who is a substantial contributor to a foundation, a foundation manager, certain family members, related business entities, government officials, and others who may hold a fiduciary capacity with regard to the foundation. A disqualified person can be held liable for an excise tax even if a transaction was completed at arms length.

[2] See IRC Secs. 4946(a)(1) and 4941(d)(1).

Supporting Organizations
IRC Sec. 509 (a)(3)

Supporting organizations, like private foundations, are often established and funded by a single individual or family. Unlike private foundations, however, supporting organizations are afforded many of the benefits of being a public charity, while avoiding the taxes and regulations imposed on private foundations by IRC Secs. 4940 through 4948.

A supporting organization which meets the requirements of IRC Sec. 509(a)(3) is distinguished from a private foundation in that it serves public, rather than private, purposes; it is this public focus which justifies the organization's status as a nonprivate foundation.

Creating a Supporting Organization

A supporting organization is typically created as a charitable trust. Occasionally, the donor will setup the organization as a nonprofit corporation under local (state) law. At least one public charity (university, hospital, museum, etc.) must be identified in the organizing document as a recipient of the new organization's support. Frequently, the creator and his or her family serve as trustees or directors of the supporting organization, along with representatives of the charities named.

Qualification as a Supporting Organization

The following three tests must be satisfied.

- The supporting organization must operate exclusively for the benefit of one or more specified public charities.

- It must be operated, supervised, or controlled by or in connection with, one or more public charities.

- The supporting organization must not be controlled (directly or indirectly) by a disqualified person.[1]

---

[1] A disqualified person is defined in IRC Sec. 4946.

Continued...

Supporting Organizations
IRC Sec. 509 (a)(3)

Tax Treatment of Supporting Organizations

Generally, a supporting organization is accorded the benefits of being a public charity, including the following.

- **Income tax deduction for gifts:** Gifts of cash to a supporting organization (as with a public charity) are deductible up to 50% of the donor's adjusted gross income in the year of contribution. Any unused deductions may be carried forward up to five years. Gifts of appreciated property held long term are deductible from the donor's taxable income at full market value, up to 30% of the donor's adjusted gross income, with a five year carry forward of any unused deductions.

- **Not subject to private foundation excise taxes:** Specifically, the prohibitions against self-dealing, minimum distribution requirements, taxes on net-investment income, excess business holdings, jeopardizing investments and prohibited expenditures do not apply to supporting organizations.

Control Issues

While many individuals focus on the tax benefits of charitable giving, other donors are concerned with the loss of control over money and property gifted to a charity. For such patrons, the private foundation is usually the preferred means of achieving philanthropic goals. The greater control found in a private foundation comes at a cost, in the form of greater tax restrictions and increased regulation.

While the creator of a supporting organization does not have the same level of control as the individual who establishes a private foundation, he or she can still have a significant voice in the organization. From a practical standpoint, the supported charities will carefully consider the opinion of the ultimate source of their support.

Family Participation

An unspoken benefit of creating a supporting organization is the opportunity for a donor to involve his or her children and/or grandchildren in directing the family's philanthropic legacy to public charities in the community. By involving a younger generation in the organization, a donor is sometimes able to convey deeply held family values, while at the same time transferring funds to charitable causes.

Continue

Supporting Organizations

IRC Sec. 509 (a)(3)

Private Foundation vs. Supporting Organization

	Private Foundation (non-operating)	Supporting Organization (IRC Sec. 509(a)(3))
Deductibility limitations		
Value of appreciated assets	Cost basis[1] at time of transfer	Market value at time of transfer
Deduction allowable in tax year		
Gifts of cash	Up to 30% of AGI	Up to 50% of AGI
Gifts of appreciated assets	Up to 20% of AGI	Up to 30% of AGI
Carryover of deduction	Maximum of five years	Maximum of five years
Tax restrictions excise taxes		
Tax on net investment income (IRC Sec. 4940)	Yes	No
Tax on self-dealing (IRC Sec. 4941)	Yes	No
Tax on failure to distribute income (IRC Sec. 4942)	Yes	No
Tax on excess business holdings (IRC Sec. 4943)	Yes	No
Tax on jeopardy investments (IRC Sec. 4944)	Yes	No
Tax on taxable expenditures (IRC Sec. 4945)	Yes	No

---

[1] A market value deduction is allowed for publicly traded stock under IRC Sec. 170(e)(5).

Agenda for Discussion

List Planning Objectives

Level of Importance

	High	Medium	Low
1. Getting the estate in order	_____	_____	_____
2. Probate avoidance	_____	_____	_____
3. Death tax reduction	_____	_____	_____
4. Care of children after death	_____	_____	_____
5. Transferring the business	_____	_____	_____
6. Providing sufficient cash flow	_____	_____	_____
7. Covering risk exposure	_____	_____	_____
8. Retirement planning	_____	_____	_____

Specific Areas Which Need Current Review

1. ___ Present wills and trusts
2. ___ Insurance program
3. ___ Current investments
4. ___ Fringe benefit package
5. ___ Business agreements
6. ___ Gifting program
7. ___ Disability income
8. ___ Long-term care
9. _____
10. _____
11. _____
12. _____

Planner Input Sheet

Planner: _____

Case No.: _____   Date: _____

Client Name: _____   Date Needed: _____

Instructions for Preparation of Proposal

Place client's name in header or footer? _____
    __ No
    __ Yes -- _____

Place page number in lower-left corner of each page?
    __ No
    __ Yes -- Begin with page number _____

File numbers to be printed (in the same order they are to appear in the report) are as
     follows:

____,____,____,____,____,____,____,____,____,____,____

____,____,____,____,____,____,____,____,____,____,____

____,____,____,____,____,____,____,____,____,____,____

Remember - If it's too long it may not get read!

    __ Add disclaimer at beginning of report.
    __ Omit disclaimer at beginning of report.

Other Instructions:

_____

_____

_____

_____

_____

_____

Receipt for Documents

The following documents are received this ___ day of _____, 20___, for the purpose of study and analysis in the personal estate planning of _____. It is understood that this material will be treated confidentially and returned as soon as the planning process is completed or sooner if requested.

Planner's Signature: _____

Address: _____ Phone No: _____

Items Received

Wills

___ Client   Dated _____   ___ Spouse   Dated _____

Trust agreements

Type: _____   Dated: _____

Type: _____   Dated: _____

Business agreements

Type: _____   Dated: _____

Type: _____   Dated: _____

Insurance and annuity contracts

Company	Policy No	Company	Policy No
_____	_____	_____	_____
_____	_____	_____	_____
_____	_____	_____	_____
_____	_____	_____	_____

Mutual Fund, Brokerage and 401(k) Account Statements (list companies)

_____   _____

_____   _____

_____   _____

Other Statements (list companies)

_____   _____

_____   _____

The policies and documents for which the above receipt was given have been returned to me.

Date: _____ Client Signature: _____

Planning Task List

Items for the Client to Accomplish

In order for the planning process to proceed successfully and smoothly, the following items need to be accomplished by the indicated dates.

❑ 1. _____

_____

_____   Due date: _____

❑ 2. _____

_____

_____   Due date: _____

❑ 3. _____

_____

_____   Due date: _____

❑ 4. _____

_____

_____   Due date: _____

❑ 5. _____

_____

_____   Due date: _____

❑ 6. _____

_____

_____   Due date: _____

Please, call if there are questions or concerns: _____

Continued...

Planning Task List
Items for the Planner to Accomplish

☐ 1. _____

_____

_____   Due date: _____

☐ 2. _____

_____

_____   Due date: _____

☐ 3. _____

_____

_____   Due date: _____

☐ 4. _____

_____

_____   Due date: _____

☐ 5. _____

_____

_____   Due date: _____

☐ 6. _____

_____

_____   Due date: _____

Client Referral

Others Who May Appreciate Our Services

One of the key sources of future business is the thoughtful referral received from a satisfied client. Are there friends, family members, or co-workers who might benefit from our services?

Name: _____

Address: _____

City/ST/Zip: _____

Telephone: _____ Work Home (circle one)

Relationship: _____

Name: _____

Address: _____

City/ST/Zip: _____

Telephone: _____ Work Home (circle one)

Relationship: _____

Name: _____

Address: _____

City/ST/Zip: _____

Telephone: _____ Work Home (circle one)

Relationship: _____

Name: _____

Address: _____

City/ST/Zip: _____

Telephone: _____ Work Home (circle one)

Relationship: _____

Name: _____

Address: _____

City/ST/Zip: _____

Telephone: _____ Work Home (circle one)

Relationship: _____

Summary of Legal Citations

- **IRC:** The Internal Revenue Code is enacted by Congress and is the "law of the land" for tax purposes.

- **Rev. Rul. and Regs.:** Revenue Rulings are issued by the IRS and Regulations are issued by the Treasury Department and are the department's interpretation of the Internal Revenue Code. The Courts are not bound to follow Revenue Rulings or Regulations if they feel the IRS or the Treasury Department is unreasonable in its interpretation of Congressional intent. In most situations, however, the Courts are strongly influenced by Rulings and Regulations.

- **PLR:** Private Letter Rulings are formally requested from and issued by the Internal Revenue Service.

- **Prop. Regs.:** Proposed Regulations are often issued while the Treasury Department is seeking input prior to finalization of the Regulations. They are not binding.

Court Decision

- **U.S. Supreme Court:** The highest court in the land. Its decisions as to interpretation of a law or its constitutionality are final and binding on all parties and all lower courts.

- **Federal Circuit Court of Appeals:** There are 13 different Federal circuits in the United States. Decisions by these courts are binding upon other lower District Courts within that circuit and upon the U.S. Tax Court, if its decision could be appealed to that Circuit Court.

- **Fed. District Court, Court of Claims and U.S. Tax Court:** The IRS can appeal these decisions.

INDEX

i

v

**Back Room
Technician**®

f you like this book, imagine what the actual software can do or you!

Back Room Technician®-Sales Edition (BRT-SE) is the leading needs analysis, client presentation and education software.

>> Designed to help you promote productivity, increase sales, acquire and retain clients, BRT is user friendly and results driven. Key features include:

  >> Over 600 reports, graphs, charts & illustrations
  >> 11 Needs Analysis Modules
  >> Live Calculators
  >> One Seamless Interface

50% More Sales. 39% Larger Transactions. Less Time!*

* Source: Independent customer survey

powered by advisys®

Notes